Ottoman Provincial Society and the *Waqf* of Jerusalem, 1703–1831

Studies in Islamic Law and Society

VOLUME 58

The titles published in this series are listed at *brill.com/sils*

Ottoman Provincial Society and the *Waqf* of Jerusalem, 1703–1831

By

Şerife Eroğlu Memiş

BRILL

LEIDEN | BOSTON

The Library of Congress Cataloging-in-Publication Data is available online at https://catalog.loc.gov
LC record available at https://lccn.loc.gov/2025048264

Typeface for the Latin, Greek, and Cyrillic scripts: "Brill". See and download: brill.com/brill-typeface.

ISSN 1384-1130
ISBN 978-90-04-74343-4 (hardback)
ISBN 978-90-04-74344-1 (e-book)
DOI 10.1163/9789004743441

This book is printed on acid-free paper and produced in a sustainable manner.

Contents

Figures and Tables

Figures

Tables

CHAPTER 1

Introduction: *Waqf*s and Daily Life in the Ottoman Provinces

1 Purpose and Scope

The study aims to identify the provincial community of Jerusalem within the city's *waqf* network. It also aims to examine the community of Jerusalem within the framework of the political and social hierarchy, the power of the local notables, and their relations with ordinary people, while at the same time dealing with how the Ottoman state apparatus operates in the rural environment. In doing so, the issues of Ottoman and Middle Eastern historiography are addressed together with many other issues in this book's research agenda, some of which are more limited in scope. These topics include, narrowly, decentralization as well as the integration and rise of local notables, which are directly related to central-provincial relations in the period discussed. In examining these processes, this book focuses on the role of the *waqf*s in the context of urban history, identity issues and, finally, the politics of everyday life.

The *waqf*s that were inherited from the Ayyubids and Mamluks, those established after the Ottoman annexation, and those established later point to the presence of an active *waqf* network in the city of Jerusalem in the eighteenth century. However, studies on *waqf*s in the city have been mostly focused on a limited number of *waqf*s or, alternatively, various *waqf*s in a short period of time.[1] This book takes those studies as a starting point but focuses on defining this *waqf* network with an integrated approach, analyzing the effect of this

1 See, for example, ʿĀrif al-ʿĀrif, *al-Mufaṣṣal fī Tārīkh al-Quds* (Jerusalem: Fawzī Yūsuf, 1961), 45; Abdullatif Tibawi, *The Islamic Pious Foundations in Jerusalem* (London: The Islamic Cultural Centre, 1978); Gabriel Baer, "The Waqf as a Prop for the Social System (16th–20th Centuries)," *Islamic Law and Society* 4, no. 3 (1997): 264–97; Haim Gerber, "A New Look at the Tanzimat: The Case of the Province of Jerusalem," in *Palestine in the Late Ottoman Period*, ed. David Kushner (Jerusalem: Yad Izhak Ben-Zvi, 1986), 30–45; Habeeb Albert Khayat, "Waqf in Palestine and Israel from the Ottoman Reforms to the Present" (PhD diss., American University, Washington, DC, 1962); Amy Singer, *Osmanlı'da Hayırseverlik: Kudüs'te Bir Haseki Sultan İmareti*, trans. Dilek Şendil (Istanbul: Tarih Vakfı Yurt Yayınları, 2004); Salīm Jūmʿā Sūwāriyya, *al-Ḥayāt al-Ijtimāʿiyya fī Madīnat al-Quds: 1750–1800* (Amman: Dār ʿĀlam al-Thaqāfa lil-Nashr wa-al-Tawzīʿ, 2009); ʿAbd al-Jalīl Ḥasan ʿAbd al-Mahdī, *al-Madāris fī Bayt al-Maqdis fī l-ʿAṣrayn al-Ayyūbī wa-l-Mamlūkī* (Amman: Maktabat al-Aqṣā, 1981).

 | DOI:10.1163/9789004743441_002

network on urban space, social relations, and central government relations, and filling the gap in the literature in this sense. By making use of unpublished archival materials about the *waqf*s of Jerusalem, it deals with a different type of connection that existed between local and wider Ottoman networks of scholars and officials. Rather than presenting a definitive analysis of the function of *waqf*s in the historical development of Jerusalem, it aims to contribute to an ongoing debate about the functions of the *waqf*, and more particularly, the *waqf* in their urban context. The archival materials used in the study, often for the first time, are carefully analyzed and systematically connected, and they reveal the network of social relations in Jerusalem developed around *waqf* institutions in the early modern period in different contexts.

In the eighteenth century, leading families among the local Muslim population in the cities of Ottoman Palestine possessed a wide variety of powers at the local level. This can be attributed to several factors, including the weakening of the central authority and the transfer of governmental offices from father to son or other close family members as inheritance.[2] As a result of this practice, the positions of many important governmental departments remained in the same family for many years, and thanks to these positions, the families that gained influence, wealth, and strength also gained the recognition of being leading families.[3] Much scholarly work has been devoted to the rise of these prominent families and to their power mechanisms in Jerusalem. Firstly, the city of Jerusalem is a very suitable city for this type of study, as it is modest in terms of the number of historically prominent families.[4] Secondly, the multitude of religious-educational *waqf*s in the city, many of which were built during the Ayyubid and Mamluk periods, allows for better observation of the role of *waqf*s in the wealth and empowerment of traditional families belonging to the class of scholars (*ʿulamāʾ*). The source of wealth and influence for the leading local families in Jerusalem was not taxation nor delegated tax-collection privileges, but their *waqf*s.[5] Thirdly, unlike other Islamic cities,

---

2 Gabriel Baer, "The Dismemberment of Awqaf in Early 19th Century Jerusalem," in *Ottoman Palestine, 1800–1914: Studies in Economic and Social History*, ed. Gad G. Gilbar (Leiden: E. J. Brill, 1990), 299–319.

3 Dror Ze'evi, *Kudüs: 17. Yüzyılda Bir Osmanlı Sancağında Toplum ve Ekonomi*, trans. S. Çağlayan (Istanbul: Tarih Vakfı Yurt Yayınları, 2000); Abu-Manneh, Butrus. "Jerusalem in the Tanzimat Period: The New Ottoman Administration and Notables." *Die Welt des Islams* 30, no. 1/4 (1990): 1–44.

4 Gabriel Baer, "Jerusalem's Families of Notables and Waqf in the Early 19th Century," in *Palestine in the Late Ottoman Period*, ed. David Kushner (Leiden: E. J. Brill, 1986), 109–11.

5 Perhaps the most obscure group of local power-holders in the provinces were the prominent figures of Arab cities, called *aʿyān*. According to the local chroniclers, these served as the

the relations between the elite families of Jerusalem and the *waqf* institution are often studied academically after the Tanzimat,[6] specifically in the 1920s and 1930s.[7]

This book covers the years 1703–1831, and the area of study is limited to the city of Jerusalem. Until the 1860s, the city of Jerusalem consisted of an area surrounded by walls, called the Old (*Qadīm*) City. However, due to the fact that the subject of this study is *waqf*s, the villages with agricultural production that provided income to the *waqf*s in the city are also included in the scope of the study in some cases. For instance, most of the cases related to the Khasseki Sultan *imāret* (public kitchen) in Jerusalem refer to peasants residing in the villages of Bayt Jālā, Bayt Liqyā, Bayt Laḥm, Bayt ʿInāb, and Bayt Ṣafāfa.

2 Methodology and Sources

The data analyses included in the study can be organized around four major problematics. The first problematic is how the Ottomans are determined as the center and Jerusalem, a provincial town, was positioned according to the center. In this framework, when the center is a big city, the space of the province comes to mind. The special features of the city of Jerusalem as distinct from the other Ottoman provincial cities are important in this context. One can discuss, in this context, the political geography of the city of Jerusalem.

The *waqf* network of Jerusalem is the second problematic of the study. *Waqf*s in Muslim societies constitute not only the basis of the system of religious institutions composed of mosques, masjids, schools (*madrasa*s) and other facilities but also real estate and other assets. These are sometimes acquired by a family over generations, donated as trusts for regular income to their families or other charitable services. The *waqf* is a system for the purpose of serving the poor, the scholars, Sufis, travelers, and volunteers in society. Based on this brief introduction, it is clear that establishing a *waqf* was an occasion of material

---

cement that kept the urban order together. Dina Rizk Khoury, "The Ottoman Center versus Provincial Power-Holders: An Analysis of the Historiography," in *Türkiye Tarihi, 1603–1839*, ed. Suraiya Faroqhi, trans. Fethi Aytuna (Istanbul: Kitabevi, 2011), 135–206.

6 See Khayat, "Waqf in Palestine," 60–127.

7 See Uri M. Kupferschmidt, "The Supreme Muslim Council, 1921–1937: Islam under the British Mandate for Palestine" (PhD diss., Hebrew University of Jerusalem, Jerusalem, 1978); Uri M. Kupferschmidt, "Palestinian Waqfs and the Supreme Muslim Council" (paper presented at the International Seminar on Social and Economic Aspects of the Muslim Waqf, Jerusalem, June 1979).

and spiritual significance for the endower and society as a whole.[8] Over time, as the economic importance of *waqf*s increased, the number of people who benefited and were provided their living from *waqf* revenues also increased, and the *waqf* institution in turn became more complex. In this section, in the context of the development of urban structures, it is our intention to present a general framework for the development of the *waqf* institution in Jerusalem in this historical process. Another question that needs to be answered in this context is whether or not *waqf*s were established by non-Muslim subjects – namely Christians and Jews – according to Islamic law, and if so, how they were established.

The third problem we deal with in the framework of the study revolves around understanding provincial society in the eighteenth century. For this, the actors in the provinces are the focus of consideration, and the relations between the *waqf* institution and these actors are defined from various angles. The argument that the eighteenth century was a period of "decline" has lost much credibility. Instead, the suggestion that "decentralization" prevails in administration is emphasized. Although the second half of the century seems to be a period when the state has lost its managerial reins, this situation is increasingly balanced by "Ottomanization" in the rural community of Jerusalem.[9] These provincial actors, oriented in different ways to the institutional framework of the empire, increased the powers of the provinces by entering the institutional umbrella of the empire, thereby transforming the traditional administrative structure of the empire. The Ottoman center, on the one hand, had no other choice but to add these local powers to its own structure in order to bring the resources in the provinces to the service of the center and, on the other hand, had to ensure the security in the provinces. However, "this articulation was not formed by a vertical assignment process from the center to the provinces, but rather a horizontal process that continued through negotiation and reconciliation."[10]

Still, the elites in the city were indeed elite: the richest, most influential, and most respected *ʿulamāʾ*, civilians, and military officers. As a class whose boundaries are not clearly drawn or fully defined, it is often not easy to decisively include or exclude some families in this class. In this study, we ask questions

8 Richard van Leeuwen, *Bir Osmanlı Şehri: Şam, Vakıflar ve Şehir* (Istanbul: Küre Yayınları, 2012), 19–22.

9 Dina Rizk Khoury, *Osmanlı İmparatorluğu'nda Devlet ve Taşra Toplumu*, trans. Ülkü Tansel, 3rd ed. (Istanbul: İş Bankası Kültür Yayınları, 2008), 3.

10 Ali Yaycıoğlu, "Sened-i İttifak (1808): Osmanlı İmparatorluğu'nda Bir Ortaklık ve Entegrasyon Denemesi," in *Nizam-ı Kadimden Nizam-ı Cedide: III. Selim ve Dönemi*, ed. Seyfi Kenan (Istanbul: ISAM, 2010), 667–709.

about establishing common characteristics of these notable families, identifying some differences between them and defining their numerical significance in *waqf* practices. Members of some prominent families gained control over their property, income, and *waqfs*, for example, through various economic, social, and political forces in *waqfs* not even established by their own families.[11] Since for centuries all *waqf* properties were considered tax-exempt, inalienable, and permanent, some well-to-do elite families tended to use *waqfs*, presumably to preserve their wealth and safely pass it on to future generations. By analyzing *waqf* records and examining the history of notable families in Ottoman Jerusalem, the study makes it clear that the *waqf* was the main source and vehicle for the continued power of Jerusalem's local elite, especially within the leading *ʿulamāʾ* families. It finds that Jerusalem's elite families not only aided the ruling dynasty's Ottomanization policies by acting as local administrators of regional imperial *waqfs*, but also established local *waqfs* that preserved their economic power by designating their descendants as administrators and beneficiaries. Thus, these prominent families consolidated their social status and increased their political influence over rival families. The basic problem of this part of the study is the detailed analysis of the relations between the elites of Jerusalem and the *waqf* institution. It explores how *waqfs* reflected the changing interests of different segments of society, such as government officials, provincial notables, merchants, peasants, and the poor. It also seeks to answer questions such as how these interests changed during the period under scrutiny and how these changes were reflected in the *waqf* endowment and its management. In this context, it also discusses the interactions between notables and commoners as mediated by the notables' control over the *waqfs*, with their revenues and properties.

The fourth problematic of the study is the functioning of the Ottoman central administration in the provincial environment. Although no attempt will be made here to engage in debates on the nature of central administration, the way in which the centre exercised the administrative reins and how far the influence of the *waqf* extended is of interest to the sources of central state archives. The questions it poses are inspired by the debates among Ottoman specialists writing in Western languages and focusing on the functioning of state power and control in the provinces, and by the signs of the existence of central state institutions in the context of their practices in relation to the institution of *waqf*. Documents written by representatives of the central government shed light on the framework and functioning of institutions, their

11 Baer, "The *Waqf* as a Prop," 264–97.

justifications, and the distribution of power over them.[12] Thus, the scope, intensity, and diversity of the relations between Istanbul and Jerusalem through the *waqf*s are addressed.

2.1 Waqfs

After providing a historical background on the city of Jerusalem in the first part of the study, and mentioning some points about the importance of Jerusalem, the main issue of the second part of the study is the *waqf*s of Jerusalem. According to Kuban, one of the researchers who emphasize the importance of *waqf*s in terms of Ottoman cities, the basic features of Ottoman city are the division of residential and commercial areas, the central role of the mosque and bazaar, the constitutional nucleus of the neighborhood unit constituting the city, social solidarity provided by the *waqf* and guild organizations, and the local notables that have grown in importance since the sixteenth century.[13] In support of Kuban's opinion, Ergenç argues, "the Ottoman city is a synthesis and in this synthesis it is possible to find the influences of Islamic elements and Central Asian Turkish civilization."[14] According to him, "What characterizes Ottoman cities and makes them superior to other Islamic cities is the development of cities by establishing *imāret*, a complex of religious and social structures."[15] Both Ergenç and Kuban[16] share the same emphasis on institutional factors as Barkan[17] and İnalcık,[18] who are among the founders of Ottoman social and economic historiography.[19] Among these studies pointing to various aspects of the *waqf*s in the history of the city, Barkan's *imāret* (complex sites)[20] and, more recently, Yediyıldız's *khayrāt* (charities system)[21] can offer insights into the place of the buildings in the physical, social, economic,

12 Van Leeuwen, *Bir Osmanlı*, 19–22.

13 Doğan Kuban, "Anadolu Türk Şehri: Tarihi Gelişmesi, Sosyal ve Fiziki Özellikleri Üzerinde Bazı Gelişmeler," *Vakıflar Dergisi* 7 (1968): 7–71.

14 Özer Ergenç, *Osmanlı Klasik Dönemi Kent Tarihçiliğine Katkı: XVI. Yüzyılda Ankara ve Konya* (Ankara: Ankara Enstitüsü Vakfı, 1995), 48.

15 Kuban, "Anadolu Türk Şehri," 54–55.

16 ibid., 54–55.

17 Ömer Lütfi Barkan, "Şehirlerin Teşekkül ve İnkişâf Tarihi Bakımından: Osmanlı İmparatorluğunda İmâret Sitelerinin Kuruluş ve İşleyiş Tarzına Ait Araştırmalar," *İstanbul Üniversitesi İktisat Fakültesi Mecmuası* 23, no. 1–2 (1962–63): 239–96.

18 Halil İnalcık, "The Rebuilding of Istanbul by Mehmed the Conqueror," *Cultura Turcica* 4, no. 1–2 (1967): 5–15.

19 Ergenç, *Osmanlı Klasik Dönemi*, 49.

20 Barkan, "Şehirlerin Teşekkül," 239–96.

21 Bahaeddin Yediyıldız, "Osmanlı Döneminde Türk Vakıfları ya da Türk Hayrat Sistemi," in *Osmanlı: Toplum*, vol. 5, ed. Güler Eren (Ankara: Yeni Türkiye Yayınları, 1999), 17–33.

and cultural life of the cities. In this study, we used the concept of "*waqf* network" to define the *waqf*s of the city in its physical, social, economic and cultural life with a similar approach.

The word "net" is defined in the dictionary as "*lattice-shaped grid, network, and spider net*,"[22] and two of these elements relate to this study. Firstly, *waqf*s are part of the symbolism of the dynamic process and the spatial alchemy that shape spatial organization within the city structure. Secondly, this process is closely related to the development of power mechanisms in Muslim societies, namely the *sharīʿa*, the administrative systems prepared by administrators and social groups, and in particular the influence of the *ʿulamāʾ*.[23] In the present study, Islamic *waqf*s, which have a decisive position in the social and economic structure of the city of Jerusalem, both in their social and economic structure, are studied in order to define a continuous interaction and communication which, we claim, is the people living in the city and the city center existing between each other and the central government. The word "system," which is sometimes included in the text, is used to mean a structure that is bordered by legal rules and controlled by bureaucratic mechanisms.

The Khasseki Sultan *imāret*, a sign of the benevolence of the Ottoman sultan and at the same time a source of power and legitimacy, is located at the center of the city, but it fulfills a very important function not only for Jerusalem but also for the periphery. It is also part of the spiritual center of the city, near the Dome of the Rock and Masjid al-Aqṣā, which constitute the core of the *waqf* network in the city.[24] These mosques, built in the Umayyad period and rehabilitated with numerous repairs and maintenance during the Ayyubid, Mamluk and Ottoman periods, have in time become the center of a

---

22 Şemseddin Sāmī, *Kāmūsu'l-aʿlām* (Istanbul: Çağrı Yayınları, 1899–1900). For a similar usage, see Van Leeuwen, *Bir Osmanlı*, 19. In a different example, Doumani defined the role of the Arafat family, one of the merchant families of Jabal Nablus, in trade, and defined regional and local economic connections with the concept of "network." See Beshara Doumani, *Rediscovering Palestine: Merchants and Peasants in Jabal Nablus, 1700–1900* (Berkeley: University of California Press, 1995), 54–95. Also see Nurcan Abacı, "SNA (Social Network Analysis) and Ottoman History: A Social Network Analysis of Mountain and Immigrant Villages of Bursa (Late Ottoman/Early Republic)" (paper presented at the 12th International Congress of Ottoman Social and Economic History, Retz, Austria, July 11–15, 2011); Joanna Innes, "'Networks' in British History," *East Asian Journal of British History* 5 (2016): 51–72.

23 See Van Leeuwen, *Bir Osmanlı*.

24 The magnificent building, known as the Haseki Sultan *Imāret* or *Takiyya*, is located in the center of the old city surrounded by walls, at the junction of the ʿAqabat al-Takiyya and Shāriʿ al-Wād, on the slope that rises to the hill just south of the Via Dolorosa, and is still standing today. See Amy Singer, *Osmanlı'da Hayırseverlik*, 1.

wide network of *waqf*s that surround the city center and are part of the organization of the administrative system and urban services. The area containing these two mosques is called al-Ḥaram al-Sharīf and includes one-sixth of the Old City. The Ḥaram area is formed by the coming together of a large number of *waqf* buildings built by various Islamic states over the centuries.[25] Although the Masjid al-Aqṣā and Dome of the Rock have not been designated as *waqf*s, they gained a central position in the city's *waqf* system over time. During the Ayyubid, Mamluk, and Ottoman periods, *waqf* properties located both within and around al-Ḥaram al-Sharīf were of great material and spiritual significance.[26] This evolution illustrates the transformation of a city into a rich *waqf* system governed by strict legal rules under Ottoman governance.

Waqf, in essence, means that a property is eternally assigned to a certain charity. The founder of the *waqf* declares the charitable cause for the *waqf* establishes the operation of the *waqf* property to generate revenue for that cause, and relinquishes his property rights, declaring it to be "God's property." The *waqf* is no longer a market commodity. Sale, grant, or pledge was strictly forbidden in any way whatsoever.[27] These properties were usually set up for the benefit of *khayrāt*, which themselves were under the *waqf* legal category. *Waqf* could refer to income and profits from an asset as well as the religious or social services using these incomes. For example, agricultural land has been converted into *waqf*, and its revenues might have been allocated for the construction and maintenance of a certain mosque, *madrasa*, or outbuilding. When *waqf*s were still new, the founder of the *waqf* or his family and descendants might have been identified as "benefactors" of the *waqf*. However, when the lineage from the endower was completely cut off, the *waqf* incomes could be allocated to a certain charity (the poor of Jerusalem, for example). At the same time, the founder could appoint a trustee for himself or his descendants. Thus, the *waqf*'s founder was able to retain the administration of the property despite the waiving of property rights.[28] This general definition of the concept

---

25 al-ʿĀrif al-ʿĀrif, *Tārīkh Qubbat al-Ṣakhra al-Musharrafa wa-l-Masjid al-Aqṣā wa-Mulakhkhaṣ Tārīkh al-Quds* (Jerusalem: Maktabat al-Andalus, 1955), see Appendix 1.

26 ʿĀrif al-ʿĀrif, *Tārīkh al-Ḥaram al-Qudsī* (Jerusalem: Maṭbaʿat Dār al-Aytām al-Islāmiyya al-Ṣināʿiyya, 1947).

27 Ömer Hilmi Efendi, *İthāf al-Akhlāf fī Aḥkām al-Awqāf* (Ankara: Vakıflar Genel Müdürlüğü Yayınları, 1977).

28 On the historical development of *waqf*s, see Fuad Köprülü, "Vakıf Müessesesinin Hukuki Mahiyeti ve Tarihi Tekāmülü," *Vakıflar Dergisi* 2 (1942): 1–36, 12–14; Bahaeddin Yediyıldız, "Müessese-Toplum Münasebetleri Çerçevesinde XVIII Asır Türk Toplumu ve Vakıf Müessesesi," *Vakıflar Dergisi* 15 (1982): 23–53, 53; Neşet Çağatay, "Türk Vakıflarının Özellikleri," in *X. Türk Tarih Kongresi, 22–26 Eylül 1986, Kongreye Sunulan Bildiriler*, vol. 4

of the *waqf* shows the basic function of the institution. Moreover, by endowing a portion of his assets to a charitable institution, the founder of the *waqf* would both receive blessings and also allocate his name to perpetuate his name forever. In some cases, he would have ensured that the remaining part of his assets would be utilised by the most virtuous and talented of his generation, usually as stated in the *waqfiyyas*, by stipulating various duties such as trustees or as beneficiaries of the endowment.[29] Makdisi noted that *waqfs* could be used "to prevent a son's extravagance."[30] Many wealthy families used the *waqf* as a tax shelter to prevent their wealth from diminishing and thus established family foundations (*ahlī* or *dhurrī waqf*). These *waqfs* combined both familial and charitable purposes.[31] The prevention of the distribution of wealth at the time of the death of the *waqf* was another, though not exclusive, material reason motivating the establishment of such *waqfs*.[32] Moreover, the *waqf* could provide a significant income both to the founder and to their descendants for generations. For example, in this study, it is claimed that the property itself was considered less important than the stable and regular income it could generate. Thus, one of the aims of the work is to provide a general framework for

(Ankara: Türk Tarih Kurumu Basımevi, 1993), 1615–27, 1615, 1617; Hüseyin Salebci, "Tarih Boyunca Vakıflar," in *11. Vakıf Haftası, 3–9 Aralık 1984: Konuşmalar ve Tebliğler* (Ankara: Vakıflar Genel Müdürlüğü Yayınları, 1985), 107–12, 108–09; Ömer Yörükoğlu, "Vakıf Müessesesinin Hukuki, Tarihi, Felsefi Temelleri," in *11. Vakıf Haftası, 3–9 Aralık 1984: Konuşmalar ve Tebliğler* (Ankara: Vakıflar Genel Müdürlüğü Yayınları, 1985), 113–24. For sources and discussion of the *waqf* in Islamic history, see Wilhelm Heffening, "Wakf," in *Encyclopaedia of Islam, First Edition*, ed. Martijn Theodor Houtsma, Thomas Walker Arnold, René Basset, and Richard Hartmann (Leiden: E. J. Brill, 1934), 4:1096–1103; Bahaeddin Yediyıldız, "Vakıf," in *Türkiye Diyanet Vakfı İslâm Ansiklopedisi*, vol. 42 (Istanbul: Türkiye Diyanet Vakfı Yayınları, 2012), 475–79; Köprülü, "Vakıf Müessesesinin," 3–9; and Bahaeddin Yediyıldız, *İslam ve Türk Hukuk Tarihi Araştırmaları ve Vakıf Müessesesi* (Istanbul: Ötüken Neşriyat, 1983), 311–14; Ahmet Akgündüz, *İslam Hukukunda ve Osmanlı Tatbikatında Vakıf Müessesesi* (Ankara: Türk Tarih Kurumu Yayınları, 1988), 11–12; Nazif Öztürk, *Menşe'i ve Tarihi Gelişimi Açısından Vakıflar* (Ankara: Vakıflar Genel Müdürlüğü Yayınları, 1983), 30–40; İsmet Kayaoğlu, "Vakfın Menşei Hakkındaki Görüşler," *Vakıflar Dergisi* 11 (1977): 47–55; Halim Baki Kunter, "Türk Vakıfları ve Vakfiyeleri Üzerine Mücmel Bir Etüd," *Vakıflar Dergisi* 1 (1938): 103–29.

29 Mehmet Genç, "Klasik Osmanlı Sosyal-İktisadî Sistemi ve Vakıflar," *Vakıflar Dergisi* 42 (2014): 15–31, 16.

30 George Makdisi, *The Rise of Colleges: Institutions of Learning in Islam and the West* (Edinburgh: Edinburgh University Press, 1981), 39.

31 Yaacov Lev, "Charity and Gift Giving in Medieval Islam," in *Charity and Giving in Monotheistic Religions*, ed. Miriam Frenkel and Yaacov Lev (Berlin: Walter de Gruyter, 2009), 45.

32 Mustafa Nuri Paşa, *Netâyicü'l-vukû'ât: Kurumlarıyla Osmanlı Tarihi*, ed. Yılmaz Kurt (Ankara: Kitabevi Yayınları, 1995), 289–93.

the development of the *waqf* institution in the context of the development of urban structures.

Recently, *waqfs* have had a significant place both in *waqf*-based research and in urban history studies. Interests in *waqf* have been diverse, and there has been a significant increase in the number of socio-economic aspects identified in *waqfs*.[33] *Waqf* documents are further investigated in this study as a source for social histories of Islamic societies. The expansion of interest in *waqfs* has inspired or obliged richer approaches to and perspectives of history, both sociological and cultural.[34] However, many important studies on *waqfs* still remain limited and incomplete, focusing on specific case studies or institutional aspects or functions. There is relatively little effort to comprehensively address the *waqf* institution in all its complexity.

33 For an overview of the activities of *waqfs* and the *waqf* system in social and economic life, see Halil İnalcık, "The Ottoman State: Economy and Society, 1300–1600," in *An Economic and Social History of the Ottoman Empire*, vol. 1, ed. Halil İnalcık and Donald Quataert (Cambridge: Cambridge University Press, 1997), 9–411, 47, 79–83; idem, Halil İnalcık, "Capital Formation in the Ottoman Empire," *The Journal of Economic History* 29, no. 1 (1969): 97–140, 132–35; Colin Imber, *Ebu's-su'ud: The Islamic Legal Tradition* (Stanford, CA: Stanford University Press, 1997), 140; Hasan Yüksel, *Osmanlı Sosyal ve Ekonomik Hayatında Vakıfların Rolü (1585–1683)* (Sivas: Dilek Matbaası, 1998); Bahaeddin Yediyıldız, *XVIII. Yüzyılda Türkiye'de Vakıf Müessesesi: Bir Sosyal Tarih İncelemesi* (Ankara: Türk Tarih Kurumu Yayınları, 2003).

34 The seminal study of Yediyıldız demonstrated that the waqf institution preserved its dynamism throughout the eighteenth century, offering an analytical framework that inspired subsequent scholarship. Building on this model, Hasan Yüksel adapted a similar approach to the seventeenth century, selecting a representative sample and examining the relevant waqfs, with particular emphasis on their contribution to urban development (Yüksel, *Osmanlı Sosyal*, 263–96). Numerous studies have followed this line of inquiry, further illustrating the close relationship between waqfs and the social, economic, and spatial configuration of Ottoman cities. See, for example, Ömer Demirel, *Osmanlı Vakıf-Şehir İlişkisine Bir Örnek: Sivas Şehir Hayatında Vakıfların Rolü* (Ankara: Türk Tarih Kurumu Yayınları, 2000); Saim Savaş, *Bir Tekkenin Dinî ve Sosyal Tarihi: Sivas Ali Baba Zaviyesi* (Istanbul: Dergâh Yayınları, 1992); Cafer Çiftçi, *Bursa'da Vakıfların Sosyo-Ekonomik İşlevleri* (Bursa: Bursa Kültür Sanat ve Turizm Vakfı Yayınları, 2004).

A recent and comprehensive literature review is provided by Nada Moumtaz in her introduction to the thematic issue titled "A Third Wave of Waqf Studies." Moumtaz argues that Western scholarship on waqf produced over the last two decades constitutes an epistemological break from earlier approaches, proposing "waves" rather than Hoexter's stage-based periodization. This "third wave," as she conceptualizes it, advances a more international, multidisciplinary, and comparative mode of inquiry, bringing together case studies that span diverse regions and historical contexts. See Nada Moumtaz, "Theme Issue: A Third Wave of Waqf Studies," *Islamic Law and Society* 25, 1/2 (2018): 1–10; Miriam Hoexter, "Waqf Studies in the Twentieth Century: The State of the Art," *Journal of the Economic and Social History of the Orient* 41, 4 (1998): 474–95.

Many research projects on *waqf*s have raised issues that require some rethinking of traditional considerations about the *waqf* institution. These traditional considerations were generally based on the assumption that the property of the *waqf* is completely out of economic circulation, where the value of the goods is determined, since sale or pledge is forbidden. From this point of view, the *waqf* property is now separated from the fluctuations in the buying and selling process and the markets, thus becoming a static and restrictive element that prevents socio-economic development in Muslim societies and even impedes the development of capitalist economic relations.[35] This picture of the *waqf* institution is narrow, limited, and ignores some of the essential features of the institution. It is important to present an objection to the "traditional" view of the *waqf* by putting forward that the institution is not outside of economic conditions, based on the historicization of the *waqf* institution. Besides, *waqf*s have dynamic functions that transcend the role of being economic assets. The interaction between these different roles in the process of historical change will be another issue for us to analyze in our work.

This work, which focuses more closely on the *waqf*, is often in contradiction with the absolute approach, which has a long history of discourse about the structure and management of *waqf*s. According to Singer, "any deviation in the *waqf*'s *waqfiyya* is blamed on corrupt administrators and the corrupt structures of the *waqf*. However, when examined carefully, the *waqfiyya* of a *waqf* is not a detailed guide that will always be valid, but a general outline."[36] However, there are different kinds of documents, registers, and collections that can be used by the *waqf* researchers to shed light on the *waqf*, its establishment over time, and its physical and economic status.[37] Based on these and other clues

35 Van Leeuwen, *Bir Osmanlı*, 19–22.

36 Singer, *Osmanlı'da Hayırseverlik*, 13–14.

37 For instance, see Suraiya Faroqhi, "Agricultural Crisis and the Art of Flute-Playing: The Worldly Affairs of the Mevlevi Dervishes (1595–1652)," *Turcica* 20 (1988): 43–70, 44; Ruth Roded, "Quantitative Analysis of Waqf Endowment Deeds: A Pilot Project," *Osmanlı Araştırmaları* 9 (1989): 61–79; Ronald C. Jennings, "Pious Foundations in the Society and Economy of Ottoman Trabzon, 1565–1640: A Study Based on the Juridical Registers Şer'i Mahkeme Sicilleri of Trabzon," in *Studies on Ottoman Social History in the Sixteenth and Seventeenth Centuries: Women, Zimmis and Sharia Courts in Kayseri, Cyprus and Trabzon* (Istanbul: Isis Press, 1999), 613–65. For some studies in which various archive sources are introduced in *waqf* research, see Kayhan Orbay, "Vakıfların Bazı Arşiv Kaynakları (Vakfiyeler, Şeriyye Sicilleri, Mühimmeler, Tahrir Defterleri ve Vakıf Muhasebe Defterleri)," *Vakıflar Dergisi* 27 (2005): 41–53, 41; Kayhan Orbay, "Vakıf Taamhoran and Fodulahoran Registers as Archival Sources for Imārets," in *Feeding People, Feeding Power: Imārets in the Ottoman Empire*, ed. Nina Ergin, Christoph K. Neumann, and Amy Singer (Istanbul: Eren Yayıncılık, 2007), 31–44; Mustafa Alkan, "Türk Tarihi Araştırmaları Açısından Vakıf Kayıtlar Arşivi," *Vakıflar Dergisi* 30 (2007): 1–34; Şerife Eroğlu Memiş, "Osmanlı Toplumsal Tarihi Kaynaklarından ḥurūfāt ya da 'Askerî Rūznāmçe Defterleri: Kazā-i Kudüs-i Şerif

found in various documents, it is possible to make some generalizations about possible motivations, such as when in the life cycle of the endower, how the properties were acquired, and under what conditions. However, it should be remembered that each *waqf* is unique in that it situates the subjectivity of the endower within a unique configuration of emotional, kinship, property and social relations. The flexibility of the *waqf* allowed the endower to pursue a variety of overlapping goals when it came to the transfer of property and the pious promotion of good deeds in preparation for the afterlife.[38]

Researchers such as Faroqhi, Hoexter, and Jennings have already shared some of the rich details of the institutions' documents in the Ottoman archives one by one.[39] In addition to this, there is a tradition of research, of which we give some examples above, producing analytical works from the more general questions about *waqfs*. Examples include the studies of Baer, Barkan, and Gerber.[40] The focus and main problematic of these researches is the *waqf*. Still, the *waqf* is generally only one form of many large-scale categories; for example, a form of holding property, a form of capital investment, a form of patronage, or a form of philanthropy.[41] Therefore, we believe that, with a similar point

Örneği," *Vakıflar Dergisi* 39 (2013): 115–46; Şerife Eroğlu Memiş, "Between Ottomanisation and Local Networks: Appointment Registers as Archival Sources for Waqf Studies, the Case of Jerusalem's Maghariba Neighborhood," in *Ordinary Jerusalem, 1840–1940: Opening New Archives, Revisiting a Global City*, ed. Angelos Dalachanis and Vincent Lemire (Leiden: Brill, 2018), 75–99.

38 Beshara Doumani, *Family Life in the Ottoman Mediterranean: A Social History* (Cambridge: Cambridge University Press, 2017), 135–36.

39 Suraiya Faroqhi, "Sayyid Gazi Revisited: The Foundation as Seen Through Sixteenth- and Seventeenth-Century Documents," *Turcica* 13 (1981): 90–122; idem, "The Tekke of Hacı Bektaş: Social Position and Economic Activities," *International Journal of Middle East Studies* 7, no. 2 (1976): 183–208; idem, "A Great Foundation in Difficulties: Or Some Evidence on Economic Contraction in the Ottoman Empire of the Mid-Seventeenth Century," in *Mélanges Professeur Robert Mantran*, ed. Abdeljelil Temimi (Zaghouan: Centre d'Études et de Recherches Ottomanes, Morisques, de Documentation et d'Information, 1988), 109–21; Miriam Hoexter, *Endowments, Rulers and Community: Waqf al-Ḥaramayn in Ottoman Algiers* (Leiden: Brill, 1998); Ronald C. Jennings, "Pious Foundations in the Society and Economy of Ottoman Trabzon, 1565–1640: A Study Based on the Judicial Registers of Trabzon (Şerʿi Mahkeme Sicilleri)," *Journal of the Economic and Social History of the Orient* 33, no. 3 (1990): 271–336.

40 Baer, "The Waqf as a Prop," 264–97; idem, "Women and Waqf: An Analysis of the Istanbul Tahrir of 1546," *Asian and African Studies* 17, no. 1 (1983): 9–27; idem, "The Dismemberment of Awqāf," 299–319; Ömer Lütfi Barkan, "Osmanlı İmparatorluğu'nda Bir İskân ve Kolonizasyon Metodu Olarak Vakıflar ve Temlikler 1: İstilâ Devirlerinin Kolonizatör Türk Dervişleri ve Zâviyeler," *Vakıflar Dergisi* 2 (1942): 279–386; Haim Gerber, "The Waqf Institution in Early Ottoman Edirne," *Asian and African Studies* 17, no. 1 (1983): 29–45.

41 Singer, *Osmanlı'da Hayırseverlik*, 14.

of view, it is most useful to evaluate the *waqf* in these multiple and overlapping contexts. In doing so, various archive resources, especially the *waqfiyyas*, are included in the study in order to follow the changes of *waqf* over time. Collectively, the study allows us to get to know the *waqf*s of Jerusalem, while trying to clarify how this institution is at the crossroads of the various dimensions of the Ottoman world.

2.2 *Society*

The third issue of the study is the problem of locating the eighteenth-century Jerusalem-urban provincial community in a particular context and highlighting its aspects that are distinct from other periods, and this is shaped around discussions of "decentralization." The studies of two academics presented a different perspective to the views that determined the eighteenth century as the century of decentralization. In his study, in which he focused on the institutions of the central government, Barbir showed that the governing emphasis was on the reorganization of the governance of states in the first half of the eighteenth century.[42] Salzmann, based on the work of Genç, offered important criticisms of the view that the applications of the tax-farming system in the eighteenth century were an indicator of a decentralization process. Salzmann mentioned that the *malikane* system, which means a lifetime tax-collecting privilege, does not result in the transfer of the state treasury, and that the management reins have not been dropped. Salzmann's argument is based on the idea that one of many strategies devised by the state elite, the privilege of collecting taxes for life, has been developed in order to take advantage of the resources of provincial political and social groups. He emphasizes that, politically, the inclusion of the provincial groups in state finances does not mean that the state loses its power.[43]

In order to test the decentralization model, we have chosen to magnify two important features of the provincial society of Jerusalem in shaping its relations with the state – within the framework of the network of relations formed around the *waqf* institution – over a period of time: the assignments to *waqf* posts and stipends, and the procedures of long-term leasing to *waqf* properties. In this context, the present study attempts to uncover how local community groups have transformed in Jerusalem, and then demonstrate how this transformation has shaped the *waqf* institution. The provincial society of Jerusalem

---

42 Karl K. Barbir, *Ottoman Rule in Damascus, 1708–1758* (Princeton, NJ: Princeton University Press, 1980).

43 Ariel Salzmann, *Tocqueville in the Ottoman Empire: Rival Paths to the Modern State* (Leiden: Brill, 2004).

became more "Ottomanized" as the segments attempting to fulfill the requirements of the Ottoman state expanded, despite the fact that the state had abandoned some administrative control throughout the transformation process and the beginning of the nineteenth century.[44] This concept, which is particularly important in terms of the study, is the fact that on the one hand, it included in the central administration and distribution networks of local people a distinctive expression of integration between the imperial center and the provinces across 150 years of decentralized "classical" administration. The state, thus, saw the formation of an integrated class of elites. On the other hand, the state saw the "localization" of members of the Ottoman bureaucracy. As Canbakal cites, "While the officials became local by making economic initiatives in the place they were appointed, the locals became Ottoman through salaries, duties, and tax-farming agreements. Marriage strengthened the ties in favor of both sides."[45] In terms of the *waqf*s in Jerusalem, this process was reflected in the new appointments to the *waqf* posts by share, the salary allocations for these duties, or the long-term leasing procedures of *waqf* properties.

Recent studies have revealed that the rise of the provincial elite may not herald the dissolution of the empire.[46] On the contrary, if we think of the transformation expressed by the concept of Ottomanization as the creation of a mixed elite composed of central officials and local notables functionally and socially intertwined, it is necessary to talk about the existence of concessionary arrangements originating from the Ottoman center that makes this possible.[47] Whether such privileges exist in the context of the *waqf*s of Jerusalem is also a question to be answered in the study. What distinguished the eighteenth century from earlier periods of the Ottoman Empire was the level of economic, social, and possibly also ideological integration between the center and the various provincial elites. In this context, the comments of Rifa'at Ali Abou-El-Haj, Ariel Salzmann and Baki Tezcan on the process are instructive.[48]

---

44 Khoury, *Osmanlı İmparatorluğu'nda Devlet*, 11–12.

45 Hülya Canbakal, *17. Yüzyılda Ayıntāb: Osmanlı Kentinde Toplum ve Siyaset* (Istanbul: İletişim Yayınları, 2009), 82.

46 Peirce and Hathaway took critical approaches to the subject. See Leslie P. Peirce, "Changing Perceptions of the Ottoman Empire: The Early Centuries," *Mediterranean Historical Review* 19, no. 1 (2004): 6–28; Jane Hathaway, "Rewriting Eighteenth-Century Ottoman History," *Mediterranean Historical Review* 19, no. 1 (2004): 29–53.

47 Canbakal, *17. Yüzyılda Ayıntāb*, 19.

48 Rifa'at 'Ali Abou-El-Haj, *Formation of the Modern State: The Ottoman Empire, Sixteenth to Eighteenth Centuries* (Albany: State University of New York Press, 1991); Ariel Salzmann, "An Ancien Régime Revisited: 'Privatization' and Political Economy in the Eighteenth-Century Ottoman Empire," *Politics & Society* 21, no. 4 (1993): 393–423; Baki Tezcan, *The*

The factors determining the developments in the eighteenth century were shaped since the second half of the sixteenth century. As a result of the military and financial crises experienced in the second half of the sixteenth century, the Ottoman State in the seventeenth century was no longer in its old position. The *tīmār* (landholding) regime, which was born from the economic and financial structure of the Middle Ages, lost its importance to a great extent and was replaced by an army equipped with firearms. Therefore, the application area of the tax-farming system widened against the landholding system.[49] The tax system, which is related to this system, became more dependent on cash taxes. The state was searching for new resources after being trampled under the burden of long and costly wars and inner turmoil in Anatolia. Many jurisdictions were turned into *muqāṭaʿa* units, and the taxes collected during a state of emergency were also made permanent.[50]

During this period (the entire seventeenth century), one can see that the measures taken by the state to protect the "Ottoman order" unintentionally prepared the rise of a new ruling power, *aʿyān* (leading local notables), in the provinces.[51] İnalcık emphasizes the tendency of provincial power-holders to cease representing the executive authority of the sultan, based on the power

Second Ottoman Empire: Political and Social Transformation in the Early Modern World (Cambridge: Cambridge University Press, 2010).

49 Mehmet Genç, "State and the Economy in the Age of Reforms: Continuity and Change," in *Ottoman Past and Today's Turkey*, ed. Kemal H. Karpat (Leiden: Brill, 2000), 99–147.

50 The effects of price movements, which are seen with the effect of silver flowing from America in Europe, and financial difficulties arising from long lasting and inefficient wars, have caused a general economic crisis. On the one hand, the Ottoman Empire had to keep up with the developments of the European states in war technology. The groomed cavalrymen were ineffective against German and Austrian infantry soldiers using firearms. As a result, the Ottoman Empire increased the number of janissaries. The number of janissaries, which was 21,094 in 1574, increased to 47,033 in 1609. In other words, there has been an increase of 123% in thirty-five years. On the other hand, the number of sipahis, which was 87,000 during the reign of Süleyman I, decreased to 45,000 in the early seventeenth century and to about eight thousand in the 1630s. Erol Özvar, *Osmanlı Maliyesinde Malikane Uygulaması* (Istanbul: Kitabevi Yayınları, 2003), 12. For more detailed information about the process, see Halil İnalcık, "Military and Fiscal Transformation in the Ottoman Empire, 1600–1700," *Archivum Ottomanicum* 6 (1980): 283–337, 53, 288; Erol Özvar, *Osmanlı Maliyesinde Malikane Uygulaması* (Istanbul: Kitabevi Yayınları, 2003), 9–17; Şevket Pamuk, *Osmanlı-Türkiye İktisadî Tarihi, 1500–1914* (Istanbul: İletişim Yayınları, 2005), 113–21.

51 Yaşar Yücel, *Osmanlı Ekonomi, Kültür, Uygarlık, Tarihine Dair Bir Kaynak: Esas Defteri (1640 Tarihli)* (Ankara: Türk Tarih Kurumu Yayınları, 1992), 657; Halil İnalcık, "Centralization and Decentralization in Ottoman Administration," in *Studies in Eighteenth-Century Islamic History*, ed. Thomas Naff and Roger Owen (Carbondale: Southern Illinois University Press, 1977), 27–52, 27.

given by the *sarıca-sekban* or *levend* troops (salaried soldiers) who they started to feed at their gates, especially since the end of the sixteenth century. The *reʿāyā* (ordinary people) were dealing not only with the increasing demands and security problems of the center, but also with the illegally collected taxes and other autonomous practices of these administrators.[52] From the end of the seventeeth century, the state appealed to the provincial power-holders in the provinces.[53] In this period, *aʿyān* assumed different roles according to the conditions of his local base: the executor of orders from the center, the protector of the *reʿāyā*, or even a supporter of the *qāḍī* (judge) against the abuses of local administrators or *de facto* administrators who guided him and other city administrators in line with local interests.[54] Abou-El-Haj emphasizes the influence of another development related to this process. In the same period, the class-based merit system of the classical period of Ottoman administration ended. Unity among the ruling elites decreased and political competition increased. This factor, which according to Abou-El-Haj, caused the governing administration to become increasingly decentralized, increased the demands on the peasant surplus product, and brought about instability in the tax system. The state began losing control in the process of harvesting the product.[55] Therefore, the decentralization that occured in the seventeenth and eighteenth centuries became dominant in the administration,[56] and localization and a restructuring of different levels and characteristics emerged in various parts of the empire.[57]

Following the path paved by Abou-El-Haj, Tezcan states that the Ottoman Empire transformed into an early modern state characterized by

52 For examples of such irregularities by rulers dating back to the early sixteenth century, see Halil İnalcık, *Osmanlı'da Devlet, Hukuk, Adâlet* (Istanbul: Eren Yayıncılık, 2000), 75–190.

53 Halil İnalcık, "Centralization and Decentralization in Ottoman Administration," in *Studies in Eighteenth-Century Islamic History*, ed. Thomas Naff and Roger Owen (Carbondale: Southern Illinois University Press, 1977), 27–52, 28; İnalcık, "Military and Fiscal"; Yücel Özkaya, *Osmanlı İmparatorluğunda Āyanlık* (Ankara: Türk Tarih Kurumu Yayınları, 1994), 8.

54 İnalcık, "Centralization and Decentralization," 28–29.

55 Abou-El-Haj, *Formation of the Modern State*, 39–42.

56 Yaşar Yücel, *Osmanlı Ekonomi, Kültür, Uygarlık, Tarihine Dair Bir Kaynak: Esas Defteri* (*1640 Tarihli*) (Ankara: Türk Tarih Kurumu Yayınları, 1992); Khoury, *Osmanlı İmparatroluğu'nda Devlet*, 3.

57 See Karl K. Barbir, *Ottoman Rule in Damascus, 1708–1758* (Princeton, NJ: Princeton University Press, 1980); Abou-El-Haj, *Formation of the Modem State*; Salzmann, "An Ancien Regime"; Karen Barkey, *Bandits and Bureaucrats: The Ottoman Route to State Centralization* (New York: Cornell University Press, 1994); Hathaway, "*Rewriting Eighteenth-Century Ottoman History*," 37.

a market-oriented economy, a financial system with a common currency, a legal system in which the *ʿulamāʾ* exercised control over the dynasty, a society in which class barriers were weakened, and a constitutional government in which power was increasingly shared by broader groups.[58] He defines early modernity as the period in which political power was shared by the wider masses – again as a result of economic transformation – and an identification between the rulers and the ruled developed. In the late medieval and early modern period, with the development of monetary economies, the privileged elite expanded to include some of the economically powerful and those historically excluded from the centers of political power, such as merchants, freelancers, and rentiers. It was the so-called openness of the ruling class with this limited expansion that led to the formation of a common identity that more directly united the rulers and the ruled over time, and that laid the foundation of the modern state by enabling the ruling classes to assert their political dominance over the masses of the people as if it were natural.[59] The third and fourth chapters of this study discuss in detail how and by which segments of society this transformation was undertaken through *waqf* in Ottoman Jerusalem.

In parts of the empire, several *aʿyān* families controlled economic and political affairs, including the Karaosmanoğulları in Western Anatolia, the Çapanoğulları in Central Anatolia, the Canikli Ali Paşaoğulları in Northeast Anatolia, Tepedelenli Ali Pasha in Epirus in Rumelia, Vidinli Osman Pasvandoğlu in the Lower Danube region (extending from Belgrade to the sea), Süleyman Pasha's family in Baghdad in the Arabian provinces, the Galilean family in Mosul, and Ali Bey in Egypt.[60] These provincial actors, who were added to the institutional framework of the empire in different ways, increased their power in the provinces, on the one hand, by entering the institutional umbrella of the empire, and on the other hand, through the transformation of the traditional administrative structure of the empire and localizing authority

58 Tezcan, *The Second Ottoman Empire*, 10.

59 Ibid, 235.

60 For detailed information, see Özkaya, *Osmanlı İmparatorluğu'nda Āyanlık*; Donald Quataert, *Workers, Peasants, and Economic Change in the Ottoman Empire, 1730–1914* (Istanbul: Isis Press, 1993), 85.; Canay Şahin, "The Rise and Fall of an Āyān Family in Eighteenth-Century Anatolia: The Caniklizādes (1737–1808)" (PhD diss., Bilkent University, 2003); Özcan Mert, *18. ve 19. Yüzyıllarda Çapanoğulları* (Ankara: Kültür Bakanlığı Yayınları, 1980); Necdet Sakaoğlu, *Anadolu Derebeyi Ocaklarından Köse Paşa Hanedanı* (Ankara: Yurt Yayınları, 1984); Robert Zens, "Pazvantoğlu Osman Paşa ve Belgrad Paşalığı, 1791–1807," in *Osmanlı İmparatorluğu'nda İsyan ve Ayaklanma*, ed. Jane Hathaway, trans. Deniz Berktay (Istanbul: Alkım, 2010), 141–65; Yuzo Nagata, *Muhsinzāde Mehmet Paşa ve Āyanlık Müessesesi* (Izmir: Akademi Kitabevi, 1999), 119–33; Jane Hathaway, ed., *Osmanlı İmparatorluğu'nda İsyan ve Ayaklanma*, trans. Deniz Berktay (Istanbul: Alkım, 2010).

in the provinces.[61] Over time, these people managed enormous resources and in some provinces monopolized the governorships. The vast majority of local dignitaries were from more modest families holding close to only one city and its environs, and before the eighteenth century, they were more oligarchic. Later, in the nineteenth century, after the banning of the *aʿyān*, who opposed the re-centralization efforts of Sultan Mahmud II, the ordinary *ashrāf* (notables) survived and were included in the new administrative structure brought by the Tanzimat. As we will discuss in this study, this segment was included in the administrative mechanisms in the period of this study.[62]

During the period under review, local military leaders controlled most major Palestinian cities and successfully monopolized regional trade. Ẓāhir al-ʿUmar and later Aḥmad Pasha al-Jazzār established political and economic power centers in the *sanjāq* of Ṣaydā, making ʿAkkā their base. They also gained significant control over southern Palestine, while Muḥammad Āghā Abū Nabbūt (1807–1818) ruled Jaffa. These three rulers achieved a semi-autonomous position within the empire, but none established a dynasty like the elite families

61 Albert Hourani, "Ottoman Reform and the Politics of Notables," in *The Beginnings of Modernization in the Middle East: The Nineteenth Century*, ed. William R. Polk and Richard L. Chambers (Chicago: University of Chicago Press, 1968), 41–68; Halil Inalcık, "Centralization and Decentralization in Ottoman Administration," *in Studies in Eighteenth-Century Islamic History*, ed. Thomas Naff and Roger Owen (Carbondale: Southern Illinois University Press, 1977), 27–52; Halil Inalcık, "Military and Fiscal Transformation in the Ottoman Empire, 1600–1700," in *Studies in Ottoman Social and Economic History* (London: Variorum Reprints, 1985), 283–337; Engin D. Akarlı, "Provincial Power Magnates in Ottoman Bilad al-Sham and Egypt, 1740–1840," *in La vie sociale dans les provinces arabes à l'époque ottomane*, ed. Abdeljelil Temimi (Zaghouan: Centre d'Études et de Recherches Ottomanes, 1988), 41–56; Bruce Masters, "Arap Vilayetlerinde Yarı Özerk Güçler," in *Türkiye Tarihi 1603–1839, Cilt III: Geç Osmanlı İmparatorluğu*, ed. Suraiya Faroqhi, trans. Fethi Aytuna (Istanbul: Kitabevi, 2011), 135–206; Dina Rizk Khoury, *Osmanlı İmparatorluğu'nda Devlet* (Ankara: İletişim Yayınları, 2009), 135–206; Ali Yaycıoğlu, "Provincial Power-Holders and the Empire in the Late Ottoman World: Conflict or Partnership?," in *The Ottoman World*, ed. Christine Woodhead (London: Routledge, 2012), 436–52.

62 Mustafa Nuri Paşa, *Netayic ül-Vukuat: Kurumları ve Örgütleriyle Osmanlı Tarihi*, vol. 2, ed. Neşet Çağatay (Ankara: Türk Tarih Kurumu Yayınları, 1979–80), 282–83; İsmail H. Uzunçarşılı, *Meşhur Rumeli Ayanlarından Tirsinikli İsmail, Yılık Oğlu Süleyman Ağalar ve Alemdar Mustafa Paşa* (Istanbul: Maarif Matbaası, 1942); Mert, *18. ve 19. Yüzyıllarda Çapanoğulları*, 1980; Inalcık, "Nature of Traditional Society," 54; Hourani, "Ottoman Reform," 60–62; Nagata, *Muhsinzāde Mehmet Paşa*, 119–33.

mentioned above.[63] It can be said that Jerusalem never entered the sovereignty of a single family or administrator.[64]

The political and socio-economic conditions that shaped the rise of local notables in Jerusalem differed significantly from those in other Palestinian cities and provincial centers of the Ottoman Empire. Until the late nineteenth century, the wealth of Jerusalem's notable families remained largely confined to the city. These notables neither owned extensive land or property in surrounding villages nor held tax-farming rights, limiting their influence in the countryside.[65] The inhabitants of Jerusalem were not the farmers who handled the city fields. Already the poor rural areas around the city were far from establishing the agricultural hinterland of the city.[66] Relations between the city and the countryside in Jerusalem, however, became more distinctive in the Tanzimat years when the dominance of the city was established.[67]

The main source of the economic power of influential families in Jerusalem was not tax-farming or *malikāne* (a lifetime tax-collecting privilege) rights, but rather mostly their religious and educational *waqf*s.[68] The *waqf*s served as instruments of political legitimacy, status, and many kinds of protection, from the personal level to the level of the sultanate.[69] The majority of the endowers in Jerusalem who were included in the scope of the study were members of the class of the *ʿulamāʾ* belonging to the local elite families of Jerusalem. These families, whose sources of economic power were largely based on religious and educational *waqf*s, played an active role in the *waqf* network of Jerusalem as founders, employees, and beneficiaries.[70] The aforementioned elite families had limited involvement in office sales. In Jerusalem, *waqf*s enhanced these families' social influence while also increasing their wealth. Charitable *waqf*s further enabled them to oversee social spaces and exert influence. Some

63 In two cases that may be exceptions to this situation, the ʿAmla family of Dayr Ghassāna and Bayt ʿŪlā established larger-scale local dynasties in Jerusalem. The ʿulamāʾ class, which made up the local political elite, had a purely civilian and much more pluralistic structure than other Palestinian cities. For detailed information, see Johann Büssow, *Hamidian Palestine: Politics and Society in the District of Jerusalem, 1872–1908* (Leiden: Brill, 2011), 317.

64 Büssow, *Hamidian Palestine*, 318.

65 Butrus Abu-Manneh, "Jerusalem in the Tanzimat Period: The New Ottoman Administration and Notables," *Die Welt des Islams*, new ser., 30, no. 1/4 (1990): 5–6.

66 Yehoshua Ben-Arieh, *Jerusalem in the 19th Century: The Old City* (Jerusalem: Yad Izhak Ben-Zvi Institute; New York: St. Martin's Press, 1984), 393.

67 Avcı, *Değişim Sürecinde*, 48–49.

68 Ze'evi, *Jerusalem*, 94–95.

69 Baer, "Jerusalem's Families," 109–20.

70 See Chapter 3.

families, profiting from long-term leasing revenues of *waqf* properties, gradually re-endowed these properties as private assets.[71]

These examples reflect results and conditions specific to Jerusalem's *waqf* practices. Contrary to the view that central control weakened and local forces gained independence, the Ottoman central government strengthened its authority over provincial cities by appointing officers and officials with strong local ties. This approach ensured system control through careful appointment policies and by allowing families to establish power bases that balanced local power structures.[72] Meanwhile, *waqf*s became a key mechanism for shaping and integrating relationship networks and institutions. They supported and supervised local networks while strengthening the economic base of state officials. The state ensured oversight of the *waqf* institution, a tool for implementing its policies, by incorporating the relationship networks of the *ʿulamāʾ*.[73]

In center-province relations, Jerusalem's elites served as "intermediaries" between state authority and local people. In daily politics, these elites, who often patronized locals, also held authority in their own right.[74] Recent studies analyze political processes from the perspective of ordinary people, viewing the empire's subjects as having agency in their own fate and challenging the idea that politics ends at the state's institutional boundaries with a monopoly by state notables. For instance, Faroqhi notes that "at least the wealthy among the provincial people" could take legitimate actions, which we might call "political," by using complaint mechanisms.[75]

The example of Jerusalem demonstrates that during the early modern period, the Ottoman State sought to preserve its authority by forging ties with provincial elites and mobilizing human resources. Despite its superficial nature, Ottoman control persisted throughout this period, as Jerusalem's local ruling elite had many reasons to remain loyal to the state. The Ottoman government supported the social and economic priorities of many leading figures. Some prominent Jerusalem families were exempt from taxes imposed by Ottoman sultans or their governors. As with the *waqf*s of the Ḥaramayn (Mecca and Medina), in certain *waqf*s controlled from Istanbul, the privileged positions of Jerusalem's prominent families were maintained in specific posts

71 Muḥammad Ali al-Alami, "The Waqfs of the Traditional Families of Jerusalem During the Ottoman Period," in *Ottoman Jerusalem: The Living City, 1517–1917*, ed. Sylvia Auld and Robert Hillenbrand (London: Altajir World of Islam Trust, 2000), 145–58.

72 Van Leeuwen, *Bir Osmanlı*, 153.

73 Ibid, 154.

74 Canbakal, *17. Yüzyılda Ayıntāb*, 19–22.

75 Faroqhi, "Political Activity," 35.

through the hereditary transfer of trusteeship from father to son[76] or the post of *naqīb al-ashrāf* appointed by the Ottoman sultan.[77]

Examining women's roles in the social system through *waqf*s offers a distinct perspective on Jerusalem's social and economic processes. Within the framework of sharīʿa and local tradition, women enjoyed a limited range of agency in property rights and personal status. Questions about what this reveal regarding social attitudes toward women, their lives in a male-dominated society, and mechanisms of social control have periodically arisen and been addressed in various contexts.

2.3 *Central Authority*

The fourth focus of this study is the nature of the Ottoman state apparatus and its operation in a provincial setting. While this study avoids engaging in debates about the central apparatus's nature, it includes documentation from central government representatives detailing how the center wields administrative control and the extent of its authority over *waqf*s. Additionally, complaints submitted by the local ruling elite to the Ottoman Imperial Council, particularly as *waqf* supervisors and auditors, will be frequently referenced. This section also explores the relationships between the local ruling elite and the society they inhabit. Unlike the countryside, Jerusalem's urban environment hosts diverse ethnic and religious groups, with religion playing a significant role in social divisions. Alongside the local Muslim population, the behavior of non-Muslims in the context of *waqf*s and social relations is another topic this study will examine.

---

76 The Ottoman central administration preferred to appoint members of the same family in place of the deceased officers, especially as clearly stated in the provisions. Butrus Abu-Manneh, "The Ḥusaynīs: The Rise of a Notable Family in 18th Century Palestine," in *Palestine in the Late Ottoman Period: Political, Social, and Economic Transformation*, ed. David Kushner (Leiden: E. J. Brill, 1986), 93–109. For instance, see VGMA, 814: 11; 814: 93; 815: 46/1; 46/2; 815: 120; 323: 23.

77 At the beginning of the seventeenth century, the *Muftī* of Jerusalem, who was the *naqīb al-ashrāf* of Jerusalem, died as the *muftī* of Jerusalem, while ʿAbd al-Qādir ibn Karīm al-Dīn al-Ḥusaynī, who was not his male heir, was running. The duty of *muftī* passed to the ʿAlamī and Jār Allāh families, one of the prominent families of Jerusalem. However, the ancestry of ʿAbd al-Qādir from the female side could continue the name al-Ḥusaynī and the Sharīf family. Ḥusaynīs held several religious duties such as *naqīb al-ashrāf* and *shaykh al-ḥaram* (officials of the two mosques Masjid al-Aqṣā and the Dome of the Rock). At the end of the eighteenth century, the Ḥusaynī regained the post of *muftī*. Apart from taking a few breaks, they continued this duty until the twentieth century. Majid Khadduri, *Arab Contemporaries: The Role of Personalities in Politics* (Baltimore: Johns Hopkins University Press, 1973), 69.

3 Microscale Review: State, Society, and the *Waqf* Institution in Early Modern Jerusalem

At the start of the eighteenth century, Muḥammad Pasha, appointed head of the *sanjāq* of Jerusalem in 1702, raised taxes and enforced their collection strictly, sparking a revolt led by the deputy *naqīb al-ashrāf*.[78] Muḥammad Ḥusaynī, from one of Jerusalem's influential families, leveraged his religious position for political activities. The *naqīb al-ashrāf* assumed control of the administration from 1703 to 1705. The rebellion, an uprising against the centrally appointed ruler, united the city's people, who closed the gates and endured hunger and siege hardships for two years.[79] In this sense, the *naqīb al-ashrāf*'s rebellion was not an ordinary rebellion that created an atmosphere of chaos.[80] The eventual failure of the rebellion caused the Ḥusaynī family to lose the administration and the post of *naqīb al-ashrāf* to the less-known Gudayya family. However, in the middle of the eighteenth century, the Gudayya family changed its name to Ḥusaynī and gave life to the Ḥusaynī family name.[81]

The second rebellion, which took place in 1825 with the support of the people, was a revolt initiated by some villagers around Jerusalem to avoid paying taxes, trying to take advantage of the weakness of the central administration. The rebels captured the city in a short time, with the support of Ibrāhīm Abū Ghawsh (Gosh), one of the bedouin Shaykhs who were influential between Ramla and Jerusalem. The Governor of Sayda, ʿAbdullāh Pasha, was able to

---

78 In Arab countries, those who were dealing with the matters of sayyids and sharifs descended from the Prophet were called *naqīb al-ashrāf*. In the Ottoman state, the position of *naqīb al-ashrāf* was established during the reign of Sultan Yıldırım Beyazıt in 1400 and Sayyid ʿAlī Naṭṭāʾ from Baghdad was first appointed to this position. *Naqīb al-ashrāf*s used to keep books containing the names of all sayyids and sharifs in the Ottoman lands through their district governors, states, *sanjāqs* and districts. Sayyids and sharifs, who checked whether they acted against the laws and customs, or the district governor in the provinces, also prosecuted and punished the fake sayyids and sheriffs. The position of *naqīb al-ashrāf* continued until the collapse of the Ottoman Empire. İsmail H. Uzunçarşılı, *Osmanlı Devleti'nin İlmiye Teşkilâtı* (Ankara: Türk Tarih Kurumu Yayınları, 1988), 164–68; Rüya Kılıç, Osmanlı'da Sayyidler ve Şerifler (Istanbul: Kitap Yayınevi, 2005).

79 For detailed information on the *naqīb al-ashrāf* uprising, see Adel Manna, "Eighteenth- and Nineteenth-Century Rebellions in Palestine," *Journal of Palestine Studies* 24, no. 1 (1994): 51–66, 54–56, 62–66.

80 Minna Rozen, "The Naqīb al-Ashrāf Rebellion in Jerusalem and Its Repercussions on the City's Dhimmis," *Asian and African Studies* 18 (1984): 250–51. For detailed information on the Ḥusaynī family, see Ilan Pappe, *The Rise and Fall of a Palestinian Dynasty: The Ḥusaynīs, 1700–1948* (Berkeley: University of California Press, 2010).

81 Rozen, "The Naqīb al-Ashrāf," 249–70; Adel Manna, "Eighteenth- and Nineteenth-Century Rebellions in Palestine," *Journal of Palestine Studies* 24, no. 1 (1994): 51–66.

suppress the rebellion in late 1826 by persuading the rebels.[82] The study starts with the first of these social movements – that is, this *naqīb al-ashrāf* uprising that took place in Jerusalem in 1703 – and ends with the administration of the Egyptian governor Mehmet Ali Pasha in 1831, which began approximately six years after the second rebellion.

The selection of these dates rests on sound reasoning, though some flexibility exists in choosing the start and end points for a local history study aiming to explain long-term social and political changes. During the period covered, these reasons manifest on two levels. Politically, the eighteenth century saw the rise of a local elite, increasingly aligned with Ottoman control while expanding their wealth and influence. As Jerusalem's provincial community became Ottomanized, Ottoman bureaucrats became localized. Economically and administratively, privileges gained through *waqfs* strengthened, laying the groundwork for new partnerships and networks. Much of this study focuses on the role of *waqfs* in the ascendancy and influence of Jerusalem's local elite. The year 1831 marks a turning point for Jerusalem, as Ibrahim Pasha, son of Egyptian Governor Mehmet Ali Pasha, occupied Syria and Palestine through a military campaign. Broadly, this period, though spanning only nine years, is seen as the start of significant shifts in the region's international standing, economic development, administrative structure, urban life, and traditional Muslim – non-Muslim relations.[83] In December 1840, Jerusalem entered the Ottoman Empire again. This period, which may be the subject of a separate study, is excluded from this study.

The arguments in this study address several key issues. The first chapter introduces Jerusalem up to 1831, situating the city within Ottoman history and detailing its administrative and physical conditions, including topography, demography, and economic resources, drawing largely on travelogues, *faḍā'il bayt al-maqdis* literature, and secondary sources for material descriptions of the city and its residents.

The study then focuses on the Muslim *waqf* network in Jerusalem, first identifying *waqfs* established after the Muslim conquest, particularly during the Ayyubid and Mamluk periods. Muslim *waqfs* founded in the city following the Ottoman conquest and recorded in eighteenth-century documents are categorized into education, religious, social-municipal, and social assistance *waqfs*. This analysis relies on *awqāf taḥrīr* (land registry of waqfs), *ḥurūfāt* (appointment records of the ruling class), *'atīq* (treasury) registers, and other edited

82 Kamil Jamil al-Asali, "Jerusalem under the Ottomans, 1516–1831," in *Jerusalem in History*, ed. Kamil Jamil al-Asali (London: Scorpion Publishing, 1989), 200–24.

83 Avcı, *Değişim Sürecinde*, 53.

works. The study classifies newly endowed *waqf*s in Jerusalem by their *waqfiyya* dates, geographical distribution within the city, and charitable purposes, while determining their revenue sources and operational procedures through analysis of local and central government archival sources.[84] In the study of *waqf*s, a geographical-vertical approach has been adopted. In the same section, *waqf*s founded by Christian and Jewish communities within the *waqf* network of Jerusalem are also included in the scope, respectively.

The third part of the study examines the relationships between state and society through the lens of Jerusalem's *waqf* practices, evaluating the privileges and titles tied to *ʿaskerī* (ruling) status, which granted access to state-organized benefits, and the role of *waqf*s in securing these advantages. It explores membership in the ruling class as both *waqf* founders and employees, noting that the pursuit of titles – whether formally or through usurpation – served as a defense against rising taxes while contributing to the Ottomanization process. This section also analyzes wealth distribution in Jerusalem linked to *waqf*s, identifying the wealthy within the context of ties between local families and the Ottoman civil service, highlighting local identity, center-provincial relations, and the state's role in distributing power in rural areas. It further investigates the supervision of *waqf*s as sources of wealth and influence, alongside the duties and privileges of Jerusalem's leading families in managing other *waqf*s. The privileged roles of these prominent families in operating *waqf* properties, their access to *surra* (grants, money, gifts) from the central government, shares from the *jizya* (poll tax), and other grants are also assessed.

The fourth chapter addresses daily politics through the interactions of Jerusalem's diverse social groups in and around the court, as reflected in *sharīʿa*

84 In the presentation titled "Vakıf İncelemelerinde Metod Araştırmaları (Research Method in *Waqf* Studies)," three types of approach styles are proposed by drilling method in order to reach a result in a short time. They include: 1 – The chronological and horizontal approach style, 2 – the geographical and vertical approach style, and 3 – the approach to the analysis of all aspects of the internal structures of the complexes and especially the socio-cultural life that took place there from the establishment to the present day. For details see Yediyıldız, "Osmanlı Döneminde," 20; Bahaeddin Yediyıldız, "Vakıf İncelemelerinde Metod Araştırmaları," in *II. Vakıf Haftası, 3–9 Aralık 1984: Konuşmalar ve Tebliğler* (Ankara: Renk Ofset Matbaacılık, 1985), 16–18. The first includes the separation of time into meaningful periods such as the Seljuk period, the Ottoman establishment period (1299–1500), and the Classical Ottoman period (1500–1585). The second includes an in-depth study of the subject in a certain number of narrow regions that could represent the entire Ottoman geography. The third includes the approach formed by the selection and examination of the complexes that will represent all of the complexes functioning in the Ottoman period. Some investigative analyses have been made according to these three research styles.

court registers, *aḥkām* (orders), and *fermāns* (imperial edicts), examining practical concerns about *waqf*s that deviate from ideal rules. It discusses relations among the central government, the public, and the local ruling elite, and, given Jerusalem's cosmopolitan nature, evaluates Christian and Jewish interventions in Muslim *waqf*s within the framework of inter-communal relations. Additionally, it considers the actions of Jerusalem's leading elites, who often acted as representatives for non-Muslims, and of non-Muslim subjects benefiting from *waqf* properties, including tenants.

In the second title in this section, the effect of the administration of the *waqf* on the administration of the city will be examined through more concrete examples. Various interventions made by different sections of society, especially the administrations of the *waqf*s, will be explained with examples. The collection of *waqf* incomes and taxes in Jerusalem will also be evaluated under a separate title. Those functions, closely related to urban autonomy and collective agency, will be examined with examples.

The Ottoman central government maintained an extensive bureaucratic network to oversee and manage provincial administrative processes, comprising officials organized in hierarchical categories and divisions, alongside administrative units and archives for processing and storing documents, collections, and records.[85] The study examines decisions and appointments related to *waqf*s, the most critical document group for understanding administrative mechanisms, using examples from sharīʿa court records, *aḥkām* (orders), *mühimme* (important matters), *ḥurūfāt* (appointment records of the ruling class), *ʿatīq* (treasury) records, and related *waqf* practices.

4 Sources

4.1 *Archival Sources*

The eighteenth-century archival sources on Jerusalem and its *waqf*s are varied, with Jerusalem's *sharīʿa* court registers serving as the primary source. *Waqfiyyas* and *waqf* registers, among the most significant archival sources for this study, were accessed from the Archives of the Palestinian State's Archive of Religious Affairs and the Preservation of Cultural Heritage (*Muʾassasat Iḥyāʾ al-Turāth wa-l-Buḥūth al-Islāmiyya*). In Turkey, records from the Ottoman Imperial Archives (BOA), the Archive of the General Directorate of Foundations (VGMA), the Archive of the General Directorate of Land Registry and Cadastre

85 Van Leeuwen, *Bir Osmanlı*, 152–53.

(TKGMA), and the Archive of the Museum of Islamic Art (IEMA) are analyzed to explore the relationship between society and *waqf*s.

The most detailed information about *waqf*s is found in Jerusalem's *sharīʿa* court registers (JS), imperial edict registers (*mühimme*), books of orders (*aḥkām*) and complaints (*şikayet*), *taḥrīr* and *waqf* accounting (*muhasebe*) books, and curriculum (*mufredat*) books. Additionally, several orders and appointment deed documents (*aḥkām* and *berevāt*) related to sultanic and local *waqf*s, sourced from the BOA and VGMA, are other key archival documents examined in this study. The details of all these sources are as follows:

4.2 Waqfiyyas (*Endowment Deeds*)

As one of the most fundamental archival sources of the *waqf*s, *waqfiyya*s contain important and detailed information about the *waqf*s on a wide range of issues.[86] The *waqf* founder's declaration specifies the purpose of the *waqf*, details the allocated income sources, the buildings comprising the *waqf*, the expenditure of income and related conditions, the number and roles of employees, their salaries, and the administration and supervision of the *waqf*. *Waqfiyya*s are the legal documents of *waqf*s, granting legal status upon approval. In the period studied, the *waqfiyya*s of newly established *waqf*s are analyzed. Jerusalem's *sharīʿa* court registers, located in the archive in the Masjid al-Aqṣā area, have digital copies preserved in the Archive of Religious Affairs and the Preservation of Cultural Heritage. These *waqfiyya*s are also compiled in separate books housed in the Archive of Religious Affairs and the Preservation of Cultural Heritage Section in Abu Dīs, with a small number of records also available in the VGMA.

4.3 *Jerusalem's* Sharīʿa *Court Registers* (*JS*)

The *sharīʿa* court registers offer a unique source for the social history of the Ottoman Empire, detailing the application and implementation of central administration policies in the provincial town of Jerusalem across all facets of daily life, including the local ruling elites, townspeople, villagers, Bedouin tribes, Christian and Jewish communities, their interrelationships, and matters such as debts, sales, price adjustments, complaints, escapes, or thefts. Every issue requiring registration, approval, or arbitration under the qadi's jurisdiction, along with decrees and orders from Istanbul, was recorded in these registries. This study, viewing the registers as a social product, highlights the interplay between the court, its records, and the fabric of social practices.

86 Köprülü, "Vakıf Müessesesi," 1–6.

However, the registers' wealth of detail can cause confusion, compounded by physical challenges like their storage conditions, gaps between volumes, or misplaced documents. In this study, which accounts for these issues, the interpretation of *sharīʿa* court registers as a key element in reconstructing socio-economic relations relies on a limited number of books, focusing on the legal and economic implications of *waqf*s, particularly transactions, disputes, and the institution's functioning as understood from the documents.

The material will not be used in any statistical or quantitative way. In order to comprehend certain developments, instead of making comparisons within the historical developments, various examples will be presented of their applications related to the *waqf*s in specific times and places.

*Waqf*s and related matters hold a significant place in Jerusalem's *sharīʿa* court registers.[87] This is primarily due to the abundance of *waqf* properties and charitable buildings in the city and the *qāḍī*'s (judge's) critical role in overseeing *waqf*s. The registers are nearly complete from the start of Ottoman rule.[88] The Jerusalem *sharīʿa* court registers comprise 565 books, with 415 in the original series and 150 in the new series. Written mostly in legible Arabic, they also contain documents like appointment deeds and imperial edicts (*fermāns*) in Ottoman Turkish. The eighteenth-century old series includes 81 registers, while the new series has ten. This study examines volumes 290, 297, 299, 305, and 306 of Jerusalem's *sharīʿa* court registers, covering the years 1222–1238/1807–1822, alongside select individual documents from the registers and accounting records.[89]

---

87 Musa Sroor, "Jerusalem's Islamic Archives: Sources for the Question of the Waqf in the Ottoman Period," *Journal of Palestine Studies* 34, no. 3/4 (2005): 82.

88 For an evaluation on all of the registries, see Jon E. Mandaville, "The Ottoman Court Records of Syria and Jordan," *Journal of the American Oriental Society* 86, no. 3 (1966): 311–19; idem, "The Jerusalem Sharīʿa Court Registers: A Supplement and Complement to the Central Archives," in *Studies on Palestine during the Ottoman Period*, ed. Moshe Ma'oz (Jerusalem: Magnes Press, 1975), 517–24; Beshara Doumani, "Palestinian Islamic Court Records: A Source for Socioeconomic History," *MESA Bulletin* 19, no. 2 (1985): 155–71, 161–64; Adel Manna, "The Sijill as a Source for the Study of Palestine during the Ottoman Period with Special Reference to the French Invasion," in *Palestine in the Late Ottoman Period: Political, Social, and Economic Transformation*, ed. David Kushner (Jerusalem: Yad Izhak Ben-Zvi; Leiden: E. J. Brill, 1986), 351–62; Khadr Salameh, "Aspects of the Sijills of the Sharīʿa Court in Jerusalem," in *Ottoman Jerusalem: The Living City, 1517–1917*, ed. Sylvia Auld and Robert Hillenbrand (London: Altajir World of Islam Trust, 2000), 103–44.

89 For an example, see JS 224: 185–187; JS 264: 149.

4.4 Ḥurūfāt *Registers*

Ḥurūfāt (appointment registers of the ruling elites), maintained within the Ottoman provincial administrative structure to record all duty assignments in a district, hold a significant place among VGMA documents, containing data spanning nearly the entire Ottoman geography.[90] In addition to the officer assignments made to the court in the relevant district, the *waqf*s found in the district, the tradesmen's guild organizations, and the official assignments related to city life are also recorded in the books.

The common point of these officers, whose appointments were recorded, is that they were members of the ruling class who worked in a district and defined as *'askerī*[91] within the Ottoman social structure

The *ḥurūfāt* registers, which record all *waqf* duty assignments, contain comprehensive data including the settlement unit, *waqf* name, endower's name, duty title, names of former and new officers, reasons for duty changes, wages, the administrator authorized to submit petitions for the position, and registration dates. These registers, rich in details about the city, city court, and tradesmen organizations, serve as a vital archival source for urban history researchers.

District names are listed alphabetically, and the registers are named accordingly. For instance, in the records of the Jerusalem District for the years 1102–1250/1690–1834, 1,644 entries are found across twenty-five books labeled *Kazā-i Kudüs-i Şerīf*.[92] By analyzing these records, this study assesses the efficiency of *waqf*s in Jerusalem, examining the appointments of *waqf* officials, the administration of *waqf*s, charitable institutions, officials' fees, and the distribution of properties and endowments within the city's structure.

---

90 In Baykara's book *Osmanlı Taşra Teşkilatı'nda 18. Yüzyılda Görev ve Görevliler (Anadolu)*, based on the appointment records in VGMA, Defter 1142 (*Muhtelif Elif ilā Yā Defteri*) from the *Ḥurūfāt Defterleri* series, the study identifies the duties and officials serving in courts, artisan guilds, and various aspects of urban life in district centers, noting the number of districts as 296. See Tuncer Baykara, *Osmanlı Taşra Teşkilâtında XVIII. Yüzyılda Görev ve Görevliler (Anadolu)* (Ankara: Vakıflar Genel Müdürlüğü Yayınları, 1990), 1–13. However, the aforementioned book does not contain records of districts starting with the letter *elif*. Therefore, considering the number of districts starting with the letter *Elif*, this number is much higher.

91 We used the term *zumre* to mean a legally defined status group and to mean estate (état/stande). Hülya Canbakal used the term in a similar way for eighteenth- and nineteenth-century Antep, while Schilcher applied it to seventeenth-century Damascus. See, Canbakal, *17. Yüzyılda Ayıntāb*, 81–92; Linda S. Schilcher, *Families in Politics: Damascene Factions and Estates of the 18th and 19th Centuries* (Stuttgart: Franz Steiner Verlag, 1985).

92 Şerife Eroğlu Memiş, *Ḥurūfāt Defterleri Kayıtlarına Göre Kudüs Vakıflarının Yeniden Değerlendirilmesi (1690–1834)* (institutional expert thesis, Vakıflar Genel Müdürlüğü, Ankara, 2012), 6–42; Eroğlu Memiş, 'Osmanlı Toplumsal', 115–46.

4.5 ʿAtīq/Atik (*Old, Treasury*) *and* Jadīd/Cedid (*New*) *Registers*

These books, housed in the VGMA, record appointments and decisions related to *waqf*s. The *ʿatīq* books, also known as treasury books, contain *waqf* appointment records prior to 1300/1882, after which they were transferred to the *cedīd* series. These records include the endower's name and nickname, the *waqf*'s location, its charities and properties, appointed or promoted officers and their fees, the *waqf*'s status as *mulḥāq* (administered by the endower's descendants) or *maẓbūṭ* (state-administered), and the registration date with a summary of the *waqfiyya*. The ledgers in the index, updated over centuries, document each new appointment with a summarized justification. Specifically, VGMA registers 163 (Jerusalem and Benghazi Index), 160 (Jerusalem *Cedīd*), and 515 (Jerusalem *ʿAtīq*) enable detailed study of the Khasseki Sultan *Waqf*, registered under numbers 3 (Ebru Anadolu), 523, and 524. Independent treasury records of other *waqf*s have been used to analyze charitable institutions, employee fees, and the allocation of employee fees within the annual expenses of *waqf*s.

4.6 Aḥkām (*Imperial Orders*) *and* Mühimme (*Important Affairs*) *Registers*

A series of books records complaints and resolutions submitted by Ottoman citizens to the Imperial Council, exercising their right to directly petition the sultan or authorized persons and institutions for grievance redress without intermediaries. Initially recorded in the *mühimme* registers, these decisions began appearing in dedicated complaint books in the second half of the seventeenth century, regardless of province. Due to factors like the weakening of central authority, increased complaint workloads, and the need to expedite resolutions, independent ledgers for each province were generally established starting in the second half of the eighteenth century, documenting solutions to complaints sent to the center. These *aḥkām* registers serve as a key source for assessing a region's social and economic conditions in local history, understanding conflicts between administrators and the public or among administrators, evaluating law applicability, and identifying legal gaps and resulting issues. They are also significant for the social history of the Palestinian region, reflecting community-administrator relations.

Some Jerusalem-related decisions appear in the Damascus series of *aḥkām* registers in the BOA, with seven registers relevant to this study's period and 175 records addressing Jerusalem's *waqf*s between 1742 and 1830. Additionally, 84 records from the Mecca, Medina, and Egypt *aḥkām* registers in the VGMA and twenty-seven records from other *aḥkām* registers are reviewed. By examining these, the study aims to uncover practical *waqf*-related issues and application difficulties reported to the Imperial Council by various societal groups. From the perspective of *waqf re'āyā*, this mechanism, primarily used by *waqf* administrators and officers, offers limited details about *waqf* charities.

In the *mühimme* registers in the BOA, copies of imperial edicts, responses to reports from across the empire, and summaries of petitions and complaints submitted to the center, along with their replies, are preserved. These special orders and general decrees, sent to provincial officials and judges, detail various administrative aspects. While *mühimme* records cover law and order, central government revenues, military regulations, foreign affairs, administrative duties, and other issues brought to the sultan's attention, imperial edicts primarily focus on cities or administrative units, occasionally mentioning petitions from specific villages. The limited number of imperial decrees related to Jerusalem's *waqfs* are included in this study.

Village operations tied to sultanic *waqfs* or large charitable-public *waqfs* are sometimes referenced in these imperial decrees. The *Sānī* Imperial Edict Indexes book, numbered 763, contains extracts of sixty-one edicts sent from the Imperial Council to the Dome of the Rock *Waqf* – one of Jerusalem's largest charitable-public *waqfs* – between 1167/1753 and 1191/1777 AH/CE, and fifty-five decree records of the Khasseki Sultan *Waqf* between 1173/1759 and 1223/1808 AH/CE. The Jerusalem Book of Khasseki Sultan, containing these extracts, numbered 523, is evaluated within this study. The central government's practices in addressing and resolving *waqf* issues, as reflected in imperial decrees sent to Jerusalem, are analyzed.

4.7 Taḥrīr (*Land Registry*) *Books and* Surra/Surre *Registers*

The title deed registers in the TKGMA record population, estimated tax revenues, and income distribution in specific administrative regions, compiled periodically by central government order to assess income from taxable sources, including agricultural production, market taxes, tolls, fines, personal taxes from ordinary people, and *jizya* collected from Christians and Jews. A portion of this income was allocated to military and administrative staff for their state service, forming the basis of the Ottoman *tīmār* (fief) system.

Many registers also included a *kānūnnāme* (sultanic decree), combining edicts and local customs to set tax rates for a given administrative unit, with its statute explaining the basis for tax assessments and recorded information, serving as a guide for the registers. Data from two books documenting the *sanjāq* of Jerusalem are used to analyze Jerusalem's *waqf* network. Additionally, books numbered 516 (967/1560 AH/CE) and 515 (1004/1595–6 AH/CE) from the General Directorate of Land Registry and Cadastre are examined. Among *waqf* records post-Ottoman conquest, the *İcmāl* (Summary) book numbered 517 (952/1545–6 AH/CE) and the *Evkāf Taḥrīr* (*Awqāf* Land Registry) book numbered

414 (registered as number 539 in the new classification) (970/1562–3 AH/CE) are reviewed. Though outside this study's chronological scope, these are used to analyze sixteenth-century *waqfs* within Jerusalem's *waqf* network, incorporating ninety-one *waqf* records from the *Waqfs* Registration Book, numbered five hundred fourteen, comprising sixteen leaves.

The *Surra* books, part of the *Awqāf Ḥaramayn Mukāta'a* Registers in the BOA, are analyzed in this study, detailing who submitted the *surra*, who delivered it from Istanbul to Jerusalem, the amounts, and the places and officials receiving shares. Alongside sultans sending *surra*, these books also identify local recipients of *surra* shares where the *waqf*'s allocation is recorded. To track changes in duties and officials among shareholders, *surra* books numbered 1971, 2224, 2546, and 2855 are selected, spaced roughly ten years apart. Additionally, records from the *Awqāf* Classification (EV.d), *Awqāf* Accounting (EV.MH), *Awqāf Ḥaramayn* Accounting Classification (EV.HMH.d) for *waqf* accounting, as well as documents from funds detailing officer appointments, the *Awqāf Mektūbī* (Letter) Classification (EV.MKT), and the *Awqāf Mektūbī Cihāt* (*Waqf* Appointment Letters) Classification (EV.MKT.CHT), are examined within the study's scope.

4.8 *Travelogues and* Faḍā'il Bayt al-Maqdis *Literature*

Travelogues are well-known as vibrant sources for the periods they describe. Evliyā Çelebi, a prominent figure in the Ottoman travelogue tradition, dedicated the ninth volume of his *Seyahatnāme* to his pilgrimage to Mecca, Medina, Jerusalem, and Hebron. In it, he notes that Jerusalem and Hebron are also called *al-Ḥaramayn*, reflecting the designation *al-Ḥaramayn al-Sharīfayn* used for Mecca and Medina, Islam's two holiest cities.[93] Evliyā Çelebi made his second visit to Jerusalem in 1082/1671–72 AH/CE, about twenty-four years after his first visit in 1058/1648–49 AH/CE. He deliberately reserved descriptions of Jerusalem for the ninth volume of his *Seyahatnāme*, uniting the four holiest pilgrimage cities in one book. After visiting Jerusalem, he traveled to Hebron, providing detailed accounts of the Ottoman administration, the prophets' graves in the *Ḥaram al-Khalīl*, and the Table of Abraham, also known as the *Simāt al-Khalīl*.[94]

About nineteen years after Evliyā Çelebi, Shaykh 'Abd al-Ghanī al-Nābulusī traveled from Damascus to Jerusalem and Hebron in 1101/1689–90 AH/CE. Shaykh 'Abd al-Ghanī al-Nābulusī (1050–1143/1641–1731 AH/CE), whose ancestors were from Nablus in Palestine, resided in Damascus and was a prominent

93 Evliyā Çelebi, *Seyahatnāme*, 1935, 488–98.

94 ibid., 495.

Ḥanafī qāḍī (judge), Ṣūfī, and prolific scholar, authoring over three hundred published books and monographs. His first of two journeys to Jerusalem, recorded in *al-Ḥaḍra al-Unsiyya fī al-Riḥla al-Qudsiyya* [The Intimate Presence on the Jerusalem Journey], took place in 1101/1689–90 AH/CE. This forty-five-day journey, including eighteen days in Jerusalem, also encompassed Hebron.[95] In his travelogue's introduction, he described Jerusalem as the most honorable city and first qibla among protected cities after Mecca and Medina, likening Jabal al-Ṭūr, the tomb of Prophet Moses, and its surroundings to the Mina valley, and comparing al-Khalīl to Mount Arafat, noting that visiting al-Khalīl completes a pilgrimage, similar to how Mount Arafat completes the hajj, offering a lesser degree of pilgrimage or reward.[96]

Among Arab travelers documenting Jerusalem, Muṣṭafā al-Bakrī al-Ṣiddīqī, who visited from Damascus in 1122/1710 AH/CE, seventeen years after al-Nābulusī, wrote *al-Ḥamrā' al-Ḥāsiyya fī al-Riḥla al-Qudsiyya* [The Marginal Notes of al-Ḥamrā' on the Journey to Jerusalem]. Additionally, Muṣṭafā al-Asad al-Lukaymī al-Dimyāṭī, from Dimyāṭ, visited Jerusalem in 1143/1731 AH/CE, documenting his journey in *Mawāniḥ al-Uns bi-Riḥlati li-Wādī al-Quds* [The Gifts of Intimacy through the Journey to the Valley of Jerusalem], published under various titles on different dates.[97]

François René de Chateaubriand, a Western traveler, visited Jerusalem as a pilgrim in 1806 and recorded his experiences in Volume III of his work, *Itinéraire de Paris à Jérusalem* [Paris-Jerusalem Journey]. Alongside details on Jerusalem's geographical, social, and economic conditions, he described Ottoman central government practices, with a particular focus on his impressions of the pilgrimage and the circumstances of his community.

Although many *faḍā'il al-Quds* works – thirty from the Mamlūk period alone – had been written, *al-ʿUns al-Jalīl bi-Tārīkh al-Quds wa-l-Khalīl* [The Noble Companionship: On the History of Jerusalem and Hebron] surpasses them in scope and design, structured by Mujīr al-Dīn in four parts. The first part, blending *faḍā'il* with the pre-Islamic and Islamic history of Jerusalem up to the mid-thirteenth century, spans over four hundred pages, emphasizing the enduring sacredness of *al-Quds* and its surrounding territory within the monotheistic tradition, particularly in Islam. Mujīr al-Dīn highlights Jerusalem's connection to Mecca, stating that a pilgrimage from *al-Aqṣā* to the *Kaʿba* ensures

95 ʿAbd al-Ghanī ibn Ismāʿīl al-Nābulusī, *al-Ḥaḍra al-Unsiyya fī al-Riḥla al-Qudsiyya*, ed. ʿAbd al-Wārith Muḥammad ʿAlī (Beirut: al-Maṣādir, 1990).

96 al-Nābulusī, *al-Ḥaḍra al-Unsiyya*, 21.

97 See Abdul-Karim Rafeq, "Ottoman Jerusalem in the Writings of Arab Travelers," in *Ottoman Jerusalem: The Living City, 1517–1917*, ed. Sylvia Auld and Robert Hillenbrand (London: Altajir World of Islam Trust, 2000), 63–73.

God's forgiveness of all sins, with *Bayt al-Maqdis* revered as equally holy in the seven heavens as on earth, where each prayer, per the Prophet, equals a thousand prayers, cleansing the worshipper of sin and restoring primal innocence.[98]

Another eighteenth-century manuscript by Ashraf Effendi, son of Müeyyedzāde Ali Effendi of Merzifon, *Mir'āt al-Ṣafā* [Mirror of Happiness], written by Abdurrahman Ashraf Effendi in 1122/1710 AH/CE, describes Mecca, Medina, Jerusalem, and Hebron as four *Ḥaram* regions in separate sections. Presented to Nevşehirli Damat İbrahim Pasha, the Ottoman grand vizier, its final section details the graves of the Prophet, Companions, and saints in these locations.[99]

In another manuscript, al-Naqshbandī al-Murādī reiterates Jerusalem's *faḍā'il*, listing its merits and religious significance for Muslims, starting with the verse of *al-Isrā'*, which he deems sufficient merit alone. He describes Jerusalem as the closest point on earth to heaven, the source of all sweet water and must, the dividing line between heaven and hell, and the site of the Day of Judgment, where seven thousand angels descend nightly to praise God at *Masjid Bayt al-Maqdis*.[100]

5 Research and Studies

Jerusalem, a holy city and significant religious center throughout history, has drawn attention from researchers across disciplines, resulting in diverse narratives, definitions, and analyses. Key studies relevant to this work include *al-Mufaṣṣal fī Tārīkh al-Quds* [A Comprehensive History of Jerusalem] by al-ʿĀrif al-ʿĀrif, which traces Jerusalem's history from pre-Islamic times to 1947 through its spatial organization, offering valuable details on the dates and periods of *waqf* structures, with many religious buildings, mostly *waqf* works, described in depth.[101] *Mamluk Jerusalem: An Architectural Study* by Michael Hamilton Burgoyne, with historical research by Donald Sidney Richards, spans six hundred twenty-three pages, featuring numerous color and black-and-white photographs, architectural illustrations, and two large fold-out plans. It explores Mamluk-era architecture in Jerusalem's Old City, covering construction

98 Al-Ḥanbalī, *al-Uns al-Jalīl*, vol.1, 226–35.

99 Ali Rıza Ayar, "Abdurrahman Eşref Efendi'nin (öl. 1738) 'Mir'ātü's-Safā' Adlı El Yazmasının Tanıtılması," in *Uluslararası Avrasya Sempozyumu, 4–7 Ekim 2017* (Amasya: Amasya Üniversitesi, 2017), 777–86.

100 Şerife Eroğlu Memiş, "'*Nebzetü'l-Menāsik*': en-Nakşibendī el-Muradī'nin Hac Rehberi'nde Kudüs Bahsi," in *Dini, Tarihi ve Edebi Açıdan Kudüs*, ed. İbrahim Çelik et al. (Istanbul: DBY Yayınları, 2018), 169–99.

101 al-ʿĀrif. *al-Mufaṣṣal.*

methods, materials, decorative techniques, historical context under Mamluk rule, and conservation suggestions, serving as a seminal source for understanding Jerusalem's Mamluk architectural heritage.

Another key work, *al-Madāris fī Bayt al-Maqdis fī l-ʿAṣrayn al-Ayyūbī wa-l-Mamlūkī* [Educational Institutions in Bayt al-Maqdis during the Ayyubid and Mamluk Eras] by ʿAbd al-Jalīl Ḥasan ʿAbd al-Mahdī, examines the education system, scholars, curriculum, and *madrasa*s of the Ayyubid and Mamluk periods in Jerusalem, providing valuable insights.[102] Mujīr al-Dīn al-Ḥanbalī's *al-ʿUns al-Jalīl bi-Tārīkh al-Quds wa-l-Khalīl* is a primary reference for the historical development of Jerusalem and Hebron before the Ottoman conquest and their *waqf* works.[103] Additionally, *Al-Quds al-Mamlūkiyya: A History of Mamluk Jerusalem Based on the Ḥaram Documents* by Huda Lutfi, first published in 1985, analyzes the social, economic, and administrative aspects of Jerusalem during the Mamluk period (1250–1517), using *Ḥaram al-Sharīf* estate records. Lutfi's study offers unique insights into daily life, emphasizing textiles and clothing in property inventories from laborers to wealthy merchants, with appendices providing data on *Ḥaram* property inventories, occupations, and geographical or ethnic origins, enriching this study's analysis.

Taking a different approach to the *Ḥaram* documents, Christian Müller's *Der Kadi und seine Zeugen: Studie der mamlukischen Ḥaram-Dokumente aus Jerusalem* [The Qadi and His Witnesses: A Study of the Mamluk Ḥaram Documents from Jerusalem] offers an in-depth analysis of the judicial system in fourteenth-century Mamluk Jerusalem. Based on nearly nine hundred documents from the *Ḥaram al-Sharīf*, mostly dated between 1391 and 1395, Müller provides deep insights into the practices of notaries and judges, offering valuable historical context for this study through details on *waqf* litigation in Mamluk-era Jerusalem. Heinz Halm's *The Reestablishment of Sunni fiqh in Jerusalem under Ayyubid Rule*,[104] and Yehoshua Frenkel's *Awqaf in Mamluk Bilad al-Sham* and *Political and Social Aspects of Islamic Religious Endowments (awqāf): Saladin in Cairo (1169–73) and Jerusalem (1187–93)* are considered for their detailed information on Jerusalem during the Ayyubid and Mamluk periods.[105]

102 Abd al-Mahdī, *al-Madāris fī Bayt al-Maqdis*.

103 al-Ḥanbalī, *al-Uns al-Jalīl*.

104 Heinz Halm, "The Reestablishment of Sunni Fiqh in Jerusalem under Ayyubid Rule," in *The Third International Conference on Bilad al-Sham: Palestine (19–24 April 1980)*, vol. 1 (Amman: University of Jordan, 1983).

105 See Yehoshua Frenkel, "Political and Social Aspects of Islamic Religious Endowments (Awqāf): Saladin in Cairo (1169–73) and Jerusalem (1187–93)," *Bulletin of the School of Oriental and African Studies* 62, no. 1 (1999): 1–20; Yehoshua Frenkel, "Awqāf in Mamlūk Bilād al-Shām," *Mamlūk Studies Review* 13, no. 1 (2009): 149–66.

For the Ottoman period, David S. Powers' "Revenues of Public *Waqfs* in Sixteenth Century Jerusalem," based on al-Ḥanbalī's work, is analyzed for its inventory of charitable-public *waqfs* of the period.[106] *Evkaf ve Emlākü'l-Müslimīn fī Filistīn* [The Pious Foundations and Real Estates in Palestine], prepared by Mehmet İpşirli and Muḥammad Tamimi based on land registry records, is available in English and Arabic. Although it covers an earlier period of the *sanjāq* of Jerusalem, it provides historical context for studying *waqfs* and real estates in the city.[107] Similarly, Wolf-Dieter Hütteroth and Kamal Abdulfattah's *Historical Geography of Palestine, Transjordan and Southern Syria in the Late 16th Century* is a geographical study based on sixteenth-century *mufaṣṣal* ledgers, serving as a key reference for analyzing the administrative organization, population, tax system, economic structure, and potential of the Palestinian region.[108]

After the Ottoman conquest, studies on Jerusalem and its *sanjāq* often focus on the nineteenth and twentieth centuries, particularly from the time of the conquest or the Tanzimat period.[109] While the seventeenth century has been partially explored, eighteenth-century Jerusalem remains under-researched. Studies on Jerusalem's *waqfs* typically examine one or a few *waqfs*, falling short of a comprehensive overview. Among post-conquest studies on the *sanjāq* of Jerusalem, Amnon Cohen and Bernard Lewis' *Population and Revenue in the Towns of Palestine in the Sixteenth Century* provides valuable insights into the administrative and socio-economic conditions of the Palestinian region.[110] Amnon Cohen's *Palestine in the 18th Century* focuses solely on the *sanjāq* of Jerusalem, employing a similar method but covering a different period.[111]

106 See David S. Powers, "Revenues of Public Waqfs in Sixteenth-Century Jerusalem," *Archivum Ottomanicum* 9 (1984): 163–202.

107 Mehmet İpşirli and M. Tamimi, *Evkâf ve Emlâkü'l-Müslimîn fî Filisṭīn* (Istanbul: İslam Tarih, Sanat ve Kültür Araştırma Merkezi, 1982).

108 See Wolf-Dieter Hütteroth and Kamal Abdulfattah, *Historical Geography of Palestine, Transjordan, and Southern Syria in the Late 16th Century* (Erlangen: Fränkische Geographische Gesellschaft, 1977).

109 Emine Erdoğan, *XVI. Yüzyılda Kudüs Merkez ve Nahiyesinde Nüfus ve Etnik Yapı* (master's thesis, Gazi Üniversitesi, 1998); Musa Sroor, *Fondations pieuses en mouvement: De la transformation du statut de propriété des biens waqfs à Jérusalem (1858–1917)* (Damascus: Institut Français du Proche-Orient; Aix-en-Provence: IREMAM, 2010); Mustafa Öksüz, *Şam Eyaleti'nin Güney Sanjaqlarında (Filistin) Nüfus (XVI. Yüzyıl)* (PhD diss., Mimar Sinan Güzel Sanatlar Üniversitesi, 2016); Salim Tamari, "Waqf Endowments in the Old City of Jerusalem: Changing Status and Archival Sources," in *Ordinary Jerusalem, 1840–1940: Opening New Archives, Revisiting a Global City*, ed. Angelos Dalachanis and Vincent Lemire (Leiden: Brill, 2018), 487–509, 490–509.

110 See Bernard Lewis and Amnon Cohen, *Population and Revenue in the Towns of Palestine in the Sixteenth Century* (Princeton, NJ: Princeton University Press, 1978).

111 See Amnon Cohen, *Palestine in the 18th Century* (Jerusalem: Magnes Press, 1973).

Baha Tanman and Ahmet Vefa Çobanoğlu's *Osmanlı Dönemi'nde Kudüs: Kent Dokusu, Mimarlık ve Çini Sanatına İlişkin Bir Araştırmanın İlk Sonuçları* [*Jerusalem in the Ottoman Period: Preliminary Results of a Study on the Urban Fabric, Architecture, and Tile Art*] offers detailed information on the architectural features and construction periods of Jerusalem's buildings, though it primarily addresses the sixteenth century.[112] Mehmet Tütüncü's *Turkish Jerusalem (1516–1917): Ottoman Inscriptions From Jerusalem and Other Palestinian Cities* includes original records and English translations of inscriptions from most *waqf* buildings in Jerusalem and other Palestinian cities.[113] This study also provides important information on the dates of construction, their builders and various features of the buildings.

Among the studies on the city of Jerusalem after the Ottoman conquest, it is worth mentioning *Ottoman Jerusalem: The Living City: 1517–1917*, published in two volumes edited by Sylvia Auld and Robert Hillenbrand. Numerous articles in the book provide detailed information on Ottoman Jerusalem.[114] In addition, Dror Ze'evi's *Jerusalem: Society and Economy in a 17th Century Ottoman Sanjāq* examines the social and economic life in the *Sanjāq* of Jerusalem in the 17th century, and the *waqfs* in Jerusalem are also included from time to time.[115]

The proceedings of the 7th International Symposium on the History of *Bilād al-Shām*, organized jointly by the *Bilād al-Shām* Historical Society, Jordan, Yarmouk and Damascus Universities on September 10–14, 2006, were published under the title of *Palestine* in Volume 3 of the proceedings book titled *Foundations of Bilād al-Sham from the Beginning of the Islamic Conquests to the End of the 20th Century*, edited by Muḥammad Adnan Bakhit. In the article titled ., "Dirāsa fī Maṣādir al-Infāq ʿalā Madāris al-Quds al-Sharīf wa-Miṣr

112 See Baha Tanman and Ahmet Vefa Çobanoğlu, "Osmanlı Dönemi'nde Kudüs: Kent Dokusu, Mimarlık ve Çini Sanatına İlişkin Bir Araştırmanın İlk Sonuçları," in *Ortadoğu'da Osmanlı Dönemi Kültür İzleri Uluslararası Bilgi Şöleni Bildirileri* (*25–27 Ekim 2000, Hatay*), vol. 2 (Ankara: Atatürk Kültür Merkezi Başkanlığı Yayınları, 2001), 511–43; Eroğlu Memiş, "Between Ottomanisation and Local Networks," 71–128.

113 See Mehmet Tütüncü, *Turkish Jerusalem* (*1516–1917*)*: Ottoman Inscriptions from Jerusalem and Other Palestinian Cities* (Haarlem, Netherlands: SOTA, 2006).

114 See articles on the topic from the volme *Ottoman Jerusalem: The Living City, 1517–1917*, ed. Sylvia Auld and Robert Hillenbrand (London: Altajir World of Islam Trust, 2000), specifically Abdul-Karim Rafeq, "The ʿUlamāʾ of Ottoman Jerusalem (16th–18th Centuries)," 45–52; Ernst Axel Knauf, "Ottoman Jerusalem in Western Eyes," 73–76; Lawrence I. Conrad, "The Khālidī Library," 191–209; Kamil Jamil al-Asali, "The Libraries of Ottoman Jerusalem," 285–89; Khadr Salameh, "Aspects of the Sijills of the Sharīʿa Court in Jerusalem," 103–44; Kamil Jamil al-Asali, "The Cemeteries of Ottoman Jerusalem," 279–84; Martin Dow, "The Hammams of Ottoman Jerusalem," 519–24; Paolo Cuneo, "The Urban Structure and Physical Organization of Ottoman Jerusalem in the Context of Ottoman Urbanism," 211–20; Klaus Kreiser, "The Place of Jerusalem in the Ottoman Perception," 53–57.

115 Ze'evi, *Kudüs*.

wa-Fātiḥa ʿalā Ḍawʾ Daftar Taḥrīr (T.D. 131) (932/1525–939/1531–1533)," written by Muḥammad Adnān Bakhīt, detailed information about the *madrasas* in Jerusalem and Egypt between 1531–1532 is presented based on the land registry book numbered 131.[116] The information on the importance of the *waqfs* of Jerusalem in social and economic life in the article titled "al-Awqāf al-Islāmiyya fī al-Quds: Dirāsa Ijtimāʿiyya wa-Iqtiṣādiyya, 1212–1700/1797–1918," prepared by Ziyād ʿAbd al-Aziz al-Madanī in the same study, has been a source of reference for this study.[117]

Butrus Abu-Mannah's *The Ḥusaynīs: The Rise of a Family in 18th Century Palestine*, edited by David Kushner, is an important source of reference on the prominent family of Jerusalem that served as *naqīb al-ashrāf* for many years.[118] In a recent study on Jerusalem, Abdalqader Steih, Ottoman Jerusalem (1700–1757), described Ottoman rule in Jerusalem in the 18th century.[119] It provides a nuanced understanding of how the Ottoman Empire integrated Jerusalem into its administrative and cultural framework.

Another study is Yehoshua Ben-Arieh's *Jerusalem in the 19th Century the Old City*.[120] This work is based on the reports of the British Consulate and the impressions of travelers who visited the region. In her pioneering study on the history of the city of Jerusalem titled *Değişim Sürecinde Bir Osmanlı Kenti: Kudüs (1890–1914)*, Yasemin Avcı describes the formation of modern Jerusalem and analyzes the *Tanzimat* reforms in Jerusalem that opened this field in Turkey. The introductory section of the study, which includes a historical background on the city, provides valuable details for this study.[121]

In the first of the studies on the *waqfs* of Jerusalem during and after the Ottoman period, Amy Singer's research titled *Kadılar, Kullar, Kudüs'lü Köylüler*, based on the *Awqāf* Land Registry Books, provides detailed information on the

116 Muḥammad ʿAdnān Bakhīt, "Dirāsa fī Maṣādir al-Infāq ʿalā Madāris al-Quds al-Sharīf wa-Miṣr wa-Fātiḥa ʿalā Ḍawʾ Daftar Taḥrīr (T.D. 131) (932/1525–939/1531–1533)," in *al-Muʾtamar al-Dawlī al-Sābiʿ li-Tārīkh Bilād al-Shām: Awqāf Bilād al-Shām min Badʾ al-Futūḥāt al-Islāmiyya ilā Nihāyat al-Qarn al-ʿIshrīn*, vol. 3, ed. Muḥammad ʿAdnān Bakhīt (Amman: University of Jordan Press, 2008), 1–42.

117 Ziyād ʿAbd al-ʿAzīz al-Madanī, "al-Awqāf al-Islāmiyya fī al-Quds: Dirāsa Ijtimāʿiyya wa-Iqtiṣādiyya, 1212–1700/1797–1918," in *al-Muʾtamar al-Dawlī al-Sābiʿ li-Tārīkh Bilād al-Shām: Awqāf Bilād al-Shām min Badʾ al-Futūḥāt al-Islāmiyya ilā Nihāyat al-Qarn al-ʿIshrīn*, vol. 3, ed. Muḥammad Adnān Bakhīt (Amman: University of Jordan Press, 2008), 309–35.

118 See Abu-Manneh, "The Ḥusaynīs," 93–109.

119 Abdalqader Steih, *Osmanlı Kudüs'ü (1700–1757)* (Istanbul: Taş Mektep Yayın Atölyesi / ORDAF, 2017).

120 See Ben-Arieh, *Jerusalem in the 19th Century*.

121 See Yasemin Avcı, *Değişim Sürecinde Bir Osmanlı Kenti: Kudüs (1890–1914)* (Ankara: Phoenix Yayınevi, 2004).

waqf lands in Jerusalem.[122] Amy Singer's *Osmanlı'da Hayırseverlik: Kudüs'te bir Haseki Sultan İmareti*, the founding period of the Khasseki Sultan's public kitchen is analyzed by comparing two *waqfiyyas*, one in Ottoman and the other in Arabic, and the practices of the *waqf* are traced from the Jerusalem *sharīʿa* court registers.[123] Her approach to the subject has been seminal for our study. Oded Peri's *The Waqf as an Instrument to Increase and Consolidate Political Power: The Case of Haseki Sultan Waqf in Late Eighteenth-Century Ottoman Jerusalem* examines the instrumentality of the Khasseki Sultan's public kitchen in Jerusalem in terms of consolidating the legitimacy of the Ottoman central administration. Oded Peri's article, "Muslim Waqf and Collection of *jizya* in late Eighteenth-Century Jerusalem," which is included in the study edited by God Gabriel Gilbar, contains information on the amount of *jizya* collected in Jerusalem and where it was allocated, which is also important for the study.[124] Another article by Oded Peri, "*Waqf* and Ottoman Welfare Policy: The Poor Kitchen of Khasseki Sultan in Eighteenth-Century Jerusalem," attempts to identify the position of the Khasseki Sultan's public kitchen in the 18th century in the context of Ottoman welfare policies. At this point, information on the various segments of society that benefited from the *imāret* is also presented, although it is not mentioned in the *waqfiyya*.[125] The article "Jerusalem's Families of Notables and Waqf in the Early 19th Century in Palestine in the Late Ottoman Period," edited by David Kushner, and the chapter "The Dismemberment of Awqāf in Early Nineteenth-Century in Ottoman Palestine 1800–1914" by Baer, are both very important for the information they provide on the relationship between Jerusalem's leading local families and *waqfs* in the 19th century.[126]

Although Abdullatif Tibawi's *The Islamic Pious Foundations in Jerusalem* has a general title in terms of *waqfs*, when the study is analyzed in terms of content, it focuses on the periods of British rule and the State of Israel.[127] In the

122 See Singer, *Kadılar, Kullar.*

123 See Singer, *Osmanlı'da Hayırseverlik.*

124 See Oded Peri, "Muslim Waqf and Collection of Jizya in Late Eighteenth-Century Jerusalem," in *Ottoman Palestine, 1800–1914: Studies in Economic and Social History*, ed. Gad G. Gilbar (Leiden: E. J. Brill, 1990), 287–98.

125 See respectively Oded Peri, "The Waqf as an Instrument to Increase and Consolidate Political Power: The Case of Khasseki Sultan Waqf in Late Eighteenth-Century Jerusalem," *in Studies in Islamic Society: Contributions in Memory of Gabriel Baer*, ed. Gabriel R. Warburg and Gad G. Gilbar (Haifa: Haifa University Press, 1984), 47–62; Oded Peri, "Waqf and Ottoman Welfare Policy: The Poor Kitchen of Hasseki Sultan in Eighteenth-Century Jerusalem," *Journal of the Economic and Social History of the Orient* 32, no. 2 (1989): 167–86.

126 See Baer, "Jerusalem's Families," 109–123; Baer, "The Dismemberment of Awqaf," 299–319.

127 See Tibawi, *The Islamic Pious Foundations.*

part of the book covering the Ottoman period, the importance of Jerusalem for Muslims, especially for the Maghribīs, the North African region that today includes Tunisia, Morocco and Algeria, is discussed, and the *waqfiyya*s of the endowment established by Ṣalāḥ al-Dīn Ayyūbid's son Mālik al-Afḍal and Abū Madyan al-Ghawth's grandson Shuʿayb ibn Muḥammad ibn al-Shuʿayb are analyzed. Another recently published study on the Maghāriba neighborhood and its *waqf*s evaluated the neighborhood *waqf*s within a "local" *waqf* network.[128]

The article titled *The Waqfs of the Traditional Families of Jerusalem During the Ottoman Period*, which is included in the first volume of the work edited by Sylvia Auld and Robert Hillenbrand, is extremely important for our study, and was written by Muḥammad Ali al-Alami.[129] In the study, detailed information about the lineages of the traditional families of Jerusalem and their instrumentalization of *waqf*s in gaining wealth, influence and power thanks to these ties are discussed. However, since the study covers the entire Ottoman period, the analysis and numerical data are expressed in a very general way. In the second volume of the work, which is devoted to architectural studies under the title of *Architectural Survey*, the architectural structures of the Ottoman period are examined one by one.[130] Of the ten buildings built in the period covering the study area, five of them were of *waqf* origin and were introduced in detail in accordance with the *waqfiyya*s. Diana Abouali's work, which deals with the relationship between Saladin Ayyubid *waqf*s and the 'Alami family, one of the leading families of Jerusalem, is also a family history research.[131] The study titled *al-Awqāf al-Islāmiyya fī al-Quds al-Sharīf: Dirāsa Tārīkhiyya Muwaththaqa* [The Islamic Endowments in al-Quds al-Sharif: A Documented Historical Study], prepared by Muḥammad Hāshim Ghūsha and published by IRCICA, is about the Muslim *waqf*s established in Jerusalem from the Ottoman conquest until 1977.[132] In the tables created on the basis of the *waqfiyya*s, systematic information is provided under various headings including information

128 See Hasan H. Güneş, *Kudüs Meğaribe Mahallesi* (Ankara: Vakıflar Genel Müdürlüğü Yayınları, 2017).

129 See Muḥammad Ali al-Alami, "The Waqfs of the Traditional Families of Jerusalem during the Ottoman Period," in *Ottoman Jerusalem*, 145–58.

130 See Yusuf Natsheh, "Architectural Survey: Catalogue of Buildings," in *Ottoman Jerusalem: The Living City, 1517–1917*, ed. Sylvia Auld and Robert Hillenbrand (London: Altajir World of Islam Trust, 2000), 963–95.

131 See Diana Abouali, *Family and Society in a Seventeenth-Century Ottoman City: The 'Alamis of Jerusalem* (PhD diss., Harvard University, 2003).

132 See Muḥammad Hāshim Ghūsha, *al-Awqāf al-Islāmiyya fī al-Quds al-Sharīf: Dirāsa Tārīkhiyya Muwaththaqa* (Istanbul: IRCICA, 2009).

on the endowments. The study, which does not include an analysis of the endowments, provides a holistic perspective on the endowments in terms of the breadth of the period it covers. Salīm Jūmʿā Al-Sūwāriyya's *al-Ḥayāt al-Ijtimāʿiyya fī Madīnat al-Quds: 1750–1800* [Social Life in the City of Jerusalem: 1750–1800] provides useful information on the settlement of *waqf*s in the urban space and their activity in all areas of social life in Jerusalem in the second half of the 18th century. The study is based on documents obtained from the registers. A similar study was prepared by Ziyād ʿAbd al-ʿAzīz al-Madanī. The 256 *waqfiyya*s in the registers between 1700–1800 are summarized under various headings.[133] The study, which provides summarized information about the endowments under certain headings, is critical in that it enables the identification and comparison of endowments. The book entitled *Dalīl Madīnat al-Quds Minārāt al-Maqdisiyya* [Guide to the City of Jerusalem: The Minarets of al-Quds], prepared by the Iḥyāʾ al-Turāth wa-l-Buḥūth al-Islāmiyya Institution, was among the reference sources in terms of reflecting the current number and status of *waqf*s.[134]

Beshara Doumani's work *Family Life in the Ottoman Mediterranean: A Social History* offers a nuanced exploration of family dynamics, property devolution, and familial roles in the Ottoman Empire, focusing on the cities of Nablus and Tripoli between 1660 and 1860.[135] By analyzing sharīʿa court records, Doumani challenges monolithic perceptions of the Muslim or Arab family, revealing significant regional variations in family structures and legal practices. His comparative approach to *waqf* underscores that it could serve multiple purposes depending on the founders' interests and the broader social and economic structure of a given society.

Ron Shaham's article titled "Christian and Jewish Waqf in Palestine during the Late Ottoman Period," is very important in terms of the information it provides on how Christian and Jewish residents of Ottoman Jerusalem established *waqf*s according to Islamic law.[136] Again, on this subject, Moshe Gil, in his work titled *Documents of the Jewish Pious Foundations from the Cairo Geniza*, focuses

133 Ziyād ʿAbd al-ʿAzīz Muḥammad al-Madanī, *Awqāf al-Quds fī al-Qarn al-Thāmin ʿAshar al-Mīlādī, 1112/1700–1214/1799* (Amman: Wizārat al-Thaqāfa, 2011).

134 See Muʾassasat Iḥyāʾ al-Turāth wa-l-Buḥūth al-Islāmiyya, *Dalīl Madīnat al-Quds: Manārāt Maqdisiyya* (Jerusalem: Wizārat al-Awqāf wa-l-Shuʾūn al-Dīniyya, 2010).

135 Beshara B. Doumani, *Family Life in the Ottoman Mediterranean: A Social History* (Cambridge: Cambridge University Press, 2017).

136 See Ron Shaham, "Christian and Jewish Waqf in Palestine during the Late Ottoman Period," *Bulletin of the School of Oriental and African Studies* 54, no. 3 (1991): 460–72.

on the understanding of philanthropy among Jews, based on the example of the Cairo Geniza Region.[137]

This study draws on a wealth of information from numerous sources to explore how the *waqf* shaped, influenced, and organized Jerusalem's society in the eighteenth and early nineteenth centuries, in a manner consistent with other cities in the Ottoman state. It utilizes previously unstudied archival sources while placing Jerusalem within its imperial context and referencing its distinctive local elements. In this context, the study begins by describing the *waqf* network, which we argue shaped, influenced, and regulated the physical, social, economic, and cultural life of Jerusalem during this period. While doing so, we seek to determine the development of Muslim *waqf*s, many established with the Islamic conquest long before the eighteenth century, particularly in the Ayyūbī and Mamlūk periods, and the contributions the Ottomans made to this development.

The *waqf*s actively serving in Jerusalem in the eighteenth and early nineteenth centuries, alongside newly established *waqf*s in the same period, are considered as a whole, with their partnerships and interactions in management, personnel, services, and practices defined within Jerusalem's social relations network. We also aim to contribute to the analysis by encouraging comparisons among the city's communities. Practically, this provides more information about the *waqf* practices of other communities. In Jerusalem, more than elsewhere, interactions between communities were strong and frequent, documented through *waqfiyyas*, correspondence, complaints, petitions, and more. We utilized unpublished archival materials from both the Ottoman imperial archives and the local archives of the Jerusalem district. Additionally, we sought to connect the documentary collections of the imperial center and local level to better understand the processes, objectives, and underlying spirit of both administrations. Ultimately, the study aims to make a significant contribution to the early modern history of Jerusalem through methodological and theoretical innovation. The *waqf* provides a unique framework, encompassing relationships between residents and their urban environment across religious boundaries.

In a broader Ottoman context, the study examines the effects of transformations in the empire's socio-economic structure on the remote district of Jerusalem. It argues that the early modern social transformation, expressed as the "expansion of the ruling elite class," was achieved in the provinces through *waqf* cadres. Records containing examples of stockpiling or trading

137 Moshe Gil, *Documents of the Jewish Pious Foundations from the Cairo Geniza* (Leiden: Brill, 1976).

waqf positions among elite households explain this expansion. Economically, long-term leasing of *waqf* properties provided the cash needed by *waqf*s during the transition to a monetary economy. Additionally, an all-embracing privilege distribution scheme from the center enabled jurisprudential transformation in *ʿulamāʾ*-owned *waqf*s. Cases like *khuluww* and *istibdāl*, previously discussed among some *ʿulamāʾ*, provided expansion and dynamism to *waqf*s in this period. The preservation of *waqf* buildings requiring repair and maintenance, and the replacement of non-income-generating *waqf* properties, ensured *waqf* continuity. Imperial orders from the period are crucial for assessing the practical effectiveness of these legal implementations. Thus, Jerusalem's social and economic transformations in the early modern period are defined through *waqf*s, with their impacts on the institution discussed from multiple perspectives.

From this point, it is appropriate to present a historical background on Jerusalem's urban space, where we will define the *waqf* network, a main focus of the study.

CHAPTER 2

A Provincial Base: Jerusalem

1 The City of Jerusalem: Charitable Endowments (*Waqf*) in Urban Everyday Life

The word "province" is defined in the dictionary as "the outer side of something, outside" in the first meaning, and as "the province outside the capital" in the second meaning.[1] Pakalın, on the other hand, states that "The cities, towns and villages outside of Istanbul, the capital, are called provinces."[2] In the definitions of the provinces as space, it is inevitably necessary to determine a center and to position the province according to this center. Based on the assumption that the capital was the center, the provinces characterized the places outside Istanbul. However, over time, the meaning of the word "province" has expanded and it had come to mean "outside the place defined as the center," which has been widely used in meanings such as village, town and Anatolia.[3]

Accepting the center as the major city raises the question of what constitutes the provinces. If the center is understood as the seat of the central government, the provinces can be seen as a broad network of interconnected regions, not a singular, indivisible entity. These provinces extend to even the smallest settlements. Here, the distinction between village, town, and city becomes significant. An urban economy is characterized by a settlement primarily driven by trade and industry, rather than agricultural production. In contrast, a village is defined by its agricultural economy and lower population density compared to a city, marked by its limited facilities, remoteness, and isolation as a provincial component of the city.[4]

In this study, Istanbul, the hub of Ottoman administration, represents the center, while Jerusalem is one of many Ottoman provinces. When Jerusalem is considered the center, the surrounding villages and towns become its provinces. Although this study focuses on Jerusalem's city center, it includes

1 Şemseddin Sāmī, *Kāmūs al-Aʿlām* (Istanbul: Çağrı Yayınları, 1899–1900), 884.

2 Mehmed Zeki Pakalın, *Osmanlı Tarih Deyimleri ve Terimleri Sözlüğü* (Istanbul: Milli Eğitim Basımevi, 1946–1956), 420.

3 Şaban Sağlık, "Malzeme ve Estetik Olarak Bir Taşra Estetiğinden Bahsedilir mi?," *Hece Öykü Dergisi*, no. 41 (2010): 68–78.

4 Berna Moran, *Türk Romanına Eleştirel Bir Bakış 2* (Istanbul: İletişim Yayınları, 2008), 322.

 | DOI:10.1163/9789004743441_003

numerous surrounding villages due to their status as *waqf* villages.[5] Conversely, if the province is viewed as a vast spatial area outside the center, existing in cooperation with or despite it, understanding the province inevitably involves analyzing the center.

To contextualize the study of Jerusalem's *waqfs*, it is useful to provide a historical background on the Ottoman provincial city of Jerusalem. First, Jerusalem's significance as a city for the three monotheistic religions and its elevated status as a *sanjāq* center following the Ottoman conquest should be highlighted. Its role within the Ottoman administrative structure, and how this position evolved over time, will be addressed under a separate heading. The historical trajectory of the city, from the Ottoman conquest to the rule of Mehmet Ali Pasha in 1831, will also be briefly discussed.

1.1 *The Importance of Jerusalem*

The city of Jerusalem was established at the intersection of the regions of Egypt, Mesopotamia, and Anatolia near the Syrian shores of the Mediterranean. It is 52 km from the Mediterranean and 24 km from the Dead Sea, which is a salty lake, 394 meters below sea level.[6] The city of Jerusalem, which is located in the west of the pit area where the lake of Lut is located and on the hilly surface of the Judea plateau, is a rugged city developed on the axis of the Kidron River, which forms the narrow mountain chain consisting of Mount Scopus and the Mount of Olives.[7]

The connection of Jerusalem with the coast is provided by Jaffa, a port city, and neighbors other centers such as Gaza and Hebron. The roads opening to the outside of Jerusalem are the roads that reach Jaffa in the west, Haifa in the north, Hebron in the south and Jericho in the east.[8]

Throughout history, Jerusalem has come to prominence as a central city of sanctity in terms of religion rather than just a commercial mobility, industrial

---

5 For example, after discussing the "decline" thesis that portrayed the Ottoman Empire as stagnant, peripheral, and a passive spectator, Beshara Doumani (*Rediscovering Palestine*, p. 3) cites how it has been challenged by the "integration" narrative since the early 1970s. However, he continues to criticize that integration narrative, which tends to relegate the interior regions of the Ottoman Empire, such as Jabal Nāblus, to the status of a "periphery's periphery."

6 Ömer Faruk Harman, "Kudüs," in *Türkiye Diyanet Vakfı İslâm Ansiklopedisi*, vol. 26 (Ankara: Türkiye Diyanet Vakfı, 2002), 323–24.

7 Erdem Demirkol, *II. Abdülhamid Döneminde Kudüs'te Kilise İmar ve İnşa Faaliyetleri* (master's thesis, Marmara Üniversitesi Türkiyat Araştırmaları Enstitüsü, Türk Tarihi Anabilim Dalı, 2007), 1.

8 ibid., 1–2.

production center, or regional focus of political power. As with other urban settlements, the main factor determining and guiding the development of the city, along with having certain administrative, military and economic functions, stems from its religious significance.[9] The economy of the city largely depended on the religious activities of urban communities, the services provided to pilgrims and visitors to the city for religious purposes.[10]

In this context, during the Ottoman period Jerusalem was also the crossroads of the Muslim, Christian and Jewish religions. Jerusalem has a great spiritual reputation among Muslims as the first *qibla*, and where the nocturnal journey of the Prophet Mohammad took place.[11] Although the name *al-Quds* is not mentioned in the Holy Qur'an, the scholars of *tafsīr* stated that either the *Bayt al-Maqdis* in Jerusalem or the Palestinian lands in which the city in question is located are generally meant by the expressions such as *"al-masjid al-aqṣā, mubawwaʾ ṣidq wa al-arāḍī al-muqaddasa."*[12] This was undoubtedly due to its association in the Qur'an and Islamic tradition with Muḥammad's miraculous nocturnal journey to Jerusalem. It is believed that the two stages of Muḥammad's journey *al-Isrāʾ* (the nocturnal journey) and *al-Miʿrāj* (ascension) took place around the western wall of *Ḥaram al-Sharīf* and the Dome of the Rock. These miraculous events in Islamic tradition have endowed the area with a special importance for Muslims. For centuries, scholars and other travelers from all over the Muslim world have come to pray at the Ḥaram and lodge in the sacred places mentioned in the verse: "Glory be to Him, who carried His Servant by night from the Holy Mosque [in Mecca] to the Farther Mosque [al-Masjid al-Aqṣā], the precincts of which We have blessed ..."[13] Apart from the interpretations of indirect references stating the sacred identity of the Masjid al-Aqṣā in the Qur'an, there are traces of it in the hadiths of the Prophet Muḥammad. In one, the Prophet states: "It is not right to go [for a special sacred journey] to any mosque except three: Masjid al-Ḥaram [Mecca], my *masjid* [Masjid al-Nabawī – Medina] and Masjid al-Aqṣā [Jerusalem]".

For Jewish communities, Jerusalem was the nucleus of the universe, the place of God's inevitable convergence with the beginning of creation, and a spiritual capital. In the eyes of Christians, Jerusalem had a great importance

---

9 Yasemin Avcı, *Değişim Sürecinde Bir Osmanlı Kenti: Kudüs (1890–1914)* (Ankara: Phoenix Yayınevi, 2004). 22–23, 31–32.

10 Ben-Arieh, *Jerusalem in the 19th Century*, 392–394.

11 Ghada Talhami, "Jerusalem in the Muslim Consciousness," *The Muslim World* 86, no. 3–4 (1996): 222–287.

12 Harman, "Kudüs," 324.

13 Qur'an 17:1.

in religious doctrine as the place where Jesus died and was resurrected.[14] As stated in Singer, pilgrims who came to Jerusalem via Jaffa and Akka established ties between religious communities around the Mediterranean or strengthened the existing ties. Jerusalem had become an international city with them, a mosaic of peoples, languages and sects. The Dead Sea in the middle of the desert attracted people to Jerusalem and formed a counter-gravity center to balance the charm of the Mediterranean. The economic, familial, and military relations with the Bedouins and the pilgrimage route to Mecca and Medina were at least as important as the local sea connections. These elements around Jerusalem gave the region a special position within the empire.[15]

The annexation of Jerusalem into Ottoman dominance meant that the city was joined by one of the political actors influential on the European scene and by a stronger army of a large region.[16] The expedition of Sultan Selim I to Syria and Egypt made the Ottomans the most powerful state of the Islamic world and gained the Ottoman sultan the title of servant of Mecca and Medina, *Khādim al-Ḥaramayn*.[17] The Sultan Suleiman I, who adopted the title of the caliphate of all the Muslims on earth, prioritized the protection of all Muslims as an extension of his policy of becoming a worldwide political power.[18] During his reign, the Ottoman central administration gave special importance to Jerusalem, and in some documents, Suleiman I was mentioned as the ruler of the Anatolian, Persian and Arab countries, and the Kaʿba and Medina and Jerusalem.[19] The city was one of the few cities in the classical period toward which the activities of the Ottoman sultans were directed. In the view of the Ottoman government, after Mecca and Medina, it was the third holiest city for Islam, namely *ūlā al-qiblatayn* (first qibla), *thānī al-masjidayn* (second mosque), and *thālith al-Ḥaramayn* (third Ḥaram).[20]

---

14 Avcı, *Değişim Sürecinde*, 31.

15 Singer, *Osmanlı'da Hayırseverlik*, 45; Amnon Cohen, "The Walls of Jerusalem," in *The Islamic World: From Classical to Modern Times; Essays in Honor of Bernard Lewis*, ed. C. E. Bosworth and Charles Issawi (Princeton, NJ: Darwin Press, 1989), 467–77; Lewis ve Cohen, *Population and Revenue.*, 84–104.

16 Cohen, "The Walls," 468.

17 Feridun M. Emecen, "Kuruluştan Küçük Kaynarca'ya," *in Osmanlı Devleti ve Medeniyeti Tarihi*, ed. Ekmeleddin İhsanoğlu, vol. 1 (Istanbul: İslam Tarih, Sanat ve Kültür Araştırma Merkezi, 1994), 32.

18 Halil Inalcık and Donald Quataert, *Osmanlı İmparatorluğu'nun Ekonomik ve Sosyal Tarihi, 1300–1600*, vol. 1, trans. Halil Berktay (Istanbul: Eren Yayıncılık, 2000), 56.

19 Kreiser, "The Place of Jerusalem in the Ottoman Perception," 211–20.

20 Angelika Neuwirth, "Jerusalem in Islam: The Entire Honorary Names of the City," in *Ottoman Jerusalem*, 77–95.

The mid-16th century marked a turning point in the attitude of the Ottoman administrative center as a whole towards the south of *Bilād al-Shām*. Astrid Meier argues that Suleiman the Magnificent's activities in Damascus should be seen in the context of practices aimed at integrating the region into an emerging Ottoman conception of state and administration. She sees the organization of the pilgrimage as the most important pillar of the ideal of integrating this area into the imperial imaginary. In the half-century after the conquest, a significant number of initiatives were undertaken by the imperial center to attract pilgrims or facilitate travel in these regions. She cites the activities carried out at the Khasseki Sultan's public kitchen, a *waqf* complex built in Jerusalem, as an important component of this ideal.[21] At the same time, physically, these buildings are landmarks of the first century of Ottoman rule.

This public kitchen in Jerusalem, alongside other *takiyya-zāwiyas* and *khanqāhs* functioning as pilgrimage *imārets* in the city, provided essential needs such as food, drink, and shelter for the poor and needy residents, as well as pilgrims, Ṣūfis, and travelers visiting the city. These *imārets* played a vital role in supporting the steady flow of pilgrims to the holy city and meeting their needs. For instance, Thierry Zarcone highlights the cultural, religious, and political exchanges between Central Asia, India, the Ottoman Empire, and particularly the Arab provinces, facilitated by Uzbek, Afghan, and Indian *takiyyas* in Jerusalem, which offered shelter and food to Central Asian and Indian Ṣūfī pilgrims.[22] Another example is the Abū Madyan al-Ghawth and ʿUmar al-Mujarrad lodges in the Maghāriba neighborhood, which served as pilgrimage *imārets* for Ṣūfī pilgrims from North Africa (present-day Tunisia, Morocco, Algeria, and Western Sahara) for centuries. In the eighteenth century, the construction of *waqfs*, caravanserais, inns, baths, and hostels along pilgrimage routes from Istanbul to Damascus, then to Medina and Mecca, and occasionally to Jerusalem and Hebron, within the structured and regular framework of pilgrimage organization, demonstrates the extent of this development.[23]

---

21 Astrid Meier, "For the Sake of God Alone? Food Distribution Policies, Takiyyas, and Imarets in Early Ottoman Damascus," in *Feeding People, Feeding Power: Imarets in the Ottoman Empire*, ed. Nina Ergin, Christoph Neumann, and Amy Singer (Istanbul: Eren Yayıncılık, 2007), 121–49.

22 Thierry Zarcone, *Kudüs'teki Orta Asyalı ve Hintli Sufi Hacılar* (Istanbul: Kabalcı Yayınevi, 2012), 43–45.

23 For analysis on the regulation of the pilgrimage route, see İsmail Hakkı Uzunçarşılı, *Mekke-i Mükerreme Emirleri* (Ankara: Türk Tarih Kurumu, 1972), 40–42; Münir Atalar, *Osmanlı Devleti'nde Surre-i Hümâyûn ve Surre Alayları* (Ankara: Diyanet İşleri Başkanlığı Yayınları, 1991), 129; A. Latif Armağan, "xviii. Yüzyılda Hac Yolu Güzergâhı ve Menziller,"

Muslim pilgrims visiting Mecca and Medina for *ḥajj* also visited Jerusalem, which has held a sacred position as a pilgrimage site since early Islamic times.[24] With the growing number of pilgrims in the eighteenth- and nineteenth-century Ottoman Empire, diverse sources and uses of pilgrimage books enriched and articulated representations. Depictions of holy sites, whether navigated, illustrated, or interpreted, enhanced the books' value while reinforcing Ottoman sovereignty over Islamic holy sites. They also responded to users' desires for protection and healing, guiding pilgrims and mediating imagination and remembrance. Consequently, a wide range of representations, from the tombs of the Prophet, Abū Bakr, and ʿUmar to the holy cities of Mecca, Medina, and Jerusalem, appeared in Ottoman pilgrimage books during the eighteenth and nineteenth centuries. These varied combinations and expansions created a new form of Ottoman religious imagery, creatively blending holy spaces with prophetic traces. Some authors who visited Mecca, Medina, Jerusalem, and Hebron for pilgrimage discussed these towns in their works, referring to the latter as part of the *al-Ḥaramayn* or *Ḥaram*-like, echoing *al-Ḥaramayn al-Sharīfayn*. However, the Damascus-Mecca pilgrimage route did not pass through Jerusalem or Hebron. Pilgrimage caravans are known to have headed south after assembling in Damascus. This does not account for the construction and activities of numerous *waqf* buildings in Jerusalem from the mid-sixteenth century, such as the *Ribāṭ Bayram Çavuş* or the *Imāret al-Khasseki Sultan*, which provided accommodation, food, and refreshments for pilgrims and the city's needy.

In addition, some prayer books include representations of the Dome of the Rock and Masjid al-Aqṣā, *Ḥaram al-Sharīf*, or Jerusalem in addition to those of the Ḥaramayn. Therefore, a triad of Mecca, Medina, and Jerusalem displays the three major Islamic pilgrimage and visitatiton sites. Jerusalem's significance as the "City of All Prophets" and Muslims' first direction of prayer, as well as the city's role in the Prophet Muḥammad's night journey and his heavanly ascension makes this three-city formula a powerful one.[25] As Morean Bahtī has demonstrated, Jerusalem also had significance as the land of gathering

Osmanlı Araştırmaları 20 (2000): 73–76; Muḥammad Adnān Bakhīt, *The Ottoman Province of Damascus in the Sixteenth Century* (Beirut: Librairie du Liban, 1982), 100.

24 Eroğlu Memiş, "'Nebzetü'l-Menāsik': 169–99, 170.

25 Sabiha Göloğlu, "Depicting the Islamic Pilgrimage Sites: Mecca, Medina, and Jerusalem in Late Ottoman Illustrated Prayer Books," in *Proceedings of the 15th International Congress of Turkish Art, Naples, 14–16 September 2015*, ed. Michele Bernardini, Alessandro Taddei, and Michael Douglas Sheridan (Ankara: Republic of Turkey Ministry of Culture and Tourism, 2018), 323–38.

(*arḍ al-maḥshar*), which can be traced through eschatological imagery.[26] For instance, the scales of justice (*mīzān*), which weigh good and bad deeds on Judgement Day, is depicted below the Dome of the Rock in this example.[27]

In addition to pilgrims, Sufis were also fascinated by the mysterious aspect of the events of *Isrāʾ* and *Miʿrāj*; they came to Jerusalem for various reasons such as "fulfilling the *sunna*, purification from sins, ascending to the level of Allah, receiving the reward of a martyr and protection from hellfire", acquiring knowledge, and *kasr al-thawāb*.[28] In this respect, the blessings of this city, which is "blessed around" in the Holy Qur'an, and its connection with the *Miʿrāj*, have always been an important center for all Muslims in general and Sufis in particular.[29]

In the Ottoman period, for Muslims, the most important religious center of Jerusalem was the *Ḥaram al-Sharīf* area where Masjid al-Aqṣā and Dome of the Rock are located. During the Ottoman classical period, a large portion of buildings such as mosques, fountains and *madrasa*s built or restored in Jerusalem were found in *Ḥaram al-Sharīf* or in the immediate vicinity. One of the most important contributions of the Ottoman administration to the *Ḥaram al-Sharīf* area was the removal of the mosaic coating on the outer wall of the Dome of the Rock Mosque and the paving of its tiles. Mixed with green and yellow, this blue-tile-plated glass gives it the look we see today.[30]

The fact that Jerusalem was included among the great *qadī*ships such as Istanbul, Edirne, Bursa, Egypt, Mecca, Medina, Damascus and Aleppo in the Ottoman administrative organization stemmed from the religious importance of the city.[31] Likewise, there is the territorial jurisdiction of Jerusalem including Hebron, Nablus, Ramla, Karek, Laccun, and Jenin District, thus extending beyond the administrative boundaries of the province.[32]

---

26 Şerife Eroğlu Memiş, "Tarihi Bir Vesika Olarak Hac Seyahatnameleri: Moralı Bahtî'nin Manzûme fî Menâsiki'l-Hacc Örneği," in *XVIII. Türk Tarih Kongresi Bildirileri, 1–5 Ekim 2018*, vol. 2 (Ankara: Türk Tarih Kurumu, 2022), 611.

27 For eschatological imagery, also see Gülru Necipoğlu, "The Dome of the Rock as Palimpsest: ʿAbd al-Malik's Grand Narrative and Sultan Süleyman's Glosses," *Muqarnas* 25 (2008): 17–105, 73–79.

28 Eroğlu Memiş, "*'Nebzetü'l-Menāsik'*," 170.

29 ibid., 173.

30 Buhl, "Kudüs," 962.

31 Avcı, *Değişim Sürecinde*, 35.

32 Kamil Jamil al-Asali, "Jerusalem under the Ottomans, 1516–1831," in *Jerusalem in History*, ed. Kamil Jamil al-Asali (London: Scorpion Publishing, 1989), 200–24, 213; Singer, *Kadılar, Kullar*, 38.

1.2 *Population in the Old City*

The Ottomans did not immediately dismiss the local administrators of a conquered place,[33] but rather established direct control only by establishing a *tīmār* (fief) system based on the registration of the financial resources and population of the region.[34] As a matter of fact, the first known *Taḥrīr* records that determine the estimated tax revenues in Jerusalem and the population of the city and village residents belong to the years 1525–6, approximately ten years after the conquest.[35] The first court registers of the Ottoman *qāḍī* in Jerusalem are dated to the year 1530–1. Therefore, it is possible to argue that the administrative structures that changed with the Ottoman administration became fully functional in the 1530s. The fact that the second *Taḥrīr* record made in 1538–9 produced more reliable and comprehensive data supports this view.[36]

The population of Jerusalem, which is estimated to have a population of around 10,000 during the Mamluk period, followed an upward trend throughout the sixteenth century, as can be seen in Table 1 below.

33 After the conquest, Sultan Selim I left the Province of Damascus and the *sanjāqs* of Jerusalem and Gaza to Mamluk Emir Janbirdī al-Ghazālī. However, after the death of Sultan Selīm I, he was killed when he started an uprising by declaring his own sovereignty (1521), and after that, Ayas Pasha was appointed to the Province of Damascus, and new administrators were appointed to the *sanjāqs* of Jerusalem and Gaza. See Yaşar Yücel and Ali Sevim, *Osmanlı Klasik Dönemi'nin Üç Hükümdarı: Fatih, Yavuz, Kanuni* (Ankara: Türk Tarih Kurumu Yayınları, 1991), 153.

34 Halil İnalcık, "Osmanlı Fetih Yöntemleri," *Cogito: Osmanlılar Özel Sayısı*, no. 19 (1999): 104–19, 115. In the newly conquered Arab lands, the *timar* (fief) order, which is the main element of the Ottoman classical socio-economic structure, is geographically encountered only in Syria, Palestine, and Northern Iraq. Most of the other Arab states (e.g. Egypt, Yemen, Baghdad, Tripoli, Tunisia, and Algeria) were organized as *salyane* (annual taxation) provinces after the conquest. See Selçuk Akşin Somel, "Arap Eyaletleri ve Günümüz Arap Devletleri: Tarihsel Bir Perspektiften Genel Bir Bakış," *Yeni Türkiye*, no. 3 (1995): 597–615, 598. In the provinces that were taxed annually, local revenues were not distributed to the cavalrymen as fief, but rather the provincial governors would pay a fixed annual amount to the center after covering all the military and administrative expenses of the province. For detailed information, see Salih Özbaran, "Some Notes on the Salyane System in the Ottoman Empire as Organized in Arabia in the Sixteenth Century," *Osmanlı Araştırmaları* 6 (1985): 39–45.

35 al-Asali, "Jerusalem under the Ottomans." Also, for research examining Jerusalem's land registry books (*tahrir defteri*), see Erdoğan, *XVI. Yüzyılda Kudüs Merkez ve Nahiyesinde Nüfus ve Etnik Yapı*.

36 Amnon Cohen, *Economic Life in Ottoman Jerusalem* (Cambridge: Cambridge University Press, 1989), 1–2.

TABLE 1 The population of Jerusalem according to *Taḥrīr* books in the sixteenth century

	932/1525–6			940–45/1533–9			961/1553–4		
	H	B	E	H	B	E	H	B	E
Muslim	616	2	1	1.168	75	34	1.987	141	16
Christian	119	–	–	136	26	42	413	25	3
Jewish	199			224	19	–	324	13	1
Total	934	2	1	1.528	120	76	2.724	179	20

Among the Muslims, who constitute the majority of the population, there were Muslims from Anatolia, North Africa, India and Central Asia as well as Arabs. The group known as Maghribī was especially large in number. Christians, on the other hand, consisted of Syriac, Jacobite, Armenian, Greek, Melkite, Serbian, Frankish and Georgian groups. The reason for the partial increase in the Jewish population in this century was that the Ottomans allowed some of the Jews expelled from Spain to settle in Jerusalem. Jews were registered in three neighborhoods from 1538.[37]

The population continued to increase in the following centuries. Simeon of Poland stated that in 1617 there were twelve local Armenians, twenty or thirty Coptics and a small number of Greeks in Jerusalem; he stated that there were four monasteries belonging to Armenians, Greeks, Franks and Serbs.[38] Another traveler, Chevalier d'Arvieux, states that in 1660, the people were Arab, Turkish and Jewish, as well as Frankish, Greek, Armenian, Maronite, Georgian, Coptic, Abyssinian and Chaldean Christians, but they were very few compared to Arabs, Turks and Jews. Evliya Çelebi, who described the city in 1671 in detail, said that there were Turkish garrisons in the inner castle and there were seventy houses. He wrote that, except for the forty houses in the suburb of David, there were 1000 houses within the city wall.[39]

It is estimated that the population of Jerusalem did not exceed 14,000 at the end of the eighteenth century. Volney, as reported in Asali, estimated the city's population between 12,000 and 14,000 in 1784. Bonne stated that

37 al-Asali, "Jerusalem under the Ottomans," 200–24.
38 ibid., 200–24.
39 Evliya Çelebi, *Seyahatnāme*, vol. 9 (1672–72) (Istanbul: Devlet Matbaası, 1935), 132–40.

the population of Jerusalem in the first years of the nineteenth century was around 12,000.[40]

As a result, it can be said that thanks to the tolerance of the Ottoman administration towards non-Muslims, the non-Muslim population of the city increased over time. Jerusalem was under the influence of various nations and cultures in the seventeenth and eighteenth centuries. There were a small number of Christians, mostly Orthodox, as well as British merchants, Armenian craftsmen, Moroccans, and Sunni Arabs who represented most of Jerusalem. In the following years, migrations to Palestinian lands led to the development of cities such as Jerusalem, Hebron, Bethlehem, Nazareth and Galilee.[41]

1.3 *Settlement in the Old City*

Until the 1860s it was surrounded by the city walls of Jerusalem, and today it is the area called *Qadīm* (Old) City. This general settlement plan of the city was established long before the Islamic era, when it was rebuilt as a Roman city by the name of 'Aelia Kapitolina' in the second century CE. This plan consists of two elements: the city walls and the main road system.[42] It is possible to observe the checkered pattern of the Roman camps and cities in Jerusalem's urban texture. The main street starts from the al-Khalīl Gate in the west, in the east intersects with the other main street in the north-south direction, and continues until the western border of the holy area called the 'quadra', the *Ḥaram al-Sharīf*.[43]

Jerusalem was surrounded by walls that were considered to be one of the typical geographical forms of Islamic cities. However, the city walls were originally built during the Roman period, and when it was rebuilt during the reign of Suleiman the Magnificent, the old line was followed.[44] There were six gates on the city walls: Herod (*Bāb al-Saḥīra, Bāb al-Wird, Bāb al-Zuhūr*), Damascus (*Bāb al-ʿAmūd*) to the north, St. Stephen Gate (*Istifān, Bāb al-Asbāṭ*), the east part of the gate of Dāwūd (*Bāb al-Ṣihyūn*) and *Bāb al-Maghāriba* (Zion Gate) in the southern part of the Jaffa Gate (*Bāb al-Khalīl, Bāb al-Ḥujjāj*) is located in the western part.[45] Although the city walls of Jerusalem are similar to the

40 al-Asali, "Jerusalem under the Ottomans," 200.

41 Işıl Işık Bostancı, *19. Yüzyılda Filistin (İdari ve Sosyo-Ekonomik Vaziyet)* (PhD diss., Fırat Üniversitesi, Sosyal Bilimler Enstitüsü, Tarih Anabilim Dalı, 2006), 135–43.

42 Adar Arnon, "The Quarters of Jerusalem in the Ottoman Period," *Middle Eastern Studies* 28, no. 1 (1992): 1–65, 3.

43 Avcı, *Değişim Sürecinde*, 22.

44 Arnon, "The Quarters," 3–5.

45 The seventh gate of the city, New Gate (*Bāb al-Jadīd*) was opened in 1890. Al-Sūwāriyya, *al-Ḥayāt al-Ijtimāʿiyya fī Madīnat al-Quds*, 30.

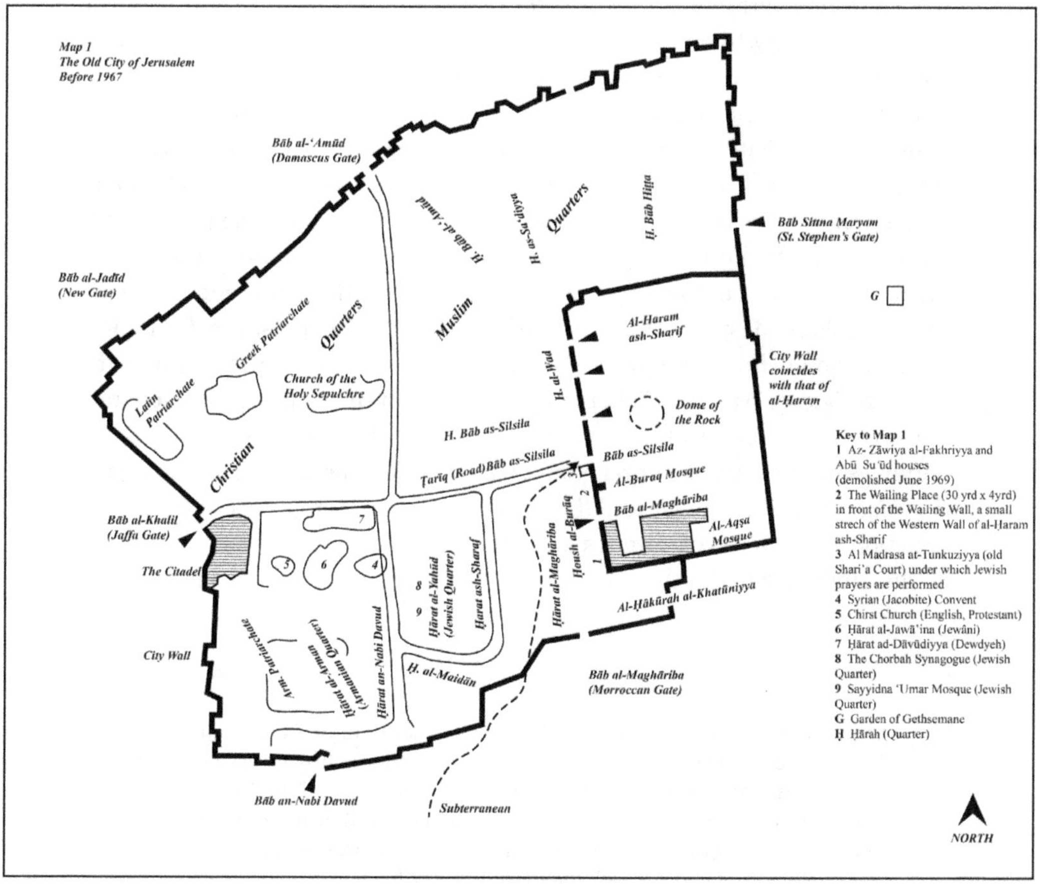

FIGURE 1 Map of the old city of Jerusalem before 1967. (Tibawi, *The Islamic Pious Foundations in Jerusalem*, 35)

Islamic cities, it is noted that they do not represent the central structure seen in the Islamic cities when they are evaluated in terms of a city settlement plan. As a matter of fact, Masjid al-Aqṣā, which is the central point of the city for Muslims and can be described as a Friday Mosque," is in the *Ḥaram al-Sharīf* located in the north-east of the city. Another Islamic structure, the Dome of the Rock Mosque, is right next to it, and both of these mosques have religious prescriptions different from an ordinary Friday mosque.[46] The area known as the *Ḥaram al-Sharīf* has not changed since about 1000 BCE, and the political power governing the city kept it as the religious center of the city, whichever

46 Avcı, *Değişim Sürecinde*, 22.

religion the government represented.[47] According to Avcı, the fact that the center of the city in almost all periods is in or around this sacred area also reinforces the superiority of the city's religious character.[48]

Until the second half of the nineteenth century, it is possible to refer to Jerusalem as a "city of religion," regarded as sacred by the three great religions of the city.[49] The most important factor that guided the development of the unique physical structure of Jerusalem was that it was the place where the members of the three great religions divided into various sects according to denomination, the direction of worship and other differences for centuries. Besides Masjid al-Aqṣā and other Islamic structures, the Church of the Holy Sepulchre, the most holy place of the city for Christians, and the Western (*Burāq*, Wailing) Wall, the religious center of the Jews, were separate religious-public spaces of the city's congregations. The vast majority of public buildings in the city were of religious character. The domed structures such as the *minaret*, the synagogue and the church, covering a large part of the reconstruction area, were voluminous and impressive and shaped the appearance of the city.[50] Likewise, the city economy largely depended on the religious

47 According to Jewish tradition, the Prophet Solomon, son of David, built the famous Solomon's temple in the center of this area, and thus the area in question became the center of Judaism. Despite the fact that Emperor Titus demolished the Temple of Solomon and the surrounding buildings in 70 AD, the sanctuary continued to exist, this time as the temple of Jupiter was built right in the middle. In the fourth century AD, the activity of the temple of Jupiter ended with the conversion of Christianity to the only legal religion, and the center of religious life in the Byzantine period shifted to the Church of the Holy Sepulchre built in the place where, according to Christian tradition, Jesus was crucified. With the beginning of Islamic rule, Masjid al-Aqṣā and the Dome of the Rock were built in that area. The star of the region, which was named *al-Ḥaram al-Sharīf* with its mosques, shined again. Tanman and Çobanoğlu, "Osmanlı Döneminde Kudüs," 511–12.

48 It was located next to the first temple where the Prophet Solomon had the palace built. According to Tanman, the sanctuary also had the feature of being a state center. In the period after that, the administrative center of the city was the castle built in the northwest corner of the sanctuary. After Jerusalem was conquered by the Muslims in 637, the administrative center shifted south of the al-Ḥaram al-Sharīf. However, during the Mamluk period, the administrative center was moved to the northwest corner of the *Ḥaram al-Sharīf* again. This time, *Madrasa Jawiliyya*, which was built between 1315 and 1320, was repaired in the fifteenth century and became the seat of the Mamluk governors. The most important feature of the *Madrasa Jawiliyya*, which continued to function for a certain period in the Ottoman period, was its dominant position in the *Ḥaram al-Sharīf* area. Tanman and Çobanoğlu, "Osmanlı Döneminde Kudüs," 513.

49 For an assessment on the issue, see Avcı, *Değişim Sürecinde*, 22–26.

50 Avcı, *Değişim Sürecinde*, 31–32.

activities of urban communities, the services provided to pilgrims and visitors to the city for religious purposes.[51]

In medieval Islamic cities, urban geographical areas were named with the names of the bazaar, ethnic-religious groups and important buildings therein. For example, the bazaar in Old Jerusalem named after wicker manufacturers (*Sūq al-Ḥuṣūr*) gave the names of the street; a neighborhood named for the glass manufacturers' bazaar (*Sūq al-Qazzāzīn*) is located in Hebron. In these bazaars, either a certain commercial product is sold or there are collective shops belonging to a certain craftsman. The Greek Orthodox District in Nazareth, the Akrad District in Hebron and the Bani Dar District, which is also the name of a family in Hebron, can be given as examples of streets or neighborhoods that are referred to by the names of ethnic-religious groups. Here, too, there were communal and/or religious groups settled in the neighborhood that determined the name of the street and the neighborhood.[52] Neighborhoods are named after their communities, along with names that indicate direction, such as up, down, east and west.[53]

Finally, prominent building names, city-wall gates, holy places and other areas have sometimes been determinant in naming the streets and neighborhoods of the city. In Arabic, the term *ḥāra* (plural *ḥārāt, ḥawārī*; meaning building) is commonly used to mean both street and neighborhood. When used as an urban term, in addition to its geographical meaning, the word also carries a social-geographic meaning of being settled by people who are united in terms of belief, ancestry, or occupation. In addition to this word, the words *maḥalla* and *ḥayy*, which mean "neighborhood" in Arabic, are frequently used in the documents. Another Arabic word *'aqaba* (to make, to build) in defining the urban geography is a term frequently used to describe the buildings in the Old City of Jerusalem. For example, while the *Bāb al-'Amūd* neighborhood in Old Jerusalem was named after the city gate with the same name, *the 'Aqaba Khanqāh* (*'Aqabat al-Khanqāh*) was named after the Khanqāh Mosque in the Old City of Jerusalem. King Dāwūd Street was given its name after the construction of the Castle in Old Jerusalem, and Saladin Street after the construction of the Tomb of Saladin.

Community neighborhoods in Jerusalem have developed around religious centers.[54] While Muslims prefer to settle to the north and west near the *Ḥaram al-Sharīf*, where the Dome of the Rock and Masjid al-Aqṣā are located,

51 Ben-Arieh, *Jerusalem in the 19th Century*, 392–94.

52 Bostancı, *19. Yüzyılda Filistin*, 135–43.

53 ibid., 135–43.

54 Ze'evi, *Kudüs*, 26; Avcı, *Değişim Sürecinde*, 20.

Christians are located near the Church of Holy Sepulchre, Armenians are located in the southwestern part of the city around the Saint James Cathedral, and the Jews were residing in areas close to the *Burāq* Wall.[55] We also know that it is not a strict or required division, but a general trend of settlement. Importantly, Muslims, Jews and Christians could buy or rent a house wherever they wanted. They were not subject to any restriction in this regard.[56] At the same time, well-organized marketplaces, controlled by the authorities, and more importantly, developed among the neighborhoods, were the most important public spaces that brought the people of the city together.[57] The fact that they preferred a certain place as a residential zone according to their religious affiliation did not mean that they did not have all kinds of organic and social connections with other groups or that they lived in a closed form. Similarly, the congregations did not only deal with their respective spiritual leaders to resolve their problems, but they also frequently applied to the *qāḍī* (judge) or *nā'ib* (deputy judge). They would have resorted to the court in order to approve business contracts, seek legal rights, or ask for confirmation of some of the old regulations.[58] Non-Muslims who resorted to the Islamic *sharī'a* court were able to complain about people from their own community or Muslims. Even those who were members of the guild organization could have been elected president.[59]

The fact that there have not been many changes between the sixteenth century and the first half of the nineteenth century, and even the names of the old neighborhoods have not changed much. According to the Land Registry Book numbered 289 and dated 1554, in the city center of Jerusalem, the Muslims were residents in the neighborhoods of *Bāb al-Qaṭṭānīn, Bāb al-'Amūd, Bāb al-Ḥiṭṭa, Rīzā'iqa, Rīna,* and *Salḥīn, Maghāriba, 'Aqaba al-Sitt, Sharq* (east); Christians were the residents of the neighborhoods of *Suryān* (Syriac), *Dayr Mar Ya'qūb, Jamā'at al-Qibtīyīn* (Copts), *Jamā'at al-Malkiyya* (Melkites), *Jamā'at al-Naṣārā*

---

55 Arnon, "The Quarters," 7.

56 Ze'evi, *Kudüs*, 26. As a matter of fact, no neighborhood was officially shown as a "Jewish quarter" or a "Christian quarter" in Ottoman records. Moreover, Muslims and non-Muslims were registered together in the same neighborhood. For example; according to the 1538–9 registry book, twelve of the eighty-one households recorded in the *Rishā* and *Ṣahyūn* districts of Jerusalem belonged to Christians and the others to Muslims. Erdoğan, *XVI. Yüzyılda Kudüs Merkez*, 32.

57 Ze'evi, *Kudüs*, 30.

58 Amnon Cohen, "On the Realities of the *Millet* System: Jerusalem in the Sixteenth Century," in *Christians and Jews in the Ottoman Empire: The Functioning of a Plural Society*, vol. 2, ed. Benjamin Braude and Bernard Lewis (New York: Holmes & Meier, 1982), 7–18, 15.

59 Ze'evi, *Kudüs*, 38.

(Christians); the Jews were residents of the *Jamāʿat al-Yahūdiyya* (east side of Jerusalem), *Masīḥ* (Messiah), *Jamāʿat al-Rīsha*. This situation is also confirmed in later period sources that the Jews lived in the neighborhoods of *Yahūdiyyān* (Judea), *al-Maslakh*, and *al-Rīsha*.[60]

In the Arabic guide prepared for Christian pilgrims approximately 350 years after the preparation of *Taḥrīr*s, the districts of Jerusalem at the end of the nineteenth century are listed as follows: *Bāb al-Asbāṭ*, *Bāb al-Ḥiṭṭa*, *Saʿdiyya*, *Bāb al-ʿAmūd*, *Ḥaddādīn*, *Naṣārā*, *Khān al-Zayt*, *Jawwālidā*, *Mawārna*, *Jāwa*, *Armanī* (Armenian), *Yahūdī* (Jewish), *Maghāriba*, *Bāb al-Silsila*, *Qaṭṭānīn*, *ʿAqabat al-Takiyya*, and *Wādī* Road.[61]

As in the districts, distinctions were also made based on congregations in the villages, although not as clearly. Just as some communities had their own villages, sometimes different communities lived together in the same village.[62]

2 The District of Jerusalem: an Administrative Organization

The Ottoman Empire was divided into large units called *beylerbeylik* or provinces in terms of administrative divisions, and these units were divided into more basic units called *sanjāqs* or *liwās*. It is not possible for the *sanjāq*, which are formed as a result of geographical and economic conditions, to be completely separated from each other in terms of administration and law. In the Ottoman administrative division, the country was administratively and

60 Ze'evi, *Kudüs*, 26.

61 Arnon, "The Quarters," 13; *ḥurūfāt* registers, which are kept according to the name of the district, contain information on the settlement units and neighborhoods according to their administrative structure. In 818 of the 1644 *ḥurūfāt* records covering the years 1690–1834, a settlement unit, region or geographical location was mentioned. In the records examined, some neighborhood, sub-district, or village names of Jerusalem are mentioned in relation to the *waqf*s and charity structures established. 620 documents related to the countryside of Jerusalem are recorded in the *ḥurūfāt* registers. Of these, 287 in Nāblus, 105 in Gaza, 104 in Ramlā, fifty-five in Jaffa (Pier), thirty-eight in Ludd, sixteen in Hebron (Khalīl), seven in Jabal ʿAjlūn, five in ʿAkkā, and four are records belonging to the towns of Jenin. The number of records regarding Jerusalem is 1,024. The neighborhoods of Jerusalem in the records are: *Bāb al-ʿAmūd, Maghāriba, Armanī, Ṣalāḥī, Ibn Yaḥūd, Bāb al-Ḥiṭṭa, Qūza, Kafara, Muṣalliyā, Ḥārat Dāwūd, Bāb al-Qaṭṭānīn, Madādīn, Yahūd, Naṣārā, Ḥārat al-Sharaf, Bāb al-Sāḥira, Jabal Shimālī, Rishā, Ifranj, Armaniyā, Jawālda, Ḥārat al-Ḥaddādīn, Qalʿūn, Qarbūn, Ṭāgh, Bāb al-Tawwābīn, ʿAkyā, ʿArāḍīn*. Also, for *Bāb al-Qaṭṭānīn*, see Annex 3.

62 Bostancı, *19. Yüzyılda Filistin*, 193–95.

militarily divided into *sanjāq* and sub-districts in judicial terms.[63] *Sanjāqs* are divided into sub-districts in military-administrative terms and into towns in administrative-judicial terms. The sub-district, located in the *qāḍī*'s area of responsibility, represented an administrative unit of a central town or city and its surroundings.[64]

When the Ottoman Sultan Selim I seized Syria, Palestine and Egypt, Gaza and Safed were the provincial outposts of the Cairo-based Mamluk Empire. Jerusalem was part of the province whose center was the city of Gaza. Palestine, which annexed the Ottoman lands at the end of 1516, was among the fifteen *sanjāqs* within the Province of Damascus. While Jerusalem and Gaza were the *sanjāqs* at the south end of the province; Gaza was in the west, on the Mediterranean coast; Jerusalem was surrounded by a desert in the east and south, and the *Sanjāq* of Nablus was in the north. In the beginning, as in the Mamluk period, the *Sanjāq* of Jerusalem was divided into the sub-districts of Jerusalem, Hebron and Banī ʿAmr.[65] As of 1538, with the abolition of the third sub-district, it was reduced to two sub-districts.[66] These two cities were also sub-district centers. However, unlike the Mamluk period, the headquarters of the *sanjāq* was not Gaza, but Jerusalem.[67] Thus, the city of Jerusalem attained an equal status with the cities of Gaza and Safed, which were administratively superior during the Mamluk period. The city of Jerusalem, which is the official seat of the *sanjaqbeys*, judges and other senior officials who were regularly sent from Istanbul, also gained a certain reputation as the place where state affairs were carried out.[68]

In the first stage, Evrenosoğlu İskender Bey was appointed to the administration of Jerusalem by Sultan Selim I, and Muntasıroğlu to the administration of Safed. On September 25, 1517, the administration of Jerusalem, Gaza and Safed was transferred to Canberdi Ghazali, who was previously the deputy judge of the Mamluks in Damascus. Taking advantage of the death of Sultan Selim I and the ascension of Suleiman the Magnificent to the throne in 1520, Canberdi

63 Musa Çadırcı, *Tanzimat Döneminde Anadolu Kentleri'nin Sosyal ve Ekonomik Yapıları* (Ankara: Türk Tarih Kurumu Basımevi, 1991), 79.

64 For details, see Tuncer Baykara, *Anadolu'nun Tarihi Coğrafyasına Giriş I: Anadolu'nun İdari Taksimatı* (Istanbul: Ötüken Neşriyat, 1988), 87; İ. Metin Kunt, *Sanjaqtan Eyalete: 1550–1650 Arasında Osmanlı Ümerası ve İl İdaresi* (Istanbul: Boğaziçi Üniversitesi Yayınevi, 1978), 17–18; Yaşar Yücel, "Osmanlı İmparatorluğu'nda Desantralizasyona (Adem-i Merkeziyet) Dair Bazı Gözlemler," *Belleten* 43, no. 171 (1979): 657–705, 665.

65 Karaman, "Filistin," 92.

66 Toledano, "The *Sanjāq* of Jerusalem," 279.

67 Singer, *Kadılar, Kullar*, 6.

68 Cohen, *Osmanlı Kudüs'ünde Loncalar*, 8.

Ghazali started a great revolt in Syria and Egypt in order to re-establish the old Mamluk administration and declared his reign with the title of Malik al-Ashrāf. As a result of the rebellion that was suppressed after a short while, Ghazali was also captured and killed (1521), and the administration of the Province of Damascus was left to the Anatolian Governor Ayas Pasha. The Safed, Gaza and Jerusalem *sanjāqs* were also separated from the *Sanjāq* of Damascus and each became an independent *sanjāq* within the Province of Damascus.[69] It was recorded as an independent *sanjāq* in the *kanunnāme* (Book of Law) prepared by Suleiman the Magnificent in 1522 and it was stated that the *sanjaqbey* was Kara Hasan Bey.[70] The sub-districts of the *Sanjāq* of Jerusalem in the Province of Damascus are shown in Table 2.[71]

TABLE 2 *Sanjāqs* and sub-districts of the Province of Damascus

Name of the district (*Sanjāq*)	Name of the sub-district (*Kazā*)
Nablus	Jabal Sāmī
	Jabal Qiblī
	Jabal Saʿb
	Jamāʿīn
Gaza	Nafs al-Ghazza (city center)
	Ghazza
	Ramla
Jerusalem	Al-Quds al-Sharīf
	Al-Khalīl
	Karak maʿa Shawbak
Safed	Nafs al-Ṣafad
	Jenin
	Ṭabarīyā
	ʿAkkā
	Sakif
	Baʿalbek

69 Enver Çakar, "Kanuni Sultan Süleyman Kanunnāmesine Göre 1522 Yılında Osmanlı İmparatorluğu'nun İdarī Taksimatı," *Fırat Üniversitesi Sosyal Bilimler Dergisi* 12, no. 2 (2002): 261–82.

70 ibid., 261.

71 Akgündüz, *Osmanlı Kanunnâmeleri*, 21.

With this law, Jerusalem, now separated from the *Sanjāq* of Damascus, was turned into an independent *sanjāq* within the Province of Damascus, and it preserved its administrative structure until 1831.[72] Between the years of 1831 and 1840, when Mehmed Ali Pasha dominated the region, the *Sanjāq* of Jerusalem was ruled from Akka, the administrative center. In 1840, after the Ottoman Empire re-established its domination in the region, it made changes in the administrative structure. In 1841, the *Sanjāq* of Jerusalem, which was reorganized to include Gaza, Jaffa and Nablus, was directly attached to Istanbul,[73] but this situation lasted for a short time, and Jerusalem was later included in the Sidon Province with a new administrative arrangement. Nablus was also separated from the *Sanjāq* of Jerusalem and turned into an independent *sanjāq* within the Province of Sidon.

The *sanjāq*, which was reconnected to Istanbul for a while during the Crimean War, was later included in the Sayda Province. With the new regulations specified in the 1864 Provincial Regulations, the Syrian Province was created in 1865, replacing Damascus and Sayda. After this date, the Jerusalem *Sanjāq* was included in the Syrian Province. However, although it was reconnected to Istanbul for a while, this situation lasted for only a short time and was included in the Syrian Province again later.[74]

Although the administrative structure was changed from time to time, Jerusalem was included in the administrative structure as an independent *sanjāq* within the province of Damascus, and this administrative structure was preserved until 1831. In the period when the province of Syria is connected, the Jerusalem *Sanjāq* has four districts, seventeen towns and 284 villages.[75]

---

72 Enver Çakar, "Kanuni Sultan Süleyman Kanunnāmesine Göre 1522 Yılında Osmanlı İmparatorluğu'nun İdarī Taksimatı," *Fırat Üniversitesi Sosyal Bilimler Dergisi* 12, no. 2 (2002): 261–82.

73 Avcı, *Değişim Sürecinde*, 60.

74 Bostancı, *19. Yüzyılda Filistin*, 125–28. The reason for the Ottoman State to constantly change the administrative structure of the Jerusalem *sanjāq* is the intervention of the Western states in the region. In order to prevent interventions, the desired success could not be achieved due to the fact that the Jerusalem *sanjāq*, which is directly connected to Istanbul, is far from the center and it was deemed appropriate to be governed from the Syrian provinces. However, this administrative structure continued until 1871. Bostancı, *19. Yüzyılda Filistin*, 126.

75 *Suriye Vilayeti Salnamesi*, 1288/1871–1872: 149–68; See also Table 3.

TABLE 3 Administrative division of the *Sanjāq* of Jerusalem under the Syrian province

Name of the sub-district (*Kazā*)	Name of the town (*Nāhiye*)	Number of the villages
Al-Quds al-Sharīf	Banī Zayd	24
(center of the district)	Banī Mūsa and Banī Salīm	12
	Banī Malik	23
	Bānī Ḥasan	9
	Wādiba	10
	Shamālī wa Janūbī Ḥāris	17
	Bīra wa Jabal al-Quds	21
Gaza	Khān Yūnus	14
	Majdal	7
	Ghazza	34
Jaffa	Yāfā	11
	Ludd	18
	Ramla	32
Al-Khalīl	Ḥalīl al-Raḥmān	14
	Amāma	5
	Bayt Jirīn	12
	ʿArqūb	21

3 The City of Jerusalem from the Ottoman Conquest to the Rule of Muhammad Ali Pasha (1516–1831)

Before the Ottoman rule, the city of Jerusalem was ruled by Muslim states such as those of the Umayyads, Abbasids, Ayyubids, Fatimids, and Mamluks for nearly a thousand years (excluding the years of the Crusaders).[76] Despite its status as a sacred place for all three monotheistic religions, the city has never shown a serious advantage in the economic field nor emerged as a political center in any period of history. It was far from the official communication and trade route connecting Damascus to Egypt via Gaza.[77] It was not on the

76 For a brief history of the city before the Ottoman rule, see F. Buhl, "Kudüs," in *İslâm Ansiklopedisi*, vol. 6 (Istanbul: Kültür ve Turizm Bakanlığı – Milli Eğitim Basımevi, 1977), 952–64.

77 Avcı, *Değişim Sürecinde*, 31–32.

traditional pilgrimage route for Muslims either.[78] At the time of the Ottoman conquest, the city of five or six thousand did not attract traffic from the Mediterranean coast.[79]

By the mid-sixteenth century, the city of Jerusalem had greatly benefited from the Ottoman administration, which began in 1517. On a broader scale, Jerusalem, with its new capital Istanbul to the north and the provincial capital Damascus, was positively influenced by the stable governance of the empire. Jerusalem had become part of the expansive Ottoman economic system; the impact of this system at the local level was the creation of a relatively more prosperous and secure trade network, fueled by the increased interest and resources brought by pilgrimage caravans to Mecca and Medina. Muslim pilgrims, on their way to or from the Hejaz, sometimes stopped near Jerusalem and even ventured into the city. Jerusalem held a unique significance in the geography of pilgrimage. Jerusalem, which is considered the holiest city after Mecca and Medina, was given many titles such as Holy Pilgrimage Gate or Right Hand of Syrian Cities.[80] Christian and Jewish pilgrims would also come. The money paid by Christian pilgrims, including the entrance fee to the Church of the Holy Sepulchre, contributed to the income of the city.[81] Pilgrims, albeit temporarily, would regularly increase the population and create demand for the city's food stocks.

The weakening of the Ottoman central administration, which became more evident in the last quarter of the sixteenth century, also affected Jerusalem negatively. The clearest indication of this was the weakening of the security of the region in general and the roads leading to Jerusalem in particular. Pilgrims who went to sacred places were sometimes attacked by Bedouins. Another development that threatened the general security and Ottoman rule in the region was the growing power and influence of Fakhr al-Dīn al-Maʿānī, one of the Druze emirs in Sidon.[82] Under these conditions, it was of great importance for the Ottoman administration to get the support of strong groups with local roots, with which the central government could cooperate in financial, military and political matters. In seventeenth-century Jerusalem, thanks to the combined military forces of the Ridwan-Farrūkh-Turabay dynasties and the relations they

78 The traditional Damascus-Cairo pilgrimage route crossed the Taberiye lake in the west to the Mediterranean coastal plains and turned south following the sea. Singer, *Kadılar, Kullar*, 11.

79 Cohen, *Economic Life*, 6.

80 Zarcone, *Kudüs'teki Orta Asyalı ve Hintli Sufi Hacılar*, 19.

81 On Jerusalem, see Cohen, *Economic Life*; Cohen and Lewis, *Population and Revenues*, 84–104.

82 Ze'evi, *Kudüs*, 22–23.

established with the Bedouins, they were appointed by the Ottoman central government as *al-amīr al-ḥajj* (pilgrimage caravan commander) or *sanjaqbey*. The members of the dynasties transferred power to members of their families until the end of the seventeenth century. During this time, the relations between the three dynasties gradually developed through political alliances, marriage and economic relations, and by the second half of the century they became a large, single dynasty.[83]

In the eighteenth century, the conditions in Jerusalem in general got worse. In 1702, Mohammed Pasha, who was appointed as the head of the *Sanjāq* of Jerusalem, caused a revolt under the leadership of *naqīb al-ashrāf* Muḥammad Ḥusaynī, one of the influential families in Jerusalem who based his political activities on religious positions due to increasing taxes and strictness in tax collection. The *naqīb al-ashrāf* took over the administration for two years. The provincial governor of Damascus was able to suppress the rebellion using military force in 1705.[84]

Once again, in the eighteenth century, the state of the central administration resulted in two new developments in Jerusalem. The first was that district governors were appointed from among the influential local families, and the second was that the prestige and power of certain families in Jerusalem grew significantly. During this century, most of the governors of the Jerusalem district were selected from the Tūkān and Nimr families.[85] Likewise, families such as Ḥusaynī, Khalīdī, and Abū al-Luṭf got stronger during this period and were effective in the administration of Jerusalem throughout the Ottoman administration. Of these families, the Ḥusaynīs were the most well-known of the influential families belonging to the *ʿulamāʾ* in Jerusalem. In addition to being *naqīb al-ashrāf* from the second half of the eighteenth century, they held positions such as *muftī* and Shaykh of Ḥaram al-Sharīf for generations, and in later periods they also carried out administrative functions such as mayor of Jerusalem. By consolidating their religious positions in the city with their economic power, they gained political effectiveness and social superiority.[86] Similarly, other influential families such as Dajjānī and ʿAlamī also attained positions of political power by being known for their knowledge of religion and Sufism.[87] Most *muftīs* were elected from the Abū al-Luṭf family and the chief clerks of the religious court from the Khalīdī family. ʿAṣalīs, on the other

83 ibid., 23; Avcı, *Değişim Sürecinde*, 41–42.
84 al-Asali, "Jerusalem under Ottoman Rule," 200–12.
85 al-Asali, "Jerusalem under Ottoman Rule," 212.
86 Avcı, *Değişim Sürecinde*, 46–47.
87 Ze'evi, *Kudüs*, 84, 87.

hand, rose by using the economic wealth they gained through their commercial activities. In these families, whose histories date back to Ottoman rule and generally to the Mamluk period, religious-public duties such as *muftī, naqīb al-ashrāf*, and Shaykhdom of the *Ḥaram al-Sharīf* remained in the same family, a generally accepted practice in this period.[88]

Another important point in terms of the subject of the study is that these families gained their economic power and influence mostly through religious and educational *waqf*s. In addition to being the main beneficiaries of the *waqf* income, they were also appointed as trustees or overseers, thus gaining influence and power in decision circles.[89] The ties between the charitable foundations in Jerusalem and the prominent people of the city were not limited to administrative duties. In the records of the Jerusalem *Ḥurūfāt* Registers, the number of the families mentioned above in the assignments made to the *waqf*s supports this evaluation.[90]

In addition, the eighteenth century witnessed the rise of local notables, who also had military power in terms of central-provincial relations. Over time, these people managed enormous resources and became monopolies in some provincial bases. The vast majority of local notables were more modest families holding only one city and its environs, and before the eighteenth century they were more notable dominated. Later, after the removal of the local notables, which opposed the re-centralization efforts of Sultan Mahmud II in the nineteenth century, the ordinary *ashrāf* continued to exist and became involved in the new administrative structure brought by the *Tanzīmāt*.

In this period when the Ottoman administrative mechanism gained a decentralized character, there was stagnation in terms of architectural activities in Jerusalem. Religious buildings in the *Ḥaram al-Sharīf* continued to be repaired frequently. Other than a few fountains built in the city, the largest building built in and around Jerusalem is the castle built on the road to Bethlehem. Similarly, there was a decrease in the number of *madrasa*s in Jerusalem. Only forty of the fifty-six *madrasa*s from the Mamluk period continued to provide education in 1672.[91] This number was recorded as forty-nine in the *Ḥurūfāt* Registers covering the years between 1690 and 1834. This situation brings to mind the possibility that the number of *madrasa*s may have been higher than needed for the city population. As a matter of fact, with the conquest, the

88 Avcı, *Değişim Sürecinde*, 47.

89 Ze'evi, *Kudüs*, 94.

90 The appointment records made from the influential families of Jerusalem to the *waqf*s of Jerusalem are examined in the third part of this study.

91 al-Asali, "Jerusalem under Ottoman Rule," 213.

Ottoman administration preferred to invest in the city in the fields of social assistance and security rather than religious educational institutions.[92]

Political developments in the first quarter of the nineteenth century also affected Jerusalem. The rebellion that included Jerusalem in 1807 was suppressed by the Governor of Sayda Süleyman Pasha, and in 1810, Süleyman Pasha assumed the defense of the *Sanjāq* of Jerusalem against the Wahhabi danger that developed in the region. The Greek rebellion in 1821 inspired mobilization in Jerusalem, especially among the Greek Orthodox, but clashes were prevented by strict measures from the authorities. In 1825, some villages around Jerusalem, who wanted to take advantage of the weakness of the central government, started a rebellion in order to avoid taxes; they captured the city in a short time with the support of Ibrahim Abū Ghawsh (Gosh), one of the Bedouin Shaykhs who were influential between Ramla and Jerusalem. Sidda Governor Abdullah Pasha was able to maintain peace by persuading the rebels in late 1826.[93]

During the rule of Egyptian governor Mehmed Ali Pasha (1831–1840), important changes occurred in Jerusalem. His strict practices, increased taxes, disarmament and compulsory military service decisions led to a series of Jerusalem-centered uprisings between 1834 and 1838. In December 1840, Jerusalem again came under Ottoman rule.[94]

As mentioned above, the population of Jerusalem was less than that of the Ottoman cities such as Damascus, Edirne, Bursa and Thessaloniki, and it was not as rich as them. With less than three thousand taxpayers in the middle of the sixteenth century, Jerusalem's population was more comparable with the cities of Çorum, Amasya, Niğde and Aksaray in Anatolia.[95] Aleppo, Damascus, and Cairo remained economic centers throughout the sixteenth and seventeenth centuries.[96] The centers of trade with Baghdad, Basra and India were Cairo and Aleppo. The presence of merchants settled in Cairo and Aleppo, who also traded with Istanbul, was an important indicator. It can be said that, towards the end of the sixteenth century, three main economic regions

92 André Raymond, "The Ottoman Conquest and the Development of the Great Arab Towns," *International Journal of Turkish Studies* 1, no. 1 (1979–80): 84–101.

93 al-Asali, "Jerusalem under Ottoman Rule," 213.

94 ibid., 213.

95 Faroqhi noted in her study that she defined a settlement as a city only as long as there were marketplaces and over 400 taxpayers. Suraiya Faroqhi, *The Ottoman Empire and the World Around It, 1540s to 1774* (London: I. B. Tauris, 2004), 355–56.

96 André Raymond, *Artisans et commerçants au Caire au XVIIIe siècle*, 2 vols. (Damascus: Institut Français de Damas, 1973–74), 1:144.

surrounded Ottoman Aleppo: Damascus, Cairo and Istanbul.[97] The city, which ranks second if not third in administrative position, was also far from main roads and waterways. While the number of manufacturing and service guilds was around 260 in Cairo and 1100 in Istanbul, it was about 60 in Jerusalem.[98]

Commercially and economically, Jerusalem did not have many sources of income. The numbers of Muslim and Jewish visitors are not known, and the number of Christians is known from the taxes paid for their visits to the Church of Holy Sepulcher. In 961/1553–54, it was predicted that approximately 120,000 coins would be obtained from the taxes of the Church of the Holy Sepulcher. The income was calculated on the basis of forty-five coins per capita paid by Christians to the church as a footfall tax. Since the church is a frequent destination for all of them, we can deduce that the average number of Christian pilgrims who came to Jerusalem every year is around 2500 with a simple calculation.[99] However, the entrance fee to the church would vary according to the proximity or distance of where the Christians came from. Also, the number of visitors decreased significantly due to the variability of the Ottoman Empire's political and military relations; hence the figure given is only an estimate.

Pilgrims and visitors gave vitality to handicrafts and trade. In addition to taxes, the sales made during the regular visits of the members of the three holy religions to the region and especially the income from handicrafts can be mentioned among the revenues of Jerusalem. Seetzen, a German traveler who visited Jerusalem at a later time, states that in 1806 the number of tradesmen and merchants operating in Jerusalem was at least 700.[100]

An institution that had a central importance in the social and economic life of Jerusalem was the market. The marketplace in Jerusalem, like many other Ottoman cities, was a well-organized shopping environment controlled by the authorities. The market sometimes guided or determined the economic lives of Christians, Muslims and Jews who were members of joint trade or craft associations. There, slaves and servants traded side by side with the local and ruling elite. Janissaries shared their meals with modest craftsmen.[101]

Making money through trade and production was almost a precondition for social mobility. The market provided shelter for fugitive slaves and unemployed soldiers. The market was also one of the main links between the city

97 Faroqhi, *The Ottoman Empire*, 356.

98 Amnon Cohen, *Osmanlı Kudüs'ünde Loncalar*, trans. N. Elhüseyni (Istanbul: Tarih Vakfı Yurt Yayınları, 2003), 5, 13.

99 Singer, *Osmanlı'da Hayırseverlik*, 159.

100 al-Asali, "Kudüs," 334–38.

101 Ze'evi, "*Kudüs*," 30.

and the surrounding villages and Bedouins. Yet the market was a strictly structured hierarchical institution, where peasants, townspeople, and Bedouins each had their own place and function, each group accepting its own role in the established order.[102]

In the Ottoman Period in Jerusalem, production was made in the branches of weaving and dyeing, leather-making, soap-making and metal atelier. While soap produced in Jerusalem was sent to Egypt, grain was sent to Egypt, Rhodes and Dubrovnik; rice came from Egypt, clothes and coffee from Damascus, and some textile products and carpets from Istanbul, Iraq and China. *Surras* sent from Istanbul and Egypt constituted the most important income source of Jerusalem. On the other hand, the money sent by Jews outside of Jerusalem to their coreligionists in Jerusalem and the financial support of the European kingdoms to the Christians were also important sources of income for Jerusalem.[103]

4 Conclusion

Consequently, during this period, the *Sanjāq* of Jerusalem as a whole, and the city of Jerusalem in particular, was regarded as a predominantly religious city, esteemed as the third holiest city in Islam within the context of the Ottoman Empire. During the zenith of the empire's power, Jerusalem witnessed significant development and enhancement initiatives, which revitalized its economic and commercial activities within a secure environment, leading to a notable increase in its population. However, when the empire entered a process of decentralisation, Jerusalem was also affected. During this era, the city's religious significance overshadowed its administrative role as a *sanjāq* center, causing the latter to diminish in prominence.[104]

By the end of the sixteenth century, Jerusalem was the most populous urban center in Palestine. However, due to the transformations in the seventeenth and eighteenth centuries, it ceded this status to Akka, which emerged as a prominent port city. Akka's harbor expanded significantly through its integration into European trade networks, enabling it to become Palestine's largest city by the eighteenth century. In the early nineteenth century, Jerusalem came under the control of İbrahim Pasha, the son of Mehmet Ali Pasha. This occupation heightened the strategic importance of the eastern regions

102 Ze'evi, "*Kudüs*," 31.

103 al-Asali, "Jerusalem under the Ottomans," 200–24.

104 Avcı, *Değişim Sürecinde*, 50–51.

of the Ottoman Empire for European diplomacy, bringing Palestine, and particularly Jerusalem, to the forefront of European political discourse and public opinion.[105]

Throughout its history, Jerusalem has been a focal point for architectural and construction endeavors. During the Mamlūk and Ottoman periods, numerous monumental structures, including mosques, *madrasas*, Ṣūfī lodges, *zāwiyas*, *ribāṭs*, and *khāns*, were erected, significantly enhancing Jerusalem's economic vitality. The city reached its historical peak under Sultan Suleiman I, marked by extensive construction, such as the restoration of the Dome of the Rock, the reconstruction of Jerusalem's city walls (1536–1540), and the establishment of *waqfs*, notably the *Khasseki Sultan imāret*, a public kitchen providing daily sustenance to hundreds of impoverished individuals. These developments highlight Jerusalem's enduring role as a center of religious, cultural, and economic activity.[106]

105 Avcı, *Değişim Sürecinde*, 51–57.
106 al-Asali, "Kudüs," 334–38.

CHAPTER 3

Waqf Networks in Jerusalem (1703–1831)

1 Muslim *Waqfs*

Waqfs have been the prominent institutions in Islamic states and societies throughout the centuries which provided philanthropic, social, municipal, religious and educational services.[1] They sustained the infrastructures for bazaar, inn and bathhouses, revive key institutions such as mosques, *madrasas* and *imārets* (public kitchens), and thus, they contribute to the development of urban and rural centers.[2] They actively engaged in daily life with all its aspects and founded a lot of establishments.[3]

In the center of three monotheistic religions, Jerusalem, Islamic *waqfs* continued to operate for centuries giving the town a *waqf*-town identity. These *waqfs* are formed around Masjid *al-Aqṣā*[4] or *Ḥaram al-Sharīf*, which was the center of administrative system and urban services organization. Christian and Jewish *waqfs* are also important components of the *waqf* system though less in number compared to Muslim ones.

In this part of the study, Muslim *waqfs* both in Jerusalem and the ones in and out of the *Ḥaram al-Sharīf* will be examined. First, the *waqfs* established before the annexation of Jerusalem by the Ottoman Empire will be discussed. Following this are the *waqfs* established during the Ottoman period until the

1 For a general evaluation related to the effects of *waqf* on socio-economic life see Köprülü, "Vakıf Müessesesinin Hukuki Mahiyeti," 1–6; Bahaeddin Yediyıldız, "Sosyal Teşkilatlar Bütünlüğü Olarak Osmanlı Vakıf Külliyeleri," *Türk Kültürü* 19, no. 129 (1981): 71–85; Bahaeddin Yediyıldız, "Vakıf Müessesesinin XVIII. Asırda Kültür Üzerindeki Etkileri," in *Türkiye'nin Sosyal ve Ekonomik Tarihi (1071–1920)*, ed. Osman Okyar and Halil İnalcık (Ankara: Meteksan, 1980), 119–24; Yediyıldız, "Müessese-Toplum," 38; Yediyıldız, "Vakıf;" İnalcık, "The Ottoman State," 47, 79–83; Imber, *Ebu's-suʿud*, 140; Ali Himmet Berki, "Hukukî ve İçtimaî Cephesiyle Vakıf," *Vakıflar Dergisi* 7 (1966): 11; Yüksel, *Osmanlı Sosyal*,153–76; Barkan, "Osmanlı İmparatorluğunda," 279–304; Ömer Lütfi Barkan, "Vakıfların Bir İskân ve Kolonizasyon Metodu Olarak Kullanılmasında Diğer Şekiller," *Vakıflar Dergisi* 2 (1942): 354–65; İsmet Miroğlu, "Türk-İslâm Dünyasında Vakıfların Yeri," in *II. Vakıf Haftası, 3–9 Aralık 1984: Konuşmalar ve Tebliğler* (Ankara: Vakıflar Genel Müdürlüğü Yayınları, 1985), 121–29, 123.

2 Halil İnalcık, "Istanbul: An Islamic City," *Journal of Islamic Studies* 1 (1990): 1–23.

3 For example see, Mustafa Alkan, *Adana Vakıfları: İnsan, Vakıf ve Şehir* (Ankara: Türk Tarih Kurumu Yayınları, 2014).

4 The lead-domed Masjid *al-Aqṣā* Mosque has recently been referred to as the *Qibla* Masjid. In the present study, we refer to the lead-domed mosque as the Masjid al-Aqṣā Mosque and the area as the *Ḥaram al-Sharīf* as it appears in Ottoman documents.

 | DOI:10.1163/9789004743441_004

eighteenth century Jerusalem. The newly established Muslim *waqfs* during the period under review will be analyzed in detail after that. Christian and Jewish *waqfs* will also be assessed under to be able to provide a wholistic description of the *waqf* network operating and affecting the social relations in the eighteenth century Jerusalem.

1.1 Waqfs *Established in Jerusalem before the Ottoman Annexation*

Over time, the Masjid *al-Aqṣā* and the Dome of the Rock mosques, which formed the center of Jerusalem's system of religious institutions, emerged as two central structures in the city. Located in the southeast of the old city of Jerusalem, Masjid *al-Aqṣā* covers an area of one-sixth of the old city.[5] Surrounded on three sides by *madrasas* and *takiyyas*, the *Ḥaram al-Sharīf* served as a central hub for prayer, Qur'an recitation, and the study of tradition and law. Hosting pilgrims, Ṣūfī dervishes, and *ʿulamāʾ* while meeting their needs in this area, where charitable activities were concentrated, were primary functions supported by *waqf* founders.

In Jerusalem, the open architectural design of the *al-Aqṣā* Mosque, combined with the natural separation of its platform from the surrounding walls, facilitated the integration of additional structures into the *Ḥaram al-Sharīf* complex.[6] The complex of *al-Aqṣā* Mosque includes the open spaces, the masjids above and below ground, prayer rooms, *minarets*, domes, *madrasas*, buildings, porticoes, public outbuildings, gates, outbuildings adjacent to the open spaces of *al-Aqṣā* Mosque, and the walls surrounding it on all four sides.[7]

---

5 The total area of the Masjid today is 144,000 m^2. All of the buildings and open spaces within the borders of al-Aqṣā Mosque are considered to have the same sanctity in terms of Islamic belief and jurisprudence. The ruling is the same whether they are above ground, as in the case of the Dome of the Rock, or below ground, as in the case of the Marwān Masjid. The buildings in the Masjid al-Aqṣā complex have various levels of height. The first level is below ground and includes water wells, water channels, and some buildings covered with soil. The second level, also below ground, includes the Marwan Masjid, the *Burāq* Masjid, the old Aqsā Masjid, the Gates of Mercy and Repentance, and the closed gates of the *Mufrad* (Single) Gate, the *Muṣawwaj* (Double) Gate, the *Muthallath* (Triple) Gate, the *Burāq* (Moorish) Gate, and the Silsila Gate. The third level is at ground level and includes the Qibla Masjid on the south side of the al-Aqsā Mosque, the main areas, the open doors and the porticoes. The fourth level rises slightly above the ground and includes the Dome of the Rock, its courtyard, the domes, the buildings and the arches surrounding them. See *Palestinian Academic Society for the Study of International Affairs* (PASSIA), *Mescid-i Aksâ Rehberi* (*Harem-i Şerîf*) (Jerusalem: TİKA Yayınları, 2013), 4–5.

6 Frenkel, "Political and Social Aspects of Islamic Religious Endowments (Awqāf)," 2–3.

7 Masjid al-Aqṣā, Dome of the Rock, Marwān Mosque, Women's Mosque (Ayyubid period), Maghāriba Mosque (Museum of Islamic Art- Ayyubid period), Burāq Mosque (Umayyad/ Mamluk period), Masjid of the Cradle of Jesus (Ottoman period) are the mosques in

The *al-Aqṣā* Mosque has fifteen gates: the Raḥma or Tawba (Mercy), Burāq (Funerals), and *Muthawwaja* (Double) Gates from the Umayyad period; the *Musallas* (Triple) and *Munfarida* (Single) Gates from the Fatimid period; the *Asbāṭ* (Tribes), *Ḥiṭṭa*, *Sharaf al-Anbiyā'* (King Faisal), *Muṭahhara*, *Sakīna* (Gate), and *Silsila* (Chain) Gates from the Ayyūbī period; and the *Ghawānima*, *Nāẓir*, *Ḥadīd*, *Qaṭṭānīn* (Cotton), and *Maghāriba* Gates from the Mamlūk period.[8]

---

al-Ḥaram al-Sharīf. The domes in the *Ḥaram al-Sharīf* are as follows: Dome of the Chain, Dome of Suleiman built during the Umayyad Period; Dome of Miʿrāj, Dome of Moses, Dome of Yusuf, and Dome of the Nativists built during the Ayyubid Period; Dome and the *Miḥrāb* of the Prophet, Dome of Khidr, Dome of Yusuf Agha, Dome of the Spirits, Dome of Muḥammadiya/al-Khalīlī Lodges, Dome of Sultan II, and the Maḥmud Dome/Prophet's Lovers Dome. Among the *minarets* in the Ḥaram, the *Minaret* of the Gavanime Gate was built during the Ayyubid Period; the *Minaret* of the Asbāṭ (Tribes) Gate/Ṣalāḥiyya Minaret, the *Minaret* of the Maghāriba (Moorish) Gate/Fakhriyya Zāwiya Lodges, and the *Minaret* of the Silsila (Chain) Gate were built during the Mamluk Period. The arches in the *Ḥaram al-Sharīf*: There are the southern and eastern arches built during the Abbasid period; the western one, whose construction is unknown; the southeastern arches built by the Fatimids; and the northwestern, northeastern and southwestern arches built by the Mamluks. There are thirty-two water sources in al-Aqṣā Mosque. These are two fountain pools, two water cisterns, eight fountains and twenty water wells, most of which have water. Among these, the fountain for ablution and the Malik ʿĪsā al-Muʿaẓẓam Water Cistern were built during the Ayyūbid Period, while the Qāytbāy Fountain and the Citrus Pool were built during the Mamlūk Period, and the Qāsim Pasha Fountain and Süleymān Fountain were built during the Ottoman Period. The *Minbar* of Nūr al-Dīn Zangī from the Ayyūbid Period and the *Minbar* of Burhān al-Dīn from the Mamlūk period are two important minbars in the *Ḥaram al-Sharīf.* The Museum of Islamic Art, now located near the Maghāriba Gate, was formerly part of the *Maghribī* Masjid and the Women's Masjid. The Wall of Burāq, located southwest of the al-Aqṣā Mosque, is also part of the al-Aqṣā Mosque. Finally, there are 26 prayer stations on the site of al-Aqṣā Mosque. They are flat areas made of stone with a surface of 1 meter above the ground. They are connected to each other by steps, and many of them have a small miḥrāb or a marker stone to indicate the direction of the *qibla*. These prayer rooms were used for prayer, preaching, and lectures. Two of these twenty-six prayer halls are of recent construction, while the others were built during various Islamic periods, especially during the Mamlūk and Ottoman periods. For detailed information on the structures, see Tanman and Çobanoğlu, "Osmanlı Döneminde Kudüs," 511–43; PASSIA, *Mescid-i Aksa Rehberi*, 4–65.

8 Today, five of these gates are closed, namely the gate called *Raḥma* or *Tawba*, the Gate of *Burāq* (Gate of Funerals), the *Muṣawwaj* (Double) Gate, the *Muthallath* (Triple) Gate, and the *Mufrad* (Single) Gate. The other 10 gates are open. Michael H. Burgoyne, "The Gates of Ḥaram al-Sharīf," in *Bayt al-Maqdis: 'Abd al-Malik's Jerusalem*, part 1, ed. Julian Raby and Jeremy Johns (Oxford: Oxford University Press, 1992), 111–20; al-Ḥanbalī, *al-'Uns al-Jalīl bi-Tārīkh al-Quds wa-l-Khalīl*, vol. 2 (Amman: Maktabat al-Muḥtasib, 1973), 27. Chateaubriand, who visited Jerusalem in 1806, mentions seven gates. These are *Bāb al-Khalīl* (Abraham Gate, Jaffa Gate, Pilgrims' Gate), *Bāb al-Nabī Dāwūd* (*Bāb al-Ṣidd al-Dāwūd*, Zion Gate), *Bāb al-Maghāriba* (Gate of the Moors), *Bāb al- Ḍarā'ib* (Golden Gate), *Bāb al-Sayyida Maryam* (Gate of the Lady Mary, Saint Stephen, Gate of the Flocks in Jewish times), *Bāb al-Zahra* (Gate of Ephraim or Herod). See Chateaubriand, *Paris-Kudüs Yolculuğu*, vol. 3, trans. Oğuz Peltek (Ankara: Milli

The name *Masjid al-Aqṣā*, meaning "the farthest one" in Arabic, derives from its reference in the Qur'an as the mosque furthest from *Makka al-Mukarrama* at the time of the Prophet's revelation. In linguistic terms, *al-Aqṣā* denotes a place distant from a known location. Its sanctity stems from the Qur'anic phrase "the farthest mosque," referring to its distance from the *Ka'ba*. Now also called the Qibla Mosque, it was the first *qibla* for Muslims and is located in the city known as *Bayt al-Maqdis*, making it the second oldest mosque after *Masjid al-Ḥarām*.[9]

The fact that it was the site of the Prophet's *Isrā'* and *Mi'rāj* is another reason for the exceptional place of al-Aqṣā Mosque in Islam. *In the first verse of Surat al- Isrā'*, Masjid al-Aqṣā is mentioned as follows: "The glory of God is supreme, who brought His servant Muḥammad from al-Masjid al-Ḥarām to al-Masjid al-Aqṣā, whose surroundings We have blessed, to show him some of Our signs one night. Without doubt, God is all-hearing and all-seeing."[10] It is stated here that Masjid al-Aqṣā is referred to as "of which surrounding was made blessed by us."

The area surrounding the *al-Aqṣā* Mosque has been understood to encompass Jerusalem and, by extension, the rest of Palestine. The wall known to Jewish communities as the Wailing Wall and to Muslims as the *Burāq* Wall is believed, in Jewish tradition, to be a remnant of the ancient temple. Following the conquest of Jerusalem in 638 CE during the reign of Caliph 'Umar, a modest mosque was constructed on the southern side of the *al-Aqṣā* Mosque area near this wall. 'Umar's decision to designate this site as a sanctuary reflected its sanctity and significance. However, no traces of 'Umar's mosque remain today, as it was dismantled during the construction of Masjid *al-Aqṣā* by the Umayyad caliph 'Abd al-Malik ibn Marwān between 90–96 AH/709–714 CE. Some historians suggest that the construction began under 'Abd al-Malik and was completed during the reign of his son, al-Walīd ibn 'Abd al-Malik. Built with fifteen naves during the Umayyad period, *al-Aqṣā* Mosque underwent numerous repairs and renovations throughout history. During the Abbasid period, Caliph Ja'far ibn Abū Manṣūr repaired it, and after an earthquake damaged the eastern and western walls, Caliph al-Mahdī restored the mosque. Another Abbasid caliph, al-Ma'mūn, renovated the central naves. In the Mamlūk period (885–923 AH/1451–1517 CE), new naves were constructed under 'Abdullāh ibn Ṭāhir, an emir of the Ṭāhirid dynasty ruling in Yemen. Extensive restoration

Eğitim Basımevi, 1949), 60. This number suggests that other gates were closed at the beginning of the 19th century.

9 Tanman and Çobanoğlu, "Osmanlı Döneminde Kudüs," 323–24.

10 Qur'an 17: 1.

work also occurred during the Fatimid period, notably under Caliph al-Ẓāhir li-Iʿzāz Dīn Allāh in 427 AH/1036 CE.

During the Crusader occupation of Jerusalem (1099–1187 CE), when the city was part of the Kingdom of Jerusalem, *al-Aqṣā* Mosque was converted into a church, and its Islamic symbols were altered. The city retained its sanctity within Christian belief during this period. This changed with Saladin's conquest in 1187 CE following the victory at *Ḥiṭṭīn*. Saladin, an Ayyūbī leader, initiated the transformation of Jerusalem into an Islamic city, extending the *waqf* policies he had implemented in Egypt to Palestine,[11] and replaced the Christian images in the city with Islamic symbols: Saladin had the pulpit that Nureddīn Zengī had ordered to be built in Aleppo before his death, especially for the *al-Aqṣā* Mosque, installed and the mihrab was cleaned, its cover was removed and the Holy Qur'an was displayed.[12] Masjid *al-Aqṣā*, which was extensively repaired and restored during the Ottoman period,[13] is described in Evliyā Çelebi's travelogue as follows:

> First of all, the eastern corner is the altar of Caliph ʿUmar. The Caliph ʿUmar worshipped here for a week as the price of conquest. Close to it is the *mihrab* of Prophet David, to the left of this *mihrab*, the Qur'an with the writing of Caliph Osman was placed on a pulpit. To the right of the pulpit there is the *Maqam* of Jesus Christ. Praise be to Allah, we visited all of them and asked for their intercession. The mosque has 800 janitors. On Fridays, the orators ascend the pulpit with a sword. That sword is the sword of Caliph ʿUmar. There are fifty *muezzins*, *müsebbih*, *muʿarrif*, *naʿt* reciters, *devirhān* and *kayyum*, and their salaries are paid from the sultan's treasury. *Surras* are sent every year. The domes of Masjid *al-Aqṣā* are completely covered with lead.[14]

As mentioned earlier, another building of central importance for Muslim *waqfs* in the Ḥaram al-Sharīf is the Dome of the Rock Mosque. It was built by

11 Halm, "The Reestablishment of Sunni Fiqh," 111–12; After the victory of *Ḥiṭṭīn*, Ṣalāḥ al-Dīn allocated the property of houses, buildings, an allocation, and temples composed of an estate to *Faqīh Ziyā' al-Dīn ʿĪsā al-Ḥakkārī*. Frenkel, "Political and Social Aspects of Islamic Religious Endowments," 4.

12 Frenkel, 'Political and Social', p. 4.

13 The most extensive restoration by the Ottomans was done by Sultan Süleyman, and afterwards, Sultan Mahmud II, Sultan Abdülaziz, and Sultan Abdülhamid II. They renewed the carpets and oil lamps of *Qibla Masjid*. For further information see, Laurent, "The Dome of the Rock," 415–24.

14 Çelebi, *Seyahatnâme*, 132.

the Umayyad Caliph ʿAbd al-Malik ibn Marwān in 71–72 AH/691–692 CE. and is considered one of the oldest and most beautiful examples of Islamic architecture.[15] The Dome of the Rock consists of a dome-shaped structure covering the *Muʿallaq* Stone, which is believed to be the *Miʿrāj al-Musharrafa* Stone (the sacred rock from which the Prophet Muḥammad ascended to the ascension), four doors entering the Dome of the Rock, sixteen windows decorated with stained glass and reveals with geometric plant motifs and Islamic calligraphy, and the *Muʿallaq* Stone.[16] The Dome of the Rock Mosque,[17] which underwent many repairs and maintenance throughout the periods of Islamic states, was also a very important structure during the Ottoman period.[18]

---

15 Tanman and Çobanoğlu, "Osmanlı Döneminde Kudüs," 512.

16 The"*Muʿallaq*" Stone is a natural rock with an irregular shape. Underneath it is a small cave called the "Masjid of the Prophets" with two altars, one deep and the other flat. Many Muslims believe that this rock is the stone on which the Prophet stepped when ascending to heaven. The virtue of this rock is that it is located within the boundaries of Masjid *al-Aqṣā*. There is also a widespread belief among the people that this stone is suspended in the air between heaven and earth. PASSIA, *Mescid-i Aksa Rehberi*, 13.

17 The main repairs and restorations made during the Abbasid period were the repair of the dome building in 216 AH / 831 CE during the reign of Caliph al-Maʾmūn and the large wooden doors built by the mother of the ʿAbbāsid Caliph al-Muqtadir Billāh in 301 AH / 913 CE. During the Fāṭimid Caliph al-Ẓāhir bi-Amr Allāh Abū al-Ḥasan b. al-Ḥakam's reign, the Dome of the Rock was extensively repaired after a major earthquake in Jerusalem in 413 AH / 1022 CE. Abū Jaʿfar ʿAbdullāh, one of the Fāṭimid caliphs, also repaired the mosque in 467 AH / 1075 CE. After the Crusaders captured Jerusalem in 492 AH / 1099 CE, they turned it into a church and called it "The Temple of the Lord (Templum Domini)." After the reconquest of Jerusalem by Ṣalāḥ al-Dīn Ayyūbī in 583 AH / 1187 CE, it was turned back into a mosque and decorated with gold ornaments. Another artifact from the Ayyūbī period is the protection wall made of wood surrounding the *Muʿallaq* Stone, which was built to prevent people from trying to take a piece from the *Muʿallaq* Stone. During the Mamlūk period, restoration and repair works were carried out during the reigns of al-Ẓāhir Baybars, Malik al-ʿĀdil al-Manṣūrī, Sultan Muḥammad b. Qalāwūn, and Amīr Muḥammad b. Sayf al-Dīn al-Ẓāhirī. For further information, Beatrice St. Laurent, "The Dome of the Rock: Restorations and Significance, 1540–1918," in *Ottoman Jerusalem*, 415–24.

18 Süleyman the Magnificent replaced the historical mosaics surrounding the collar on which the dome of the Dome of the Rock rises with specially prepared tiles brought from Istanbul between 955–969 AH/1548–1561 CE. He also had the building of the Dome of the Rock undergo a general renovation, had new windows opened in the Dome of the Rock and copper ornaments put on its doors. Sultan Abdülmecid commissioned extensive repairs to the Dome of the Rock and restored the building to its former structure in 1270 AH/1853 CE. Later, in 1291 AH/1874 CE, Sultan Abdülaziz had a large chandelier installed between the door on the *qibla* side and the pulpit and the dome was covered with lead. Sultan Abdülhamid II ordered the *Sura Yasin* to be written outside the Dome of the Rock in the *thuluth* calligraphy in 1293 AH/1876 CE. Laurent, "The Dome of the Rock," 415–424.

1.1.1 Ayyubid Period

With the conquest of the city by Saladin, the restoration and repair of Islamic *waqfs* and monuments in Jerusalem began. Buildings, agricultural lands and other real estate were taken from the Latin Church and directed to the needs of the Muslim community. Saladin also appointed an *imam* to the Dome of the Rock and allocated him a house, a garden and a field. Two years later, on 15 Ramadan 585 AH/ 27 October 1189 CE, he established a Sufi Khanqah in Jerusalem called *Ṣalāḥiyya*, which was located at the residence of the Latin Patriarch.[19]

When Saladin heard about the Third Crusade, he confiscated the Church of Saint Anna to strengthen the city's defenses and founded a *madrasa* on 13 Rajab 588 AH/ 26 July 1192 CE. Saladin built this *madrasa* in (583 AH/1187 CE) after taking Jerusalem from the Crusaders.[20] The date of the endowment of the *madrasa* is given in the sources as 588 AH/ 1192 CE. Accordingly, the *madrasa* became operational five years after its construction. This is clearly recorded on the inscription placed on the door of the *madrasa*: "In the name of Allah, the Merciful and the Compassionate. Every blessing you have is from Allah. This blessed *madrasa* was endowed by Mawlānā Malik Nāṣir Ṣalāḥ al-Dīn wa-l-Dunyā to the Shāfiʿī jurists in the year 588."[21] This *madrasa*, one of the important centers of knowledge built by Sultan Saladin, is the first and most important *madrasa* established in Jerusalem during the Ayyubid period.[22] The

19 Properties endowed by the adjacent quarter for the expenses of *Khānqāh al-Ṣalāḥiyya*: a mill, bake house, a monastery known as New Monastery and ones adjacent to it, a large underground cellar known as Patriarch's Cellar and a mansion; Patriarch Bathhouse, an underground cellar and Patriarch Pool, adjacent *rabʿ* having two floors (above and below), *Māmilā* Water Pool outside the wall of Jerusalem and a water channel in the city walls which carried the water of Māmilā Water Pool to the Patriarch Bathhouse. The *Waqf* of *Khānqāh al-Ṣalāḥiyya* included the land known as *wādī*. Frenkel, "Political and Social," 1–20.

20 Bedrettin Basuğuy, *Selahaddin-i Eyyubi Devrinde İlmi Faaliyetler* (Istanbul: Hivda İletişim, 2009), 28.

21 Johannes Pedersen, "Mescit," in *İslâm Ansiklopedisi*, vol. 8 (Istanbul: Milli Eğitim Bakanlığı Yayınları, 1993), 81–86.

22 As for the Ṣalāḥiyya *Madrasa*, it consisted of the land known as Jismāniyya, the land known as ʿAyn Silwān, the Ṣahyūn Bath known as the Bath of Mount Zion, the public bath at the gate of al-Asbāḥ, a bakery, a vegetable garden, a property in the countryside known as Ṣand Ḥanna, a residence and an adjoining house south of the *madrasa*, a mill opposite, gardens, a water source, a small church known as Probātīkā, and shops in the bazaar. Frenkel, "Political and Social Aspects of Islamic Religious Endowments (Awqāf)," 4–5. In the records of the Land Registry Books, as cited in Powers, the assets of the *waqf* that provided income for the *madrasa* were recorded as 104 shops, twelve houses, fifteen sofas, a bakery and a mill, an inn, a hammām, ʿAyn Silwān, revenues from the village of Bi'r

madrasa was called Ṣalāḥiyya as well as Nāṣiriyya. In time, it became famous as Ṣalāḥiyya with its first name. Although the *madrasa* was endowed to the followers of the Shāfiʿī *madhhab*, this should not be taken to mean that only Shāfiʿī jurisprudence was taught. In addition to Shāfiʿī jurisprudence, Ḥanafī and Ḥanbalī jurisprudence were also taught.[23]

Finally, before leaving the city for Damascus in Shawwal 588/October 1192, Saladin ordered the *Qāḍī* of Damascus, Bahāʾ al-Dīn ibn Shaddād, to establish a hospital in Jerusalem. Although Ṣalāḥ al-Dīn's death in Damascus on March 4, 1193 CE prevented him from seeing this hospital, numerous Mamluk and Ottoman documents mention the Ṣalāḥiyya Bīmāristān in Jerusalem.[24]

The beneficiaries of these *waqfs* established in Jerusalem were also clearly defined in their endowments. The *Khānqāh* al-Ṣalāḥiyya was established for young, middle-aged or elderly, married or single, Arab or Persian (non-Arab foreigners such as Turks or Iranians) Sufis.[25] The Ṣalāḥiyya *Madrasa* was established as a school of Islamic jurisprudence of the Shāfiʿī sect for students of the righteous jurisprudence to be calm and learn knowledge. Sultan Saladin's purpose in establishing a *madrasa* and a *khanqāh* was to give the city an Islamic identity by enabling Sufis and students of Islamic law to migrate to and settle in a newly conquered town.[26]

As a result, although Sultan Saladin's *waqf* policy in Egypt and Jerusalem was a continuation of Nūr al-Dīn Zengī's policy in Central and Northern Syria, it nevertheless ushered in a new era in the history of Cairo, Palestine and Jerusalem. As a victorious sultan, Saladin both ended the Christian rule in these regions and established a new political and religious order. Compared to the limited number of religious *waqfs* established in Jerusalem before the

---

Ayyūb, two olive groves, rents, the hamlet of Kastāsābila, and revenues from an unnamed village. Powers, "Revenues of Public Waqfs," 166. For information on the agricultural lands of the foundation in Jerusalem in the eighteenth century, see JS 210:173 (Islamic Court, Jerusalem).

23 The *madrasa*, which had a great influence on the scholarly movements of its period, maintained its place in the history of thought until the late Ottoman period. Prominent scholars of the period such as Bahāʾ al-Dīn Ibn Shaddād (d. 632/1234), Majd al-Dīn ibn Jaḥbal (d. 597/1200), Fakhr al-Dīn ibn ʿAsākir (d. 620/1223) and Abū ʿAmr ibn Ṣalāḥ (d. 643/1245) taught at this *madrasa*. Basuğuy, *Selahaddin-i Eyyubi*, 28.

24 Frenkel, "Political and Social," 4–5; İpşirli and Tamimi, *Evkaf ve Emlākü'l*, 45; al-ʿĀrif, *al-Mufaṣṣal*, 178–9; Cohen, *Jewish Life*, 199.

25 JS 214: 114.

26 For the detailed analysis of the aforementioned *waqfiyya* record see, Frenkel, "Political and Social," 10–15.

Crusader Kingdom, the number of religious institutions and *waqf*s established under Saladin increased considerably.[27]

At the same time, with the arrival of the Ayyubids in Jerusalem, Saladin re-established Sunni Islamic institutions to replace the Shiite institutions established by the Fatimids. These Sunni structures established during the Ayyubid and later Mamluk periods were supported by the Ottomans and their continuity was ensured. These structures can be defined in terms of their functionality: *Sharīʿa* courts, the control and management of *waqf*s, the functioning of mosques, *madrasa*s, Sufi lodges, and the provision of some educational and health services.[28] In addition to their spiritual functions, the economic and administrative aspects of the buildings and the management of the foundations attached to them were also considered within this framework. All appointments were made by the central government in order to increase both control and efficiency.

The financial resources to sustain these Sunni structures were mostly created in the post-Crusader period, especially in the case of Jerusalem and Hebron. The status of villages, their cultivability, groves, and valuable city properties came under the control of the conquering sultans. The majority of these were endowed to finance mosques, *madrasa*s, lodges, and the like. The Masjid *al-Aqṣā* mosque in Jerusalem and the *Khalīl al-Raḥmān* mosque in Hebron were the most prominent structures, with numerous villages endowed with substantial revenues. In addition to these, the Shāfiʿī Ṣalāḥiyya *madrasa* and the Sufi *Khānqāh* al-Ṣalāḥiyya and Ṣalāḥiyya *Bīmaristan* and the Prophet Moses *Maqām* (Mausoleum), which were established during the Ayyubid period, also had very large endowments.[29]

According to Frenkel, Sultan Saladin used *waqf*s as an important tool in his efforts to gain political and military power in Egypt and Syria, systematically converting property belonging to his enemies into *waqf*s.[30] As in the Zengid

27 Thanks to the *waqf* and land system implemented by Saladin, a large number of *waqf*s from Palestine have been identified before the Crusader period.

28 Frenkel, "Political and Social," 1.

29 Al-Alami, "The Waqfs of the Traditional Families of Jerusalem," 147. In his study based on the records of TTD (131 (932/1525–26); 342 (970/1562/63; 522 (980/1572–73)), Powers states that there is no record of any charitable foundation from the pre-Ayyubid period (1099–1187). During the Crusader period, Muslim places of worship were converted into churches or destroyed. More than half of the charitable foundations that survived until the Ottoman period date from the Baḥrāynī Mamlūk period. Powers, "Revenues of Public Waqfs," 184.

30 "Saladin defined his two great goals as the liberation of the Nile Valley from the Ismaili-Fatimid heresy and the cleansing of Jerusalem from the infidels." Frenkel, "Political and Social," 1.

dynasty, Saladin established *waqf*s to strengthen his own position, while other emirs and sultans established *waqf*s to reward their supporters and finance important social groups.[31]

Saladin not only supported religious structures in Jerusalem and Cairo with the *ribāṭ* and *madrasa*s he established, but also provided facilities such as meeting the housing needs of newcomers after the conquest. In this context, *waqf*s constituted a fundamental source for Saladin's monetary and social policy. With the redevelopment of Armenian and Latin properties, he depleted both the economic resources and the social support of his enemies. By seizing these resources and then distributing them to the poor and the scholars, he was able to ensure the social support of these groups. He also frequently rewarded the founders of Islamic religious structures by establishing *waqf*s. By allocating *waqf* revenues to these individuals, he gained the support of many different groups. With these methods, Saladin ensured that Muslims from many different ethnic groups settled in the lands under his control. In this way, the religious status of the places conquered by his armies was filled. These newcomers were devoted to Islam in general and to Saladin personally. They called the victorious Sultan "al-Malik al-Nāṣir" meaning the greatest *mujāhid* and the greatest victor in the Holy War against the enemies of Sunni Islam. Thus, Saladin effectively reinforced his image as a pious sultan by reinforcing the Islamic requirement. His control over properties and the *waqf*s he established served as a powerful tool both to legitimize his position as a strong leader and to attract nomads to the lands under his rule.

The *waqf*s established by Sultan Saladin in Jerusalem played a vital role in the social and economic life of the city for centuries. Historical sources from the Mamluk and Ottoman periods show that generations of Muslim rulers following Saladin either added new properties to Saladin's *waqf*s or established new ones. Nevertheless, these *waqf*s shaped the Islamic character of Jerusalem.[32]

In 587/1191, Saladin also established the al-Khātūniyya *Zāwiya* (*al-Khātūniyya* Sufi Lodge) south of the *al-Aqṣā* Mosque for a well-known scholar. The *amir*s of the Ayyubid state also established similar institutions in 589 AH/1193 CE, 593 AH/1197 CE, and 598 AH/1202 CE, and others were established in the 7th and 9th centuries AH.[33] According to al-Mujīr al-Dīn al-Ḥanbalī (d. 927/1521), thirty-one of these *madrasa*s and Sufi lodges were directly connected to the

31 The Zangid Dynasty (1127–74) supported religious institutions in Syria and their scholars. In addition to converting Christian places of worship into Islamic buildings, the Zangids used *waqf*s to provide financial support to members of religious organizations who came to them. The Zangids allocated considerable resources to build and maintain madrasas and hangahs in the areas under their control.

32 Frenkel, "Political and Social," 16.

33 Pedersen, "*Mescit*," 54.

Ḥaram al-Sharīf, twenty-nine were next to it, and sixteen were partially distant. Forty of these institutions were specifically named as *madrasas*, one as *Dār al-Qur'ān* and one as *Dār al-Ḥadīth*. In the same period, there was also the al-Malik al-Nāṣir *Madrasa* in Hebron.[34]

In addition to these, Ḥanafīyya,[35] Afḍaliyya (Afḍaliyya Madrasa; Afḍaliyya Darsiyya),[36] Maymūniyya,[37] Badriyya[38] were the *madrasas* established during the Ayyubid Period and staff were appointed in the 18th century. Some of

---

34 ibid., 54.

35 Founded by al-Malik al-Muʿaẓẓam ʿĪsā, the Ḥanafiyya *Madrasa* is also known as *Madrasa* al-Muʿaẓẓamiyya. al-ʿĀrif, *al-Mufaṣṣal*, 240. The *madrasa* was endowed for the education of Ḥanafī jurisprudence, and although the date of the endowment was 606/1209 AH, the construction of the *madrasa* continued until 614/1217 AH. In his study on the social and economic life of Jerusalem in the second half of the 18th century, Salīm Jūmʿā Sūwāriyya, based on the registers, identified eleven records regarding the appointment of officials to the *madrasa*. Sūwāriyya, *al-Ḥayāt al-Ijtimāʿiyya*, 201–4. In the Jerusalem *ḥurūfāt* registers, there are nine records of appointments to the *madrasa* between Dhū al-Ḥijja 1143 and Jumāda al-Awwal 1163/1731–50 CE.

36 The *madrasa*, recorded as the Afḍāliyya *Madrasa* in the Jerusalem *ḥurūfāt* registers, was named after its founder, Malik al-Afḍal Nūreddīn Abū al-Ḥasan ʿAlī ibn Sulṭān Ṣalāḥ al-Dīn. After building the *madrasa*, Malik al-Afḍal endowed it in 589 AH/1193 CE to the Mālikī jurists who came to Bayt al-Maqdis and began to reside there. Al-Malik al-Afḍal endowed this *madrasa* and the neighborhood of Maghāriba, known as Ḥārat al-Maghāriba, to the *fuqahā'* and students from various parts of North Africa. The *madrasa* played an important role in the intellectual movements in Bayt al-Maqdis during both the Ayyūbī and Mamlūk periods. The record of the *madrasa*, also called Darsiyya Afḍaliyya in addition to Afḍaliyya *Madrasa* in the Jerusalem *ḥurūfāt* registers, states that it was required for the *'ulamā'* of the Mālikiyya school of jurisprudence. VGMA, 1109: 6/37. In another record of the *madrasa*, the name "*Madrasat al-Maʿrūf al-Mālikiyya al-maʿrūf bi-Qubbat al-Afḍāliyya*" is used. VGMA, 1107: 2/78. The *madrasa* continued its presence in scholarly life until the end of the 18th century, and today it has taken the form of a house where poor people from the Maghrib live. Basuğuy, *Selahaddin-i Eyyubi*, 29.

37 The Maymūniyya *Madrasa*, located near Bāb al-Sāḥira, was originally built as a church, known by the Greeks as the Church of Dayr al-Majdaliyya. Amīr Fāris al-Dīn Abū Saʿīd al-Maymūn b. ʿAbdullāh al-Qasrī established the *madrasa* as a foundation in 593/1196. al-ʿĀrif, *al-Mufaṣṣal*, 239. Again, ten records were found in the Jerusalem *ḥurūfāt* registers between Rajab 1123–Rabīʿ al-Awwal 1149/1711–1736, in which officials belonging to the al-Luṭfī family, one of the leading families of Jerusalem, were also assigned to the *madrasa*, which was established before the Ottoman period.

See VGMA, 1112: 1/91; 1107: 2/216.

38 The Badrīyya *Madrasa* was located in Ḥārat al-Manzibān near the Lu'lu'iyya *Madrasa*. The *madrasa* was built in 610/1213 and endowed by Badr al-Dīn Muḥammad b. Abū al-Qāsim al-Ḥakkārī. al-ʿĀrif, *al-Mufaṣṣal*, 240. ʿAbd al-Mahdī, *al-Madāris fī Bayt al-Maqdis*, 359. A shaykh and a janitor were appointed for the *madrasa* in the *ḥurūfāt* registers. VGMA, 1140:245/12. al-Sūwāriyya also identified a record of the appointment of a *nāẓir*, *mashā'ikha*, *bawwāb*, and *saqā* for the madrasa in the registers. al-Sūwāriyya, *al-Ḥayāt al-Ijtimāʿiyya*, 200.

the other artifacts of the Ayyubid period in and around *Ḥaram al-Sharīf* are recorded as Qubbat al-Yūsuf, Qubbat al-Naḥwiyya, Qubbat al-Miʿrāj, and the Olive Prayer Hall.[39] In another study on the subject, it is stated that among the charitable *waqf*s established during the Ayyubid period, the Shāfiʿī Ṣalāḥiyya *Madrasa*, Sufi Khānqāh al-Ṣalāḥiyya, and the Mausoleum of the Prophet Mūsā were the most important great charities were the most important great charities of the period.[40]

1.1.2 Mamluk Period

After the Ayyubids, Jerusalem was ruled by the Mamluks (1250–1517). During the Mamluk period, the city of Jerusalem was part of a state that extended from Egypt and western Arabia to central Anatolia. Cairo was the throne city of the Mamluk sultanate, while Damascus and Aleppo were the most prominent provincial cities. In other words, under Mamluk rule, the city of Jerusalem was geographically close to the central government.[41] However, it is difficult to say that its proximity to the center gave Jerusalem any political or economic advantage. Jerusalem was seen as a suitable "place of exile" for commanders during the Mamluk period, as it lacked a strong headquarters or fortress that could be the basis for a possible uprising and was cut off from the environment.[42] The last years of Mamluk rule in particular were characterized by deteriorating security conditions in Jerusalem and the region and a decline in the local economy.[43] The same period of decline applied to other cities in Egypt and Syria.[44]

The Mamluks paid great attention to Jerusalem, the third city considered holy by Muslims, and focused on construction activities, which made it possible for Jerusalem to become an Islamic city again. Eighty of the 150 important historical monuments in Jerusalem today belong to the Mamluk period. The increase in construction activities in Jerusalem during this period can be attributed to the Mamluk sultans' efforts to establish themselves in the society, religious purposes, and the Mamluk emirs' endowment of their properties by

39 Tanman and Çobanoğlu, "Osmanlı Döneminde Kudüs," 517–22; See, Appendix 8.

40 al-Alami, "The Waqfs of the Traditional Families," 146; Powers, who utilizes al-Ḥanbalī's travel narrative in addition to the books of the *Tahrīr* of *Awqāf*, mentions six charitable foundations in Jerusalem during the Ayyūbī Period (1187–1250). Powers, "Revenues of Public Waqfs," 166.

41 Robert Hillenbrand, "Introduction: Structure, Style, and Context in the Monuments of Ottoman Jerusalem," in *Ottoman Jerusalem*, 1–25, 1–3.

42 Singer, *Kadılar, Kullar*, 6.

43 Avcı, *Değişim Sürecinde*, 35.

44 Raymond, *Osmanlı Döneminde*, 16.

appointing their children or relatives as trustees in order to prevent confiscation after their deaths.[45]

In the Mamluk period, the undeniable presence of *waqf*s as a source of wealth and influence in social life manifested itself in every aspect of urban and rural life. Frenkel evaluates the *waqf*s established by the Mamluk ruling class as a means for the ruling elite to establish both prestige and dominance over society, in addition to their philanthropic purposes. Here, the ruling elite's decisive influence in both the control of culture and the shaping of the social structure was emphasized.[46] To achieve this goal, rulers could not limit their activities to public control or monitoring of society. They had to invest in buildings that consolidated their position. Islamic *waqf*s served as signs of the exalted position of the endower in the urban space. These *waqf*s were employed to institutionalize the social hierarchy and to demonstrate the relationship between the *waqf* and the recipient. In this way, *waqf*s reflected the mindset of the rulers.[47] This was not only ensured by military officials. To ensure this, sultans and rulers needed religious buildings financed by *waqf*s. Without the support of other parts of society, it was not possible to talk about the hegemony of the Mamluk rulers as a whole. In this sense, the *waqf* gave the impression of being a social institution that supported the entire Islamic society without any discrimination. In practice, most of the beneficiaries of *waqf*s belonged to the Mamluk ruling class.[48]

The Mamluk ruling elite built a series of structures both for the benefit of religious institutions and for the general public, and Islamic *waqf*s financed both their construction and their day-to-day operation. The prominent presence of these structures and their significant imprint on the landscape cannot be ignored by historians writing centuries after the fall of the Mamluk sultanate.[49]

Of the two different periods of the Mamluk Period,[50] twenty-five charitable *waqf*s were established in the Baḥrī Mamluk Period (1250–1390) and eleven

45 André Raymond, *Osmanlı Döneminde Arap Kentleri*, trans. Ali Berktay (Istanbul: Tarih Vakfı Yurt Yayınları, 1995), 33.

46 Frenkel, "Awqāf in Mamlūk Bilād al-Shām," 149–53. For the opposite opinion, see Moshe Gil, *Documents of the Jewish Pious Foundations from the Cairo Geniza* (Leiden: Brill, 1976), 11.

47 R. S. Humphreys, "The Expressive Intent of the Mamlūk Architecture of Cairo: A Preliminary Essay," *Studia Islamica* 35 (1972): 69–119, 79–80.

48 For the detailed information related to social groups benefitted from Mamluk *waqf*, see Frenkel, '*Awqāf* in Mamluk', p. 154–156.

49 Frenkel, "*Awqāf* in Mamlūk Bilād al-Shām," 156.

50 Medieval historians divide the Mamlūk State, which was established in Egypt in 1250 and lasted until the Ottoman conquest in 1517, into two periods. The first one between 1250–1382 was called "Baḥrī" because the majority of the Mamlūk sultans were raised in the

charitable *waqfs* were established in the Burjī Mamluk Period (1390–1517).[51] The *Encyclopaedia of Islam* notes that the number of *madrasas*, Ṣūfī lodges, *khanqāhs*, and *ribāṭs* established during the Mamlūk period was significant. Numerous foundations were also created to support the many religious *madrasas* founded by the Baḥrī and Burjī Mamlūks.

There were more than fifty *madrasas* and around twenty sufi lodges, *khanqāhs* and *ribāṭs* in Jerusalem during the Mamluk period. Some of the *waqfs* built or repaired in Jerusalem during the Mamluk period are Qarīmiyya *Madrasa*,[52] Bayram Pasha Fountain (Sabīl Shaʿlān, originally from the Shaʿlān Ayyūbī period and repaired under Mamlūks), Fakhrīyya *Madrasa*, Qāḍī Burhān al-Dīn *Miḥrāb* and *Minbar* (*Minbar* al-Sayf), Tankiziyya *Madrasa* and Khanqāh, Sūq al-Qaṭṭānīn,[53] and Jāwiliyya *Madrasa* (built 715–720 AH/1315–1320 CE), renovated in the early fifteenth century and later serving as the Mamlūk governors' residence (Dār al-Niyāba). This *madrasa* retained this function in the Ottoman period until 1870, after which it became the Nizāmiyya Barracks. Charitable institutions established by Baḥrī Mamlūks included *Ribāṭ* ʿAlāʾ al-Dīn Amīr ʿAlam al-Dīn Sanjar al-Dawādār, Sitt Tunshuq Palace by al-Ṣāliḥī, *Khanqāh* Dawādārīyya (d. 695/1295) by Amīr ʿAlāʾ al-Dīn Aydoğdu (d. 666/1267),[54] *Madrasa* al-Wajīhiyya endowed by Shaykh Wajīh

barracks on the island of al-Rawḍa on the Nile and resided there; the second one between 1382–1517 was called "Burjī" Mamlūks because the majority of the Mamlūk Sultans resided in the bastions of Qalʿat al-Jabal. Kazım Yaşar Kopraman, "Mısır Memlûkleri (1250–1517)," in *Doğuştan Günümüze Büyük İslâm Tarihi*, vol. 6 (İstanbul: Çağ Yayınları, 1986), 444.

51 Powers offers information related to founder of the *waqf*, the name of the *waqf*, its establishment date and its properties in Jerusalem *waqfs* which were recorded as philanthropic *waqfs* from the first years of Ottoman's Jerusalem control covering forty-seven years.

52 Although it is not known when the Qarīmiyya *Madrasa* was founded, it is estimated that it was established around 700 AH / 1301 AD. al-Ḥanbalī, *al-Uns al-Jalīl*, 38.

53 Al-Ḥanbalī (*Al-Uns al-Jalīl*, 35) states that the Dengiziyya (Tenkiziyya, Tankiziyya) *Madrasa* was established as a foundation by Amīr Tankiz al-Nāṣirī, the Nāʾib of Damascus, in 729 AH/1328 CE. The *Evkāf Tahrir* Register numbered 522 states that a copy of the *waqf* was written in 730 AH/1328 CE, while Powers states that the inscription on the door of the *madrasa* indicates that the date of the *waqf* is 729 AH/1328 CE. See Powers, "Revenues," 169. In the Jerusalem *ḥurūfāt* registers, it was found that ten appointments were made to the *madrasa* between Rabīʿ al-Awwal 1137–Dhū al-Qaʿda 1228/1724–1813 CE.

54 It was determined that six appointments were made between Shaʿbān 1111–Jumādā al-Awwal 1160/1699–1748 CE regarding the lodge, which is referred to as the Dawādārīyya *Madrasa* in the Jerusalem *ḥurūfāt* registers. In a record titled as Dawādārīyya *Madrasa* Lodging from the Ḥanafiyya *Madrasa Mulḥaqāt*, it is indicated that the foundation was from the Ḥanafiyya *Madrasa Mulḥaqāt*. VGMA, 1160: 116/40; 1107: 2/227; 1107: 2/283; 1091: 77/5; 1112: 1/76; 1112: 1/155; 1112: 1/156; 1112: 1/189.

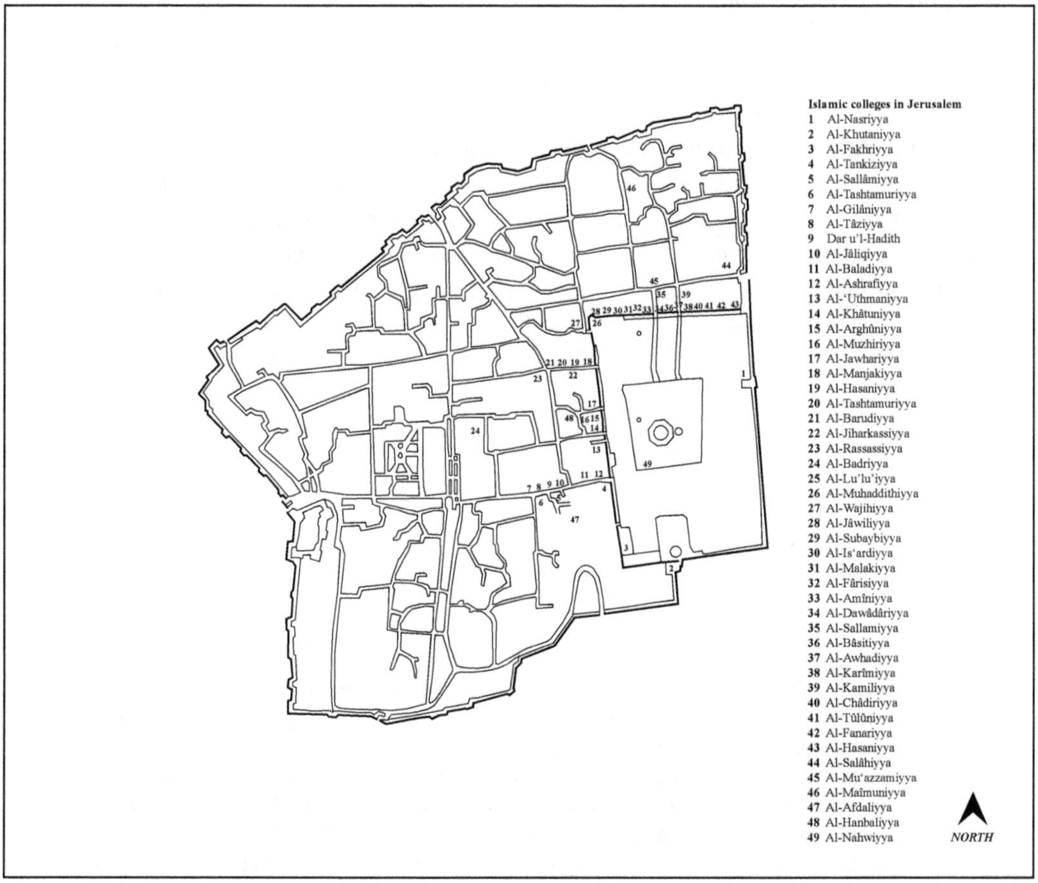

FIGURE 2 Map of *madrasas* in Jerusalem during the Mamluk period
Note: The identification of the *madrasas* in Jerusalem during the Mamluk period is based on the map prepared by Donald P. Little. See Donald P. Little, "Jerusalem under the Ayyūbids and Mamlūks, 1187–1516 AD," in *Jerusalem in History*, ed. Kamil Jamil al-Asali (London: Scorpion Publishing Ltd., 1989), 190.

al-Dīn Muḥammad ibn 'Uthmān al-Tanūkhī in 701/1302, *Madrasa* al-Jālikiyya by Amīr Rukn al-Dīn Baybars in 707/1307, and the Karīmiyya, Sallāmiyya[55]

55 There are three different records regarding the al-Salāmiyya *Madrasa* located in Ḥaṭṭ al-Dawūd in Jerusalem in the *Evkāf Tahrir* Book No. 522. According to the aforementioned record, one-third of the foundation revenues were allocated to the *madrasa*, which was endowed with the revenues of Jabā'a Village. The salaries of the *madrasa*'s residents and staff were distributed as follows: fifteen *dirhams* per month for the Qur'ān teacher; seven and a half *dirhams* per month for each of the six students; and twenty *dirhams* per month for the *muḥaddith* reciting *ḥadīth* from Ṣaḥīḥ al-Bukhārī during the blessed three months. The annual cost of the attendants' salaries totaled 780 *dirhams*,

and Amīniyya[56] *Madrasas* established in 715–720 AH/ and 1315–1320 CE. The most spectacular of the buildings built by the emirs are the aforementioned Tankiziyya *Madrasa*, built by Amīr Tankiz al-Nāṣirī, the viceroy of Damascus, in 729 AH/1329 CE, and Sūq al-Qaṭṭānīn.[57]

The Ashrāfiyya *Madrasa*, completed by Mamlūk Sultan Qā'itbāy in 887 AH/ 1482 CE, was destroyed by an earthquake in 1545.[58] The *madrasa*, which overlooks the *ḥaram* of Masjid *al-Aqṣā* with large windows cut from three sides in Jerusalem, was renovated in line with the detailed explanation made in its *waqfiyya* and al-Ḥanbalī's recipes, and took its final form after the visit

---

and the remaining two-thirds of the *waqf*'s income was conditional on the *waqf*'s family and descendants. When the *waqf*'s descendants were completely cut off, the *waqf* revenues would be divided into four and distributed as follows: one-quarter to the sick in the Ṣalāḥī Bīmāristān; one-quarter to the poor in the Manṣūrī *Ribāṭ* for the provision of bread; one-quarter to *Sīmāt al-Khalīl*; and one-quarter to the *Zāwiyat al-Sallāmiyya al-Kubrā*. Powers, "Revenues," 182. As quoted in Powers, the revenues of the villages of al-Baṭīḥ, Jirās, the hamlet of Bayt Rāfā, the hamlet of 'Adāsa, and the villages of Ba'alīl and Bīra al-Kubrā were endowed for the *madrasa* founded by Shaykh Mujadd al-Dīn 'Abd al-Malik b. Abū Bakr al-Mūṣilī. Powers, "Revenues," 183. Although there is an appointment record for the al-Salāmiyya *Madrasa* in the Jerusalem *Ḥurūfāt* registers, the "Dār al-Qurrā' al-Salāmiyya Foundation," which is more frequently mentioned in the records and has the same place of establishment, is considered to be the same foundation. VGMA, 1107: 2/14; 22, 60, 63, 136, 206; 1109: 6/158; 553: 38/11. Al-Ḥanbalī, on the other hand, states that the name of the *madrasa* was also referred to as "Mawṣiliyya" *Madrasa*. al-Ḥanbalī, *al-Uns al-Jalīl*, 42.

56 The *madrasa*, which is located on the right side of the Fayṣal Gate entering the Ḥaram, was endowed by Amīn al-Dīn 'Abdullāh in 730 AH/1329 AD. Al-Ḥanbalī, *al-Uns al-Jalīl*, 38.

57 Tanman and Çobanoğlu, "Osmanlı Döneminde Kudüs", p. 519–528; Tomar, "Kudüs", 334; Pedersen, "Mescit," 54; "Üç Kitaplı Kentler - 19. Yüzyıl Fotoğraflarında Kudüs ve Kutsal Topraklar" (İstanbul: Suna ve İnan Kıraç Vakfı, İstanbul Araştırmaları Enstitüsü, Eylül 2008), 42–47.

58 al-Ḥanbalī, *al-Uns al-Jalīl*, 325; The *madrasa*, located inside the Ḥaram, between the Osmāniyya *Madrasa* and the Baladiyya *Madrasa* from the north, was built in 875 AH / 1470 CE during the reign of Sultan al-Malik al-Ashrāf Abū al-Naṣr. al-'Ārif, al-Mufaṣṣal, 255.

of al- Qā'itbāy to Jerusalem.[59] Bāsiṭiyya (Khānqāh al-Bāsiṭiyya),[60] Fārisiyya,[61] Jīlāniyya,[62] Khanqāh al-Jawhariyya (Madrasa al-Jawhariyya),[63] Khātuūniyya,[64]

59 Burgoyne, *Mamluk Jerusalem*, 589–605.

60 The construction of the Bāsiṭiyya *Madrasa*, which was started by Shaykh al-Islām Shams al-Dīn Muḥammad al-Harawī, was completed by Qāḍī Zayn al-Dīn 'Abd al-Bāsiṭ b. Khalīl al-Dimashqī upon the death of the Shaykh al-Islām. Al-Ḥanbalī, al-Uns al-Jalīl, 39. The *madrasa*, to which the revenues of Ṣūr Bāḥir Village were endowed, was also named after the woman who founded it. The endowment of the *madrasa*, which was established as a *waqf*, is dated 834 AH/1430 CE. Powers, "Revenues," 182. In the Jerusalem *ḥurūfāt* registers, five appointment records are found between Jumādā al-Awwal 1108–Sha'bān 1143 AH/1696–1731 CE for the *madrasa*, which was referred to as Bāsiṭiyya *Madrasa* and Hankāh-i Bāsiṭiyya *Madrasa* in two ways.

61 The Fārisiyya *Madrasa* was founded by Amīr Fārisī b. al-Amīr Quṭlū Malik b. 'Abdullāh. According to Powers, Mujīr al-Dīn also mentions a *waqfiyya* dated 755 AH/1354 CE for the *madrasa*, to which the revenues of the town of Ṭūl Karīm were endowed. Powers, "Revenues," 178–79. In the Jerusalem *ḥurūfāt* registers, seven appointments were made to the *madrasa* between Ṣafar 1120 and Rajab 1138/1708–1726 CE.

62 In the Jerusalem *ḥurūfāt* registers, nine appointment records of the *madrasa* were identified between the dates of Dhū al-Qa'da 1123–Jumādā al-Awwal 1201/1711–1787 CE.

63 As mentioned above, the word "khānkāh" was used instead of "ribāṭ" in the sixteenth century, and both words mean "Sufi *khānqāh*." There is also a very fine distinction between *khānkāh* and *madrasa*. As quoted by Powers, the "Jawhariyya *Madrasa- khānkāh*" *waqf*, which is referred to as *khānqāh* in some records and as a *ribāṭ* in others, is sometimes recorded as both a *khānqāh* and a *madrasa*. Powers, "Revenues," 183. In the Jerusalem *ḥurūfāt* registers, similar to Powers, it is recorded as both the *khānqāh* al-Jawhariyya *Madrasa* Foundation (VGMA, 1109: 6/22) and the *Khānqāh* al-Jawhariyya Foundation. See VGMA, 1107: 2/264; 1109: 6/24; 1109: 6/27. Two appointments to the *madrasa* were recorded between Muḥarram 1131–Sha'bān 1143/1718–1731 CE. Established by Jawhar al-Qunqabāy al-Zimām in 843 AH/1439 CE, the foundation was endowed with the revenues of the villages of Bayt Zaytūn, Kūfiyya, Taqū', and Ṭūl Karīm. Powers, "Revenues," 183. The *madrasa* is located at Ḥadīd Gate, opposite the *Madrasa* of Arghūniyya. Al-'Ārif, *al-Mufaṣṣal*, 254.

64 *Madrasa-Zāwiya* Khātūniyya was founded by 'Ujul Khātūn, the daughter of Shams al-Dīn Muḥammad b. Sayf al-Dīn, al-Kāzāniyya al-Baghdādiyya. 'Ujul Khātūn endowed the revenues of Baṭn al-Jamal village for the needs of the *madrasa* in 755 AH/1354 CE. It was later completed by Isfahān Shāh, daughter of Amīr Kāzān Shāh, in 782 AH/1380 CE. Powers, "Revenues," 179. In the Jerusalem *ḥurūfāt* registers, twelve assignment records for the *madrasa* were found between Jumādā al-Ākhira 1136–Muḥarram 1147/1724–1734 CE.

Madrasa al-Qādirīyya,[65] *Madrasa* al-Tāziyya,[66] *Madrasa* al-Mālikiyya (Qubbat al-Mālikiyya),[67] Manjikiyya,[68] Muṣliyya,[69] ʿUthmāniyya,[70]

65 Miṣr Khātūn's father built the Qādiriyya *Madrasa* in 836 AH/1432 CE, and the revenues of an inn were also endowed for the needs of the *madrasa*. Powers, "Revenues," 182. According to Mujīr al-Dīn, the *madrasa* was endowed by Naṣr al-Dīn Muḥammad al-Ghādirī after the death of his wife Miṣr Khātūn. The *madrasa*, which has no endowment, was built in 836 AH/1432 CE during the reign of al-Malik al-Ashrāf Barsbāy. Al-Ḥanbalī, *al-Uns al-Jalīl*, 40. The Qādiriyya *Madrasa* is located between the Kirmīmiyya and Ṭūlūniyya *Madrasas*, between Ḥiṭṭa Gate and Asbāṭ Gate. Al-ʿĀrif, *al-Mufaṣṣal*, 253. In the Jerusalem *ḥurūfāt* registers, an appointment record dated Ramaḍān 1130/1718 CE was found for the *madrasa*.

66 The *Madrasa* Tāziyya built by Amīr Tāz is known as Tāziyya on Dāwūd Street, near the Chain Gate. The village of Mīnā, with its bakery, mill, shops, and other revenues, was endowed for the expenses of the *madrasa*. Powers, "Revenues," 179. In the Jerusalem *ḥurūfāt* registers, an appointment record dated Shawwāl 1121/1709 CE was found for the *madrasa*.

67 The Mālikiyya *Madrasa*, built by al-Malik Quṭluqtimur in 757 AH/1356 CE, is located between the Asʿardiyya and Fārisiyya *Madrasas*, and the *Ḥaram* is entered from the right side of the *madrasa* through the Gate of Honor. Al-ʿĀrif, *al-Mufaṣṣal*, 246. The *madrasa* was built during the sultanate of al-Nāṣir Muḥammad b. Qalāwūn by al-Ḥājj Malik al-Jūkandār. Al-Ḥanbalī, *al-Uns al-Jalīl*, 38. However, Malika, the daughter of al-Sayfī Quṭlūkhum al-Nāṣirī and the sultan's wife, endowed the assets that would provide income for the foundation in 745 AH/1344 CE. Powers, "Revenues," 177. The revenues of the village of Dayr al-Bazūʿ were endowed. In the Jerusalem *ḥurūfāt* registers, seven assignment records for the *madrasa* were found between Muḥarram 1127–Ṣafar 1134/1715–1721 CE.

68 The endowment of the Manjakiyya *Madrasa*, founded by Amīr Manjak Pasha b. ʿAbdullāh (Meḥmed al-Sayfī Manjak al-Ashrāfī), is dated 730 AH/1329 CE. Powers, "Revenues," 176. However, Mujīr al-Dīn al-ʿUlaymī al-Ḥanbalī gives the construction date of the *madrasa* as 741 AH/1340 CE. Some sources state that Amīr al-Manjak came to Jerusalem to build the *madrasa* for Sultan al-Malik al-Nāṣir al-Ḥasan, but upon al-Malik's death in 762 AH/1361 CE, he built the *madrasa* in his own name. Powers, "Revenues," 176. In the Jerusalem *ḥurūfāt* registers, there are three appointment records for the *madrasa* between Rabīʿ al-Ākhir 1118–Dhū al-Qaʿda 1123/1706–1711 CE. If the *Hankāh-i Manjakiyya*, which is also identified in the records, is considered to be the same foundation, the number of appointments increases to four. VGMA, 1112: 1/30.

69 The *waqf*, which is referred to as *Hankāh-i Mawṣiliyya Madrasa* Foundation or Mawṣiliyya *Madrasa* in the records, has nine appointment records between the dates of Rajab 1119–Shaʿbān 1143/1707–1731 CE.

70 The *madrasa*, which is referred to as the ʿUthmāniyya *Madrasa* in the Jerusalem *ḥurūfāt* Books, is also known as the Isfahāniyya *Madrasa*. The *madrasa*, to which the villages of Kafr Ṣūr and Ṭūlkarm were endowed, was founded by Isfahān Shāh Khātūn (Khān). Powers, "Revenues," 183. The madrasa, built in 840 AH/1436 CE, is located near the Sulṭāniyya *Madrasa*. Al-Ḥanbalī, *al-Uns al-Jalīl*, 36.

Shaykhūniyya,[71] Awhādiyya,[72] Jīlāniyya,[73] Khātūniyya,[74] Argūniyya,[75] Es'ardiyya,[76] Lu'lu'iyya,[77] Tashtimūriyya,[78] Tulūniyya,[79] Fānāriyya,[80] Zemāniyya,[81]

---

71 Amīr Sayf al-Dīn Qatīsha b. 'Alī b. Muḥammad, one of the leading high-ranking officials of Damascus, established the Shaykhūniyya Lodges in 761 AH/1359 CE. The endower stipulated that the management of the *waqf* was to be entrusted primarily to himself and after his death to his son Shaykhūn. According to Powers, the lodges, named after the endowment's son Shaykhūn, were one and the same institution, also known as the Shaykhūniyya *Madrasa*. Powers, "Revenues," 179. The entire income of the village of Qalūniyya, a few kilometers north of the village of 'Ayn Kārim, was endowed to the Shaykhūniyya *Madrasa*. Singer, *Kadılar, Kullar*, 95. In the Jerusalem *ḥurūfāt* registers, an appointment record for the madrasa dated Jumādā al-Awwal 1201/1786 CE was found.

72 It was endowed by al-Malik al-Awḥad Najm al-Dīn Yūsuf b. al-Malik al-Mu'aẓẓam 'Īsā b. al-'Ādil in 697 AH/1297 CE. Al-Ḥanbalī, al-Uns al-Jalīl, 39. The *madrasa* is located on the south side of the city, in the Bāb al-Ḥiṭṭa, and east of the Dawādārīyya and Bāsiṭiyya *madrasas*.

73 The *madrasa*, which was also called "Khālidiyya *Madrasa*" during the period we examined, is located in the neighborhood of the Ghaylāniyya Tomb, which is near the Tāziyya *Madrasa* on the west side. Religious sciences were taught in the *madrasa* built in 753 AH/1352 CE. Kāmil Jamīl al-'Asalī, *Ma'āhid al-'Ilm fī Bayt al-Maqdis* (Amman: Jāmi'at 'Ummāl al-Maṭābi' al-Ta'āwuniyya, 1981), 142.

74 Located between the gates of *Bāb al-Ḥadīd* and *Bāb al-Qaṭṭānīn*, the *madrasa* is flanked by *Ḥaram al-Sharīf* to the west and the Arghūniyya *Madrasa* to the south. Al-'Ārif, al-Mufaṣṣal, 250. The *madrasa* was endowed in 755 AH/1354 CE by 'Ijal Khātūn, the daughter of Shams al-Dīn Muḥammad b. Sayf al-Dīn al-Kāzānī al-Baghdādī. Al-Ḥanbalī, *al-Uns al-Jalīl*, 36.

75 Located in Bāb al-Ḥadīd, the *madrasa* is adjacent to the Khātūniyya *Madrasa*. Sayf al-Dīn Arghūn al-Kāmilī endowed the *madrasa* in 758 AH/1356 CE.

76 The *madrasa* was endowed by al-Ḥājj Majd al-Dīn b. Yūsuf al-As'ardī in 770 AH/1368 CE. Al-Ḥanbalī, *al-Uns al-Jalīl*, 38. The *madrasa* is also written as *Madrasa* al-*Khānqāh* al-As'ardiyya in various records in the registry. See JS 242: 366; JS 244: 125.

77 To the south of the Lu'lu'iyya *Madrasa* in Line Marzubān is the Badriyya *Madrasa*. The *madrasa* was endowed by Amīr Lu'lu' Ghāzī al-Malik al-Ashrāf Sha'bān in 775 AH/1373 CE. al-Ḥanbalī, *al-Uns al-Jalīl*, 46.

78 Founded by al-Ashrāf al-Sayfī Ṭashtamur al-'Alā'ī in 784 AH/1382 CE, the *madrasa* is located on the road between the *Bāb al-Silsila* gate and the *Ḥārat al-Sharaf* road beyond the Barakat Khātūn Tomb. al-'Āṣalī, *Ma'āhid*, 136.

79 Located to the west of the Fanāriyya *Madrasa*, between *Bāb al-Ḥiṭṭa* and *Bāb al-Asbāṭ*, it can be traced back to Shihāb al-Dīn Aḥmad b. al-Nāṣirī Muḥammad al-Ṭūlūnī al-Ẓāhirī. The *madrasa* is believed to have been built before 800 AH/1398 CE. al-Ḥanbalī, *al-Uns al-Jalīl*, 40.

80 It has the same founder as the Ṭūlūniyya *Madrasa* and was established by Shihāb al-Dīn al-Ṭūlūnī in approximately 800 AH/1398 CE. It is located opposite the Ṭūlūniyya *Madrasa* from the east. al-'Ārif, *al-Mufaṣṣal*, 252.

81 According to Mujīr al-Dīn al-Ḥanbalī, the *Ribāṭ/Madrasa* al-Zamāniyya was endowed by al-Ḥājj Shams al-Dīn Muḥammad b. al-Zamān in 881 AH/1476 CE. The *madrasa* is

Ḥusniyya,[82] Muzhiriyya[83] were the other *madrasas* established in Mamluk Period.[84]

1.2 *Muslim* Waqfs *in Jerusalem during the Eighteenth century*

Following the Ottoman conquest, *madrasas* and mosques inherited from the Ayyūbī and Mamlūk periods were preserved, with their core functions maintained through repairs and official appointments. These activities in the eighteenth century can be traced through *Ḥurūfāt* (Ruling Elite Appointment) Registers in the VGMA, covering 1102–1250 AH/1690–1834 CE.[85]

Waqfs established between 922 AH/1522 CE and 1025 AH/1615 CE followed the *qāḍī*'s legal school, as in Ayyūbī and Mamlūk times. For instance, the *waqf* of Mālikī Sa'd al-Dīn Taqī al-Dīn ibn al-'Alamī adhered to Mālikī jurisprudence, while that of Ḥanafī Zayn al-Dīn ibn Jamāl al-Dīn 'Abdullāh al-Dā'irī (al-Khālidī) was set up by a Shāfi'ī *qāḍī*. After this period, all *qāḍīs* appointed in Jerusalem were Ḥanafī, and regardless of the endower's legal school, *waqfs* adopted a standardized Ḥanafī form. For example, a Shāfi'ī *muftī* from the

located to the west of the *Ḥaram*, opposite the 'Uthmāniyya *Madrasa*. al-Ḥanbalī, *al-Uns al-Jalīl*, 36.

82 Endowed by Emir Ḥusām al-Dīn Abū Muḥammad al-Ḥusn ibn Naṣr al-Dīn in 837 AH/1434 CE, the *madrasa* is located north of the Nāẓir Gate, near the *Madrasa* al-Manjikiyya and above the *Ribāṭ* of 'Alā' al-Dīn al-Baṣīr. Al-Ḥanbalī, *al-Uns al-Jalīl*, 275.

83 The Muzhiriyya *Madrasa*, located to the west of the Ḥadīd Gate and the Arghūniyya *Madrasa*, was endowed by Zayn al-Dīn Abū Bakr Muḥammad ibn Aḥmad ibn 'Abd al-Khāliq ibn 'Uthmān ibn Muzhir al-Anṣārī in 893 AH/1487 CE. However, the construction of the endowment building was completed in 885 AH/1480 CE. al-'Ārif, *Mufaṣṣal*, 255; al-Ḥanbalī, *al-Uns al-Jalīl*, 37. Half of the revenues of the village of Bayt al-Sāḥūr were endowed for this *madrasa*. JS 264: 38–39.

84 In his study on Ayyubid and Mamluk *madrasas*, 'Abd al-Jalīl Ḥasan 'Abd al-Mahdī also mentions the *madrasas* of Bārūdiyya, Baladiyya, Jaharkasiyya, Ḥanbaliyya, Muḥaddithiyya, and Ṣabībiyya. It is conceivable that these *madrasas*, which are not included in our records, may have been destroyed over time. 'Abd al-Mahdī, *al-Madāris fī Bayt al-Maqdis*, 71–110.

85 When previous records were examined, most were related to religious and educational *waqfs*. Additionally, numerous records documented *waqf* donations, such as mosques, *zāwiyas*, shrines, *khānqāhs*, *maqāms*, and *marqads*, established in the names of revered figures like prophets, *ṣaḥāba*, and *awliyā'*. Educational *waqfs*, primarily *madrasas*, were mostly constructed during the Ayyubid and Mamluk periods. In Jerusalem, regarded as holy by the three Abrahamic religions, the abundance of religious and educational institutions serving as centers of *taṣawwuf* and culture holds significant meaning. For detailed information related to registers see, Appendices 1–12; Şerife Eroğlu Memiş, *Ḥurūfāt Defterlerinde Kudüs-i Şerīf Kazası: Vakıflar, Görevliler ve Görevler* (İstanbul: Yeditepe, 2017).

Jārullāh family restructured his *waqf* (originally established in 1031 AH/1622 CE) in 1032 AH/1623 CE to align with this new order.[86]

For Ottoman sultans, safeguarding the *Ḥaram al-Sharīf*, home to Masjid *al-Aqṣā* and the Dome of the Rock, Jerusalem's foremost Muslim religious center, was a primary religious duty. Many religious structures built or repaired during the Ottoman classical period were located in or near the *Ḥaram al-Sharīf*. A notable Ottoman innovation was replacing the mosaic exterior of the Dome of the Rock with blue, green, and yellow tiles, giving the mosque its current appearance. Compared to the Mamlūk period, Ottoman architecture in the *Ḥaram al-Sharīf* features smaller buildings. Another key difference is the Ottoman shift toward prioritizing social and municipal services over religious and educational structures. Investments focused on improving security, water supply, constructing a new covered bazaar, and enhancing the welfare of Jerusalem's residents. The Ottoman administration likely aimed to demonstrate its superiority in a newly conquered region, with the reconstruction of Jerusalem's walls serving as a tangible expression of this distinction and the new administration's prioritie.[87]

At the same time, it should be noted that compared to the Mamluk period, Ottoman architecture in *Ḥaram al-Sharīf* is represented by much smaller buildings.[88] Another noteworthy difference compared to the Mamluk period is the change in the Ottoman priorities in the city and the prioritization of social and municipal services. Instead of religious and educational buildings, emphasis was placed on the infrastructure investments needed in the city.[89] Allocations and donations to the city budget were concentrated in areas such as improving security conditions, providing water, building a new covered bazaar, and improving the welfare of the people of Jerusalem. The Ottoman administration wanted to concretely demonstrate its superiority to the people of a newly conquered region, and it is likely that the reconstruction of the walls of Jerusalem was also conceived by the Ottoman administration as a way to show the distinction between the two administrations and to express the priorities of the new administration.[90]

The reconstruction of city walls and fortress brought the sense of security for the residence twenty years after the conquest. The most significant security problem of the Jerusalem and its surrounding before the Ottoman conquest

86 al-Alami, "The Waqfs of the Traditional Families of Jerusalem," 156.
87 Avcı, *Değişim Sürecinde*, 36.
88 Avcı, *Değişim Sürecinde*, 39.
89 Raymond, "The Ottoman Conquest," 84–101.
90 Cohen, *Economic Life*, 469.

was the Bedouin raids which disturbed both city-dwellers and the passengers coming to town. In addition, the fear of the possibility of the restart in the Crusaders was another factor in the requirement of the construction of the wall. Moreover, the wish was to terminate the economic and demographic regression of Jerusalem and create secure environment for providing stability in the town in the last period of Mamluk administration.[91] Besides, the superiority was wished to be shown perceptibly to the people of newly conquered area, and thus, the reconstruction of Jerusalem walls by Ottoman administratives could be an indicator of the differences between two administrations and the displaying of the priorities of the new one.[92] The repair and extention of waterways, laying pipes from Artas village in the South of Bethlehem to Jerusalem, contributed to the water provision to fast growing towns. A total of six (four in the *Ḥaram al-Sharīf* and two of them around the *Ḥaram al-Sharīf*) fountains were established for meeting the water needs for the residents.[93] A big water storage facility was constructed below the Sultan Pool outside the city walls in order to provide water for visitors and hajj caravans coming to Jerusalem and to sustain reservoir for water supply system of the town.[94]

The reconstruction of the bazaars and the establishment of a big *waqf* (Khasseki Sultan or al-Khassekiyya) provided a serious recovery in economy and the quality of the town with its people.[95] Established by the Khasseki of Suleiman the Magnificent, Hürrem Sultan, the complex was composed of a large *imāret* (public kitchen), *madrasa*, mosque, shops and *tabhāne* (hostel). It was the biggest *külliye* (complex) established in Palestine at that time and it was supported by the neighbouring income of the tens of villages.[96] Khasseki Sultan constructed a big *waqf* to compensate the expense of the complex and she allocated many villages and extensive lands in Syria and Palestine especially around Ramla. After her death (1558) Sultan Suleiman added land of four

91 Avcı, *Değişim Sürecinde*, 37–38.

92 Cohen, *Economic Life*, 469.

93 Myriam Rosen-Ayalon, "On Süleyman's Sabīls in Jerusalem," in *The Islamic World: From Classical to Modern Times; Essays in Honor of Bernard Lewis*, ed. C. E. Bosworth, Charles Issawi, Roger Savory, and A. L. Udovitch (Princeton: Darwin Press, 1989), 589–607.

94 Cohen, *Economic Life*, 3–4.

95 Ze'evi, *Kudüs*, 4–5.

96 Singer, *Kadılar, Kullar*, 69.

villages around Sayda to this *waqf*.[97] The *waqf* was the prominent social welfare institution during the Ottoman classical age activating the town economy.[98]

The *Maqām* of the Prophet Dāwūd on Mount Zion and the Asʿadiyya Lodges on the Mount of Olives should also be mentioned among these works. Some other *waqf* structures built or renovated in Jerusalem during the Ottoman period are as follows: Yūsuf Āghā Prayer Hall, Sinānbar Prayer Hall (*Miḥrāb* and *Maṣṭabat* al-Sinānbar, located between the *Bāb al-Maghāriba* and Masjid *al-Aqṣā*. Although it is known to belong to the Ottoman period, the date of its construction and the name of its builder could not be determined), Bayram Pāshā Fountain (the fountain was built during the Shaʿlān-Ayyūbī period and was repaired during the Mamluk and Ottoman periods), Qāsim Pāshā Fountain and Pool (Sabīl Bāb al-Maḥkama, built by Qāsim Pāshā during the reign of Sulaymān the Magnificent). In addition to these known works, some of

TABLE 4 Charitable *Waqfs* established in Jerusalem (1099–1572),[a] (1591–1703)[b]

Period	**Date**	**The number of established philanthropic *waqfs***
Before Ayyubids	1099–1187	0
Ayyubids	1187–1250	6
Bahrī Mamluk	1250–1390	25
Burjī Mamluk	1390–1517	11
Ottoman	1517–1572	4
	1591–1688	154
	1688–1703	5
Total		204

a As mentioned earlier, Powers ("Revenues," 163–202), based on the *Awqāf* Land Registry Books No. 131 (932 AH/1525–26 CE), 342 (970 AH/1562–63 CE), and 552 (980 AH/1572–73 CE), provides information on the name of the *waqf*, its founder, the date of its establishment, and its assets regarding the *waqfs* of Jerusalem, which were recorded as charitable *waqfs* within a period of forty-seven years from the first years of Ottoman rule over Jerusalem. In the study, fifty-eight *waqf* records in Jerusalem were identified in these three records.

b Ghūsha, *al-Awqāf al-Islāmiyya*, 550–786

97 Kemal Abdülcelil el-Aselî, "Kudüs," in *Türkiye Diyanet Vakfı İslâm Ansiklopedisi*, vol. 26 (Ankara: Türkiye Diyanet Vakfı, 2002), 334–338.

98 Ze'evi, *Kudüs*, 31.

which have survived to the present day, there are many fountains, *sabīls*, *ribāṭs*, prayer halls, and similar foundation works.[99]

In the 17th century, Evliyâ Çelebi said about the Ottoman *waqf* works, "I have traveled to 18 sultanates and kingdoms in fifty years, and nowhere have I seen so much charity." During the Ottoman period in Jerusalem, a civilization of foundations was established thanks to various works built for the purposes of helping the needy, which Islam praises, and for the purposes that people want to be remembered with good deeds both in this world and in the next.[100] As can be seen in Table 1, in the early years of the Ottoman period (1517–1572), four charitable foundations and fourteen family (*dhurrī*) *waqf* were established in Jerusalem.[101] The number of charitable *waqfs* established in Jerusalem between 1591–1688 is 154.[102] Until 1703, the beginning of the subject of this study, five more charitable *waqfs* were added to this number.[103]

In this part of the study, in addition to the *waqfs* inherited by the Ottomans, we will try to identify the *waqfs* established after the Ottoman conquest and recorded in the 18th century *Ḥurūfāt* and *ʿAtīq* (treasury) books, their distribution in the city and the services they provided. For this purpose, the Muslim *waqfs* in the city of Jerusalem between 1703–1831 will be discussed under the headings of educational and training institutions, religious, social and municipal institutions, respectively, and the records identified will be evaluated in tables.

1.2.1 *Waqfs* for Educational Purposes

When the Ottomans annexed Jerusalem, there were more than fifty *madrasas* in the city and there were dozens of scholars and hundreds of students in these *madrasas*. All of the *madrasas* were established as *waqfs*, which meant the administration and continuation of the *madrasas* were provided by the

99 Tanman and Çobanoğlu, "Osmanlı Döneminde Kudüs," 517–30.

100 Ufuk Gülsoy, Vahdettin Engin, et al., *Bir Medeniyetin İzdüşümü: Vakıflar* (İstanbul: VGM Yayınları, 2012), 250.

101 Powers, "Revenues," 163–202. Powers provides information on the name of the *waqf*, its founder, the date of its establishment, and its assets regarding the *waqfs* of Jerusalem, which were recorded as charitable *waqfs* over a period of forty-seven years from the first years of Ottoman rule over Jerusalem. As presented in the study, fifty-eight *waqf* records were identified in these three books.

102 In the study published by IRCICA in Istanbul, 154 of the 327 *waqfs* were recorded as charitable (56 *nuqūd waqfs*) and 173 as *dhurrī* (three *nuqūd waqfs*). See Ghūsha, *al-Awqāf al-Islāmiyya*, 550–612.

103 Among 47 *waqfs*, five of them were *waqf khayrī*, while 1 of them was cash (*nuqūd*) *waqf*. Ghūsha, *al-Awqāf al-Islāmiyya*, 780–86.

*waqf*s.[104] Stipulations related to these educational institutions established as *waqf* were openly mentioed in the *waqfiyya*s by the endower. The endower stated how the operation of the institution would be implemented and these conditions would not be changed. The appointment of officials belonged completely to the endower and they either directly appointed the instructors and other personnels or put stipulations in the *waqfiyya* as to the appointment.[105]

If the schools and *madrasa*s in Ottoman State were accepted as today's formal educational institutions, mosques and *zāwiya*s were among the informal educational institutions, because they contributed to the education disregarding the age.[106] There were also many *zāwiya*s, *ribāṭ*s and *khānqāh*s in Jerusalem contributing to the education. Yet, the center of the education in the city was the Mosques of Masjid *al-Aqṣā* and the Dome of the Rock in the *Ḥaram al-Sharīf*. Besides, there were large and small libraries in *Ḥaram al-Sharīf*. In addition, there were private libraries of *ʿulamāʾ* in their houses. These institutions both supported the development of cultural life and made Jerusalem an important center of knowledge in Islamic world. Educational institutions concentrated mostly on religion and partly linguistic and literary studies. Natural sciences, philosophy and logic were not in the curriculum, however, astronomy and arithmetics were sometimes taught.[107]

With the annexation of the Ottomans, *madrasa*s and Sufi lodges were maintained. Fundamentally, at least four *madrasa*s were established during the Ottoman period.[108] This richness in cultural life proceeded in the sixteenth century. The primary focus of this part of the study is on the educational *waqf*s established in Jerusalem before the period under review, categorized under formal educational institutions such as *madrasa*, school or *muallimhāne, dār al-ḥadīth*, and *dār al-kurrā*. Libraries are also examined under this heading. Additionally, mosques and *zāwiya*s are assessed as religious service *waqf*s, emphasizing their educational functions.

104 al-Asali, "The Libraries of Ottoman Jerusalem." 285.

105 Yediyıldız, "Vakıf Müessesesinin," 157–59.

106 Yediyıldız, *XVIII. Yüzyılda*, 217.

107 For further information see, al-Alami, "The *Waqf*s of the Traditional Families of Jerusalem," 285–87.

108 Kāmil Jamīl ʿAsalī, *Ajdādunā fī Tharā Bayt al-Maqdis: Dirāsa Athariyya Tārīkhiyya li-Maqābir al-Quds wa-Turābihā wa-Ithbāt bi-Asmāʾ al-Aʿyān al-Madfunīn Fīhā* (Amman: al-Majmaʿ al-Malakī li-Buḥūth al-Ḥaḍāra al-Islāmiyya, 1981), 46.

1.2.1.1 *Madrasas*

Madrasas were named diversely, such as *dār al-ʿilm, medrese-i hāne, medrese-i münīfe, medrese-i refīʿ al-bunyān*. As mentioned elsewhere, the fundamental functions of the repair, maintanence and appointments to *madrasas* and mosques proceeded in the Ottoman Empire. Most of the *madrasas* given in Table A1 were established in the Ayyubid period and many of them in Mamluk period. *Madrasa* Khassekiyya[109] and Si'irdiyya[110] were founded in the Ottoman period and the appointment records were kept according to the *berāts* (appointments deeds) given by the Ottoman State as followed in the *Ḥurūfāt* Registers. *Madrasas*, exceeding the number of fifty and being established in the Mamluk period, should not be regarded as the sign of wealth. Most of the *madrasas* were small and the payment to their officials was modest.[111] The modesty of the payment can also be followed from the *Ḥurūfāt* Registers.[112] In addition, in the period under the study, it is discerned through the examined registers that Ottoman administration continued to appoint officials to the many *madrasas* which were established in the period of Ayyubids and Mamluks, make their payment and meet their need.[113]

---

109 The only *madrasa* of which the copy of deed of trust was available in VGMA was Khasseki Sultan *Madrasa* and it was established by Khasseki of Sultan Süleyman. Details related to the *madrasa* in its deed of trust in 964 AH/1557 CE were: "Bu evkaf cümlesinden bir kısmı da: mezkūr cāminin etrafında binā ettiği elli beş adet odalardır. Bunları da dindar mü'minlerin sālihlerine ve muvahhid müttakīlerden mücāvir olanlara, nefislerini tabiat kirlerinden temizleyen zāhidlere; ahkām-ı şer'iyyeyi ihlāl etmeksizin şeriat ipine tutunanlara vakfetmiştir. Bunlar sünnet usulünce taata devam ederler, gece gündüz ayakta ve oturukça oldukları halde Allahı zikrederler, Mescidlere kapanıp rükū' ve secde yaparlar, bu evsāfı hāiz olanlar bu odalarda gece ve gündüz sākin olup gizli ve āşikār sūrette vākıfın ruhu için dua ederler." VGMA, 608–2: 235/178. The *madrasa* was composed of fifty-five rooms and the conditions were openly stated of who would stay, and what kind of study and prayer they would conduct. There were twelve appointment records in Jerusalem *ḥurūfāt* registers as to the madrasa in Muḥarram 1111–Rabīʿ al-Ākhir 1141 AH/1689–1728 CE. The Khasseki Sultan *Madrasa* was also registered as Khassekiyye *Madrasa*.

110 *Madrasa Khānqāh* Siʿirdiyye, established by Abdülgani el-Siʿirdî, was identified only in the *Evkâf Tahrir Defteri* (no. 342) in 952 AH/1545–46 CE. Powers, "Revenues," 180. In the Jerusalem *ḥurūfāt* registers, there was one appointment to the *madrasa* in 1112 AH/1700–01 CE.

111 Tomar, "Kudüs," 332–34.

112 For the payments of *madrasa* officials see, Şerife Eroğlu Memiş, Kudüs-i Şerif (İstanbul: Yeditepe Yayınevi, 2017), 154–58.

113 Related to the Amīniyya, Barqūqiyya, Zamāniyya, Muzhiriyya, Dīniyya, Ṭablūniyya, and Qāmiriyya *madrasas*, as mentioned in Powers's study, no record exists in the *ḥurūfāt* registers. The Wajīhiyya, Jāliqiyya, Jawliyya, and Karīmiyya *madrasas*, built during the Baḥrī Mamluk period, are not mentioned in Jerusalem *ḥurūfāt* registers or Powers's study. Tomar, "Kudüs," 332–34. Complexes established during the Burjī Mamluk period and not mentioned by Powers include: the Mawṣiliyya *madrasa* (d. 797 AH/1394–95 CE)

1.2.1.2 *Schools/Muallimhāne*

In the Ottoman State, children in the level of primary schools generally go to the schools named as *dārü't-ta'lim, dārü'l-'ilm, mekteb-i etfāl ve sıbyan mekteb-i lātīf-i dil-gūşa*, while in some registers they were called as *muallimhāne*.[114] The *waqf* of the primary schools are sometimes remembered with the names of the founder, quarter, closer masjid or mosque. When there was no school in the quarter, the children went to a division of quarter masjid or house of the teacher (*mu'allim-i sıbyān, muallim* or *hoca*) or to a suitable place. When the schools were not available in the villages, this services was given in the mosque of the village or by the imam of the masjid.

There were appointment registers one to a school and two to *muallimhānes* in the eighteenth century Jerusalem *Ḥurūfāt* Registers. These were: Qarqashandī Mosque and School[115] in Afranj Quarter, close to the Dayr al-'Amūd, in Jerusalem; the second one was in the Qal'ūn Quarter in Dayr al-Zanjīl Village endowed by Riḍwān Bey; the *waqf* of Shaykh Muḥammad Qarqashandī. It included a room of a house and a mosque as well as a *muallimhāne*.[116] Finally, Bayram Çavuş's *Waqf Muallimhāne* was in *Bāb al-Qaṭṭānīn* Quarter.[117]

---

that was founded by Abū Bakr 'Alī al-Shaybānī for Khwāja (Tājir) Fakhr al-Dīn al-Mawṣilī, the *Madrasa* al-Jahārkasiyya (Sharkasiyya), endowed by Amīr Jahārkas al-Khalīlī, and the Ṣubaybiyya *madrasa*. According to the Jerusalem *Esās* accounts: there were appointments of officials to the *madrasa waqfs* of Ummiyya (VGMA, 515: 36/12), Baladiyya (VGMA, 515: 53/11), Muḥammadiyya (VGMA, 515: 51/53), Qarnābāl (VGMA, 515: 56/15), *Waqf* al-*Madrasa* al-'Uthmāniyya (VGMA, 515: 54/57), Farhādiyya (VGMA, 515: 56/58), Mārūniyya (VGMA, 515: 65/68), Balāsiyya and Ismā'īliyya (VGMA, 515: 65/69), Jahārkasiyya (VGMA, 515: 65/70), Zayniyya (VGMA, 515: 73/79), Maḥmūdiyya (VGMA, 515: 73/80), al-Aghrāwī (VGMA, 515: 76/84), Āmidiyya (VGMA, 515: 81/95), Māsikiyya (VGMA, 515: 91/134), Kabāriyya (VGMA, 515: 93/142), and Ṣafiyya (VGMA, 515: 100/168), which were not registered in other accounts. For detailed information, see Table A1.

114 Cahit Baltacı, *XV–XVI. Asırlarda Osmanlı Medreseleri: Teşkilât ve İşleyiş* (İstanbul: İrfan Matbaası, 1998), 6.

115 The mentioned school was the Jahārkasiyya *Madrasa Waqf* in the Afranj Quarter near Dayr al-'Amūd. In the Jerusalem example, the name of the Jahārkasiyya Mosque could be applied to the school. As a prominent Egyptian family, the Jahārkasiyya had the privilege of serving as scribes in Masjid *al-Aqṣā*.

116 Located in Jerusalem, in the quarter of Bāb al-Qaṭṭānīn, Bayram Çavuş *Waqf Muallimhāne* was recorded in the registers. VGMA, 1111: 54/6; 1107: 2/5. In the mentioned registers, a *muallim-i sıbyan* was appointed to the *waqf*.

117 In another record, Rıdvan Bey *Waqf Shaykh* Mehmed Jahārkasiyya in Jerusalem, in the Qal'a Quarter in the *qarya* of Dayr al-Zanjīl, was endowed as a *dār al-suknā*, and buildings of a masjid and *muallimhāne* were mentioned. VGMA, 1112: 1/26. Since it was not mentioned in another record, it is unclear whether this was a second *waqf* by him or a school-*waqf*, as noted above. Also, the locations of the *awqāf* in the two records were different.

1.2.1.3 Dār al-Ḥadīth (*House of* Ḥadīth)

Composed by the words of *dār* and *ḥadīth* meaning place, house and space, which are also called as *Dār al-Sunna, Dār al-Sunna al-Nabawiyya,* or *Dār al-Sunna al-Muḥammadiyya.* In addition, they are named with various adjectives in the documents such as *dārü'l-hadīs-i bī hemtā, dārü'l-hadīs-i refīʿātü'l-kubāb.*[118] In the first period of Islam, educational activities were mostly conducted by masjids and mosques. Being used as a prayer place, masjids were functioned as a classroom. In masjids, scholars called as *muḥaddith* (expert in hadith) could give lessons, also, the places were left to the *ḥadīth* classes of the prominent *muḥaddith* who came to the city for their scholarly travels. The scholars who were the authority in their field were able to give lessons, however, generally they took permission from the political authority. Due to the rising number of courses and students, there came the need of new institutions out of mosques. While schools were constructed for the children in the period of Umayyads, *madrasa*s were opened as in the Abbasid period. Yet, as to the importance of *hadith,* private education institutions were generally called as *Dār al- Ḥadīth* which gave expert-level education in *ḥadīth.* They were giving today's graduate education, in a way.[119]

According to Mujīr al-Dīn (d. 927 AH/1521 CE), forty of the *madrasa*s and Sufi lodges established in Jerusalem during the Ayyubid period were particularly *madrasa*s, one of which was *Dār al-Qur'ān*, while another was *Dār al-Ḥadīth.*[120] A *Dār al-Ḥadīth waqf* was recorded in the *Ḥurūfāt* registers in the *Khaṭṭ Dāwūd* Quarter in Jerusalem.[121] Powers also mentions a *Dār al-Ḥadīth* in Jerusalem established by Amīr Sharaf al-Dīn ʿĪsā ibn Badr al-Dīn Abū al-Qāsim.[122] ʿAbd al-Mahdī, in his study on *madrasa*s from the Ayyubid and Mamluk periods, refers to two *Dār al-Ḥadīth* named al-Ḥakkāriyya and al-Tankiziyya. While describing his *Dār al-Ḥadīth* (endowed in 666 AH), al-Ḥakkārī noted that it was located west of the *Ḥaram al-Sharīf,* near the Silsila Gate and around the Jālikiyya Tomb on the western side, adding that the endower was Amīr Sharaf al-Dīn ʿĪsā ibn Badr al-Dīn Abū al-Qāsim al-Ḥakkārī. This could indicate that the two *waqf*s were the same *waqf.* The endower, also described as *aʿyān*

118 Nebi Bozkurt, "Dârü'lhadis," TDV *İslâm Ansiklopedisi,* vol. 8 (İstanbul: Türkiye Diyanet Vakfı, 1993), 527–29.

119 Yusuf Küçükdağ, "Konya Şehri'nin Fizikī ve Sosyo-Ekonomik Yapısı," *Makaleler, I* (Konya, 2004). 360.

120 Pedersen, "*Mescit,*" 54.

121 There were six appointments in the aforementioned *waqf*s in Shawwāl 1117 and Jumādā al-Ūlā 1137/1705–1724 CE. VGMA, 1107: 2/15, 62, 63, 136, 201; 1119: 110/49.

122 Powers, "Revenues," 171.

al-umarā' (a leading ruler), was engaged in literature. The endower, who died in 669 AH, dedicated *Dār al-Ḥadīth* for the education of *ḥadīth*.[123]

1.2.1.4 Dār al-Qur'an (*House of* Qur'an)

The word was the combination of *dār* and *Qur'an*, sometimes *qurrā'* meaning house of Qur'an which denotes an institution where the Qur'an was read and taught. It also refers to a place where the children having a certain level of Qur'an education and studying *qirā'a* (reading).[124] In some records, it was recorded as *Dār al-Qurrā' al-Jannat-Numā'* (House of Qur'ān Showing Heaven), *Dār al-Qurrā' bi-Bahā'* (Priceless House of Qur'ān). In these institutions, ten different reading style of Qur'an was taught by *Shaykh al-Qurrā'*. The instructors of Qur'an were the *mu'allims* and writing instructors were *mukattibs*. First separate *madrasas* apart from the mosques for high-level Qur'an education were *Dār al-Qur'an*.[125]

Dār al-Qur'ān al-Sallāmiyya (or *Madrasa al-Sallāmiyya*, as in some registers) was endowed by Sirāj al-Dīn 'Umar ibn Abī Bakr Abū al-Qāsim al-Sallāmī in 761 AH.[126] For the needs of the *madrasa*, the revenues of al-Batīḥ Jirās, Mazra'a of Bayt Rafā' and 'Adāsa, and the villages of Ba'līl and Bīra al-Kubrā were endowed.[127]

1.2.1.5 *Libraries*

Social and civil services in Ottoman State was operated through *waqfs*. There were book and library *waqfs* for the scholars and students, also, for the need of people in the quarters.[128] There were many libraries with miscalleneous dimensions in *Ḥaram al-Sharīf* and *madrasas* in Jerusalem. Masjid *al-Aqṣā* and the Dome of the Rock libraries in *Ḥaram al-Sharīf* were significant knowledge centers. In addition, there were private libraries of *'ulamā'* in their houses.[129] It is possible to examine libraries in Jerusalem under the headings of

123 'Abd al-Mahdī, *al-Madāris fī Bayt al-Maqdis*, 187–90. It is noted in the registers that the Tankiziyya (Sayfiyya) *Dār al-Ḥadīth*, established by Amīr Sayf al-Dīn Tankiz ibn 'Abdullāh al-Nāṣirī in 729 AH, was a separate building from Tankiziyya *Madrasa*.

124 Ferit Devellioğlu, *Osmanlıca: Türkçe Ansiklopedik Lūgat* (Ankara: Aydın Kitabevi Yayınları, 2002), 167.

125 Nebi Bozkurt, "Dârü'lkurrâ," TDV *İslâm Ansiklopedisi*, vol. 8 (İstanbul: Türkiye Diyanet Vakfı, 1993), 543–45..

126 'Abd al-Mahdī, *al-Madāris fī Bayt al-Maqdis*, 187–93.

127 Powers, "Revenues," 183.

128 İsmail E. Erünsal, *Osmanlı Vakıf Kütüphaneleri: Tarihi Gelişimi ve Organizasyonu* (Ankara: Türk Tarih Kurumu Yayınları, 2008).

129 Al-Alami, "The Waqfs of the Traditional Families of Jerusalem," 285.

civic and private ones. The Masjid *al-Aqṣā* and the Dome of the Rock libraries were among the first in public libraries having many books such as rare, hand-written Qur'ans and Islamic studies, Arabic grammer, history, mathematics and astronomy.[130] The most special collection of the library was the ornamental Qur'ans endowed by sultans, princesses and administrative elites. It was the tradition of the Mamluk Sultans that Qur'ans were endowed to *al-Aqṣā* and the *waqf*s were established for the Qur'an prayers (*qurrā*s). Ottoman State proceeded this tradition and endowed Qur'an to *al-Aqṣā* library and appointed *qārī*s.[131] In the seventeenth century, *yedd-i emīn-i kutub* (librarian) was appointed for the books in the Dome of the Rock. In the seventeenth century, al-Shaykh Bashir al-Khalīlī conducted the duty of *tawliya* and after his death, this duty was transferred to his sons, al-Shaykh İbrahim and al-Shaykh Abdürrahman, by equally sharing the payment.[132]

The second, *madrasa* libraries had a significant place in civic libraries in Jerusalem and the first one was the *Madrasa* Fakhriyya. There were approximately 10.000 volumes of books of the *madrasa* libraries established by *Qāḍī* al-Fakhr al-Dīn in 732 AH/1339 AD. The collection including maunscripts related to astronomy and other religious sciences was vanished.[133] The Amīniyya *Madrasa* Library was stated to be covered the ancestors of *al-Imām* family. Among them, the works of *Madrasa* Shaykh Muḥammad Ṣāliḥ al-Imām, a nineteenth-century *madrasa*, held an important place. Lastly, the Ashrāfiyya *Madrasa* Library, constructed by Mamluk Sultan Qā'itbāy in the fifteenth century, existed until the seventeenth century. Additionally, there were libraries belonging to the *madrasa*s Qādirīyya and Wafā'iyya, and Zāwiya al-Bukhāriyya (*Takiyya* Uzbakiyya), which had smaller collections.[134]

The third, libraries belonging to Christian monastery had a rich collection as of Byzantine Period having works in fifteen different languages.[135] The collection mostly focused on the religious topics and Christian beliefs, including questions related to the prayers, Bible copies, history of saints, and the lives of apostles. Additionally, there were collections about relations between Christian groups and Islamic state administrators. Among them, there were instructions regulating the lives and stating the rights and duties of communities belonging to administrators such as *fermān* (imperial edict), *berāt* (appointment

130 ibid., 285–86; Sūwāriyya, *al-Ḥayāt al-Ijtimā'iyya fī Madīnat al-Quds*, 266.
131 Al-Alami, "The Waqfs of the Traditional Families of Jerusalem," 285.
132 al-'Asalī, *Ma'āhid al-'Ilm*, 369, 371.
133 al-'Ārif, *al-Mufaṣṣal*, 451.
134 al-Asali, "The Libraries," 285–86.
135 For further information see, al-Asali, "The Libraries," 285–86.

deed), judicial decisions. The libraries belonging to Christian monasteris having the richest collections were: Greek Orthodox Patriarchate and Monastry; Latin Patriarchate and St. Saviour Monastry; Armenian Patriarchate and St. James Cathedral and Monastry; Assyrian Orthodox Monastry, and St. Mark Monastry.[136]

Private libraries belonging to Mamluk and Ottoman period were mostly endowed by the *ʿulamāʾ* in the Ottoman period. For instance, Immat Khalīfa ibn Ibrāhīm, one of the scholars of the sixteenth century, endowed his books to the students with the deed of trust (dated 1550) then to the *Madrasa* of Argūniyya.[137] In Islamic countries, the books were kept in the wooden boxes called *khizāna*. Books were not allowed to be out of the *madrasa* or mosque. *Iwan*s were used as a reading room in a *madrasa*. The books were sorted as to their subjects. The copies of Qur'an were on top of the list and following them, religious titles such as *tafsīr* and Islamic law. The conditions stipulated in the *waqfiyya*s were essential in the use of the books. The principal responsible of the *waqf* library was the *nāzir* or the *mutawallī* of the *waqf*. There were appointment of assistants to the big libraries.[138]

All in all, in this part of the study, the *madrasa*s being abundant in number in the period of Ayyubids and Mamluks also continued their fundamental functions through repairs, maintanence and appointment of officials in Ottoman period. *Madrasa* al-Khassekiyya, established within the Khasseki Sultan Complex were among the prominent educational institutions of the Ottoman period. Although school/*muallimhāne* and *dār al-hadith* and *dār al-qur'an waqf*s and libraries were few in numbers, they were important educational institutions.

1.2.2 The *Waqf* of Religious Services

Apart from the authorized appointment of the officials from center to the religious institutions in Ottoman State, religious services were conducted by the diverse *waqf* officials. The prosecution of the establishment of all kinds of mosque, masjid, sufi lodge, *zāwiya* and shrine; the payment of the officials working there; the repair and maintanence of them reciting of *khatm*, parts of the Qur'an, *sūra*s, and *mawlud*s were mentioned among the religious services. The *waqf* founders in the eighteenth century, the period when the registers were intensified, gave importance to religious institutions and services. These *waqf*s allocated shares for the aforementioned services.

---

136 ibid., 287–88.

137 For further information see, al-Asali, "The Libraries," 288–89.

138 al-Asali, "The Libraries," 289.

This section provides information on *masjid*s and mosques in Jerusalem, followed by definitions of religious service-based *waqf*s, including Ṣūfī lodges, *zāwiyas*, *khanqāhs*, and *ribāṭs*. Thirdly, mausolea, tombs, and shrines, often categorized together, will be examined. *Tilāwa* and prayer *waqf*s, significant in the registers, will be discussed under a separate heading.

1.2.2.1 Masjid

The term *masjid* derives from the Arabic root *sajada*, meaning to bow and place the forehead on the ground in reverence, and refers to the place where this act occurs. In Ottoman *waqf* sources, *masjid*s are described with complimentary adjectives such as *mābed-i münīf, mābed-i güzīn, mābed-i laṭīf, mābed-i dil-furūz*, and *mābed-i naẓīf*. These are prayer spaces established in neighborhoods, distinct from larger mosques lacking a *minbar*, and are generally small. *Masjids* in neighborhoods typically served as places for the five daily prayers. People gathered in larger mosques for Friday and feast prayers, *kandil* (blessed) nights, and Ramadan evenings. Many in Ottoman society either established a *masjid*, covered its expenses, or added a *minbar* to convert it into a mosque through the *waqf*s they founded.

*Masjid*s established in the quarters, generally, were the places where people performed five time prayers. People gathered in particularly big mosques in Friday and feast prayer, *kandil* (blessed) nights and Ramadan evenings. Most of the people in Ottoman society, either established a *masjid* or met expenses of *masjids* or putting minbār for making them mosque with the *waqf*s they established.[139]

There was no obvious distinction in the use of mosque and *masjid* in the *Ḥurūfāt* records. Sometimes they were recorded as mosque and sometimes as *masjid*. Probably, as in the case of *Masjid al-Aqṣā*, they were recorded with their old name. In some examples, the structures which was turned into mosque with putting *minbār* (previously *masjid*) were recorded with their old names.[140] There were twenty-seven appointment records related to eighteen diverse *masjids* in Jerusalem *Ḥurūfāt* records.[141] Primarily, the *masjid*s bearing the names of prophets and *ṣaḥāba* were attention-grabbing. Among those named after prophets: *Lūṭ, Yūsha*ʿ, and an unidentified *masjid* (possibly misrecorded as Leshmevī/Lishmevī); and from companions: *ʿAyyāsh ibn Abī Rabīʿa, Salama ibn al-Akwa*ʿ, and *Abū ʿUbayda ibn al-Jarrāḥ* had *masjid*s carrying their names.[142]

139 For example see, VGMA, 627: 62/231; VGMA, 733: 53/23.
140 For example see, VGMA, 552: 37/23.
141 See, Table A2.
142 See VGMA, 1112: 1/83; 1110: 131/54.

1.2.2.2 *Mosques*

The word mosque comes from Arabic root verb of *jam*ʿ, which means collecting and gathering, also, the place of worship in which people perform Friday prayer having *minbār* for preacher for the sermon.[143] The fundamental function of the mosques are its being a place where Muslim performed their religious deeds in peace.

There were Friday mosques which were divided according to having one or two *sharafa* in the small and big Ottoman cities.[144] These were also referred to as the Grand Mosque. People from surrounding villages gathered there not only for Friday prayers but also on other significant occasions, such as festivals. At times, Friday and festival prayers were held in a *musalla* (*namazgāh*, open-air prayer area) due to its spaciousness. Typically, the *imām* and preacher of the Grand Mosque led these prayers in the *musalla*.

Beyond their primary function, mosques served as centers for various branches of education, particularly religious instruction. Over time, they became practical extensions of *madrasa*s. In addition to worship and education, mosques were key social spaces, forming the core of towns and cities.[145] They were the places where economic, administrative, juridical and military decisions were taken, therefore, mosques sometimes became a military camp, treasury, embassy and court. They fulfilled the functions of library, questhouse, hospital and parade ground. These services went beyond in time and complexes (*külliye*s) were emerged. In this way, mosques came to be main institution in which many other ones were born out of,[146] thus, all the social formations constructed around the *masjid*, mosque and complexes.[147]

The Mosque of ʿUmar al-Khaṭṭāb (*Jāmiʿ al-ʿUmarī*) in Jerusalem is said to have been established by the Umayyads at the site where Caliph ʿUmar performed his first prayer in Jerusalem following the Muslim conquest in 16 AH/637 CE. There were administrative appointments to the Masjid *al-Aqṣā* and the Dome of the Rock *waqf*s such as *mutawallī* (trustee), *nāzır* (inspector), *kātib* (clerk),

143 Osman Nuri Ergin, *Türk Şehirlerinde İmaret Sistemi* (İstanbul: Cumhuriyet Matbaası, 1939), 198–223; Nebi Nebi Bozkurt, "Cami," TDV *İslâm Ansiklopedisi*, vol. 7 (İstanbul: Türkiye Diyanet Vakfı, 1993): 46–56, 49–53; Sāmī, *Kāmūsü'l-Aʿlām*, 1341.

144 Suraiya Faroqhi, "Kentlerde Toplumsal Yaşam," in *Osmanlı İmparatorluğunun Ekonomik ve Sosyal Tarihi*, ed. Halil İnalcık and Donald Quataert, vol. 2 (İstanbul: Eren Yayıncılık, 2000), 699–730, 700.

145 H. Sadi Selen, "16. ve 17. Yüzyıllarda Anadolu'nun Köy ve Küçük Şehir Hayatı III," in *Türk Tarih Kongresi* (Ankara: Türk Tarih Kurumu Basımevi, 1948), 589–97, 595.

146 Ergin, 221–23; Bozkurt, "Cami", 51–53.

147 Özer Ergenç, "Osmanlı Şehrindeki Mahallenin İşlev ve Nitelikleri Üzerine," *Osmanlı Araştırmaları* 4 (1984): 69–78.

jābī (revenue collector). In another group, among the big *waqfs* such as Khasseki Sultan, Sultan Suleiman, Ahmed Pasha, Mustafa Pasha, Sinan Pasha, they allocated payment for reading of Qur'an, *hadith* and short *suras* inside the Dome of the Rock Mosque. Thirdly, there were appointments of officials from the Dome of the Rock *Waqf* for reading of Qur'an, *hadith*, short *suras*. In the aforementioned registers, there was no identification of *waqf* name. Lastly, there were records of the *waqfs* near the Dome of the Rock include the Yāʿqūbiyya Mosque, Ḥanābila Mosque, Qarqashandī Mosque, and Shaykh Ḥusayn (al-Riḍā) Mosque in Jerusalem, which are among the most frequently mentioned in the records.[148]

1.2.2.3 Takiyyas (*Sufi Lodges*)

Takiyya, as a term, means the place for the members of the sufi order to sit up and perform the rituals, and it is a break from the word one-on-one, which means based in Persian and "place to endure."[149] Early on, Sufi lodges were known as *zāwiyas*. Having been considered as the center of Sufi life and thought, also, the institution of the sufi orders, the lodges were mentioned with the sect they belonged to in some places as in the case of *kalenderhāne*, *mevlevīhāne* and *kādirīhāne*. In Mawlawī understanding, central and big *zāwiyas* were called *āsitāne* and others were *zāwiyas*. In some places, dervishes who stayed in the lodges continuously conducted the inner services in the lodges which were adjunct to the division (having the function of *masjid*) where the shaykh resided with his family. The expenses of the lodge was met by the *waqfs* and the dervishes endowed their gain to their dervish convent.[150]

The establishment and operation of *takiyya* and *zāwiya* mostly happened by the *waqf* to a great extent. Their expense was mostly met by the *waqfs*.[151] A part of the expenses was provided from the income of products from orchard, garden and fields around the *zāwiyas*.[152]

In addition, the main purpose of the pilgrims was to reach Mecca and Medina, and Jerusalem was one of the main destinations on the road. There were many denotations to Jerusalem, as it was the holiest city after Mecca and Medina, such as "Holy Hajj Gate" or "The Right Hand of Syrian towns".[153] The

148 See Table A3. Mosque Records of Jerusalem (1703–1831)

149 Pakalın, *Osmanlı Tarih Deyimleri*, 445.

150 Mustafa Kara, "Tasavvuf," in *Doğuştan Günümüze Büyük İslâm Tarihi*, ed. Hakkı Dursun Yıldız, vol. 13 (İstanbul: Çağ Yayınları, 1989), 529–64.

151 Ahmet Yaşar Ocak, "Zaviyeler," *Vakıflar Dergisi* 12 (1978): 247–69, 262.

152 Hasan Basri Öcalan, *Bursa'da Tasavvuf Kültürü* (*XVII. Yüzyıl*) (Bursa: Gaye Kitabevi, 2000). 184, 208.

153 Zarcone, *Kudüs'teki Orta Asyalı ve Hintli Sufi Hacılar*, 19.

city was also close to the pilgrimage route. Sufi lodges in Jerusalem, which can be called public kitchens for the pilgrims, particularly, Uzbek, Afghan and Indian Sufi lodges played a significant role in cultural, religious and political exchange in the Middle Asia, India and Ottoman Empire and specific to the Arabian towns. Their impact was important in the interpretation of Naqshbandī and Qādirī doctrines.[154]

These Sufi lodges mostly resided by the Central Asian and Sufis had close relations.[155] The Ottomans supported the Uzbek Sufi lodges with which they shared a common culture, however, they did not share the same closeness to Indian lodges as they were foreign to their culture. Central Asian languages were spoken, studied, and even taught in Uzbek lodges.[156]

Over the centuries, many Sufis who established some *takiyya*s affiliated with well-known Sufi orders such as Qādirīyya, Shādhiliyya, Naqshbandiyya, Mawlawiyya, and Qalandariyya had also visited Jerusalem. However, it is possible to say that Evliya Çelebi, who visited Jerusalem in the seventeenth century and wrote that there were dervish lodges affiliated to 70 different Sufi orders and that the most important ones belong to ʿAbd al-Qādir al-Jīlānī, Aḥmad al-Badawī, and Jalāl al-Dīn al-Mawlawī exaggerated this number.[157]

1.2.2.3.1 Uzbek Sufi Lodge

It is known that Uzbek sufi lodge (*Khanqāh al-Uzbek, Uzbekiyye Zāwiya*) linked to the Sufi order of Naqshbandiyya located in the northwest of Ḥaram al-Sharīf was established in the beginning of the 13th century. The repaired epitaph on the *tevhidhāne* entrance of the *zāwiya* 1236 (1820) was the rare Ottoman language in the Ottoman structures and end with "Yapıldı Hankāh-ı Özbek açıldı ehl-i irfāne."[158] The Jerusalem *sharīʿa* court registers record that the *waqf* was established by the Chief Doorkeeper Ṣūfī Osman Agha ibn ʿAbd al-Muʿīn, son-in-law of Jerusalem's Governor Mehmed Pasha, in Shawwāl 1024 AH (October–November 1615 CE), through the endowment of substantial immovable property and money. It is noted that a large house in Istanbul and 1,000 Sulṭānī gold coins were endowed to cover the expenses of the *takiyya*, comprising a mosque and four cells for the Ṣūfī order. Not only the Ṣūfīs residing

154 Ibid., 25–26.

155 Zarcone (ibid., 43–44) expressed that there was a Sufi lodge network in Jerusalem. Uzbek and Indian lodges were carrying the cultural and religious traditions of India and Middle Asia to the world of Turkey and Arabia and, thus, they were an advanced station of Turkish and Indian Sufism.

156 Zarcone, ibid., 45.

157 Çelebi, *Seyahatnāme*, 239; See Table A4. Kudüs Kenti Tekke Kayıtları (1703–1831).

158 Tanman and Çobanoğlu, "Osmanlı Döneminde Kudüs," 524.

in the lodge but also their descendants benefited from the *waqf*'s income.[159] The lodge was considered as a place of worship and a place of worship not only for Arabs but also for guests and pilgrims from Turkistan.[160] In one of the *waqfiyyas* of the lodge, there were obligations for four Naqshbandis staying in the cells such as growing a beard and being well-groomed. In the records, it is also expressed that in the periods when the Sufis, who were the members of Naqshbandi order, were not in Jerusalem, the income of the *waqf* would be used for *arwam* (Rumī/Anatolian); in other words, for the Ottoman Turks and the poor Sufis having the same qualifications. When there was no one in Jerusalem from the Ottoman lands, half of the *waqf* would be given to four travellers from Sufi sect; if it was not possible, it would be given to four Sufis from any orders.[161]

Shaykh Muḥammad Ṣāliḥ al-Uzbekī (d. 1144 AH/1731–32 CE), who imbued the lodge with its Uzbek identity, expanded and developed it through the mid-eighteenth century. From that period, the structure became known as the Naqshbandiyya Lodge. Following the shaykh's death in 1144 AH/1731–32 CE, Jerusalem's governor Pervānezāde Agha ordered the construction of a dome over his grave. After Muḥammad Ṣāliḥ al-Uzbekī, his son Shaykh Ḥasan led the lodge. Severely damaged in the mid-nineteenth century, the lodge was restored with Ottoman State support in the first half of the twentieth century and has since been referred to as the Uzbek Ṣūfī Lodge.[162]

1.2.2.3.2 Afghan Sufi Lodge

This institution is related to the Uzbek lodge in Jerusalem. The term *Afghān* referred to a broad ethnic group, now primarily identified as Pashtun (including *Abdālī/Durrānī* and *Gilzā'ī* tribes), living in the northwest periphery. In the early eighteenth century, many from this region were called Pashtun, while those south of the Hindu Kush were labeled *Balūchī*s, *Fārisī*s, or Indians. Additionally, Transoxanians (from what was known as Little Turkistan), Turcomans from Afghan Turkistan, Uzbeks, and Fārisīs (Tajiks) were also termed "Afghān." The Afghan lodges in Istanbul and Jerusalem, led by shaykhs from Khorasan and Kandahar, reflected this diversity. Pilgrims from these regions were often recognized as Sulaymānī, referring to the Sulayman

159 For Frederick de Jong, the founder of the lodge is ʿUthmān al-Bukhārī according to a deed of trust on Muḥarram 10, 1133 AH/1720 CE. Frederick De Jong, "The Sufi Orders in Nineteenth and Twentieth-Century Palestine," *Studia Islamica* 58 (1983): 149–81, 167.

160 Tütüncü, *Turkish Jerusalem*, 4.

161 Yusuf Natsheh, "al-Zāwiya al-Naqshbandiyya (1033/1623–24)," in *Ottoman Jerusalem*, 904–13, 905–06.

162 For epitaph of which its date was erased see, Tütüncü, *Turkish Jerusalem*, 143.

region on the modern Afghanistan-Pakistan border, considered the origin of Pashtuns.[163]

The Afghan Sufi lodge was constructed in the first half of the seventeenth century on land belonging to the Uzbek lodge. During that period, the site was designated for Sufis of the Qādirīyya order, not for Afghan pilgrims or dervishes. Its *waqfiyya*, dated 1633 CE, states that it was endowed to Qādirīyya dervishes devoted to Shaykh Muḥyī al-Dīn ʿAbd al-Qādir al-Jīlānī, who gave his name to the order. The *waqf* epitaph of the lodge, also dated 1633 CE, refers to this Sufi saint as "our father and master, the father of scholars, the sultan of saints." The deed of trust mentions eleven cells allocated for impoverished members of the Qādirīyya Sufi order in various sections of the lodge.[164] In the eastern side, there were some buildings known as "Osman Bey es-Sufi el-Mısrī dormitories"; in the North, there was Naqshbandi Lodge endowed by Osman Bey.[165]

The Qādirī Sufi lodge served Qādirīs throughout the eighteenth and nineteenth centuries, however, there was no mention of Afghan dervishes in the documents related to the lodge. In a register belonging to 1731, it is seen that the Shaykh of the lodge was Muḥammad Ṣāliḥ ibn al-Shaykh Ḥilmī al-Qādirī, and the lodge retained the name "Qādirīyya Sufi Lodge." At that time, another document dated 1776–77 affirmed this denotation. In the list of Qādirī Sufi Lodges prepared in the nineteenth century Ottoman Empire, the name of the place was called the "Āsitane of Shaykh Yusuf" and there was no mention of Afghan dervishes. However, even at this period, the lodge was known for its hospitality as one of the lodges that pilgrims were invited to, and it was described as the "Sīdī ʿAbd al-Qādir Mosque near the Ḥaram al-Sharīf" and was quickly understood to be a Qādirī Sufi lodge."[166]

From the *waqf* decisions (1809–1810) which ordered that Afghan Sulaymani dervishes staying in Qādirī Sufi lodge would be given bread and olive oil daily, one can see that there were Afghan dervishes in Jerusalem at the beginning of the nineteenth century.[167] This Sufi lodge, mentioned by prominent ʿAbd al-Ghanī al-Nābulusī, at the end of the seventeenth century, should not be confused with Madrasa al-Qādirīyya.[168] As Nābulusī (also a member of Qādirī Sufi order) was hosted in the *madrasa*, it indicated that this place was both an educational institution and a guesthouse. Beyond any doubt, a Qādirī Sufi lodge

163 Zarcone, *Kudüs'teki Orta Asyalı ve Hintli Sufi Hacılar*, 111–15.

164 Natsheh, "al-Zāwiya al-Naqshbandiyya," 917–26.

165 Zarcone, *Kudüs'teki Orta Asyalı ve Hintli Sufi Hacılar*, 111–15.

166 ibid., 116.

167 ibid., 116.

168 For more information see, VGMA, 515: 95/149.

which was mentioned by Nābulusī coincided with *madrasa*-lodge having the same name.[169] According to a foreign observer, Uzbek Lodge and Qādirī Lodge performed as "Afghan and Uzbek soup kitchens" and they were remembered with these names.[170]

1.2.2.3.3 Indian Sufi Lodge

It was first mentioned in *al-Uns al-Jalīl* by Mujīr al-Dīn which was written through the end of fifteenth century: "The Indian Lodge is located outside Bāb al-Asbāṭ. It is an old site. Prior to its current association, it was initially endowed to the poor of the Rifāʿiyya order."[171] In the record, there was a Indian Lodge out of the Lions Gate of the Masjid *al-Aqṣā*. Its name was written as *Zāwiya al-Hunūd* in the inscription that informs the establishment of the *takiyya*. However, the inscription, whose date is not read even though it is located on the upper part, belongs to the eighteenth century and the seventeenth century at the earliest.[172] Zarcone states from the evidence in other documents that a *takiyya* around *Bāb al-Sāhira* hosted Indian travelers in 1712, and this is the current Indian Takiyya. There is a register related to lodge in Jerusalem's *Esās* Records belonging to the eighteenth century: "Vakf-ı Tekye-i eş-Şeyh Seyyid Şihab ve Şeyh Farid ve Şeyh Merdem Bahaeddin ve Seyyid Celal meşruta Hindiyān der-Kuds-i Şerif."[173]

The records also include the information that the Ottoman State provided official aid (*surra*) to some Indians.[174] As a matter of fact, twenty-two coins share were allocated to the *Zāwiyat Hunūd* together with Umar Mosque in the *surra* book record dated 1113.[175] There are also provisions in the Damascus *Aḥkām* Registers that include the issues regarding the lodge in question.[176]

169 Rafeq, "Ottoman Jerusalem," 66–67.
170 Arnon, "The Quarters of Jerusalem," 20, 38, 46.
171 al-Ḥanbalī , *al-Uns al-Jalīl*, 167.
172 Zarcone, *Kudüs'teki Orta Asyalı ve Hintli Sufi Hacılar*, 122.
173 VGMA, 515: 94/145.
174 The notebook is registered as "Defter-i Taksimāt-ı Surre-i Şerīfe-i Hakāniyye-i Rūmiyye-i Cedīde-i berā-yı ahāli-i Kudüs-i Şerīf şerrefallahu teālā ilā yevmi'l-āhirati der. vācib-i sene-i sālis 'aşar ve mi'e ve elf." BOA, EV.HMK.SR: 556/2b.
175 Although there is a record related to the *Zāwiya* of Indians in *Surra* register numbered 1113, there was no Indian among the employments. The reason could be that; either they were not mentioned with the information related to their being Indian or the service of the *Zāwiya* conducted by local people. BOA, EV.HMK.SR. 556: 27–28.
176 For example; in Safer 1156 (March–April 1743) it was ordered that one of the *Hindī Shaykhs*, Shaykh Maqṣūm would be appointed as shaykh to *Zāwiya-i Hindiyān* in Jerusalem, and all of his expense on his way to duty would met by "... mevāli-i ʿizām -zīdet fezā'ilühum-ve mefāhirü'l-kuzāt ve'l-hükkām, ma'denü'l fezā'il ve'l-kelām kadılar ve nā'ibler -zīde

In 1799, the lodge (described by Persian word *khanqāh*) was administrated by Shaykh Shahbāz al-Hindī and mentioned by his name. The lodge was also known as Shaykh Farīd Hindī Sufi Lodge and *Takiyya* Hindī in this period. It was not certain that to which Sufi order the lodge belonged to; yet, in 1849, the lodge was described as an "Indian place belonging to Kalenders". At the end of the nineteenth century, it was mentioned as "Indian Imāret" with other lodges of the town.[177]

1.2.2.3.4 *Mawlawī* Sufi Lodge

This was built within the city walls in the highest area of Jerusalem, where the population is concentrated. The *Mawlawī* sufi lodge is located in Saʿdiyya District, on Ibn Jarrah Street, which crosses the *al-Mawlawiyya* Street between Damascus Gate and Herod Gate in the north of the city.[178] The *Mawlawī* order entered Jerusalem during the Mamluk period, however, there was no reminiscences of *khanqāh* from that period.[179] Since the Ottoman conquest, the *Mawlawī* order has also existed in Ottoman Jerusalem. Yavuz Sultan Selim gave 500 coins to Dervish Ahfeshzāde, who was the head of the *Mawlawī* dervishes living in the city.[180] In the sixteenth century, the Mawlawī *khanqāh* was established by Jerusalem Brigade Commander Hudavendigār Bey. In one of the rooms on the upper floors, there is an inscription that "Hüdavendigar Beg, the Commander of the Jerusalem Liva in 995/1586, ordered the construction of this place, which is called the *Mawlawī khanqāh*."[181]

Until the seventeenth century, the *Mawlawī postnishīn* of Jerusalem was assigned by the *Mawlawī postnishīn* in Tripoli. This convention continued until

---

fazlühüm- ve mefāhirü'l-emāsil ve'l-akrān mütesellimler ve kethüdā-yerleri ve yeniçeri serdārları ve sāir aʿyān ve zābıtān -zīde kadruhüm ..." BOA, ADVNS.AHK.ŞM (1): 29/3.

177 Arnon, "The Quarters of Jerusalem," 20.

178 Muḥammad Hāshim Mūsā Ghūsha, *Ḥārat al-Saʿdiyya fī al-Quds* (Ramallah: Sharikat Maṭbaʿat Bayt al-Maqdis, 1420/1999).

179 The presence of the *Mawlawī* order in Jerusalem was apparent until the death of Jalāl al-Dīn al-Rūmī al-Kunawī al-Balkhī in 672 AH/1273 CE. According to al-Ḥanbalī, in his work *al-Uns al-Jalīl*, there was a district in Mamluk-period Jerusalem known as *Mawlawī* Quarter. Although, as with other Sufi sects, there were signs that the *Mawlawī* order existed in pre-Ottoman Jerusalem, their existence declined between 936 AH/1529–30 CE and 968 AH/1560–61 CE.

180 Mu'assasat Iḥyā' al-Turāth wa-l-Buḥūth al-Islāmiyya, *Dalīl Madīnat al-Quds: Minūḥ al-Maqdisiyya* (Jerusalem: Mu'assasat Iḥyā' al-Turāth wa-l-Shu'ūn al-Dīniyya, 1431/2010), 112.

181 Mehmet Tütüncü, "Kudüs Mevlevîhânesi Tarihi ve Mimarisi," in Uluslararası Düşünce ve Sanatta Mevlânâ Sempozyumu Bildirileri, Çanakkale, 25–28 Mayıs 2006 (Çanakkale: T.C. Kültür ve Turizm Bakanlığı, 2006), 699–723; Tütüncü, *Turkish Jerusalem*, pp. 192–93.

the death of Shaykh ʿAbd al-Jalīl al-Sunaynī al-Ḥanafī al-Tarābulusī, the eldest of the most competent family of the *Mawlawī* order in Tripoli, in 1102/1690. Afterwards, the *postnishīn* appointments were made directly from Istanbul by the Ottoman administration.[182]

The *Mawlawī* Ṣūfī order received greater support than other orders. According to Evliyā Çelebi, who visited Jerusalem in 1082 AH/1671 CE, as recorded in his travelogue: "If a person or a member of the *ʿulamāʾ* entered the *Mawlawī* order in Jerusalem, 500 coins were given to each of them."[183] This donation, which can be seen as an incentive, was unique to the *Mawlawī* order, indicating state support in Jerusalem. In the seventeenth and eighteenth centuries, senior officials provided revenue to existing lodges, enabling the *Mawlawī* order to persist and expand across many Ottoman regions. Repairs to *Mawlawī* lodges, constructed by viziers, beys, and pashas, were funded from the treasury by the sultan's decree, and since the seventeenth century, *Mawlawī* dervishes were treated as a state institution, unlike other orders. Consequently, with the end of Ottoman rule, the income of the *Mawlawīkhāne* in these regions declined and gradually depleted. As seen with the *Mawlawīkhāne* in Jerusalem, though it remained standing as a structure, it could not sustain its daily operations like other orders.[184]

There are five *waqfiyya*s of the *Mawlawīkhāne* of Jerusalem that have survived until today. Three of the *waqfiyya*s were *nuqūd* (cash) *waqf*s, and were dedicated by Hüdaverdi Beg Ebū Seyfeyn Ğazi b. Muḥammad Ağa. The first *waqfiyya* belonged to the year 995/1586. Accordingly, five hundred *sultani* were endowed to the *Mawlawī* Sufi lodge.[185] Other *waqfiyya*s were endowed for the

182 Ghūsha, *Ḥārat al-Saʿdiyya*, 358.

183 ibid., 360.

184 *Mawlawī* existence in Jerusalem was based on pre-Ottoman administration. However, as in the other *waqf*s, there was no support from people or contribution to it and the order did not penetrate Jerusalem in time. Even today, a Naqshbandiyya and Qādiriyya lodge existed in Jerusalem, but the *Mawlawī* order used a house and not an official *zāwiya*. For further analysis, see Hasan Hüseyin Güneş and Mehtap Kuş, "Kudüs Mevlevihanesi ve Vakfiyeleri Üzerine Metodik Bir İrdeleme," in *11. Uluslararası Sultan Divani Mevlevilik Sempozyumu Bildirileri, Afyon, 2013* (Afyon: Afyonkarahisar Valiliği, 2013), 118–26.

185 Seventy-five of this amount in gold was allocated to five *Mawlawī* dervishes, one of whom was a shaykh, to recite the *Mathnawī*. Daily, two *akçe*s were assigned to each of two *muezzins* present in the *zāwiya*, one *akçe* daily to the doorkeeper, two *akçe*s daily to the *ferraş*, and provisions were made for those managing the oil lamps. It also includes the annual profit from the endowed funds for the trustee, 400 *kurūsh* equivalent to 600 *sultaniye*, endowed to Abū Sayfayn in 995 AH/1586–87 CE, and payments for the officials of the *Mawlawīkhāna*. Ghūsha, *Ḥārat al-Saʿdiyya*, 705.

needs of the residents in the *zāwiya* with the income from a fruit garden close to Damascus Gate.[131] In this third *waqfiyya* of Hüdaverdi dated 996/1587, 3 Muharram dedicated two hundred *sulṭānī* for the Jerusalem *Mawlawī* Lodge.[186] In the period covered by the study, an official was appointed as the imam of a *mathnawīkhān* to the *Vakf-ı Hüdaverdi Bey* as the former governor of Jerusalem.[187] The fourth *waqf* was established in 1048/1638 by Muḥammad Effendi b. Ibrahim, one of the Sublime Porte's scribes. With the *waqfiyya*, he endowed 440 *esedī kurūsh* to the residents of the *Mawlawī* poor in the *Mawlawīkhāne*.[188] The last *waqf* was established in 1033/1623 by the commander of Jerusalem, Muḥammad Pasha Ebū'l-Fūl, son of Süleyman Beg bin Kubad. He endowed his vegetable garden, which is located near *Bāb al-ʿAmūd*, which is the entrance gate from the north side of Jerusalem, and which contains trees such as almond and rose trees, for the *Mawlawī* dervishes residing in the *Mawlawī* lodge. When the conditions could not be implemented, he wanted it to be spent on poor Muslims.[189]

In the period examined within the scope of the study, the *Qādiriyya*, *Bistāmiyya*, *Khalwatiyya*, *Naqshbandiyya*, *Shādhiliyya*, and *Rifāʿiyya takiyya*s were also active in Jerusalem. In the *Ḥurūfāt* Registers, twelve appointment records belonging to six different *takiyya*s were recorded. Of these: Sayyid Shahbaz, Shaykh Mezīd, Shaykh Muḥarram Sināʿ al-Dīn, and Sayyid Jelāl *Takiyya*,[190] Ṭarīq *Rufāʿiyya Takiyya*,[191] and *Maghribī*s *Takiyya* are the Sufi lodges with the highest number of records.[192]

186 He allocated this amount to the trustee of the *Mawlawīkhāne*, Dervish ʿAbd al-Qādir Çelebi. Dervish ʿAbd al-Qādir Çelebi benefited from this money at a rate of 1.5 units each. Consequently, an annual sum of 30 *sultaniye* would be allocated to the drummer (2 *akça* daily) and the *neyzen* (2 *akça* daily). Olive oil would be purchased with three *sultaniye* to illuminate the *Mawlawīkhāne*. Ghūsha, *Ḥārat al-Saʿdiyya*, 705; idem, *al-Awqāf al-Islāmiyya*, 530–31.

187 VGMA, 515: 44/36.

188 Ghūsha, *Ḥārat al-Saʿdiyya*, 705.

189 Ghūsha, *Ḥārat al-Saʿdiyya*, 705.

190 VGMA, 515: 94/145.

191 VGMA, 160: 62.

192 The structure referred to as a lodge in the *ḥurūfāt* records was identified as a *zāwiya* in the Maghāriba Quarter. Two *zāwiyas* were established as *waqf* in the Maghāriba Quarter. The first was founded by Shaykh ʿUmar ibn ʿAbdullāh ibn ʿAbd al-Nabī al-Maghribī al-Maṣmūdī in 3 Rabīʿ al-Ākhir 703/1313 for the benefit of the Maghāriba Quarter's residents. This *zāwiya* was the first *waqf* established by a Maghribī for the Maghāriba Quarter. It consisted of two floors, with a masjid on the upper floor. Destitute Maghribīs were housed there, and their needs were provided for. For the *waqf* deed, see VGMA, 583: 27/20. The endower was buried in the Mamilla (*Maʿman Allāh*) cemetery, where prominent scholars had been

1.2.2.4 *Zāwiya/Ribāṭ/Khanqāh*

Zāwiya means "corner" in Arabic and as a term, it is a house established in town, province, village or road, and where shaykhs and dervishes belonging to certain Sufi orders lived, guests were hosted and fed free of charge.[193] They are also called *ribāṭ, khanqāh, khāni-qāh, buk'a, düveyre, itikafhāne, meşīhathāne, dār-ı tevhīd, dār-ı rahat, tevhīdhāned-i zāwiya, zikrullahhāne, madrasa* until the fourteenth and fifteenth centuries. Later on, they took names such as *tekke, āsitāne, mevlevīhāne, dārü'r-rāha*.[194] The lodges are also mentioned with some praising titles, including *zāwiya-i ma'mūre, zāwiya-i latīfe*.

Takiyyas and *zāwiyas*, which developed with religious and social thoughts besides Sufism, served as places of *dhikr* and worship of religious orders, places of spiritual treatment and social assistance, and guesthouses for their members and passengers. In addition, among the *takiyyas* and *zāwiyas*, which were regarded as a kind of educational institution, there were also those who provide literature, philosophy, music and vocational education.[195]

---

interred since the time of Ṣalāḥ al-Dīn. See al-Ḥanbalī, *al-Uns al-Jalīl*, 397, 580. The second *zāwiya* in the quarter was established by Shu'ayb ibn Muḥammad ibn Shu'ayb, the grandson of Abū Madyan al-Ghawth, renowned for his knowledge and philanthropy among the Maghribī residents of Jerusalem. The *waqf* deed recorded under account number 583 in the VGMA (Vakıflar Genel Müdürlüğü Arşivi) is documented in Arabic on lines 27 and 20. An English translation of the deed is provided in Tibawi, *Islamic Pious Foundations in Jerusalem*, 11. The endower, commonly known as Abū Madyan, is referred to in the *waqf* deed as: "Şeyh-i sālih Ebi Medyen Şuayb ibn Şeyh Salih Ebi Abdullah Mehmed ibn Şeyh İmām-ı Ebi Medyen Şuayb el-Mağribī el-Osmanī el-Mālikī". VGMA, 583: 28/21. In other documents related to *waqf*, the endower was remembered with prayers such as "kuddise sırrahu, kuddise sırrahü'l-azīz, radiye, radiyallahu 'anh, kaddesallahu sırrahu." For example see, BOA, ŞD. 2296.40.26; BOA, ŞD.d. 2296.40.30; BOA, ŞD.d. 2296.40.36; BOA, ŞD.d. 2296.40.40; BOA, ŞD.d. 2299.02.01. The endower, in deed of trust, endowed all the income of 'Ayn-ı Kārim in Jerusalem. The endower endowed his *waqf* to all residents of Jerusalem and the ones coming to Jerusalem and all the Maghribīs. Secondly, he endowed a certain space which was located in the edge of Silsila Door (*Bāb al-Silsila*) known as *Umm al-Banāt* Bridge in Jerusalem ("bir eyvān ve iki oda ve bir saha ve kendine mahsus bir mürtefak ve bu mürtefakın altında kemer yapılı bir mahzeni müştemil ve dört tarafının hudūdu"). The endower endowed this place as *Suknā Zāwiya* for the accommodation of men coming to Maghāriba Quarter. In the deed of trust, it was particularly mentioned that the women visitors or men and women residents in the Maghāriba Quarter had no right to residency (*suknā*).

193 Ocak, "Zaviyeler," 248.

194 Kara, "Tasavvuf," 394.

195 Şamettin Başol, *Kentleşme, Ekonomi ve Sosyal Hayat Yönleriyle 17. Yüzyıl Bursa Vakıfları* (PhD diss., Gazi Üniversitesi, Sosyal Bilimler Enstitüsü, Tarih Anabilim Dalı, Ankara, 2008), 158.

It is possible to talk about only a difference of origin between *zāwiyas*, *khanqāh* and *ribāṭ*. Namely, while the *ribāṭ* is used for the buildings where the *ghāzī* fighters live; but this word is also used by Sufis who are involved in spiritual warfare.[196] In the early period of the Ottoman Empire, the fortified places where veterans who fought voluntarily for *jihad* and war along the borders lived were called *ribāṭ*. On the other hand, these three terms are mostly used in similar meanings. These three terms also refer to the Sufi *khanqāh*s, which accept foreigners and thus assume the role of a guesthouse. *Ribāṭ* in Jerusalem also functioned as guesthouses for pilgrims.[197] Having acquired a mystical character, the *ribāṭ*s became *zāwiya*s and caravansaries in time.[198]

In an earlier period, Ocak evaluates that *zāwiya*s in the Middle East countries and Jerusalem were more related to the development and organization of the Sufi movements[199] rather than the purpose of a settlement activity.[200] In the fourteenth and fifteenth centuries, some defects appeared in the lodges and these lost their real functions and started to take the form of institutions belonging to only a number of orders. Thus, after the thirteenth century, instead of *zāwiya*s in villages and cities, *takiyya*s as Sufi lodges continued their functions.[201]

---

196 Pedersen, "Mescit," 58.

197 ibid., 58.

198 Ocak, "Zaviyeler," 248.

199 ibid., 253.

200 *Zāwiya*s were established by nomad Turks settled in Anatolia. They became important cultural institutions and a center of organization and settlement among Turks. In the first years of Ottomans' foundation, and through the entire fourteenth and fifteenth centuries, they were a focal center for the transfer of nomadic Turcoman tribes to conquested lands. They served in *zāwiyas* and supported the facility with other tools. See, Barkan, "Osmanlı İmparatorluğunda Bir İskān," 295–97. In this context, executive *umarā'* – such as viziers, governors, and *sanjāq* governors – along with high-ranking palace officials like *mīrāhūr*, *hazinedarbaşı*, *kilarcı*, *'ulamā'*, *mashāyikh*, and *fuqahā'* played key roles in settlement and colonization efforts. State officials established villages, hamlets, and quarters within their own *dirlik*. They provided facilities to ensure the welfare of the *re'āyā*, who formed the majority of the Turk-Islamic population, and took measures to support them. In this way, the *re'āyā* served as the backbone of these founding efforts. Barkan, "Osmanlı İmparatorluğunda," 279–386. Likewise, they did important deeds such as opening *zāwiyas*, establishing *masjid* and lodges, developing the places as a cultural, social and financial centers with the first ruler's exemptions and *berat*s as dervishes or shaykhs (*Abdalān-ı Rūm*) (or *Baba*) did in Anatolia connected to different sufi sects.

201 Ocak, "Zaviyeler," 278.

In the records included in Table A5, fifty-five appointment records for twenty-two different *zāwiya waqf*s were identified.[202] The records highlight the *waqf zāwiya*s of Lu'lu' Ghāzī,[203] Bistāmiyya (*Waqf Zāwiya* of Shaykh ʿAbdullāh al-Bisṭāmī),[204] *Qādiriyya* (known also as *Baba* of *Shaykh al-Islām* Asʿad Effendi, Asʿadiyya)[205] as having the most appointments. The *Zāwiya Qādiriyya* was endowed by Jerusalem's district governor, Mehmet Pasha, as his final charitable project. No records indicate Mehmet Pasha's birth or death dates, with the earliest mention of him in Jerusalem appearing in his daughter's marriage contract. His activities are documented in the Jerusalem *Sharīʿa* Court Registers and surviving inscriptions. The *waqfiyya* inscription of the *Zāwiya Qādiriyya* dates its construction to 1043 AH/1663 CE, stating: "In the name of God, the Merciful, the Compassionate. This *zāwiya* belongs to our master and *sayyid*, the Sultan of masters, Shaykh ʿAbd al-Qādir Jīlānī. May God bless his secret.

---

202 Fakhriyya *Khanqāh*, which was mentioned as a *zāwiya* in Powers, was a *madrasa* in the Jerusalem *ḥurūfāt* account. The *Zāwiyat* al-Maghāriba was registered as the Maghāriba Lodge. *Zāwiyat al-Shaykhūniyya* was recorded as a *madrasa*, and no records were found for the *zāwiya*s called *Zāwiyat al-Adhhamiyya*, *Zāwiyat al-Mihmāziyya*, or *Zāwiyat al-Tawāshiyya* in the sources cited by Powers ("Revenues," 166–189). In Jerusalem Esās registers, there are records of zāwiyas with other names: *Zāwiyat al-Qamariyya* (VGMA, 515: 41/27); *Zāwiyat al-Adhhamiyya* (Shaykh Ibrāhīm Adhham) (VGMA, 515: 72/77); *Zāwiyat al-Shaykh ʿAlāʾ al-Dīn ʿAlī* (VGMA, 515: 76/83); *Zāwiyat al-Maghāriba* (VGMA, 515: 79/89); *Zāwiyat al-Ṭāhiriyya* and *Zāwiyat al-Qāsimiyya* (VGMA, 515: 84/106); *Zāwiyat al-Ṣadriyya* (VGMA, 515: 89/122) and "*Vakf-ı Zaviye-i Köstendilī Şeyh İbrahim Efendi ʿan meşayih-i tarikat-ı Rufai der civarı Ḥaram al-Sharīf*" (VGMA, 515: 101/171). See, Table A5.

203 *The Madrasat-Zāwiya and Ribāṭ al-Lu'lu'iyya* in Bayt Sāwīr village were established by Lu'lu' Ghāzī. The *waqf* deed was registered in 775/1354 in the *Evkāf Taḥrīr* registers (no. 522). Powers, "Revenues," 180–81. In Jerusalem's *ḥurūfāt* accounts, there were thirteen appointment registers for the Bedr al-Dīn Lu'lu' Ghāzī *Waqf*, which was associated with a *shaykh* in the *Bāb al-ʿAmūd quarter*. Additionally, *there were four registers for the Zāwiyat al-Lu'lu' Ghāzī*, one register for the *Masjid al-Shaykh Lu'lu'*, and two registers for the *Masjid Zāwiyat al-Shaykh Lu'lu' Waqf*. Based on these registers, it can be inferred that the *waqf* established by Lu'lu' Ghāzī was referred to as a *zāwiya*, with a mosque nearby or the *zāwiya* itself functioning as a mosque. Three officials were appointed between Ṣafar 1192 and Jumādā al-Awwal 1239/1778–1824 CE.

204 *Zāwiyat al-Bisṭāmiyya* was established before 770/1368–69 CE by Shaykh ʿAbdullāh al-Bisṭāmī. Powers, "Revenues," 180–81. Three officials were appointed to the *zāwiya*, named after its founder, between Jumādā al-Ākhira 1126 and Ṣafar 1212/1714–1797 CE, according to the records.

205 In the examined records, *Zāwiyat al-Qādiriyya* had the most entries, with seventeen official appointments between 1109 and 1184/1697–1770 CE. The *Zāwiya* was named in variant such as "Tūr-ı Zīnada Zāwiya-i Esʿad Bey Vakfı, Şeyhülislam Esʿad Efendi, Esʿad Efendi, Esʿadiyye, Kādiriyye." Thus, it is understood that the *zāwiya* was founded by Shaykh al-Islām Asad Effendi.

Year 1043/1663." In the endowment document, Mehmet Pasha, in the presence of witnesses, designated the lodge in the *Ghawānima* district as a *waqf* for the *Qādirī* dervishes, providing immovable properties and cash to cover its expenses.

The common feature of the *khanqāh*s listed in Annex 8 and in the records, particularly *Khanqāh al-Jawhariyya*,[206] *Bāsiṭiyya*,[207] *Jarrāḥiyya*,[208] *Ṣalāḥiyya* (*Khanqāh Malik Ṣalāḥ al-Dīn, Khanqāh al-Ṣalāḥī*)[209] devoted by Malik Ṣalāḥ al-Dīnis also the existence of *madrasa*s established in their name. This situation brings two possibilities to mind. First of all, the *madrasas* in question may be referred to as both *madrasa* and *khanqāh* in the records. Secondly, in these *madrasas*, there were also places where people or travelers who have subscribed to a certain Sufi thought could stay. In the Jerusalem *Esās* (Treasury) Registers of the same period, Khanqāh al-Ḥilya,[210] *Khanqāh al-Khātūniyya*,[211] *Khanqāh al-Fakhriyya*[212] were the other *khanqāhs* to which they are appointed.[213]

206 In sixteenth century, *khanqāh* was used instead of *ribāṭ*, and both words means *Sufī khanqāh*. There is a slight difference between *khanqāh* and *madrasa*. As conveyed from Powers, *khānqāh* was sometimes recorded as *ribāṭ* or *waqf* or both khanqāh and *madrasa*. Powers, "Revenues," 183.

207 The establishment of the *madrasa* was commenced by Shaykh al-Islām Shams al-Dīn Muḥammad al-Harawī, upon his death, Qāḍī Zayn al-Dīn ʿAbd al-Bāsiṭ ibn Khalīl al-Dimashqī completed it. The income of Ṣūr Bāhir village was endowed and got the name of founder *qāḍī*. The *madrasa* which was established as *waqf* dated back to 834 AH/1430 CE. Powers, "Revenues," 182. In the same record, *Bāsiṭiyya Khānqāh* was diversely recorded as a *madrasa*, *zāwiya*, and *khanqāh*.

208 The *Jarrāḥiyya* were located outside Jerusalem, and salaried personnel were appointed. The *zāwiya* was named after Emir Ḥusām al-Dīn al-Ḥusayn ibn Sharaf al-Dīn ʿĪsā al-Jarrāḥī, one of Sultan Ṣalāḥ al-Dīn's emirs (Powers, "Revenues," 170).

209 Previously known as Dār al-Baṭrak under Malik Ṣalāḥ al-Dīn, the *Ṣūfī Khānqāh* was established near (bi-jiwārin min al-qumāma) the Church of the Prophet ʿĪsā. As cited in Powers, although the deed of trust was dated H. 585/M. 1189, the *khānqāh* was established in 483 AH/1090–1091 CE (Powers, "Revenues," 167). The income of the *waqf* was raised before Sultan Ṣalāḥ al-Dīn departed from Jerusalem. In the examined records, the *khānqāh* was referred to as *Zāwiya Ṣalāḥiyya* and *Zāwiyat Khānqāh Ṣalāḥiyya*.

210 See, VGMA, 515: 38/18.

211 See, VGMA, 515: 72/78.

212 See, VGMA, 515: 92/139.

213 See, Table A6.

Ribāṭs in Jerusalem during the period of this study included Çavuş,[214] *Bayram* Çavuş,[215] Ribāṭ al-Kurd,[216] *Ribāṭ al- Manṣūrī*[217] and *Ribāṭ al-Mardīn*.[218] In Jerusalem *Ḥurūfāt* registers, there were appointments to *Ribāṭ-ı Sānī Waqf, Ribāṭ al-Tamjūn*, and *Ribāṭ al-Hujūr Waqfs* in *Bāb al-Qaṭṭānīn* Quarter without mentioning the position. Besides, in the *sharīʿa* court registers belonging to the second half of the eighteenth century, there were records related to *Ribāṭ al-ʿUmarī, Ribāṭ al-Ḥajj Qāsim*, and *Ribāṭ al-Ḥajja Fāṭima* in *surras* sent to Jerusalem.[219] In Jerusalem *Esās* (Treasury) Records belonging to same period, there were appointments of officials to the *Waqf of Ribāṭ al- Ḥamawī*[220] and *Ribāṭ al-Kalāmiyya*[221] *Waqfs*.[222]

1.2.2.5 Merkad, Türbe, Maqām (*Tomb, Shrine, Mausoleum*)

These three words mean grave or tomb, however, there is a slight difference. *Merkad* means tomb and grave in the dictionary[223] while a *türbe* is a tomb for a prominent person and secondly, and it refers to a roof above the grave.[224]

---

214 It was home to the Takarana family today al-Sūwāriyya, *al-Ḥayāt al-Ijtimāʿiyya.*, 261.

215 In other *ribāṭs* in *ḥurūfāt* accounts, appointments were made to the *Ribāṭ al-Thānī Waqf* (VGMA, 1112:1/157), to *Bayram* Çavuş *Ribāṭ* (VGMA, 1160:116/59), and to *Ribāṭ al-Tamjūn Waqf in Bāb al-Qaṭṭānīn* (VGMA, 1119:110/4). As mentioned in Powers (Revenues, 173), a record pertaining to *Ribāṭ ʿAlāʾ al-Dīn al-Baṣīr* in the Jerusalem *esās* registers, among the earliest records, indicates that *Çavūsh* ibn Muṣṭafā was an active statesman in Jerusalem. Bayram Çavuş was appointed by Qānūnī Sulṭān Sulaymān as an overseer for the construction of city walls. He established Bayram Çavuş *Ribāṭ* in Jerusalem in 947 AH/1540 CE and built a shrine for himself near the *ribāṭ*. Dow, "The Hammams," 284. There was also school in *ribāṭ* for the education of children. In this school, the *müeddib-i etfāl* was Muḥammad ibn Hoca and resided in the houses given in return for his service. JS 263: 37.

216 In the second half of the eighteenth century, a share from the *surra* was given to share holders who was settling in *ribāṭ*. JS 261: 320.

217 *Ribāṭ al-Manṣūrī* (*Ribāṭ Qalāwūn*) was established by Malik al-Manṣūr Qalāwūn al-Ṣāliḥī, a Baḥrī Mamlūk Sulṭān, in *Bāb al-Nāẓir* in *al-Ḥaram al-Sharīf* in 681 AH/1282 CE for the destitute coming to the city (al-Ḥanbalī, *al-Uns al-Jalīl*, 43). Khalīl's son Muṣṭafā and his brother Muḥammad ʿĀrif were appointed as *müeddib-i etfāl* with a half share (JS 255:175). There was one appointment to *Ribāṭ al-Manṣūrīn* in the Jerusalem *ḥurūfāt* accounts. VGMA, 1109: 6/25.

218 There were three appointment records for the *Ribāṭ al-Mardīnī Waqf*, located in *Bāb al-Ḥiṭṭā* quarter in Jerusalem, documented in three different forms in the Jerusalem *ḥurūfāt* accounts. VGMA, 1112: 1/188; 1140: 245/7; 1107: 2/12.

219 al-Sūwāriyya, *al-Ḥayāt al-Ijtimāʿiyya*, 265.

220 See, VGMA, 515: 84/105.

221 See, VGMA, 515: 87/112.

222 See, Table A7.

223 Devellioğlu, *Osmanlıca*, 621.

224 ibid., 1115.

Maqam is defined as a place where the person who was accepted as *velī* (saint) or the grave of a prominent individual.[225]

While there are usually dome on the *merkads*, there is a *mihrab* for those who pray. Some offices consist of a room or an open space, while others consist of two or three buildings. Most of the tombs in Jerusalem during the Ottoman Period were open to visitors.[226] Although many of them have disappeared in Jerusalem, especially in the Old City, there are still many *merkad*s, tombs and mauseloums that still exist today. There are graves with around fifty prominent figures and many different burial places.[227] Some features of *merkad*s, tombs and authorities in Jerusalem can be listed as follows: *Merkad*s were generally built as burial places of well-known people. In some examples, they were built as part of a *madrasa*, lodge, or mosque. But their main function is that they are tombs. Most of the *merkad*s are located on the *Bāb al-Silsila* road. *Merkads* of *Türkan Khatun*,[228] *Saʿdiyya*, *Geylāniyye*,[229] *Tashtimūriyya*[230] and *Avhādiyya*[231] were in that group.[232] Secondly, in Jerusalem, the *merkad*s of the people who were buried in a room of *madrasa*s, sufi lodges or *ribāṭ*s established in reference to the founders of the *waqf* or individuals were also called with the same name. For example: The tombs in *Khātūniyya Madrasa*, *Amīniyya Madrasa*, and *Jarrāḥiyya*, *Wafā'iyya*, and *Kirāmiyya* Ṣūfī lodges were of this type. Additionally, some mausoleums are identified by the authority, grave, or mosque associated with them, such as Shaykh Ḥaydar Tomb and Shaykh Rayḥān Mosque. Furthermore, certain standalone shrines or groups of shrines were constructed in open fields or within buildings, their owners often unknown, with most belonging to martyrs of war. Such tombs were also located within the *Badriyya* and *Muʿaẓẓamiyya Madrasa*s.

225 Muʿallim Nācī. Lughāt-i Nācī (İstanbul: Çağrı Yay., 2006), 817.

226 Dow, "The Hammams of Ottoman Jerusalem," 283.

227 ibid., 283.

228 The shrine, located in *Bāb al-Silsila* and founded in 753 AH/1352 CE, was attributed to Türkan Hatun the daughter of Toktay who was the son of Uzbek Selçuk. ʿAsalī, *Ajdādunā*, 63.

229 The Jīlāniyya Shrine was constructed at the behest of Ibn al-Ṣāḥib al-Jīlānī, known as Ḥājj Jamāl al-Dīn Pahlawān ibn al-Amīr Shams al-Dīn Qarad Shāh ibn Shams al-Dīn Muḥammad al-Jīlānī. Powers, "Revenues," 178.

230 The *Ṭashtīmūriyya* Shrine, comprising a shrine, madrasa, and public fountain, was established by one of the Mamlūk emirs, Amīr Ṭashtīmūr al-ʿAlī, in 753 AH/1352 CE. The late Amīr Ṭashtīmūr was buried in the shrine in 786 AH/1384 CE. Powers, "Revenues," 181.

231 Malik al-Awḥad Najm al-Dīn Yūsuf ibn al-Malik al-Nāṣir Ṣalāḥ al-Dīn Dāwūd ibn al-Malik al-Muʿaẓẓam ʿĪsā was buried in a marqad in the north of the *Ḥaram*, close to *Bāb al-Ḥaṭṭ* in 697 AH/1298 CE. al-Sūwāriyya, al-Ḥayāt al-Ijtimāʿiyya, 43.

232 Dow, "The Hammams," 283.

Tombs, shrines, and mausoleums in Jerusalem which were defined with its general features, were abundant in number, thus, in this study, the ones in Jerusalem *Ḥurūfāt* records are given in tables whereas the ones having too much records will be briefly elucidated.[233] When Table A8 regarding the mausoleums and *merkads* included in the Jerusalem *Ḥurūfāt* Books were examined, 23 appointment records for 10 different posts were identified.

In the first group of these, the *merkads* built in the name of the Prophets attract attention. David, Saint Prophet, Moses, Jesus were mentioned as prophets with *merkads* in the records. Another notable aspect of the merkads in the analyzed records is their association with specific locations, such as mosques or *masjids* where some merkads were situated (e.g., *Waqf of Dīb Nabī ibn Yāsīn Mosque and Merkad, Merkad and Masjid al-Taymī, Salama ibn al-Akwaʿ Tomb and Masjid Waqf*), and others linked to Ṣūfī lodges (e.g., *Waqf of Shaykh ʿUmar Lodge and Merkad*). Among the mausoleums, those dedicated to prophets are most prominent. Prophets mentioned in the records include Yaʿqūb, Shuʿayb, Ṣāliḥ, Mūsā, Yūnus, Lūṭ, ʿAnbar, ʿĪsā, Lāwī, Shām, Yaḥyā, and Yūshaʿ. A striking detail is the mention of three distinct locations for Nabī Ṣāliḥ. Additionally, the mausoleum records in Jerusalem indicate a higher prevalence of sayyids and sayyidas compared to merkads and tombs.[234]

When examining Table A9, compiled from tomb records in the Jerusalem *Ḥurūfāt* Books, twenty-two distinct tombs are identified. The first group consists of tombs dedicated to prophets, including Ṣāliḥ, Binyāmīn, Dāwūd, Shamūʾīl, Dhū al-Kifl, Rubīl (also recorded as Rubayl or Rūbīn), Yūnus, and Lūṭ,[235] İsmail,[236] Üzeyir[237] and İshak[238] are mentioned as Prophets with tombs in the records. In the records, the *ṣaḥāba* ʿUbayda ibn Sāmit and Shaykh Maḥmūd al-Muttaṣī are noted, alongside mausoleums of saints such as Shaykh Māʾ and Shaykh Nāẓir Qudsī al-ʿUzayr. Similar to *merkads*, some tombs are associated with nearby mosques or *masjids*, such as the *waqfs* of Malik Sayf al-Dīn ibn ʿĀṣir and Badr al-Dīn, the Sayf al-Dīn ibn ʿĀṣir Tomb and Masjid,

---

233 See, Table A8, Table A9.

234 In Jerusalem *Esās* registers, there are appointments of officials to the shrines such as *Sayyidi Kalamud* and *Sayyidī Ḥammādī*. VGMA, 515: 81/92; 90/125.

235 See, VGMA, 515: 43/34.

236 See, VGMA, 515: 87/117.

237 See, VGMA, 515: 87/113.

238 See, VGMA, 515: 91/132.

and the *Waqf* Tomb and *Mosque of Yaʿqūb*. Records also mention the *Jālikiyya*[239] and *Geylāniyya* Tombs.[240]

A notable observation in the records is the interchangeable use of *merkad*, tomb, and mausoleum to describe the same structure. For instance, the Mausoleum and *Merkad* of Maryam, Shaykh Yaʿqūb Tomb and Mausoleum, and Shaykh Aḥmad al-Mattā are recorded as both tomb and mausoleum. This indicates that *merkad*, tomb, and mausoleum were used synonymously by record-keepers. Additionally, comparing the data on *merkad*s and tombs in the table, it is evident that the same building is sometimes labeled as a *merkad*, a tomb, or an office.

Tombs established during the Ottoman period and still existing today include those of Bayram *Çavūsh*, Muḥammad al-ʿAlamī,[241] Muḥammad al-Uzbekī, Muḥammad al-Khalīlī, Muḥammad ibn Budayr, and the tombs in *Amīniyya Madrasa* belonging to the *al-Imām* family.[242] However, these tombs are not recorded in the Jerusalem *Ḥurūfāt* Registers. Comparing Dow's list of shrines visited by travelers in the seventh and fifteenth centuries with the Jerusalem *Ḥurūfāt* registers reveals records for the Shaykh Ḥaydar Tomb in Old Jerusalem and the Tomb of Shaykh Mūsā al-ʿAlamī. Among tombs located outside the city walls, only the Tomb of ʿUbayda ibn Sāmit, a *ṣaḥābī*, is documented.

Consequently, the *Ḥurūfāt* Registers related to Jerusalem, which Evliyā Çelebi hyperbolically described as "the *āstāna* (a major Ṣūfī lodge) of one hundred twenty-four thousand prophets," contain numerous records of *merkad*s, tombs, and mausoleums associated with prophets. Beyond prophets, the registers include many records of *merkad*s, tombs, and mausoleums of *ṣaḥāba*, saints, scholars, and religious figures. However, these structures, despite subtle distinctions, are often used interchangeably, labeled as *merkad*, tomb, or mausoleum. As a result, some records identified here are duplicates.

---

239 Rukn al-Dīn Baybars al-Jālikī al-Ṣāliḥī, from the Emir of Damascus, was buried in 707 AH/1307 CE at the shrine. Al-Sayyid Mūsā ibn al-Shaykh Ṣunʿullāh Effendi al-Khālidī was appointed to a 1/6 share of the shrine's duties of *tawliyya*, *nizāra*, and *şeʿal*. He was appointed with a payment of 10 *zolota* daily, taking the duty from al-Sayyid Abū al-Hawā ibn al-Sayyid Muḥammad. See al-Sūwāriyya, *al-Ḥayāt al-Ijtimāʿiyya* (Istanbul: Maṭbaʿat al-ʿUthmāniyya, 1431 AH/2010 CE), 65.

240 The endower of the shrine was al-Ḥājj Jamāl al-Dīn Pehlevānī ibn al-Amīr Shams al-Dīn Qaradsha ibn Shams al-Dīn Muḥammad al-Jīlānī, and it was built in 753 AH/1352 CE. Al-Sūwāriyya, *al-Ḥayāt al-Ijtimāʿiyya*, 67.

241 See, VGMA, 515: 97/155.

242 Dow, "The Hammams," 284.

1.2.2.6 *Tilāwa/Tilavet (Reading Qur'an) and the Prayer Waqfs*

Some people who established *waqfs* in the Ottoman society put conditions in their *waqfiyyas* regarding this issue in order to ensure that the Qur'an, *mawlid* or prayer was read for them while they were alive or after their death. Among the conditions of endowers: there are conditions such as reciting the whole or a partial Qur'an every day on behalf of one's own or family members or praying. In order to ensure that these conditions were fulfilled continuously after their death, *waqf* owners had allocated income or provided various opportunities to those who would fulfill these duties in their *waqf*. Thus, professions such as *kāri-i cuz/eczā* (reciting some part/parts of Qur'an),[243] *kāri-i yasin/mulk/tebāreke, kāri-i ma teyessera* (reciting the verses Yasin, Mulk, Tebareke, short verses)[244] who were mostly in education and worship institutions and earn their living by reading the Qur'an, verses and praying had emerged in the Islamic world.

One of the most important worship for the Muslims is to prayer meaning to beg and to want a desirable deed, to ask for forgiveness and mercy from God. For this reason, salient part of the endowers allocated income from *waqf* to the people called *duagū* or *duahān*. They were generally existed in the tombs, lodges, mosques and masjids dealing with prayer for endowers, their family members and their past.[245]

A significant practice for Muslims is the observance of blessed days and nights through worship. One such occasion is the night of *mawlid*, marking the birth of the Prophet on the twelfth day of Rabīʿ al-Awwal, the third month of the Hijri calendar. The Ottomans commemorated this night using a poem

243 *Juzhāns* were the official reading fascicles in mosques before performing prayer. The verb "khāndan" in Persian means to read and to call. Fascicle (Turkish: *cüz*, Arabic: *juz*) is one of twenty parts of the Qur'an. Pakalın, *Osmanlı Tarih Deyimleri*, 318. There were fascicle readers in mosques according to their size. The most determined and hardworking person became the chief reader. After the morning prayer, apart from Friday, they read fascicle and endowed them to the mosque community and founder. The one who read fascicles of Qur'an (*eczā-yı şerīfe*) were recorded in Turkish as *eczāhān*.

244 *Qāriʾ* means reader. As an official, it means reader of the Qur'an. Yediyıldız, *İslam ve Türk Hukuk Tarihi Araştırmaları*, 57. In Jerusalem *ḥurūfāt* account, besides the *kāri-i kur'ān*, there were *kāri-i ma teyessere* (the official for reading chapters from Qur''an), *kāri-i aşır* (the official reading at least 10 verses after the prayer), *kāri-i tefsir* (the official reading the Qur'an with its explanations), *kāri-i hadis* (the official reading hadith mentioning the Prophet's *sunna*) and *kāri-i mevlid-i şerif* (the official reading slamic memorial). In larger *waqfs* and events, such as *Salawāt al-Nabī* and *Khusraw al-Rūmī*, where multiple *qāriʾ*s were appointed, they were collectively referred to as *qurrāʾ* (readers). Al-Sūwāriyya, *al-Ḥayāt al-Ijtimāʿiyya*, 68. For instance see, VGMA, 1160: 116/7; 1160: 116/98.

245 Pakalın, *Osmanlı Tarih Deyimleri.*, 479.

by Süleyman Çelebi (d. 1422), a dervish of the *Khalwatiyya* order, known as *mawlid al-sharīf*. This religious tradition, which gained profound importance in the Ottoman Empire by the late fifteenth century, was deeply ingrained in the public conscience. Consequently, many *waqf* founders appointed specialized officials, such as *mawlidkhān*s and *ḥāfiẓ*, to celebrate this religious holiday in various mosques across the empire.[246]

Records show that the *waqf* staff was appointed for reciting Qur'an and prayers in 145 appointment records in 52 different records in the Jerusalem *Ḥurūfāt* and *Esās* Registers. The first thing that draws attention in the records is the allocation of various charity fees for reading the Qur'an or various *sura*s in the Dome of the Rock and Masjid *al-Aqṣā* and for prayers. The *waqf*s that made allocations to the Dome of the Rock and Masjid *al-Aqṣā* were determined to be mostly charitable *waqf*s such as Sultan Suleiman I *Waqf*, Khasseki Sultan *Waqf*, Sinan Pasha, Küçük Ahmed Pasha and Mustafa Pasha *Waqf*.

Another point that draws attention in the appointments is that after the endowers passed away, they established *waqf*s for the purposes such as reciting the Qur'an and praying for their souls and determined wages for the officers. The pharmacy made for the parts of the Qur'an recited for the soul of Turgut Agha after the morning prayer in the Dome of the Rock, which is included in the records; The appointment of *aşırhan* (reciting ten verses from Qur'an) for the spirit of Umar Effendi in the Dome of the Rock. This is the type of recordings from Sultan Suleiman I *Waqf* for the *juzhān* (reciting parts from the Qur'an) assignments for the spirit of Sultan Suleiman in the Dome of the Rock mosque.[247] Apart from the matters mentioned here, in some records, in addition to wages, various allocations were made from the pay-taker such as the right to settle in a house (*süknā*) or the rent of a shop to the officials who fulfill the conditions of reading the Qur'an and praying.[248]

---

246 Yediyıldız, *XVIII. Asır*, 4.

247 In the Jerusalem *Esās* Register in VGMA belonging to the same period, there were many officials of *tilāwa* and prayer *waqf*s. For example: Vakf-ı Eczāhānān-ı Turgut Ağa der Sahratullah Müşerrefe (VGMA, 515: 47/45); *Vakf-ı Eczāhānān-ı İbrahim bey bin Karaman der Sahratullah* (VGMA, 515: 47/46); *Vakf-ı Eczāhānān-ı Zeyneb Hatun der Sahtarullah* (VGMA, 515: 46/30); *Vakf-ı Eczāhānān-ı İbn-i Ibade der Sahratullah eczāhānān-ı vakt-i zuhur der Kudüs-i Şerif* (VGMA, 515: 49/49); *Vakf-ı En'ām-ı Müezzinān veled-i Çelebi Efendi Defterdār* (VGMA, 515: 87/115); *Vakf-ı Eczāhānān-ı Medrese-i Belediyye el-mezbūr* (VGMA, 515: 52/53); *Vakf-ı evlad-ı Mehmed Bey Türbesi Eczahānları* (VGMA, 515: 90/129); *Vakf-ı Eczāhānān-ı Hamza Kaşif* (VGMA, 515: 92/135).

248 For example see, "Kudüsde Mecelle Sūkı Beyti'l-Me'bezde bir vakıf menzilin süknāsına kırāat-ı ma teyessera içün vakf ve şart olan süknāya mutasarrıf olan Şeyh Abdullah ve Şeyh Abdullatif ve Muḥammad Nahefī hüccet ile mutasarrıflar olub bī berāt olmakla kadısı Ahmed arzıyla buyuruldu." VGMA, 1160: 116/128; "Kudüsde kırāat ma teyesserahu

During the period covered by this study, several newly established family *waqfs* allocated revenues for Qur'an recitation. Sharīfa bint Ṣāliḥ al-ʿAsalī stipulated in her *waqfiyya* that the imāms of Masjid *al-Aqṣā* recite the Qur'an in Masjid *al-Aqṣā* using the income from her mansion in *Khaṭṭ Dāwūd*.[249] Additionally, ʿAbdullāh ibn Ibrāhīm al-Dāwūdī mandated that the Sūrat al-Fātiḥa be recited between the two sermons every Friday at Masjid *al-Aqṣā*, with one recitation dedicated to his soul.[250] Another endower, Muḥammad Sunʿ Allāh al-Khālidī, designated the monthly income of his waqf, 18 *kurūsh*, to be distributed among four individuals who would recite the Qur'an monthly, completing it three times during Ramaḍān, with the reward dedicated to the soul of the Prophet, the endower, and his mother.[251] Khalīl Sharaf al-Dīn ibn Abū Jibna, another endower, stipulated that 12 *zoloṭa*[252] from the annual *waqf* income be given to *Takārīn* Ṣūfis in the Jerusalem *Ḥaram* for reciting two parts of the Qur'an, with one dedicated to the Prophet and the other to himself.[253] Finally, ʿAbdullāh ibn Ibrāhīm al-Dāwūdī also required an annual recitation of *mawlid* for the Prophet, funded by 20 *fidda Miṣriyya* from the *waqf* income.[254]

Finally, the reciters of the verses of *Yā Sīn*, *Fātiḥa*, and *Mulk*, appointed to collect wages from the *Kısmet-i Askeriye* (share of the office), draw attention.[255] The term *Kısmet-i Askeriye*, in the event of the death of a person belonging to the ruling elite in the Ottoman Empire, refered to the division of his inheritance to his successors according to religious law.[256] In the Ottoman Empire, the division of the inheritance of the members of the ruling elite among the inheritors was fulfilling the military chiefs on behalf of the *kadıasker* (chief

---

Hattı Davud Aleyhisselamda Bābü't-Tevvahīn mahallesinde bir bāb dükkān ile yine kıraatı ma teyesserahu mevkūfe Hattı Davud Aleyhisselamda Bāb-ı Meğaribede dahi bir bab dükkāna mutasarrıf ..." VGMA, 1112: 1/130; "Merhum Husrev Rumī ma tayessere Kur'an üzerine vakf eylediği eczahānānlardan beş seneden beru Şeyh Abdulkadir el-'Alemī mutasarrıf olub, kusuru yoğiken haricden Derviş Halil nām kimesne bir tarīkle berāt itdürüb küllī gadr itmeğin merkum Şeyh Abdulkadir el-'Alemiye berāt kayd şod." VGMA, 1160: 116/7.

249 JS 243: 183–184.

250 JS 213: 91–94.

251 JS 250: 18–20.

252 Polish origin, steel money called *Zolota* was imitiated and coined by English and Banadigas. Ottomans, too, coined money like this. el-Madanī, "al-Awqāf al-Islāmiyya fī al-Quds," 62.

253 JS 250:129–133.

254 JS 244:182.

255 See, Table A10.

256 Sadık Tural, "615 Numaralı İstanbul Askeri Kassam Defterinin Değerlendirilmesi," *İ.Ü.SBE İktisat Tarihi* (Istanbul: İstanbul Üniversitesi İktisat Fakültesi Yayınları, 1380 AH/ 1961 CE), 45.

judge).[257] During their term of office, the taxes collected by these officials, called *Kismet-i Askeriye*, were kept in the ballot box in the place where they were found. The revenues of *Kismet-i Askeriyye* contained here has been evaluated in this context.

In this part of the study, based on the records of the Jerusalem *Ḥurūfāt* (Appointment) and *Esās* (Treasury) registers, masjid, mosque, *zāwiya*, *takiyya*, *khānqāh*, *ribāṭ*, *merkad*, tomb, mausoleum, reciting Qur'an and prayer *waqf*s were examined respectively. From the records examined, it was observed that instead of building new religious institutions in Jerusalem, endowers enabled them to continue their services by making *waqf*s to those established before. In this case, it can be said that there were mosques or *masjids* in almost every neighborhood in Jerusalem in the eighteenth century, which started to develop and institutionalize rapidly since the conquest, therefore such structures were not needed much. There were a total of 673 appointments for religious institutions and services in the eighteenth century. The ratio of this to the *waqf*s established for all service areas is 58%. As can be seen, in the relevant period, officials were assigned to the *waqf*s for the religious field rather than other fields. It should also be emphasized that as a matter of fact religion was effective on people, in daily work and activities during this period.

Various ammunition expenses of the *waqf*s for religious service purposes were also covered by *waqf*s. Some of the expenses encountered under the conditions of the *waqf*s are as follows: Purchasing the wax called *şemʿ-i asel* for the illumination of the mosque, supplying olive oil called *revgan-ı zeyt* to be burned in the oil lamps, repair and restoration of mosques, maintenance and repair of waterways, burning of the lamps of the mosque minarets. Expenses such as buying wax to be laid are included in this scope.

The various equipments of the *waqf*s providing religious services were met by *waqf*s. These expenses mentioned in the deed of trust were: the purchase of *şemʿ-i asel* (a kind of wax) for the lightening of mosque, provision of *revgan-ı zeyt* (olive oil) for lighting oil lamps, repair and maintanence of the mosques, repair and restoration of waterways and lighting of the oil lamps of mosque *minaret* and the purchase of wicker for laying in the mosque.[258]

257 Ercan Özyürek, *158 Uluborlu Şeriyye Sicil Defteri ve Bu Sicilin Uluborlu Kent Tarihindeki Yeri, 1311–1313* AH*/1890–1892* CE (master's thesis, Süleyman Demirel Üniversitesi Sosyal Bilimler Enstitüsü, Isparta: Süleyman Demirel Üniversitesi Yayınları, 1423 AH/2002 CE), 13–14.

258 VGMA, 1112: 1/184; 1110: 131/12; 1110: 131/75.

1.2.3 Social and Municipal Service *Waqfs*

The largest part of the municipal services in Ottoman cities were handled by *waqfs* and guilds. For supplying the water need of the towns and even the villages, the *waqf* founders built fountains and water-well in the various quarters. *Waqfs* procured the servants for dealing with oil lamps to light the streets, cleaner for sweeping the streets, also, constructed public bathhouses for the cleanliness of people, established public toilets for the cleaning of the city, made the city ensured the continutiy of all these service through repairs and renovations.[259] As in the institutions such as mosque, school and *madrasa*, *waqfs* reimbursed the repairs of lightening, cleaning and repairments of the streets.[260]

Besides, the establishment of bridges, lighthouses and towers and allocation of cervanserais on the accommodation places in the large road connections were provided by the *waqfs*. These *waqfs* were aimed to ease the travel of merchants and pilgrimages, security of road and feeding and hosting the poor and needy.[261]

In the eighteenth century, a new *waqf* founder in Jerusalem, Qāsim Bey al-Turjumān, stipulated that a portion of the *waqf* income be allocated for purchasing olive oil for the oil well in Masjid *al-Aqṣā* and for acquiring two *riṭl* of lighting oil during Ramaḍān for the Ḥanābila Mosque.[262] Sunʿ Allāh al-Khālidī also specified that part of the income from his *waqf* be used to purchase olive oil for the well in Masjid *al-Aqṣā*.[263] Another endower, ʿAbdullāh Samūm, required the purchase of two *riṭl* of lighting oil for illumination during Ramaḍān in the Mālikiyya and Burāq mosques.[264] The Ottoman State mandated that 7.5 *fidda* from the income generated by soap transportation be allocated to purchasing *farsh* (carpets) for the Dome of the Rock.[265]

Imārets, or public kitchens, were also important social service institutions. Of the four holy cities of Islam, Mecca, Medina and al-Khalīl were already equipped for regular grain distribution at least as far back as the Mamluks. However, the example of al-Khalīl is the most well-known example from the pre-Ottoman period. Ibrahim's Table, attributed to the Prophet Abraham, served the poor and needy for centuries. While these services were considered an act of philanthropy, special meals and banquets on Fridays and feast

259 Yediyıldız, *XVIII. Yüzyılda*, 242, 245.
260 ibid., 245.
261 ibid., 245.
262 JS 207: 120–121.
263 JS 207: 344–345.
264 JS 23: 6–7.
265 JS 277: 3.

days, which also included a measure of sanctity, were standard practices in the *imāret*. The Khasseki Sultan *Imāret* in Jerusalem, which was built as a link in the chain of *waqf-imāret* complexes of the Ottoman Empire, was built to feed the poor and needy, as well as the pilgrims and sufis visiting the area. With the construction of the Khasseki Sultan *Imāret* in Jerusalem, the Khalil Ibrahim Table (*Simāt al-Khalīl*) in Hebron, along with those in Mecca and Medina, played an important role in this organization. The continuity of the services offered here also preserved the image of the Ottoman sultan in the eyes of Muslim states. In this context, the *imāret*s in Jerusalem and al-Khalīl were quite large, and they were used to ensure the continuity of the pilgrims coming to the holy cities and to provide the necessary services to the pilgrims.[266]

Another important service provided by the social service *waqf*s was the *dārüşşifā*s (healing houses or hospitals) allocated to all people. In this context, considering the Jerusalem sample, *Bīmāristan Ṣalāḥiyya* established by Sultan Melik Saladin provided important services as a hospital.

In this part of the study, social and municipal *waqf*s will be examined under the headings of fountain/public fountain, bathhouse, soup kitchens and *bīmāristan/māristan waqf*s, subsequently all of which are detected in Jerusalem *Ḥurūfāt* Registers.

1.2.3.1 *Sabīls* (*Fountains*)

Turning now to the waterways, there were many fountains and water sources in Ottoman cities. It was a toilsome work to bring water outside the town and distrube it to the fountains in streets and houses, also, mosque, *masjid*, *madrasa*, inn and bathhouses where the water was highly used. The construction, repair, maintanance and water distribution of Ottoman waterways and facilities actualized in proper and constant organization.[267]

Sultan Süleyman's most important construction activity was the repairment of waterways which brought water from Bethlehem and Hebron to Jerusalem, the renovation of the pools where the water of the town was distributed and establishment of six fountains, five of which were inside the walled city.[268] The channel, which had vital importance for this desert climate, brought water to fountains and bathhouses of the town besides the fountains which were inside

266 For an assessment of the importance of the *imāret* in Hebron in the context of pilgrimage, see also Şerife Eroğlu Memiş, "A Table in the City of Hebron in the XVIIIth Century: Simāt al-Khalīl," *Journal of Historical Research* 40, no. 69 (1442 AH/2021 CE): 188–233.

267 M. Mehdi İlhan, *Osmanlı Su Yollarının Sevk ve İdaresi* (Canberra: Australian National University Press, 1430 AH/2009 CE), 41–66.

268 al-Asali, "Jerusalem under the Ottomans," 40.

the walled city water pipes that were laid in ancient times were repaired during the general construction held during the reign of Sultan Suleiman and there built a *waqf* for the maintanence. The new public kitchen *waqf* created source for the town's water need.[269] In a decree (H.1147), it is stated that "... *Kudüs-i Şerīfde vākiʿ Mescid-i Aksā ve Sahratullaü'l-ʿulyāya cennet mekān firdevs-i āşiyān Sultan Süleyman Hān -eskenehullāhu Teʿālā fī ğurafi'l-cinānın- icrā buyurdukları suyunyolları tamire muhtac olmağla ... söz konusu suyollarının tamirinin ise ... Vālide-i Sultan -dāmet ismetuhā vezādet iffetuhā- nın tarafı vakf-ı şerīflerinden taʿmir ve itmām ve tekmīline mübāderet olunub ...*", indicating that the damages of the groups of urban, *fellāh* and shepherds and other brigands and bandits would be prevented because the villages, which were aligned with the channels, bringing water to the town and the officials were contentious. The conflict about the water was among the city dwellers, villagers and the Bedouins who were coming and going to the region.[270]

There are two records belonging to two different fountain *waqfs* among *Ḥurūfāt* registers. Most of the records are about the fountains in Nablus and only the Fountain of Dawud Pasha is cited as in the center of Jerusalem.[271] The second one is in the Masjid *al-Aqṣā* related to the appointment of an employee to the *Delü Hüseyin Pasha Sebīlī*.[272]

1.2.3.2 *Hammams (Public Bathhouses)*

There were six bathhouses actively serving in Jerusalem in the Ottoman period. These were *Hammam al-ʿAyn* (Spring Bathhouse),[273] *Hammam al-Shifa* (Shifa Bathhouse),[274] *Hammam al-Batrik* (Patriarch Bathhouse),[275] *Hamam al-Sultan*

269 Cohen, *Osmanlı Kudüs'ünde*, 31–51; the name of the *waqf* is Vakf-ı Kanātü's-Sebīl in the registers.

270 VGMA, 323: 88.

271 VGMA, 1109: 6/39.

272 VGMA, 1112: 1/38.

273 Spring Bathhouse, as known in the Ottoman period, was named as *Yeni Hamam* in the period it was established or Tankiz Bathhouse, with the founder's name. Dow, "The Hammams of Ottoman Jerusalem," 520; Cohen and Lewis, *Population and Revenue*., 97.

274 Shifā' Bathhouse, built by Tankiz (sometimes referred to as *ʿĀshūra'* Bathhouse), derived its name from the belief that *zamzam* waters overflowed and mixed with the waters of Shifā' Bathhouse (10th of Muḥarram). Thus, it was believed that the water was healing and beneficial for skin diseases. Taufik Canaan, "Water and 'The Water of Life' in Palestinian Superstition," *Journal of the Palestine Oriental Society* 9 (1347 AH/1929 CE): 57–66, 66.

275 Patriarch Bathhouse, also known as a bathhouse, was known as *Ḥammām al-ʿAmūd* in Ottoman *tahrir* accounts. Dow, "The Hammams of Ottoman Jerusalem," 520.

(Sultan Bathhouse),[276] *Hamam al-Sayyida Maryam* (Mariam Bathhouse)[277] and *Hammam al-Jamal*[278] (Camel Bathhouse).[279] Spring Bathhouse, located in the Cotton Producers Bazaar (*Sūq al-Qattānīn*) and *Shifā'* Bathhouse were established by the Mamluks and at least two of them from the rest were actively functioned in the Ottoman period.[280]

All the bathhouses in Jerusalem in the Ottoman period were parts of the *waqfs* which were establihed with aim of philanthropy and had an important place among the properties bringing income for the *waqf* charitable buildings. The bathhouses allocated all their income to the *waqfs* of the Dome of the Rock and the Masjid al-Aqṣā whereas the income of the Mariam and Patriarch Bathhouses endowed to the *Khanqāh al-Ṣalāḥiyya* and lastly, the income of Sultan Bathhouse allocated to the expenses of the public kitchen of Khasseki Sultan *Waqf* in Jerusalem.[281]

1.2.3.3 Memşās (*Public Toilets*)

With meanings including *helā, kenif, abdesthane* in the dictionary, *memşā*[282] is used for *public toilets* in the registers. There were two appointment register related to officials being responsible for *memşā ebārık* (pitchers and pots used in the toilet) repaired by Receb Pasha from the *Waqf* of the Dome of the Rock mentioned in Jerusalem's *Ḥurūfāt* registers. In these registers, it is understood that the officials' payment appointed to these matters was paid from the income of the Dome of the Rock *Waqf*.[283]

276 It was established at the corner of Mujāhidīn and al-Wād roads, circa 974 AH/1557 CE, by *Khāṣṣakī Hürrem Sulṭān* and named Sulṭān Bathhouse. Dow, "The Hammams of Ottoman Jerusalem," 519.

277 Maryam Bathhouse, also known as Virgin Mary Bathhouse, derives its name from the legend that Maryam bathed there. In fact, it was named after *Bāb al-Asbāṭ* (Lions' Gate), located nearby, and called *Bāb al-Asbāṭ* Bathhouse. Dow, "The Hammams of Ottoman Jerusalem," 520. As a Late Ottoman Period bath, it was established at the end of the nineteenth century.

278 The bathhouse, named Camels Bathhouse, derived its name from a belief that a spirit appeared in the shape of a camel. Due to its proximity to the Shrine of Dāwūd in the Early Modern Ottoman period on Mount Ṣahyūn, it was also called Dāwūd Bathhouse.

279 Çelebi, *Seyahatnāme*, 488.

280 Dow, "The Hammams of Ottoman Jerusalem," 519.

281 Dow, "The Hammams of Ottoman Jerusalem," 520.

282 Sāmī, *Kāmūsü'l-A'lām*, 1405.

283 "Kudüs-i Şerīfde Receb Paşa'nın ta'mir eylediği memşānın ebārıkına vakf olan Sahratullah Vakfı'ndan altı akçe ile gassal-ı şadırval Salih Lu'lu' fevtinden oğulları Receb ve Muḥammad ve Halil ve Salih ve 'Atāya iştiraken inayet. Fī gurre-i Receb sene 1136." VGMA, 1107: 2/341; 1119: 110/25.

1.2.3.4 Imārets (*Public Kitchens*)

In the Ottoman State, the feeding of people and the poor was among the important duties of the rulers. For this reason, many of the rulers made an effort to feed people, particularly the poor through banquests or *imārets* (public kitchens). This feature supported by the cooperation understanding of Islam was highly developed in the Ottoman society and as a result, statesmen and rich people established *imārets* which was regarded as large public kitchens. In the use of Ottoman, the word *imāret* was utilized as a complex and a soup kitchen, in this part, it was used as a soup kitchen (*imāret-i dārü'z-ziyāfet* or *imāret-i dārü'l-it'am*).[284] Principally four groups of people benefited from the *imārets*: the students of *madrasa*, the personnel of charitable institutions such as the mosque, shrine, the poor of the town and the passerbys.[285] The *imārets* sometimes sent food to the neighbours. The *imārets* were the social aid institutions assisted by the *waqfs* and founded by the philanthropists.[286] For this reason, all the expense of the *imārets* was provided by the various income sources identified by the founder of the *waqf*.

The examples of Ottoman soup kitchens giving food to the scholars and students in Jerusalem was detected in the mosque, *madrasa*, schools and shrines constructed during the Ayyubid and Mamluk period. The purpose of the scholarships given to the students and *'ulamā'* in Mamluks' big *madrasas* and schools were the provision of fundamental livelihood. Yet, it is not certain whether there was an operating kitchen; also the amount of food was allocated to one person.[287]

Khasseki Sultan's public kitchen was the biggest *waqf* in Palestine up to that time aiming to provide social aid for the ones living in Jerusalem. It was located in the westside door of Bāb al-Nāzir reaching to 'Aqabat al-Takiyya in the south side. Sitt Tunshuk Palace belonging to Mamluk Period (est. 1388) was the transference of soup kitchen-lodge by the wife of Suleiman the Lawgiver, Hürrem Sultan. This facility on the pilgrimage road is one of the chain of soup kitchens which was built Hürrem Sultan in Mecca and Medina, referred in the Architect Sinan's *tezkires*.[288]

284 Ergin, *Türk Şehirlerinde İmaret Sistemi*, 5–16; Ekrem Hakkı Ayverdi, *Osmanlı Mīmārīsinin İlk Devri*, vol. 1 (Istanbul: İstanbul Fetih Cemiyeti Yayınları, 1385 AH/1966 CE), 84–88; İnalcık, "Istanbul," 10–11; Singer, *Kadılar, Kullar*, 124–2.

285 Meier, "For the Sake of God Alone," 123.

286 For the *soup kitchens*' role in social welfare, see Oded Peri, "Waqf and Ottoman Welfare Policy," Journal of the Economic and Social History of the Orient 35 (1412 AH/1992 CE): 171–85, 167–182; Singer, *Osmanlı'da Hayırseverlik*.

287 Singer, *Osmanlı'da Hayırseverlik*, p. 174.

288 Tanman and Çobanoğlu, "Osmanlı Döneminde Kudüs," 529.

The *imārethāne* which was built by Kanuni Sultan Süleyman's Khasseki, *Hürrem* Sultan, in 1552 was a complex consisting of shops, hostels, *madrasa* and mosque.[289] In the *waqf*iyya, Hürrem Sultan is described like this:

> "the pearl of the crown of majesty and glory, the beginning of the crown of honor and glory, the queen of queens, the angelic state, the sultan's attitude, the exalted person, the self-exalted, the honorable of the elders, the hopes of the honorable women, the honor and the glory of the male and female Muslims, the mother of Emir Mehmed, the son of Sultan Suleyman, who is the mother of the Sultan, who is the Ayşe of the time, the Fatma of the period, the star of the apparent, the pearl of the sultanate."[290]

The endowed charitable goods in *al-Sitt* Quarter, one of the quarters of Jerusalem were: a mosque endowed for the Muslim's prayer; a rich kitchen across the mosque, a clean, neat dining hall, an oven, a courtyard, a cellar, a storehouse, a woodhouse, also, a soup kitchen for food distribution to the poor, needy and weaks; a *madrasa* composed of fifty-five rooms around the mosque for pious Muslims, ones on the path of God, devotees cleaning their souls from bad deeds; belonging to without disregarding the *sharīʿa* law. Th *waqf* khan served for the visitors and passengers coming from the other places.[291] Tens of villages neighbouring the town, even the ones in north such as Tripoli directly paid their taxes to the *waqf* officials.[292]

---

289 There are two different forms of the deed of trust for Khasseki Hurrem Sultan. The first was in Ottoman Turkish, written on 30 Jumādā al-Ūlā 959 AH/24 May 1552 CE; the second was in Arabic, in mid-Shaʿbān 964 AH/9–18 June 1557 CE. Singer, *Osmanlı'da Hayırseverlik*, 53. For an evaluation related to deed of trusts see, St. H. Stephan, "An Endowment Deed of Khāṣṣakī Sulṭān, Dated 30 Jumādā al-Ūlā 959 AH/24 May 1552 CE," *Quarterly of the Department of Antiquities in Palestine* 10 (1414 AH/1994 CE): 170–94.

290 VGMA, 608/2: 235/178.

291 VGMA, 608/2: 235/178.

292 Items whose income was transferred to the ʿimāra by Khasseki Hurrem Sultan: income from the village of ʿAmyūn in the district of Kūrā of Ṭarābulus al-Shām governorate, Shaykh Tūtmāj Khān and adjacent shops, a plot of land, soap factories of al-Saʿdiyya and al-ʿAwāmīd, four watermills in Rashīn village, four *raʿiyya* watermills in Bistānīn village, three Ṣahyūn windmills, taxes from Kaykūba hamlet, and Ludd village in Gaza *sanjāq* For details, see VGMA, 608/2: 235/178; Singer, *Osmanlı ʿda Hayırseverlik*, p. 56–63. Besides, between 1550–1557, Sulṭān Süleymān issued ten title deed (*mülknāme*) and the ownership of the properties which would be endowed to soup kitchen by Hürrem Sulṭān was transferred. See, Amy Singer, "The Mülknāmes of Khāṣṣakī Hürrem Sulṭān's Waqf in Jerusalem," *Muqarnas* 14 (1417 AH/1997 CE): 96–102.

During the establishment of Khasseki Sultan's public kitchen (964/1557), the Agha of Babussaâde (chief eunuch), Cafer Agha, was the absolute official related to the issues of this public kitchen. There is an appointed *mutawallī* in the complex in Jerusalem, having a clerk and a revenue collector (*cābī*). A sunni or Ḥanafī person was appointed to the mosque both as *imam* and muezzin. Head of the *imāret*, the *shaykh*, was responsible for the coordination of food preparation, *vekil-i harç* for expenses and providing provisions, *anbārī* for storehouse and *kilārī* for cellar.[293]

Most of the poor in the town got food daily from the public kitchen of the *waqf* with some *ʿulamāʾ* who were not that needy. It is stipulated that in the morning and evening, four hundred people composing of poor, weak, needy and helpless coming to dining hall would be given two hundred bowls of food. Thus, two people had a bowl of food. In addition, it is also stipulated that each of them would be given a bread called *fodula*.[294] It was *qāḍī* to decide whether the person had right to have a bowl of food (*tāse mineʾt-taʿam*).[295] The endower stipulated that an outsider could not take food except for the public kitchen's personnel.[296]

Besides its social role, this *waqf* had a crucial role in the economy of the town. The officials of the *waqf* operated mills, the machines of olive and sesame

293 For the more detailed information related to soup kitchen officials see, VGMA, 523: 23–38; 524: 2–29; Singer, *Osmanlı'da Hayırseverlik*, 64–68.

294 According to Singer, *fodula* is used for the plain loaves made by flour, salt and water. Each of the *fodula* after baking should have been 90 *dirham* in terms of standard weight. See, Singer, *Osmanlı 'da Hayırseverlik*, 69. If it is considered that 1 dirham is approximately 3 gram, the weight of 1 loaf is approximately 270 grams. See, Halil İnalcık, "Weights and Measures," in *An Economic and Social History of the Ottoman Empire*, ed. Halil İnalcık and Donald Quataert, vol. 1 (Cambridge: Cambridge University Press, 1417 AH/1997 CE), 988. Yet, Emecen gives room to different names including *Fudūla*, *Fodula*, and *Fodla* and states that they were flat breads distributed as to ratio in a basket to the officials with their payments mostly in the soup kitchens, Ottoman palace kitchens, and certain palaces and ovens of Janissaries. Feridun M. Emecen, "Fodula," *TDV İslâm Ansiklopedisi*, vol. 13 (Istanbul: Türkiye Diyanet Vakfı Yayınları, 1416 AH/1996 CE), 167–70. The *waqf* of sultans and his close subjects' record of *fodula* distribution and consumption was registered properly. There are approximately 40 *Fodūla* Registers (Nu: 1004–1043) in VGMA. These accounts were kept in the period of Fatih (Nu: 1018) proceeding to nineteenth century. They had different serieses based on location, *selātīn* complexes, and some big *waqfs*. Şerife Eroğlu Memiş, "Feeding the Poor: Fodula and Taʿāmiyya Records of Sulṭān Süleymān's ʿImārets in Istanbul and Damascus," *Middle East Studies Association 44th Annual Meeting*, Washington, DC, 1432 AH/2011 CE.

295 About the *Waqf* of Khassekiye see, Singer, *Osmanlı'da Hayırseverlik*; Stephan, "An Endowment Deed of Khāṣṣakī Sulṭān," 170–94; Peri, "The *Waqf* as an Instrument," 47–62.

296 VGMA, 608/23: 235/178.

oil and oven. Many guilds sent most of the products to *waqf*. These officials and supervisiors determined the economy of the town to a great extent.[297]

As different from the other sultanic complexes, the fundamental unit of Hürrem Sultan's *waqf* was its *public kitchen*. Thus, it differentiated itself from others in Jerusalem. For centuries, Muslim administrators contributed to mosques, *madrasas* and sufi lodges in Jerusalem. The Dome of the Rock and the Masjid *al-Aqṣā* were the prayer centers surrounded by *madrasas* and Sufi lodges. The founders of the *waqfs* substantially supported praying, reciting Qur'an, studying tradition and law, also, hosting dervishes and *ʿulamāʾ*. Public Kitchen of Hürrem Sultan was the typical sample of the Ottoman enterprise though it was unique. There were many *waqfs* distuributing food to the dervishes, students or visitors. However, it is seen that it was the only operating public-kitchen in Jerusalem and there would be no other.

There was an allocation of *fodula* for the *waqf* officials or other needies in the new *waqfs* established in Jerusalem in eighteenth century which was provided from Khasseki Sultan *Imāret*. It is registered that there would be distribution of 48 *fodula* and soup (taken from Khasseki Sultan *Imāret*) to the residents in the *Zāwiya* Maghāriba,[298] twenty-four loaves of bread to Shaykh Ali Agha al-Tilmisānī al-Maghribi,[299] a loaf of bread and a bowl of soup to Çelebi Mustafa Agha[300] and to the subservient of the Dome of the Rock Shaykh Nūra Abdullah,[301] eight loaves of bread from public kitchen to Sayyid Halil ibn Abdullah al-Sirrāj,[302] daily fifteen loaves of bread to the imam of the Shaykh Luʾluʾ Mosque al-Sayyid Mustafa ibn Muḥammad al-ʿAfifī,[303] six loaves of breads to water-bearer in Maghāriba Mosque in the Masjid *al-Aqṣā*,[304] daily twenty-four loaves of bread to the water-bearer of the public fountain, close to the Bāb al-Nāzir in the Masjid *al-Aqṣā*, founded by Jerusalem *kaimakam* (deputy governor) Mustafa Agha,[305] nine loaves of bread to the water-bearer of the public fountain in the Masjid al-Aqṣā and the *mutawallī* of the *Waqf* of *Küçük Pasha*.[306] Besides, there were allocations to *aʿyān* (leading local notables) and *ʿulamāʾ* (scholars) in Jerusalem though they were not needy. *Naqīb al-ashrāf* Abdullah Effendi, Jerusalem Mufti Hasan Effendi, and Necmeddin Effendi,

297 Ze'evi, *Kudüs*, 13–14.
298 JS 256: 20.
299 JS 272: 97.
300 JS 214: 113.
301 JS 256: 35.
302 JS 215: 57.
303 JS 216: 65.
304 JS 214: 65.
305 JS 277: 114.
306 JS 252: 93.

Ahmed Effendi al-Shihābī and Abu al-ʿAlā Effendi al-Muvakkıt can be cited among these.[307]

Besides allocations from Khasseki Sultan public kitchen, some of the *waqfs* established in the eighteenth century stipulated that there would be purchase and distribution of bread (14 *rıtl*[308]) to the poor and miserables who were residents in Qasım Bey al-Turjumān Mansūrī Riwāk and to the residents and miserables in Bāb al-Dawud.[309] Muḥammad Sunʿ Allāh al-Khālidī stipulated that income from the *waqf* established for the *Takārīn* poor be allocated for distributing food to the impoverished *Takārīn* residing near the ʿUthmāniyya *Madrasa*.[310] In another *waqfiyya*, the endower specified that four *riṭl* of bread be purchased and distributed during Ramaḍān to the poor and destitute, with half a *riṭl* for the destitute in Bāb al-Dāwūd, half a *riṭl* for residents of the Riwaq of the ʿUthmāniyya *Madrasa*, and three *riṭl* for the poor.[311] The *waqf* of Khalīl ibn ʿAbd al-Laṭīf in Hebron allocated 40 *zoloṭa* for orphans, 60 *zoloṭa* to the *waqf* of the Dome of the Rock, and 33 *zoloṭa* to the lodge.[312] The 1150 AH/1737 CE *waqf* account of the Maghāriba *Waqf* covered expenses for food preparation and distribution to dervishes and bread distribution to the poor in the *waqf* village of ʿAyn Kārim in the Maghāriba Quarter.[313] Additions and repairs ensured the longevity of Khasseki Sultan's *Imāret*, enabling it to provide services for centuries.[314]

1.2.3.5 Bīmāristan (*Hospital*)

The only hospital of Jerusalem under Ottoman administration was close to the central church, Holy Sepulchre, and the central bazaars naming Ṣalāḥiyya Bīmāristan. The word *bīmāristan* is in Persian meaning hospital and mental hospital. The hospital under the name of its founder, Saladin was not a structure that was newly added to the town in the period under study; it was connected to the Saladin *Waqf*.[315]

---

307 JS 259: 97.

308 "Rıtl, takrīben okkanın sülüsüne muʿādil eski māyiʿāt ölçüsü, litre." Sāmī, *Kāmūsü'l-Aʿlām*, 666.

309 JS 207: 120–121; For further information related to the ones fed by soup kitchen such as ʿulamāʾ, *ashraf*, and *aʿyān* in the eighteenth century, see Peri, "*Waqf* and Ottoman Welfare," 182; Singer, "The Privileged Poor," 257–269.

310 JS 218: 253–254.

311 JS 213: 91–94.

312 JS 271:71–72.

313 JS 229:121.

314 Today, the soup kitchen serves as an orphanage, vocational school, and meal center; its cauldrons and the list of food distribution is displayed in Museum of Islamic Arts in the *Ḥaram al-Sharīf*. Tanman and Çobanoğlu, "Osmanlı Döneminde Kudüs," 529.

315 Cohen, *Osmanlı Kudüs'ünde*, 77; Ze'evi, *Kudüs*, 32.

Although there was no information related to social groups having treatment and to the institution, as mentioned in Ze'evi, in a Jerusalem *sharīʿa* court register indicating a need of restoration for *bīmārhane*, the *mutawallī* of the Ṣalāḥiyya Bīmāristan *Waqf* went to the court stating that some parts of the hospital needed repair on 6 Shaʿban 1045, (15 January 1636). Upon this, the *qāḍī* employed a *naqīb al-ashrāf* and chief architecture to examine the building. The team reported that there was a need of new doors in the stair and *beytü'l-merzā* (division for sick) and *beytü'l-mecānīn* (division for mental patients) needed serious restoration; whereas *beytü'l-mugtesel* (laundry/bathhouse) and *beytü'l-kehhālin* (division of eye diseases) needed partial restoration.[316] Therefore, it is understood that *Bīmāristan* sustained care for both diverse physical disease and the mental ones.

Ze'evi states that the reason why travellers and pilgrims did not mention hospitals was Christian and Jewish groups had different, smaller hospitals.[317] It can be deduced that the social group that the hospital provided service was the urban Muslim groups in Jerusalem. In Jerusalem *Ḥurūfāt* Registers, apart from *bīmārhane*, there was seven appointments (between Shaʿban 1085 and Rajab 1168) of officials to the hospital recorded as Māristan *Waqf*, Bīmāristan *Waqf* from *Khanqāh* Malik Saladin *Waqf* (*Bīmāristan-ı Salāhī, Melik Salāhaddin Bīmārhanesi*).[318]

Helping the poor and the needy in the Ottoman society was sometimes done through alms and sometimes through the *waqfs*. These *waqfs* aimed to help the poor and the needy, sustain their economic power and enchance their social conditions. The *Waqfs* of *Sadakāt al- Hukmiyya*,[319] *Mısriyyūn*,[320] *Fukarā Benī an-Nakī Zümresi* (Group for the Poor of Bani Naqi) and *Ağmā Zümresi* (Group for Blind) are of this nature.[321]

In conclusion, the *waqfs* of fountain, bathhouse, public toilet, inn, public kitchen, *bimārhane* in the Old city of Jerusalem are examined in the light of Jerusalem *Ḥurūfāt* (Appointment) and *Esās* (Treasury) Registers. It is noticed

316 Ze'evi, *Kudüs*, 32–33.

317 Ze'evi, *Kudüs*, 33. For example Cháteaubriand visiting Jerusalem in 1806 mentioned a Christian hospital built by Turks: "Today, an old Christian hospital where Turkish patients stayed in draw my attention. They showed me a chaldron named Saint Helena. Formerly, each Muslim applied to this hospital got two bread and vegetables with olive oil. On Fridays, they have honey or rice with pine resin; but not anymore. It seems certain signs convenient to Holy Bible only stuck to the doors of hospital." François René de Chateaubriand, *Kudüs Yolculuğu*, trans. O. Peltek, vol. 3 (Ankara: Türk Tarih Kurumu Yayınları, 1368 AH/1949 CE), 56.

318 For example see, VGMA, 1109: 61.

319 VGMA, 515: 84/107.

320 VGMA, 515: 86/116; 1160: 116/4.

321 VGMA, 1108: 1/55; 515: 129/131.

that *waqf*s realized the large part of social and municipal services in Jerusalem. Yet, when the appointment registers, especially for *imārethane* and *bimāristan*, are assessed, these registers are few. This case indicates that, as in the sample of Khasseki Sultan *Waqf*, there can be autonomous registers related to such magnificent *waqf*s. Also, as the appoinment of officials were preffered to be *bilā-berat* (without appointment deed), this was not reflected in the registers.

1.2.4 Other *Waqf* Registers

This part aims to detect the name of individual *waqf*s in Jerusalem's *Ḥurūfāt* registers (Table A11). As these registers are not used with qualifications such as mosque, *masjid* and *tomb* in the *waqf*s of the prophet, companians, mystics, they will be dealt under the individual *waqf*s. Yet, these *waqf*s are assessed with the *waqf*s referred as the same names such as mosque, *masjid*, shrine, *maqam* etc.

Brief information related to some *waqf* accounts is available in Jerusalem's *Ḥurūfāt* registers. Some part of them includes endowed properties such as village, arable field, house, shop and product of *ʿushr* (tithe), and the other part composes of registers only mentioning the name of the charitable *waqf*s (whether they are *madrasa, shrine*, etc.) such as *Fakhriyya, Geylāniyya, Kāmiliyya*. The allocations to the imams of the *Waqf* of Dome of the Rock such as "*ehl-i hayrāt-ı Sahratullah-ı Müşerrefe eimmelerine mahsus üç hane ve bir hanın on beş dükkān Evkafı*" are described in detail in the registers.[322]

In conclusion, the *waqf* registers, in the frame of Jerusalem's *Ḥurūfāt* and *Esās* registers, are examined under the titles of educational, religious, municipal, social and other *waqf*s, respectively. Brief information related to the *waqf*s which are abundant in number have been arranged in the Appendices as tables. The charitable institutions in the center of Jerusalem operated in educational, religious, municipal, social services and social aid. The number of the *waqf*s raised in parallel with the population and produced services in every field.

All in all, it can be stated that there is an extensive *waqf* network which was formed around *Ḥaram al-Sharīf* including the Mosques of the Dome of the Rock and the Masjid *al-Aqṣā*. Gaining prominence in the Muslim *waqf* network in time, this area has a great significance in Ayyubids, Mamluk and Ottoman periods, also, in and out of *Ḥaram al-Sharīf* with its *waqf* property addressing to financial and moral terms. This chapter, prepared by the registers above, shows

322 VGMA, 1160: 108.

TABLE 5 The number of *waqfs* by years (1703–1831)

Years	Number of the *waqf*	1703–1750	1703–1750	Years	Number of the *waqf*	1751–1800	1751–1800	Years	Number of the *waqf*	1801–1831	1801–1831
1703	4	20	125	1751	2	39	122	1801	2	10	50
1704	1			1752	6			1802	1		
1705	3			1753	1			1803	3		
1707	1			1756	7			1805	1		
1708	4			1757	8			1807	1		
1711	3			1758	6			1808	1		
1712	3			1759	2			1809	1		
1713	1			1760	7			1811	4	29	
1714	4	27		1761	1	42		1812	6		
1715	2			1762	6			1813	3		
1717	1			1763	5			1814	7		
1718	2			1764	1			1815	1		
1719	4			1765	2			1816	3		
1720	1			1766	4			1817	1		
1721	2			1867	4			1818	3		
1722	7			1768	10			1819	1		
1723	4			1769	3			1820	1	11	
1724	7	38		1770	6			1821	3		
1725	4			1771	1	14		1823	1		
1726	1			1773	3			1824	3		
1727	2			1775	2			1826	1		
1729	6			1778	7			1830	1		

TABLE 5 The number of *waqf*s by years (1703–1831) (*cont.*)

Years	Number of the *waqf*	1703–1750	1703–1750	Years	Number of the *waqf*	1751–1800	1751–1800	Years	Number of the *waqf*	1801–1831	1801–1831
1730	5			1779	1			1831	1		
1731	4			1782	2	9		Yazılmamış	3	3	3
1732	5			1783	1			Toplam	300	300	300
1733	4			1786	3						
1734	1	30		1788	1						
1735	1			1790	2						
1736	4			1791	1	18					
1738	6			1792	1						
1739	2			1793	2						
1740	3			1794	4						
1741	6			1795	2						
1742	2			1796	2						
1743	5			1798	1						
1744	2	10		1799	2						
1745	1			1800	3						
1746	2										
1747	1										
1748	1										
1749	1										
1750	2										

that *waqf* takes place in every sphere of social life in Jerusalem as a system of *waqf* which covers the ruined and vanished *waqfs*, charities and services.

1.3 *Newly Established* Waqfs *in Jerusalem (1703–1831)*

We have divided the *waqfs* established in the Old City of Jerusalem into two parts: those that were established during our research period (1703–1831) and those that existed before, and are still active in our period. First of all, we tried to deal with the *waqfs* that were established during the Ayyubid and Mamluk times, mostly for educational and religious service purposes. Between 1703–1831, which is our period of study, 300 *waqfs* were established in Jerusalem.[323] However, it will be seen that these *waqfs*, which will be examined in detail in the following parts, are those established before 1703, which are more influential in the socio-economic and cultural life of the city of Jerusalem. In fact, we will see that those established before the Ottoman Empire were the biggest *waqfs*.

In this part of the study, first of all, the chronological distribution of the *waqfs* established in the period in our field of study will be discussed. Afterwards, their qualifications will be examined in legal terms. Another important dimension of the *waqfs* is the sources of income of the *waqf*, which, from a different perspective, closely concerns the urban society and even the rural areas outside the city. It is possible to divide the sources of income, which will be examined under the titles of movable and real estate, into two as city center and out of town.

1.3.1 Chronological Distribution

In the period examined within the framework of the study, 300 *waqfs* established in Jerusalem in different years were distributed in different numbers and rates from 1703 (1115 AH) to 1831 (1247 AH). In the period covered by the

---

323 Scanning the existing records and the independent *waqf* books prepared in the Archive of *Iḥyāʾ al-Turāth wa'l-Shuʾūn al-Dīniyya Muʾassasat Iḥyāʾ al-Turāth wa'l-Buḥūth al-Islāmiyya* for most of the endowment records examined within the scope of the study. For the list of endowments recorded in a separate book. see Annex 17. This number also includes fifteen *waqfs* registered for the period within the scope of work in VGMA. In addition to these is the work of Ghūsha, who prepared the *waqfs* established in Jerusalem until 1591–1977 with systematic data (under the titles of date, *waqf, mawqūf, khātimat jihat al-waqf,* source and type). One can also benefit from the studies prepared by al-Madanī, who analyzed the *waqf* records between the years 1700–1800 in a similar systematic framework. Due to the fact that the information provided by the *waqfs* has not paid attention to share ownership, less reference has been made to the work of al-Madanī (al-Madanī , *Awqāf al-Quds*).

research, the first *waqf* is dated 1115 /1703 CE.[324] The last *waqf* in the relevant period is dated 1247/1831.[325] The distribution of the *waqf*s by years is shown in Table 5.

In the examination made taking into account the *waqfiyya*s and the foundation dates in the relevant period, no *waqf* established for thirty-one Hijri years could be identified.[326] In thirty-five years, only one *waqf* has been established. According to the data in Table 5, the first two years when the *waqf*s were established are 1183/1768 and 1172/1757. In the first of these dates, ten *waqf*s were established and eight *waqf*s were established in the second. The number of years when seven *waqf*s were established in a year is five.[327] Comparison of such individual data may not always lead us to correct results. For example, is the reason for not establishing *waqf*s in years when there were no *waqf*s because the political environment or the economy was really weak? Or is it a natural situation that nobody wanted to establish a *waqf*? Or is it that the documents of the *waqf*s established in those years could not be reached? It is very difficult to explain them correctly with the resources and data available. For this, new research and longer-term comparisons are needed on the subject.

When we look at the ten-year breakdown of the *waqf* numbers, we see a table as follows; twenty *waqf*s were established in the first decade of the eighteenth

324 *Waqf* of ʿUmar Shakkī Makkī, JS 201: 231.

325 *Waqf* of Nasab bint al-Ḥājj Yūsuf al-Nuʿāṣī, JS 316.

326 These Gregorian years are: 1706, 1709, 1710, 1716, 1728, 1737, 1754, 1755, 1772, 1774, 1776, 1777, 1780, 1781, 1784, 1785, 1787, 1789, 1797, 1804, 1806, 1810, 1822, 1825, 1827, 1828, 1829. These data should not mean that no *waqf*s were established in Jerusalem in the relevant years. Because new information and documents can be accessed in researches from other sources. For example, in the study of al-Madanī, it is seen that he identified endowments belonging to some years (H. 1160, 1170, 1187, 1195, 1200, 1212) given above. These endowments are recorded as follows: Ghurra Muḥarram 1160/13 Kānūn al-Thānī 1747, Shaykh Isḥāq bin Nūr al-Dīn al-Jāʾūnī (CS 235: 180–181); 10 Rabīʿ al-Thānī 1160/13 April 1747 by Ḥusayn Çelebi bin ʿAbd al-Nabī Bölükbaşı (JS 235: 217–219); Faḍlī al-Ṭayyib bin Yūsuf al-Ḥakīmī (CS 235: 262–263) on 17 Jumādā al-Thānī 1160/10 June 1747; al-Ḥājj Ṣāliḥ bin Salīm al-Ḥanīkāt on Ghurra Ramaḍān 1160/6 September 1747 (CS 235: 320–322); 14 Shawwāl 1170/19 June 1757, Ḥāmid bin ʿAbdullāh Babahıyyə (JS 241: 39–41); Ākhir Jumādā al-Ūlā 1187/10 July 1774 by Fāṭima bint Aḥmad Baʿīsa (JS 255: 46–47); Ākhir Jumādā al-Ūlā 1187/10 July 1774, al-Ḥājj ʿAlī al-Maghribī (JS 255: 47); 12 Jumādā al-Thānī 1187/1773 Fāṭima bint Muḥammad (JS 255: 53–54); Fāṭima bint as-Siknācı in 1195/1781 (JS 262: 59); 1195/1781 Yūsuf bin Muḥammad al-Kalandavī (CS 262: 73); Muḥarram 1195/28 Kānūn al-Thānī 1780, ʿAbdullāh al-Dāwūdī (JS 262: 108–109); Muḥarram 1200/4 Tishrīn al-Thānī 1785, Aḥmad bin Muḥammad al-Khaṭṭ al-Ramlī (CS 266: 96–97); 9 Rabīʿ al-Thānī 1200/1 February 1786, Muṣṭafā Effendi al-Shihābī and Fayḍ Allāh Effendi bin Aḥmad al-Shihābī (CS 266: 158–159); Awsāṭ Dhū al-Ḥijja 1212/17 May 1789 Al-Sayyid Ghāzwān Fayḍ Allāh al-ʿĀlamī (CS 279: 145–146); and Ākhir Dhū al-Ḥijja 1212/17 May 1798, Muḥammad bin ʿAbd al-Qādir al-Wazna (al-Vezne) (JS 279: 147).

327 These are the Hijri years: 1722, 1724, 1760, 1778, and 1814. See Table 5.

century, twenty-seven in the second decade, thirty-eight in the third ten, thirty in the fourth decade, and ten in the fifth decade. Therefore, 125 *waqfs* were established in the first half of the century. Thirty-nine *waqfs* were established in the first decade of the second half of the eighteenth century, forty-two in the second decade, twenty-three in the third decade, eighteen in the fourth decade, and ten *waqfs* in the fifth decade. Therefore, 122 *waqfs* were established in the second half of the century. In the period until Mehmet Ali Pasha's annexation of Jerusalem, that is, ten *waqfs* were established in the first decade of the nineteenth century, twenty-nine in the second decade and eleven in the third decade. Therefore, fifty *waqfs* were established in the first half of the nineteenth century. Thus, while the number of foundations established in the two half of the eighteenth century was very close to each other, this number decreased considerably in the first half of the nineteenth century. The reasons for this situation should be sought in the political and socio-economic characteristics of the period. *Waqfs* should also be affected by the weakening of the central authority and the deterioration of public order. In this period, reasons such as the damage to some *waqf* structures, the unfair demand for money from *waqf* villages, the misappropriation of *waqf* properties by the officials had affected the social and economic situation of the people, and the number of the *waqfs* decreased in the eighteenth century and considerably decreased in the early nineteenth century.[328]

1.3.2 Categorization of the *Waqfs*

According to Islamic law, *waqfs* should aim for a charitable cause, directly or indirectly. For this, the income or the right of use of the *waqfs* is stipulated in different ways for charitable purposes.[329] *Waqfs* are divided into two categories as *khayrī* (charitable/public) *waqfs* and *dhurrī* (family, descendants, ordinary) *waqfs* according to the allocation method of income.[330]

---

328 These issues will be examined in detail in the fourth part of the study under the title of applications regarding the *waqfs*.

329 Hilmi Efendi, *Ithaf-ül-ahlāf*, 25; Akgündüz, *İslam Hukukunda*, 162.

330 In some studies dealing with eighteenth century *waqfs*, the category of semi-familial *waqfs* has been added as a third category. Semi-familial *waqf* is defined as the sharing of the income of the *waqf* between the family of the endowers or third parties who have savings and the charity institution. Yediyildiz, *XVIII. Century*, 14; Akgündüz, *İslam Hukukunda*, 270–72; Alkan, *Waqfs*, 26–29. On the other hand, al-Madanī, evaluating the eighteenth century Jerusalem *waqfs*, evaluated the *waqf* established by Muḥammad Sunʿullāh Effendi bin Khalīl Effendi al-Khālidī in 1123 AH/ 1711 CE as semi-familial *waqf*. With the income to be obtained specified in the *waqf*'s endowment, the trustee of the *waqf* should buy and put olive oil for the lighting oil well in Masjid al-Aqṣā; to distribute 22 cents to the poor; 22 piasters should be given to 4 people in exchange for reading *Sūrat al-Fātiḥa* and *hatim*; placing water in the water dispenser of the *waqf*, again by the

1.3.2.1 *Charitable* Waqfs

It is standard that the direct allocation of the entire income of the *waqf* should be for charitable purposes. The founder of the *waqf* does not expect any material benefit other than divine grace and sometimes fame or social influence from the *waqf*, which, after turning a few of his properties into the *waqf*, the proceeds from them allocate to public institutions established either by himself or by others.[331]

During the period covered by the study (1703–1831), 6% of the *waqfs* established in Jerusalem are in the charitable category (18 *waqfs*), 94% are in the family *waqf* (282 *waqfs*) category. The establishment dates of 1% of these *waqfs* (3 *waqfs* in total) are not known exactly.[332] The charitable *waqfs* established in Jerusalem within the scope of the study are both local and quite modest in terms of their number and the assets they had endowed.

Technically, the *waqf* covers goods or items endowed to generate income to support a particular person. The range of real estates that can be endowed is also diverse and extensive: As a whole building can be a single room, a large land, a small parcel, an orchard, a single tree, there may also be commercial enterprises such as mills, looms, printing houses or baths. Weapons and horses that can be used in war can be endowed as well as property such as the Qur'an, carpets, mosques and mausoleums.[333] Among the modest charitable *waqfs* established in Jerusalem during the period under study, Shaykh Abū al-Wafā' al-ʿAlamī endowed various books to students of knowledge residing in the Ṣalāḥiyya *Khanqāh*, marking one of the earliest such *waqfs*.[334] Dervish Muḥammad Mīrālāy endowed a Qur'an to the dervishes of the Uzbekiyya *Zāwiya*.[335] al-Ḥajj Muḥammad ibn ʿUmar al-Shāmī dedicated a prayer rug for the niche of the Dome of the Rock.[336] Qāsim Bey al-ʿAlaybeyzāde provided two

---

trustees; Adding lighting oil to the Masjid *al-Aqṣā minarets*; It stipulated that 4 *rıtl* bread should be purchased and exchanged for the poor and the needy in the *Shaykh* Mansur *Riwaks*. In addition to these charitable conditions, he stipulated the income of the *waqf* for himself while he was alive, his sons and daughters after his death, and their children until they were cut off. When their descendants were cut off totally, he stipulated that the *waqf* revenues would belong to the Dome of the Rock and Masjid *al-Aqṣā*. JS 207: 120–121; al-Madanī, *Awqāf al-Quds*, 40.

331 Yediyıldız, *XVIII. Yüzyılda*, 14–17.

332 The first of the endowments kept as files in the Archive in Abū Dīs in Jerusalem, 196 numbers on page 429 of the registry record; The second is File number 10/214: 2/25/13 and the third is File number 10/235: 34/13. For detailed information, see Ghūsha, *al-Awqāf al-Islāmiyya*.

333 Yediyıldız, "Vakıf Müessesesinin," 117.

334 JS 202: 375, 1116/ 1704; See also for a list of books. al-Madanī, *Awqāf al-Quds*, pp. 139–141.

335 JS 221: 48.

336 JS 293: 188.

Qur'ans to the poor and Qādiriyya dervishes in Jerusalem.[337] The wife of Ḥasan Pasha endowed a wicker mat for the niche of Masjid *al-Aqṣā*.[338] Muḥammad Effendi al-Turk, Muṣṭafā ibn Khalīl al-Bosnī, and Sulaymān Pasha endowed prayer rugs for the Dome of the Rock.[339] Shaykha al-Khamūriyya al-Jaghba[340] and Jerusalem's deputy governor Muḥammad Agha also endowed Qur'ans for the Dome of the Rock.[341] Shams al-Dīn Khātūn bint ʿAbdullāh al-Rūmiyya dedicated two candlesticks, one small and one large, for the Dome of the Rock.[342]

Other charitable *waqf*s included that of Muḥammad Sunʿ Allāh Effendi ibn Khalīl Effendi al-Khālidī, who established a public fountain in *Khaṭṭ Dāwūd* for all Jerusalem residents to drink from, endowing a shop and a pool to support it.[343] In 1126 AH/1714 CE, al-Ḥajja Ṣāliḥa bint al-Ḥajj Muḥammad al-Rakaṭ dedicated a storied house to charity in the *Bāb Ḥiṭṭa* District.[344] The *qāḍī* of Jerusalem, Aḥmad Effendi al-Ḥaṭenī, endowed his house with twelve-*qarārit* shares in *Bāb al-Qaṭṭānīn* for the *Sabīl al-Qubba* (*Bāb al-Maghāriba* fountain), located near Masjid *al-Aqṣā* opposite *Bāb al-Maghāriba*.[345] Aḥmad al-Kūtāhī allocated half the income from a *waqf* shop to the fountain he endowed in Masjid *al-Aqṣā* in the *Bāb al-Qaṭṭānīn* Quarter.[346] Ḥasan Effendi al-Dajjānī (al-Ḥusaynī) endowed nine public toilet facilities near the Maghāriba neighborhood by *Bāb al-Ḥaram*, along with a pool equipped with two copper taps for ablution, serving Masjid *al-Aqṣā* and *Jāmiʿ al-Mālikiyya* (Maghāriba Mosque).[347] Khayr al-Dīn ibn al-Ḥajj Rajab Çelebi dedicated his three-story house and vegetable garden in the *Bāb al-ʿAmūd* Quarter, along with six-*qarārit* arable land in *Arḍ al-Misrāra*, to the *Ḥaramayn al-Sharīfayn*.[348] Muḥammad ibn al-Ḥajj ʿAbdullāh Agha endowed his house to the Abū Madyan al-Ghawth *Zāwiya* in the Bāsağa Sharaf Quarter.[349] Finally, Fāṭima bint Muḥammad endowed her house,

337 JS 290: 1.

338 JS 290: 4.

339 JS 290: 4; JS 290: 38.

340 JS 290: 1.

341 JS. 308: 124.

342 JS 232: 532.

343 JS 208: 105. The endower also stipulated that the water carrier would put a lamp for two piastres and would be paid six *kurush* each day for the service of the waterways.

344 JS 209: 253; The endower devoted half a share of the house in question to the staff of the water carrier built by ʿAbd al-Ḥayy al-Dajjānī, located near the Tomb of Nabi Dawūd.

345 JS 59: 43.

346 JS. 220: 33–34. The endower also stipulated that three *kurush* from the rental income of the shop be given to the officer who put water in *sabīl*.

347 JS 220: 145–146.

348 JS, 237: 246; File 21: 1194/13.

349 JS 218: 487.

TABLE 6 Where the income of the *waqf* was stipulated after the generation of the endower was cut off in *dhurrī waqfs*

1	*Zāwiya* of Abū Madyan al-Ghawth[a]	8
2	For the Maghribi residents in the *Zāwiya* of Abu Madyan al-Ghawth	1
3	*Al-Ḥaramayn al-Sharifayn*	14
4	*Madrasa* Aminiyya and to the Shāfiʿīte Prayers in the *Ḥaram al-Sharīf*	1
5	*Zāwiya* Asʿadiyya	2
6	*Khanqāh* al-Ṣalāḥiyya	4
7	*Ḥaram al-Quds al-Sharif*	1
8	Servants (*khuddām*) of the Dome of the Rock	2
9	Servants (*khuddām*) of the Masjid *al-Aqṣā*	1
10	*Zāwiya* Qādirīyya	1
11	Waterways (*Qanāt al-Sabīl*)	3
12	Dome of the Rock[b]	116
13	*Minaret* of the Dome of the Rock	1
14	Waterways of the Dome of the Rock	1
15	Dome of the Rock and Masjid *al-Aqṣā*[c]	43
16	Dome of the Rock and the Masjid al-Abraham	1
17	Dome of the Rock, Masjid *al-Aqṣā*, waterways, the poor and the miserable	1
18	Scholars of al-Quds	2
19	The poor of al-Quds	3
20	The poor of al-Quds and the dervishes in the Qādirīyya Sufi Loge	1
21	To the poor and miserables in al-Quds	1
22	*Madrasa* students in al-Quds	3
23	Readers of the Holy Qur'an	2
24	Readers of short verses from the Holy Qur'an	1
25	*Maqām* al-Nabi Musa[d]	2
26	*Maqām* al-Nabi Musa and Masjid *al-Aqṣā*	1
27	*Maqām* al-Nabi Dawud	4
28	The Impovershed Maghribīs	1

a E.g. *Waqfiyya* of *Bashir al-Maghribi*. JS 245: 55–56

b E.g. *Waqfiyya* of *Abdullah ibn İbrahim ad-Dāwudi*. JS 244: 182; JS 245: 40

c E.g. *Waqfiyya* of *Āmine bint Abdullah al-Jibālī*. JS 236: 55

d E.g. *Waqfiyya* of *Abdullatif Efendi*. JS 249: 63–66. In the *waqfiyya* the endower stipulated that half of the income of the *waqf* would be given to the Tomb of Nabi Musa and the other half to the employees of the *Zāwiya* of Muḥammad al-Qırmī when he was cut off from his offsprings.

TABLE 6 Where the income of the *waqf* was stipulated (*cont.*)

29	Staff of the Dome of the Rock and then, the poor and the miserables of al-Quds	2
30	Staff of the Dome of the Rock	1
31	Masjid *al-Aqṣā*	19
32	*Mujāwirīn* in Masjid *al-Aqṣā*	1
33	Blind and poor *mujāvirīn* in Masjid *al-Aqṣā*	1
34	*Huffaz mujāwirīn* in Masjid *al-Aqṣā*	2
35	Staff of the *Riwaq al-Mansūrī* in Masjid *al-Aqṣā*	1
36	Mujāvirīn in the *Riwaq* of *Madrasa* Sultaniyya in Masjid *al-Aqṣā*	1
37	Imams in Masjid *al-Aqṣā*	1
38	For the waterways and water cups in Masjid *al-Aqṣā*	1
39	Masjid al-Abraham	15
40	To the poor and miserable of the Masjid al-Abraham	1
41	Masjid al-Nabawi	9
42	Niche of the Dome of the Rock	3
43	Niche of Masjid *al-Aqṣā*	1
44	Tomb of Nabi Musa and the staff of *Zāwiya* of Shaykh Muḥammad al-Qirmī (equally)	1
45	Shrine Cover of Nabi Musa and then, to the poor and Muslims in al-Quds	1
46	Bimāristan Ṣalāḥiyya	1
47	Mosque of Sidi	1
48	Table of Abraham (*Simāt al-Khalil*)	3
49	Table of Nabi Musa and the Dome of the Rock	1
50	Waterways	3
51	*Madrasa* Tashtimuriyya and the *Shāfiʿī* imams in Masjid *al-Aqṣā*	1
52	Unspecified	7
Total		300

consisting of three rooms, an *īwān*, a kitchen, and a cistern on Abū Shamāt Street, to the poor of Jerusalem.[350]

Among the *waqfs* established in Jerusalem in the eighteenth century, there were also *nuqūd waqfs* established for charitable purposes. The first of these

350 JS 255: 53–54. In the *waqfiyya*, it was also stipulated that 360 *Misri* of the *waqf*'s income be given to a person who would read one part of the Qur'an in the Jerusalem Ḥaram, and that 10 *zolotas* be given by the hand of trustees in return for reading 7000 words of *kalimat al-tawḥīd*.

*waqf*s was established in 1151 AH/ 1738 CE by the Guardian of Damascus, Jerusalem and Gaza and Nablus and Commandor of Hajj Caravan, Damascene, Vizier Hüseyin Pasha ibn Abbas by endoweing 500 *Esedi kurūsh*. With this *nuqūd* endowed to *Ḥaram al-Sharīf*, it was also required to buy rose and wood water for incense. The second *waqf* was established by the District Governor of Jerusalem, al-Hajj Mustafa Agha, by endowing 40 *lira zeheb* for the public fountain he built at the *Nāzir* Gate in Masjid *al-Aqṣā*. The third *waqf* was established by Muḥammad Effendi's daughter, Āmine, known as ibn Hoca, in 1185 AH/ 1771 CE by dedicating 10 *kurūsh* to buy and put lamps to the lit in the Dome of the Rock *minaret*. In the last *waqf*, 10 *dirhams* were endowed by Khalīl in 1231 Hijri / 1816 AD for the beneficience of Masjid *al-Aqṣā*.[351]

1.3.2.2 *Dhurrī* (*Family*) Waqfs

The entire income of the *waqf* is allocated to the endower's family or designated third parties without serving a charitable purpose. Only after the extinction (*inqirāḍ al-nasl*) of the endower's family or the designated third parties does the income of the last two of these *waqf*s fully support charitable causes.

When evaluating the family *waqf*s established in Jerusalem during the study's period, 282 out of 300 foundations are descendant *waqf*s, accounting for approximately 94%. Comparing this ratio with similar studies from the same period reveals consistent results.[352]

When the generations of the endowers ceased in 293 of the 300 *waqf*s mentioned above, the *waqf* income was to be allocated to the *waqf*s detailed in Table 6, including the Dome of the Rock, Masjid *al-Aqṣā*, Khalīl al-Raḥmān *Waqf*s, As'adiyya Ṣūfī Lodge, *Zāwiya* of Abū Madyan al-Ghawth, *al-Ḥaramayn al-Sharīfayn*, Amīniyya *Madrasa*, Tashtimūriyya *Madrasa*, *Khanqāh* al-Ṣalāḥiyya, *Bīmāristān* al-Ṣalāḥiyya, and the *waqf* of waterways.

The difference between family and charitable *waqf*s has led to the adoption of different approaches by the persons studying on the subject. Family *waqf*s do not benefit the poor or the public. They are set up to ignore normal inheritance shares. In addition, they are criticized in many ways as they facilitate the exploitation of state property that is obtained as income or tax source without having property rights.[353] However, in many verses of the Qur'an, it was essential that the goodness started from the closest family members and

351 JS 290: 1.

352 In his study on Adana *waqf*s in the eighteenth century, Alkan stated that the proportion of family *waqf*s was 71.07%, semi-family *waqf*s 7.17%, and charitable *waqf*s were 21.52%. Alkan, *Adana Vakıfları*, s. 26–29.

353 For the studies indicating that the "*khayrī*-ahlī" distinction in *waqf*s emerged in the modern period, see Singer, *Osmanlı'da Hayırseverlik*, 39–40.

the distinction between charitable and family *waqfs* has significantly shaped scholarly approaches to the subject. The first and most fundamental critique of family *waqfs* is that, unlike charitable *waqfs*, they are not intended to serve the poor or the broader public; the second critique is that they are primarily established to circumvent established inheritance regulations. In addition, they have been criticized for enabling the appropriation of state revenues or tax-derived assets without formal property rights. Yet, the Qur'an consistently emphasizes that acts of benevolence should begin with one's immediate family and progressively extend outward to those in greater need, reflecting a moral imperative that harmonizes familial duty with broader social responsibility. For example, Verbit, in his study in which the provisions of the *waqfs* belonging to the ninth century are studied, includes many examples showing that *waqfs* established as family *waqfs* are authentic and necessary. Even *waqfs* that initially designated family members as beneficiaries stipulated that the needy should benefit from the *waqf* income once no family members remained. During times of disaster and disease, when lifespans were generally short, beneficiary family members often died out within one or two generations. The ultimate beneficiaries were then the local poor, devoted poor, or beggars in holy cities like Mecca, Medina, and Jerusalem. Thus, all *waqfs* were fundamentally charitable. For this reason, the *qāḍī* of the *sharīʿa* court ruled that family *waqfs* were authentic and necessary. As shown in Table 6, most *waqfs* established in Jerusalem in the eighteenth century faced challenges in applying the *waqfiyya* conditions. They stipulated that *waqf* income be directed to the poor and destitute in Jerusalem, the needy, *Bīmāristān Ṣalāḥiyya*, or waterways.

Al-ʿAlamī notes that the popularity of the *waqf* among Jerusalem's traditionally influential families stemmed from its ability to achieve the endower's core objectives. The first advantage was securing property rights through long-term leases and transferring these rights to future generations as designated by the endower. The second was the broad autonomy allowing the endower to maintain control during their lifetime and determine post-mortem beneficiaries, making the *waqf* attractive to Jerusalem's prominent families. In his study of 112 family *waqfs* established by six distinguished Jerusalem families throughout the Ottoman period, al-ʿAlamī found that in 100 *waqfs*, the founders appointed themselves as sole beneficiary and trustee during their lifetime. This demonstrates that converting private property to a *waqf* did not compromise the endower's control or influence. In contrast, among the thirty charitable *waqfs* established by these families, only three endowers appointed themselves as sole beneficiary and trustee while alive, highlighting a cautious approach to the two *waqf* types. Family *waqfs* were created for the endower's specific purposes, while charitable *waqfs* served broader altruistic goals, as per Ḥanafī jurisprudence. Charitable *waqfs* appointed trustees from both within and outside the family, whereas family *waqf*s typically favored a family member, preferably male heirs, as trustees.[354]

Some family *waqf*s established in Jerusalem during the study's period also included provisions for charitable purposes. For instance, Sharīfa bint Ṣāliḥ al-ʿAsalī stipulated in her *waqfiyya* that the *imām*s of Masjid *al-Aqṣā* recite the Qur'an in Masjid *al-Aqṣā* using income from her mansion in Khaṭṭ Dāwūd.[355] Meanwhile, ʿAbdullāh ibn Ibrāhīm al-Dāwūdī required the preacher of Masjid *al-Aqṣā* to recite *Sūrat al-Fātiḥa* between the two sermons every Friday, dedicating one recitation to the soul of the Prophet Muḥammad and one to himself.[356] Another endower, Muḥammad Sunʿ Allāh al-Khālidī, allocated the income of his *waqf* to four individuals who would recite the Qur'an monthly and complete three *khatm*s during Ramaḍān, with the *thawāb* (spiritual reward) dedicated to the souls of the Prophet, the endower, and his mother.[357] Khalīl Sharaf al-Dīn ibn Abū Jibna stipulated that 12 *zoloṭa* from his *waqf* income be given to the *Takārīn* Ṣūfīs within the *Ḥaram al-Sharīf* in Jerusalem for reciting two parts of the Qur'an, one for the soul of the Prophet Muḥammad and the other for his own soul as spiritual gifts.[358] Finally, ʿAbdullāh ibn Ibrāhīm al-Dāwūdī allocated 20 *fidda Miṣriyya* annually from his *waqf* income for reciting *mawlid* in honor of the Prophet.[359]

1.3.3 Geographical Distributions in the City

Waqf charitable buildings scattered around the districts of Jerusalem are described in detail in the *waqfiyyas* and their expenses are covered by the *waqf*s. On the other hand, the properties assigned to charitable buildings of this *waqf* were also scattered in Muslim, Christian or Jewish quarters in the city. This can be seen in Annex 18, which is prepared regarding the distribution of assets and charitable buildings of the *waqf*s established by Muslims, according to neighborhoods, endowers endowed assets from every neighborhood, especially houses and shops.

1.3.3.1 *Charitable Goods* (*Khayrāt*)

Charitable good, one of the two main elements of the *waqf*s, is defined as usufruct with the same in the books where the provisions of the *waqf* are explained. In the same way, a usufruct is called an institution that benefits the

354 Al-Alami, "The Waqfs of the Traditional Families of Jerusalem," 155.

355 JS 243: 183–184.

356 JS 213: 91–94.

357 JS 250: 18–20.

358 JS 250: 129–133.

359 JS 244: 182.

society directly, namely, the *waqf* mosque, school, library, *madrasa*, hospital, nursing houses for the poor etc.

Basically, in order for an asset to be endowed, it is necessary that it should carry the qualifications of a *waqf* asset and be allocated to a benefactor according to the *sharīʿa* law. Otherwise, it is not possible to register the *waqf*.[360] The institutions that the society directly benefited from are well defined in the *waqfiyyas* and are described in two ways.[361] The first of these gives detailed information about where, when and how the endower built charitable goods by himself.[362] In the second, if the endower establishes a *waqf* for an existing charitable building, it is described where the charity was built by whom and its current situation.[363]

Of the 300 *waqfs* established in Jerusalem in the eighteenth century, while eighteen are in the category of charitable and 282 are in the family *waqf* category. Only four of these charitable *waqfs* had charitable buildings of their own, the first of which was built by Muḥammad Sunʿ Allāh ibn Khalīl Effendi al-Khālidī.[364] The second one was a fountain located near Tankiziyya *Madrasa*

---

360 Efendi, *Ithaf-ül-ahlāf*; *Ahkāmu'l-Evkāf*, 20–26.

361 Yediyıldız, *XVIII. Yüzyılda*, 91–92.

362 The *waqfiyya* of Muḥammad Sunʿullāh Effendi bin Khalīl Effendi al-Khālidī. JS (208: 105). The endower gives detailed information about the reason that it has established in Khaṭṭ Dāwūd Quarter in its *waqfiyya*.

363 The *waqfiyya* of al-Ḥājja Ṣāliḥa bint al-Ḥājj Muḥammad al-Rakkāt. JS 209: 253. Here, it is said that the endower devoted half of its assets in Bāb Ḥuṭṭa Quarter to the water dispenser built by his wife ʿAbd al-Ḥayy al-Dajjānī, located near Maqām Nabī Dāwūd.

364 Also known as Khālidī fountain, it is registered in the Jerusalem *sharīʿa* court registers for *sabil* as Muḥammad Sunʿ Allāh Effendi ibn Khalīl Effendi al-Khālidī *Waqf*. While the first of the *waqfiyya* dated Rajab 1125 / July 1713 contained detailed information about the saint, the second *waqfiyya* dated 1136/4 September 1724 and the properties dedicated to the public fountain were explained in detail. *Waqfiyyas* were very important in terms of being the only source related to cause. The first *waqfiyya* that contains information about the *sabil* is a short *waqfiyya* of 320 words. Details such as the definition of the structure, its boundaries, the conditions regarding the personnel and wages of the endower and the purpose of the fountain were included in the *waqfiyya*. JS 208: 105–106. The second *waqfiyya* consists of 2500 words and the expenses of the public fountain were covered by the endower, the properties of the *waqf* in the old city of Jerusalem; twelve houses, five shops, one vegetable garden, three houses with varying shares, two vegetable gardens, a shop, a soap factory, a bakery, a large roaster where coffee and peanuts were roasted were recorded. JS 218: 407. All these properties were recorded in the endower's seven endower charters established on different dates in the same century. The first of these is dated 18 Shawwal 1123/29 November 1711 and the last *waqfiyya* is dated 12 Shawwal 1136/4 July 1724. Among the conditions of the endower specified in the second *waqfiyya*, the trustee of the *waqf* required the water supply for the fountain, copper bowls and their protection, and repair and maintenance of the fountain if needed. JS 208: 105. In addition, the appointment of two officials for the public fountain of the trustee; It stipulated that the first of them should serve as a *saqa* and be given two *mısrī* wages per day, open the fountain every

and it was built by Kazim Bey ibn Rajab al-Tarjuman on 1131/1718.[365] Sabīl al-Ḥusaynī, also known as Sabīl al-Qubba al-Naḥawiyya, was constructed in the eighteenth century.[366] The fountain's inscription indicates it was built by Ḥasan ibn al-Dānī al-Ḥusaynī between 1137 AH/1724–25 CE. Examination of the registers from the same period reveals two records identifying al-Ḥusaynī as *al-Qāḍī al-Quds*. The first record confirms that the *waqf* officially assumed the role of *al-Qāḍī al-Quds* on 1137 AH/20 October 1724 CE.

In the second record, there is a *waqfiyya* dated 1137/1725 and with this *waqfiyya*, it was stipulated that a pool would be built for the renovation of 9 *kenifs* (public toilets) located around *Madrasa* Fakhriyya in the west of *Ḥaram al-Sharīf* and for ablution. It had been stipulated that these would be built for the benefit of the employees of Masjid *al-Aqṣā* and the Mosque of Mālikiyya and the students in the *Ḥaram al-Sharīf*. The name of the *waqf* is recorded as al-Sayyid Hasan Effendi Danizāde *al-Ḥusaynī* in the *waqfiyya*. It is introduced with the first names such as "*el-şecere el-tahire el-zekiyye*," which indicates that he was the descendant of the Prophet.[367] Finally, Sabīl Mustafa Agha, also known as Sabīl Shaykh Budayr,[368] was built on 1153/1740–1 by the governor of Jerusalem *Sanjāq* Mustafa Agha.[369] In the *waqfiyya*, al-Hajj Mustafa Agha had endowed 40 *zangirli* (gold *lira*) for the fountain that he built next to the Bāb al-Nāzir in the *Ḥaram al-Sharīf*.[370] It was stipulated that the *mutawallī* of

morning and turn it off every evening, the other one should serve in the fountain and do the lighting services, and a daily fee of seven *mısrī*. JS 218: 470. Endower also required the allocation of eight *mısrī* per month for the purchase of lighting oil for the fountain.JS 208: 105; 218: 470. For detailed information about the architectural features of the *sabil*, see Auld and Hillenbrand, eds., *Ottoman Jerusalem*, 963–65.

365 The properties endower donated for the expenses of the fountain; four houses in the Jewish Quarter, six shops in the Jewish Quarter, three houses in Risha Quarter, two houses in Khaṭṭ Dāwūd and two shops in Bāb al-ʿAmūd. The endower stipulates that every year fifty cents of the *waqf*'s income would be spent by the trustee for the endower's *sabil*. JS 213: 95.

366 Auld and Hillenbrand, eds., *Ottoman Jerusalem*, 2:966.

367 JS 220: 145–6.

368 See Van Berchem, *Corpus Inscriptionum*, 195–96; al-ʿĀrif, *al-Mufaṣṣal*, 97; Burgoyne, "The Gates," 146. However, when the biography of Sheikh Budayr is examined, there is no connection between the fountain in question and Sheikh Budayr. See Mannaʿ, "The Sijill," 351–62. Hillenbrand attributes this to the fact that the Zāwiya Wafāʾiyya, where Shaykh Budayr lived and owned, is located in the western part of the Ḥaram al-Sharīf near the Nāẓir Gate. Auld and Hillenbrand, *Ottoman Jerusalem*, 2:974–81. Another name given by Van Berchem is "ʿUthmān Bey al-Fikārī Fountain." The public fountain was rebuilt by the order of ʿUthmān Bey al-Fikārī.

369 JS, 230: 210.

370 According al-ʿĀrif (al-Mufaṣṣal, 318) Mustafa Agha ruled Jerusalem for more than twenty years between 1144–65 /1731–51. Mustafa Agha agreed with the peoples of the villages of al-Biʾra, Bayt Ḥanīnā, Bayt Iksā (all north Jerusalem) not to attack visitors to the Holy City. He contributed to other construction projects in the city, such as organizing the

the *waqf* should be given 4 *zangirli* annually. He made the management of the *waqf* as a condition to Isa al-Kurdī bin Muḥammad while he was alive, to his son after his death and to the oldest and most mature son of his sons. When Isa al-Kurdī died without any offspring from his generation, he made the administration of the *waqf* a condition to the *mutawallī* of the Masjid *al-Aqṣā Waqf*. The endower also stipulated that the *saka* (water carrier) should be given 14 loaves of bread daily from Khasseki Sultan's Public Kitchen, that the *saka* would clean the fountain weekly and if he did not fulfill his duty, the task would be given to another person. It had also stipulated that the *nāzir* (inspector) of the *waqf* would be the *al-Qāḍī al-Quds* over the *mutawallī*.[371]

On the other hand, books endowed as movable property are classified as charitable goods rather than assets, since their usufruct is realized through direct use in kind, not through revenue generation. Beyond the previously examined public libraries, this section analyzes *waqfiyyas* recording endowed books and examines private libraries established within the chronological and thematic scope of the present study during the period fallig into the field of study.

It is recorded that during the period in the field of study, people from the *ʿulamāʾ* class in Jerusalem dedicated their private libraries, sometimes to institutions such as *madrasas*, mosques, Sufi lodges, and sometimes they endowed their books together with the house they lived in and asked those in need to benefit from such books. As the examples given below, people from the *ʿulamāʾ* class only devoted their books on the condition that they would benefit from them as long as they lived and then they would be supervised by other generations.

According to the information in the *waqfiyyas* registered in the Jerusalem *sharīʿa* court registers, three of the eleven *waqfs* endowed one Qurʾan.[372] In another *waqfiyya*, two Qurʾans were endowed.[373] Among the seven other *waqfs*, Shaykh Abū al-Wafāʾ al-ʿAlamī endowed books on various subjects, particularly *tafsīr*, *ḥadīth*, and *ʿaqāʾid*, in his *waqfiyya* dated 1117 AH/1705 CE.[374] The endower stipulated that the books would belong to him during his lifetime, and after his death, they would pass to his two sons, Shaykh Jawdat Allāh and Sayyid Abū al-Faḍl, then to their sons and subsequent male descendants until the line ended. Upon the extinction of his male lineage, he designated that the

---

construction of the small domed building built in the Naqshbandiyya Zāwiya and the reconstruction of the water-filled castle moat with Sultan Maḥmūd Khan's decree dated 1144/1731–2.

371 JS 230: 210; For the architectural features of the fountain, see Auld and Hillenbrand (eds.), *Ottoman Jerusalem*, 2:979.

372 Endowed by Asʿad Bey, Shaykhat al-Ḥamūriyya al-Jaghba, Quds Mutasallim Muḥammad Āghā. See respectively. JS 290:1; 308: 124.

373 Endowed by Qāsim Bey al-ʿAlāybeyzāde. See JS 290: 1.

374 See JS 202: 375; For the list of books, see al-Madanī, *Awqāf al-Quds*, 139–41.

books be given to the *Khanqāh al-Ṣalāḥiyya*. If the conditions of the *waqf* were not applicable, the endowed books were stipulated to the *madrasa* students in Jerusalem. He made the management of the *waqf* a condition for himself as long as he was alive, and for his children after his death. In addition, it has only made it necessary for himself to increase and decrease the *waqf*'s income, to add or remove something from the *waqf*.[375]

Secondly, approximately 600 manuscripts forming the core collection of the Khālidī Library were endowed by al-Ḥajj Muḥammad Sunʿ Allāh al-Khālidī in 1133 AH/1721 CE. Thirdly, the library established by Shaykh Sharaf al-Dīn Muḥammad ibn Muḥammad al-Ḥalīlī in Jerusalem at the *Zāwiya al-Muḥammadiyya* stands out for its extensive collection. A list of the books he endowed is included at the end of his *waqfiyya*, dated 1139 AH/1727 CE. Scholars could access this library, which boasted a rich collection of around 7,000 volumes. Shaykh Sharaf al-Dīn Muḥammad specified in his *waqfiyya* that none of the books were acquired through seizure, theft, or deception. He designated the *waqf* for his own soul during his lifetime, then for his sons and their descendants, and subsequently for the scholars of the *Zāwiya al-Muḥammadiyya* and Shāfiʿī scholars. The endower also set strict conditions for borrowing: a borrower had to be known for honesty, belong to one of the four *madhhab*s (legal schools), and reside in Jerusalem; books were not to be lent to individuals known for losing or damaging them.[376]

Fourth, the Ḥanafī *mufti* of Jerusalem, Ahmad bin Muḥammad al-Muwakkit, also donated a precious library in Jerusalem in 1181 AH/ 1767 CE. He devoted the library to *madrasa* students.[377] Again, Al-Ḥajj Muḥammad Sunʿ Allāh al-Khālidī and Ṭurfanda Khātūn bint al-Shaykh Najm al-Dīn al-Khayrī, *Muftī* of Jerusalem, endowed a large number of Qur'ans and various books in their *waqfiyya* dated 1201 AH/1786 CE. The endower stipulated that *waqf* revenues be allocated first to the three sons of Muḥammad Sunʿ Allāh al-Khālidī, then to their sons and subsequent male descendants and relatives, to their daughters only when the male line was entirely extinguished, and finally to Jerusalem scholars when the family lineage ceased.[378] At the same time, the *waqf* was committed to Muḥammad Effendi, Musa Effendi and Umar Effendi, the brother of the two, and after those two, it had been stipulated on the most mature sons after them.

375 al-Madanī, *Awqāf al-Quds*, 141.

376 Erünsal, *Osmanlı Vakıf Kütüphaneleri*, 208, 519.

377 al-Asali, "The Libraries," 288; Erünsal, *Osmanlı Vakıf Kütüphaneleri*, 253.

378 JS 267: 151–153. For a list of books, see al-Madanī, *Awqāf al-Quds*, 428–35. In addition, many books were brought from various Arab countries, especially from Egypt, to be sold in booksellers. Members of the Khālidī family in Jerusalem had been involved in such a commercial activity since the beginning of the eighteenth century and they had sold many books they bought from Cairo in Istanbul. See Conrad, "The Khālidī Library," 196.

It was also stipulated that the books belonging to the *waqf* would not be borrowed for more than three days.[379]

The *muftī* of Jerusalem, al-Ḥajj Ḥasan ibn ʿAbd al-Laṭīf al-Ḥusaynī, endowed in his *waqfiyya* dated 1201 AH/1786 CE: 26 volumes of *tafsīr* (commentary), over 70 volumes of *ḥadīth*, 44 volumes of *taṣawwuf* (Sufism), 18 volumes of *balāgha* (rhetoric), approximately 122 volumes of *fiqh*, 15 volumes of *mīrāth* (inheritance law), about 27 volumes of *ʿaqāʾid* (theology), 43 volumes of *ṣarf* and *naḥw* (grammar), 32 volumes of lexicons and *dīwān*s (poetry collections), around 12 volumes of *ṭibb* (medicine), and 51 volumes of *ʿubūr* (scientific texts, likely referring to *ʿulūm* or miscellaneous scholarly works).[380] The endower stipulated that the *waqf* benefit himself during his lifetime, then pass to his brother al-Ḥajj ʿAbdullāh, *Naqīb al-Ashrāf*, and his son after his death, followed by their sons, descendants, and relatives. Subsequently, it was designated for all *madrasa* scholars and students in Jerusalem. He also required that books not be removed from the library without being recorded by the *murattib* (arranger).[381]

Finally, Shaykh Muḥammad al-Budayrī al-Qudsī endowed his house and library through a *waqfiyya* dated 1206 AH/1792 CE. As cited in al-ʿAsalī, the library contained 1,000 manuscripts. The *waqf* established a library in the Wafāʾiyya Ṣūfī Lodge in Jerusalem. According to al-ʿĀrif, the library, located at the Nāẓir Gate, one of the entrances to the *Ḥaram al-Sharīf*, housed around 1,000 books.[382] There were many manuscript rare books among the books written on various subjects.[383]

In addition to the library *waqf*s, libraries with rich collections were inherited, one by Muḥammad Zāda in 1151 AH/1739 CE, and another by the Shāfiʿī *muftī* of Jerusalem, ʿAbd al-Muʿtī al-Ḥalīlī, as described in al-ʿAsalī.[384] Some of the *waqf*s established in Jerusalem in the eighteenth century provided income for a charitable *waqf* established before them.[385] New *waqf*s had also been established to support the *waqf*s that could not cover their expenses.[386]

---

379 al-Madanī, *Awqāf al-Quds*, 435.

380 JS 267: 158–160. For detailed information about the books, see also. Al-Madanī, *Awqāf al-Quds*, 473–55; al- Sūwāriyya, *al-Hayāt al-Ijtimāʿiyya*, pp. 266–71.

381 al-Madanī, *Awqāf al-Quds*, 455–56.

382 Al-Sūwāriyya, *al-Ḥayāt al-Ijtimāʿiyya*, 272–75; Erünsal, *Osmanlı Vakıf Kütüphaneleri*, 265.

383 al-ʿĀrif. *al-Mufaṣṣal*, 390. Microfilms of the works in the library are available at the University of Jordan Center for Documents and Manuscripts. In addition, the study on the manuscripts in the Budayri Library was published by Khadr Salameh in two volumes arranged according to the subject and the author. For a sample list of estates, see also as-al-Sūwāriyya, *al-Ḥayāt al-Ijtimāʿiyya*, 272–75.

384 For detailed information, see al-Asali, "The Libraries," 288.

385 For example, the endower Qāsım ibn Rajab al-Tarjumān, who was a translator at the Jerusalem *Sharīʿa* court, stipulated that 50 *kurūsh* from the income of his *waqf* would be spent on the *sabil* he endowed (JS, 213: 95).

386 For example, the endower Ḥāmid bin ʿAbdullāh Bābāḥiyya stipulated the income of the *waqf* he established to the expenses of Jāmiʿ al-ʿUmarī (JS, 241: 39–41).

The charitable goods that are scattered in the neighborhoods of Jerusalem are not just the ones recorded in these *waqfiyyas*. It has been revealed that the charitable buildings such as mosques, masjids, schools, *madrasas*, *zāwiyas*, *takiyyas* and Sufi lodges established during the Ayyubid and Mamluk periods as well as ealier Ottoman periods continued to provide active and functional services between 1703 and 1831.

1.3.3.2 Waqf *Assets* (*Akar*)

Charity institutions and organizations need continuous income in order to maintain their physical existence, to function properly and to provide services to the society without interruption. Here, movable or real estate income sources, which are devoted to meet the expenses of charities and to ensure the fulfillment of the *waqf* requirements, are called '*akar* (assets)'. These goods are operated in a variety of ways, and the revenues generated were allocated to charities or distributed directly to the poor.[387] It is possible to describe the wages and income obtained by operating assets as movable or immovable properties that are endowed to be spent for a charity.[388] In other words, assets provide income for charity organizations to serve their *waqf* purposes.[389] The *waqfiyyas* contain rich, explanatory information about charity-type structures as well as their income sources. This information explains the type, locality, qualifications, number (amount) of assets and the method of generating income. Identifying sources of income in the *waqf* studies is the main factor in analyzing the economic structure of the *waqf* and the region where it is established. In addition, the size of the *waqf* established allows us to make inferences about the scarcity or the abundance of its financing. The type, amount, and return of income sources owned by the *waqfs* depend on the social and economic status of the *waqf* founder and the size of the *waqf*. In addition, these determinations can be used as a tool to determine the economic status of the *waqf* founders. Based on this, in the period examined in this section, the sources of income of the *waqfs* established in Jerusalem, their geographical distribution in the city and their numerical rates will be determined.

It will be appropriate to mention some of the findings of the *waqf* assets established in Jerusalem during the period under consideration before moving on to the numerical data. Above all, there was a much thicker line between

387 Among these sources of income, which were called assets and were endowed; lands, some villages, all kinds of agricultural enterprises, farms, fields, gardens, buildings used as dwellings, shops or other structures built for economic purposes, and properties such as animal skins, ships, cash. Berki, *Vakfa Dair*, 2.

388 Pakalın, *Osmanlı Tarih*, 32.

389 Öztürk, *Menşe'i ve Tarihi*, 83.

TABLE 7 List of *waqf* assets established in Jerusalem (1703–1831)

Property types	Type of the charitable goods			No.	Total	Ratio (%)	General total	General ratio %
City center	Unmovable goods	Dwellings	*Dār/Dur* (house)	225	496	64,93	691	90,45
			Shared house	250				
			Bayt (room)	3				
			Shared room	3				
			Room	5				
			Floor	3				
			Shared Floor	1				
			Eyvan (iwan)	2				
			Shared cistern	1				
			Istabl (stable)	1				
			Warehouse	1				
			Shared coffee warehouse	1				
		Commercial buildings	Shop	53	112	14,66		
			Shared shop	37				
			Coffeehouse	1				
			Weaving shop	1				
			Store	7				
		Industrial enterprises	*Mahmas* (grinder)	2	29	3,80		
			Ma'sara (mill)	1				

TABLE 7 List of *waqf* assets established in Jerusalem (1703–1831) (*cont.*)

Property types	Type of the charitable goods			No.	Total	Ratio (%)	General total	General ratio %
			Oven	4				
			Shared oven	6				
			Mill	1				
			Shared mill	2				
			Fahūre (potter)	1				
			Imalathane (workshop)	4				
			Shared workshop	8				
		Agricultural Field and enterprises	bāğ (vineyard)	2	48	6,28		
			bāḫçe (garden)	16				
			share of a garden	21				
			garden with a şadırvan (fountain)	1				
			share of land	7				
			mezrā'a (small agricultural plot)	1				
	Movable goods	Animal kinds	Beehives	1	1	0,13		
		Nuqūd	*Nuqūd* (cash/money)	5	5	0,65		

TABLE 7 List of *waqf* assets established in Jerusalem (1703–1831) (*cont.*)

Property types	Type of the charitable goods			No.	Total	Ratio (%)	General total	General ratio %
Central village and mezra'as'	Real estate	Dwellings	House	4	8	1,04	73	9,55
			Mansion	2				
			Floor	2				
		Agricultural Field and Enterprises	Land	4	65	8,51		
			Shared land	7				
			Arz Hissesi (shared estate)	1				
			Vineyard	3				
			Garden	3				
			Shared garden	1				
			Vegetable garden	1				
			Mezra'a	14				
			Share of mezra'a	28				
			Olive grove	1				
			Olive grove share	1				
			Cistern	1				
Total				764	764	100		

the city and the countryside in Jerusalem.[390] The inhabitants of Jerusalem were not farmers who cultivated the urban fields. The poor rural areas around the city were far from forming the agricultural hinterland of the city.[391] In the study conducted on *waqf* assets, the ratio of assets in rural areas to all assets remained at 9.55%. The rate of assets in the center was 90.45%. These rates indicate that *waqf* assets are concentrated in the city center. Secondly, the shareholding in the *waqfs* established in Jerusalem in the period examined had a very serious ratio. For example, the number of areas cultivated by the *waqfs* established by six families during the Ottoman period (103), houses in the city (215) and shops (224), 66% of the cultivated areas, 71% of the houses and 85% of the shops were found to be shareholdings.[392] The process of establishing a *waqf* in Jerusalem also increased this shareholding rates. It is not technically possible for outsiders hope to purchase the entire ownership by buying the shares of the *waqf*. The early Islamic *fiqh* imams were not in agreement on shared ownership. Mālikīs opposed this practice, and notably, the prominent Ḥanafī Imam Abū al-Ḥasan al-Shaybānī, whose views were widely adopted by the Ottomans, did not endorse foundations established in this manner. Nevertheless, Ḥanafī judges in Ottoman Jerusalem accepted this process and deemed it legitimate. The data in Table 7, based on *waqfiyyas* from the study's period, corroborates al-ʿAlamī's findings, showing that shared assets constituted 50.47% of all properties, highlighting the prevalence of share ownership during this time.

Table 7 collectively presents the income sources of *waqfs* established in Jerusalem, though the income or benefits they generated could not be fully recorded. This is due to several reasons: First, not all *waqfs* began generating income simultaneously. Second, as most *waqfs* were family-oriented, their assets remained in family possession, often yielding no income or being irregularly managed by their *mutawallīs*. Third, many endowed roofed properties required repairs over time, and several could not be restored or rebuilt. This section distinguishes between real estate or property income sources while also noting income potentials. Finally, it seeks to assess the role of *waqfs* in Jerusalem's economy by detailing the operational procedures of income-generating *waqfs* through execution or management.

As can be seen in Table 7, 99% of 764 items assets were immovable and 1% were movable properties. 64.93% of the immovable properties in the city center, 1.04% of the dwellings in the villages and arable fields attached to the

390 Mannaʿ, "Continuity and Change," 75.

391 Ben-Arieh, *Jerusalem*, 393.

392 Al-Alami, 'The *Waqfs*,"154.

center, 6.28% in the city center, 8.51% of the agricultural enterprises in the central villages and arable fields, 14%, 66 of them were commercial buildings and 3.80% were industrial enterprises. 0.13% of movable assets consist of beehives and 0.65% of cash money. If we add to this number those who were endowed without a number and those whose assets cannot be identified (6 foundations), this number will increase more.

1.3.3.2.1 Immovable Goods

Immovable properties, which constitute an important source of income for the *waqf* institution, are known today as real estates.[393] In the provisions of the *waqf*, it means the goods that cannot be transferred and bonded without deteriorating their current situation.[394] It includes lands and buildings and trees fixed to them. In the early days of Islamic law, in order for income sources to be included in the *waqf*, it had to be real estates that were the property of the endower. However, the changing social, economic and social conditions have expanded the scope and type of income sources subject to the *waqf*.[395] We have classified the immovable properties endowed in Jerusalem as residences, commercial buildings, industrial establishments and agricultural enterprises.

1.3.3.2.1.1 *Dwellings*

Since dwellings, which mean the place of residence, are considered as an income generating real estate, they have become the subject of the *waqf*. Generally, four types of dwellings are encountered in *waqfiyyas*. These comprise stations (*menzils*), palaces, waterside mansions (*yalis*), and small dwellings referred to as '*oda*' or '*hane*'.[396]

During the period covered by the study, residential properties endowed as *waqf* in Jerusalem were categorized into five groups, described using terms such as house, *bayt*, room, floor, layer, and mansion, often expressed in the Arabic form *dār*/*dūr* in *waqfiyyas*, depending on their characteristics and functions. Among these, *dār*/*dūr* is the most frequently used term. Typically constructed as two-story buildings, these houses included features listed in some *waqfiyyas*: downstairs and upper floors (rooms), *īwān*, *qaʿa* (a reception area, akin to a sofa), a courtyard called *saḥḥa* or *saḥḥa samāwī* (open courtyard), kitchen, vestibule, water cistern, *ḥammām* (bath), *tāqa* (window), *bāyika* (cellar for storing

393 *Türkçe Sözlük*, p. 730.
394 Hilmi Efendi, *Ithaf-ül-ahlāf*, 39–41.
395 Yediyıldız, "XVIII. Asır," 5.
396 ibid., 9.

grain and olive oil), *liṭrā'* (noted as a subordinate space in some records), and *istabl* (stable).[397] There were also sections such as the barn and a water cistern for collecting snow and rain water is available in almost all houses.[398] Houses with sections such as pools and cloisters were also endowed.[399] Besides, the houses were in a garden surrounded by walls and mostly trees with and without fruits were described in the *waqfiyyas*.[400] In some *waqfiyyas*, houses with back gardens were also defined.[401] Information on the current status of the endowed houses such as arched,[402] devastated[403] or rented through *khuluww*[404] is also provided. The word *khuluww* was used for some houses endowed in the *waqfiyyas*.[405] This means that houses rented with the *khuluww* method could be reendowed through the transfer of the right of *khuluww* to the others.

In the period we are examining, the houses were the highest rate of endowments among all sources of income in the *waqf*s of Jerusalem. In the period covered by the study, only one house or a house share was devoted to 150 out of 300 newly established *waqf*s. In total, 225 houses, 250 share houses, five rooms, one floor, three *bayt*, three shared *bayt*, three layers, one shared layer, one *iwan*, one *iwan raqaba* and one shared cistern were endowed.[406] As stated above, the fact that the number of shared houses is more than fully owned houses shows that the fragmentation of property rights in Ottoman Jerusalem was at a significant level. Secondly, it points out that the rate of house ownership was high in Jerusalem. Endowers have devoted their houses to provide income for

397 For examples, see JS 212: 7–8; 223: 372; 231: 251; 247: 80–81. For detailed information on the characteristics of the houses in Jerusalem in the second half of the eighteenth century, see also al-Sūwāriyya, *al-Ḥayāt al-Ijtimā'iyya*, 87–92.

398 See JS 207: 343–344; 209: 249; 218: 22–23; 214: 144.

399 See JS 213: 51–52; 260: 25.

400 SeeJS 221: 301; 223: 288–289; 225: 203; 229: 252.

401 See JS 253: 130; 255: 45; 256: 59; 257: 71.

402 See JS 247: 19; JS 272: 147; JS 275: 93.

403 See JS 248: 61.

404 See File No. 2/21/: 1194/13; JS 285: 89; 295: 232; 301: 109; 314: 123.

405 *Khuluww*, which means "empty," has very different meanings as a legal term. The most comprehensive of these is the right of beneficial interest (usufruct) obtained in return for a certain amount of money given in favor of that *raqaba* on the account of an asset. This certain amount can be given for the purpose of repairing the said asset or for another purpose. For detailed information, see Akgündüz, *İslam Hukukunda*,506–15. The word *khuluww*, which is also mentioned in many documents in the registries, was recorded as a rental method. When these examples are combined with the examples in the *waqfiyyas*. It is understood that the right of *khuluww* was endowed, not the *raqaba* of the endowed house.

406 See Annex 18.

charities and to provide assistance to their families and relatives. At the same time, the ease of setting up a house *waqf* must have increased the number of such *waqfs*. Considering that some of the houses were rented, it can be said that house *waqfs* contributed to the solution of the settlement problem in the city. There were also the *waqfs* in which a larger mansion than the house was endowed.[407]

The residence rights of the houses endowed in Jerusalem had been allocated to various people. The residence rights of the houses were mostly allocated to the sons of the endower,[408] who are referred to as *'mevkūfun ʿaleyh'*[409] in the *waqfiyya*, and even a little after his death to his wives[410] and daughters until they get married.[411] In this case, according to the condition of the endower, mostly family members, close relatives,[412] and sometimes officials such as the prayer, preacher of the neighborhood[413] or the other staff of the *waqf* could live

407 al-Ḥājj Sulaymān Bey bin ʿAbd al-Jawād al-Aṣalī devoted a vineyard consisting of figs, olives, and two cisterns and a palace bordered by the Hārūsh vineyard in the land of Sīmār. JS 251: 139–141. Shaykh Muḥammad Najm al-Dīn ibn al-Shaykh Muḥammad Badr al-Dīn Effendi al-Jamāʿa endowed a neighboring palace to the Badr al-Dīn bin al-Jamāʿa Waqf outside Jerusalem. File 10/195/65/13.

408 Al-Ḥajj Ṣāliḥ ibn Badr al-Dīn al-Ḥūsh (Ḥawsh-Ḥawāsh) stipulated that the children of the *waqf* must reside in the house he endowed in the Bāb Khuṭṭa neighborhood, as per his *waqfiyya* dated 1185/1771. JS, 254: 324.

409 Ömer Hilmi Efendi, *Ithaf-ül-ahlāf*, 25–26.

410 During the period between 1703 and 1800, 13 endowers allocated the right of residence to their spouses until their death. See, JS 217: 34; 230: 24; 241: page not specified; 242: 184; 245: 4; 249: 63–64; File 2/21: 1194/13; JS 250: 18–20; 254: 139; 254: 306–307; 273: 13–14; 277: 23–25; 279: 145–146. One of the endowers in question, Sulaymān ibn Ṭāhā al-Dajjānī stipulated that his wife Sayyida bint Ḥasan would reside in the house of the *waqf* and that she be provided with 10 *fidda* from the income of the *waqf* every day. JS 277: 23–25. In another *waqfiyya*, ʿAbd al-Laṭīf Efendi al-Ḥusaynī, who was the deputy governor of Jerusalem, *naqīb al-ashrāf*, and the shaykh of the Ḥaram al-Sharīf, stipulated that his wives Fāṭima bint ʿAbd al-Ḥayy al-Dajjānī and Āmina bint Ibrāhīm Çelebi al-Namrī would reside in the *waqf* house. If his wife married after his death, this right would end immediately. See, JS 249: 63–64; File 2/21: 1194/13.

411 In the period between 1703 and 1800, twenty-one endowers allocated the right of residence to their daughters until their marriage. See JS 202: 12; 207: 122; 217: 359–360; 223: 311–313; 223: 372; 223: 425; 330: 177; 218: 563; 225: 73; 230: 147; 243: 147; 243: 275; 247: 71–72; 250: 22; 250: 39–40; 254: 74; 254: 457; 255: 116; 255: 120–122; 260: 70–73; 277: 182.

412 E.g. Aḥmad Agha ibn ʿAbd al-Wahhāb allocated the right of residency of his storied house, which he endowed in the Sharaf Quarter, first to his neighbor Fāṭima and then to his brother's daughter Fāṭima bint ʿAbdullāh. JS. 261: 108–109.

413 E.g. JS 243: 183–184.

in that *waqf* house without paying any fee.[414] The right of residence of most of these houses, the rents of some, the sale of some of them and the amount of their rents[415] were all stated as a *waqf* condition. In seven *waqf*s, while the rental income of the houses was allocated to the charity conditions, the income to be obtained from the sale of a house was also allocated for another *waqf*.[416]

It was determined that five rooms were endowed in the Jerusalem *waqf* records.[417] As understood from the *waqfiyya*s, the rooms that were endowed located in the city center. Residences called so-called *hujurāt* or rooms were usually built on floors and in rows of equal size, uniform shapes for the purpose of renting. It can be said that the cells were a series of single-storey masonry rooms. These small, single-story dwellings, designed to accommodate one or two individuals, could serve as permanent residences for low-income inhabitants, or as temporary lodgings for single laborers, porters, merchants, travelers, and visitors arriving from various regions. In these rooms, any person from the groups mentioned above could live by paying a cheap rent.[418]

In the account register dated 1153/1740 of the Maghāriba *Waqf*, which is a charitable *waqf*, the rental income of eighteen houses, most of which are located in the Maghāriba Quarter, vary between three and eighteen *zolota*s per year.[419] In the same record, the annual rental income of a house inhabited by Jews is thirty-five *zolota*, while the annual rental income of houses adjacent to the *waqf*, whose number is not specified, is stated as 232 *zolota*. In the account register dated 1168 AH/1755 CE for the *Waqf* of Shaykh Khalīl al-Jāʿūnī, a family *waqf*, all nineteen income-generating assets were houses. Four of these, described as *dār*, were larger, with annual rental incomes ranging between

414 E.g. JS 243: 183–184.

415 ʿĀfifa Khātūn bint Hibbat Allāh Çelebi al-Namrī stipulated in her *waqfiyya* that the *waqf* house in the Sharaf Quarter be leased. From the rental income of the house in question, five kurush was allocated to her four daughters Ṣāliḥa, Fāṭima, Nafīsa, and Ḥasība, whose father was ʿAbd al-Ḥayy al-Dajjānī. JS 223: 107. Ḥusayn ibn Badr al-Dīn Qimīʿ stipulated the rent of two houses and one īwān he donated in the Sharaf Quarter to his sons. JS 230: 200.

416 E.g. JS 223: 107; 230: 200.

417 These are: A new room near the Patriarch Bath in the *waqfiyya* of al-Shaykh Jūd Allāh Efendi ibn al-Shaykh Muṣṭafā al-ʿAlamī (JS 213: 51); Muḥammad Sunʿ Allāh Efendi ibn Khalīl Efendi consisted of two rooms adjacent to *Dār al-Ḥadīth Waqf* in the Maghāriba Neighborhood in al-Khālidī *Waqf* and two rooms in the Maghāriba *Waqf*, which was also endowed by another waqf of the same endower. See JS 213: 91–93; 218: 47.

418 Gerber, *Economy and Society*, 151.

419 JS 224: 185–187.

thirty-five and fifty *zoloṭa*.[420] The rental income of smaller houses or rooms, expressed by the word *bayt*, ranges from one to thirteen *zolota*. Of the houses specified in the accounting record with their features, the fee for the workshop house is stated as twenty-four *zolotas* per year and *sefaki* house fee as forty-two *zolotas* per year. It has been noted that the house whose income belongs to the workshop in the Sharaf District was rented with the method of *khuluw al-shariʿ*. The annual rental income of this *waqf*, in which the *waqf*'s income was based entirely on houses, was recorded as 396 *zolotas*. When the house rental incomes in the accounting records of the two charitable and family *waqfs* are compared, it has been determined that the majority of the *waqf* income was based on the rental revenues of the houses. These accounting records also indicate that the annual incomes from different house rents varied according to the location and size of the houses.

1.3.3.2.1.2 *Commercial Buildings*

It is known that charity institutions and the properties, which provide income to these institutions, formed the core of the Ottoman city.[421] Although charitable establishments form the center of settlements in rural areas, their impact on development and settlement is limited since *waqf* assets are mostly based on agricultural revenues. In urban centers, commercial and public buildings such as inns (hans), bathhouses (hammams), bakeries, mills, candle workshops, dye houses, slaughterhouses, headhouses, festival and marketplace areas—each constructed to serve a particular social, professional, or commercial group and to generate revenue for charitable institutions—formed the nucleus of a newly established city or neighborhood.[422] With this structuring, both the development of Ottoman cities and commercial dynamism of the cities are provided.

In the relevant period in Jerusalem, 112 commercial enterprises in the city center were transformed into *waqf* properties. The ratio of these among all movable and real estate assets is 14.66%. Commercial businesses, which are reflected in the documents within the scope of the research, are shops with and without shares, bakeries, coffee houses and stores.

1.3.3.2.1.2.1 *Khans* (Inns)

Khan refers to accommodation places built in settlements or trade routes, or to multi-storey and multi-room trade places where the same occupational groups

420 JS 264: 149.

421 Ergin, *Türk Şehirlerinde İmāret*, 18.

422 Barkan, *Osmanlı Devleti'nin Sosyal*, 109.

generally gather.[423] The *khans*, which are built as a courtyard with portico surrounded by cells used by craftsmen, merchants and travelers, are an organization with wooden and extraordinary (upper/lower) floors, halls, water wells, toilets and all outbuildings gathered in a courtyard. The inns are known by the names of the goods they collect and distribute such as *Khan* of Silk and Rice *Khan*. The ground floors of the inns consist of warehouses, and the upper floors consist of rooms built for trading and accommodation.[424] In big cities, commercial shopping was usually done in covered inns. Inns were among the sources of income for the *waqfs*. However, maintenance and repair costs of the inns were also covered by the *waqfs* to which they were affiliated.

There is no established *khan* in Jerusalem during the period under review. In a *waqf* record, a soap factory with a share of twenty-one carat 1/5 was established in *Khan al-Zayt* near *Akbāt Khan*.[425] *Khan al-Zayt* is located in Wādī al-Tawwāḥīn.

1.3.3.2.1.2.2 Stores

Seven stores were endowed in Jerusalem during the period under review. Three of them were located under the endowed house, and four of them were self-contained. Of the stores, all of which were devoted to family savings, two were in Naṣāra Quarter,[426] two were under the big house in the Khaṭṭ Marzubān,[427] and the remaining three were in the *Khaṭṭ al-Tawwāḥīn*.[428]

1.3.3.2.1.2.3 Shops

They are the workplaces where craftsmen or small craft owners manufacture or sell. In the Ottoman period, the shops were mostly wooden or masonry single-storey buildings. Towards the end of the nineteenth century, shops began to be seen in the main trade centers, made of brick and two floors, but always illuminated from one direction, at a height not exceeding five or six

---

423 Raymond, *Osmanlı Döneminde*, 174.

424 Ergenç, *XVI. Yüzyılın*, 29–37; Çiftçi, *Bursa'da Vakıfların*, 101.

425 In the same period, *Khān* in Khaṭṭ Dāwūd in Jerusalem, Bāb al-Shawwāyīn Khān in Khaṭṭ Marzubān; Jībāliyya Khān located near 'Alā' al-Dīn al-Baṣīr Bath in Shaykh Muḥammad al-Kirīmī Quarter; in the Bāb al-Qaṭṭānīn Quarter, there was the Shi'āra Khān, which was built in 964/1556 and located in the Khāssekī Sulṭān *Waqf* 'Imāra Khān and Wicker Bazaar. For detailed information, see al-Ḥanbalī, *al-Uns al-Jalīl*, p. 53; al-Madanī *Awqāf al-Quds*, 312.

426 JS 217: 359–360.

427 JS 205: 108–110.

428 File 2/21: 1194/13.

meters. Shops were commercial spaces that were usually lined up on both sides and side by side in a street. Some of these were located inside the covered bazaars, *sūqs* and inns.

Bazaars with shops were named according to the group of tradesmen working there. Bazaars in the Ottoman city occupied a physical area varying between 6% and 10% of the urbanized area. Trade and craft areas would be concentrated in one or more streets lined with shops and workshops, leaving out dwellings absolutely. The life arteries of the Ottoman city were thrown in the bazaar more than anywhere else, production and "economic value" meant more than a place of shopping. In the cities, bazaars, inns, *arasta* and shops were commercial centers.[429]

During the period covered by the study, Jerusalem's bazaars included *Sūq Bāb al-Ḥuṭṭa* (Ḥuṭṭa Gate),[430] *Sūq Bāb al-ʿAmūd* (Damascus Gate),[431] *Sūq Bāb al-Qaṭṭānīn* (Cotton Producers),[432] were located at the gates opening to the *Ḥaram al-Sharīf*. The *Sūq al-Yahūd* (Jewish Bazaar),[433] *Sūq al-Ṭabbākhīn* (Cooks),[434] *Sūq al-Ṣāgha* (Jewelers)[435] and *Sūq al-Ḥaṣīr* (Wickers)[436] Bazaars were mentioned in the *waqf* bazaars.[437] While defining the locations of the shops devoted in Jerusalem in the relevant period, they were defined according to their locations in the said bazaars.[438] *Khan al-Zayt* Bazaar was also an important bazaar with *waqf* shops.[439] In addition to these bazaars, besides the

429 Raymond, *Osmanlı Döneminde*, 162–174.

430 The market located at *Ḥuṭṭa Gate,* one of the gates opening to the *ḥaram*, is separate from all the bazaars in the city. al-ʿĀrif, *al-Mufaṣṣal*, 468.

431 Located in the *Bāb al-ʿAmūd* Quarter, the bazaar was between the *Khān al-Zayt* Bazaar in the south and the Damascus Gate in the north. al-ʿĀrif, *al-Mufaṣṣal*, 468.

432 The bazaar in the *Bāb al-Qattānīn* District was located to the west of the *Ḥaram*. At the end of the bazaar, on the west side, there is the *ʿAyn Bath*. al-ʿĀrif, *al-Mufaṣṣal*, 468.

433 It is located in the Jewish Quarter. The Bazaar extends from the north to the Merchants Bazaar known as the Grand Bazaar, and from the south it is close to Nabī Dawūd. al-ʿĀrif, *al-Mufaṣṣal*, 467.

434 The bazaar in *Khaṭṭ Dāwūd* extends to the Harāfiş Stairs in Cebīliyye Arch. Al-Ḥanbalī, *al-Uns al-Jalīl*, p. 53.

435 The bazaar stretches from the mosque gate to *Dār al-Qur'an*. Al-Ḥanbalī, *al-Uns al-Jalīl*, p. 53.

436 The Wickers Bazaar borders the Bazaar from the east and the Butchers Bazaar from the south. al-ʿArif, *al-Mufaṣṣal*, p. 468.

437 For detailed information about the bazaars, see Al-Ḥanbalī, *al-Uns al-Jalīl*, p. 50–53; al-ʿĀrif, *al-Mufaṣṣal*, p. 467–468; Sūwāriyya, *al-Hayāt al-Ijtimāʿiyya*, 55–56.

438 E.g. JS 207: 129–130; 218: 156; 218: 253; 223: 161; 227:144; 255: 120–122; 276: 141; 298: 208; 314: 123.

439 E.g. JS 239: 50; 456: 36.

Merchant Bazaar in Jerusalem, there were also bazaars known as the Spice Bazaar and Butchers Bazaar, which were called by the relevant profession. In addition, all of the bazaars from the *Ḥaram al-Sharīf* to the castle were referred to as the Grand Bazaar in the records.[440]

During the study's period, fifty-three shops in Jerusalem were endowed as *waqf*. Additionally, thirty-seven shop shares were endowed with varying ownership fractions.[441] Notably, twelve *qīrāṭ* shop shares with *khuluww* rights were endowed near the Karīmiyya *Madrasa Waqf* on the bazaar's border,[442] three *qīrāṭ* shops with *khuluww* rights on the bazaar border in *Khaṭṭ Dāwūd*,[443] and three *qīrāṭ* shop shares with *khuluww* rights in the adjacent *Khaṭṭ* Bazaar.[444] Furthermore, a coffee shop in *Khaṭṭ Marzibān*[445] and a weaving shop in Bāb al-ʿAmūd Quarter were endowed, with their specific types noted.[446]

Among all assets endowed, shops rank second among all assets with a rate of 14.66%. As a result, endowers have dedicated their considerable number of shops, especially located inside the bazaars and khans, to generate income for their *waqf*s to continue their services.

In the Accounting Register dated 1168 AH/1755 CE of the *Waqf* of Shaykh Khalīl al-Jāʿūnī's wife, established as a family *waqf*, no commercial structures are listed among the *waqf* revenues. In the Accounting Register of the Maghāriba *Waqf*, a charitable *waqf*, dated 1153 AH/1740 CE, eight shop revenue items were recorded: a shop in the Grand Bazaar paid 11 *zoloṭa* per month, a shop in Bāb al-Tawwāḥīn paid 8 *zoloṭa* per month, a shop opposite the Qishqish (Qoshqosh) house paid 13 *zoloṭa* per month, four *ḥaddād* (blacksmith) shops with unspecified locations paid 3 *zoloṭa* per month each, a shop occupied by Dervish Meḥmed paid 3 *zoloṭa* per month, and a shop occupied by Badr paid 4 *zoloṭa* per month. The rental income of the shop registered as the Sulaymān shop was not specified, but a shop inhabited by Jews recorded a rental income of 35 *zoloṭa* per month. While *waqf* shop rents generally ranged from 3 to 13 *zoloṭa* per month, similar to *waqf* house rents, the 35 *zoloṭa* per month for the shop occupied by Jews, with an unspecified location, stands out as notably high.

---

440 E.g. JS 254: 518.
441 For detailed information, see Table 7.
442 See JS 246; 252: 35–36.
443 See JS 251: 139–141.
444 See JS 220: 161.
445 See File 2/21: 194/13.
446 See JS 221: 331.

1.3.3.2.1.2.4 *Hammams* (Public Baths)

Baths are social in terms of public cleanliness, industrial in terms of producing hot water with certain technical equipment, and economic institutions in terms of having a very high income in the city and *waqf* economy.[447] The construction of baths and fountains in the *kulliye* (complex), which was the most central structure of the Ottoman city, was earlier than other institutions. There are two main reasons for this. The first is the cleaning of the workers in the construction of the complex,[448] and the second is the contribution of the income to be made to this *imāret*. There is no bathhouse in Jerusalem dedicated to the period that falls within the study area.

1.3.3.2.1.3 *Industrial Enterprises*

Industrial enterprises that provide income to the *waqf*s in Jerusalem were small sized organizations. Industrial enterprises, which were endowed as a total of 29 items, constitute 3.80% of *waqf* income sources. In this sector, there were *maʿsara, mahmas, karhane*, mill, bakery, and potter.

1.3.3.2.1.3.1 *Maʿṣara* (Press House)

Also called *mengenehāne*, it refers to a press used for producing sesame and olive oil. One *maʿṣara* was endowed in Jerusalem, located in a ruined state in the *Ḥayādira* Quarter, established by Shaykh Muḥammad Sunʿ Allāh ibn Khalīl Effendi. Al-Suwāriyya noted two separate presses in *Khaṭṭ Marzibān* and *Rīsha* Quarter, recorded in registers from the second half of the eighteenth century.[449]

1.3.3.2.1.3.2 *Maḥmaṣ* (Grinder)

Primarily used for grinding coffee, two *maḥmaṣ* were endowed in Jerusalem. The first, near the bazaar in *Khaṭṭ Dāwūd*, was endowed by Muḥammad Bey ibn Aḥmad Bey ibn al-Amīr.[450] The second, renovated with *khuluww* rights adjacent to the *Afḍaliyya Madrasa*, was endowed by *Naqīb al-Ashrāf*, ʿAbd al-Laṭīf Effendi.[451]

---

447 Eyice, "Hamam," 402.

448 Yediyıldız, "XVIII. Asır," 28.

449 For detailed information, see al-Sūwāriyya, *al-Hayāt al-Ijtimāʿiyya*, 61.

450 See JS 246.

451 See JS 281: 12–14.

1.3.3.2.1.3.3 *Kārhāne* (Workshop)

Businesses that could be defined as workshops were usually endowed with all the tools and materials belonging to a craft or professional organization. The revenues of such businesses that were rented out were transferred to the *waqf* institution. Workshops were mostly used or rented by artisans who produced goods.

During the period in question, four workshop *waqf*s owned by individuals and eight workshop shares were turned into *waqf*s. While only one of these was a brickworks, the others were soap works. The soap produced by processing olive oil in Jerusalem during the Ottoman period was exported to Egypt.[452]

Shaykh Sharaf al-Dīn Muḥammad ibn Muḥammad al-Khalīlī endowed two soap factories in the Bāb al-ʿAmūd neighborhood.[453] Unlike other workshops, the brick workshop, located in the Khān al-Zayt bazaar south of Abū Shamāt Street, was dedicated by al-Ḥajj Muṣṭafā ibn al-Ḥajj Kuwaydar.[454] Additionally, a workshop in the Bāb al-ʿAmūd Quarter was endowed to Jerusalem's deputy *Naqīb al-Ashrāf*, ʿAbd al-Laṭīf Effendi.[455]

The first two shared workshops are soap factories in the Naṣāra Quarter, one with 12 *qīrāṭ* shares and the other with one *qīrāṭ* and 1.5 shares, endowed by Muḥammad Sunʿ Allāh Effendi ibn Khalīl Effendi al-Khālidī. The third shared workshop, located in the Khān al-Zayt Bazaar, was established by Muḥammad Sunʿ Allāh Effendi ibn Khalīl Effendi al-Khālidī with a twenty-one *qīrāṭ* and 1/5 share. The fourth workshop, with six *qīrāṭ* shares in the Sharaf Quarter, was endowed by Jerusalem architect Ibrāhīm Çelebi ibn Ḥibbat Allāh al-Namrī. A workshop with 9/10 and half *qīrāṭ* shares on Muṣliḥ Bukhāra al-Sharaf Street was also endowed by Ibrāhīm Çelebi ibn Ḥibbat Allāh al-Namrī. The sixth shared workshop, with 4 *qīrāṭ* shares across two villages, was dedicated to Jerusalem architect Ṣādiq ibn Ibrāhīm al-Namrī. The seventh, located opposite the Castle, was endowed by Ḥamūda Basha ibn Aḥmad al-Qandiljī with a six *qīrāṭ* share. The eighth, a workshop with 8 *qīrāṭ* shares in the Bāb al-ʿAmūd Quarter, was endowed by Muḥammad ibn Badr ibn Muḥammad. All workshops were endowed for family disposition.

1.3.3.2.1.3.4 Mills

Referred to as *ṭāḥūn* and *āsiyāb* in the documents, mills were endowed along with their millstone (*ḥajar*), vineyard, barn, and all outbuildings. These

452 al-Asali, "Jerusalem," 200–24.
453 See JS 221: 331.
454 See JS 239: 50; 456: 36.
455 JS, 28: 12–14.

structures housed tools for grinding grain into flour, with wheel-shaped millstones powered by water or wind to crush the grains into flour.[456]

In Jerusalem, one foundation mill and two shared mills were recorded. Though less common, these mills, referred to as *ṭāḥūn* and *āsiyāb*, were significant investment assets, generating income for *waqfs* through rentals. As high-capital enterprises, they were not widely owned. The *khuluww* right of the first mill in the Armenian Quarter was endowed by Jerusalem's *Naqīb al-Ashrāf*, Ḥasan ibn ʿAbd al-Laṭīf al-Ḥusaynī. The second mill, in the Jewish Quarter, was dedicated by Barīra bint al-Ḥajj Shahāda Abū Laḥya with a twelve *qīrāṭ* and 1/6 share. The third, a 1/4 *qīrāṭ* share of the Murād Pasha Mill on the Bāb al-Qaṭṭānīn line, was endowed by Maḥbūba Khātūn, daughter of ʿAlaybeyzāde.

The annual rental income of the mill recorded in the Maghāriba *Waqf*'s accounting register was 36 *zoloṭa*, an average amount compared to shop rents from other *waqfs*. A provision in the Damascus *Ahkām* Register granted Jerusalem's Jewish community the right to use any mill, but restricted certain "irregular" individuals to a specific mill; their objections were overruled to maintain this restriction. This indicates that different religious communities could jointly access mills. The high consumption of bread, a staple for Ottoman society and particularly Jerusalem's residents, necessitated broad accessibility to mills.

1.3.3.2.1.3.5 Pottery House

Pottery, produced in houses referred to as *fakhūra* in the documents, was a developed craft in Jerusalem, primarily for storing water and olive oil and, secondarily, for sale to pilgrims visiting the city. In the *waqfiyya* record, Alfiyya bint Yūsuf al-Jibālī endowed a pottery house for the benefit of the *Zāwiya* Nabī Dāwūd.[457]

1.3.3.2.1.3.6 Bakery

These are commercial enterprises that meet the basic needs of the people in cities regarding bakery products such as bread and pastries. It is an essential social institution like a bath and a mill. These businesses are leased to finance the *waqfs*. In addition, ovens can be named according to the product they produce, such as donut bakery. Four furnaces and six furnace shares in Jerusalem were registered among the *waqf* assets. The emphasis was on the shares owned in the ovens whose type was not specified.[458] In the Accounting Register of the

456 Yediyıldız, "XVIII. Asır," 12.

457 See JS 243: 36–37.

458 For detailed information, see Table A13.

Maghāriba *Waqf*, it was stated that there was an unproductive bakery in the Maghāriba Neighborhood and no rental income was recorded.[459]

1.3.3.2.1.4 *Agricultural Lands and Enterprises*

Among the sources of income of *waqf* institutions, agricultural land and enterprises constituted the most important sources of agricultural production.[460] These revenues consisted of agricultural areas and businesses such as land, vineyards, gardens, farms, villages, arable fields and mills. Agricultural income sources were generally located around the city or in villages close to the city. These sources of income explained the relationship between the city and its surroundings on the one hand, and on the other hand, it revealed the connection of *waqf* institutions in the city with the provinces. In this case, while the charity or condition of the *waqf* was in the city center, all or part of the main income generating resources could be outside the city. Especially in large-scale *waqfs*, there were income collectors assigned to collect the income of one or more villages in order to collect the income of the *waqfs* in the provinces and villages.

Most of the lands and gardens owned by the *waqfs* were rented and the rental income from these real estates was transferred to the various expenses of the *waqf*. The crops of some of the vineyards and gardens grown on them were endowed, and income was provided to the *waqfs* in this way. In the relevant period, 44 *waqfs* in Jerusalem had included various agricultural areas and businesses among their real estates. The ratio of this number from *waqf* assets to 300 *waqf* is 13.2%. In other words, 13.2% of the *waqfs* established in Jerusalem chose their income from real estate properties, agricultural fields and enterprises. In this way, a total of 44 units of agricultural areas and businesses in and around Jerusalem had turned into a *waqf*. On the other hand, while the number of agricultural lands and enterprises devoted in the city center was 48 and its ratio to all mites was 6.28%, this number was 65 in the central villages and arable fields and 8.51% for all assets.

1.3.3.2.1.4.1 Lands

In *waqfiyyas*, lands refer to agricultural fields within or around Jerusalem, varying in size. Some *waqf* records specify field sizes, while others describe boundaries using the phrase *qiṭʿat arāḍī*. According to the documents, seven *waqf*

459 See JS 224: 185–187.

460 Yediyıldız, "XVIII. Asır," 7.

lands were located in Jerusalem's center, fourteen were in surrounding villages, fourteen were shared lands, and one share of supply was registered.[461]

In addition to fiefs, classified as *mīrī* land (state-owned land with certain farmer rights), Jerusalem's land ownership system included lands endowed for public benefit, religious purposes, or individuals by their owners. *Waqf* lands formed a small portion of cultivated land in the *Sanjāq* of Jerusalem, constituting 2.49% of all *waqf* assets. The Ottomans preserved Mamlūk *waqf*s and added new ones during the sixteenth and seventeenth centuries. Apart from fiefs and *waqf*s, there were some estates, mostly in towns and villages and around them.[462] From this point of view, the rate of land *waqf* in Jerusalem seems relatively low. This rate is 2.49% when looking at all *waqf* assets. The *Waqf* trustee of the Dome of the Rock, Ibrāhīm ibn al-Shaykh ʿAbd al-Qādir al-Danaf (al-Anṣārī), and the district governor, *Naqīb al-Ashrāf*, noted that some lands were acquired through inheritance.[463]

1.3.3.2.1.4.2 Vineyard, Garden and Vegetable Garden

These agricultural areas, distinguished by function and size, are separately defined in *waqfiyyas*. Vineyards and gardens were significant revenue sources for Jerusalem's *waqf*s. Vineyards, referred to as *karm-i ʿinab* and *bund-i kürüm* in documents, were small fields, typically a few acres (ranging from one to twenty-five acres), growing fruits like grapes, pomegranates, figs, and citrus. Gardens, meaning small vineyards and orchards, were often wetlands or areas near settlements suitable for vegetable cultivation. Vegetable gardens, termed *ḥaqūra*, were dedicated to growing various vegetables.[464] Vineyards and gardens were generally enclosed areas located in or around the city. Some *waqfiyyas* specify types of fruit and vegetable gardens, with olive, apricot, fig, walnut, and date orchards being common in Jerusalem.[465]

While two vineyards were endowed in the center of Jerusalem in the relevant period, sixteen gardens expressed with the word "*ḥaqūra*" and twenty-two shared gardens were endowed. In the central villages and arable fields, three

---

461 Regarding the location of the lands, see Table 10; See also, e.g., al-Shaykh ʿAbdullāh Efendi ibn al-Shaykh Ibrāhīm al-Danaf (al-Anṣārī) endowed land in ʿĪsāwiyya village. JS 252: 68. ʿAbdullāh ibn Ibrāhīm Ṣāliḥ al-Dāwūdī likewise devoted land to a scarcity in the village of ʿĪsāwiyya. JS 252.

462 Ze'evi, *Kudüs*, 3.

463 See respectively. File 3/34: 210/13; JS 281: 12–14.

464 Alkan, *Adana Vakıfları*, 134.

465 E.g. JS 227: 179; JS 250: 130.

vineyards,[466] three gardens and a shared garden were dedicated.[467] In addition to these, a vegetable garden with a fountain was endowed.[468]

Although olive groves in Jerusalem were also endowed in gardens, they were also stated in two *waqfiyyas*. The first of these was the olive grove in the Yūsufiyya Land,[469] the second was the olive grove in the Bayt Safāfā Village, which was devoted with six *qirat* 1/6 share.[470]

Beside the gardens, there are also several acres of land devoted to vegetable cultivation, surrounded by stone walls or ditches.[471] In the relevant period, a orchard in Jaffa and its incomes were donated by al-Shaykh Şerefeddin Muḥammad ibn Muḥammad al-Khalíli and whose limits were specified in his *waqfiyya*.[472]

In the Accounting Register of the Maghāriba *Waqf*, the annual rental income of the garden near Shaykh ʿAyd is recorded as 7 *zolota*, while the rental income of the garden in the village of ʿAyn Kārim was 30 *zolota* and the annual income of another garden in the village of ʿAyn Kārim was recorded as 8 *zolota*.[473] It was stated that a garden in the accounting record was unproductive.

1.3.3.2.1.4.3 *Mezraʿa* (Arable Lands)

Among agricultural sources of income were the *mezraʿa* and cultivated fields, which were typically located at a greater distance from inhabited areas. The term *mezraʿa* refers to an extensive tract of arable land—ranging from one to one hundred hectares—without a permanent settlement on it,[474] and was used to describe either abandoned villages or lands reclaimed and cultivated by neighboring communities.[475]

During the period in question, while only one *mezraʿa* was endowed within the city center of Jerusalem, the number increased considerably in the surrounding areas and nearby villages, reaching fourteen *mezraʿas* and

466 The first of these vineyards was established in Bekaa Valley and was defined as "Khuluww-ı medresetu'l-belediyye, Khuluww-ı sūkü'l-kattānīn ve karyetü'l-Ceyb Vakf-ı Sultan Īnāl." This shows that the aforementioned bond was rented from these *waqfs* in the *Khuluww* method. JS 221: 331.

467 For the locations and numbers of vineyards and orchards, see Table A14.

468 JS 229: 50.

469 JS 221: 331.

470 File 2/21: 1194/13.

471 For the eighteenth century see Yediyıldız, *XVIII. Yüzyılda*, 99.

472 JS 221: 331.

473 JS 224: 185–187.

474 Yediyıldız, *XVIII. Yüzyılda*, 100.

475 İnalcık and Quataert (eds.), *The Ottoman State*, 454.

twenty-eight *mezraʿa* shares (*hissas*).[476] As shown in Appendix 19, numerous *mezraʿas* were endowed in regions such as the Bekaʿa Valley, the Tabl Valley, the village of ʿIsāwiyya, Bayt Ṣafāfa, Arḍ-i Miṣrāra, the village of Bayt Iksā, the village of Abū Sūr, the village of Jayb, the Seyfī Mencik estate, the Mount of Olives (Jabal al-Zaytūn), the Ṣalāḥiyya estate, Wādī al-Jawz, Karm al-Aswad, the Simār land, the Qadūm Valley, the Deyr-i Sinne (Sene) estate, and Sawāna. The proportion of these thirty-four *mezraʿas*—endowed in various shares and numbers outside the city—within the total of other extra-urban *aqārāt* amounted to 46 percent.

1.3.3.2.1.4.4 Water Tank

Among the outbuildings of agricultural enterprises in Jerusalem, pools, water closets, and water channels were common, indicating irrigated agriculture in the region. During the relevant period, a water tank in ʿArḍ al-Miṣrāra was endowed as part of the *waqf* of Muḥammad Ṣāliḥ Effendi ibn ʿAbd al-Ghanī al-Imām.[477] Most houses in Jerusalem featured a water cistern for storing rainwater and snow, likely due to vineyards and orchards serving as water sources in homes with gardens.

1.3.3.2.2 Movable Goods

The question of whether movable goods – items that can be transported – could be endowed was a significant issue in *waqf* law.[478] Early Islamic jurists deemed the endowment of movable properties inappropriate, but changing economic and social conditions led to a reinterpretation within Islamic legal frameworks. Imam Muḥammad ibn al-Ḥasan al-Shaybānī, a student of Abū Ḥanīfa, authorized the endowment of movable properties. Abū Ḥanīfa's students, Imam Yūsuf and Imam Muḥammad, permitted such endowments provided they were linked to real estate, while another Ḥanafī jurist, Imam Zufar, considered *waqfs* of movable goods valid regardless of real estate affiliation.[479] Among the movable goods subject to the *waqf*, movable goods such as money, gold, books, animal skin, ships, household items, agricultural tools, craft tools can be counted.

Household goods, couple tools, cash money, gold and various goods were recorded as movable properties in the *waqfiyyas* of Jerusalem *waqfs*. Among

476 For detailed information, see Table A13 and A14.

477 JS 297: 86.

478 Yediyıldız, 'XVIII. Asır', p. 5.

479 For detailed information on the *waqf* of movable goods, see Akgündüz, *İslam Hukukunda*, 202–233.

the income sources of the 300 *waqfs* established in the city in the years that entered the study period, movable goods were also endowed. Their numbers were 6 and their ratio to all assets was 0,78%. When this ratio is considered, *waqfs* of movable goods came in the last place among the properties established in Jerusalem. The book *waqfs* excluded from this number which did not generate income for the *waqf*.

1.3.3.2.2.1 *Nuqūd* (*Cash*) Waqfs

Cash *waqfs* had been a subject of debate since the 16th century when it became widespread. Although its origins are not clearly known, it is accepted that cash *waqfs* were introduced by the Ottomans.[480] In *waqfs* established before the Ottomans, the first condition was that only immovable property could be endowed and that the endowed property could be used indefinitely. Since cash is a movable wealth, it is clearly more difficult to preserve in the long term. For this reason, monetary wealth or precious metals were excluded from the *waqf* system.[481] By the 16th century, Ottoman scholars had affirmed the legitimacy of *nuqūd* (cash) *waqfs* through treatises and *fatāwā* they issued. However, some Ottoman jurists, such as Çivizāde and Birgivī, opposed the endowment of cash.[482]

Since it is forbidden to take interest (*ribāʿ*) in Islamic law, the cash *waqf* seemed legally impossible, was severely condemned and questioned. One of those who approached the debate from a utilitarian point of view, *Shaykh al-Islām* Ebussuud Effendi (d.1574) allowed the establishment of cash *waqfs* on the grounds they were already widely practiced (*tecâmül ve teʿârüf*), contributed to public welfare (*istihsān*), and had been previously sanctioned by earlier judges.[483] Ömer Lütfi Barkan highlighted that, from the second half of the 16th century onward, there was a notable increase in the allocation of cash assets (*nukūd tahsīsī*) in public endowments (*âmme vakıfları*) established by prominent figures among the populace, particularly in traditional real estate properties such as caravanserais, bathhouses, homes, vineyards, and gardens. This trend led to intensified debates in the 16th and 17th centuries over which movable assets could be endowed, with a particular focus on cash *waqfs*.[484]

---

480 J. E. Mandaville, "Usurious Piety: The Cash Waqf Controversy in the Ottoman Empire," *International Journal of Middle East Studies* 10, no. 3 (1979): 289–308.

481 Timur Kuran, "The Provision of Public Goods under Islamic Law: Origins, Impact, and Limitations of the Waqf System," Law & Society Review 35, no. 4 (2001): 841–98, 846.

482 Özcan, *Osmanlı Para Vakıfları*, 36–38, 47–50.

483 On cash foundations see Imber, *Ebu's-Suʿud*, 142–46; Çizakça, "Cash *Waqfs*," 313–54.

484 Barkan, "Edirne Askerī," 34.

In the Ottoman Empire, income from endowed cash was typically generated through a method known as *mu'āmele-i şer'iyye* (a legally sanctioned commercial transaction), and these proceeds were spent in accordance with the stipulations of the *waqfiyya*. The management of endowed funds, much like other revenue sources of a *waqf*, was governed by the specific regulations set by the founders themselves. In this regard, nearly every *waqf* founder repeated a similar formula in their endowment deeds regarding the investment and utilization of the endowed capital. The standard wording was as follows: "With a strong mortgage (*rehn-i kāvi*) and a reliable guarantor (*kefīl-i mel'ī*), or one of the two, it shall be lawfully invested (*mu'āmele-i şer'iyye*) at a rate of ten and a half (per hundred), under the supervision of the trustee (*mutawallī*), and each year it shall be profitably invested (*istirbāh*) and lawfully utilized (*istiğlāl*) in a permissible manner (*'alā vechi'l-halāl*)." In simple terms, this clause meant that the endowed cash would be lent at a 15% return to generate income for the *waqf*.[485]

From the 15th century onwards, the Ottomans added a new quality and practice to the *waqf* culture with this new type of cash *waqfs*. In addition to the real estate *waqfs* established by high state officials such as sultans and viziers, they also made legal arrangements to enable the non-wealthy segments of society to convert their small cash savings into *waqfs*. For instance, the oldest cash *waqf* that Mandeville[486] could reach in Ottoman history was in Edirne and was established by Yağcı Hācī Muslihuddin in 1423. The *waqf* here consisted of a few shops and 10,000 akçe; the condition of the *waqf* was that the shops would be rented out and the cash would be used as a 10% *ribh* and the Quran would be read in the *Kilise Camii* (Church Mosque) every day for 1 aķçe with the proceeds. Again, it is seen that cash *waqfs* were also used by the palace in the same century. Uzunçarşılı also narrates a *waqf* established by Fatih Sultan Mehmed by endowing 24,000 gold coins and stipulating that its interest (*nemā*) would be used as a subsidy to protect the Janissaries' meat needs from inflation.[487] This not only paved the way for individuals with modest budgets to establish *waqfs*, but also expanded the supply of credit in a society where interest was prohibited, enabling individuals to borrow the money they needed for small-scale consumption and production. During the 16th century, the number of cash *waqfs* in Istanbul increased considerably.[488] Recent studies also

485 Yediyıldız, "XVIII. Asır," 23.

486 Mandaville, "Usurious Piety," 290.

487 Uzunçarşılı, *Kapıkulu Ocakları*, 1:254.

488 Ömer Lütfi Barkan and Ekrem Hakkı Ayverdi, *İstanbul Vakıfları Tahrîr Defteri: 953 (1546) Târîhli* (Istanbul: İstanbul Fetih Cemiyeti İstanbul Enstitüsü, 1970).

suggest that over time, the ratio of cash *waqfs* to real estate *waqfs* increasingly favored cash *waqfs*, a trend that persisted until the 19th century when their establishment became more frequent.[489]

The evidence from eighteenth-century Jerusalem, however, challenges this perspective. Cash *waqfs* constituted a mere 0,65% of all endowments established in the city during this period, with only five documented instances. As previously noted, the first charitable cash *waqf* was founded in 1151 AH/1738 CE by Ḥusayn Pasha ibn ʿAbbās, Guardian of Damascus, Jerusalem, Gaza, and Nablus, and *Amīr al-Ḥajj*, who endowed 500 Esedī *kurūsh*.[490] The second was established by al-Ḥajj Muṣṭafā Agha, deputy governor of Jerusalem, with a donation of 40 *līra zahab*.[491] The third, endowed in 1185 AH/1771 CE by Amīna bint Muḥammad Effendi, allocated 10 *kurūsh* for purchasing and maintaining lamps to illuminate the *minaret* of the Dome of the Rock.[492] The fourth, established by Khalīl in 1231 AH/1816 CE, contributed 10 *dirhams* to Masjid *al-Aqṣā*.[493] The fifth and final cash *waqf*, with an undated *waqfiyya*, was founded by Muṣṭafā Effendi, Qāḍī al-ʿAsākir al-Sulṭāniyya, who designated an unspecified sum for charitable purposes.[494] Notably, the revenue from these new cash *waqfs* constituted only a small fraction of Jerusalem's overall *waqf* resources, highlighting their limited economic impact in the city during this period.

Singer observes that cash *waqfs* remained underdeveloped in the Arabic-speaking regions of the empire that had been Muslim prior to the Ottoman conquest,[495] a situation likely influenced by the divergent opinions of various *madhāhib* (legal schools).[496] In Jerusalem, however, these cash *waqfs* were founded by members of the Ottoman ruling elite appointed to the city, indicating that these *waqfs* were managed by a competent group capable of addressing both confessional sensitivities and legal complexities.

As a result, it was seen that in the period examined, there were almost all kinds of investment vehicles, movable and real estate among the sources that

489 Murat Çizakça, "İktisat Tarihi Açısından Vakıflar," *Vakıflar Dergisi* 80, no. Yıl Özel Sayısı (2018): 75–92, 75.

490 JS 228: 224.

491 JS 230: 210. In addition, fourteen loaves of bread to be bought from the Khasseki Sultan *Imāret* was allocated to the person who puts water in the fountain of the *waqf*.

492 JS 254: 161.

493 JS 290: 1.

494 JS. 196: 429.

495 Singer, *Osmanlı'da Hayırseverlik*, 22. See also for detailed information. Mandaville, "Usurious Piety," 298.

496 For a comment mentioned in Yediyıldız (*XVIII. Century*, 117), see footnote 339; Faroqhi, *Osmanlı Dünyasında*, 193.

financed the income and maintenance of the *waqf*s established in Jerusalem. Houses have stood out among the *waqf* income sources in the city. In a way, this situation drew the main chart of the *waqf* economy in the relevant period and region.

1.3.4 Operating Procedures of *Waqf* Income Sources

The *waqfiyya*s in Jerusalem during the study period specified rental methods within the *waqf* system, primarily *ijāra wāḥida*, *ḥikr* (or *ḥukr*), and *ijāratayn*, with annual or long-term leasing (*ijāra tawīla*) being the most preferred for evaluating *waqf* properties.[497] *Ijāra wāḥida*, also known as *ijāra ṣaḥīḥa* or *ijāra maʿrūfa*, involved a single rental transaction and was widely used for leasing both land and *waqf* properties. The prevalence of dwelling *waqf*s established during this period likely influenced this preference. Long-term leases typically involved a lump-sum advance payment and a low rental fee, often for up to 90 years, to cover debts or repair costs, with the fee remaining stable despite theoretical variability. Endowers typically stipulated leases of one to three years.[498] *Muqāṭaʿa* (*ḥikr* or *ḥukr*), a form of ground rent, required tenants to maintain buildings and trees on the land, resembling a debt transfer where tenants handled *waqf* repairs. However, such payments often became substantial debts owed to the *waqf*. Recorded in Jerusalem registers as *khuluww al-sharʿ al-marsad ʿalā* (repaired property), these leases were theoretically repurchaseable but, in practice, transferable, inheritable, or even endowable to another *waqf*.[499] When properties lacked tenants for long-term leases or repairs, *waqf* trustees sought judicial approval for *istibdāl*, exchanging properties to meet cash needs or invest elsewhere.

This part of the study, which aims to examine these practices regarding the transactions of *waqf* properties in Jerusalem, will consist of three parts. Firstly, the methods of operation of these properties will be examined. Then, the *khuluww* method will be defined in the leasing of *waqf* properties and some examples related to the applications will be given. In some *waqf*s, the examples of *istibdāl* applied in accordance with the *waqfiyya*s and other land management methods, *ḥikr*, will also be mentioned.

---

497 Demirel, *II. Abdülhamit*, 104.

498 In the eighteenth century, al-Madanī noted that the income sources of newly established Jerusalem *waqf*s were leased for a maximum of one year in fifty-eight waqf charters and up to three years in forty-nine *waqf* charters. This represents approximately 43.5% of all *waqf*s (calculated from 256 *waqf*s in al-Madanī). For detailed information, see al-Madanī, *Awqāf al-Quds*, 130–498.

499 Baer, "Jerusalem's Families," 109–23.

1.3.4.1 Ijāra Wāḥida *and* Ijāra Tawīla

Since the Ottoman annexation, Ḥanafī jurisprudence governed the leasing of lands, houses, and shops in Jerusalem, with *waqf* properties typically leased for one to three years during the study period, predominantly as annual *ijāra wāḥida* (single lease).

Numerous records document this practice. For instance, women named Ḥadīja and ʿĀʾisha, who paid the annual rent for Khān al-ʿUsārī from the Khasseki Sultan *Waqf* in Jerusalem's Yahūd district in Tripoli, operated the *khān*.[500] In another case, Meḥmed ibn al-Ḥārūn seized a mill, an annual rental asset of the Meḥmed Pasha *Waqf*, for several years without paying the requested two-year rent.[501] Similarly, al-Ḥajj ʿAlī endowed a house in Jerusalem leased annually to al-Ḥajj Meḥmed for charity, but the latter failed to pay and embezzled the rent, as reported by Sayyid Aḥmad, Sayyid Dāwūd, Sayyid Khalīl, and Sayyid Ibrāhīm.[502] Records also note that roofed properties like inns, baths, and shops from the Khalīl al-Raḥmān and Dome of the Rock *Waqf*s were leased annually, with tenants receiving a yearly *temessük* (official lease document). However, Jerusalem's judges faced complaints from *waqf* trustees to the Imperial Council, alleging that they leased *waqf* properties to favored individuals, violating decrees and harming the *waqf* for years.[503]

While rural *waqf* land leases were not expected to exceed three years, in practice, the same individuals cultivated village or arable lands for generations. For example, Fayḍ Allāh al-ʿAlamī leased a vegetable garden and room in the Naṣāra neighborhood from his father Muṣṭafā Effendi al-ʿAlamī's *Waqf* for 60 years. Dāwūd ibn Aḥmad Qudsiyya leased a house in Bāb al-ʿAmūd from his father's *Waqf*, Karīmiyya ibn Fakhr al-Dīn Qudsiyya, for 12 years as its trustee.[504] In some other *waqf*s, the lease period was 90, 60, 30 and 15 years.[505]

Inner-city lands were often converted to *muqāṭaʿa* or long-term leases (*ijāra tawīla*). Registers contain numerous such cases. As cited in al-Madanī, a dilapidated plot in the Khān al-Zayt Bazaar from the Bīmāristān Ṣalāḥiyya *Waqf* was rebuilt by Asʿadiyya Ṣūfī Lodge trustees in Mount of Olives, Fayḍ Allāh, ʿAbd al-Raḥmān, and Jawdat Allāh al-ʿAlamī, and leased long-term.[506] A vineyard was leased long-term by Abū al-Hudā and Ṣāliḥ, trustees of the Shaykh Aḥmad al-Ḥakkārī *Waqf* and sons of Shaykh Muḥammad al-ʿAfīfī, a prominent

500 BOA, ADVNS.ŞM (1): 7/1.
501 BOA, ADVNS.ŞM (4): 178/2.
502 BOA, ADVNS.ŞM (7): 91/2.
503 VGMA, 814: 279.
504 al-Madanī, *Awqāf al-Quds*, 118.
505 al-Madanī, *Awqāf al-Quds*, 118–19.
506 al-Madanī, *Awqāf al-Quds*, 117.

Jerusalem family.[507] ʿAbd al-Razzāq al-Luṭfī, trustee and inspector of the Ṣalāḥiyya *Madrasa Waqf*, leased its wheat storage area for 30 years.[508]

Though annual leases were common for vineyards, fields, gardens, vegetable gardens, and plots, some *waqfs* adopted long-term leasing. Records note unpaid rents for such properties. For instance, after the death of the *dhimmī* Andrīyā ibn Ibrāhīm, who leased three gardens from the Dome of the Rock *Waqf* long-term, a known Jerusalem resident seized them, embezzling 585 *kurūsh* (five years' rent). The *mutawallī*, Sulaymān, petitioned the Imperial Council to reclaim the assets.[509] Similarly, vineyards, gardens, and plots in ʿAyn Kārim village, leased long-term for the Abū Madyan al-Ghawth *Waqf*, went unpaid at 75 *kurūsh* annually by *dhimmī* tenants, prompting the *mutawallī* to petition the Imperial Council.[510]

Long-term leases facilitated urban development by enabling structures on *waqf* plots. For example, Shaykh Mūsā ibn ʿAbd al-Wahhāb built a house on a plot from the Ibrāhīm al-Namrī *Waqf*, a former Jerusalem head architect. After Shaykh Mūsā's death, known individuals seized the house, which was meant for his sons, Sayyid Ibrāhīm and Sayyid ʿAbdullāh.[511]

1.3.4.2 Khuluww *al-Sharʿ*

Khuluww, meaning "empty" in its literal sense, carries diverse legal meanings, primarily referring to the right of usufruct over a property's *raqaba* (underlying ownership) in exchange for a payment, often for repairs or other purposes. As noted by Akgündüz, the Circassian Mamlūk Sultan Qānṣūh al-Ghawrī (r. 850–922 AH/1446–1516 CE) applied *khuluww* to *waqf* shops called *jamlūn* in Egypt, transferring tenancy rights to merchants for a fee, with each shop appraised separately.[512]

According to al-Madanī's study of Jerusalem *Sharīʿa* court registers, between 1700–1800 CE, 25 family *waqfs* and 17 charitable *waqfs* in Jerusalem were leased via *khuluww*.[513] Families such as ʿAsalī, Daqāq, Jāʿūnī, Ashā, and Dajjānī leased

507 al-Madanī, *Awqāf al-Quds*, 117.

508 al-Madanī, *Awqāf al-Quds*, 118.

509 BOA, ADVNS.ŞM (4): 163/1.

510 BOA, ADVNS.ŞM (4): 163/2.

511 BOA, ADVNS.ŞM (7): 100/1.

512 For detailed information, see Akgündüz, *İslam Hukukunda*, 506–15.

513 Ten of the charitable applications in the *khuluww* method were from the Dome of the Rock *Waqf*, and the others were *Bīmāristān* Ṣalāḥiyya; ʿAlāʾ al-Dīn al-Baṣīr; *Zāwiya* Shaykh Muḥammad al-Kirīmī; Barakat *Khān*; Ḥusayniyya *Madrasa*; Kāmiliyya *Madrasa*; Āminiyya *Madrasa*. It has been determined that it is implemented jointly by Sulṭān Ḥammām *Waqfs* of Khāssekī Sulṭān Waqf and Ḥalīl al-Raḥmān and Ṣaḥrat Allāh *Waqfs*

properties using *khuluww*, while social-purpose leases were made by Jāʿūnī, Muwakkīt, *Muftī*, and ʿAsqar families.[514] As stated in Madani, the trustee of the Amīniyya *Madrasa Waqf* leased its properties via *khuluww* for repairs.[515] In another example, also with the *qāḍī*'s permission, the Kāmiliyya *Madrasa* leased properties for maintenance via *khuluww*.[516] These cases show that charitable *waqf*s could use *khuluww* with *qāḍī* approval.

Jerusalem registers indicate that individuals could hold multiple *khuluww* contracts simultaneously. For example, one *khuluww* was leased from the Dome of the Rock *Waqf* for repairing a mill wall in Khaṭṭ Dāwūd, while another was leased from the ʿAbdullāh al-Muwakkīt *Waqf* for maintenance.[517] Assets leased via *khuluww* included houses, coffeehouses, bakeries, *madrasas*, and baths.[518] The most expensive *khuluww* lease, a house from the Tāj al-Dīn al-Dajjānī *Waqf*, cost 1,220 *zoloṭa*.[519] A coffeehouse from the Dome of the Rock *Waqf* cost 660 *zoloṭa*, and the lowest was 27 *zoloṭa*.[520] *Khuluww* rights were also traded; for instance, Shaykh Fayḍ Allāh Effendi of the *Ḥaram al-Sharīf*, Ismāʿīl Bostancı, and Ibrāhīm Hindī sold *khuluww* rights for a coffeehouse via *marsadan khuluwwan*[521] method for 550 *zoloṭa* to fund repairs for the Dome of the Rock *Waqf*.[522] Salmān and Badr ibn Muḥammad Quṭayna purchased *khuluww* rights for a *waqf* oven from Muḥammad al-Muwakkīt for 27 *zoloṭa*.[523]

(and also by Ṣaḥrat Allāh and *Ḥaramayn Sharīfayn Waqf*s). al-Madanī, *Awqāf al-Quds*, 119–20.

514 For detailed information, see al-Madanī, *Awqāf al-Quds*, 119–23.

515 JS 201: 7.

516 JS 213: 82.

517 al-Madanī, *Awqāf al-Quds*, 119–120.

518 al-Madanī, *Awqāf al-Quds*, 119–120.

519 al-Madanī, *Awqāf al-Quds*, 119–120.

520 al-Madanī, *Awqāf al-Quds*, 122.

521 *Marsad* literally means a place or method of watching and waiting. In *waqf* law, it refers to a long-term lease. This method allows leasing properties for nine or ten years under a long-term rental agreement, provided the *waqf*'s benefit is preserved. Though rooted in the Ḥanbalī law school, it is also accepted in the Ḥanafī law school and Ottoman practice. Legally, *marsad* applies when a *waqf* lacks income, needs repairs, and cannot be leased for cash rent. In such cases, the trustee borrows a sum to repair the *waqf* property, making the *waqf*'s legal entity the debtor to the creditor. The repaired building is leased to the creditor at a rental fee, with the rent offsetting the debt, under a conditional repair-lease contract called *marsad*. In practice, buildings or similar structures, whether funded by the trustee's loan or the creditor's direct expenditure, remain *waqf* property. The *waqf*'s debt is repaid through rent, and the tenant who covers repair costs can use the repaired *waqf* property for a minimal fee. Akgündüz, *İslam Hukukunda* ve Osmanlı, 499.

522 al-Madanī, *Awqāf al-Quds*, 122.

523 al-Madanī, *Awqāf al-Quds*, 122.

Baer identified 63 documents from Jerusalem registers (1805–1814 CE) recording *khuluww*, *ḥikr*, *ijāra tawīla*, and *istibdāl* transactions. A 1228 AH/1813 CE document notes a dilapidated soap factory in Khān al-Zayt leased long-term for 24 *zoloṭa* annually, with repair costs covered via *khuluww*. The tenant built a *khān*, coffeehouse, bakery, and shops, and after their death, heirs sold the *khuluww* rights, splitting the long-term rent. New tenants, with *qāḍī* approval, restored the soap factory, incurring 23,755 *kurūsh* in costs, raising the property's value to 31,755 *kurūsh* from 8,000 *kurūsh*.[524] This illustrates *khuluww*'s prevalence in early nineteenth-century Jerusalem.

Jerusalem *Sharīʿa* court records from the study period show frequent *khuluww* leasing. In 1226 AH/1811 CE, Khālidīzāde as-Sayyid Muḥammad Ḥusayn Effendi, trustee of Shaykh Maḥmūd al-Khālidī *Waqf*,[525] sought to renew a *khuluww* contract for a two-floor, two-room house, citing insufficient *waqf* income for repairs. The *qāḍī* approved, forming a commission that estimated repair costs at 1,700 *qurūsh*. The *khuluww* right was granted to Sayyid Dāwūd Effendi al-Khālidī, with pre-repair rents of 4 *zoloṭa* for the upper floor, 2 *zoloṭa* for the large house, and 2 *zoloṭa* for two small rooms (totaling 8 *zoloṭa* annually), giving him full disposal rights.[526]

In 1229 AH/1814 CE, the trustee reported non-payment of 6 *zoloṭa* pre-repair rent, but Ḥusayn, who repaired the properties, proved a 1,500 *kurūsh* repair cost, verified by witnesses including chief architect ʿAbd al-Raḥmān al-Namrī, Khalīl Abū Ḥandān, Muṣṭafā Samāra, and Ḥasan al-Balāṭ.

In a record dated 1229 AH/1814 CE, Sayyida Ismāʿ bint Shaykh Muḥammad Sunʿ Allāh al-Khālidī, through her deputy ʿAbd al-Ḥamīd Effendi al-Jāʿūnī, imam of the Dome of the Rock *Waqf*, sold the *khuluww* right of a bakery in Bāb al-ʿAmūd to Muṣṭafā Effendi for 500 *zoloṭa*, with the *qāḍī* requiring repairs and 12 *zoloṭa* annual pre-repair rent. A month later, Ismāʿ claimed non-payment, but Muṣṭafā Effendi proved spending 200 *zoloṭa* on repairs.[527] About ten days later, Sayyida Ismāʿ appealed again, via Jerusalem's chief architect, declaring she endowed her house in Khaṭṭ Dāwūd for *ḥadīth* readers, demanding repairs of its dilapidated parts via *khuluww*. The *khuluww* price was set at 30 *zoloṭa* before the *qāḍī* approved the sale.[528]

In another example from 1229 AH/1814 CE, a bakery from the Dome of the Rock *Waqf* held a *khuluww* contract. Trustee Ḥasan Agha reported to the court

524 Baer, "Jerusalem's Families," 115.
525 JS 297: 159–160.
526 JS 297: 33–34.
527 JS 297: 121–122.
528 JS 297: 129–130.

that the oven's walls and roof were dilapidated, requiring significant repair costs. He sought to repair and lease the oven via *khuluww*, noting that the previous *khuluww* holder, ibn Sahnā, neglected it, causing its ruin and loss of income. The *qāḍī* approved the *khuluww* re-lease, stipulating 12 *zoloṭa* annual pre-repair payment to the *waqf*, demonstrating *khuluww*'s renewability.[529]

Among *waqf* properties established between 1703 and 1831 CE, *khuluww* rights for shops and houses were also endowed. In his *waqfiyya* dated 1214 AH/1799 CE, ʿAbd al-Laṭīf Effendi, Jerusalem's deputy governor and *naqīb al-ashrāf*, endowed the *khuluww* right of a grinder adjacent to the Afḍaliyya *Madrasa Waqf*.[530] In the 1229 AH/1814 CE accounting record of Qāsim Bey al-Turjumān *Waqf*, 70 *kurūsh* was recorded as the annual *khuluww* income from a *waqf* house.[531]

These examples indicate that the *khuluww* leasing method was prevalent for Jerusalem *waqfs* between 1703–1831 CE. *Waqfs* unable to fund repairs and maintenance adopted *khuluww* due to insufficient income or trustee negligence, leading to short-term property fragmentation and long-term disposal. Baer notes that this "lease from the tenant" model caused *waqf* disintegration, as tenants subdivided and resold or endowed their rights, resulting in long-term *waqf* dismemberment.[532] At the end of the day, *waqf* properties were rented out into small parts, and tenants gradually resold or endowed their rent rights.[533]

1.3.4.3 Muqāṭaʿa (*Ḥikr/Ḥukr*)

The term *muqāṭaʿa* holds various meanings in Ottoman society and denotes different practices in *waqf* law. Here, *muqāṭaʿa* refers to a long-term lease contract for *waqf* land, allowing tenants to construct buildings or plant trees, with the condition of permanence (right to remain fixed) and ownership of the property. The annual rental fee from this contract is called *ijāra-yi zamīn* or *muqāṭaʿa-yi zamīn*, alongside *muqāṭaʿa*. Lands leased this way are termed *muqāṭaʿalī vakıf* (endowments under *muqāṭaʿa* contracts). In Ottoman practice, *muqāṭaʿa* was used for this contract, while Islamic jurisprudence texts employed terms like *ḥukr*, *ḥikr*, *ḥakar*, *iḥkār*, *taḥkīr*, and *istiḥkār*. These texts also used *muḥtakir* or *mustahkir* for the person engaging in *ḥikr*. In Jerusalem, these practices were expressed as *ḥukr*.

529 JS 297: 135–136.

530 JS 281: 12–14. In the endowments examined within the scope of the study, *khuluww* of a total of 16 mites were endowed. For detailed information, see Annex 18.

531 JS 297: 34.

532 Baer, 'Jerusalem's Families', pp. 109–123.

533 Baer, 'Jerusalem's Families', pp. 109–123.

A key challenge for *waqfs* was securing funds to rebuild properties damaged by natural disasters like fires and earthquakes or deteriorated over time. As these properties were significant income sources, their reconstruction was vital for sustaining *waqf* services. Trustees had options like securing an interest-free loan (*qarḍ-i ḥasan*), borrowing via a *muʿāmala sharʿiyya* contract, or covering repairs by deducting employees' salaries (*raqaba*).[534] However, these methods were often inadequate. If no one leased ruined *waqf* buildings or vacant lands through *ijāra wāḥida* (single-payment rent) by offsetting expenses against rent, the *waqf* lost income. This prompted scholars to seek solutions. Scholars, alongside trustees and others involved in *waqf* affairs, developed the *muqāṭaʿa* system – despite some disadvantages – because it attracted tenants, developed idle *waqf* lands, and provided stable income for *waqfs*.[535]

Before the *ijāratayn* (double rent) system, *waqfs* with insufficient budgets relied on *muqāṭaʿa*, which favored tenants, to repair or rebuild properties damaged by fires and earthquakes. After *ijāratayn* emerged, trustees preferred it for leasing ruined properties, as it benefited *waqfs* more than *muqāṭaʿa*.[536] When no tenants leased under *ijāratayn*, *muqāṭaʿa* was used instead. Thus, *ijāratayn* did not eliminate *muqāṭaʿa*, which continued, though less frequently. *Sharīʿa* court registers from the 18th century, when *ijāratayn* was prevalent, show *waqf* lands leased under *muqāṭaʿa* contracts. Although Ḥanafī scholars generally deemed long-term leasing (*ijāra tawīla*) of *waqf* properties illegitimate, they permitted it due to necessity and urgent needs.

The *muqāṭaʿa* method was applied for long-term tenancies of land or roofed properties in Jerusalem's *waqfs*. For example, after Shaykh Mūsā ibn ʿAbd al-Wahhāb, who built a large room on land from the former Chief Architect Ibrāhīm's *Waqf*, died, the room was to transfer to as-Sayyid Ibrāhīm and as-Sayyid ʿAbdullāh. However, known individuals intervened and objected. A petition by the endower's sons prompted the Imperial Council to issue an order clarifying that the room built by Shaykh Mūsā on *waqf* land belonged to his sons after his death.[537]

---

534 '*Muʿāmala sharʿiyya*' is a financial arrangement in which a sales contract is introduced to ensure that the borrowed amount, to be repaid in the future, originates from a sale transaction. For more detailed information, see Süleyman Kaya, "XVIII. Yüzyıl Sonlarında Üsküdar Vakıflarının Gelir Kaynakları", *Divan: Disiplinlerarası Çalışmalar Dergisi*, 15/29 (2010): 95–132.

535 For *muqāṭaʿa* in *waqf* law and Ottoman practice, see Muḥammad Emin Durmuş, *Osmanlı Vakıf Hukukunda Mukâtaa*, İktisat Yayınları, İstanbul 2021.

536 Süleyman Kaya, *Osmanlı Hukukunda İcâreteyn* (Istanbul: Klasik Yayınları, 2014).

537 VGMA, 34/1: 39/15.

In a document dated 1226 AH/1811 CE, al-Ḥajj Mubārak al-Maghribī sued Shaykh Aḥmad al-Maghribī, trustee of the Sādād al-Maghāriba *Waqf*. The trustee claimed the plaintiff, who leased property on *waqf* land, did not pay 4 *zoloṭa* in rent. Al-Ḥajj Mubārak stated he paid 4 *zoloṭa* over two years, at 2 *zoloṭa* annually. After hearing witnesses, the *qāḍī* ruled the *muqāṭaʿa* fee was 4 *zoloṭa* per year.[538]

1.3.4.4 Istibdāl (*Substitution*)

Istibdāl, the sale and replacement of *waqf* property, was a complex procedure for the *waqf* institution, inherently inalienable and built on the principle of perpetuity. During the era of the founding imams of the Ḥanafī school, debates on *istibdāl* focused on the validity of a founder's stipulation permitting it – whether such a condition created an authorizing ruling. The opinions of Abū Ḥanīfa's two prominent students diverged. Abū Yūsuf held that if the founder included an authorizing condition for *istibdāl* in the *waqfiyya*, both the condition and the endowment remained valid. Imam Muḥammad, however, argued that while the endowment was permissible and valid, the condition was null and void, meaning the founder's stipulation for *istibdāl* had no legal effect. In the post-formative period of the Ḥanafī school, where *istibdāl* conditions were widely accepted and even considered a matter of consensus, questions arose about applying *istibdāl* to *waqf*s lacking such stipulations. Jurists were torn between the necessity of *istibdāl* for *waqf*s ruined by war, fire, earthquakes, and the risk of exploitation by malicious actors, leading to differing stances. In practice, if a *qāḍī* deemed *istibdāl* to serve the public interest (*maṣlaḥa*), he could authorize it, not based on the *waqfiyya* but through the general administrative authority (*wilāyat al-ʿāmma*) vested in his office.[539]

Significant studies address the practical application of *istibdāl* in the Ottoman State. Kenan Yıldız's study, *1660 İstanbul Yangını ve Etkileri: Vakıflar, Toplum ve Ekonomi* [The Great Fire of 1660 in Istanbul and Its Effects: Endowments, Society, and Economy], examines expropriations during the construction of the Eminönü New Valide Mosque, completed after a fifty-seven-year delay following the 1660 fire, known as *Ḥarīq-i Akbar*, one of Istanbul's largest. A notable aspect involves the use of *istibdāl* for expropriating Muslim *waqf* properties during the mosque complex's expansion, alongside transferring dilapidated churches and synagogues in Galata, Kumkapı,

538 JS 305: 3.

539 For *istibdāl* in *waqf* law and Ottoman practice, see Hatice Kübra Kahya, "İstibdāl Uygulamaları Işığında Osmanlı Vakıf Hukukunun Dönüşümü" (PhD diss., Istanbul University, 2021), 17–102.

Langa, and Zeyrek as compensation in *istibdāl* transactions, later granted to Ḥatice Turhan Sultan.[540] Osman Safa Bursalı's doctoral dissertation, *Ebedi Fakat Tamire Muhtaç: Osmanlı Hukukunda Vakıf Malın Tamiri* [Eternal Yet in Need of Repair: The Restoration of Waqf Property in Ottoman Law], explores the legal framework for repairing *waqfs* within the problematic application of jurisprudential knowledge. Its final section examines the sale and *istibdāl* of irreparable ruined *waqfs*.[541]

As reported in al-Madanī, between 1700–1800 CE, seventeen *waqf* assets were forfeited via *istibdāl*, three from charitable *waqfs* and fourteen from family *waqfs*. Among charitable *waqfs*, assets of the *Zāwiya* Muḥammad al-Qırımī,[542] Bīmaristān Ṣalāḥiyya[543] and Jāmiʿ al-ʿUmarī[544] *Waqfs* in Tibāna Quarter were replaced by the *istibdāl* method.[545] In an example from the Imperial Council's orders, the trustees of Khalīl Effendi and Ḥoca Ṣāliḥ ibn Shihāb al-Dīn Kātib Effendi *Waqf* in Jerusalem sought *istibdāl* for a house on a *waqf* plot in Bāb al-ʿAmūd Quarter and another in Shaykh al-Biqāʿ Neighborhood. The *qāḍī* ruled that *istibdāl* must strictly adhere to the issued *fatwā*, ensuring no deviation in valuation.[546] This case highlights the critical role of both a *fatwā* and judicial approval in ensuring compliance with Islamic jurisprudence (*fiqh*) during *waqf* property expropriation.

2 Christian *Waqfs*

Under Islamic law, Jews and Christians were allowed to establish *waqfs* as long as they served religious purposes. According to the Ḥanafīs, it is permissible for a Muslim and a *dhimmi* to establish a *waqf* for the Bayt al-Maqdis, for the *dhimmi* poor, and for similar charitable purposes. On the other hand, the *waqf* of a *dhimmi* on a mosque and the *waqf* of both a *dhimmi* and a Muslim on churches, synagogues, their repair and construction, the Bible and the Torah are invalid. If a *dhimmi* endowed something to a mosque or a church, and then allocated its income to the poor or other charitable causes, the endowment

540 Kenan Yıldız, *1660 İstanbul Yangını ve Etkileri: Vakıflar, Toplum ve Ekonomi* (Ankara: Türk Tarih Kurumu, 2017).

541 Osman Safa Bursalı, *Ebedi Fakat Tamire Muhtaç: Osmanlı Hukukunda Vakıf Malın Tamiri* (PhD diss., Marmara University, Institute of Social Sciences, Istanbul, 2019).

542 al-Madanī, *Awqāf al-Quds*, 122.

543 al-Madanī, *Awqāf al-Quds*, 122.

544 al-Madanī, *Awqāf al-Quds*, 23.

545 See also for detailed information: al-Madanī, *Awqāf al-Quds*, 122–23.

546 BOA, ADVNS.AHK.ŞM (4): 85/3.

would be valid, but the condition of spending it on the church or mosque would be invalid.[547]

In practice, for endowments made to churches and synagogues, the method of endowing the Christian or Jewish poor and poor clergy was adopted. Otherwise, it was accepted in practice that *waqf*s could not be made directly to monasteries and churches. In addition, hospitals, fountains and similar *waqf*s of non-Muslims, which were also considered charitable by Muslims, were considered absolutely permissible.[548]

In this part of the study, firstly, the approach towards the establishment of *waqf*s by Christians in Ottoman practice will be analyzed. Then, information on the *waqf*s established by Christians in Jerusalem will be presented. Finally, after providing brief information on the religious buildings belonging to Christians, some examples of the practices will be discussed.

2.1 *Christian* Waqfs *in the Ottoman Empire*

Under Ottoman rule, some Christian organizations were supported by the *waqf*s. Most of the time, the property belonging to monasteries was also included in these *waqf*s, providing the state with an important source of income through the taxes they paid.[549] Allowing the property of monasteries to be transferred to the records of the *waqf*s through legal regulations provided them with protection and also pleased the monks, who continued to be exempt from taxation. Eugenia Kermeli shows that the Ottomans, under the leadership of the pragmatic *Shaykh al-Islām* Ebussuud Efendi, recognized some traditional monastic foundations in the Balkans and Thrace, which were equivalent to family *waqf*s, where monks were substituted for families.[550] In this method developed by Ebussuud, the monks in a monastery are treated as family. As in a family *waqf*, they could establish *waqf*s for the benefit of poor family members, as well as for the poor, travelers, and permanent members of the monastery (which in practice meant other monks) and their children. This practice, developed by Ebussuud, follows Ḥanafī inheritance law, but redefines the monks as a family. Thus, he instructs them to establish foundations in their own names and not in the name of the monastery, while at the same time recognizing their collectivity, a fundamental element of the Byzantine monastic tradition.[551]

547 Akgündüz, *İslam Hukukunda*, 173–4.

548 Verbit, *A Ninth Century Treatise*, 366–77.

549 See Van Leeuwen, *Notables and Clergy*, 34–36, 168–70; Van Leeuwen, "The Maronite *Waqf*," 259–76; Gil, *Documents*, 8–10.

550 Kermeli, "Ebū Suʿūd's," 147.

551 Kermeli, "Ebū Suʿūd's," 152–53.

On the other hand, Ebussuud, realizing the implications of the concessions made by this edict, hastily issued a *fatwā* restricting similar requests from other monasteries. When asked whether monks could endow flocks, vineyards, orchards, mills, for the benefit of the poor and travelers, Ebussuud replied that it was permissible as long as it was not for the benefit of the church and as long as no cultivable land was donated. In this *fatwā*, Ebussuud recognizes the poor and travelers as beneficiaries of a waqf that is not established on cultivable land. Up to this point, he complies with Ḥanafī rulings prohibiting the endowment of cultivable land, and on his own terms. Only then does he allow the priests to be considered a collective group with the same privileges as the heirs of a family endowment; provided there is a record in the land registry confirming this, the priests can receive the property of deceased priests without any interference by the local authorities.[552]

Alexander Fotić, basing his claim that Christian foundations were permitted under the Ḥanafī interpretation of the *Sharīʿa* with reference to Ahmed Akgündüz, states that "the Arabic term *waqf* was used in the Ottoman Empire to refer to every *waqf* (*teberru*) in the most general sense, regardless of whether the founder was Muslim or non-Muslim (Christian, Jew), but rather for religious purposes, for the sake of Allah."[553] According to Ahmed Akgündüz, a Christian could bequeath his property to churches or monasteries; moreover, 'he could bequeath it for the public good and for other purposes that, according to Islam, were considered to be for the pleasure of God, such as fountains and hospitals.'[554] Ahmed Akgündüz's view, accepted by Alexander Fotić, that "a Christian could bequeath his property to monasteries or churches as long as it ultimately benefited the poor," was also found in the edicts of various monasteries.[555] In a similar practice, it was stated that the Church of Mar Ya ʿqub of the Armenian nation in Jerusalem was to "spend the income of the assets located in the Suleymān Bey neighborhood in the Yalova accident of the *Sanjāq* of Izmit, which is the property of Mar Ya'qub Church of the Armenian nation, for the sustenance and maintenance of the poor of Mar Ya'qub Church."[556]

On the other hand, Richard Van Leeuwen argues that in Ḥanafī law, the conditions for *waqf*s established by Christians did not fundamentally differ from those established by Muslims.[557] The main restriction for these *waqf*s was that their income had to be *kurbet* (for the sake of Allah). *Waqf*s were permitted if

552 Kermeli, "Ebū Suʿūd's," 153.

553 Fotić, 'The official explanations', p. 53.

554 Akgündüz, *İslam Hukukunda*, p. 173–4.

555 Bkz. Kermeli, 'Ebu Suʿud's'.

556 For the *waqfiyya* dated 18 Muharrem 1322 belonging to the *Keyf Orkpiskopos Waqf* in Yalova, see VGMA, 593: 169/161.

557 Van Leeuwen, *Notables and Clergy*, 30.

the beneficiaries were declared to be the poor. However, Christian *waqf*s could never be established for the benefit, repair or maintenance of mosques, for the expansion of religious buildings, or for the livelihood of clergy or monks. After all, "these designs were incompatible with the Muslim understanding of piety."[558] Moreover, according to Richard van Leeuwen, "the restrictions on the establishment of Christian *waqf*s in the Ottoman Empire were essentially aimed at preventing the clergy and the church as an institution from gaining a strong independent economic foothold." Indeed, while these *waqf*s were tolerated in the empire and efforts were made to regulate them, they never fell under the umbrella of specific privileges granted to *dhimmis* by the Ottoman administration.[559]

2.2 *Christian* Waqfs *in Ottoman Jerusalem*

Jerusalem is sacred for Christians because Christianity was born there, Jesus Christ was born and raised here and Mary lived there. Temples, monasteries and churches were built here, and over time these lands were considered sacred for all Christian denominations. The common sanctuaries of the region, which are considered sacred by all Christian denominations, are the Church of the Holy Sepulcher, the tomb of Mary, the place considered to be the tomb of Jesus Christ, the cells of the Apostles, various monasteries and the Church of Nativity. The common holy places of Christians in Jerusalem, especially the Church of the Holy Sepulcher and the Church of Nativitiy, are called, in Ottoman documents, *Makāmāt-i Mubāraka* (Holy Places).[560]

In Ottoman practice, religiously defined communities within the framework of the *millet* system enjoyed judicial autonomy, especially in certain personal matters such as marriage and divorce.[561] In these matters, the laws of the various communities were applied in their own communal courts. On the other hand, in personal matters such as inheritance and guardianship, the *shārī'a* courts were the competent judicial authority. In these matters, the state courts and the community courts tried simultaneously.[562] Matters related to religious *waqf*s, on the other hand, did not fall within the jurisdiction granted autonomy to the community. Christians and Jews were obliged to establish *waqf*s before

558 Van Leeuwen, *Notables and Clergy*, 30.

559 Van Leeuwen, *Notables and Clergy*, 31.

560 Demirkol, *II. Abdülhamit*, 39; Buzpınar, "Makamat-ı Mübareke Meselesi ve Kırım Harbi," 182.

561 Küçük, "Osmanlı Devleti'nde Millet Sistemi," 208–16; Karpat, "Millets and Nationality."

562 On *dhimmi* law in Islam, see Bozkurt, *Gayrımüslim Osmanlı Vatandaşlarının Hukuki Durumu*, 7–9.

the *sharīʿa* courts. These courts had exclusive jurisdiction over the establishment and internal management of *waqfs*.[563]

Christian subjects, like Muslims, established both charitable and family *waqfs*. They had various reasons for this. First of all, the founders established *waqfs* to ensure the security of their property and to prevent its confiscation by the state authorities.[564] It was generally expected that the integrity of a property endowed as a Muslim *waqf* in a *sharīʿa* court would be safeguarded by the authorities, aligning with the public purposes designated for Muslims. The aim was to ensure that Muslims would not damage a *waqf* ultimately intended for charitable purposes in Muslim hands. Among Christians, al-Kassār, Ibn Wahba, al-ʿĪsā, and Ibn ʿAwd stipulated that their *waqf* beneficiaries included the poor, sick, widows, and orphans – encompassing Muslim poor – wherever they were located.[565]

Another possible reason for the establishment of a *waqf* was tax exemption. Before it was endowed, *waqf* property was purely private property and theoretically not exempt from taxation under law. Once endowed, the revenues of *waqf* properties belonged to the *waqf*. The only exceptions to this were small plots of land (less than a thousand square meters) in towns and villages, bounded by walls or fences and adjacent to houses.

The factors discussed above, such as security of tenure and tax exemption, applied to both public and family *waqfs*. However, there were different considerations for each type of *waqf*. Public *waqfs* can be believed to have been established as a solution to specific problems faced by religious institutions, especially in Jerusalem. As mentioned above, public institutions (including churches) were not recognized by law as "Legal Entities" and could not register property in their own names, which forced them to find legal constructs to secure their property rights. As in the case of the Protestant Church, church properties lacking an official status were specifically used to overcome this practice by registering church heads as representatives of the community in churches. In addition to the above-mentioned factors, the purpose of the establishment of public *waqfs* by the non-Muslims was the desire to do charity, which is rooted in Christianity and Judaism. The desire to do charity was personal and private and not necessarily initiated by the church apparatus. Within Christianity, a *waqf* established for religious purposes represents a desire to gain a special reward. As was the practice in the Ottoman Empire, the

563 Gerber, The *Jews of the Ottoman Empire in the Sixteenth and Seventeenth Centuries*, 32–3.

564 On properties confiscated by tax-farmers, see Gerber, *The Jews*, 138.

565 Cohen, *Economic Life*, 465.

use of a *waqf* for this purpose merely meant the formal channeling of an existing religious motivation into an institutional channel.[566]

On the other hand, the motivation for the establishment of family *waqfs* by non-Muslims is much more difficult to identify, and other mechanisms need to be taken into account in this context, such as inheritance law, wills and gifts. Studies of family *waqfs* established by Muslims have shown that the founder of the *waqf* was able to ensure that the property he had accumulated during his lifetime would not be divided or traded after his death.[567] The *waqf* also provided the founder with an opportunity to overcome inheritance laws that were not in line with social reality. This was done by identifying beneficiaries through the *waqf*, defining the distribution among them, and establishing a model for authorizing the transition between generations of beneficiaries. As mentioned above, non-Muslims also accepted certain structures, such as the authorization of distribution typical of Muslim *waqfs*. The aim was to circumvent the law of inheritance. The desire to keep the property in the hands of the cognate family, which is one of the most basic features of the patriarchal social structure, was also present among non-Muslims who adopted this structure.[568]

In Christianity, unlike Judaism and Islam, religious law does not cover all areas of life. Catholic canon law, for example, does not include special laws on inheritance. In this regard, Christians have historically accepted the civil law of the places they inhabited. In Palestine, Christians also practiced Islamic law. However, in matters such as marriage and divorce, the Church has in practice established its own law. The application of Islamic law has been useful in avoiding potential conflicts with Muslim authorities.[569]

Goadby, as quoted in Ron Shaham, pointed out that members of the Greek Orthodox community tended to use Islamic law because church law from Byzantine sources was in Greek and difficult to apply. Armenians had a strong tradition of using the law of any state as long as it was morally acceptable. Greek Catholics also seemed to apply Muslim law.[570] As a rule, Palestinian Christians in the 19th century divided their inheritance according to the principles of *sharīʿa* law. This explains the similarity between their attitude towards family *waqfs* and that of the Muslim majority. The same motivation for avoiding inheritance law typical of Muslims was also present among Christians. Gifts and wills were not satisfactory means to avoid inheritance restrictions.

566 Shaham, "Christians and Jewish," 467–70.

567 Gerber, *The Jews*, 113.

568 Shaham, "Christians and Jewish," 467–469.

569 Shaham, "Christians and Jewish," 470.

570 Shaham, "Christians and Jewish," 471–72.

The gift, as an undesirable step, forces the owner to give up the property he or she owned while alive, while the will, as in existing inheritance practices, cannot prevent the division of property in the sense that it implies a full property right for the beneficiaries.[571] For these reasons, the foundation was used. For these reasons, the *waqf* was applied.

In Christianity, the use of *waqf* was not considered a religious issue. That is to say, Christianity allowed many matters to be judged according to civil law. With the approach of the modern era in Europe, a tendency emerged for Christian religious endowments to be subject to the civil laws of the state. Religious-charitable *waqf*s were placed within a civil institution called "charitable *waqf*." The property rights of the church began to be institutionalized within the framework of the rules of law rather than the rules of *fiqh*.[572] This is important in explaining Christian foundations in Palestine. In a broader context, the adoption of *waqf* by *dhimmi*s under Ottoman rule can be seen as the use of legal institutions and the conditions of the ruling majority.[573] The adoption by non-Muslim subjects of the institution of *waqf*, especially the family *waqf*, which initially existed neither in Christianity nor Judaism, is not surprising. It merely demonstrated the existence of one of the numerous forms of cultural interaction in a cosmopolitan society.[574]

2.3 *Newly Established Christian* Waqfs *in Jerusalem (1703–1831)*

In the *waqf*s established by the *dhimmi*s, the endowments were drafted in accordance with the Ḥanafī method and the conditions they stipulated were as valid as those of Muslims. The following is an example of a *waqfiyya* of a *waqf* established by one of the members of Armenian community resident in Jerusalem. The reason for including this example is to describe the process of establishing a *waqf* established by non-Muslim subjects as a legal text. The *waqfiyya* approved by the judge in the Jerusalem *shārī'a* court was established on the basis of the Ḥanafī jurisprudence adopted in the Ottoman practice. The authenticity, features and boundaries of the dedicated property were specified, the founder of the foundation and its conditions were also listed. It concludes with the manner in which the endowed property was acquired, witnesses to the

571 Jews had no option to take their own interests forward to overcome inheritance law. Because Jewish law only granted such a right to sick and bedridden persons (*mattenat shekhiv me-ra*). In Judaism, the term "will" as commonly used means to be healthy individuals (*mattenat bari*) and therefore it was perceived as a regular gift that the giver would have throughout his life.

572 Singer, *Osmanlı'da Hayırseverlik*, 27–31.

573 Goitein, *A Mediterranean Society*, 142.

574 Shaham, "Christians and Jewish," 471.

purchase and sale, the appointment of the registration trustee, the date, and the testimony of members of prominent families of Jerusalem. In this *waqf*, the procedures and principles of the Muslim founders were preserved. The income of the endowment was made conditional on the Armenian clergy and the poor; it was not established directly in the name of the Dayr Mar Yaʿqub.

In 1113 AH/1701 CE, the *waqf* of Patriarch Minas of the Armenian community, approved by Muṣṭafā, the *qāḍī* of Jerusalem, was registered at the Jerusalem *Sharīʿa* Court. Avanis *Tarjumān*, an Armenian Christian cleric appointed as proxy by Patriarch Minas and residing at Dayr Mār Yaʿqūb Church in Jerusalem, purchased an endowed house from Ḥājj ʿAlī Agha, trustee of the Sayyid Khalīl *Waqf* and Ṣaḥrat Allāh *Waqf*. Avanis's representation was verified by witnesses in court, including Agha Nisābiyya, Meḥmed ʿAlī al-ʿUjmiyya, and Bālī al-Armanī. The property was acquired by Ḥājj ʿAlī Agha per *sharīʿa* law in a transaction dated Jumādā al-Ūlā 1111 AH/November 1699 CE. The house, still standing in Jerusalem's Rīsha Neighborhood, was described as comprising three *bayt*s, one *bayt* for the deaf, a kitchen, *murafaq*, *saḥḥa samāwiyya* (open courtyard), *ṣahrīj* (cistern), and *ḥawsh* (courtyard), with its boundaries detailed in the *waqfiyya*. Established under Ḥanafī law, the *waqf* emphasized the house's righteous acquisition, as customary. Ḥājj ʿAlī Agha sold the house to Avanis, the trustee, for 800 silver *kurūsh* (each equivalent to 30 *qiṭʿa Miṣrī*) in a *sharīʿa*-compliant sale. The same document records both the purchase and endowment. On behalf of Patriarch Minas, Avanis, as proxy, took delivery, witnessed by the court. The text states: "Minas Batrik annahū waqafa wa ḥabasa bi l-wakālat al-madhkūra mā huwa li-muwākilihī l-madhkūr," that is, Batrik Minas endowed the property purchased by his proxy Avenis *Tarjumān*. Patriarch Minas designated the house for Armenian priests at Dayr Mār Yaʿqūb Church, then the Armenian clergy, followed by the Armenian clergy's poor, and, upon their extinction, the Armenian Christian poor worldwide. The *waqf* stipulated that its income first maintain the house, with supervision assigned to Patriarch Minas during his lifetime, then to the Armenian Patriarch overseeing the clergy. Qāsim Beg al-Tarjumān was appointed trustee for registration. The endowment was dated 1 Shaʿbān 1113 AH/1701 CE, followed by nine witnesses, none from non-Muslim communities. The first witness was Muḥammad Sunʿ Allāh al-Khālidī, from the prominent Khālidī family and among Jerusalem's *ʿulamāʾ*, alongside Meḥmed, Qāsim, Abū al-Wafāʾ, Muṣṭafā, Abū al-Ghanem, Faḍl Allāh, Maḥmūd, and Sardār.[575]

575 See JS 199, See Appendix 5.

In his study based on Ottoman period registers, Muḥammad Ali al-Alami states that nine *waqfs* were established by Christians between 1698–1737, 16 between 1737–1785, and twelve between 1785–1834.[576] In other words, approximately 37 *waqfs* were established in the years covered by this study. Salīm Jumʿa al-Sawāriyya, citing Jerusalem registers, documents four *waqfs* established by Christians in the second half of the 18th century. In the first, Anṭūn ibn al-Yāqūt was appointed trustee of his grandfather Yūsef's *waqf*. Another record names Yāqūt ibn al-Bāliḥ al-Qibṭī as trustee and administrator for a *waqf* founded by the Coptic Christian community in the Qaṭṭānīn neighborhood near Jaffa Pier. Some Christians endowed *waqfs* for Dome of the Rock employees; for instance, Isṭifān, interpreter for the French (*Efrenj*), endowed 12 *qīrāṭ* shares of a house in the Naṣāra neighborhood for its workers. Another record shows a house in the Naṣāra neighborhood endowed for the Christian poor. Finally, a *waqf* was established for foreigners in the Qaṭṭānīn Bazaar, where cotton merchants were located near Dayr al-ʿAmūd.[577]

In the 19th century, thirteen Christian *waqfs* were established in Jerusalem. The number of charitable *waqfs* is nine.[578] The first Christian *waqf* during the study period was established by al-Muʿtām Anṭwān ibn Ḥannā Marqas al-Ifranjī. He endowed a house in the Ḥaddādīn Quarter, stipulating that its revenues be primarily allocated to the *imārat* (maintenance), with any surplus returned to the *waqf*. He designated himself as trustee during his lifetime, his son Yūsuf after his death, and the Ifranjī priests if his lineage ended. If the *waqf* conditions could not be fulfilled, the trustee was to be as-Sayyid Yūsuf Effendi al-Shihābī of the Dome of the Rock. The second *dhurrī waqf* was founded by Fāris ibn al-Wahba Abū Saʿīb al-Ifranjī in 1236 AH/1821 CE, endowing land in Jerusalem. He stipulated that he serve as trustee while alive, followed by the Shaykh of *Ḥaramayn al-Sharīfayn*. If the *waqf* conditions could not be met, the revenues were to support the employees and residents of *Ḥaramayn al-Sharīfayn* and all prophets. The third *waqf* was established by Jarīs ibn Ḥannā ʿUlūshiyya al-Ṣāniʿ al-Rūmī in 1249 AH/1833 CE, endowing a shop in Jerusalem. He designated himself as trustee during his lifetime, followed by his sons, then Greek priests, and subsequently the imam of the Jerusalem *Ḥaram*.

576 Al-Alami, "*The Waqfs of the Tradtional*," 152.

577 Al-Sūwāriyya, "*al-Hayāt al-Ijtimāʿiyya*," 52–53.

578 For the list of the foundations in question, see Aḥmad Ḥāmid Ibrāhīm al-Quḍāt, *Naṣārā al-Quds fī al-Qarn al-Tāsiʿ ʿAshar: Dirāsa fī Sijillāt Maḥkamat al-Quds al-Sharʿiyya* (MA thesis, Yarmouk University, Faculty of Arts, Department of History, 1427/2006), 247–63.

If the *waqf* conditions could not be implemented, the poor under the *qāḍī*'s responsibility were to be the beneficiaries.[579]

Established in the first half of the 19th century, the first of three charitable *waqf*s in the study period was founded by al-Namiyya ʿAzīza al-Rūmiyya in 1240 AH/1824 CE, endowing a house in the Naṣāra neighborhood with its revenues dedicated to the Greek Church. The second *waqf* was established by an Armenian priest in 1242 AH/1827 CE, stipulating that income from copper, silver, gold, and *nuqūd* be allocated to Dayr Mār Yaʿqūb Church. The third *waqf*, founded by al-Kasīs Jirjis Miḥnā al-Rūmī in 1242 AH/1827 CE, endowed pottery jugs, gold, and *dirhams*, with the income designated for the Greek poor.[580]

In the *Ḥurūfāt* records of the period, eleven appointment records for four different churches are identified. The first record appoints a tax collector, paid 10 coins daily, to gather revenues from immovable properties in Āmid for the Armenian Maryākūb Church *Waqf*.[581] Similarly, for the Jaghdar Church *Waqf* and Karyādira Church *Waqf* in Diyarbakır, the first appointment lacks a specified fee, while the second assigns a daily fee of 10 coins.[582] These appointments of collectors for church properties in Diyarbakır likely reflect their distance from Jerusalem.

Finally, a Shaykh was appointed to do the work of non-Muslim subjects in *Kamāme* and other churches.[583] The church, which is called *Qiyāma*[584] by Muslims and local Christians, and is called Saint Sepulchre by the Christians of the world. The church, which is also referred to as *Kamāme* in the *Ḥurūfāt* records. It located in Khaṭṭ Darjāh in the Naṣāra Quarter, and is believed to be the site of Jesus's tomb according to Christian tradition, near a rocky hill outside old Jerusalem's walls.[585] According to *Evliyā Çelebī*, the doors of the *Kamāme Church* were opened only once a year, during the Feast of Easter. On each day of the three-day ceremonies, the doors were opened by the *mutasarrıf* of Jerusalem, the *qāḍī*, the *Shaykh al-Islām*, and armed Ottoman soldiers. On these days, approximately five to ten thousand Christians would gather in the church, and a fee of ten gold coins was collected from visitors.[586] One-tenth of

579 See al-Quḍāt, *Naṣārā al-Quds*, 247–63.
580 ibid., 247–263.
581 VGMA, 1112: 1/92; 1108: 1/14; 1108: 1/60; 1125: 64/2; 1111: 54/5; 1109: 6/59.
582 VGMA 1119: 110/3.
583 VGMA, 1107: 2/291.
584 While the word qiyāma means resurrection after death, khamāma means rubbish. Demirkol, *II. Abdülhamit*, 39.
585 Demirkol, *II. Abdülhamit*, 39.
586 Evliya Çelebi, *Seyahatnāme*, XI, 246.

the gold collected was allocated to the administration of the *mutasarrıf*, while the doors remained sealed at all other times.[587]

In addition to these, other churches belonging to the Christian community in Jerusalem during the period covered by this study are as follows: Dayr Mār Ilyas, one of the churches of the Greek community in Jerusalem, is located south of Jerusalem on the road to Bethlehem and has resident clergy.[588] Another church, Dayr Zaytūna, is located near the Holy Prophet David. On the eastern side, it was located behind the Church of Mar Yaʿqub. The churches of *Elma, Fitomas, Katerina* and the Patriarch, also in the Christian neighborhood, belonged to the Greek community.[589] Among the churches belonging to the Assyrians, Dayr Asūriyān in the Ṣahyūn al-Jawāniyya neighborhood and Dayr ʿAdas in the Banī Zayd neighborhood in northern Jerusalem, repaired in 978 AH/1570 CE.[590] Dayr Martūmā, located in Ṣahyūn al-Jawāniyya, was situated at the start of a street in the Nabī Dāwūd neighborhood in the late 18th century.[591] Dayr al-ʿAmūd, an Ifranjī Latin church, lies north of the Naṣāra neighborhood.[592] The Georgian churches Dayr Zangil and Dayr Miṭrī are also in the Naṣāra neighborhood.[593]

3 Jewish *Waqf*s

The *Ḥaram al-Sharīf*, the oldest holy center of Jerusalem, was also a holy place for Jews. For the Jews, Jerusalem was considered different from other cities because of its holiness, and it was considered a place chosen by God. The city became a kingdom and a center of worship during the time of David.[594] David, who laid the foundation of temple in Jerusalem and started its construction, willed its completion to his son Solomon. After his father's death, Solomon completed the temple and then built the city of Jerusalem with its twelve neighborhoods. He built palaces and surrounded the city with walls. From time to time, the Jewish community, which had been overflowing and rebelled against the prophets sent to them, came under the rule of the Roman state, which burned and destroyed Jerusalem and Masjid *al-Aqṣā* in 63 BC.

587 Demirkol, *II. Abdülhamit*, 39.
588 al-ʿArif, *al-Mufaṣṣal*, 517.
589 al-ʿĀrif, *Tārīkh al-Ḥaram*, 102.
590 al-ʿĀrif, *Tārīkh al-Ḥaram*, 146.
591 al-ʿArif, *al-Mufaṣṣal*, 535.
592 Al-Sūwāriyya, "*al-Hayāt al-Ijtimāʿiyya*," 54.
593 Al-Sūwāriyya, "*al-Hayāt al-Ijtimāʿiyya*," 54.
594 Harman, "Kudüs," 326.

In 20/24 BC, Herod, the Roman governor of Palestine, who was a descendant of the Israelites, expanded and rebuilt the *al-Aqṣā* Mosque and rebuilt Jerusalem. In 70 AD, the city of Jerusalem was completely burned and destroyed by the Roman commander Titus, and only the western wall called the 'Wailing Wall' remained standing. Jews pray in front of the Wailing Wall, believing that it is a part of the Temple of Solomon, which according to Jewish tradition, was the first Jewish temple.[595]

The number of the *waqf*s established during the Ottoman period in Jerusalem, which was also considered exceptional by Jews, is quite low. Before moving on to the reasons for this situation, we will try to define philanthropy in Jewish societies through the terms *sedaqa* and *hekdesh*. Subsequently, the views on *waqf*s to be established in the Ottoman period in terms of both Jewish law and Islamic law will be presented. After giving examples of various *waqf*s established by Jews in Jerusalem, evaluations on the *waqf*s established in the 18th century will be given.

3.1 *Philanthropy in Judaism*

The use of a specific word (*sedaqa*) meaning justice or righteousness to refer to mandated charitable giving in Judaism dates back to at least the 2nd century AD.[596] In Judaism, however, the religious centralization of charity was mandated. According to historian Mark R. Cohen, "in-depth study of the experiences of the truly poor and the workings of charitable institutions has been hampered by the idealized assumptions about Jewish generosity and the universal praise of the poor detailed in the Bible, Talmud, Midrash and other medieval sources."[597] According to Amy Singer, the practice of *sedaqa* in Jewish communities in Arabia is poorly understood. The linguistic similarity between the Islamic word for charity and the Jewish word *sedaqa* suggests that Jews may have had some influence on Muslims in thought and practice. There were many Jews in the early Muslim community. Moreover, Muslims had long-standing close relations with the Jewish communities in Arabia.[598]

Extensive evidence of Jewish charitable institutions and practices from the later period is found in the Cairo Geniza.[599] Public philanthropy in the Geniza District, which was more communal in scale, had features that distinguished

595 Tibawi, *The Islamic Pious*, 17–19.
596 Singer, *Osmanlı'da Hayırseverlik*, 27.
597 Cohen, *Poverty and Charity*, 347–60.
598 Singer, *Osmanlı'da Hayırseverlik*, 27.
599 Goitein discussed the practices of the Jews in Cairo and Fustat during the Fatimid period. See Gil, *A Mediterranean*, 91–143.

Jews from their Muslim neighbors, especially in terms of its emergence: it covered a limited area, which could be called food charity. Adam Sabra notes that "there was no state-funded social welfare system in Mamluk Cairo. Although some aid was provided by religious foundations to hospitals and schools, there was no regular distribution of food to the poor by the state."[600] Social aid in the period under study is different in one aspect. Namely, as has been the case in the Abrahamic religions for centuries, social aid, which is primarily expressed by the Hebrew word *misva* (*mishva*), is first and foremost a religious activity. In the study, it is stated that the foundations of social solidarity were established by the Jewish community long before the spread of Islam through such practices.

In the orderly binary structure of the complex economy of Jewish philanthropy in the Geniza Region, as described by Cohen, the distinction between voluntary, private (personal) philanthropy and compulsory, public (impersonal) philanthropy found in modern social welfare did not exist. Individuals responded to requests for help from the poor, the poor were given the money they requested, religious foundations were established for the purpose of getting out of poverty, and thus made a direct contribution to social welfare.[601] However, social assistance in Geniza society was, at least in theory, voluntary, even if it was felt obligatory, emerging from a religious mindset that aimed to please God by fulfilling His commands.[602]

In Fustat, on the other hand, there is no evidence of any official taxation in support of social welfare or public services as a means of combating poverty. At this point, Fustat differs from Alexandria. In Alexandria, as in the Jewish communities in Ramla in Palestine and later in Europe, a meat tax was levied on the community.[603] If it was not taxed, where did the money for social welfare in Fustat come from? Jewish religious foundations, "*heqdesh*" (*heqdesh*, *qodesh* as it was called in the Geniza region, meaning holy), ran side by side and sometimes together with social welfare. In the pre-biblical period, *heqdesh* originally took the form of consecrated property donated for the protection of the Jerusalem Temple and its officials. It also included the purchase of sacrificial animals for worship. In the post-biblical period, the scope of the *heqdesh* was expanded and made available to synagogues and the poor.[604]

600 Sabra, *Poverty and Charity*.
601 Cohen, *Poverty and Charity*, 198–199.
602 ibid., 199.
603 ibid., 190.
604 ibid., 200.

Moshe Gil discusses Jewish endowments (*heqdesh*) according to their origins and evolution and, on a broader level, the relationship between *hekdesh* and *waqf* as found in the Geniza documents.[605] He notes that the charitable endowment organizations in the Geniza region resemble the Islamic *waqf* in some respects. Practices such as accommodation for the poor (*ʿaniyye-i ha-ʿir*), *imārets* (*tamḥui*), and charity (*quppa*) that he identified in the Geniza region are similar. On the other hand, while similar in essence to Islamic endowments, Jewish *heqdis*/endowments differ in some important respects. First of all, there are no family *waqfs*, which are defined as *ahlī* waqfs in Islam. The Jewish foundations in the Geniza Region, like the Holy Temple in the pre-Biblical period and the synagogues thereafter, are almost entirely in the service of communal needs. A very modest amount of *waqf* income, mostly in the form of rents or income from property endowed to the community, goes directly to charity, such as the distribution of food and the provision of daily necessities to individuals. Gil states that about 10% of the income of the *heqdesh* was used directly to meet the needs of the poor. A very large proportion of the *heqdesh* income was spent on the salaries or wages of scholars and officials, on the education or salaries of poor or orphaned children (76.3%), or on the maintenance and repair of synagogues (about 14%). Expenditures on synagogues included lighting fees.[606]

The similarity between the religious foundation institutions of the three monotheistic religions, a point emphasized by Gabriel Baer, facilitated the adoption of the Muslim institution by non-Muslims. On the other hand, the establishment of the *waqf* before the Muslim *qāḍī* court was at odds with the traditional judicial sovereignty of the Jewish community court. Indeed, in the sources we find conflicts among rabbis and arguments for and against the establishment of a *waqf* by a Jew before a Muslim *qāḍī* court. Some rabbis rejected the legal validity of the *waqf*, arguing that it violated Jewish inheritance law. Other rabbis argued that a Jewish foundation established in a non-Jewish court was valid on the grounds that the law of the land was binding (*dina de-malchuta dina*).[607] According to this concept, if the law of the country conflicted with Jewish law, the principle developed during the Persian-Sassanid

605 Gil, *Documents of the Jewish*, 1–36, 102–17.

606 This practice in *Hekdesh* stands in sharp contrast to practices in late medieval and early modern European Jewish societies, as it is not unusual for the needs of the poor, especially those of the poor sick, to outweigh the needs of synagogues. For detailed information, see Cohen, *Poverty and Charity*, 199–217.

607 "The law of the country is considered law." See Shilo, "Wills," 453–64.

period that the law of the country was the law was applied. Accordingly, the Jewish population was obliged to obey the laws of the country in which they resided, as long as they did not interfere with or prohibit the observance of religious commandments. In the Middle Ages, this extended from tax and financial law to civil law.[608]

3.2 *Jewish* Waqfs *in Ottoman Jerusalem*

As in the case of Christian foundations, Jewish foundations did not fall within the jurisdiction of the autonomy granted to the community. Jews were also obliged to establish foundations before the *sharīʿa* courts. As mentioned earlier, these courts had exclusive jurisdiction over the establishment and internal management of foundations.

In addition to legal or administrative constraints, these founders were also aware of some practical advantages associated with the use of the *waqf* institution. There were two reasons why foundations established by Muslims were also adopted by non-Muslim subjects. These were the security provided for the founder's property and the prevention of confiscation by state authorities. These reasons are particularly relevant for Jews as well as Christians, who, as *dhimmi*s, felt less secure.[609] Studies mention that Jews established foundations to prevent the confiscation of their property by tax collectors. Jews who died childless established charitable foundations specifically to prevent their inheritance from ending up in the state treasury (*bayt al-māl*). Thus, for example, ʿAmiel made the revenues of his endowment ultimately conditional on the mosques in the *Ḥaram al-Sharīf* in Jerusalem. It should be recalled at this point that *waqf* affairs regarding the beneficiaries of the *waqf* were managed by the *qāḍī*, who, as agents of the state, were responsible for the continuity of the *waqf*. In addition, the founders of *waqf*s imposed conditions that were in line with Muslim religious and moral norms. For example, Dabās' *waqf* confirmed that beneficiaries of the *waqf* who engaged in adultery, usury, wine drinking and gambling would be deprived of their share of the rights.[610]

Public institutions could not register property in their own name, which forced them to find legal frameworks to secure their property rights. One device used to circumvent this prohibition was to register the property as a foundation and the public institution as the beneficiary. In this context, the foundation established by Niego is a case in point. The house, which was donated as

608 Riemer, "Yahudi Kimlikleri," 42, http://www.sabahulkesi.com/category/sayi-42/.

609 Shaham, "Christian and Jewish," 468; Cohen, *Poverty and Charity*, 210–11.

610 Cohen, *Economic Life*, 465.

his private property, was in fact purchased with a donation from his baroness, Klara Hirsh, to the Jewish community of Jaffa. Although not mentioned in the *waqf*, Niego acted in court as a representative of the community and not as a private individual. The administrative body organized by the *waqf* also reflects community participation in the management of the *waqf*. This method was also used by Jewish public institutions in Jerusalem.[611]

According to Amnon Cohen, the main motivation behind the foundations established by Jews in Jerusalem in the 16th century was to prevent the confiscation of their properties by powerful individuals, the state or religious structures. To give an example of Jewish foundations established in Jerusalem in the 1530s, three Jews who owned land in Jerusalem endowed their agricultural lands in order to prevent the confiscation of their lands. A Jewish woman who was the wife of Shamila bin Yaʿqub, inherited from her father an orchard of figs, apple trees and grape vines in the village of Bayt Iksa, Mansur bin Abdallah,[612] another Jewish traveler who came to Jerusalem from Damascus, endowed an orchard in which he had a 25% share,[613] and the third, Musa bin Judah, endowed an orchard in the village of Beit Safafa in which he had a 25% share.[614] All three of them adopted this method and stipulated that the revenues of their endowments would belong to the Dome of the Rock Mosque when they ceased to be descended from their children, and that the trusteeship of their endowments would be entrusted to the trustees of the *Ḥaram al-Sharīfayn* endowments. Although there is no detailed information in the endowments of the foundations in question, Amnon Cohen suggests that the fact that all three *waqf*s adopted the same method is based on the possibility that there was a practice in the period under scrutiny whereby the revenues of the endowments could only revert to the Dome of the Rock when they were discontinued by descent.[615]

Amnon Cohen, on the other hand, attributes the establishment of foundations, especially by Jewish women, to the idea that women were less secure than men. This also helped to keep their property within the family.[616] In the 16th century *waqf* established by Rifqa bint Suleiman, the *waqf* endowed all of her property (clothing, household furniture, an orchard in the Bekaa lands,

---

611 Shaham, "Christian and Jewish," 469.
612 Cohen, *Jewish Life Under Islam*, 210. See also Cohen, *A World Within*, 30.
613 Cohen, *A World Within*, 32. Other shareholders of the garden are also Jewish.
614 ibid., 32.
615 Cohen, Jewish *Life*, 210.
616 ibid., 211.

and a house in the Jewish Quarter) in the presence of the *qāḍī*. She stipulated the disposition of the endowment's income to herself while she was alive, to her daughter after her death, and to her daughter's children after her daughter's death. When she ceased to be a daughter, she made it conditional on the poor of the Jewish community.[617] A similar foundation was established by Hanna bint Harun on August 29, 1532. In fact, this practice existed a century earlier. Namely, the foundation established by Bannita binti Barakat during the Mamluk period was continued during the Ottoman period. In her endowment of a house, she endowed the income of the foundation to her son, and then to his children and descendants. When his descendants ceased to exist, she stipulated that the income of the endowment would be given to the poor of the Jewish community. If the conditions of the endowment became unenforceable in time, she stipulated that the proceeds of the endowment be given to the Dome of the Rock Mosque.[618]

In two other endowments established by Jews, Muslim institutions are again recorded as the ultimate owners of the endowment's revenues. In the first of these, Musa bin Davud bin Yaqub, a Rabbanite Jew from Mosul, endowed his house in Sharaf (formerly Akrād) Quarter on 6 Safar 949/22 May 1542. He stipulated that the income from the endowment should be paid to himself while he was alive and to his son and his son's sons after his death. When he ceased to be a son, he stipulated that the proceeds be divided equally among the Dome of the Rock Mosque and Khalil al-Rahman *Imāret*. The *waqf* stipulated the trusteeship of the *waqf* to himself as long as he was alive and to his sons after his death. The *waqf* allocated 50 *dirhams* to be given by the trustee to the Dome of the Rock and Masjid *al-Aqṣā* mosques.[619] Approximately six years after this *waqf*, Suleiman bin Daud, another Jewish resident, established a *waqf* in which the *waqf* stipulated that the income from his four shops should be given to the poor Jews living in Jerusalem and the pilgrims coming to Jerusalem, and then to the poor Muslims in Jerusalem. If the conditions of the *waqf* could not be implemented, it was made conditional on *Simāt-ı Ibrahim*. In this case, the proceeds of the endowment were endowed for the benefit of the Jewish community rather than the family.[620] The last foundation, as reported in Amnon Cohen, was established by Esther bint Ibrahim. She endowed her two houses

617 Cohen, *Jewish Life*, 211. In medieval Egypt, "many charitable foundations were established by women." Goitein, *A Mediterranean*, 113.

618 Cohen, *A World Within*, 54.

619 Cohen, *Jewish Life*, 212.

620 ibid., 212.

in the Jewish Quarter and stipulated that the income from the endowment would benefit herself while she was alive, her son Ibrahim after her death, and then her children. When she ceased to be descended from her children, Jerusalem.[621]

When the Jewish foundations, some examples of which are given above, are compared to Muslim foundations, the purpose of the foundation is similar in most of them. In addition to similarities such as the desire to protect the assets owned by the *waqfs* from all kinds of confiscation and the desire to keep the *waqf* income within the family, it has been observed that in Jewish *waqfs*, as in Muslim *waqfs*, the *waqf* income was directed to a charitable purpose when the *waqf's* offspring ceased to exist. According to Amnon Cohen, although this may be considered as an attempt to increase the strength and protection of the *waqf*, from the perspective of Islamic law, the possibility that the *waqf* would one day serve a charitable purpose was the basis for its registration by the *qāḍī*.

3.3 *Newly Established Jewish* Waqfs *in Jerusalem (1703–1831)*

In his study based on the Jerusalem *sharīʿa* court registers, Muḥammad Ali al-Alami states that the number of foundations established by Jews in Jerusalem is quite small. In the period covered by the study, the number of newly established foundations was found to be three.[622] The authorization to establish foundations, which was limited according to Islamic law, and the disapproval of the establishment of foundations according to Islamic law by some rabbis are thought to be effective in this. However, while there were a small number of Jewish foundations before 1290/1873 CE, this number increased considerably after 1870. Muḥammad Ali al-Alami, who attributes the small number of foundations before 1873 to the small Jewish population, has shown that after 1870, a large number of foundations were established by the Jews who settled in Palestine due to the protection of property rights and the right of use.[623]

As mentioned earlier, there are numerous examples of the re-endowment of another *waqf's* property in *waqfs* established in the 18th century when the traditional families of Jerusalem were strong. Similarly, the cultivated fields around Jerusalem, which were given on long-term lease and emphasized as part of the properties of the waqfs established during the Ayyubid and Mamluk periods, were also re-endowed. In some cases, properties that had been endowed by foundations established by ancestors of the same family

621 ibid., 212.

622 Al-Alami, "The *Waqfs* of the Traditional," 152.

623 ibid., 152–53.

and leased for long periods of time were also reendowed. There are also many instances in other family *waqf*s where a large number of non-owned properties were endowed.[624] Similarly, Christians and Jews followed the same path in Jerusalem during the last century of the Ottoman rule, when their influence increased, and re-established endowments with endowed properties that had been leased to them for long periods of time. For example, between 1882 and 1919, the number of Jewish foundations reached 348.[625] This use came to an abrupt end during the British Mandate in Palestine. This institutional dynamism indicates that, in the late Ottoman period, the Jewish community's capacity to establish *waqf*s had developed significantly.[626]

In the period under study, Jewish settlements were centered around four synagogues in the Jewish Quarter. Three of these had a Sephardic core. The first was the Eliyahu Synagogue, built by Yohanan Ben Zakkai in the early 17th century. The second was the synagogue founded in the 18th century, variously called the Middle or Kehal Katan or the Synagogue of Zion. The third synagogue was the Stambuli Synagogue, built in the middle of the 18th century and founded in 1764 by Jews who immigrated to Jerusalem from Constantinople.[627] These synagogues were central to Jewish life in Jerusalem between 1721 and 1836, when the walled Ashkenazi lands were destroyed. However, due to the Ottoman ban on synagogues being taller than mosques, these synagogues did not become monumental buildings in the city as places of Jewish worship.[628] The Great Synagogue, the main place of worship for Ashkenazis, was founded in the 18th century by Ashkenazi Rabbi Judah Hassid. In 1857 it was destroyed by a fire.[629]

4 Conclusion

This third part of our study discusses the history of *waqf*s in the province, detailing the many services provided by the *waqf*s, their properties and how these properties exploited. There is also a discussion of Christian and Jewish *waqf*s in the city. It utilizes a wealth of information gleaned from myriad

624 ibid., 153.
625 ibid., 152–54.
626 ibid., 151.
627 Cueno, "The Urban Structure," 216–17.
628 ibid., 217.
629 For detailed information about the synagogue, see Cueno, "The Urban Structure," 217.

sources to situate Jerusalem within its imperial context while also referring to its particular, local elements.

Waqfs were an important means of transferring values rooted in tradition and a system of religious symbols to space, but they were also an important tool for determining the status of properties, sanctifying them, and determining and protecting their position in the urban fabric. *Waqfs* also functioned as a mechanism to coordinate between private interests and private initiatives and the interests of the urban community. It is through these functions that *waqf* networks created the model underpinning urban development.

CHAPTER 4

Between the Ruling and Ruled: Notables and the *Reʿāyā* in Jerusalem's Waqf Network

Recent studies have revealed that the political history of cities in the early modern period is inextricably linked to the history of the relationship between the urban elite and the central authority.[1] The rise of provincial elites in the Ottoman Empire from the 17th century onwards also marked a new phase of center-periphery integration. The 17th and 18th centuries began to be considered not in the context of decline and dissolution, but as a "restructuring" in terms of the Ottoman administrative mechanism and center-periphery relations.[2] This restructuring, expressed by the concept of Ottomanization,[3] involved, on the one hand, the inclusion of the local population into the administrative and distribution networks of the center, and thus the formation of a class of elites integrated into the system, and, on the other hand, the "indigenization" of members of the Ottoman bureaucracy.[4] What distinguished the 18th century from previous periods of the Ottoman Empire was the level of economic, social and, possibly, ideological integration between the center and various provincial elites.[5]

In this context, this part of the study aims to answer questions such as the following: What was the situation in Jerusalem in the 18th century? Who were

1 See Canbakal, *17. Yüzyılda Ayıntāb*, 82; Yaycıoğlu, "Provincial Power".

2 See Karl Barbir, "The Changing Face of the Ottoman Empire," 253–67; Abou-El-Haj, *Formation of the Modern State*; Salzmann, "An Ancien Regime Revisited"; Khoury, *Osmanlı Imparatroluğu'nda*; Barkey, *Bandits and Bureaucrats*; Hathaway, *Osmanlı İmparatorluğu'nda İsyan*, 37. For critical comments on the subject see Peirce, "Changing Perceptions," 6–28, 29–53.

3 The eighteenth century saw fundamental changes in the relationship between the Ottoman State and the elites in its various provinces. Moreover, these changes varied from province to province. Some historians have argued that a large segment of local elites became Ottomanized in the eighteenth century. In their view, this *Ottomanization* served as an antidote to the dissolution of centralized control that had become so pervasive in the late 1700s. Jane Hathaway (*The Politics of Households: 'Egypt in the Seventeenth Century'*), while not using the term *Ottomanization*, argues that a distinctly Ottoman elite political culture was transferred to Egypt, but spread to the secondary administrative circles of the Ottoman provinces. Masters (*The Origins of Western Economics*) sees this group as an emerging Ottoman upper class, while Khoury (*In the Ottoman Empire*, 55–60) describes the process as Ottomanization.

4 Canbakal, *17. Yüzyılda Ayıntāb*, 82; Yaycıoğlu, "Provincial Power," 667–709.

5 Salzmann, "An Ancien Regime"; Abou-El-Haj, *Formation of the Modern State*.

 | DOI:10.1163/9789004743441_005

the social groups that acquired new roles among the rulers and the ruled? How did the Ottoman state apparatus function in the provinces? For this purpose, first, Jerusalem's society will be defined within its changing dynamics. Second, the positions of the identified segments of society within the Jerusalem *waqf* network will be identified. Third, we will look at the privileges and titles brought about by the status of *ʿaskerī* (ruling elite), which means having a share in the system of privileges organized by the state, and the effectiveness of *waqfs* in gaining these privileges and titles. At this point, the issue of being a member of the ruling elite, both as a founder of a *waqf* and as an employee of a *waqf*, will be analyzed. The demand for titles, and the way in which this demand was met, either officially or through extortion, was a defensive reaction to increasing taxes, as well as their contribution to the process of Ottomanization, which will be another issue discussed in this context. Again in this section, the distribution of wealth in Jerusalem will be analyzed in the context of the identities of individuals and especially the relations between local families and the Ottoman civil service. Thus, this chapter aims to discuss local identity and center-periphery relations and to draw attention to the role of the state in the distribution of power in the provinces.

1 Urban Conditions and Social Structure

Describing the 17th century *Sanjāq* of Jerusalem as "a battlefield between various layers of property," Amy Singer identifies the layers of property as the state, the military-administrative elite, the local elite, and the productive peasants. According to Singer, "the same situation existed in the 16th century, but the distribution of power between the contending parties was different. The local elite played a minor role in the conflict. The state and the peasants, with the help of the *qāḍī*, were able to maintain their power against the military-administrative elite. In the 18th century, the empowered local elite, sometimes in collaboration with the military-administrative elite, were oppressing the people through the activities of the bullying."[6]

Albert Hourani, on the other hand, has analyzed the local elite as leaders of the urban population in Arab cities into three groups that, through their mediation between the people and the administration, assumed a delimited political role.[7] The first is the *ʿulamāʾ*, the traditional spokespersons of Islamic cities, who derived their power from their religious status. The *ʿulamāʾ* class

6 Singer, *Kadılar, Kullar*, 166–67.

7 Hourani, "Ottoman and the Politics of Notables," 48–49.

were the intermediaries that ensured the legitimacy of state actions in the center as well as in the provinces. In Istanbul, the *ʿulamāʾ* derived their power and influence from appointments to high religious offices by the central government, whereas in the provinces, the *ʿulamāʾ* came from local families with pre-existing political influence. If not serving as *qāḍī, muftī, naqīb*, or *nāʾib*, they were often members of prominent local families. Beyond the authority of their positions, they amassed significant wealth through families with generations of religious prestige, their roles as *waqf* administrators, or ties to the commercial bourgeoisie. Local garrison leaders formed the second group, controlling armed forces and, like the *ʿulamāʾ*, were essential to administration, enjoying some autonomy. The third group comprised local rulers – *aʿyān*, *agha*s, and *amīr*s – who were either members of families with traditional military and political power or individuals controlling agricultural production through *malikāne* rights.

Albert Hourani's theoretical perspective on urban elites can be discussed, albeit in outline form, for the city of Jerusalem.[8] However, it is important to emphasize that the local elite in Jerusalem mostly possessed the qualities attributed to the first group, that is, they came from the *ʿulamāʾ* class. ʿAdel Manna attributes this to the fact that the local garrisons in the city were smaller units, unlike those in Damascus, Aleppo and Cairo. Those who commanded the military units there did not have the chance to gain access to the power that would enable them to be included in the elite class.[9] However, the abundance of educational and religious buildings in the city must also have contributed to the influence of the *ʿulamāʾ* class. This study, which will evaluate Jerusalem's *ʿulamāʾ* class among the local elites, is based on the classification under the headings of the military-administrative elite (ruling elite); the empowered local elite (local elite); and the common people, as indicated in Singer's assessment of 18th-century Jerusalem, as mentioned above.

The political and socio-economic conditions that characterized the rise of the city's notables in Jerusalem were very different from those in other Palestinian cities. Until the second half of the 19th century, the wealth of Jerusalem's notables was generally confined to the city. The notables of Jerusalem did not own large tracts of land or property in the villages, nor did they have the right of alimony. This lack prevented them from exerting much influence in the countryside.[10] The notables of Jerusalem were not farmers who cultivated the urban fields. In fact, the poor rural areas around the city were far

8 Avcı, *Değişim Sürecinde*, 45.

9 Manna', "Contunuity and Change," 71.

10 Abu-Manneh, "Jerusalem in the Tanzimat Period," 5–6.

from constituting the city's agricultural hinterland.[11] The relations between the city and the countryside in Jerusalem took on a different character only during the Tanzimat years, when the city's dominance became apparent.[12] As mentioned earlier, the economic power of the influential families in Jerusalem was mostly generated by religious and educational *waqf*s. As founders, employees and beneficiaries, they played an active role in Jerusalem's *waqf* network.

On the other hand, Marshall G. S. Hodgson and other scholars have emphasized that the evolving relationship between the establishment of *waqf*s and political legitimacy was increasingly exploited for personel gain from the 10th and 11th centuries onwards.[13] With the weakening of the central administration, the power of local elites increased. The selection of those who would be appointed to salaried positions in the institutions supported by the *waqf*s was exploited and used to acquire loyal servants and protect the existing ones among the learned and respected people who served as spiritual and informational advisors to the government with a patronage approach.[14] It should also be noted that in provincial cities, the Ottoman administration needed urban leaders as intermediaries between the central administration and the local population. Consequently, the social and economic priorities of many prominent people were supported by the Ottoman state.

In this part of the study, which aims to understand and define the relationship between Jerusalem society and the *waqf* institution, Jerusalem society will be defined within its changing dynamics. Secondly, the positions of the defined segments of society within the *waqf* network in Jerusalem will be identified. For this purpose, firstly, the Ottoman state administrators or their representatives and the influential families of Jerusalem will be analyzed under the title of "administrator-local elites". Finally, information on the people of Jerusalem will be presented under the heading of *reʿāyā*.

1.1 *Ruling and Local Elites of Jerusalem*

In this part of the study, the prominent administrators of the city of Jerusalem who were active in decision-making mechanisms within the Ottoman social structure will be discussed. First of all, the concept of "ruling elite" will be used for high-level Ottoman officials. The local actors of the city of Jerusalem will also be considered as "local elites." On the other hand, a significant number of

---

11 Ben-Arieh, *Jerusalem in the 19th Century*, 393.

12 Avcı, *Değişim Sürecinde*, 48–49.

13 Marshall G. S. Hodgson, *The Venture of Islam: Conscience and History in a World Civilization*, vol. 2 (Chicago: University of Chicago Press, 1974), 214.

14 Singer, *Osmanlı'da Hayırseverlik*, 33.

local Jerusalemites were appointed to various positions due to their personal or family ties in the city or neighboring areas. This blurs the boundaries between the ruling elite and the local elite. Ehud Toledano defines the Palestinian or Syrian ruling elites discussed under this heading as "Ottoman local elites."[15]

In the case of the city of Jerusalem, it is seen that an upper stratum, which had a say in the city administration and was separated from the public, came to the fore. In this period, the most important members of this layer were the members of the *qāḍī* (judge) and his *nā'ib*s (deputy judge); *mutasallim* (deputy governor) of the *Sanjāq* of Jerusalem, *kethudā-yeri* (high officer of the Porte's cavalry),[16] *serdar* (commander of the janissaries) and the *aʿyān* (local notables) as well as *işeris*[17] (agents) as stated in some of the documents.[18]

---

15 Ehud Toledano, "The Emergence of Ottoman-Local Elites," 145–162. For the ruling and local elites of the seventeenth century Jerusalem see Ze'evi, *Kudüs*, 71–72.

16 Although *kethüdā yeri* is among those addressed in the edicts, there is no record of this official's participation in the city administration in practice during the period we examined. Mustafa Akdağ states that the Janissary *serdār* and *kethüdā* positions emerged as two official roles following the Bayezid rebellion in 1558, after which the *Kapıkulları* (Janissaries and *Altı Bölük Halkı*) established garrisons in Anatolian cities. They have engaged in different jobs such as trade and farming. As a result of this situation, in the city centers, after the *yeniçeri serdārı* engaged in the work of janissaries, the *qāḍī, subaşı, city kethüdā* and other dignitaries, along with the "Altı Bölük Halkı", the "Kethüdā yeri" handled their affairs. Oğuzoğlu, "Change in the Ottoman State Order (1299–1918)," 44.

17 Mustafa Ali, who wrote in the late sixteenth century, clearly determines that the *iş erleri* are from the local elite. According to the scholar, these people had no fear of being dismissed because they did not take their authority from the sultan's *berāt*. (Yusuf Oğuzoğlu, "Change in the Ottoman," 51). Hülya Taş, on the other hand, refers to those who are tasked with doing the work of the town with the term "iş erleri", and with the determinations in the *Qāḍī* Registries, in this group, as a representative of various provincial officials and draws attention to the weight of the local elements as the *ayan-ı belde*. The *iş eri* refers to different people in different contexts. At the end of the official counted at the beginning of the *fermāns*, the term *iş erleri* refers to other persons connected to the subject that led to the writing of the edict. (For example, shopkeeper *kethüdās*, experts). Taş, "Merkezi Mutlak Yönetim," 199. Cohen, on the other hand, said the edicts sent to Jerusalem routinely contained *iş erleri* apart from the *sanjāq* rulers and religious leaders, who sent reports on their respective posts to the capital. He stated that the *iş erleri*, whom he described as a less memorable address, had a duty to collect taxes, appoint a new *sanjāqbeyi*, or report changes to the official rates of various coins in circulation. Cohen, *Osmanlı Kudüs'ünde*, 8.

18 "... Üsküdar'dan Kudüs-i Şerīfe varınca; yol üzerinde vākıʿ olan mevāli-i ʿizām zīdet fezā'ilühum ve mefāhirü'l kuzāt ve'l-hükkām, mā'denü'l-fezā'il ve'l-kelām kadılar ve nā'ibler zīde fazlühüm ve mefāhirü'l-emāsil ve'l-akrān mütesellimler ve kethüdā-yerleri ve yeniçeri serdārları ve sāir aʿyān ve zābıtān zīde kadruhüm tevkī'-i refīʿi hümāyūn vāsıl olunmak ma'lūm olup ki Meşāyih-i Hindiyye'den kıdvetü's-sulehā-i's-sālikīn Şeyh Maksum -zīde salāhuhā- Kudüs-i Şerīf'de vākıʿ Zāviye-i Hindiyān'a şeyh olup ol tarafa āzim olmağla şeyh-i mūmā-ileyh her kangınızın taht-ı kazāsına varup dāhil olur ise mü'emmen ve mahfūz mahallerde kondurup ve gider oldukda yanlarına yarar kulaguz

The head of the board, authorized by the central state, was the *qāḍī* to be the subject of matters concerning the issues governed by the city of Jerusalem. Besides, there were *qāḍī*s of all four Islamic schools of jurisprudence: but the chief judge was a member of the official school of jurisprudence of the Ottoman State, i.e. Ḥanafī. He was a senior member of the scholarly class, appointed annually from Istanbul. The other *qāḍī*s, from the Shāfiʿī, Mālikī and Ḥanbalī sects, could be chosen from among the local *ʿulamāʾ*. The fact that Jerusalem had *qāḍī*s from all four schools of jurisprudence shows the religious importance of this provincial city, which was otherwise quite modest.[19] The *Qāḍī* of Jerusalem was under the supervision of the chief judge in Damascus, who belonged to the scholarly class and the Ḥanafī school of jurisprudence.[20] Although his authority was restricted because the judicial affairs of the *reʿāyā* of the *Ḥaramayn* were handled by the deputy inspectors of this *waqf*, the *qāḍī* was the complaint authority for both the ruling and the ruled.[21]

The *Qāḍī* of Jerusalem held a high position and his jurisdiction extended beyond the administrative boundaries of the *sanjāq*. The *nāʾib*s of the *Qāḍī* of Jerusalem, usually appointed from among the local *ʿulamāʾ*, administered the judiciary in all the towns in the region, from Jenin and Nablus in the north to Gaza in the south. The deputy inspectors of the *Ḥaramayn* were also local. Thus, in addition to the *qāḍī*, there were local people who ruled in the city. Likewise, the *naqīb al-ashrāf* of Jerusalem, the *muftī*, the chief clerk of the *sharīʿa* court, and the officials of other institutions in the city were superior to those occupying the same positions in neighboring cities. Indeed, most of the edicts sent to the *sanjāq* were preceded by the words "to the honorable pillar of the judges, the absolute Sharīʿa judge of al-Quds al-Sharīf, our master Mulla Effendi, may Allah perpetuate his virtues, to the *muftī*, the leader of the great scholars, to the *Naqīb* Effendi, the branch of the holy genealogy, the leader of the honorable and prominent, the mutasallim, *alaybey*, *kethüdā-yeri* (high officer of the Porte's cavalry), commander of the janissaries, *mutawallī* of the *Waqf* al-Khalīl and other scholars, righteous and the ordinary people of Jerusalem." The names of the *qāḍī*, *muftī* and *naqīb* would be mentioned first, and the name of the *mutasallim* would be mentioned after them.[22]

---

koşup emn ü sālah yerlerine irsāl ve īsāle ihtimām-ı tāmm eylemek bābında fermān-ı ālişān yazılmışdır. [Fī] Evāhir-i Safer Sene 1156." BOA, ADVNS.AHK.ŞM (1): 29/3.

19 Singer, *Kadılar, Kullar*, p. 37.

20 Bakhit, *The Ottoman Province*, 123.

21 Singer, *Kadılar, Kullar*, p. 38.

22 JS 256: 27. For the salutations in the provisions see "Kudüs-i Şerīf Mollasına ve Kudüs-i Şerīf Sancağı Mütesellimine hüküm ki ..." BOA, ADVNS.AHK.ŞM (1): 41/3; (2):13/3; (2): 31/4; (3): 58/4. "...[ ] ve Kudüs-i Şerīf Kadısına ve Mütesellimine hüküm ki; ..." BOA,

In the classical period, the rotation of officials (*qāḍīs* and *beys*) in the provinces prevented any collaboration with local notables as much as possible. In this way, the state was able to protect the society from organized opposition movements and abuses to a great extent.[23] In the period we are analyzing, it is observed that the state involved the *aʿyān* (local notables) and *ashrāf* (nobles) more in the administration.

Following the unraveling of *tīmār* (fief) system in the seventeenth and eighteenth centuries, many *sanjāqs* were assigned as *arpalık* to higher officials in Istanbul or to commanders of a fortress on the frontiers. A state official or a commander who held such a *sanjāqs* did not usually reside in this province but instead appointed a *mutasallim* to administer on behalf of him. As the head of the administrative officers in the city, *mutasallim* appointed as deputy to take over officially the administration of the province in the names of governors or *beys*, until they reached their posts, or to administer in their absence and especially to collect the *khass* (sultanic) revenues.[24] Even when governors were resided in their provinces, *muhassils* (deputy tax collectors) were appointed to collect *khass* revenues in remote areas or taxes that were gathered irregularly, and deputies were particularly used to collect fines. It would appear that this practice of appointing surrogates became widely established because the *beys* were required to remain on the Hungarian front both summer and winter.[25] Thus, the expansion of the practice of *arpalik*, the consequent administration and tax collection of *sanjāqs* by *mutasallims* and *muhassils* and finally the appointment of *sanjāq beys* from among the local notables, appear to have

ADVNS.AHK.ŞM (1): 186/2; (2): 96/1; (3): 46/1; (3): 110/4; (6): 170/1). "Kudüs-i Şerīf Monlasına, Gazze Sancağı'na vākı' Remle Nāhiyesi nā'ibine ve Kudüs-i Şerīf Sancağı Mütesellimi [ ] ve Gazze sancağı Mütesellimi [ ] zīde kadruhümāya hüküm ki;..." BOA, ADVNS.AHK.ŞM (1): 252/4; (3): 60/4.

23 Abacı, "Osmanlı Kentlerinde Sosyal Kontrol," 103. See also Jennings, "The Office of the Vekil."

24 The origin of this practice dates back to the seventeenth century. A person appointed as *beylerbeyi* or *sanjāqbeyi* was appointing someone to formally take over the administration until he came to his office, to manage the *sanjāq* in his absence, or to collect the personal *khass* income of especially remote places. And even if the *beys* lived in their own provinces, they were appointing officials to collect the special income of remote land or the taxes. These officers were also used to collect fines. These deputies, who were responsible to governors of *sanjāqs*, were known as *subaşı* and *voyvodas* in the fifteenth and sixteenth centuries. After the classical period, it is observed that this proxy management practice has been spread extensively and these deputies have taken the name of *mutasallim*. İnalcık, "Centralization and Decentralization," 30–31.

25 İnalcık, "Centralization and Decentralization," 30; Çadırcı, *Tanzimat Döneminde*, 23.

been the most important operative factors which resulted in the rise of prominence of local notables in provincial administration.[26]

In the seventeenth and eighteenth centuries, it was common practice for every district to have a *voyvoda*,[27] and in the imperial orders submitted to the Province of Damascus *voyvoda*s were also cited among the provincial administrators together with the *mutasallims*.[28] *Voyvoda* administered the *khass* belonging to the treasury or which were assigned to royal ladies; *ze'āmet*s or *tīmār*s assigned to palace and government officials; and villages belonging to the *awqāf*. Apart from the collection of revenues, *voyvoda*s were also responsible for local security and maintenance of *sekban* (mercenary) troops.[29] In an imperial order submitted to the Province of Damascus it was stated that although the *re'āyā* of the *waqf* lands of Lud which were the assets of the *Waqf* of Khasseki Sultan Public Kitchen was exempted from the *'urfī* (customary) taxes such as *cürm-i cināyet* (homicide tax), *resm-i arūsāne* (marriage tax), *kul ve cāriye müjdegāneleri* (slave and concubine taxes), the governor of the *sanjāq* as well as the *mutasallim* and *voyvoda* were interfered in the *waqf* revenues. Since these unnecessary interventions, contrary to the law and ordinary practices (*mugāyir-i kanūn-ı qadīm ve'l-'urf*), were devastating the situation of *waqf re'āyā*. For this, two separate imperial orders were sent and the intervention of the members of ruling elites to the *waqf* revenues was prohibited.[30]

---

26 İnalcık, "Centralization and Decentralization," 30. For further information about this process see Akdağ, "Osmanlı Tarihinde Āyanlık," 51–61.

27 Mustafa Akdağ states that in addition to the *voyvoda*, these people were also called *zābit* and *nāib* until the beginning of the 15th century. On the subject, see Akdağ, *Türkiye'nin İktisadi*, 263.

28 "... kadı ve nā'ib ve mütesellim ve voyvoda ve subaşı ve sāir ehl-i örf tāifesi yanlarına varmayup ve hilāf-ı vākı' mevādd isnādıyla fukarāyı gamz ve tecrīm itdirmeyüp zulm ü te addī itmemeleriçün muhkem tenbīh ve te'kīdi hāvi kanūn üzre emr-i şerīf yazılageldiği derkār olunmağla ..." BOA, ADVNS.AHK.ŞM (3): 18/1.

29 İnalcık, "Centralization and Decentralization," 35–36.

30 "Kudüs-i Şerīf kadısına [ ] ve [ ] kadılarına [hüküm] ki: Bābü's-sa'ādetim Ağası nezāretinde olup Kudüs-i Şerīfde vākı' merhūm ve mağfurün-lehā Sultan Süleyman Hān ve Haseki Sultan tābet serāhümānın cāmi'-i şerīf ve tekye ve imāret-i āmireleri Evkāfından taht-ı kazānıza tābi Lūt kazāsı ve tevābi-i karyeleri mefrūzü'l-kalem ve maktu'ü'l-kadem min-külli'l-vücūh serbest olup vākı olan cürm-i cināyet ve resm-i arūsāne ve kul ve cāriye müjdegāneleri ve sāir bād-ı hevālarına mīr-mirān ve mīr-livā ve mütesellim ve voyvoda ve serdār ve sāir ehl-i örf tā'ifesi taraflarından hılāf-ı kanūn bir dürlü dahl ve ta'arruz olunmak īcāb itmez iken vāliler ve mütesellim ve voyvoda ve sāir ehl-i örf tāifesi taraflarından rüsūm-ı serbestiyete hilāf-ı kanūn fuzūlī müdāhale ve re'āyā-yı vakfı ahz u haps teklīfi ile te'āddī ve ahvāl-i fukarā diger-gūn ve perākende ve perīşān olmalarına bā'is ve bādī olmalarıyla rüsūm-ı serbestiyesine ehl-i örf tāifesi taraflarından hılāf-ı kanūn bir dürlü dahl ve ta'arruz olunmamak bābında hükm-i hümāyūn virilmek recāsına bundan akdem Ağa-yı Bābü's-sa'āde-i esbāk Ali Ağa arz itmeğin. İmdī Selātīn-i İzām Evkāfı karyeleri

In the period under scrutiny, the role of *aʿyān* was both a way to become an *aʿyān* and an investment tool accessible to those with wealth. In this period, the *aʿyān* held a large portion of the *mīrī* land under the *çift-hāne* system as *muqāṭaʿa*. Apart from this, they were also the customary authorities (administrators) in the places where they held tax-farming.[31]

In the documents, *serdār* (commander of the janissaries) as the Agha of Jerusalem and the Janissary Officer were also stated among the members of the ruling elite of the *sanjāq*.[32] The Agha of Jerusalem was responsible for preventing the city-based tyranny and providing security. However, it should not be forgotten that all the janissaries in the city did not constitute the force of law enforcement and a significant portion of them were engaged in agricultural production.

The *aʿyān-ı vilāyet* (local notables) constituted an important part of the social stratum active in urban administration. In the eighteenth century these local notables as it was also called as *vucūh-ı belde* (city elders) included the scholars such as *hākim al-sharīʿa* (in other words, the *qāḍī*), the *muftī*, *mudarris* and religious order *shaykh*s and *naqīb*s; captains such as *kethudā-yeri* (high officer of the Porte's cavalry) and the janissary sergeant and those who dismissed or retired and their children; traders of valuables such as *bezzāz* (tradesman), *kimhācı* (silk merchant), jewelry traders; artisan leaders such as *kasabbaşı* (butcher's counter), *bakkalbaşı* (grocery counter), and *marketbaşı* (merket counter); and the *kethudā*s (chamberlains).[33]

Aʿyān (local notables) and *ashrāf* (nobles) consisted of groups with different status, wealth and social standing. In each *sanjāq* and district, there was

---

mefrūzü'l-kalem ve maktu'ü'l-kadem min-külli'l-vücūh serbest hāriçden kat'a dahl olunmak cā'iz değildir kanun amel olunmak için Hudāvendigār-ı esbak ammi-zādem merhūm ve mağfūrün-leh Sultan Mahmud Hān tābe serāhü zamānında emr-i şerīf virilüb tecdīdin recā itmekle vech-i meşrūh üzre amel olunmak emrim içün yazılmışdır. Fī Evā'il-i Şevval Sene 1173." BOA, ADVNS.AHK.ŞM (2): 156/1.

31 For example, it was recorded with a petition that the residents of villages in Jerusalem and Ramla of the Khasseki Sultan *Imāret Waqf* in Jerusalem, did not pay their taxes due to the drought that took place in 1061, 62 and 63 and when the tax-farmer Mehmed wanted to collect these in the beginning of Rabīʿ al-Awwal 1065. A provision was given that such revenues should be collected by the *mutawallī* al-Hajj Khalil. BOA, ADVNS.AHK.ŞM (1): 289/4. For another example, see BOA, ADVNS.AHK.ŞM (1): 212/5.

32 BOA, ADVNS.AHK.ŞM (1): 29/3; 245/4; (2): 156/1; (2): 286/3; (2): 314:5.

33 The increase in the proportion of ruling elite in this social group happened in the seventeenth century. See also about the scope of the *aʿyān*. Özer Ergenç, "Osmanlı Klasik Dönemindeki Aʿyān ve Eşrāf Üzerine Bazı Bilgiler," Osmanlı Araştırmaları 3 (1982): 105–18, 106. İnalcık, "Centralization and Decentralization," 37–38; Göçek, *Rise of the Bourgeoisie*, 136, endnote 54; Şahin, "The Rise and Fall," 29; Mert, *18. ve 19. Yüzyıllarda*, 195–96.

also a ranking of the *aʿyān* from senior to junior. Therefore, it can be said that those who excelled in terms of wealth and reputation were among those who, together with the *qāḍī* and others, made decisions on behalf of the city.[34]

Apart from these, the city *kethudā* (chamberlain), *pazarbasi* (the bazaar master) and the deputy *naqīb al-ashrāf* were among the *aʿyān*. The city chamberlain and bazaar master were in charge of determining and allocating the city's expenses, which were distributed to the people of the district every six months or a year.[35] They constituted a kind of board that acted under the presidency of the *qāḍī* and convened in the *qāḍī*'s office when necessary.[36]

The central government held these urban decision-makers accountable, authorized them, and held them responsible at the same time.[37] It can be said that the state expected them to act in unison, especially in matters concerning the entire district or *sanjāq* such as the collection of taxes, the elimination of banditry, and the provision of soldiers and ammunition (or money) demanded by the center.[38] These individuals, who originated from the *ahl al-sharīʿa* (*ʿulamāʾ*), *ahl al-ʿurf* (*umarā*), and *aʿyān*, were also the center's instruments of social control in urban administration.

As the scope of the definition suggests, not all city elites had a direct say in the administration. Local elites had a say in many administrative areas in which the imperial center did not directly intervene, and local officials were in a position to decide how the provisions would be implemented, even in matters that were directly decided at the seat of power.[39] Likewise, along with the *qāḍī* (judge) and *muhtasib* (market superintendent), the urban elites, as representatives of the people, were involved in determining the time of harvest, which was also the basis for annual taxation, as well as the value of money and

34 Akdağ, "Osmanlı Tarihinde Āyanlık," 51–61.

35 Cohen, *Osmanlı Kudüs'ünde*, 3–6, 9, 38.

36 İnalcık, "Centralization and Decentralization," 41.

37 Faroqhi, at the end of the sixteenth century, reconsidered these people who were active in the city administration in Çorum as urban decision-makers. See Faroqhi, *Osmanlı Dünyasında Üretmek*, 315–40, 320–27.

38 See "... imdī siz ki mevlānā ve mütesellim ve sāir mūmā-ileyhumāmsız [vücūh-ı ahāli] belde-i mübāreke-i mezkūrede īʿfā-yı nizām istemeyüp duā-yı enʿām içün merkūm Ali fī-mā-baʿd vakten mine'l-evkāt bir vechile mahkemeye takrīb ve idhāl olunmaması husūsına ihtimām ve dikkat olunması matlūb-ı şāhānem oldığı maʿlūmunuz oldukda mazmūn-ı emr-i şerīfimi mahfūza kayd ve mazmūn-ı sınıfı üzre ale'd-devām ʿamel itdiğin birle merkūmun vakten mine'l-evkāt bir vecihle mahkemeye uğratılmaması emrine dāʿī ve müstemirren iʿtinā ve nezāret ve mezīd-i ihtimām ve hırāseten bi-gāyet-i hazer ve mücānebet olunmak bābında. Fī Evāhir-i *Zi'l*-kaʿde Sene [1]210" BOA, ADVNS.AHK.ŞM (5): 54/3); VGMA, 324/83–84.

39 Canbakal, *17. Yüzyılda Ayıntâb*, 199.

prices.[40] Many officials were appointed through the intervention of the *aʿyān* and the *ashrāf* and elected unanimously. In the appointment of *waqf* employees and *mutawallīs*, if not specified in the *waqfiyya*, the person agreed upon by the local elite was also appointed to these positions.[41] When two people competed for the same office, the approval of the *muhtar* (elected) and the *aʿyān* played an important role in determining who would be given the office. When faced with a request for intervention in disputed cases, the central administration accepted the local decision: "[whichever] of the *aʿyān* of the city had the consent and gratitude" remained in charge.[42]

In 18th-century Ottoman Jerusalem, the leading *ʿulamāʾ* families among the local Muslim population gained perhaps the most significant power and held a wide variety of positions at the local level. Throughout the period under study, local prominent families across the Ottoman Empire built their wealth through tax-farming, or tax collection rights. Initially sold by the government at auction for a short period of time, tax-farming were quickly transformed into long-lasting concessions and eventually into *mālikānes* (lifetime leases or de facto private property).[43] As already mentioned, however, the tax-farming was not the main source of enrichment for Jerusalem's elite families. In most cases, religious and educational *waqfs* established by dignitaries and *ʿulamāʾ* from the imperial center, rulers and their dynasties, and local notables were the main source of wealth.

---

40 Ze'evi, *Kudüs*, 144. See also. Ergenç, "Osmanlı Klasik," 111.

41 Ergenç, "Osmanlı Klasik," p. 109–10. In the first example of appointments to foundations, it was recorded that the newly appointed officer was appointed with the approval of the city's leaders in the following provisions instead of the officers who died childless. A similar situation applies to Jerusalem. "... medīne-i Kudüs-i Şerīf'de Hazret-i Dāvud en-Nebī -aleyhi's-selām- Zāviyesi'nin yevmī iki akçe ile bā-berāt-ı ʿālī yolunda cihete mutasarrıf Şeyh Abdurrahman Şemseddin-zāde bundan akdem bilā-veled fevt ve es-Sayyid Ali bin Arif yolunda mezkūreye müstehak oldığı medīne-i mezkūre ahālisinden erbāb-ı vukūfdan Şeyh Ali bin Muḥammad ve Ahmed bin Mustafa nām kimesneler ihtiyārlarıyla müstehak oldığını Mahmud Paşa Mahkemesi nā'ibi Mevlānā es-Seyyīd Mehmed Şemseddin iʿlām itmekle mūcebince işbu bin iki yüz sekiz senesi Şaʿbān'ında tevcīh olundığı ..." BOA, ADVNS.AHK.ŞM (5): 13/1. "... Kudüs-i Şerīfde vākiʿ Evkāfdan ve Kudüs-i Şerīf mimarlığının nısfı Hacı Ahmed bin Receb ve nısfı āheri İbrahim bin Hebbetullah üzerinde olub mezbūr İbrahim bundan akdem nısf hissesin evlādlar üzerlerlerine berāt itdirmekle minvāl-i muharrer üzere mestūr ve mukayyed olub lākin zikr olunan nısıf mimarlığa mutasarrıf olan merkūm Hacı Ahmed müddet-i vefīreden beru fevt olmakla cümle aʿyān ve eşrāfın ittifakıyle bā-hüccet-i şerʿiyye Nureddin halīfe mutasarrıf olub sadākat ve istikāmet üzere umūrun ru'yet idegelüb ..." VGMA, 814: 89.

42 Ergenç, "Osmanlı Klasik," 110.

43 İnalcık, "Centralization and Decentralization," 41; İnalcık, "Military and Fiscal," 331–33. See Marcus, *The Middle East on the Eve of Modernity*, 57–58.

So how did Jerusalem's leading figures establish their influence within the *waqf* system? To some extent, of course, through their wealth. However, this is far from being the main reason for this situation. Their social prestige and influence, as well as tradition, solidified and reinforced their position within the *waqf* system. This high position played a crucial role in their appointment as *mutawallīs* and other important officials of charitable *waqfs*. As seen in many examples, the privileged positions held by their grandfathers years ago, due to their position in society, the coercive power of custom and the influence of tradition, have been preserved by the *qāḍī* by being passed down from generation to generation within the same family.

So how did the notables of Jerusalem establish their influence in the *waqf* system? Gabriel Baer in his article "Jerusalem's Families of Notables and the *Wakf* in the Early Nineteenth Century," discusses the connection between *waqf* institutions and the notable families of Jerusalem. His analysis is limited to a time period of around ten years of court records (*sijill*) between the years of 1805 and 1814. First, he examines the *waqfs* founded by the notable families between this time periods and later examines the *waqf* founded by people other than the notables but which the notables are a part of, either through being *mutawallī* or having hereditary rights to certain posts within these *waqf* institutions. He gives a detailed list of all the families, their positions in the *waqfs* and their relationship with the *waqfs*. Then he goes on to a lengthy discussion of dismemberment and alienation of *waqfs*. Baer notes that normally the *waqf* endowments are eternal and inalienable but the practices evolving in the late Ottoman period have brought new ways of changing the status of *waqf* properties.

At the same time, Muḥammad Ali Alami examines the issue from a different perspective in his article "The *Waqfs* of the Traditional Families of Jerusalem during the Ottoman Period," First, he gives an extended historical background of the notable families and depicts their whereabouts in the Crusader and Post-Crusader period in Jerusalem and compares the structural differences with regards to the *Awqāf* in the Ayyubid, Mamluk and Ottoman periods. He also analyzes the relationship between the notables' wealth and *waqf* endowments and gives tables of specific endowments belonging to families of notables. Baer clarifies the reason for this relationship stating that these families have gained administrative powers, ownership, and revenue from the existing non-family *waqfs* because of their economic, social and political powers. Baer also describes four ways in which notables become related to the *waqfs*: the first is through endowment, as being the endower, and the second being *mutawallīs* and other officials to the existing major *khayrī waqfs*. Third, *waqfs* are endowed by their ancestors. Fourth is from gaining a post within the *waqfs*.

On the other hand, Alami advocates that since the beginning of the Ottoman period, *waqfs* were a way to finance religious institutions such as mosques and schools. In line with Baer's argument, al-Alami also states that there was a relation between the notables and the *waqf* institutions but these *waqf* institutions were a way for notables to gain influence and wealth, so they almost gained their notable position because of their association with *waqfs*. However, Baer argued that notables were related to *waqfs* because they were already notables. This point distinguishes their arguments from a basis of causality. Both authors have placed emphasis on different concepts. While al-Alami has focused on the endowment of the non-owned properties as *waqf*, Baer has examined the dismemberment processes. Even though both of these concepts are somewhat demonstrating an unconventional practice or a misuse of the *waqf* institution their arguments were not convincing as they have not provided a sufficient picture for the usage of these *waqfs* for personal gain.

In this context, to be able to create a much stronger and convincing fusion, together with the analysis of their points, we have tried to add the role of Ottoman state in this relationship. That is, in addition to their wealth and tradition, their social dignity and influence have maintained and strengthened their position within the *waqf* system. Their high position played a crucial role in the appointment to *khayrī* (public) *waqfs* as *mutawallīs* (trustees) and other important officials.[44] Certain positions had become the prerogative of certain families and could be sold, but the social consensus limited the sale of these positions to other prestigious family members. Clearly, social status and family connections played an important role in obtaining rights to *waqf* property. Tenants acquired such rights for reasons that required financial resources, such as the repair and renovation of *waqf* properties or the planting of trees. However, these rights were not transferred as a result of public tension. The *mutawallī* of the charitable or spiritual *waqfs* had a say in the selection of beneficiaries. Other revenues from the government were the *surra* and the *jizya* tax levied on non-Muslims. The notables were often placed in well-paid, prestigious jobs and, in rare cases, appointed as *qāḍī* and chief clerk. The tax exemption granted to the *'ulamā'* and the notables allowed them to save a large part of their income and to build up a substantial surplus, which was often invested in other businesses.[45]

Most of the families that increased in number and rose to high positions in Jerusalem with the Ottoman annexation were families that lived in Jerusalem before the Ottoman rule or were identified with Jerusalem. The most notable

44 Baer, "Jerusalem's Families," 118–19.

45 Ze'evi, *Kudüs*, 94–95.

of these families are the Dajjānids. Ahmad Dajjānī (d. 1562), who was regionally recognized as the famous Sufi of the *Maqam* of the Prophet David, is the person on whom the family traces its lineage.[46] The families of al-Jāʿūnī and al-Nammār (Ḥasan ibn al-Nammār) are noted as architects and administrators of *waqf* institutions. The families of al-Maʿarrī, Daqāq, Quṭb (descended from the Ṣūfī writer al-Quṭb al-Khalīlī), al-Zuhaymān, ʿAbd al-Laṭīf, Tarjumān, Quṭayna, Tirḥī, Wahba (Shaykh Makkī), Ḥujjāj, al-Shihābī, and Abū Suʿūd (of Syrian descent) had established themselves as Jerusalem's high religious elite by the third century of Ottoman rule (18th century). During the same period, the Ibn Ḥubaysh (Budayrī) family, originating from Acre, joined Jerusalem's elite. The Darwīsh, Murād, and Ḥallāq families, of Ottoman origin, also settled in Jerusalem in the 18th century. Additionally, Moorish families from the Maghāribī community, along with Banī Ghānim (from the Ayyūbī period) and the Mamlūk-era Dankiz, Arghūn (now Rajabī), and Tunbukha (now al-Sayfī) families, were among the influential families of Ottoman Jerusalem. While not exhaustive, these family names provide a historical overview of Jerusalem's elite families.[47]

The most important of these influential families belonging to the *ʿulamāʾ* class in Jerusalem was the Ḥusaynī family.[48] From the second half of the 18th century onwards, Ḥusaynīds, who held the posts of the *muftī*, *naqīb al-ashrāf*,[49] and the Shaykh of the *Ḥaram al-Sharīf* for generations, and later held administrative functions such as the mayor of Jerusalem, were the best example of a family that gained political influence and social superiority in the city by matching their religious positions with their economic power. It had become a generally accepted practice in this period for both administrative and religious-public positions such as the posts of the *muftī*, the *naqīb al-ashrāf*, and the Shaykh of the *Ḥaram al-Sharīf* to be held by the same family. However, a certain official procedure was also followed for appointments to

46 Al-Alami, "The Waqfs of the Traditional Families," 148.

47 ibid., 148–49.

48 Khadduri, "Arab Contemporaries," 69.

49 In Arab countries, those who were engaged in the affairs of the *sayyids* and *sharifs* descended from the Prophet and were called *naqīb al-ashrāf*. In the Ottoman Empire, the office of *naqīb al-ashrāf* was established in 1400 during the reign of Sultan Yıldırım Beyazid and Seyyid Ali Nattâ from Baghdad was first appointed to this office. The *naqīb al-ashrāfs* kept books containing the names of all *sayyids* and *sharifs* in the Ottoman lands through their district governors in the provinces, *sanjāqs* and districts. The *naqīb al-ashrāf* or his district governor in the provinces, who supervised whether the *sayyids* and *sharifs* acted contrary to the laws and customs, would also prosecute and punish the inauthentic *seyyids* and *sharifs*. The office of *sayyids* and *sharifs* continued until the collapse of the Ottoman Empire. Uzunçarşılı, *İlmiye Teşkilâtı*,164–68; Kılıç, *Osmanlı'da Sayyidler*.

the office of *naqīb* and the approval of Istanbul was sought. In a study based on Jerusalem *qāḍī* registers, Abu-Manneh states that the *qadi* appointed the next person to the office of *naqīb al-ashrāf* after consulting with the prominent people of the city.[50] However, this appointment was only temporary and was finalized with the approval of the governor of Damascus and the *naqīb al-ashrāf* in Istanbul.[51] As can be seen, although the *naqīb al-ashrāf* was responsible for protecting and representing the rights of the *sayyid* and *sharif*s, he was not elected by the *sayyid* and *sharif*s, but in accordance with the opinion of the city elders. In addition to his main responsibilities, the *naqīb al-ashrāf* also served as the representative of certain *waqf*s and as a witness in matters concerning the city's notables.[52]

However, in addition to these duties, the *naqīb* was also part of the city administration. Local administrators sometimes sought his advice and assistance in matters outside their normal duties. For instance, in 1776, the governor of Damascus sent a letter asking for the *naqīb*'s help in collecting the *jizya* from non-Muslims or, as in 1798, asking for the Bedouin Beni Hasan tribe to pay taxes. In another example, in the curriculum book written in 1195 AH/1780 CE, in addition to the *qāḍī*, the *naqīb al-ashrāf*, the Shaykh of the *Ḥaram al-Sharīf*, chief clerk, and other prominent people of the city were also present during the exploration and measurement procedures required for the repairs of the al-Aqṣā Mosque, the Dome of the Rock, and other holy sites.[53] Therefore, the religious-social priorities provided by the position of *naqīb al-ashrāf* and its prestige in the eyes of the administration made the city's notables take a special interest in who would be appointed to this position.[54]

During the study period, the al-Ḥusaynī family was prominently represented in Jerusalem's religious and administrative elite. ʿAbd al-Laṭīf Effendi ibn ʿAbdullāh Effendi al-Ḥusaynī served as deputy *naqīb al-ashrāf* and Shaykh al-Ḥaram, contributing to three *waqf*s.[55] His son, Ḥasan Effendi ibn ʿAbd al-Laṭīf

50 Abu-Manneh, "The Ḥusaynīs," 96.

51 Avcı, *Değişim Sürecinde*, 48.

52 Ze'evi, *Kudüs*, 86.

53 "Sādır olan emr-i ʿālī mūcibince Kudüs-i Şerīfde vākiʿ Mescid-i Aksā ve Sahratullah-ı Müşerrefe ve sāir emākin-i mübārekelerin üzerlerine cānib-i şerʿden Kātibbaşı Ali Efendi, Nakībü'l-eşrāf ve muʿavin-i bi'l-iftā Şeyhü'l-Harem Efendiler ve sāir ehl-i vukūf mağrifetleri ve filan kulları mağrifetiyle begān begān keşf u mesāhā olunub işbu müfredāt defteri ... Rebiu'l-ahir 1195."

54 Abu-Manneh, "The Ḥusaynīs," 97.

55 When Sayyid ʿAbd al-Laṭīf Effendi passed away in 1188/1775, he left four sons: ʿAbdullāh, Ḥasan, ʿAbd al-Samad, and Muṣṭafā. ʿAbdullāh inherited his father's roles as *naqīb al-ashrāf* and *shaykh al-ḥaram*. His brother Ḥasan, who also founded the aforementioned *waqf*, became the Ḥanafī Muftī of al-Quds. All three emerged as the most influential authorities

al-Ḥusaynī, the *muftī* of Jerusalem, established four *waqf*s.[56] Additionally, ʿUmar Effendi al-Ḥusaynī, named as *naqīb al-ashrāf* in his 1229 AH/1814 CE *waqfiyya*, founded two *waqf*s. In total, the al-Ḥusaynī family established nine modest family *waqf*s during this period.[57]

In the eighteenth century, the Ḥusaynīds were followed by their biggest rivals, the Khālidīds, who held other prestigious positions in the city, such as the position of *nāʾib*s (deputy judges) and chief clerk in the Jerusalem's *sharīʿa* court.[58] During the period covered by this study, nine *waqf*s were established by Muḥammad Sunʿ Allāh Effendi ibn Khalil al-Khālidī al-Abbāsī Shaykh al-Quds; nine by Musa Effendi ibn al-Ḥajj Muḥammad Effendi Sunʿ Allāh al-Dīrī al-Khālidī served as the chief clerk of the Sharīʿa Court in Jerusalem;[59] and one by Muḥammad Ali al-Khālidī in 1227 AH / 1812 CE. Thus, a total of twelve *waqf*s were established in Jerusalem by members of the al-Khālidī family during the period analyzed.

Similarly, other influential families, such as the ʿAlamī and Dajjānī, were renowned for their expertise in religion and Sufism, which they leveraged to gain political influence. Sources indicate that, except for the ʿAlamī family, these families generally traced their lineage to a prominent scholar, *qāḍī*, or other respected religious figure or official. The exception is the Ḥanafī Amīr Mūsā ibn Sulaymān al-ʿAlamī, founder of the ʿAlamī family, who served as Governor of Jerusalem from 793–795 AH/1391–1393 CE.[60] The ʿAlamīds identified with the ʿAlamīds of Morocco, who claimed descent from al-Ḥasan ibn ʿAlī ibn Abī Ṭālib through their ancestor, the Sufi Ibn Mashīsh, a respected figure among Moroccan gentry. Members of the ʿAlamī family also held positions as *qāḍī* or *nāʾib* in the *sharīʿa* court for many years.

During the period under study, ten *waqf*s were established by members of the ʿAlamī family in Jerusalem. The first *waqf* was founded by

---

in the city, which remained under the control of the Ḥusaynī family. Abū Mannā, "The Ḥusaynīs," 95. During the eighteenth century, the office of the Muftī of Jerusalem, previously held by various *ʿulamāʾ* families, was managed by six generations of the Ḥusaynī family following its transfer to Shaykh Ḥasan.

56 Sayyid ʿUmar, along with Shaykh Ṭāhir, represents the third generation of the Ḥusaynī family. Upon the death of Shaykh Ḥasan in 1809, his nephew Shaykh Ṭāhir assumed the post of Muftī, while Sayyid ʿUmar, the founder of the *waqf* and grandson of Shaykh Ḥasan, became Shaykh al-Ḥaram. In 1800, he was also appointed as *naqīb al-ashrāf*. Abū Mannā, "The Ḥusaynīs," 100.

57 JS 220:161.

58 Al-Asali, "Jerusalem," 217.

59 Shaykh Mūsā al-Khālidī, a local rival to the Ḥusaynīs, is a well-educated scholar. Abu-Manneh, 'The Ḥusaynīs," 99.

60 Al-Ḥanbalī, *Uns al-Jalīl*, 164–5.

al-Shaykh Abū al-Wafā' al-ʿAlamī in 1116 AH/1704 CE.[61] The second was established by al-Shaykh Jūd Allāh Effendi ibn al-Shaykh Muṣṭafā al-ʿAlamī in 1130 AH/1718 CE;[62] the third by al-Shaykh Ṣalāḥ ibn al-Shaykh ʿAbd al-Laṭīf al-ʿAlamī in 1141 AH/1728 CE;[63] the fourth by al-Shaykh ʿUthmān Effendi ibn ʿAlī Effendi al-ʿAlamī in 1150 AH/1737 CE;[64] the fifth by ʿAbd al-Raḥmān Effendi ibn al-Shaykh ʿAbd al-Raḥīm al-ʿAlamī in 1150 AH/1737 CE;[65] the sixth by Faḍl al-Dīn ibn al-Shaykh Muṣṭafā al-ʿAlamī in 1153 AH/1740 CE;[66] the seventh by ʿAbd al-Bāqī al-ʿAlamī in 1167 AH/1748 CE;[67] the eighth by al-Shaykh Fayḍ Allāh (Fayḍī Effendi al-ʿAlamī, naqīb al-ashrāf al-Quds) in 1167 AH/1754 CE;[68] the ninth by ʿAlī Effendi ibn ʿAbd al-Laṭīf al-ʿAlamī in 1177 AH/1764 CE;[69] and the tenth by al-Shaykh Aḥmad ibn al-Shaykh ʿAbd al-Bāqī al-ʿAlamī in 1197 AH/1782 CE.[70] Almost all members of the ʿAlamī family were nicknamed al-shaykh and *effendi*. In addition, the founder of the *waqf* in 1754, al-Shaykh Fayḍ Allāh, also bore the title *naqīb al-ashrāf* of Jerusalem. All these *waqf*s, modest in assets, were family *waqf*s.

The Jār Allāh family (Ibn Abī al-Luṭf, also known as Luṭfī),[71] from which the majority of the *muftī*s of Jerusalem was elected, established three endowments during the period covered by this study. The first was established by Abī al-Luṭf Effendi, *Muftī* al-Shāfiʿiyya, in 1115 AH/1703 CE and a house in Dāwūdiyya Gate was endowed.[72] The second, by al-Shaykh Muṣṭafā ibn Ṣāliḥ al-Luṭfī in 1123 AH/1711 CE, endowed a house and an olive grove vegetable garden in Bāb Ḥiṭṭa, part of ʿUmar al-Luṭfī's estate.[73] The third, by al-Shaykh ʿUmar ibn al-Shaykh Ṣāliḥ al-Luṭfī in 1134 AH/1722 CE endowed a house and a garden with pomegranate, apricot, mulberry, grape, and various fruit trees in Bāb Ḥiṭṭa.[74] In the latter two endowments, revenues were designated for *Ḥaramayn al-Sharīfayn* after the family lineage ended.

The Imām family, a prominent Jerusalem family, established three *waqf*s. The first was founded by Ḥajar bint al-Shaykh Muḥammad Ṣāliḥ al-Imām in

61 JS 202: 375.
62 JS 213: 51–52.
63 JS 221: 602.
64 JS 227: 179.
65 JS 229: 52.a.
66 JS 230: 168.
67 JS 236: 117–118.
68 JS 403: 376.
69 JS 247: 48–49.
70 JS 256: 134.
71 Ze'evi, *Küdüs*, 87.
72 JS 202: 295.
73 JS 207: 129–130.
74 JS 218: 18.

1178 AH/1764 CE, endowing a house in the Sharaf neighborhood.[75] She designated the income of this family *waqf* to herself during her lifetime, then to her daughter Nafīsa bint Ḥajj Ḥusayn al-Tanbāgha, her descendants, and Ḥajj Ḥusayn al-Tanbāgha's descendants, and, upon their extinction, to the blind neighbors of Jerusalem's *Ḥaram*. Muḥammad Ṣāliḥ Effendi ibn ʿAbd al-Ghanī al-Imām established two *waqfs* in 1230 AH/1815 CE. The first endowed six hamlets in Bayt Iksā, five in Abū Sūr, one in Sayf Manjik, eight and two in Bayt Ṣafāfā, one in Miṣrāra, and a water tank in Miṣrāra.[76] He stipulated that the revenues of the *waqf* should be given to the scholars of Jerusalem in the event of the endower's extinction. The second endowed a house on Bazbazat Street, a house near Bistāmiyya Lodge in Banī Zayd, and vegetable gardens in Ṭūriyya and Bāb Ḥiṭṭa.[77]

The ʿAsalī family gained prominence through commercial wealth, establishing seven family *waqfs* with modest assets.[78] In the period under study, seven *waqfs* were established by members of the ʿAsalī family. The first two *waqfs* were established by Ṣafiyya Khātūn bint ʿAbd al-Jawād al-ʿAsalī[79] and Sharīfa Khātūn bint Ṣāliḥ al-ʿAsalī.[80] Two *waqfs* were established by al-Ḥajj Sulaymān Bey ibn ʿAbd al-Jawād al-ʿAsalī,[81] two by Aḥmad Agha al-ʿAsalī al-Dizdār[82] and one by Muḥammad Beg ibn Ḥasan Beg al-ʿAsalī.[83] All of them were family *waqfs*, and their assets were quite modest. Similarly, other influential families, such as al-Dajjānī, were known for their knowledge of religion and Sufism and used their positions to gain political influence.[84]

Al-ʿAlamī's study of *waqfs* by the Ḥusaynī, Khālidī, ʿAlamī, Jār Allāh, Nāmrī, and Imām families during the Ottoman period shows similar patterns for the period 1703–1831 CE, though with some differences.[85] When this study was

75 JS 248: 54–55.
76 JS 297: 86.
77 JS 298: 169.
78 Ze'evi, *Kudüs*, 84, 87.
79 JS 207: 144.
80 JS 207: 144; JS 243: 183.
81 JS 251: 139–141; JS 255: 116.
82 JS 251: 39; JS 261: 20.
83 JS 301: 109.
84 Ze'evi, *Kudüs*, s. 84.
85 See Table 8. For further information, see Al-Alami, "The Waqfs of the Traditional,"145–58. In his work, Al-Alami identified that mentioned six families established 142 *waqfs* in the Ottoman period. Thirty of these *waqfs* were *khayrī* while 142 of them were *zhurrī*. Again, 124 of them were established by the male members of the families, as women *waqf* founders were eighteen in total. The number of properties of which endowers endowed their properties as their own was registered as 624. The number of *waqfs* encompassing books were 9. For further information, see Al-Alami, "The Waqfs of the Traditional," 152.

TABLE 8 *Waqf*s endowed by the leading local families of Jerusalem (1703–1831)

Family names	Number of the *waqf*s	Type of the *waqf*		Gender		Total revenue	*Waqf*s having books	Time period
		Khayrī	*Dhurrī*	Men	Women			
Ḥusaynī	9	–	9	9	–	18	2	1174/1761–1229/1813
Khālidī	12	1	11	12	–	65	1	1123/1711–1227/1812
ʿAlamī	10	1	9	10	–	30	1	1116/1704–1197/1782
Jarullah	3	–	3	3	–	5	–	1115/1703–1134/1722
Nimrī	3	–	3	3	–	52	–	1172/1758–1221/1806
Imam	3	–	3	2	1	27	–	1178/1764–1230/1815
Total	40	2	38	39	1	197	4	1116/1704–1233/1818

compared with the *waqf*s established by these families during the period covered by our study (1703–1831), similar results were reached, but some differences were also identified. First of all, the six families in question, who established numerous *waqf*s throughout the Ottoman period, also established new *waqf*s during the period covered by this study. Although modest in number, these *waqf*s endowed the largest amount of land in Jerusalem. On the other hand, when compared to the data cited in Muḥammad ʿAlī al-ʿAlamī, the number of *waqf*s established by the Jārullah and Imām families decreased. The number of charitable *waqf*s and the number of women founders of *waqf*s also decreased significantly.

In addition to the aforementioned share ownerships of the *waqf*s established by the leading families of Jerusalem, what is noteworthy in the aforementioned *waqfiyya* documents is the ownership of the family *waqf*s established by the *waqf*s during the period under review. In the application of Islamic law, the early *imāms* based the validity of the *waqf* on the absolute ownership of the endowed property. The Shāfiʿī, Ḥanbalī and Ḥanafī *imāms* did not even agree that the endower could endow his own share in the case of shared ownership. However, there are numerous examples of the re-endowment of another *waqf*'s property in *waqf*s established by prominent families of Jerusalem in the

18th century.[86] In two extreme examples, in endowments established by the al-Khālidī family (dated 1213 AH/1799 CE and 1255 AH/1839 CE), properties that did not originally belong to the *waqf* but had been rented out for long periods were listed one by one and then re-endowed.[87] Similarly, in an earlier *waqfiyya* of the family (dated 952 AH/1545 CE),[88] they re-endowed the cultivated fields around Jerusalem, which had been rented out for a long period of time, with special emphasis on the fact that they were part of the properties of the *waqfs* established during the Ayyubid and Mamlūkid periods. In other cases (e.g., al-Khālidī 1255 AH/1839 CE and al-Ḥusaynī 1249 AH/1834 CE), properties that had been endowed by *waqfiyyas* established by ancestors of the same family and leased for long periods of time were also re-endowed.

The reason for this situation is that the aforementioned properties belonged to previous *waqfs* but were leased to the *waqf* for a certain period of time. The close ties of Jerusalem's leading families with the great charitable and endowment *waqfs* provided them with opportunities such as long-term leases, as was the case here. It should be emphasized that these long-term leases were used in similar ways by Christians, Muslims and Jews. Other religious groups followed suit in the last century of the Ottoman rule in Jerusalem, when their influence increased, and re-established *waqfs* with the *waqf* properties given to them on long-term leases.[89]

In addition to the six families previously mentioned, other notable families include Dāwūdī, Jāʿūnī, Quṭb, Quṭayna, Khaṭīb/ʿAfīfī (from families prominent in pre-Ottoman Jerusalem), Kuwayda, Anṣārī, al-Saʿdī (families prominent in pre-Ottoman Jerusalem), al-Ḥujjāj, al-Nashāshībī, al-Qudsiyya (prominent families in pre-Ottoman Jerusalem), al-Shihābī, al-Budayrī, and al-Nusayba (prominent families in pre-Ottoman Jerusalem).[90] In his study on *waqfs* established in Jerusalem during the Ottoman period, Muḥammad Hāshim Ghūsha expanded the list of traditional families founding *waqfs* to 54. Conversely, Baer, in his study of Jerusalem's elite families as founders, managers, and beneficiaries of *waqfs* between 1905 and 1914, identified fourteen families frequently mentioned in the registers. Considering these studies, the Table 9 below presents the number of *waqfs* established by prominent households in Jerusalem.[91]

The table related the number of *waqfs* endowed in Jerusalem by the elite families during the period under review as follows:

86 Al-Alami, "The Waqfs of the Traditional," 153.
87 JS 280: 87. The founder was Mūsā ibn Muḥammad al-Khālidī.
88 JS 17: 66. The founder was Musa ibn-i al-Dairi (al-Khālidī).
89 Al-Alami, "*The Waqfs of the Traditional*," 154.
90 Al-Alami, *idib.*, s. 152–153.
91 Al-Alami, "The Waqfs of the Traditional," 149.

TABLE 9 The number of *waqf*s established by elite families of Jerusalem (1703–1831)

No	Family name	*Khayrī* (public)	*Dhurrī* (family)
1	Akl (Akkal)	–	1
2	ʿAlami (al-Alam, Suʿūdī)	1	7
3	Asali (ibn Rabiʿ)	–	7
	Jarullah	–	1
4	Jaʿūni	–	13
5	Dajjani (Dāwūdī)	–	3
6	Dervish	–	2
7	Abu al-Lutf (Jarullah)	–	2
8	Abu Usʿūd (Dāwūdī, Abu Hāmid)	–	1
9	Abu Jibna	–	1
10	Ansari (Denef, Dāwūdī, Ibn Dāwūd)	–	9
11	Asmar (Tantūra)	–	2
12	Ibn Ganīm	1	2
13	Gūshe (ʿIsha, Abu al-Wafa)	–	4
14	Khālidī (Dayrī (2))	1	13
15	Khatib (Jamāʿa, Ibn Jamāʿa, Qutāhī)	–	1
16	Ḥusaynī (Qudsiyya (2) Juda, Abu al-Wafa)	–	11
17	Hujaj (al-ʿĀrif, Sharaf)	–	1
18	Hūshe (Havāsh)	–	1
19	Imam (Ibn Kādı as-Salt)	–	4
20	Qalibu	–	1
21	Qamal (Ibn Abu Sharif)	–	1
22	Qashmīrī	–	2
23	Quttīna (Qutayna)	–	7
24	Qutb	–	9
25	Quvaydar	–	3
26	Maghribī	–	12
27	Muwaqqıt (Muhaddis)	–	5
28	Nammar (Nimrī)	–	3
29	Nemrī (Ibn Nemr)	–	4
30	Nashashibi (Bani Qudsiyya, Fewāz)	–	1
31	Nuʿāji	–	2
32	Rasās	–	5
33	Saʿdī al-Mālikī (Muna, Hijāzī)		2
34	Semūm	–	3
35	Serenda	–	2

TABLE 9 The number of *waqfs* established by elite families of Jerusalem (1703–1831) (*cont.*)

No	Family name	*Khayrī* (public)	*Dhurrī* (family)
36	Shiihābī (Shihābeddin)	–	2
37	Turjuman	–	7
38	Terhī	–	2
39	Wahba (Shekkī Mekkī)	–	4
40	Zuheiman (Awlad al-Zuheiman)	–	1
Total		3	162

The families, as in the examples given in this study, are mostly from the *ʿulamāʾ* class and they took charge in active and long-term duties in the administration of a variety of religious-educational *waqf* in the Ottoman period.[92] The Ottoman center had to integrate these local powers in its own contexture to offer the local sources to the service of centre and to provide security in locality. Yet, this integration "is formed with a horizontal process continuing over negotiation rather than vertical appointment process from centre to locality".[93] In the period covered by this study, the ratio of the number of *waqfs* established by Jerusalem's leading families, most of whom belonged to the *ʿulamāʾ* class, to all *waqfs* is 55%. This ratio is meaningful in terms of showing the activity of Jerusalem's leading families as founders of *waqfs*.

1.2 *The* Reʿāyā (*Ordinary People*)

This section of the study aims to define the population of Jerusalem during the period under review, focusing on the *reʿāyā*, the plural of *raʿiyya*, which dictionaries define as "people subject to a ruler's administration who pay taxes known as *tekālīf-i emīriyye* (extraordinary tax)."[94] The reʿāyā encompassed all Muslim and non-Muslim subjects obligated to pay taxes but excluded from

92 For further information about families and their other duties in *waqf*, see: Eroğlu Memiş, "Ḥurūfāt Defterleri Kayıtlarına Göre," 145–85; Şerife Eroğlu Memiş, "*Waqfs* as a Tool for the Rise of Local Notables in Jerusalem During the Eighteenth Century," paper presented at the Middle East Studies Association 46th Annual Meeting, New Orleans, 2013.

93 Yaycıoğlu, "Sened-i İttifak (1808)," 667–709.

94 Şemseddin Sāmī, *Kāmūsü'l-Aʿlām*, 666.

state administration,[95] categorized into urban dwellers (merchants, craftsmen, or *ehl-i ḥiref*), peasants, and farmers.[96]

Peasants in the Palestine region, all Arabs and forming the majority, were divided into tribes, such as Qays and Yaman, based on customs and traditions. Villages were typically split among large families, each led by a *shaykh*, with multiple *shaykhs* if several tribes coexisted.[97] Palestinian peasants were relatively more open compared to those elsewhere in the Ottoman Empire, frequently encountering strangers in Jerusalem. In villages like Bethlehem and Bayt Jālā, Christian pilgrims were a constant presence, while Muslims visited local shrines. The *fellāḥīn* (peasants) were shaped by local customs, climate, geography, agriculture, their native language, and Jerusalem's unique urban center, influencing their multifaceted world.[98]

In 18th-century Jerusalem, "Ottomanization" held little relevance for most inhabitants, including artisans, workers, and migrants, who faced limited social mobility due to insufficient wealth to become even minor intermediaries. Some ascended socially by joining political households or entering the lower tiers of the education system. The proliferation of *waqf*s, funded by sultanate and provincial treasuries, supported a small portion of this group. Otherwise, it was rare for commoners to rise to the ranks of the *ʿulamāʾ* or mid-level notables.[99]

Artisans and craftsmen were organized into guilds, with around 70 professions across approximately 60 guilds in Ottoman Jerusalem, spanning production, service, and trade. Each guild's internal hierarchy and activities were managed by a guild head (*shaykh al-ḥirfa*), appointed by the local *qāḍī*, serving as the primary link between the largely autonomous guild and the administration.[100] This was the regular and main channel of communication between the guild, which was autonomous in other respects, and the administration.

95 Mardin, *Din ve İdeoloji*, 85.

96 Akdağ, *Türkiye'nin İktisadi*, 119–27.

97 Bostancı, *19. Yüzyılda Filistin.*

98 Singer, *Osmanlı'da Hayırseverlik*, 166–67.

99 Khoury, *Osmanlı İmparatroluğu'nda*, 144.

100 Cohen, *Economic Life*; Lewis and Cohen, *Population and Revenues*, 84–104. See also for the study, which assessed the appointment records of representatives of trades organizations operating in Jerusalem in the eighteenth century. Şerife Eroğlu Memiş, "Ḥurūfāt ya da ʿAskerī Rūznāmçe Defterlerinde Eṣnāf Teşkilātı Atama Kayıtları ve Önemi: Kaza-i Kudüs-i Şerîf Örneği," in *Osmanlıdan Günümüze Filistin Sempozyumu: Bildiriler*, vol. 1 (Ankara: Türk Tarih Kurumu, 2013), 41–71.

2 The Endowers and Their Status in Ottoman Jerusalem's *Waqf* Network

Charity was shaped by a combination of status, economic power, gender and group solidarity. These factors influenced not only the means of raising the income needed to establish a *waqf*, but also the choice of the city, the location, the date, and the management of the *waqf*. In this section of the study, the titles and nicknames, social status and gender of the founders of *waqf*s in the period covered by the research (1703–1831) will be analyzed in order.

2.1 *Titles and Nicknames of Endowers*

A nickname is a name given to a person or a family apart from their own name and pronounced in front of their name, deriving from a characteristic of that person or family.[101] The leading local Muslim families of Jerusalem used two main linguistic tools to distinguish themselves from other social groups. The first is the unchanging family name that is passed down from generation to generation. Other members of the non-elite Muslim community did not have such family names.[102]

The naming conventions and structures of traditional Jerusalem families during the study period exhibit distinct characteristics rooted in historical practices. In the Ayyūbid and Mamlūk periods, the form *awlād* (sons of) was prevalent, as seen in names like Awlād al-ʿAlamī, Awlād al-Dāʾirī, and Awlād Abū al-Luṭf. The form Banī (tribe of) was also used, such as Banī Jamāʿa and Banī Qudāma. The Sunnī *madhhab* of each family was consistently appended to their names, predating Sultan Baybars' policy of appointing officials from their respective sects.[103]

During the Ayyūbid and Mamlūk eras, two titles were commonly attached to first names. The first, Abū (father of), was paired with a specific name: every Muḥammad was Abū ʿAbdullāh, Ibrāhīm was Abū Isḥāq, Sulaymān was Abū Rabīʿ, and ʿAlī was Abū al-Ḥasan. The second, al-Dīn (of the faith), was similarly standardized: Muḥammad was Kamāl al-Dīn or Shams al-Dīn, Ibrāhīm was Burhān al-Dīn, Sulaymān was ʿAlāʾ al-Dīn, ʿAlī was ʿAlāʾ al-Dīn, and Yūsuf was Jamāl al-Dīn or Ṣalāḥ al-Dīn. Ibn Taghrī Birdī traces these naming conventions to the 5th century AH, likely amplified by the Seljūk migration and influx of non-Arab Turkmen, where emphasizing first names provided an Islamic veneer for non-Arab middle names. This practice was swiftly adopted locally. Family names like ʿAlamī, Shihābī, and Kamāl often originated from ancestors'

101 *Türkçe Sözlük*, 956.

102 Büssow, *Hamidian Palestine*, 375.

103 Al-Alami, '*The Waqfs of the Traditional*', 148.

titles, such as ʿAlāʾ al-Dīn Sulaymān, Shihāb al-Dīn Aḥmad, and Kamāl al-Dīn Muḥammad.

At the onset of Ottoman rule, family naming practices evolved. Sunnī *madhhab*-related names, including those tied to Ḥanafī jurisprudence, were gradually abandoned, with most families dropping this usage by the late 16th century, except for non-Ḥanafī families like the Shāfiʿī Imām and Jār Allāh. Another change was the addition of the suffix *yāʾ* (indicating belonging, read as *ī*), simplifying family names into a single word. For example, awlād al-Dāʾirī al-Khalīdī al-Ḥanafī became Ṭāhirī and later al-Khālidī, and awlād al-ʿAlamī al-Mālikī became al-ʿAlamī. This simplification, after nearly five centuries, is attributed to non-Arab Ottoman rulers.[104]

Another development in the formation of family names was the addition of the letter *yāʾ* at the end of family names, which indicates belonging, and the reading of the letter ī. Thus, each family name was expressed with a single word. For example, the name awlād al-Dāʾirī al-Khalīdī al-Khanafī became only Ṭāhirī and later al-Khālidī, and the name awlād al-ʿAlamī al-Mālikī became only al-ʿAlamī in reference to the family. This significant simplification of family names, which had been in use for nearly five centuries, can be attributed to the non-Arab Ottoman rulers.

It was observed that the names of the founders of *waqf*s during the period analyzed in this study were mostly expressed with the letter *ī* added to the end of their family names. In total, 34 founders of *waqf*s were named in 98 waqfs with the letter *ī* added to the family name and family names such as Ḥusaynī, ʿAlamī, ʿAsalī, Tirḥī, and Khālidī. Again, the nicknames of the founders of the *waqf* expressed with the letter *abū* added to the family name are six. Similarly, while the number of foundation founders whose family names are expressed with the expression *bi-ibn* is eleven, this number is 3 for family names expressed as *awlād*. Female *waqf* founders are recorded as *bint* or *zawja*.

At the beginning of the 18th century, some families changed their names completely in order to strengthen or establish a connection with the notables. Thus, at least three unconnected families adopted al-Ḥusaynī as their family name. The Awlād Abū al-Wafāʾ became ʿAbd al-Laṭīf al-Ḥusaynī; a branch of the Qudsiyya family became Yūnus al-Ḥusaynī and then the awlād al-Qāḍī al-Sāyiḥ al-Imām al-Ḥusaynī. The al-Dīnīn, on the other hand, abandoned the traditional family name altogether and took the name al-Khālidī. The aim here was to strengthen the family's alleged ties with the Companion Khālid ibn al-Walīd. In the same period, the ʿAlamīds who did not change their family names identified themselves with the ʿAlamīds of Morocco. The ʿAlamīds

104 *Al-Alami, 'The Waqfs of the Traditional,' 148.*

in Morocco claimed that they traced their ancestry back to al-Ḥasan ibn ʿAlī ibn Abū Ṭālib, who held a respected position among the Moroccan gentry and whose ancestors were traced through the Ṣūfī Ibn Mashīsh. On the other hand, al-Murtaḍā al-Zubaydī made a clear distinction between the ʿAlamīds of Morocco and the ʿAlamīds of Jerusalem.[105] The family names given here are the family names of the city's prominent members. While these names represented a family membership in the network of leading families of the city, these were also means of separating themselves from the local community and reinforcing their leading positions.

Second, various titles were used by Jerusalem's leading families to distinguish themselves from the rest of society.[106] In his study on Haifa, Mahmoud Yazbak has identified the importance of titles as an important indicator of social status in late Ottoman *sharīʿa* court registers.[107] In his study based on the Haifa registers, Yazbak identified 24 different titles indicating various social groups.[108]

Pasha, *beg*, and *effendi* are functional titles indicating three main positions in the Ottoman official hierarchy. However, *beg* and *effendi* were sometimes used as epithets signaling social status. The title *pasha* was used as the highest military and administrative position and was never used for religious officials. The Arabic word *al-afandiyyā* was used for the leading *ʿulamāʾ* families of Jerusalem. As is well known, this is a title of exaltation. A white turban or a green turban worn by the descendants of the Prophet (*ashrāf*) was the attire of members of the *ʿulamāʾ* class.[109]

Moreover, in official documents, members of these families were differentiated from the *reʿāyā* with various admonishing epithets and prayers and titles due to their duties within the ruling caste. First of all, the title of the *qāḍī*, the highest member of the *ʿulamāʾ* in the city, was *mawlānā*. *Mawlānā* was a title used for those who held the rank of *mawlawī*, which is the rank of *qāḍī*, and it means "our lord". In addition to these, *imām*s and orators were called *khalīfa*, *faqīh*, *mullā*. The word *khalīfa* is the title given to Muslims after the Prophet who became the imam and leader of Muslims. However, in the Ottomans it was generally used for *imām*s, those who knew the *sharīʿa* and taught and practiced the practical knowledge of the religion. *Faqīh* is the name given to scholars of *fiqh* (Islamic law). The title *mullā* was the form of the word *mawlānā*. The common characteristic of all these titles is that they are words

105 ibid., 148.
106 Büssow, *Hamidian Palestine*, 375.
107 Yazbak, "The Islamic *Waqf*," 2, 47–69.
108 ibid., 118, 235–42.
109 Büssow, *Hamidian Palestine*, 376.

that indicate the special place of *ʿulamāʾ* and the religious officials in society, the importance and respect given to them.

Members of the *ahl al-ʿilm* (*ʿulamāʾ*) were closely related to each other. In many cases, a person whose father was a judge, the *mudarris* or prayer-preacher would himself be drawn to the same profession. Because of their wealth and prestige, they had close relations with the *ahl al-ʿurf* (*umarāʾ*) and big merchants. Their nobility and high status is once again evident in their bearing the title *çelebi*. Ergenç has determined from the registry records of the late 16th and early 17th centuries that the word *çelebi* was used "as the title of those who were the sons of the members of the sciences, religious officials, and great merchants and who perpetuated the social status, cultural values and wealth of their fathers."[110] It signifies erudition, nobility, wealth and respectability. Canbakal, too, defines the title *çelebi* as a civilian epithet that does not indicate a distinction between ruling elite and ordinary people. She noted that some of the individuals she identified as *agha* and *beşe* could also be referred to as *çelebi* in other documents.[111] The epithets occasionally used in the case of Jerusalem are shown in Table A15.

2.2 *Social Status of the Endowers*

In studies on Ottoman social structure, Ottoman society is divided into two major classes.[112] The *ʿaskerī*, usually defined as the ruling elite or the ruling class and sometimes as those who collected taxes separately from the *reʿāyā* (ordinary taxpaying population), was a service-based nobility consisting of those who held religious or administrative power by virtue of a sultan's decree, namely officials, civil servants, and *ʿulamāʾ* attached to the palace and the army.[113] In return for their loyalty and service, the sultan would bestow them with salaries and certain monopolies over land and resources.[114] The second was the aforementioned *reʿāyā*, which included all Muslim and non-Muslim citizens who were obliged to pay taxes but did not participate in state administration.[115]

In the Ottoman Empire, efforts were made to preserve the social structure created within the framework of the state's economic and administrative policy.[116] As İnalcık puts it, "it was the basic rule of the state to keep its subjects away from the ruling elite. Only those who were actually raiding on the borders and those who entered the *ʿulamāʾ* class through a regular education

110 Ergenç, *XVI. Yüzyılın*, 242.
111 Canbakal, *17. Yüzyılda Ayıntāb*, 81–85.
112 Mardin, *Din ve İdeoloji*, 89–94; Ergenç, "Osmanlı Klasik," 107.
113 İnalcık, 'The Nature of Traditional," 44. See also Rafeq, "Changes in the Relation," 22.
114 Khoury, *Osmanlı Imparatroluğu'nda*, 69.
115 Mardin, *Din ve İdeoloji*, 85.
116 Yüksel, *Osmanlı Sosyal ve Ekonomik*, 22.

in a *madrasa* could receive the sultan's license and become members of the ruling class."[117]

Following the 16th century's peak of expansion and centralization, the ruling class expanded in the 17th and 18th centuries. In the second half of the 17th century, there were three ways to become part of the military elite: Obtaining the right to an income with or without a specific service, claiming descent from the Prophet Muḥammad, and joining a military unit.[118] In the period covered by this study, the transition to the expanding and localized military caste in the city of Jerusalem was largely through new positions as *waqf* officials. In this context, before moving on to the *waqf* officials to be discussed, the founders of *waqf*s belonging to the "ruling class" will be identified.[119]

2.3 *Endowers Belonging to the Members of the Ruling Elite in Jerusalem*

Although it is possible to divide the Ottoman social structure into two groups with a rough classification, Bahaeddin Yediyıldız and Hasan Yüksel, in their studies based on 17th and 18th century *waqfiyyas*, evaluated the founders of *waqf*s in four main groups. In this framework, the ruling class is grouped under the headings of courtiers, military-administrative (*ahl al-ʿurf*), civil servants (*kalemiyye*), and scholars (*ʿilmiyye*). In addition, shaykhs and dervishes (members of *tariqa* and Sufism), who had a privileged position in Ottoman society, and the *sayyids* (*sādāt*), who constituted the privileged group based on nobility as in other Islamic states, were also classified within the ruling elite.[120] It should be noted here that the wives and daughters of administrators and individuals who were given titles such as *beg*, *pasha*, *mullā*, and *mawlānā*, and

---

117 In the Ottoman Empire, "berāt-ı hümāyūn ile hitābet ve imāmet ve emānet ve kitābet ve tawliya ve cibāyet ve nezāret ve meşīhiyyet ve cüz'ü tesbih-hān ve bunun emsāli mansıb tasarruf edenler askerīdir ve berāt-ı şerīfle doğancı ve yayacı ve derbendci ve köprücü ve ulakçı ve yağcı ve otakçı ve haymana ve çeltükçü … kadı ve nā'ibleri ve şehir kethüdāları ve tekālif-i örfiyyeden muʿāf olanlar askerīdir." Apart from these, "evlād-ı askerī ve sādāt, muʿtak ve muʿtakaları … askerīnin zevcātı askerīdir." See Ergenç, *Osmanlı Klasik*, 214.

118 Canbakal, *17. Yüzyılda Ayıntāb*, 81–82.

119 The *ʿaskerī* definition of the beginning of seventeenth century was not left on paper, although there was the possibility of going through changes with time, *Ḥurūfāt* or *Askerī Rūznāmçe* books, which contain the first half of the nineteenth century, support the continuity of the structure. The *Ḥurūfāt* or *ʿAskerī Rūznamçe* Books, which were kept on the basis of the Ottoman provincial organization's district administrative structure, contain all sorts of duty ranks of the related district and records of the military class serving in a district. Regarding the *waqf* officials that became a part of military class through their duties, 96% of the Jerusalem district records are about the appointments to *waqf*s.

120 Yüksel, *Osmanlı Sosyal*; Yediyıldız, *XVIII. Yüzyılda*. For similar analyses see Alkan, *Adana Vakıfları*; Eroğlu Memiş, "17. ve 18. Yüzyıllarda Edirne'de," 67–87.

women with the title *khātūn*, were also included. In addition, *waqf* employees are also included in this group.

2.3.1 Members of the Palace

This group, which includes the sultans and their relatives, includes the sultans who established *waqf*s in Jerusalem, as well as the mother of the sultans, their wives and daughters. During the reign of Suleiman the Magnificent, a total of six fountains were built in Jerusalem, five within the *Ḥaram al-Sharīf* and one around the Ḥaram, to meet the clean water needs of the city's residents.[121]

In addition, the *waqf* complex founded in 1552 by Hürrem Sultan, the wife of Suleiman the Magnificent, is one of the most important works that came to life in Jerusalem during the Ottoman period. The complex in question consisted of a public kitchen, *madrasa*, mosque, shops and *tabhāne*s. The complex, which was the largest *waqf* established in Palestine up to that time, was supported by the revenues of dozens of villages neighboring the city, and these villages, which were exempt from the excise tax, paid their taxes directly to the *waqf* officials.[122] Hürrem Sultan, who established a large *waqf* to cover the expenses of the complex, allocated many villages and large areas of land in Syria and Palestine, especially around Ramla, to this *waqf*. After her death in 1558, Sultan Suleiman added the land of four more villages around Sidon to this *waqf*.[123] Although Hürrem's public kitchen was a typical example of Ottoman attempts, it was unique in Jerusalem. There had been many *waqf*s that distributed food to the *madrasa* students, Sufi dervishes or guests. However, at the time of its establishment, it was observed that there was only one public kitchen in Jerusalem and no similar institutions were opened. In addition to these *waqf*s, in the period examined (1703–1831) no records of *awqāf* were established by the members of the palace in Jerusalem.

2.3.2 Members of the Military-Administrative Class (*Sayfiyya -Ahl al-ʿUrf*)

Ahl al-ʿurf is used for the group that includes the highest state officials and the lowest-ranking state officials other than the sultan. This group, whose duty was to ensure the sultan's authority in the country, is also referred to as *ahl al-sayf* (men of the sword) because they carried swords.[124]

---

121 Rosen-Ayalon, "On Süleyman's Sabīls," 589–607.

122 A copy of the *waqfiyya* of Khasseki Sultan *Waqf* is present at *Waqf* Records Archive (Vakıf Kayıtlar Arşivi) while the original is at the Archive of the Museum of Islamic Arts (IEMA). IEMA, 2962; VGMA, 608–2: 235/178, See Appendix 3; Singer, *Kadılar, Kullar*, 69.

123 al-Asali, "Kudüs," 334–38.

124 Yüksel, *Osmanlı Sosyal*, 24.

When the status of the founders of the *waqf* belonging to the *ahl al-ʿurf* group is analyzed, it is seen that their status is directly proportional to the hierarchy at the administrative level. As they moved from the lowest to the highest level of the state, their reputation, influence, responsibilities, and wealth increased. Regardless of the level of the state, the *ahl al-ʿurf* was obliged to govern the state in accordance with the orders of the sultan. If they were found to be deficient or wrong, they were dismissed; if necessary, they were even beheaded, and their property was confiscated.[125]

In Jerusalem, 500 Asadī *kurūsh* were endowed by Ḥusayn Pasha ibn ʿAbbās, "Guardian of Damascus, Jerusalem, Gaza, Nablus, and the *amīr al-ḥajj al-shāmī*, vizier," in 1151 AH/1738 CE.[126] With this cash *waqf* for the *Ḥaram al-Sharīf*, the purchase of rose and wood water for incense was also stipulated. The second *waqf* was established by the deputy governor of Jerusalem, al-Ḥajj Muṣṭafā Agha, by endowing 40 *zahab* (golden liras) for the fountain he built in Bāb al-Nāẓir in Masjid al-Aqṣā.[127]

Muḥammad Agha, *mutasallim* (deputy governor) of Jerusalem endowed a Qur'an for the Dome of the Rock,[128] while the Qāsim Bey as the commander of the fief holders in the province endowed one to the poor and the dervishes in the Qādirīyya Sufi Lodge[129] and Esed Bey also endowed another Qur'an to the dervishes in the Qādirīyya Sufi Lodge.[130] Suleyman Pasha endowed a prayer rug for the Dome of the Rock.[131] Dervish Muḥammad Miralay, on the other hand, dedicated a Qur'an for the dervishes of Uzbek Sufi Logde.[132] In the eighteenth century, considering the small number of *khayrī* (public) *waqf*s, it is seen that the ruling class of the *ahl al-ʿurf* group formed more modest and charitable *waqf*s.

The *subaşı* (police superintendent) was among the members of *ahl al-ʿurf* on a local basis. Among them, Muḥammad ibn ʿAlāʾ al-Dīn, a *subaşı* in Jerusalem and an assistant to the *qāḍī*, endowed a house in the Naṣāra neighborhood, two vegetable gardens in the Saʿdiyya neighborhood, and a vise for processing olives.[133] Among the other endowers of this class were those who had some military titles, such as Ḥāsib Ḥasan ibn Sulaymān as the commander of janissaries

125 Yüksel, *Osmanlı Sosyal*, 26.
126 JS 228: 224.
127 JS 230: 210. In addition, fourteen portions of bread to be taken from the Khasseki Sultan *İmāret* was endowed to the person adding water to the *waqf*'s *sabil*.
128 JS 308: 124.
129 JS 290: 1.
130 JS 290: 1.
131 JS 290: 38.
132 JS 221: 48.
133 JS. 250: 126–127.

(*bölükbaşı*),[134] Ḥusayn Çelebi ibn ʿAbd al-Nabī as the commander of janissaries (*bölükbaşı*),[135] ʿAbd al-Mawlā al-ʿAbd al-Bāqī as the artilleryman (*topçu*),[136] and ʿAlī ibn Muḥammad as the sergeant (*çavuş*).[137] Among the endowers , the number of *waqf*s established by *aghas*[138] and members of the janissary quarry with the title of *beşe* is also significant.[139] In conclusion, members of the *ahl al-ʿurf* and their relatives have an important place among the founders of *waqf*s.

2.3.3 Scholars (*Ahl al-ʿIlm*)

When we look at the members of the *ahl al-ʿilm* (scholars) class, the group that was trained in *madrasas* in the Ottoman Empire and fulfilled duties related to religion, justice, and education in line with the general character of the state was called the scholars' class. Among the people who belonged to this group and established *waqf*s were *shaykh al-islām*, chief judges (*qaḍāʾ ʿaskar*), judges (*qāḍī*s), *muftī*s, *mudarris*es, and shaykhs.[140]

In addition to the *waqf*s established mostly by members of the *ʿulamāʾ* families mentioned under the heading of Jerusalem's local elite, this section will discuss other founders of *waqf*s belonging to the scholarly class. There is no record of a *waqf* whose founder was a *shaykh al-islām* in the period under study. The number of *waqf*s established by *qāḍī*s in Jerusalem is only one. In the charitable *waqf* established by the *qāḍī* of Jerusalem, Aḥmad Effendi al-Ḥatnī, the income of a 12-*qīrāṭ* house in Bāb al-Qaṭṭānīn was endowed for the Dome of the Rock fountain (Bāb al-Maghāriba fountain) located in the area of Masjid al-Aqṣā and opposite Bāb al-Maghāriba.[141] Chief Judge (*qaḍāʾ ʿaskar*) Muṣṭafā Effendi, on the other hand, endowed a cash *waqf* for the charities of the public.[142]

As a *muftī*, a *waqf* was established by the Shāfiʿī *Muftī* of Jerusalem, Muḥammad Ṣāliḥ Effendi al-Ḥusaynī al-Ḥalwatī ibn ʿAbd al-Ghanī Effendi al-Imām, known as *ash-shahīr bi-ibn Qāḍī al-Ṣalṭ*"[143] In this *waqf*, a shop in

134 JS 235: 123.

135 JS 235: 217–219.

136 JS 223: 372.

137 JS 230: 187.

138 On ʿAbdullāh Āghā ibn al-Ḥājj Muḥammad al-Maghribī, see JS 235: 318. ʿAbd al-Raḥmān Āghā ibn Muḥammad Karam: JS 257: 65. Yūsuf Āghā ibn Ḥusayn ibn al-Ḥājj ʿAlī al-Jāʿūnī: JS 302: 93; 397: 25.

139 ʿAbdullāh Āghā ibn al-Ḥājj Muḥammad al-Maghribī: JS 235: 318. ʿAbd al-Raḥmān Āghā ibn Muḥammad Kirm: JS 257: 65. Yūsuf Āghā ibn Ḥusayn ibn al-Ḥājj ʿAlī al-Jāʿūnī: JS 302: 93; 397: 25.

140 Yediyıldız, "Müessese-Toplum," 152.

141 JS 59: 43.

142 JS 196: 429.

143 JS 298: 208.

Khaṭṭ Dāwūd, 12 independent shops in the Bāb al-ʿAmūd neighborhood, 6 shops in the western branch of Bāb al-ʿAmūd, a coffee shop known as Dāwūdī Coffeehouse in the Ḥaddādīn neighborhood, and a floor on the coffee shop road were endowed. Secondly, Muḥammad al-Ḥusaynī ibn al-Shaykh ʿAbd al-Ghanī, the Muftī of Jaffa Jetty, established a *waqf* for the *imām* of Masjid al-Aqṣā. In his *waqfiyya*, he endowed the *khuluww* of a house located in Khaṭṭ Dāwūd, Bāb al-Silsila neighborhood, adjacent to the Tashṭīmūriyya *Madrasa Waqf*.[144] Both of the endowers were the members of the family of *Qāḍī* al-Ṣalṭ.

In Ottoman society, the scholarly class included not only those who graduated from *madrasas*, such as *mudarris*, *qāḍīs*, *muftīs*, and *imāms*,[145] but also *qāḍī nāʾibs*, *kassāms*, sultan's teachers, *sayyids*, and *sharīfs* who were descendants of the Prophet Muḥammad, as well as *naqīb al-ashrāfs* and court officials such as the chief physician, physicians, *munajjims* (astrologers), and *hünkār imāms* (sultan's preachers).[146]

The number of *waqfs* established by the *naqīb al-ashrāfs* of Jerusalem in the period covered by this study is large. In 1143 AH/1730 CE, the Jerusalem *naqīb al-ashrāf* Muḥibb al-Dīn Effendi, who was not a member of the al-Ḥusaynī family, established a *waqf* in which he endowed his house.[147] In the second, Shaykh Fayḍ Allāh Effendi al-ʿAlamī endowed six *qīrāṭ* of shares of a shop in the Naṣāra neighborhood.[148] Later, ʿAbd al-Laṭīf Effendi ibn ʿAbdullāh Effendi al-Ḥusaynī established three *waqfs* in Jerusalem as the deputy *naqīb al-ashrāf* and *Shaykh al-Ḥaram*.[149]

All three *waqfs* were established after his appointment as *naqīb al-ashrāf*. In his first *waqfiyya* dated 1174 AH/1761 CE, he endowed a house in Bāb al-Ḥiṭṭa near the Shaykh al-Bisṭāmī *Zāwiya*.[150] He stipulated the revenues and management of the *waqf* to himself while he was alive, to his daughter Nasība Khātūn after his death, then to his sons, his progeny, and his *aʿqāb*, and if he had no sons, to his daughters, and when their progeny ceased, to the Shaykh Muḥammad al-Qırımī *Zāwiya*. The second *waqf* was established in 1180 AH/1766 CE, and the assets of the *waqf* are listed as a two-story house consisting of *ḥaramlik* and *salāmlik* sections (households were divided into two separate sections: the *salāmlik*, housing the male members, and the *ḥaramlik*, where the women and

144 JS 295: 232.

145 Yusuf Halaçoğlu, *XIV–XVII. Yüzyıllarda Osmanlılarda Devlet Teşkilatı ve Sosyal Yapı* (Ankara: TTK Yayınları, 1995), 102.

146 İsmail Hakkı Uzunçarşılı, *Osmanlı Devleti'nin İlmiye Teşkilâtı* (Ankara: Türk Tarih Kurumu Yayınları, 1988), 359–74.

147 JS 223: 288–89.

148 JS 403: 376.

149 JS 249: 63–64; File 2/21: 1194/13; JS 281: 12–14.

150 JS 243: 122.

children dwelt) and dwellings on Sitt Ascent, and the large two-story house that Muḥammad Agha Murād received from his heir. He stipulated that the income of the *waqf* should be distributed to himself while he was alive, then to his sons, then to his daughters when they were no longer descended from him, then to his uncle Sayyid Muḥibb al-Dīn Effendi when they were no longer descended from him, and then to the employees of the Nabī Mūsā Tomb and Shaykh Muḥammad al-Qırımī *Zāwiya* equally when they were no longer descended from him. In his last *waqfiyya* dated 1210 AH/1795 CE, the endower stipulated a *khuluww* of a mill that extracted olive oil and a furnace stove, stones, and tools in the village of Jabal Tūr.[151]

He stipulated 6 *zoloṭa* from the income of the *waqf* to the *mujāwirīn* (people who stay in a city for a period exceeding that of a guest). He stipulated the other endowment revenues to himself as long as he was alive, then to his sons, then to their minor children, then to his daughters when the generation from the sons ceased, then to *Simāṭ* (Public Kitchen) Nabī Mūsā when the generation from them ceased, and if the conditions were not applied, to the poor and needy. All three of the endowments briefly summarized here are family endowments and are quite modest in terms of their assets. Finally, ʿUmar Effendi al-Ḥusaynī, *naqīb al-ashrāf* of Jerusalem, established a foundation in 1229 AH/1813 CE.[152] In this *waqfiyya*, he endowed a house at the beginning of Ẓāhiriyya Ascent, three empty shops in Khaṭṭ al-Bazaar adjacent to the Afḍaliyya *madrasa*, and a house at the beginning of Sitt Ascent. He endowed the income of the *waqf* to the *Maqām* (Mausoleum) al-Nabī Mūsā and Masjid al-Aqṣā after he ceased to be descended from his children. Thus, with the above-mentioned *waqf*s, a total of four family *waqf*s were established by the members of the Ḥusaynī family in the period analyzed. A *waqf* was established by Ṣūfī al-Ḥajj ʿUthmān ibn al-Ḥajj Aḥmad al-Shahīr bi-Ibn al-Ḥāmid.[153]

Many *waqf* officials who worked in *waqf* institutions and received salaries in return for their services were also from the scholars' class. Among them, religious officials such as *imām*, *muʾadhdhin*, preacher, and pulpit preacher were at the forefront.[154] In the period under review, Shaykh *al-Ḥaram* ʿAbd al-Wahhāb Effendi, *sanjaqdar* of Masjid al-Nabawī Shihāb al-Dīn Effendi,

---

151 JS 177: 177–178.

152 Sayyid ʿUmar and Shaykh Ṭāhir, third-generation representatives of the Ḥusaynī family, assumed key roles after Shaykh Ḥasan's death in 1809. Shaykh Ṭāhir, Ḥasan's nephew, took over the *muftī* position, while Sayyid ʿUmar, Ḥasan's grandson and founder of the mentioned *waqf*, assumed the role of Shaykh al-Islām. And in 1800 he was appointed also as the *naqīb al-ashrāf*. See Abu-Manneh, "The Husasynīs," 100. For the details of the *waqfiyya* see JS 220: 161; File 2/21: 1194/13.

153 JS 218: 156.

154 Ziya Kazıcı, *Osmanlı'da Toplum Yapısı* (İstanbul: Bilge Yayıncılık, 2003), 70–71.

Shaykh al-Ḥaram of Quds Shaykh ʿAlī al-Khalīlī, and the Shaykh al-Maghāriba ʿAbd al-Salām al-Maghribī established *waqfs*.[155]

Again in the period under review, *khādim* al-Masjid al-Aqṣā and Dome of the Rock, al-Shaykh ʿAbd al-Qādir ibn al-Shaykh Mūsā al-Quṭb al-Muwakkīt,[156] the *muḥaddith* Aḥmad Effendi ibn al-Shaykh Aḥmad Effendi,[157] *khādim* al-Masjid al-Aqṣā, al-Shaykh ʿAbd al-Qādir ibn al-Shaykh Mūsā al-Quṭb al-Muwakkīt[158] and Muḥammad Hasan al-Nashāshibī,[159] Ibrāhīm ibn al-Shaykh ʿAbd al-Qādir al-Danaf (al-Anṣārī),[160] the trustee of the Dome of the Rock, Muṣṭafā ibn Muḥammad ʿUjān as lightener (*sirāj*);[161] Muhammad Beşe ibn Muṣṭafā,[162] the lamp keeper and janitor, Tomb of the Nabī Dāwūd, Ṣāliḥ al-Dajjānī[163] are some of those who established *waqfs* as *waqf* officials.[164]

In the period covered by this study, nine *waqfs* were established as *Shaykh al-Quds* by Shaykh Muḥammad Sunʿ Allāh Effendi ibn Khalīl Effendi al-Khālidī al-ʿAbbāsī, a member of the scholarly class and the chief clerk of the Jerusalem Court from the Khālidī family. Information on the *waqf*, which had a large number of assets, is given in Table 12. The only charitable *waqf* established by the endower was established in 1125 AH/1713 CE and endowed a shop, a pool, and a water fountain for people in Jerusalem to drink water in Khaṭṭ Dāwūd.[165] One of the two *waqfs*, established in 1201 AH/1786 CE by al-Ḥajj Muḥammad Sunʿ Allāh ibn al-Shaykh Muḥammad Sunʿ Allāh al-Dīrī al-ʿAbbāsī al-Khālidī and Ṭurfanda bint al-Shaykh Najm al-Dīn al-Khayrī, *Muftī* of Quds, endowed Qur'ans and various books.[166] In the *waqfiyya*, which was of a generational nature, the books were stipulated to the three sons of Muḥammad Sunʿ Allāh al-Khālidī, and after them to their minor sons and their minor sons' sons; when the generation ceased from the sons, only to their daughters; and when the generation ceased from them, to the scholars of Jerusalem. Secondly, two *waqfs* were also established by Mūsā Effendi ibn al-Ḥajj Muḥammad Effendi Sunʿ Allāh al-Dīrī al-Khālidī, as described in his *waqfiyya*, in the capacity of

155 JS 232: 205; Dosya 3/233: 156/12; JS 207: 82–83; JS 218: 486; 222: 76.
156 JS 228: 3–4.
157 JS 250: 137–138.
158 JS 250: 39–40.
159 File 3/21: 126/13; 10/147: 9/15/13; JS 314: 123.
160 File 3/34: 210/13.
161 JS 378: 3.
162 JS 300: 135.
163 JS 307:124.
164 JS 228: 3–4; JS 250: 137–138; JS 250: 39–40; Dossier 3/21: 126/13; 10/147: 9/15/13; JS 314: 123; File 3/34: 210/13; JS 378: 3; JS 300: 135; JS 307:124.
165 JS 208: 105.
166 JS 267: 152–154.

the chief clerk of Jerusalem's *sharīʿa* court.[167] The *waqf* endowed a house with shares[168] in Sharaf Quarter and a house and a wooden house on Darj al-ʿAyn Street.[169] Finally, a *waqf* was established by Muḥammad Ali al-Khālidī, a member of the Khālidī family, in 1227 AH/1812 CE, and this *waqf*, which was modest in terms of its assets, was also a *dhurrī* (family) *waqf*. Thus, a total of 12 *waqfs* were established by members of the al-Khālidī family in Jerusalem during the period under study. Qāsim bin Rajab, a member of the scholarly class and a translator at the Jerusalem Court, endowed a large number of assets in his family *waqf*, which was established in 1131 AH/1719 CE.[170]

In the endowments, titles such as *mullā*, *mawlānā*, and *effendi* were used when referring to members of the scholarly class. The use of these titles by members of the *ʿulamāʾ* class may be taken as a sign that they had a respected place in society. Founders with the titles *effendi* and *mullā*, whose occupational group is not clear, also occupy an important place in the *ʿulamāʾ* class.

The number of *waqfs* established by Jerusalem's elite, most of whom were known by family names, was recorded as 164. Most of the founders shown in Table A15, who are referred to by various family names (e.g., Kashmīrī, Ḥijāzī, ibn al-Mughsila, Abū Jibna) and whose titles are not explicitly mentioned, are also considered to have belonged to the scholarly class.

2.3.4 The Script Office (*Ahl al-Qalam*)

The fourth group, the scribes, were the bureaucrats of the state. The highest positions to which the script office would be promoted were the office of the bookkeeper, the office of *reʾīs al-kuttāb*, the office of the Rumeli bookkeeper, and other bookkeeper and engagement offices of various grades. The *defterdār* was the supreme supervisor of financial affairs, the guardian, and responsible for the state treasury.[171] In the *waqfs* of the period under study, no *waqfs* were established by members of the script office class, which constituted a part of the ruling elite. In the 17th century, since the administrative center of the state was Istanbul and almost all bureaucratic affairs were carried out there, there were no *waqfs* from the script office class in Jerusalem.

---

167 Mūsā Effendī was the son of his predecessor, Muḥammad Sunʿullāh al-Khālidī. Shaykh Mūsā al-Khālidī, a local rival of the Ḥusaynīs, was a well-educated scholar. Abu-Manneh, "Husasynīs," 99.

168 JS 280: 87–89.

169 JS 280: 87–89; JS 283: 118–119.

170 JS 213: 95.

171 Yediyıldız, "Türk Hayrât Sistemi," pp. 463–65.

Finally, among the local officials or members of the ruling elite, such as the architect and the chief architect, Ṣādiq ibn Ibrāhīm ibn Nimr,[172] the architect of Jerusalem, established one of the most numerous *waqf*s.[173] *Başağa* Muḥammad ibn al-Ḥajj ʿAbdullāh Agha, on the other hand, endowed his house in Sharaf Neighborhood to *Zāwiya* of Abu Madyan al-Ghawth.[174]

2.4 Awqāf *Endowed by the Ordinary People of Jerusalem*

According to the documents analyzed, there were no peasants among the founders of *waqf*s in the period covered by this study. As for merchants and artisans, there are only two of them. Considering the three founders who were recorded as *dabbāgh* (tanner) and craftsmen, as well as the three founders who were recorded without a family name and whom we consider to be from the *reʿāyā*, their ratio is 1.67%.

In conclusion, farmers in the period covered by this study were not in a position to establish *waqf*s. Likewise, merchants and artisans were generally not in a good economic position to establish *waqf*s. Therefore, the number of *waqf* founders among the latter is quite limited. This situation of the *reʿāyā*, who represented a very small fraction of *waqf* founders in Ottoman Jerusalem, was due to their poverty. In one way or another, the city's wealth was concentrated in the hands of members of the ruling elite, or at least some of its constituent groups.

But we should not forget another factor: trade, especially foreign trade, was in the hands of non-Muslims. And they established *waqf*s in favor of their religious communities according to the rules of Islamic jurisprudence, as recorded in the second part of the study under the headings "Christian and Jewish *Waqf*s in Jerusalem."

---

172 The family of Ḥasan ibn Nammār, one of the influential families of Jerusalem, whose prominence grew from the early Ottoman period, served as the architects, builders, and *nāẓirs* (inspector) of the *waqf*s of Jerusalem. See al-Alami, "The *Waqf*s of the Traditional Families," 148.

173 *Waqf*'s assets: three houses in Nāṣāra neighborhood, a weaving shop under one of these houses, three additional houses in Nāṣāra neighborhood, two shops under one house, a bakery near a house formerly a *khān*, two-storeyed and standard houses above the *khān* house in Sharaf neighborhood, the *khān* above the house of ʿĀnifat al-Dhakar, the house known as Sulaymān house in the Jewish neighborhood, recorded as a storeyed house with three cisterns known as Mūsā house, a storeyed house in Ḥayādir quarter, a house known as Maṣbana house under the house of ʿĀnifat al-Dhakar, two vegetable gardens in Rīsha quarter, a vegetable garden in Raḥba ibn ʿIzz al-Dīn district, two shops in Kaṭṭ Dāwūd, a house in Jawwālda quarter, and a house known as Nuḥḥās house in Ḥayādir quarter. See JS 242: 133–36.

174 JS 218: 487.

2.5 *Charitable Women in Ottoman Jerusalem*

Benevolent and generous women in the Ottoman Empire established *waqfs* to help the needy, sick and helpless in different cultures and eras. In addition to their social efficiency and prestige, *waqfs* provided legal sanction and protection for women to own property, to manage and benefit from their property while they were alive, and to transfer it to their designated heirs.

Islamic law guarantees certain property-related rights for women: the right to control their *mahr* (dowry), the right to inherit, the right to own and manage property, including *waqfs*, and the right to donate property as a *waqf*. If a woman possessed sufficient capital, she could establish a *waqf*. Islamic law generally prohibits differentiation in status, rights, and obligations based on gender. There were no legal restrictions preventing women from establishing *waqfs*, whether they were part of the court circle or not. Examples of women who founded *waqfs* demonstrate they followed the same legal procedures as men.[175]

However, financial constraints could limit women's ability to establish *waqfs*; the size of a woman's *waqf* depended on her financial resources. These limitations stemmed from inheritance laws, which allocated women half the share of men in the same family, as well as social and cultural norms that restricted women's ability to earn income or acquire capital.[176]

Charity was a prominent activity for the Ottoman Empire's prestigious and wealthy women, who were often recorded as compassionate benefactors, generous ladies aiding the poor, needy, sick, and unfortunate across various cultures and eras. Benevolence was likewise a field of activity held in high esteem.[177]

It is unclear to what extent women founders of *waqfs*, referred to in Ottoman Turkish with titles like *sāḥib al-waqf wa al-khayrāt* or *sāḥiba al-khayrāt wa al-ḥasanāt tālibat al-ṣadaqāt wa al-mabarrāt*,"[178] were able to exercise these

175 Ülkü Bates, "Women as Patrons of Architecture in Turkey," in *Women in the Muslim World*, ed. Lois Beck and Nikki Keddie (Cambridge, MA: Harvard University Press, 1978), 243–60, 257; Margaret L. Meriwether, "Yeniden Kadınlar ve Waqf Üstüne: Halep, 1770–1840," in *Modernleşmenin Eşiğinde Osmanlı Kadınları*, ed. Madeline C. Zilfi (Istanbul: Tarih Vakfı Yurt Yayınları, 2000), 140–50.

176 For further information about inheritance issue in Islamic law see, J. Schacht and Aharon Layish, "Mīrāth," in *Encyclopaedia of Islam*, Second Edition, ed. C. E. Bosworth, E. van Donzel, W. P. Heinrichs, and Ch. Pellat, vol. 7 (Leiden: Brill, 1993), 106–13.

177 Justin McCarthy, *The Population of Palestine: Population History and Statistics of the Late Ottoman Period and the Mandate* (New York: Columbia University Press, 1990), 1.

178 Other titles addressed to *Khasseki Sultan* in the endowment deed: "... iş bu din ve şerʿī mecellenin, bu mūteber ve güzel vesīkanın sahibi, azāmet ve celāl tācının incisi, saʿādet ve ikbal tācının gurresi, kraliçeler kraliçesi, melek halli, sultan tavırlı, zatı yüce, sıfatı temiz,

rights. However, among women, peasant women do not seem to have been able to inherit usufruct rights in agricultural property. Urban women belonging to the middle and upper artisan classes, on the other hand, are mentioned in all regional court records as heirs, property managers, founders of *waqf*s, and actual buyers and sellers of immovable property.[179]

At the apex of Ottoman society, charity, as embodied in sultanate *waqf*s, was shaped by the founder's identity as a member of the sultan's family and their limited circle, as well as by gender and status roles within the court. A comprehensive study of 14th- to 17th-century sultanate *waqf*s, based on secondary sources, indicates that the choice of *waqf* types was not heavily gendered.[180] This means that women in the Ottoman court were not systematically prohibited from founding institutions of a certain nature. There were women who patronized all kinds of construction, whether religious or non-religious, in other words, mosques, caravanserais, libraries, fountains or fortresses. A good example of this is Hürrem Sultan in Jerusalem with her complex of *imāret* (public kitchen), *madrasa* and many other buildings.[181] Whether or not they were used to establish *waqf*s, women acquired their property through dowries, inheritances, gifts and salaries from men. In this respect, they were similar to wealthy women in many periods and places throughout history. Sincerely generous women benefactors distributed the income they received from men on a large scale.

In different parts of Islamic societies and in different periods, women owned businesses, lent money and traded. Despite Islamic law, their exclusion was related to inheritance. Women received only half of the inheritance of men in the same family. This may have limited, but did not destroy, the possibilities

kadri celil, güzel eserli, büyüklerin zübdesi, muhterem kadınların umdesi, erkek ve kadın müslümanların ismeti, zaı-i ve şanı yüce, zemanın Aişesi, devranın Fatıması, saltanat-ı zāhirenin yaldızı, hilāfet-i bahirenin incisi, Melik-i Samed olan Allah'ın dürlü ātıfetlerine nāil olan Sultan Süleyman'ın oğlu emir Mehmed'in anası Vālide Sultan Hazretleri ..." VGMA, 608–2: 235/178.

179 Mary Ann Fay, "Kadınlar ve Vakıflar: 18. Yüzyıl Mısır'ında Mülkiyet, İktidar ve Toplumsal Cinsiyetin Nüfuz Alanı," in *Modernleşmenin Eşiğinde Osmanlı Kadınları*, ed. Madeline C. Zilfi (Istanbul: Tarih Vakfı Yurt Yayınları, 2000), 28–47, 33.

180 This information is not based on the detailed research of endowment deeds or other sources but relied on the work of M. Çağatay Uluçay, *Padişahların Kadınları ve Kızları* (Ankara: Türk Tarih Kurumu Yayınları, 1980) and other notes about the *waqf*s in the Ottoman Empire. Additionally, Singer and van Leeuwen stated that there is no compiled list of *waqf*s which covers all the *waqf*s in Ottoman Empire set up by dynasty members. Richard van Leeuwen, *Bir Osmanlı Şehri: Şam – Vakıflar ve Şehir*, trans. H. Ebru Aksoy (Istanbul: Küre Yayınları, 2012), 19–22, 114.

181 For example, for the *waqf* that Khasseki Sultan's property and *waqf*s found in İstanbul see VGMA, 608 /2: 222/177.

of establishing *waqfs*, because women also inherited. Women in the Ottoman court circle, on the other hand, were provided with financial resources. They were granted land, income, regular salaries and generous gifts depending on the individual. However, when the sultan died, women did not inherit his property. The source of income for women other than the mother of the new sultan was limited to the salary tied to the Old Palace. The sisters and daughters of the new sultan would acquire a status that provided them with a substantial income, which the sultan's concubines would also aspire to.[182]

Another financial constraint on women in establishing *waqfs* was that they could not share in the spoils of conquests and victories.[183] In the first 250 years of the Ottoman Empire, the spoils of war added to the wealth of the sultans and their armies. Women were only allowed to get their hands on this wealth as recipients of the sultan's bestowals and as heirs of their warriors, within the scope of salary-gift-inheritance-dowry.

Although not restricted from founding any type of *waqf*, some women chose to establish charitable *waqfs* specifically for women. Hürrem Sultan's first major *waqf* in Istanbul, near the Avrat Pazarı neighborhood, may reflect a deliberate choice to legitimize this sultanate complex, the first built by a woman in Istanbul.[184] Kösem Sultan, the mother of Murad IV (reigned 1622–40) and İbrahim (reigned 1640–48), had established a *waqf* to cover the dowries of poor girls.[185]

In the period under study, women in Jerusalem exercised their rights within a system of family politics, employing strategies to gain influence and power. Muhammad Ali al-Alami's study on *waqfs* by Jerusalem's leading families (Ḥusaynī, Khālidī, ʿAlamī, Jār Allāh, Nāmrī, and Imām) during the Ottoman period records 142 *waqfs*: 30 charitable and 112 family *waqfs*, with 124 founded by men and 18 by women.[186] During the period analyzed in this study, women founders of *waqfs* belonged to prominent families in Jerusalem.[187] For instance, Ṣafiyya Khātūn bint ʿAbd al-Jawād al-ʿAsalī endowed two houses, stipulating income distribution among family members, as did Sharīfa Khātūn bint Ṣāliḥ al-ʿAsalī for houses in Khaṭṭ al-Dāwūd.[188] Afīfa Khātūn, daughter of Hibbat Allāh Çelebi al-Nāmrī, Jerusalem's chief architect, endowed a house's income to herself, her son Ṣāliḥ and his three descendants, then her brother's

182 Fay, "Kadınlar ve Waqf," 33–34.
183 Singer, *Osmanlı'da Hayırseverlik*, 109–10.
184 VGMA, 608 /2: 222/177.
185 Peirce, *The Imperial Harem*, 202.
186 For further information, see Al-Alami, "The Waqfs of the Traditional," 152.
187 See Table A1.
188 JS 207, 144; 243, 183–83.

descendants.[189] Five *kurūsh* from the rental income was allocated to her four daughters – Ṣāliḥa, Fāṭima, Nafīsa, and Ḥasība – by her husband ʿAbd al-Ḥayy al-Dajjānī. As can be seen from these examples, women generally had a higher status and gained more autonomy and power in historical perspectives where governance was centralized and the official mechanisms and structures of bureaucratic states were embodied in the hands of households rather than states.[190] Fayy sees this as a cross-cultural phenomenon that has attracted the attention of not only historians of Islamic societies such as Leslie Pierce, but also historians of European women such as Sara Maza and Suzanne Wemple.[191]

*Waqf*s give legal sanction and protection to women's ownership of property and their desire to manage and benefit from their property while they are still alive. In the 18th century, most women who established *waqf*s established family *waqf*s rather than charitable *waqf*s, which were intended to benefit religious institutions first-hand or to provide bread to the poor. The advantage for the founder of a family *waqf* was that she could benefit from the income of the *waqf* during her lifetime, and she could also bequeath it to her heirs after her death. Many founders, including women, included a provision in the *waqf* deed that their heirs would benefit from the *waqf*'s revenues until the end of their lineage. Only then could the *waqf* revenues be allocated to the religious purposes specified in the *waqfiyya*.[192]

According to the records of the Jerusalem *Sharīʿa* Registry, 300 *waqf*s were established in Jerusalem between 1703 and 1831. The number of male founders was 243, while the number of female founders was 56. The number of founders whose founder is unknown is just one. This shows that the ratio of male founders to the total number of founders was 81% in the period analyzed,

189 JS 223, p. 107.

190 Fay, "Kadınlar ve Waqf," 33.

191 ibid., 33.

192 For example, in her *waqfiyya* dated 1124 AH/1712 CE, Fāṭima bint Muḥammad stipulated that the income of her house in Wādī al-Tawwāḥīn, which she endowed, should first be given to herself, then to her brother's son Muḥammad ibn Ḥamdān Khayr Allāh al-Khilwānī and Muḥammad ibn ʿAbd al-Raḥmān al-Duwayk, then to their children, their descendants, and their descendants' descendants, and when their descendants cease to exist, to the Dome of the Rock, and if the conditions are not met, to the poor and needy. See JS 207: 340. In another *waqfiyya* dated 1136 AH/1724 CE, Āmina Khātūn bint al-Sayyid Yaḥyā al-Shahīr ibn Qāḍī al-Ṣalt bequeathed the income of a new shop in Batrīk Ḥammām on Baraka Yolu in Nāṣāra Quarter and a twelve-*qirāṭ* half-share shop opposite Kamīm Ḥammām in Nāṣāra Quarter to herself during her lifetime and to her sons after her death. When her sons' descendants cease to exist, she designated it to the descendants of Abū al-Faḍl, then to the descendants of her brother ʿAbd al-Ghanī, and when their descendants cease, she made it conditional on the *Khānqāh* al-Ṣalāḥiyya.

while this ratio was 18.67% for women. The rate of *waqf*s with unknown founders is 0.33%. Of the women's *waqf*s, 51 were established by women alone, one by two sisters,[193] one by a mother and a daughter,[194] one by a mother and two daughters,[195] one by two sisters and a brother,[196] and the last one by a man and a woman.[197]

Almost all of the assets endowed by women were located in the city center. Secondly, the general situation in the *waqf*s established in Jerusalem during the period under study is also evident in the *waqf*s established by women. That is to say, the share ownership in the assets endowed by women *waqf*s is very significant. Roughly defined as urban *dār/dūr* (plural), these can be defined as houses, shops, and agricultural properties, mostly consisting of upper and lower floors. Property types include spaces, various types of shops and *tabaqāt* (living units in apartment-style houses) and *bayt* (rented apartments), as well as mills, courtyards, gardens, gardens, coffee houses and fertile agricultural lands.[198]

TABLE 10 The kinship of women who established *waqf* in Jerusalem (1703–1831)

*Waqf*s established only by women	50
with mother	2
with sister	1
with two relatives	–
*Waqf*s established by women with men	
with son	1
with brother	1
with non-kin men	1
Total	56

193 The endowment deed of Nāṣiḥa Khātūn and Rāji'a Khātūn bint Muḥammad Āghā Samūm is dated 1135 AH/1723 CE, see JS 218: 147.

194 For the endowment deed of 'Ā'isha bint Yūsuf Zalāṭayma and her daughter Khadīja bint al-Ḥājj Ḥasan, see JS 249: 31.

195 For the endowment deed of Mu'ayyida bint Ḥusayn al-Tawwābīnī and her daughters Sa'da, 'Ārifa, and Ṣāliḥa, and her granddaughters 'Abd Rabbih and 'Alī ibn Yūsuf, see JS 227: 192.

196 Al-Ḥājj 'Īsā, 'Ā'isha, and Ẓarīfa, children of Muḥammad al-Ṭanbāgha, see JS 242: 146.

197 Al-Ḥājj Muḥammad Sun'ullāh ibn al-Shaykh Muḥammad Sun'ullāh al-Dīrī al-'Abbāsī al-Khālidī and Turfanda Khātūn bint al-Shaykh Najm al-Dīn al-Khayrī, *Muftī* of Jerusalem. JS 267: 151–53.

198 For a detailed information see Table 11.

TABLE 11 The number of women endowing variety of properties

1	House (*dār*)[a]	20
2	Joint venture house	42
3	Joint venture *bayt* (room)	1
4	Shop	3
5	Joint venture shop	1
6	Vegetable garden	1
7	Joint venture vegetable garden	4
8	Coffee house	1
9	Olive grove	1
10	Vegetable garden	4
11	Joint venture land	1
12	Joint venture mill	2
13	Cash (*nukūd*)	1
14	Straw	1
15	The Qu'ran and other books	1
16	Candelabra	1
Total		85

a The term *mesken* is defined as a kind of settlement or residence by Raymond. See, Raymond, "The Ottoman Conquest," 84–85. In the way of its use in Jerusalem *waqf* records, *dār/dūr* (*plural*) composed of up and down *beyts* (rooms) and built with two floors, *eyvan*, *kā'a* (where the quests were met, like living room), yard or open-air yard, kitchen, *dehliz*, *sahrīcü'l-ābar* (draw well cistern for collecting the water of rain and snow), *hamam* (bathroom), *taka* (window), *ıstabl* (barn), *bāyke* (store for gaining cereals and olive oil), *edebhane* (referred as *mürtefak* in some records) and a barn in endowment deeds. Cistern is almost found in every house in order to collect the water of snow and rain. There are some endowed houses having pool and hall. Additionally, houses had gardens surrounded with walls and there were trees bearing or not bearing fruit. In some endowment deeds, there were houses with backyards. There is information whether the right of the *khuluww* (continuous tenantry), vaulted or wreck was under the endowment deed.

Most of the women who established *waqf*s in Jerusalem during the period under study, 39 out of 56 women, endowed only houses called *dār*, which are detailed in various ways in the endowments and are also called mansions. In addition, the number of women's *waqf*s who endowed two houses was one, while the number of women's *waqf*s who endowed three and four houses was three, and the number of women's *waqf*s who endowed seven houses was only one. Some women endowed a single property, a *bayt* (room), while others endowed mansions consisting of many spaces. Comparing the above data on the endowments of *waqf*s established by Jerusalem women with the endowments of *waqfs* established by women in 18th-century Egypt, it is clear that Jerusalemite women established much more modest *waqfs*. Compared to Egyptian women who invested their capital in *wakālas* and inns,[199] *rab*ʿs (apartments built on top of a *wakāla* and rented to merchants), warehouses (*hawāṣil*, singular *khāṣil*), and types of shops (*hawānīt*, singular *khānut*), Jerusalemite women established a room. In addition to one-*bayt* or story houses, they mostly endowed houses with vegetable gardens, water reservoirs, water wells, kitchens, *murtafaq* (toilet outside the house), open courtyards, and sometimes vegetable gardens or olive groves, as detailed in their *waqfiyyas*.

In order to place women's property ownership in a broader economic context, it is first necessary to situate women's economic activity within the broader economy, and then to compare women's wealth and investment decisions with those of men. 18th century Egypt was at the crossroads of trade routes to Asia, Africa and Europe. Trade was at the heart of Egypt's wealth, with the long-distance trade in coffee and spices followed by domestic production and export of cloth. While weaving was the most important craft activity in 18th century Egypt, the greatest fortunes in the Egyptian commercial economy were derived from trade with distant countries, firstly in coffee and spices, and secondly in weaving.[200] Looking at the economic activities of Jerusalem in the same period, Jerusalem did not have many sources of income in commercial and economic terms. The most important revenues of the city were the visits of pilgrims, Sufis and travelers. In addition to taxes, Jerusalem's revenues also included the sales made during the regular visits of members of the three holy religions to the region and especially the revenues from the production of souvenirs. On the other hand, the money sent by Jews from outside Jerusalem to their co-religionists in Jerusalem as a kind of *zakat* and the financial support provided by European kingdoms to Christians were also important sources of income for Jerusalem.[201] In Jerusalem, where commercial and economic life was limited compared to Egypt, the fact that women invested their capital in dwellings is significant in the context of the economy of the time as a city visited and settled by pilgrims, Sufis and travelers, and in terms of the forms of investment used by men and women.

199 In the Ottoman era, *wakāla* and *khans*, like warehouses (*khawāsil*), were buildings consisting of shops (*khawānit*) on the ground floor and a stratum of shops (*hawānit*) on the upper floor where merchants lived. Raymond traces the term *vekâle* from the medieval period and concludes that in 18th-century Cairo, the word "*vekâle*" was used more frequently than "*han*", replacing the older terms *funduq* and *kaysariyye*, although the meanings appear to be the same. See Raymond, "The Ottoman Conquest," 84–101.

200 Fay, "Women and Waqf," 37.

201 Al-Asali, "Kudüs," 334–338.

The first of the seven *waqfs* established by women for purely charitable purposes in Jerusalem during the period we have examined was established by al-Ḥajja Ṣāliḥa bint al-Ḥajj Muḥammad al-Rakāt, who endowed half of the shares of her house in the Bāb al-Ḥiṭṭa neighborhood to the employees of the water fountain built by ʿAbd al-Ḥayy al-Dajjānī.[202] The endower also stipulated that the income of the *waqf* be spent on charity. The second *waqf* that established a charitable endowment was the *wāqifa* Shams al-Dīn Khātūn bint ʿAbdullāh al-Rūmiyya. The endower stipulated that two candlesticks, one small and one large, be lit at the altar of the Dome of the Rock.[203] The third *waqf* was established by Āmina Khātūn bint Sayyid Yaḥyā, known as *Qāḍī al-Ṣalṭ*, who endowed a Qur'an for the Dome of the Rock.[204] The fourth endowment was established by the endower Āmina bint Muḥammad Effendi bi-ibn al-Khawāja, who endowed 10 *kurūsh* to buy and light oil lamps for the *minaret* of the Dome of the Rock.[205] Another *waqf*, Fāṭima bint Muḥammad, stipulated that 360 Miṣrī from the income of her house on Abū Shāmāt Street, consisting of three *bayt*, *īwān*, kitchen, and cistern, be given to the person who recites 1 *juz* of the Qur'ān in the Jerusalem *Ḥaram* every year, and that 10 *zoloṭa* be given by the trustee in return for the recitation of 7000 words of *tawḥīd*.[206] In the *waqfiyya* of the *waqf* established by Laylā Zawjat Ḥasan Pasha, a mat was endowed to be laid on the *miḥrāb* of Masjid al-Aqṣā.[207] In the last *waqf*, the *wāqifa* Shaykha al-Ḥamūriyya al-Jaghbā endowed a *muṣḥaf* for the Dome of the Rock.[208]

The founder of the first of the 49 family *waqfs* established by women in 18th-century Jerusalem was Maḥbūba bint ʿAlī Bey al-ʿAlaybeyzāde, and her endowed properties were: a house on the line of Wādī al-Tawwāḥīn, a house in the quarter of Bāb al-ʿAmūd, a mill (known as the Mill of Murād Pasha) on the line of Bāb al-Qaṭṭānīn, a house in the quarter of Ḥaddādīn, a house in the quarter of Zirāʿana, 2 *bayt* in the Arch of Ḥiḍr, shop and kitchen in the Arch of Ḥiḍr, a shop in the direction of *qibla* in the Bazaar of Ṭabbāḥīn, a house in Khaṭṭ Tawwāḥīn, a house in the Street of Arch of Ḥiḍr, a house in Sharaf Quarter in the Square of Aḥmad Bey, a *bayt* in the Quarter of Naṣāra.[209]

The second largest *waqf* was established by ʿĀʾisha bint Ḥasan al-Badawī Zawjat ʿAlī Ṭanṭāsh, and the assets of the *waqf* are recorded as a house in the

202 JS 209: 253.
203 JS 232: 532.
204 JS 254: 1.
205 JS 254: 161.
206 JS 255: 53–54.
207 JS 290: 4.
208 JS 290: 1.
209 JS 276: 141.

Bāb al-ʿAmūd neighborhood near the Mawlawiyya Lodges, a house in the Bāb Ḥiṭṭa neighborhood, a vegetable garden with shares near the Arch of Ḥiḍr, a house, 16 squares of land near the Ḥiḍr Arch house, and an empty vegetable garden adjacent to the Turgut Agha *Waqf*.[210] After women, houses and shops, other properties include vegetable gardens, olive groves, mills and coffee houses.

In sum, the Ottoman concept of benevolence had clear gendered aspects. Court women could establish *waqf*s in a manner appropriate to their position, but their ability to do so depended on the financial resources available to them, in other words, on the sultan. The choice of where and what to endow was not without restrictions; it was decided according to the needs and rules of dynastic investment. Changes over time increased the options available to women, because *waqf*-making was not a static activity.

3 Socio-economic and Demographic Characteristics of *Waqf* Officials in Jerusalem

Since *waqf* officials performed their duties with a sultan's certificate, they were members of the ruling class and called *ahl al-murtaziqa* since they held the sultan's appointment deed.[211] They were also referred to as *mutawallī* (trustee), *nāẓir* (supervisor), *jābī* (tax collector), *kātib* (clerk), *mudarris* (teacher), *shaykh*, or *dervish*, among other titles. The title of *sayyid* could also be added to these designations. In the 17th and 18th centuries, during the process of "Ottomanization" and the restructuring of relations between the Ottoman central government and the populace, *waqf* officials held a significant place within the expanding and evolving definition of the "ruling class." As previously noted, membership in the ruling class entailed certain privileges based on service or real or perceived qualifications, subject to approval by the capital or provincial authorities. These privileges included tax exemptions, salaries, or other benefits, which often coincided with social recognition. For instance, descendants of the Prophet, *ʿulamāʾ*, and shaykhs were respected across all societal segments.[212] Thus, from a popular perspective, the acquisition of new titles was a way of being included in this system of privileges. In this context, many practices in the 17th and 18th centuries, such as new allocations of duties to *waqf*s and the division of duties in shares, brought individuals tax

210 JS 299: 21.
211 Yediyıldız, "Müessese-Toplum," 143–64.
212 Canbakal, *17. Yüzyılda Ayıntāb*, 84.

exemptions as well as the prestige of a recognized status in the eyes of the state. However, the increasing demand for titles of office, which Canbakal characterizes as a dimension of the process of "title plunder, the rush for titles", led to the granting of titles of nobility to sometimes unworthy individuals from various backgrounds.[213] From the state's point of view, the fulfillment of title requests and the issuance of nobility certificates for a fee both generated revenue and contributed to the strengthening of the state by purchasing the loyalty of individuals to the state through these documents.

Here, we discuss the ruling class membership as *waqf* officials only in terms of the material benefits it brings and the authority it creates when it is linked to office-holding and supported by the state's coercive power. Under the heading of titles and epithets of officials, foundation officials with the title of *sayyid* in Jerusalem will be analyzed separately from the titles and epithets discussed in the section on *waqf* founders.

3.1 Waqf *Officials with the Title* Sayyid *in Jerusalem*

In Ottoman society, individuals were known by titles or nicknames depending on their professional, religious or social characteristics. There is a wealth of sources that provide detailed information on the *waqf* officials of the city of Jerusalem and their titles and nicknames. Especially between 1690 and 1854, thanks to the large number of documents, it has been possible to at least genealogize some of the officials.[214] The findings regarding the founders of *waqf*s in the period analyzed in this study are also valid for *waqf* officials. As explained above, *waqf* officials were also positions that were passed down from generation to generation by the elite families of Jerusalem.

At the onset of Ottoman rule, significant changes occurred in the naming conventions of traditional families. The most notable development was the addition of the suffix *ī* to family names, simplifying them into a single word. For example, awlād al-Dā'irī al-Khalīdī al-Ḥanafī became Ṭāhirī and later al-Khālidī, and awlād al-ʿAlamī al-Mālikī became al-ʿAlamī. This simplification, after nearly five centuries of use, is attributed to non-Arab Ottoman rulers. One or more titles or epithets could appear before or after a name. For instance, the role of *juzhān* (Qur'ān reciter) and *duʿāʾgū* (prayer leader) for the Dome of the Rock and the Egyptian *Waqf* of Aḥmad Pasha was assigned to Mawlānā

213 Canbakal, *17. Yüzyılda Ayıntab*, 83.

214 Documents on the titles and epithets of *waqf* officials can be found primarily in the *ḥurūfāt registers*, as well as in *sharīʿa* court registers, *aḥkām* and accounting books, and *waqfiyyas*. For detailed information on the *waqf* officials of the Jerusalem, see, for example, Eroğlu Memiş, *Hurūfāt Defterleri*, 145–85.

Sayyid Shaykh Fayḍ Allāh al-ʿAlamī for one *akçe* per day and five *kurūsh* per year via a charter.[215] The name of the person appointed was usually referred to as "al-Sayyid."[216] The epithets "al-Shaykh" and "al-Ḥājj" were also frequently mentioned in the records. In some records, family names like ʿAlamīzāde or Jār Allāhzāde were used, but appointees were often identified with their father's name.[217] It is certain that separate studies could be conducted on titles and epithets, of which there are dozens. Here, however, the subject of *sayyidship*, which shows different characteristics, will be discussed.

Among *waqf* officials, the prevalence of the *sayyid* title is high due to its associated privileges. Ottoman society occasionally encouraged *sayyids* to serve in *waqf* institutions, where their characteristics made their involvement almost essential. According to the *Ḥurūfāt* books, 291 (43%) of the 673 officials of all Jerusalem *waqfs* bore the *sayyid* title, with 251 recorded as *sayyid* and 40 as *al-sayyid*. Of these, 152 trustees in 100 records were *sayyid*, and 21 *mutawallīs* in 19 records were *al-sayyid*. This pattern extends to officials of lodges, *madrasas*, and mosques. For example, Sayyid Muḥammad al-Ḥusaynī was appointed as trustee, *nāẓir*, *shaykh*, and *jābī*[218] of the Jabībiyya *Madrasa*, and Sayyid Muḥammad al-Ḥusaynī as *mutawallī*, *nāẓir*, and *shaykh*[219] of the Tāziyya *Madrasa*. Sayyid ʿAbd al-Bāqī ibn Sayyid ʿAlī al-Luṭfī was appointed as *bawwāb* (gatekeeper), *shaʿʿāl* (lamplighter), and *farrāsh* (caretaker),[220] and Sayyid ʿAbd al-Bāqī ibn Sayyid ʿAlī al-Luṭfī as *jābī*[221] and deputy inspector[222] for the *Khanqāh* Musliyya *Madrasa Waqf*. It is noteworthy that all the officials of the Muṣliyya *Madrasa Waqf* were named *sayyid*.[223] Officials from the ʿAlamī family at the Asʿadiyya[224] and Yaʿqūbiyya[225] Lodges all bear the title of *sayyid*. Among the appointments made to the Jāmiʿ ʿUmarī *Waqf*, all of the members of the Dajjānī family bear the title of *sayyid*.[226] *Waqf* officials from elite Jerusalemite families, including Ḥusaynī, ʿAlamī, Jār Allāh, Dajjānī, Jāʿūnī, Dāwūdī, Surūrī, ʿAfīfī, Maghribī, Khālidī, and Bisṭāmī, were recorded with the

215 VGMA, 1119: 110/49.
216 For detailed information on *sayyidhood* in the Ottoman Empire, see Kılıç, *Osmanlı'da Sayyidler*.
217 VGMA, 1112: 1/155, 156, 157; 1112: 1/189.
218 VGMA, 1107: 2/95.
219 VGMA, 1107: 2/97.
220 VGMA, 1107: 2/ 254.
221 VGMA, 1107: 2/255.
222 VGMA, 1107: 2/256.
223 See VGMA, 1107: 2/51; 1107: 2/59; 1107: 2/279; 1107: 2/288; 1091: 77/14; 1109:6/7; 1108: 1/23.
224 See VGMA, 1110: 131/114; 1125: 64/10.
225 See VGMA, 1108: 1/68; 551: 99/36.
226 See VGMA, 1111: 54/32; 552: 37/20.

sayyid title. The number of *sayyids* among *waqf* officials increased in the early 18th century across the Ottoman Empire, particularly in Jerusalem.[227] Some lodge and *madrasa* officials, previously without *sayyid* titles, were registered as *sayyids* from the early 18th century, as seen in appointments for the Küçük Aḥmad Pasha *Waqf* for Qur'ān recitation at the Dome of the Rock.[228] There may be two reasons for this change in the lineage of the endower. The first is marriage, and the other is the possibility of false *sayyidhood*, which was seen throughout the Ottoman Empire.[229]

When we look at the practices regarding the appointment of officials in Jerusalem, we see many different examples and it would be erroneous to make a definitive judgment. First of all, it is common to see grandfather, father and grandson appearing in the same document with the title of *sayyid* among the Jerusalem *waqf* officials. For example, the clerk for the *waqfs* of the Nabī Ashmāwīl Masjid and Lodges in villages and hamlets, the scribe for the *Waqfs* of the Tomb of al-Ghaylāniyya, the scribe and *shaykh* for the Asʿadiyya Lodges, *Madrasa* Ḥamrā, and trustee of the Ghaylāniyya *Waqf* was recorded as "Sayyid

227 As a matter of fact, it is mentioned that there were quite a number of inauthentic *sayyids* in Anatolia and that the state was working on their control and annulment. See Özkaya, *XVIII*, 228–29; Kılıç, *Osmanlı'da Seyyidler*; B. S. Amoretti and L. Bottini, eds., *The Role of the Sādāt/Ashrāf in Muslim History and Civilization, Special Issue, Oriente Moderno 18* (1999). Moreover, the fact that the *Naqīb al-Ashrāf* registers were kept throughout the Ottoman Empire created a serious obstacle for inauthentic *sayyids*. See Cahit Baltacı, "Osmanlılar Döneminde Nakībü'l-Eşrāflık Müessesesi ve Nakībü'l-Eşrāf Defterleri," in *Proceedings of the IV. Milli Türkoloji Kongresi, 23 October 1981* (Ankara: Ankara Üniversitesi Dil ve Tarih-Coğrafya Fakültesi, 1981). There is also a *Naqīb al-Ashraf* Book of Jerusalem dated 1180 AH / 1766 CE 1766 in the Palestine Archive in Abu Dīs.

228 See VGMA, 1107: 2/36; 2/28, 29, 219; 1119: 110/34, 43; 1139: 87/19; 1108: 1/16. The officials who were recorded as *shaykh* at the beginning of the century were recorded as *sayyid* from the middle of the century.

229 Scholars of the Arab lands were the first to draw attention to the false claims of sayyidhood in the Ottoman Empire. In the 18th and 19th centuries, many studies on Bilād al-Shām and Egypt pointed to a common phenomenon: The increase in the number of *sādād* through marriage into *sayyid* families and the fabrication of false genealogies. Herbert L. Bodman, *Political Factions in Aleppo, 1760–1826* (Chapel Hill: The University of North Carolina Press, 1963); Michael Winter, "The Ashraf and Niqabat al-Ashraf in Egypt in Ottoman and Modern Times," *Asian and African Studies* 19 (1985); Abdul-Karim Rafeq, "Changes in the Relation." Studies by Establet, Pascal and Rafeq, as cited in Canbakal, show that the population of the *sādād* in Damascus almost doubled in the first half of the 18th century. By the 19th century, according to one contemporary observer, "everyone in Syria and Egypt was called as *sayyid*." Canbakal, Hülya, *17. Yüzyılda Ayıntāb: Osmanlı Kentinde Toplum ve Siyaset* (Istanbul: İletişim Yayınları, 2009), 100.

Fayḍ Allāh al-ʿAlamī ibn Sayyid Muḥammad Shahhāra ibn Sayyid/Shaykh Fayḍ Allāh al-ʿAlamī."[230]

As noted, they traced their lineage to the Prophet's uncle, Abū Ṭālib. In another example, the *Madrasa* Ḥamrā *Waqf* records the official as Sayyid ʿAbd al-Ṣamad, Abū Suʿūd, and Sayyid Muṣṭafā ʿAlī as brothers of Sayyid Muṣṭafā Khalīfa.[231] In the case of Sayyid Muḥammad and Ibrāhīm ibn Shaykh ʿAbd al-Qādir Dāwūdī, appointed as elementary school teachers to the Bayram Çavuş *Waqf*'s *Muʿallimkhāne* (elementary school), the *sayyid* title appears before their names but not their father's, raising questions about scribal errors, spelling variations, or shifts in the epithet's meaning, an issue requiring further study.

Regarding titles or professions paired with the *sayyid* title, notable examples include: among the 232 *mutawallī*s of Jerusalem's *waqf*s in the *Ḥurūfāt* books, 173 bore the *sayyid* title, often alongside titles like *ḥajj*, *shaykh*, *mullā*, *effendi*, and *agha*. *Waqf* officials such as shaykhs and *nāẓir*s were also recorded as *sayyid*, with the majority of lodge *shaykh*s, tombkeepers, *mudarris*es, and their assistants (*muʿīd*s) identified as *sayyid*.[232]

In conclusion, the *sayyid* title denoted individuals with a blood relation to the Prophet, holding an exceptional place in Ottoman society. *Sayyid*s were prevalent among *waqf* officials, as frequently noted in archival documents. Some abuses occurred to exploit state exemptions, and there is a slight possibility that the title was used as a mark of respect for prominent officials.[233]

3.2 *Appointment, Dismissal, and Term of Office of the* Waqf *Officials*

Issues such as the appointment, term of office, dismissal, and handover of *waqf* officials were primarily governed by the conditions set by the endower in the *waqfiyya*. Consequently, *waqfiyya*s often include detailed descriptions of officials' personal and quantitative characteristics, such as their number. Appointments contravening the endower's terms were annulled in Jerusalem's provisions.[234]

---

230 VGMA, 1125: 64/8; 64/9; 64/10; 1114: 10/1; 10/2.

231 VGMA, 1124: 64/14.

232 For detailed information. Eroğlu Memiş, *Hurūfāt Defterleri*, 145–160.

233 Canbakal, "On the 'Nobility'".

234 See VGMA, 814: 29. In a different example, although in the *waqfiyya* of Shaykh al-Islām al-sābiq al-marḥūm al-sayyid Muṣṭafā Effendi ibn al-marḥūm Shaykh al-Islām al-sābiq al-marḥūm al-sayyid Fayḍ Allāh Effendi Awqāf, the duty of *ders-i ʿāmm* was conditioned to a Ḥanafī *imām*, because the duty was assigned to a Shāfiʿī person by a deed that led to a court complaint. VGMA, 815: 29. In a different provision, it was decided that Ḥājj Ṣāliḥ and other individuals appointed to the *tawliya* and *shuʿāl* of the Maghribī *Waqf* should be

Specific conditions were typically set for *waqf* officials, particularly *mutawallīs*, but also for others in most, if not all, *waqfiyyas*. For example, ʿAbd al-Raḥmān ibn al-Khawāja Muḥammad al-Nuʿāʿī stipulated that the trusteeship of his *waqf* be entrusted to himself during his lifetime, then to his children after his death per the *al-arshad fa al-arshad* (most competent to most competent) method, and subsequently to competent persons appointed by the *qāḍī*.[235] In another case, Fāṭima bint Muḥammad designated the trusteeship to herself during her lifetime and to *mawqūf ʿalayhā* (beneficiaries) after her death.[236]

Generally, in Jerusalem's endowments during the study period, conditions for *mutawallīs* and other officials included *al-arshad fa al-arshad* for *mawqūf ʿalayhā*, their children, only sons, only daughters, brothers, and so forth. Some duties were stipulated for specific individuals or offices.[237] In other words, the lineage, knowledge, skills, and physical characteristics of *waqf* officials were made subject to certain conditions. However, within the family, distinctive qualities such as those were from the first generation or second generation, women, men, the most righteous and the most mature were those some separatist qualifications as were were also sought.[238]

The fact that a significant portion of the *waqfs* established in the city of Jerusalem were *waqfs* that were vested in the children led to the selection of officials directly from among the family members. The orders regarding the selection of officials stipulated that the position should be assigned to the son first,[239] or if there was no son, to his brother, or if there was no brother, to a relative.[240] Despite the stipulation that the person appointed to a new post

---

removed from their positions, and the position should be assigned to '*şart-ı vākıf üzere müstehik ve cümlenin muhtārı olan Şeyh Abdulaziz*' on the condition that any seizure is prohibited. VGMA, 317: 221.

235 JS 202: 12–13.

236 JS 207: 340.

237 For example, endower al-Ḥājjah Ṣāliḥa bint al-Ḥājj Muḥammad al-Rikāt has given the *tawliya* of her *waqf* to ʿAbd al-Ḥayy al-Dajjānī. See JS 209: 253. Endower Aḥmad al-Kūtāhī have given the *tawliya* of his *waqf* to Mālikī *imām* of Jerusalem. See JS 220: 33–34.

238 For example, Mūsā ibn al-Ḥājj Ṣāliḥ Kutayna stipulated in his *waqfiyya* dated 1152 AH/1739 CE that the trusteeship of his *waqf* should be entrusted to his *irshād* offspring. JS 230: 4.

239 With the imperial edict sent on 1177 AH/1763 CE, it was ordered that the duty of the deceased person should first be entrusted to his children. VGMA, 523: 8.

240 For instance, see "Kudüs-i Şerīfde vākiʿ Mescid-i Aksā ve Sahratullah-ı Müşerrefe Evkāflarından ve gerek taraf-ı saltanat-ı seniyyeden belde-i mübāreke ahālīlerinden irsāl olunan surreden ve zikr olunan Evkāfın gerek sikke ve gerek Osmanī surre ve cihāt-ı sāireden cüz'iyye ve külliyye her birine … sükkānı üzerlerinde olub berevāt-ı Padişahī ile mutasarrıf olanlardan biri fevt oldukda evlādına evlādı olmadığı sūretde karındaşına yahud karındaşı olmadıkda akrabasına virilüb bu sūretde fevt olan gerek ricāl ve gerek nisā

should be capable and competent, it is observed that ignorant people were sometimes appointed to posts. In fact, this issue was mentioned in the decrees sent to the provinces and it was insisted that *waqf* duties be assigned to competent people.[241] On the other hand, it was also stated that some people wanted

---

her bilā-veled fevt olduklarında Evkāftan düşen cihāt mütevelli bulunanların arzlarıyla ve cānib-i ʿaliyyeden giden surreye mutasarrıf olanlardan bilā-veled fevt oldukda Kādı-i Kudüs-i Şerīf arzıyla erbāb-ı istihkākdan olanlara virilüb ferağ ve intikālātı dahī vech-i meşrūh üzere mütevelli-i vakf bulunanların ve surre ashābı Kādı-i Kudüs-i Şerīf arzlarıyla ferāğat olunub refʿ iktizā eyledikde yine ber-minvāl-i meşrūh virilüb İstanbul'da sākin ve Kudüs-i Şerīfe varmayub baʿzıları cihāt-ı vakf ashābının menzili yoğ iken açıktan arz-ı hāl ve sehven berāt ile ahālīnin cihāt ve surreleri kimesneye kayd olunub şurūt-ı merkūma ... olunmak bābında sākin-i belde-i tayyibe fukaraları arz-ı hāl ve vech-i meşrūh üzer emr-i ʿālişān ... ve Haremeyn-i Şerifeyn Muhasebesine ve .. Kalemine kayd olunması niyāziyle istidʿā itmeleriyle ... mezkūr içün zikr olunan evkāf-ı şerīfelerden hayāt-ı mahlūlīyye vākiʿ oldukda evlādlarına ve bilā veled vākiʿ oldukda müstehikkīne virilmek üzere mütevelli arz ve ʿĀsitane-i Saʿādete gelüb arzlarıyla tevcih olmak bābında ... emr-i ʿālī sādır olduğunda mahallinden vaz u der kenār olunmakla minvāl-i meşrūh amel ve hareket ve surre ve cihāt mahlūlü vākiʿ oldukda evlād-ı ve evlādı olmadığı sūretde akrabasına ve bilā akraba vākiʿ oldukda müstehikkīne virilmek .. mütevelli-i vakf arzı ve surre vāki oldukda Kudüs-i Şerīf kadısı arzıyla virilüb ve ferağ ve intikāl dahi minvāl-i meşrūh üzere virilüb arz-ı hāl ile virilmek ve iş bu şurūta murāca'a olunub arzlarıyla sādır olan emr-i ʿālīşān mūcibince idare ve Haremeyn-i Şerifeyn Muhasebesine ve Mukāta'a Kalemine dahī kayd olunub muğāyir-i emr-i ʿālīşāna bir ferd hareket itdirilmemek bābında hükm-i hümāyun virilmek ricāsına i'lām eylemeğin mevāhim-i hükm ve bu fermān-ı ali sādır olmağın vech-i meşrūh üzere emr-i şerīf-i ʿālīşān yazılmak içün iş bu tezkire virildü. 11 Rebiuʿl-evvel 1148." VGMA, 814: 11.

241 For example, see "Hattı Hümāyūn yazıla ki; İftihāru'l-havass ve'l-mukarrabīn mu'temedi'l-mülūk ve's-selātīn muhtāru'l-izzu ve't-temkīn bi'l-fiil Dāru's-Saʿādeti'ş-Şerīfe Ağası olub Haremeyn-i Şerifeyn Evkāfı nāzırı olan Hacı Beşir Ağa -dāme ʿuluvvehu- Dīvan-ı Hümāyūn'a arz gönderüb taht-ı nezāretlerinde olmağla Kudüs-i Şerīfde vāki' Evkāfdan ve Kudüs-i Şerīf mimarlığının nısfı Hacı Ahmed bin Receb ve nısfı āheri İbrahim bin Hebbetullah üzerinde olub mezbūr İbrahim bundan akdem nısf hissesin evlādlar üzerlerlerine berat itdirmekle minvāl-i muharrer üzere mestūr ve mukayyed olub lakin zikr olunan nısıf mimarlığa mutasarrıf olan merkūm Hacı Ahmed müddet-i vefīreden beru fevt olmakla cümle aʿyān ve eşrāfın ittifakıyle bā-hüccet-i şer'iyye Nureddin Halife mutasarrıf olub sadākat ve istikāmet üzere umūrun ru'yet idegelüb mezbūr İbrahim nā-ehl olduğundan başka ihaneti dahi zahir iken bazı mütegallibeye iştirāken hissesine bir mikdar bir müddet mutasarrıf ve birkaç seneden beru gayb olduğundan müstakil ve mezbūr Nureddin hidmet-i lāzımesin ru'yet idüb kusuru yoğiken merkūm İbrahim iki nefer evlādları Abdulvehhab ve Sadık namān kimesneler ā ... berat itdirmesi mūcib-i özr olub başkaca fi'l-asl pāresi ... mecnūn ve sağīr ve nā-ehl ve hevā ve heveslerin olub umūr-ı mimarlığa ... istiğdād ve istihkāklar dahi olmamağın üzerlerinde olan nısıf hisse ref'lerinden ve nısıf hisse mukaddemā fevt olan merkūm Ahmed mahlūlünden bā-hüccet-i şerʿiyye mutasarrıfı olan hidmetinde mevr ve saʿī ve cümle ahali ... Nureddin Halīfeye tevcīh buyurulmak bābında aʿyān ve eşrāf ve ahalinin iltimaslarıyla hālā Kudüs-i Şerīf kadısı Bekrizāde Mehmed Efendi ve mütevelli-i vakf arz itmeleriyle mūcibince zikr olunan mimarlığın nısfı olan İbrahim reflerinden ve nısfı dahi Hacı Ahmed bin Receb

to be appointed to these posts in order to be exempt from the local taxation even though they were not qualified. Especially in the first half of the 19th century, such evaluations are frequently encountered.[242]

As for the official procedures followed in the appointment of *waqf* officials, first of all, in some *waqf*s, the *mutawallī*s would apply to the *qāḍī* with the *mutawallī*'s petition or a *tezkere*, and after the court desicion issued by the *qāḍī* and the issuance of the *rüʾūs tezkeresi* (appointment certificate) from the related Imperial Council's office in Istanbul, the appointment deed would be issued. Some records indicate certificates were obtained with "the supply of the *qāḍī*, the sign of the *Shaykh al-Islām*, or the *iʿlām* of the Anatolian Chief Judge."[243]

Other appointments were made with a *ḥujja* (certificate) or *murāsala* (application). Even in provincial centers such as Jerusalem, it is understood that this was common and that applications were made to Istanbul only for the renewal of the appointment deed or the resolution of the dispute.[244] In fact, it is observed that many *waqf* officials continued their duties with *qāḍī*'s favor or their father's or grandfather's appointment deeds (without renewal of the *berāt*).[245] Generally, those whose official *berāt*s were registered in the

mahlūlünden Nureddin Halife'ye tevcīh ve ināyet buyurulmak ricāsına i'lām itmeğin mūcibince tevcih olunmak bābında fermān-ı ʿāli sādır olmağın vech-i meşrūh üzere berāt-ı ʿālīşān virilmek içün işbu tezkire virildi." VGMA, 814: 89.

242 Demirel, *Osmanlı Vakıf-Şehir*, 128.

243 It was decided that the officials commissioned in endowments of the late Shaykh al-Islām Feyzullah Effendi in different cities should not be changed unless there is a petition of the *mutawallī* or a Shaykh al-Islām order of the trustee: 'Şeyhülislam -melikü'l-azizü'l-ʿallām- Hazretlerinin nezāretlerinde olub, sābık şeyhülislam -merhūm ve mağfurun leh- Feyzullah Efendi'nin Haremeyn-i Muhteremeyn ve Kudüs-i Şerīf ve Şām-ı Şerīf ve İstanbul'da ve Erzurum'da olan hayrātlarının cihāt-ı mahlūl olub, ... ferāğı iktizā itmedikde Evkāf-ı mezbūrede mütevelli olanların arzı olmadıkça tevcih ve der-kenar olunmamak bābında fermān-ı ʿāli ... ve mahalline kayd olunmağın ināyetleri ricāsıyla vakf-ı mezbūr mütevellisi fazīletlü es-Sayyid Murtaza Efendi Hazretleri arzı ve hālen ve bi'l-fiʿil nāzır-ı vakf hazretleri işaret-i ʿāliyye buyurmaları işaretleri mūcibince kaydına şerh virilmek içün Haremeyn Muhasebesine kayd ve Anadolu Muhasebesine ilm u haber virilmek bābında fī 2 Zi'l-hicce sene 1162 fermān-ı ʿāli sadır olmağın vech-i meşrūh üzere şerh virilmişdir fermān devletlü sultanımındır. Fī 11 Cemaziye'l-evvel sene 1163.' VGMA, 814/ 103; 1110: 131/81.

244 For appointments made "Hüccet-i şerʿiyye mūcibince" see VGMA, 1107: 2/7; 2/243; 1119: 110/43; 1109: 6/26; "berī olmakla görevlinin istememesi üzerine bā takrir" for the appointment. VGM 1108: 1/16. In an interesting example "bā hüccet mutasarrıf iken [görevi] kapulanmağla refʿinden" another official was appointed. VGMA, 1142: 84/20.

245 For example see '... Bābü's-Saʿādet'ş-Şerīfem Ağası nezāretinde olan Evkāfdan Kudüs-i Şerīfde vākiʿ müteveffiye Khasseki Sultan -tābet serāhā- Evkāfının kitābet ciheti yevmī beş para vazīfe ile nısf hissesine es-Sayyid Mustafa ve es-Sayyid Ahmed babalarından

Anatolian Accounting Office and in the Daily Books of the Ruling Elite (*'Askerī Rūznāmçe*), known *as Ḥurūfāt* books, received appointment deeds granted to the Ottoman ruling elite.[246]

Authorized administrators for appeals included the *qāḍī*, *nā'ib*, and *mutawallīs*. For *waqfs* legitimized by higher authorities, presentations were made by officials like the grand vizier, *Shaykh al-Islām*, or *aghas* of *Bāb al-Sa'āda* or *Dār al-Sa'āda*.[247] In Jerusalem's *Ḥurūfāt* books, appointments

---

intikal ile bā-berat-ı şerīf-i 'ālişān mutasarrıflar olup nısf kitābet hıdmeti kemāl-i sadākat ve istikāmet üzre idāre …' BOA, ADVNS.AHK.ŞM (3): 66/3. Başka bir örnekte ise; vākıfın şartı gereği babadan dededen berat ile sahip olunan su taşıyıcılık görevinin aynı aile üzerinde olduğu kaydedilmiştir:. '… ashāb-ı hayrātdan müteveffā ile al-Hac Ahmed Mezīd medīne-i mezbūrede mutasarrıf oldığı mülk menzilinde tasarruf ve süknāsını tescīl-i şer'ī ve teslīm ile almak birle vakf ve şart ve ta'yīn eylediği vakfiye-i ma'mūlun-bihāsında mukayyed ve berāt-ı şerīfemle saka olan evlād-ı Hicāzī hıdmetleri mukabelesinde yedlerinde olan hucec-i şer'iyye ve senedāt mūcebince müddet-i vāfireden berü eben-an-ced zabt idegelmişler iken …' BOA, ADVNS.AHK.ŞM. (2): 50/1.

246 There have been many provisions in Jerusalem that frequently emphasize the issues that need to be considered in the appointments of officials due to the difficulties experienced in practice. i.e.: "Haremeyn-i Muhteremeyn Evkāfı Nāzırı Beşir Ağa Dīvān-ı Hümāyūna arz gönderip taht-ı nezāretlerinde olmakla Kudüs-i Şerīfte vāki' Mescid-i Aksā ve Sahratullah-ı Müşerrefe ve Hz. Halilurrahman Evkāfı Celīlelerinden olmak üzere mütegallibe ve hayābireden bazı kimesneler birer ber-takrip ile askerī ve divan berātlarıyla hilāf-ı şart-ı vākıfa muğayir-i kānūn-ı muhdes vazīfe ihdās idüp bu vecihle vakf-ı şerīfe gadr-i külli ve vakfın ibtāline bāis ve bādī olmalarıyla taht-ı nezāretlerinde olan Evkāftan vezāif ve galleye mutasarrıf olanların askerī ve divan beratlarıyla mademki arzlarıyla Haremeyn-i Şerifeyn muhasebesinden muhreç tezkire mūcibince maliye tarafından berāt-ı şerīf-i 'ālīşān olmadıkça askerī ve divan beratıyla ve āher tarīk ile kimesneye vazīfe virülmeyüp talep idenler men' ve def' itdirülüp mütevelli-i vakf muhdes vazīfe talebiyle rencīde ve ta'ciz itdirilmemek bābında bundan akdem mute'addid evāmir-i 'aliyye sādır olduğu Haremeyn-i şerifeyn muhasebesine mestūr ve mukayyed olub şurūtundan olduğu der-kenar olunduktan derkenarı ve şurūt-ı vākıfı mūcibince amel ve hareket itdirilüp şerefyaftā-i sudūr olan emr-i 'āli ta'yīn ve icrā ve hilāf-ı bir fertten def' ve hareket itdirilmemek bābında hükm-i hümāyūn i'tā buyurulmak ricāsına i'lām itmeğin mūcibince hükm deyū fermān-ı 'ālī sādır olmakla vech-i meşrūh üzere emr-i 'ālīşan yazılmak için iş bu tezkire virildi. Fi 7 Rebi'u'l-evvel sene 1175." VGMA, 814. For a *tezkere* example containing earlier provisions (1120/ 1708–1709) see VGMA, 321: 273/2. Another provision dated 1163/1751 mentioned of similar issues. See VGMA, 229; 814/106–1.

247 In Jerusalem, inspection of large public *waqfs* such as Masjid al-Aqṣā, Ṣaḥrat Allāh, *Ribāṭ* al-Manṣūrī, Khalīl al-Raḥmān, etc., were managed by Dār al-Sa'āda Aghas. The issues relating to *waqfs* in question were reported to Istanbul by these aghas. In *aḥkām* registers, these issues reported by aghas were resolved through decisions. This situation was stated in *aḥkāms* as; "… İftihārü'l-havās ve'l-mukarrebīn mu'temedü'l-mülūk ve's-salātīn muhtārü'l-izzi ve't-temkīn bi'l-fi'il Dārü's-sa'ādeti'ş-şerīfe Ağası olub hālā Ḥarameyn-i şerifeyn Evkāfı Nāzırı olan Beşir Ağa -dāme uluvvehū- Dīvān-ı Hümāyūna arz gönderüb

were typically made at the *qāḍī*'s request, occasionally the *nā'ib*'s,[248] and rarely by other officials like *mutawallīs* or *nāẓirs*.[249] Appointments to the *Waqf* of *Madrasa al-Ḥamrā* were made at the *Shaykh al-Islām*'s request.[250]

Appointment proposals by *qāḍī*, *nā'ib*, *mutawallī*, or *nāẓir* were based on two grounds:[251]

1. First and New Appointments: Indicated by *mujaddad* (reappointment) or *tajdid* (renewal), these included appointments due to necessity or post vacancies. If an official left without reason, the new appointment was also *mujaddad*. Other renewals occurred due to *berāt-i zāyi*ʿ (lost deed)[252] or *bī-berāt olmağla mücedded berāt ināyet* (granted a new appointment deed because it was performed without an official appointment deed).[253]
2. Vacancies: If not specified, vacancies arose from:
   a. Death: *fawt* for Muslims, *murd* for non-Muslims.
   b. Dismissal: *raf*ʿ.
   c. Abandonment: *maḥlūl*, *kaf-i yad*, or *qaṣr-i yad*.
   d. Relinquishment: *farāgh*.

Between 1703 and 1831, of 673 transfers of Jerusalem *waqf* officials, 340 (50.52%) resulted from death, and 88 (13.08%) involved duty transfers while the official was alive, suggesting 51% served lifelong tenures, consistent with Ottoman life-long tenure norms. Family-based *waqfs* played a significant role. Non-death changes included consensual transfers, abandonment, and *raf*ʿ (often due to old age), followed by deed renewals due to loss, burning, or other reasons. Thirty-two appointments were made for unspecified "vacant" posts.[254] An order from Istanbul regarding the *tawliyya* of the *Waqf* of Ṣalāḥiyya Tīmāristān

taht-ı nezāretlerinde olan Kudüs-i Şerīfde vākiʿ Mescid-i Aksā ve Sahratullahü'l-Müşerrefe Evkāf-ı Şerīfleri ..."

248 See e.g. VGMA, 551:99/47–48; 552:37/9;552:37/15.

249 For an example, see VGMA, 1111: 54/56. In a provision dated Jumādā al-Awwal 1163 AH / April 1750 CE it was decided that in *waqfs* where the inspectorship was stipulated to Shaykh al-Islām, no appointments should be made without a *mutawallī* petition. "... Şeyhülislam melikü'l-azizu'l-ʿallām hazretlerinin nezāretlerinde olub, sābık şeyhülislam merhūm ve mağfūrun leh Feyzullah Efendi'nin Haremeyn-i Muhteremeyn ve Kudüs-i Şerīf ve Şām-ı Şerīf ve İstanbul'da ve Erzurum'da olan hayrātlarının cihāt-ı mahlūl olub, ferāğı iktizā itmedikde Evkāf-ı mezbūrede mütevelli olanların arzı olmadıkça tevcīh ve der-kenar olunmamak bābında fermān-ı ʿāli ve mahalline kayd olunmağın ..." VGMA, 814: 103.

250 VGMA, 1110: 131/73.

251 Baykara, *Osmanlı Taşra*, 10–11.

252 See e.g. VGMA, 1107: 2/57.

253 See e.g. VGMA, 1107: 2/293, 320.

254 See Table 12.

TABLE 12 Reasons for change in the *waqf* employees of Jerusalem according to *ḥurūfāt* registers

No	Reasons for the change of officer	Number of the records
1	After death (*fevt mahlūl*)	340
2	Renewal (*mujaddad/tajdīd*)	55
3	Vacancy (*mahlūl*)	32
4	Suspension from duty (*ferağ*)	54
5	Through petitioning (*arz-ı hāl*)	1
6	By appointment deed (*bā-berāt*)	3
7	By old appointment deed (*Bā-berāt-ı ʿatīk/Berāt-ı atīk mūcebince*)	2
8	By hujjat (*Bā-hüccet/Hücceti mūcibince*)	4
9	By official letter (*Bā-takrīr/Ber-mūceb-i takrīr*)	2
10	By generation rank (*batn tertibi*)	1
11	Due to waste of appointment record (*berātı zāyiʿ*)	28
12	Suspension due to death without children (*bilā-veled diğerinin rızasıyla*)	1
13	Vacancy of death without children (*Bilā-veled fevt mahlūlünden*)	15
14	Lack of appointment deed (*Bī-berat/ bilā-berat/beratı olmamakla*)	37
15	Suspension for desertion (*Firar itmekle refʿinden*)	4
16	Suspension (*Refʿinden*)	10
17	Dismissal (*kasr-ı yed*)	20
18	Voluntary discharge (*rızasıyla kasr-ı yed*)	7
19	Suspension for treason (*gadr itmekle refʿinden*)	5
20	Renewal due to the changes in the throne (*ibkā*)	5
21	Demand (*ihtiyaç olmağla*)	1
22	Necessity (*lazım olmağla*)	6
23	As per the condition of the endower (*şart-ı vākıf*)	1
24	By the petition of the judge (*Kadı arzıyla*)	1
25	By official letter of mutawallī (*mütevelli tezkiresi*)	1
26	Due to the imperial edict of the candidate (*yedindeki ferman gereği*)	1
27	Vacancy (*yokluğundan*)	1
28	Unspecified reason (*sebep belirtilmeyen*)	33
Total		673

in Jerusalem provided detailed information on appointment, promotion, dismissal, and employee shares and currencies over the years.[255]

Waqf officials would serve in their appointed positions until the end of their lives. However, upon the complaints of the people,[256] *waqf* officials who were not competent,[257] who came to office irregularly,[258] who committed irregularities while in office,[259] who neglected their duties, who did not perform their duties properly and who committed crimes were dismissed after the investigation, if the allegations were true. In addition, they could voluntarily withdraw from their duties.

In cases of duty changes through waivers or transfers, many *kasr-i yad* (voluntary relinquishments) were consensual, with officials often transferring duties to their children or others due to old age (*pīr*) or physical inability to continue.[260] Dismissals (*rafʿ*) also occurred due to officials relocating, undertaking military service, demonstrating incompetence, or suffering from physical ailments or disabilities.[261]

255 See BOA, ADVNS.AHK.ŞM (3): 139/1.

256 See, e.g., the Shafiʿī *kābāt* of the Jerusalem Court, which was refused and assigned to a new person due to his incompetence. VGMA, 1128:68/32; VGMA, 814: 89.

257 "… taraf-ı âherden vechen mine'l-vücûh dahl ve taʿarruz olunmak îcâb itmez iken Kudüs-iŞerîf sâkinlerinden Seyyid Ali Cârullah nâm kimesne hîleye sâlik ve gûnâ gun tezvîrat ile bundan esbak tevliyet-i merkûmu mezbûrûnun üzerlerinden ref' itdirmek sevdasıyla daʿvâya tasaddî ve mahalline havâle olundukta Harem-i Şerîf şeyhleri ve sâirlerinden istifsâr ve … olunub sâdâd-ı merkûmdan tevliyet-i mezbûre kadîmu'l-eyyâmdan eben-an-ceddin mutasarrıflar olub umûr-ı tevliyet-i ru'yete ve … Ali Cârullahın bu misillü hîle ve tezvîrât âdet-i müstemirresi olub kat'a tevliyet-i mezkûrede alâka ve medhâli olmamağın .. ve merkûmûnun … ta'ciz olduğun cümlenin ihbârıyla hâla Kudüs-iŞerîf kadısı Ahmed Efendi i'lâm itmekle …" VGMA, 814: 49/2. For other provisions on the same subject, see VGMA, 814: 70; 814: 49/1.

258 See, e.g. BOA, ADVNS.AHK.ŞM (1): 150/3; (5): 54/3.

259 See, e.g. BOA, ADVNS.AHK.ŞM (2): 154/2.

260 See, e.g. VGMA, 814: 90; 815: 16.

261 For e.g., "İftihârü'l-havâss ve'l-mukarrabîn mu'temedi'l-mülûk ve's-selâtîn muhtâru'l-ʿizzu ve't-temkîn bi'l-fiʿil Dâru's-Saʿâdeti'ş-Şerîfe Ağası olub Haremeyn-i Şerifeyn Evkâfı nâ.zırı olan Hacı Beşir Ağa -dâme ʿuluvvuhû- Dîvan-ı Hümâyûn'a arz gönderüb taht-ı nezâretlerinde olmağla Kudüs-iŞerîfde vâkiʿ Mescid-i Aksâ ve Sahratullah-ı Müşerrefe Evkâfından yevmî 10 Osmanî ş-Şeyh Mehmed Dahne Evkâfına beş Osmanî ile Sahratullah-ı Müşerrefe imâmeti Abdülkadir Efendi üzerinde iken gıyâbında hilâf-ı vâkiʿ ferâğından olmak üzere ahâli-i Kudüs'den Abdulvehhab nâm kimesne imâmet-i mezkûr evlatları üstüne berât itdürüb gadr ve kusur eylediğinden ref'inden kemakân merhûm Abdülkadir Efendiye ibkâ ve tevdî olunub …" VGMA, 814: 93.

It is also observed that trustees, who were among the *waqf* officials, were dismissed as a result of spending the *waqf* revenues for their own interests.[262] In addition, there are cases of dismissal due to the officials' struggles with each other and their acts of cruelty against each other.[263] Then, it is also known that the determination of whether the sons of the endowers were from the sons or not was made by consulting prominent residents, from the inhabitants of that city (Jerusalem) or *aʿyān* and *ashrāf* and the people's favoritism'.[264]

The term *bā-berāt* in records indicates that an official received a sultan's certificate, registered in the *Rūznāmçe* (Daybooks). Some appointments, however, were made with a *qāḍī*'s certificate without a sultan's *berāt*, relying on local *qāḍī* records.[265] Especially in places far away from Istanbul, the system functioned in this way and there is mention of a ruling class whose names did not even reach the *qāḍī*. In the records analysed for Jerusalem, it was found that many of the officials in the *waqfs* were working without a certificate.[266] Moreover, when the sultans changed, the certificates of all officials were renewed.[267] However, it has been determined that this situation was not taken into consideration in the Jerusalem *Ḥurūfāt* books, with few instances of officials continuing under *ibqāʾ* (retention) records.[268]

---

262 For e.g., "Kubbetü's-Sahra ve Halilürrahman Evkâfları mütevellisi vakıf kurâlarının 1184 senesine mahsûben zimmetine 2750 kuruş; 1185 senesine mahsûben … tevliyet-i mezbûru zabt ve ta'şir eyleyen Mirmiran İbrahim Paşa zimmetine kezâ 2.750 kuruş geçirmesiyle …" a decree was issued for the collection of these sums. (VGMA, 815: 82). This is how it is ruled in another application: "… hatt-ı hümâyûn ile vakfı şerîfin sadâkat üzere hizmet etmek şartı ile mütevellisi olan Ali Ağa 14 seneden beri mütevellisi olub küll-i imâreti işletmeyüb ve mu'tad olub fukarâya nafakaları virilmedikden gayri suyollarını dahî taʿmîr itdirmeyüb umûr-ı vakfın mücidd-u sâʿyî olduğundan vakf-ı şerîfi zarar olmağla ref' olunub sülehâdan el-Hac Mehmed Ağa vakfı şerîfe sadâkat üzere hidmet ve vakfın müsâid olduğu mertebe vakfı ta'mîr idüb imâreti işletmek ve fukarâya nafakalarını virmek şartıyla tevcih olub …"

263 See, the previous example.

264 BOA, ADVNS.AHK.ŞM (1): 44/2; 155/1; 174/3; 191/3; 232/1; (2) 50/1; 173/4; 180/2; 183/4; 184/4; (3): 68/2; 76/2; 102/3; 115/4; 121/4; (4): 29/4; 128/2; 135/2; (5): 19/1.

265 Baykara, *Osmanlı Taşra Teşkilâtında*, 6.

266 See Table 10.

267 Halil İnalcık, *Osmanlı İmparatorluğu Klasik*, 108–14.

268 *Ibkā*, in the dictionary, means allowing those whose services are appreciated to remain in their positions for another year before the end of this period among the civil servants whose appointments are made every year for a period of one year, and has the Arabic meaning of *bākī*, continuous, perpetuating. Pakalın, *Osmanlı Tarih Deyimleri*, 12. The records indicate that people continued in their existing positions, that is, the appointments remained with the same people.

As a result, in the *waqf*s of Jerusalem, there was an understanding of the duties of *waqf* officials that started with the conditions of the *waqfiyya*, lasted for a lifetime and generally passed from father to son.

3.3 *The Number of Officers and Population Size*

In the performance of the functions of the *waqf* institution, it should be noted that in addition to the qualifications of the *waqf* officials, the number of officials is equally important. In Ottoman society, it is known that the number of these officials, who belonged to the ruling class, was quite high. Despite this, there was no direct census or determination of the number of *waqf* officials in the city of Jerusalem or throughout the Ottoman Empire.[269] Despite the negativities mentioned above, the number of officials in *waqf*s and what influenced the formation and change of this number over time are issues that should be emphasised. In addition, the distribution of the number of officials according to institutional and occupational differences is also one of the issues that need to be known.

Regarding the number of *waqf* officials, important sources are *waqfiyya* records, *waqf* accounting books, and sometimes *sharīʿa* court records. The first and most important factor in the determination and assignment of the number of *waqf* officials is the endowers. Because the number of officials is mentioned separately by the *waqf*s in the conditions of the *waqfiyya*. However, this number is valid for the *waqf* date of the endowment, and it was observed that the *waqf* officials were shared among their children over time.[270] For example, in Khasseki Sultan's *Waqf* dated 964 AH/1557 CE, the number of officials is stated as 46.[271] Again, in the accounting book of Khasseki Sultan *Waqf* dated 1154 AH/1741 AD, the number of officials was 369.[272]

269 Demirel, *Osmanlı Vakıf-Şehir*, 131.

270 See e.g. VGMA, 556:37/11.

271 VGMA, 608–2: 235/ 178.

272 VGMA, 524: 2–29 For example, although the original *waqfiyya* did not include Qur'an reciters, they were added to the list of beneficiaries of the *imāret* at the end of the 16th century. See here TSAD 7301: 1. During the period covered by the study, this number has further increased. " 'An Cemâʿat-i Eczâhânân-ı merhûm ve mağfurûn leh Sultan Süleyman Han der karye-i Hamam", " 'An Cemâʿat-i Eczâhânân-ı Câmi-i Ahmar Ömerî der Şâm-ı Şerîf", " 'An Cemâʿat-i Eczâhân der Vakfı Ömer", " 'An Cemâʿat-i Eczâhân der Makâm-ı Hazreti Dâvud en-Nebî Aleyhisselam." A large number of officials are recorded under these headings. VGMA, 523: 23–38. These duties, which are not mentioned in the *waqfiyya*, suggest that they may have been created later. Still, in a record dated 965/1557–8, the main mosque of Damascus mentioned here "hudemâ-i ʿimâret-i ʿâmire ʿan gurre-i Receb ila gâye-i Zi'l-Hicce 965 ma'a mevâcibât-ı eczâhânân ve hudemâ-i câmi-i şerîf der Şam." Again, in a ledger dated 990 AH/1582–3 CE dated the end of the 16th century, the mosque is recorded

The second factor affecting the number of officials is the state's limiting the number of officials such as preachers, although not as much as the endowments, or the creation of new officials.[273]

The third factor affecting the number of attendants is that after the death of the first attendant, the children who succeeded him shared the office in more than one share. Therefore, the number of officials of that *waqf* increases. For example, the position of Shaykh, *mutawallī* and inspector of the *Zāwiya* of Prophet Dāwūd Lodge, whose appointment record is given below, was divided into thirteen shares. The share of the deceased officer was shared among his uncle's sons.[274]

In addition, the socio-economic, demographic and political conditions of the Ottoman Empire also affected the number of officials. In the 15th and 16th centuries, the expansion of the empire's territory through new conquests facilitated the employment of the human element and provided employment opportunities for the growing population. However, as the Empire reached its widest borders, it is observed that the number of employees within the *waqf* institution increased due to the decrease in employment opportunities for the growing population.[275]

---

under the name Aḥmar. However, only their salaries are recorded in this record. Amy Singer, "The Privileged Poor of Ottoman Jerusalem," in *Pauvreté et Richesse dans le monde Musulman Méditerranéen World/Poverty and Wealth in the Muslim Mediterranean World*, ed. *Jean-Paul Pascual* (Paris: Maisonneuve et Larose, 2003), 265.

273 Demirel, *Osmanlı Vakıf-Şehir*, 132.

274 "Kudüs-i Şerîfde Hz. Davud Aleyhi's-selâm Zâviyesinde bâ-mu'ayyene ile meşîhat-i şerîfe ve tevliyet-i evkâf –ı münîfe ve nezâretinin mutasarrıfı olan Seyyid Şeyh Muhammed ed-Dâvûdî bundan akdem fevt olup yerine müteveffâ-yı mezbûrun emmîzâdeleri olup ve hidmet-i şerîfeler 13 sehim itibar olunarak sihâm-ı mezkûrdan iki sehmi Derviş ve Ahmed ve Osman ve Halil ve Muhammed Taha ve Şakir ebnâ-yı Süleyman Taha'ya ve bir sehmi Muhammed ve Araka ve Ahmed ebnâ-yı Ali Araka ve bir sehmi Abdulvehhab bin Salihe ve bir sehmi İbrahim bin Mustafa'ya ve bir sehmi Abdülcelil ve Hüseyin ve Abdülkadir ebnâ-yı Abdulhay'a ve iki sehmi Muhammed bin Ahmed Fethullaha ve bir sehmi Muhammed ve Ahmed ibney Yahyaya ve bir sehmi Yusuf ve Ahmed ibney Vefaya ve nısf sehmi Ebu Bekir ve Osman ve Davud ve Abdurrahman ebnâ-yı Abdullah bin Halil'e ve nısf sehmi Ebu Bekir ve Osman ve Davud ebnâ-yı Hasan'a ve bir sehmi Hasan ve Hüseyin ve Halil ebnâ-yı Mahmud'a ve nısf sehmi Hasan Enis bin Halile ve nısıf sehmi dahî Davud ve Ahmed ibney Şeyh Muhammed'e, müteveffâ-yı mezbûrun mahlûlünden meşîhat ve tevliyet ve nezâret-i mezkûre ber-vech-i meşrûta merkûmûna tevcîh ve yedlerine bir kıt'a berât-ı'âlîşan virilmek bâbında Kâdîsı Mevlâna Muhammed Şeyh Efendi arz itmegin rûznâmçe-i 'askerîye nazar olundukda... ...tevliyet-i mezkûre 13 sehim itibarıyla bâlâda bast ve beyân olunan sihâmlar merkûmûna tevcih buyuruldu fî Zi'l-ka'de 1244 Yevm 17." VGMA, 556: 37/11.

275 As individually as this increase can be detected in Jerusalem *waqf*s, it is known that the same increase existed throughout the empire.

In some appointments, instead of a person who left the office for various reasons, a new official was appointed for all the duties he held. In the case of newly appointed officials, in line with the provisions sent by the central administration, firstly the son of the deceased person, and in the absence of a son, his brother-in-law, *emmizāde* (cousin) and other family relatives were appointed to the position in question.[276] In another instance, Shaykh Khalīl, brother of the previous officer who was died without his son, was appointed for the vacant duties of *Madrasa* Geylāniyya.[277]

Official numbers varied by *waqf* unit. A mosque-based *waqf* required at least an *imām* and *mu'adhdhin*, with larger ones employing orators, preachers, *juzhān*, *farrāsh*, and trustees. Masjid al-Aqṣā and Dome of the Rock, central to Jerusalem's *waqf* network, had numerous *imāms*, *mu'adhdhins*, and others. The Khasseki Sultan *Waqf*, with a mosque, public kitchen, *madrasa*, and *tabkhāna*, had approximately 495 officials by 1840, with significant increases in Qur'ān reciters (*qārī*, *juzhān*, *du'ā'gū*, *dawrkhwān*, *ikhlāṣkhwān*).[278]

In addition to these issues, it can be said that the size and wealth of the *waqf* was also effective in the number of *waqf* officials.[279] In almost all of the newly established local and modest *waqf*s in the period covered by this study, only a *mutawallī* was appointed as the *waqf*'s officer in accordance with the *al-arshad fa l-arshad* method, and the *waqf*'s officer consisted of a *mutawallī*.[280]

---

276 "... harābe müşrif olub ta'mīr ve külliyen inşāya muhtac olduğundan ahāli-i nahiye sākinlerinden Sayyid İsmail bin Sayyid Ahmed türbe-i şerīfi ta'mir ve termīm idüp ber-vech-i hasbī tawliya ve nezāretine dahī bā-berāt-ı 'ālī yani mezbūr İsmail fevt mahlūlünden sulbī oğulları Sayyid Hüseyin, Sayyid Osman, Sayyid Muḥammad Said ve Sayyid Halil, Sayyid Abbas, Sayyid Mustafa nām karındaşlara babaları berātı mūcibince merkūmūna ber-vech-i iştirāken tevcīh buyuruldu. Cemāziye'l-evvel 1241, yevm 25." VGMA, 556: 37/6.

277 "Kudüs-i Şerīf'de vāki' Geylāniyye Medresesinde yevmī bir pāre ile kātib ve yevmī bir pāre ile müsebbih ve yine Fārisiyye Medresesinde yevmī 3 akçe ile meşārik ve yine ... Dāvudda bir pāre ile kāri' ve bir bāb hāne ile Cāmi-i ... (Meğāribe) Receb ve Şaban ve Ramazan-ı Şerīfde kāri-i hadīs ve Kur'an ve ... meşrūta diğer haneye ve Fārisiyye Medresesinde ... ile şeyh ve kā'immakām-ı mütevelli ve kātib Şeyh Feyzullah fevt karındaşı Şeyh Halile ināyet." VGMA, 1091: 77/3.

278 For detailed information see VGMA, 523: 10–18.

279 It is understood that the Khasseki Sultan *İmāret Waqf*, the largest of the Ottoman-era Jerusalem *waqf*s, was also large in terms of the number of staff.

280 An exception to this is in his *waqfiyya* dated 1125/1713, Muḥammad Sun'ullāh Effendi ibn Khalīl Effendi al-Khālidī established to water carrier of the sābil two *qit'a ma'sara*, to see the service of the waterways and to situate lamps of six *kurūsh* each. JS 208: 105. In his *waqfiyya* dated 1131/1719, the same endower stipulated that eighteen cents from the *waqf*'s income be given to four people who read the Qur'ān and Fātiḥa each year. JS 213: 91–94. In another *waqfiyya* dated 1136/1723, the endower stipulated that eighteen cents from the *waqf*'s income should be given to three people who read *sab'a sharīf* every night

In contrast, large public *waqfs* like Masjid al-Aqṣā, Dome of the Rock, Khasseki Sultan, Ṣalāḥiyya, Maymūniyya, Ḥusniyya, and Ḥātūniyya *Madrasas* had many officials. Between 1121–1149 AH/1709–1737 CE, Masjid al-Aqṣā and Dome of the Rock had about 461 officials,[281] while this number was 369[282] in the Khasseki Sultan *Waqf* between 1099–1154 AH/1687–1742 CE and 495[283] between 1155–1255 AH/1742–1840 CE.

The Jerusalem *Atīq* (Treasury) Book recorded 28 officials for *Khānqāh* Ṣalāḥiyya, 32 for Ḥusniyya *Madrasa*, 30 for Muḥammadiyya *Madrasa*, 27 for Ṣalāḥiyya *Madrasa*, and 19 for Maymūniyya *Madrasa*, totaling 890 officials across 160 *waqfs*.[284] These numbers are meaningful in terms of showing the extent of the number of officials in charitable *waqfs* in the 18th century. The qualitative increase in the number of *waqf* officials due to various reasons, especially exemptions and social status, expanded and localized the Ottoman ruling elite in the provinces of Jerusalem.

The *Zāwiya* of Nabī Dāwūd's *tawliyya*, *naẓāra*, and *mashyakha* duties, split into 13 shares upon an official's death, exemplify this increase.[285] Similarly,

---

between the *maghrib* and *'ishā'* prayers at Masjid al-Aqṣā and then read *Fātiḥa* for the Prophet and his followers. JS 218: 470. In his *waqfiyya* dated 1137/1723, Aḥmad al-Kutahī required that 3 cents of the *waqf*'s income be given to the water carrier (*sāqā*) that put water in *sabīl* near Masjid al-Aqṣā. JS 220: 33–34. In the *waqfiyya* dated 1153/1740 al-Ḥājj Muṣṭafā Āghā 'Kaimmakam-ı Kuds' have stipulated that fourteen breads taken from *Imārat-i Amire* should be given to the water-carrier to the *sabīl* in Masjid al-Aqṣā that Bāb al-Naẓīr the endower has built. JS 230: 210. In his *waqfiyya* dated 1184/1770 Shaykh Muḥammad Kutayna ibn Shaykh 'Abd al-Raḥmān Kutayna, in return for Qur'ān recital in the Jerusalem *Ḥaram*, the readers should be paid 16 *zolota* annually (JS 254: 505–506); in her *waqfiyya* dated 1187/1773 Fāṭima bint Muḥammad stipulated 360 miṣrī from *waqf*'s revenues annually to the reader of one *juz'* from Qur'ān in Jerusalem's *Ḥaram*, and 10 *zolota* to the reader of 7000 *'kelime-i tevhid'*. JS 255: 53–54. In his *waqfiyya* dated 1185/1771 'Abd al-Raḥmān Āghā ibn Muḥammad Karam, two *kurūsh* from *waqf* revenues should be given to the reader of *Tabāraka* chapter for the soul of the *waqf* (JS 257: 65); 1206/1791 dated *waqfiyya* of 'Abd al-Laṭīf ibn Salama Zuheyman, stipulated that every year in the month of Ramaḍān a fee should be given to someone in return for the *khaṭm* of Qur'ān and gifting it to the soul of Prophet Muḥammad and other prophets (JS 273: 36–37). In the period covered by the study, in majority of the *waqfs* established in Jerusalem the number of officials was limited to the *mutawallī* of *waqfs*. In some cases inspector appointments were made along with that of the *mutawallī*. JS 218: 253.

281 *Haremeyn-Kudüs Cihât Defteri*, 1121–1149. Bkz. BOA, EV.HMH.d: 1632/15–32.

282 VGMA, 524: 2–29.

283 VGMA, 523: 10–38.

284 VGMA, 515: 33–101.

285 VGMA, 556: 37/11.

Khasseki Sultan *Waqf*'s public kitchen janitorial duties, initially assigned to one person for 4 dirhams daily, employed five by 1155–1255 AH/1742–1840 CE.[286]

Masjid al-Aqṣā and Dome of the Rock *Waqf*s had 461 officials in 1121 AH/1709–1710 CE, rising to 777 by 1177 AH/1763–1764 CE, including Maghāriba *Waqf* officials.[287] Therefore, from the data mentioned above, we can conclude that by the middle of the century, the number of officials in the largest charitable *waqf*s of Jerusalem was approximately 1600. When these numbers are added to the assumption that the newly established *waqf*s in Jerusalem during the period covered by this study (1703–1831) had at least one official, it can be concluded that the number of officials could range from approximately 1800 to 1900. When this number is compared to the population of the city of Jerusalem at the same time, it seems possible to arrive at a ratio of the number of *waqf* officials in Jerusalem to the city's population. According to Volney, the population of the city in 1784 ranged between 12,000 and 14,000, while Bonne stated that the population of Jerusalem in the first years of the 19th century was around 12,000.[288] Assuming the population of Jerusalem to be 12,000 and the number of officials to be approximately 1,800, the average number of officials per *waqf* is found to be 15%.

Comparatively, Istanbul's Fatih *Imāret* had 496 officials, aligning with Khasseki Sultan *Imāret*'s 495 in 1155–1255 AH/1742–1840 CE. Empire-wide, the average officials per *waqf* was 14.6 in the 17th century and 14.7 in the 18th century, suggesting consistency with Jerusalem's data.[289] This means that studies conducted at the macro level with the sounding method were able to reflect the micro level, at least in the case of Jerusalem. The *waqf*s of major cities such as Istanbul, Bursa and Edirne should also have a higher average than Jerusalem.[290]

The distribution of officials in the *waqf*s of Jerusalem according to their professions has not been clearly defined. The fact that *waqf* officials undertook more than one task or that some of them were mentioned collectively made this distinction difficult.[291] Nevertheless, according to our findings, common

---

286 VGMA, 523: 20.

287 BOA, EV.HMK.SR: 1971.

288 al-Asali, "Jerusalem under," 220.

289 Yüksel, *Osmanlı Sosyal*, p. 124; Yediyıldız, *XVIII. Yüzyılda*, 127.

290 Because Barkan specified the number of staff in the seven *waqf* as 1821, it seems to confirm this idea. See Barkan, "Şehirlerin Teşekkül," 239–296.

291 For example. In 1139/1726, al-Sayyid Abdulghanī al-ʿAlamī was appointed to the duties of '*bevvāb, şeʿāl, ferrāş, muezzin, mukebbir* and *kennās*' in the assignment made to Yakubiyya Mosque. VGMA, 1128: 68/1.

roles included *mutawallī*, *shaykh*, *imām*, tombkeeper, lodge official, *duʿāʾgū*, *juzhān*, *dawrkhwān*, *muʾadhdhin*, preacher, and *mudarris*.[292]

By institution, mosques, *imārets*, *madrasas*/schools, and *zāwiyas* ranked highest in official numbers. Pre-Ottoman *waqfs*, with high incomes, and 16th-century Ottoman *waqfs* also had many officials, with Masjid al-Aqṣā, Dome of the Rock, Khasseki Sultan, and Ṣalāḥiyya, Maymūniyya, and Ḥusniyya *Madrasas* leading.

3.4 *Official Fees and Inflation*

In Ottoman society, one of the largest groups of people who were dependent on their salaries for their livelihood was the *waqf* officials. The salaries of this group of officials were determined by a large and diverse group of people rather than by a centralized or single hand. The wages were determined by the founders of the *waqf*, the wage rates in the society, the income of the *waqf*, the continuity of the income and those who had a say in the Ottoman administration.

The salaries of the officials are referred to as *vazīfe'* (salary) in the language of the *waqf* and sometimes as *nân paresi* or "grandfather bread" among the officials. The wages of the officials were determined as daily (*yawmī*), monthly and yearly, and the payment could be in cash or in kind. In addition, the services rendered for free were mentioned as *ber vech-i hasbi*,[293] as well as in the form of *nısf* (1/2), *sülüs* (1/3), *rub*ʿ (1/4) and *sümün* (1/8) in shares.[294] Depending

292 For a detailed examination of *waqf* officials in Jerusalem between 1690–1834 according to the *ḥurūfāt* records see Eroğlu Memiş, *Hurūfāt Defterleri*,145–184.

293 For the '*ber vech-i hasbī*' duties of *cābī*, *şeʿal and imām* for the for the Lu'lu' Gāzī Waqf, the appointment deed of Shaykh ʿAbd al-Wahhāb, whose deed was lost, was renewed on 1234 AH/1818 CE. VGMA, 555: 25/19. His own son Sayyid Ḥalīl was appointed to the same posts free of charge from Shaykh ʿAbd al-Wahhāb's fervor. VGMA, 556: 37/9.

294 For example, Shaykh ʿAbd al-Raḥīm was appointed to the 2 *akçe sulus* share of the Maymūniyya *Madrasa*. VGMA, 1107: 2/140. Two of his sons were appointed to the 4 *akçe sulus* share of the 4 *akçe kitāba* of the Dāwūd Pasha Fountain *Waqf* with their father's certificate after their father voluntarily withdrew. In another example, upon the deduction from the fee of the *kāri-i ḥadīth* of the Salâhiyye *Madrasa*, which was 1 pare Mıṣrī, with the consent of the mutasarrıf official, Seyyid Ishāq al-Jāʿūnī was appointed to the sülūs share of the payment. VGMA, 1110: 131/97. The shares of the duties of the Evkâf of Prophet Mūsā, Prophet Yūnus, and Prophet Lūṭ—namely, the sümûn-i meşîhat, the rubʿ nezāret, and the hisse-i tevliyet—were assigned to the son of the deceased's brother, Shaykh Ismāʿīl ibn Yūnus. VGMA, 1139: 87/2. Sayyid Mūsā al-ʿAlamī, son of Sayyid ʿAbdul Ghanī, son of Sayyid Mūsā al-ʿAlamī, son of Sayyid ʿAbdul Ghanī, son of the deceased official, was appointed to the position of *thumun* share *tawliyya* and *thumun* share *mashyakha* of Prophet Ashmawil *Awqāf*. VGMA, 1125: 64/11.

on the time, different currencies such as *dirhams*, *akçe*, *kurush*, and gold,[295] as well as in-kind payment conditions such as wheat, salt, or bread were also set.[296] In some appointments, the *suknā* and/or *ijār* of a house[297] or the *ijār* of a shop

---

295 In the *waqfiyya* of the Haseki Sultan *Waqf*, all stipends assigned to officials are recorded in *dirham*. For instance, the *tawliya* (administrative) stipend of the *waqf* is stipulated as 30 *dirham*. (VGMA, 608–2: 235/178). Mevlānā Sayyid Shaykh Fayżullāh al-ʿAlamī, who was appointed as *juzhān* in the Dome of the Rock of the Küçük Aḥmad Pasha *Awqāf* and as *duʿāgū* in the *Miṣriyyūn Awqāf*, was assigned a daily stipend of "1 akçe and annually 5 *kurūsh*."(VGMA, 1119: 110/43). Apart from this example, the appointment registers of Jerusalem preserved in the *Hurūfāt* registers indicate that stipends were most often recorded as *akçe, akçe-i ʿOsmānī*, or simply *ʿOsmānī*. The cases in which payments were made in *Miṣrī* coin appear primarily in *surra* records, such as the following register. "From the exalted imperial authority (*ṭaraf-ı salṭanat-ı ʿaliyye*), the distinguished *surra sharīf* sent annually, to the group of *khaṭībs* of the Masjid al-Aqsā, assigned each year to es-Sayyid Jārullāh, who held the position by means of a *ḥujja sharʿiyya*, and upon his death transferred—with a *ḥujjat al-taqrīr*—to his brother, the mudarris Sayyid ʿAlī." (VGMA, 1109: 6/28). Stipends recorded in *Miṣrī pare* coins also appear as follows: From the Sultan Süleyman Khān *Awqāf* of the Dome of the Rock, appointments were made for *juzhān* positions with stipends of 1, 1.5, 2, and *nīm pare Miṣrī* (VGMA, 1109: 6/96, 97, 99). In the Ṣalāḥiyya *Madrasa Waqf*, the stipend for the shaykh was 1 *pare Miṣrī* (VGMA, 1107: 2/215; 2/277), and 1 *pare Miṣrī* was given to the *qāriʾ al-ḥadīth* (VGMA, 1128: 68/45; 1112: 1/129; 1110: 131/97). In the *Zāwiya-i Hangāh-i Ṣalāḥī*, the *bevvāb* (gatekeeper) was appointed with 1 *pare Miṣrī* (VGMA, 552: 37/30; 554: 25/1). In the Mescid-i ʿUmarī *Waqf* located in the Jewish quarter, the *imām*'s stipend was recorded as 2 *pare Shāmī*. (VGMA, 1112: 1/176). In the *waqf* established in 1153 AH/1740 CE by al-Ḥājj Muṣṭafā Agha, Kāʾimmakām of Quds, the *tawliya* stipend was stipulated as 4 *zeheb*. (KŞS 230: 110).

296 Upon the death of the individual who held the positions of *shaykh-i sajjādanişīn* and nāẓır of the Esʿad Efendi Zāwiya *Waqf* located in Ṭūr-i Zeytā, Sayyid Shaykh Muṣṭafā al ʿAlamī was appointed to the post with a stipend of "4 akçe plus taʿāmiyye." (VGMA, 1110: 131/92). In another example, the stipend of the *duʿāgū* appointed from the Khasseki Sultan *Awqāf* was recorded as "half a *batman* of wheat." (VGMA, 1107: 2/307; 1119: 110/21). In *al-Quds al-Sharīf*, at the *Masjid al-Aqsā* courtyard adjacent to the *Ṣakhratullāh* structure, the stipend for the *tawliya* and *nazāra* duties of the Halwat al-Bakrī Masjid *Waqf* is recorded as "taʿāmiyya." (VGMA, 1111: 54/98). A decree (*fermān*) sent from Istanbul in 1169 AH/1755 CE stipulates that for Muṣṭafā Efendi, the *khaṭīb* of Masjid al-Aqsā, "half a *ğarara* (half a sack) of wheat" be provided in addition to his daily stipend. This order, however, was rescinded by another decree issued on 2 Rabīʿ al-Ākhir 1172 / 3 December 1758. (VGMA, 723: 488).

297 For example, in the *waqf* of Shaykh Kemaleddin bin Sharif, the stipend of the *qārīʾ* who was to recite in the Masjid al-Aqsa was recorded as "one bāb of residential property (mulk süknā)." (VGMA, 1113: 35/3). The stipend of the person responsible for reciting the "qirāʾat al-ajzāʾ al-sharīf" in the same *waqf* was likewise recorded as "one residential house." (VGMA, 1113: 35/3). Both positions were granted to Shaykh ʿAbd al-Haqq ibn ʿAbd al-Raḥmān Khatīb, a relative of the founder. In al-Quds al-Sharīf, in the quarter of Hārrat al-Sharaf, the stipend of the official who recited "qāriʾ mā tayassara" was registered as "one bāb house." (VGMA, 1119: 110/6). Likewise, in the same neighborhood, the stipend of the

was allocated as an official's salary.[298] In addition, especially in documents related to *waqf* officials who did not have a *waqfiyya*, the phrase *bā mu'ayyene*, which means appointment or allocation but without specifying the amount, can also be found.[299]

It is possible to precisely determine the daily, monthly and yearly wages of officials, which are usually specified in the endowments.[300] The wages of the officials specified in *waqfs* such as Khasseki Sultan, Masjid al-Aqṣā and the Dome of the Rock are specific.[301] Apart from these, in some of the records with shares and the phrase *bā-muayyene* as mentioned in some of the records, it is not possible to determine how much he was paid.[302] A second important point is that *waqfs* established in different centuries cannot be compared with

---

qārī' who recited "qārī' mā tayassara" near the residences of Shaykh Muḥammad Palasī and Shaykh Ismā'īl Azraq was recorded as "one bāb house." (VGMA, 1107: 2/377). The stipend of *tawliya* and *nazāra* duties in the *waqf* of the Shaykh Abu Fakih Mosque (Shaykh Abū Faqīh Cāmi') was also recorded as "two pieces of residential property." (VGMA, 1107: 2/170). In the records presented here, even in cases where the term *süknā* (right of residence) is not explicitly stated, it may be understood that the houses were either occupied directly by the official or rented out, with the rental income serving as the stipend.

298 In the Hatt-i Dāvud quarter, the stipends of those who recited the "qirā'at al-mā tayassara" were recorded as "one bāb of shop rent (dükkān icāresi). VGMA, 1107: 2/ 139, 278.

299 In the records of the *Hurūfāt* Registers of Jerusalem, the stipends of 78 appointments were recorded as "bā-mu'ayyana." For example, in the Imādiyya *Madrasa Waqf* located near the Karbun quarter, the positions of *tawliya, nazāra, dersiyya, mashīha, kitaba*, as well as half of the *imāme* and half of the tomb guardianship for the *shaykh-i barīrān ḥikāk*, were assigned to Sayyid Aḥmad, Sayyid Muṣṭafā, and Sayyid Muḥammad Ṣāliḥ with a specified stipend (*nısıf hissa*). (VGMA, 1112: 1/102). In two other entries, the stipend was recorded as "nısıf mu'ayyana." In the first of these, the half of the *imāme* position of the Jāmi'-i 'Umarī *Waqf* in the Rīsha quarter was assigned jointly to the brothers Sayyid 'Abdurraḥmān, Sayyid Muṣṭafā, Sayyid Aḥmad, and Sayyid Muḥammad with a specified half-stipend. (VGMA, 552: 37/20). In the second entry, half of the *mashīhat* position of the Tomb of Gaylāniyya was assigned with a specified half-stipend to Shaykh 'Abdullah Dāvūdī's sons: Shaykh Muṣṭafā, Shaykh Muḥammad Nūrullāh, Shaykh 'Abdurraḥmān, and Shaykh Muḥammad Ṣarrāf. (VGMA, 1113: 35/13).

300 For example, the salaries of the Khasseki Sultan *Waqf*'s attendants were determined on a daily basis in its endowment deed. VGMA, 608–2. In the Accounting Record of the Maghāriba *Waqf*, wages are recorded as monthly. JS 224: 185–187. In the accounting record of the al-Shaykh Khalīl al-Jā'ūnī *Waqf*, wages are recorded as annual. JS 264: 149.

301 In the 18th century, for the fees of Khasseki Sultan *Waqf* officials, see VGMA, 523–524; for the fees of Masjid al-Aqsa and Dome of the Rock *Waqfs*, see BOA, EV.HMH.d:1632.

302 For example, in the Fārisiyya *Madrasa*, the stipend for the positions of *kā'im al-maqām* of the *mutawallī, shaykh*, nā'ib al-nāẓir, and *madrasa kātib*, which were assigned to the Ammizāda figures Shaykh Ḥalīl, Shaykh Feyẓullāh, and Shaykh Mūsā, was recorded with the phrase "bā mu'ayyana," without specifying a precise amount. (VGMA, 1107: 2/163). In the *Khangāh* Bāsitiyya *Waqf*, half of the *mashīhat* share was assigned to Shaykh 'Umar,

each other. *Waqf*s that are close to each other in terms of their establishment periods can be compared in terms of the salaries of their officials.[303] However, in this case, the assignment of officials' fees in various currencies that were in circulation as a result of Jerusalem's special status due to its holiness.

The amount or unit of remuneration of the officials was adjusted according to the prevailing prices of the period. For example, in the pre-Ottoman and early Ottoman periods, the *dirham* was used as the basis, whereas in the later period, the *akçe* came to be widely used.[304] In addition to *akçe* and *dirham*, gold was rarely used,[305] and wheat and salt were commonly used in kind.[306]

First of all, in the city of Jerusalem, where *waqf*s of various sizes existed over a long period of time, there are significant differences in the salaries of *waqf* officials. One of the *jābī*s (tax collectors) working in two different *waqf*s could receive ten and the other two; one of the *muezzin*s could receive nine and the other 1 *akçe*. In very general terms, it is observed that most of the officials

---

the son of the deceased official's brother, corresponding to a third share (sulūs hissa). (VGMA, 1107: 2/1193). However, the exact amount of the stipend was not specified.

303 For example, among the charitable conditions of the *waqf* established by Muhammad Sunʿallāh Efendi ibn Halil Efendi al-Khālidī in H. 1131 / M. 1719, it was stipulated that the *waqf*'s nāẓir should allocate 18 *kurūsh* annually from the *waqf*'s revenue to four *qārī*s who recite the Qur'ān and Fātiḥa. (KŞS, 213: 91-94). This meant that each of these officials effectively received 4.5 *kurūsh* per year for their service. In another *waqfiyya* of the same founder, dated 1136 AH / 1723 CE, it was stipulated that the muezzin stationed in the Silsila *minaret* should receive 16 *kurūsh* annually. (KŞS, 218: 470). The *waqf* established by al-Shaykh Muhammad Qutayna ibn al-Shaykh ʿAbdurraḥmān Qutayna in 1184 AH/ 1770 CE included a condition that an annual stipend of 16 zolota be distributed through the mutawallī for recitation of the Qur'ān in the *Ḥaram* of Jerusalem. (KŞS, 254: 505-506). The comparison of stipends for officials in *waqf*s founded in the eighteenth century, including some examples mentioned above, highlights the allocation of payments in various currency units. This suggests that, as a result of Jerusalem's cosmopolitan character and the pilgrims who traveled there, multiple currency types were in circulation. At the same time, it can be concluded that stipends in newly established *waqf*s were generally fixed on an annual basis.

304 While in the sixteenth century, the salaries of Khasseki Sultan *Waqf* officials were recorded in *dirham* in the *waqfiyya*, in the eighteenth century the salaries of officials were paid in *pare* and *akçe*. E.g. see VGMA, 1107: 2/ 240. The *Fetihhān* fee was paid as 5 akçe (in some records as 5 *Osmānī akçe*). E.g. see VGMA, 1107: 2/321; 1109: 110/5. In the appointment records in *ḥurūfāt* registers, for the payments of officials that were not about tasks or usufruct, nearly all payments were made with *akçe*. See Eroğlu Memiş, *Ḥurūfāt Defterleri*, pp. 145–165.

305 For example, the pharmacist who would recite the Holy Qur'an for the soul of the late Turgut Aga at the Dome of the Rock was appointed with an annual salary of 6 "*sikke-i hasene*". VGMA, 1160: 116/3.

306 For example, the *duʿāgū* fee for the Khasseki Sultan *Waqf* was paid in half a *batman* of wheat. VGMA, 1119: 110/21.

whose salaries are mentioned in the records received between 0–5 *akçe* per day.[307] The sources show that the highest paid officials were, in order, the trustees, *jābī*, *imam*, *muezzin*, orator, *nāzır* and *juzhān*s.

If the wages are evaluated in very general terms, it is seen that most of the officials listed in the records were charged between 0–5 akçes per day. In the sources, it was seen that the ones who received the most wages were *mutawallī*s, *jābī*, imam, *muezzin*, orator, and readers of verses from the Qur'an respectively.[308] In addition to all these, a more comprehensive study should be conducted to answer the question of how much the salaries of the officials were and what kind of differences occurred after the implementation of the *waqfiyya*. Furthermore, it should be investigated whether the salaries assigned at the *waqfiyya* remained the same after a long period of time, and if so, what kind of problems they caused.

The fees of the *mutawallī*s generally varied from one *akçe* or one *dirham* to 30 *akçe* and 60 *dirham* on a daily basis. As for the fees of *mutawallī*s appointed annually, they varied between 0–5 kurus. In the 18th and 19th centuries, some mosque *imām*s were paid a daily salary of 2–4 *akçe* and an annual salary of 10–20 *kurūsh*. Contrary to the natural difference in wages that can be seen in *waqf*s established in the same centuries, there were gaps between the wages allocated in shares and the annual or daily wages allocated over time. For example, in 1156 AH/1743 CE, there was a huge difference in wages between an *imām* who was paid two *akçe* (10 *kurūsh* per year) and one who was paid 1440 *kurūsh* per year. In an appointment record dated 1146 AH/1733 CE, there was a *mutawallī* who was paid 1 *akçe* per day (5 *kurūsh* per year),[309] while in an accounting record dated 1740, seven years later, the *mutawallī* share of the Maghāriba *Waqf* was 153 *zolota* per year, which was more than the other. Thus, while fixed fees did not retain their value, shared fees maintained their value as long as the sources of income could be preserved. Despite all these differences, it should be noted that a significant number of fees were close to each other.

Another issue regarding the remuneration of officials is the status of the remuneration of those who received remuneration from the same *waqf* in relation to each other. Generally, although there are very different practices among *waqf* officials, the sons[310] in the case of family *waqf*s, and the *mutawallī*s in

307 See respectively. VGMA, 1110: 131/ 13; 1108: 1/15; 1111: 54/32; 1107: 2/329.

308 For a table prepared on the fees see Eroğlu Memiş, *Hurūfāt Defterleri*, 145–65.

309 VGMA, 1109: 6/52.

310 In the accounting record of 1168 AH/1755 CE for the *waqf* of al-Shaykh Ḥalīl al-Jā'ūnī, 75 *zolota* and 372 *zolota* were allocated as the share of Sayyid 'Abdurraḥīm ibn [son], and 45 *zolota* was allocated as the share of Sayyid 'Abdullāṭīf. (JS, 264: 149).

others receive higher salaries than the other officials.[311] On the other hand, there may be *mutawallīs* who serve without pay,[312] and the amount remaining after the *waqf's* expenditures usually belongs to the *mutawallī*, who is the son of the *waqf*.[313] Apart from the *mutawallīs*, *imāms*, *mudarris*, teachers and *shaykhs*, who were usually in charge of mosques, *madrasas*, schools and lodges, have similar characteristics.

Salary proportions within *waqf* revenues varied. In 1153 AH/1740 CE, the Maghāriba *Waqf's* income was 1,150 *zoloṭa*, with 710 *zoloṭa* in expenses, including 153 *zoloṭa* for the *mutawallī*, 94 *zoloṭa* for the clerk, and 400 *zoloṭa* for the *naqīb al-zāwiya*, totaling 647 *zoloṭa* (56% of income).[314] The Shaykh Khalīl al-Jāʿūnī *Waqf* (1168 AH/1755 CE) allocated 74% of expenses to family revenues.[315] For Khasseki Sultan *Waqf* (1276–1280 AH/1860–1865 CE), official salaries were 4,110 *kurūsh* (19% of 21,884 *kurūsh* expenses), with readers at 2,379 *kurūsh* (11%) and *sādāt-i mudarrisīn* at 1,070 *kurūsh* (5%).[316] From this, it can be concluded that the proportion of attendant fees in all expenses was 35%. Barkan's empire-wide analysis found 90% of mosque and 52.5% of public kitchen expenses were official salaries.[317]

In conclusion, *waqf* positions, offering salaries, tax exemptions, and social prestige, were highly valued in Jerusalem, with family affiliation playing a key role in securing them. Further research is needed to assess salary changes post-*waqfiyya* and their long-term impacts.

---

311 For example, while the *mutawallī* of the Khasseki Sultan *Waqf* received a daily stipend of 30 *akçe*, the *jābī* received 6 *akçe*, the kātib 10 *akçe*, the imam 4 *akçe*, the chief cook 7 *akçe*, the potter 3 *akçe*, and the gatekeeper 4 *akçe* for their duties. (VGMA, 523: 10–38).

312 In another example, appointments for the positions of *tawliyya* and *nazāra* were made on a *hasbī* basis for the *waqf* known as the Masjid *Waqf* of Najmaddīn Abū Muḥammad ʿAbdurraḥīm al-Ṭabarī (VGMA, 551: 99/29), including the Seyyid Shāhbāz, Shaykh Mazīd, Shaykh Muḥarrem Senāʿu-d-dīn, and the Seyyid Jalāl Sufi Lodge. (VGMA, 1160: 116/92).

313 During the period covered by this study, in most of the newly established *dhurrī waqfs* in Jerusalem, after the conditions specified in the *waqfiyya* had been fulfilled (such as repairs, charitable obligations, etc.), the remaining *waqf* revenues were also allocated to the children of the *waqf*, including the *mutawallī*.

314 JS 224: 185–187.

315 JS 264: 149.

316 Singer, "The Privileged Poor," 257–69.

317 Barkan, "Şehirlerin Teşekkül," 239–43.

4 *Waqfs* as a Source of Wealth and Influence and the Local Elite of Jerusalem

In Ottoman cities, one of the institutional means of gaining access to the assets of others was through the administration of *waqfs*. Özer Ergenç reveals that the trusteeship and supervision of *waqfs* in 16th century Anatolian cities was distributed among prominent families.[318]

First of all, *waqfs* financed and organized most of the important public services that the state did not or could not provide before the modern period. *Madrasas*, institutions of worship and charity (mosques, sufi lodges, *zāwiyas*, hospitals, public kitchens), and various urban and commercial facilities (fountains, waterways, baths, inns, caravanserais) were all under the management of *waqfs*. Therefore, being a member of the *waqf* administration in any city meant having a say, in one way or another, over the city's budget allocated to basic public functions. This was even more important in smaller settlements where there were few or no *waqfs* established by outsiders, including the sultan.[319]

In addition to their role in providing public services, *waqfs* were the only institutionally active participants in the money market. The *mutawallī* could lend the income from the *waqf* assets, while the income from the interest was used to cover the various expenses of the *waqf*. Positions such as the management of *waqfs* brought with them many opportunities for profit.[320] In this case, Jerusalem's elite families at the center of the city's *waqf* network had a privileged position. In this competition, being in the center of the city and thus having access to the city's information networks had its own benefits.[321]

In fact, each religious institution or school and its associated *waqfs*, as unified administrative and financial entities, offered families the opportunity to increase their economic and political means. Initially, the management of these *waqfs* was usually entrusted to a prominent religious scholar, and later the management of the *waqf* was transferred to one of his descendants with the approval of the Sultan. The edicts sent from the capital were also recorded in court records. Through this process, which was repeated for years, the name of the institution became synonymous with the name of the family. The family in question reaped great benefits from this relationship, and in addition to the social prestige gained, administrative and religious positions associated with

318 Ergenç, "Osmanlı Klasik," 111; Canbakal, *17. Yüzyılda Ayıntāb*, 88.

319 Canbakal, *17. Yüzyılda Ayıntāb*, 189.

320 Bakhit, *The Ottoman Province*, 129–130; Lapidus, *Muslim Cities in the Later Middle Ages*, 61, 77; Canbakal, *17. Yüzyılda Ayıntâb*,192.

321 Canbakal, *17. Yüzyılda Ayıntāb*, 192.

the institution were also monopolized by this family. The fact that traditional families managed certain *waqf*s for many years provided the benefit of renting *waqf* properties for long periods of time, and over time these rented properties became the personal property of family members or were transferred to the control of private *waqf*s.[322] Moreover, since merit was not required in the services provided, it is not possible to comment on the quality of the services. A detailed analysis of the relationship between Jerusalem's elite and the institution of *waqf* from this perspective constitutes the main problem of this section of the study.

In this section of the study, the administrative organization of Jerusalem *waqf*s will be discussed first. Then, some examples of prominent family members as administrators of the family *waqf*s will be presented. Information on the wealth and influence of these families as administrators of the charitable-public *waqf*s will also be presented with various examples. Finally, various other duties that families performed in relation to the institution of *waqf* will be discussed.

4.1 *The Administrative Organization of* Waqfs

In the Ottoman Empire, which had established its central authority in every field, the administration of *waqf*s was a set of systems directed towards the same service, but managed separately by different administrators.[323] Until the establishment in 1826 of the The Ministery of *Awqāf*, the administration of *waqf*s, which lacked a central organization, was carried out according to the conditions determined by the endowers.[324] The *mutawallī*, on the other hand, is the person who manages and administers this administration in accordance with the conditions of the *waqfiyya* and the provisions of the *sharīʿa*.[325] For the *waqf*s of Jerusalem, apart from the *mutawallī*, the *qāḍī*, the *nāzir* and, after the establishment of the Directorates of al-*Awqāf* in the Province, the director of al-*awqāf* had a say in this organization. However, in almost every period, the *mutawallī*s served as the primary administrators of the *waqf*.

The *mutawallī*s, who were the primary administrators of the *waqf*s, were determined by the founders of the *waqf*s themselves during the lifetime, and the general and specific conditions related to this issue were clearly recorded in the endowment deeds. These conditions remained valid for those who would

322 Al-Alami, "The Waqfs of the Traditional Families," 147.

323 Demirel, *Osmanlı Vakıf-Şehir*, 142.

324 About the roots of the *waqf*s and The Ministry of Foundations see, Köprülü, *İslam ve Türk*, 351–408; Akgündüz, *İslam Hukukunda*, 224–243.

325 Pakalın, *Osmanlı Tarih Deyimleri*, 640.

become *mutawallīs* after the death of the *waqf* founder. This is because the first *de facto mutawallī* was the founder of the *waqf*. In this respect, there is no major difference between the sultan, vizier or others.[326] Although it is known that the *waqfs* mostly appointed the *mutawallīs*, it is also seen that the *waqf* himself, his children and close relatives were the first among the *mutawallīs*.[327] Therefore, the *mutawallīs* of the *waqfs*, more than half of which were established by prominent families of Jerusalem, were also prominent administrators of the city and distinguished members of the scholarly and Sufi circles. Since the duty of trusteeship was vested in the offspring, they formed a family of *mutawallīs* as their generations continued. Apart from these, some endowers (high-level state administrators) allocated the duties of trusteeship of their endowments to certain families or offices.[328]

---

326 For example, Hürrem Sultan stipulated to the governor that as long as she is alive, the right of *tawliya* of her *waqf* in Jerusalem was given to herself and after her death to the one who "is just and trustworthy." VGMA, 608/23: 235/178.

327 For example, in an endowment deed (1115 AH/1703 CE), ʿAbd al-Raḥmān ibn al-Khwāja Muḥammad al-Nuʿājī stipulated *tawliya* to himself as long as he was alive then to children of the endower with the way of "el-erşed fe'l-erşed" and then to the deserving with the consent of the *qāḍī* of Jerusalem. JS 202: 12–13. As an exception, in an endowment deed (1136 AH/1723 CE), Shaykh Muḥammad Sunʿullāh Efendi ibn Khalīl Efendi al-Khālidī left the *tawliya* of *waqf* to himself as long as he was alive and then to the male children. JS 218: 253. In another example, Ḥusayn ibn Ḥasan Ḥarb stipulated (1157 AH/1744 CE) the *tawliya* of *waqf* to his daughter. JS 233: 3. Fāṭima Khātūn bint al-Ḥājj ʿĪsā Mujāhid stipulated (1178 AH/1764 CE) the *tawliya* of *waqf* to her brother Muṣṭafā after herself. JS 247: 80–81.

328 For example, the duties of shaykhship and murattibship of the *Waqf* of Ḥaḍrat Mūsā, Ḥaḍrat Yūnus, Ḥaḍrat Lūṭ *Maqām-i Sharīf* were given to Jerusalem *shaykh al-ḥaram*. VGMA, 1107: 2/120–121. In another example, the late Abū al-Faḍl endowed the properties, including a *bāb* of windmill – Muḥammad Pasha was the *mutaṣarrif* in Jerusalem – and the *waqf tawliya* was stipulated to the Shāfiʿī *muftī* of Jerusalem. In an order in the provisions, it is recorded that Aḥmad, one of the inhabitants of Jerusalem, intervened with the *muḥaddith* and Shāfiʿī muftī, al-Ḥājj ʿAbdullāh, who fulfilled the duty of trusteeship. It was ordered that the interventions to the *waqf* staff would be prevented. It has also been stated that this duty had been carried out by generations of family members since the *waqf* was established. BOA, ADVNS.AHK.ŞM (4): 14/4. Lastly, the leaving of *tawliya* and the income of the *Waqf* of ʿAlī Āghā in Jerusalem to the children and the emancipated and after his lineage was extinct, to the *mutawallīs* of the *Waqfs* of Ḥaḍrat Khalīl al-Raḥmān and Ṣaḥrat Allāh al-Musharrafa was stipulated. When there were no children to carry out the duty of *tawliya*, the duty was given to the *mutawallī* of the *Waqf* of Khalīl al-Raḥmān, Muḥammad Khalīfa. Yet the residents of Jerusalem, Sayyid Bashīr, Sayyid Ismāʿīl, and Sayyid Ḥasan objected to that and they demanded right. BOA, ADVNS.AHK.ŞM (4): 1/1. In another decree on the same topic, a *waqf* was endowed with the appointment of *mutawallī* and the income was left to the children and when the lineage was extinct, they were left to the *mutawallī* of the *Waqf* of Khalīl al-Raḥmān. Upon the death of *mutawallīs*, Sayyid Muḥammad Muṣṭafā and Shaykh Maḥmūd unjustly restrained the

Mutawallī appointments were made by individuals or groups such as the *nāzir, qāḍī*, the family of the endower and *ahl al-wuqūf* (neighbors). In the appointment records in the Jerusalem *Ḥurūfāt* books, it is found that *mutawallīs* were usually appointed upon the request of the *qāḍī* and sometimes upon the request of the *nā'ib*,[329] while occasionally officials other than the *mutawallī* and the *nāīb* were appointed upon the request of the *mutawallī* with an appointment deed.[330]

The issue of who the *mutawallīs*, who undertook important socio-cultural and religious duties, were in the scale of the city of Jerusalem is an important issue that will be examined in the next subheading. In the meantime, if the qualifications were required of the trustees are to be mentioned, first of all, the *mutawallīs*, who protected the *waqf* against all kinds of usurpation and encroachment, kept the *waqf*'s assets in a productive state and increased its revenues,[331] undertook different duties of the *shaykh*, imam, preacher, *nāzir* in addition to their duties as *mutawallīs*.[332]

A significant number of the *mutawallīs* were literate, scholarly, and had an understanding of administrative and financial affairs and were naturally the most prominent members of Jerusalem society. In the words of archival documents, they were required to have qualifications such as "*ehl-i kalcın, din ve diyaneti zāhir, iffet ve emānet sahibi*" (a member of the ruling elite, a person of religion and religious faith, chastity and trust'),[333] "*muhasebe virüb*

waqf. BOA, ADVNS.AHK.ŞM (4): 105/3. In the last decree of the same *waqf*, Shaykh Muṣṭafā and Shaykh Maḥmūd Muḥammad objected to the *mutawallī* of the Khalīl al-Raḥmān who possessed the *tawliya* and the income and they tyrannized. BOA, ADVNS.AHK.ŞM (5): 90/2.

329 VGMA, 551:99/47–48; 552:37/9;552:37/15.

330 VGMA, 1111: 54/56.

331 Yediyıldız, "Müessese-Toplum," 171–180.

332 E.g., the *mutawallī* and *shaykh* appointed to Sayyid Shahbāz, Shaykh Mazīd, Shaykh Muḥarram Sinā' al-Dīn, and Sayyid Jalāl Sufi Lodge in 1115 AH/1703 CE (VGMA, 1160: 116/92); the *mutawallī* and *nāẓir* appointed to the *Madrasa* Foundation in Kafara Quarter, *Khanqāh* Ḥallāja in 1116 AH/1704 CE (VGMA, 1107: 2/2); the trustee and *nāẓir* appointed to the Dār al-Ḥadīth Foundation in Khaṭṭ Dāwūd in 1116 AH/1704 CE (VGMA, 1107: 2/2); the official appointed to the Dār al-Ḥadīth Foundation in Khaṭṭ Dāwūd in 1117 AH/1705 CE was both a trustee and a shaykh (VGMA, 1160: 116/92); to the trusteeship, supervision, and *mashīkha* with a partial share in 1117 AH/1705 CE (VGMA, 1107: 2/15); to the "*Madrasa* al-Mâlikiyye al-Ma'rûf bi Kubbet al-Efdâliyya and Zâviye-i Mefârikiyye-i Seyyid Ömer al-Mücerred Abu'l-Madanī al-Gavsî ve Tevâbi'i Vakıfları" in Khaṭṭ Dāwūd in 1117 AH/1705 CE, he was appointed to the duties of *tawliya, naẓāra, mashīkha, tabrīz*, and turban. VGMA, 1107: 2/78.

333 For example, Muḥammad al-Jarīrī was appointed as *mutawallī* to the *waqf*s of Maghāriba for being "pious, trustable and honest". JS 203: 186. Shaykh Khalīl al-'Izrāwī was appointed

almaya kādir, evlād ise ālim, aslah, erşed ve ekber" (the one who is able to see accounting, and the son of *waqf* is the scholar, the most righteous, the most mature and the oldest in age).[334] In addition to the duties of the *mutawallīs*, these qualifications enabled them to perform several duties at once.[335]

When we list the duties of the *mutawallīs* of the *waqfs* of Jerusalem, we can see that they were primarily responsible for managing the *waqfs*' assets and properties in the best way possible or granting them on rent,[336] collecting the revenues of the *waqf*, using the revenues for the salaries of the officials and other expenses according to the conditions of the *waqfiyya*, protecting the *waqf*'s assets and service buildings,[337] and supervising the officials. The *mutawallīs* also dismissed and appointed the officials, kept the accounting of the *waqf*, and signed and certified it in the presence of the *qāḍī*.[338]

They were even authorized to create other wards in the city.[339] In fact, in an edict dated 1178 AH/1764 CE, it was even stated that "In order that the *qadis*

---

as *mutawallī* and *nāẓir* for being "pious and honest" to the Waqf of Jāmiʿ ʿUmarī in Latron. JS 249: 65–66.

334 For example, Sulaymān Ṣūfī al-Raṣāṣ was appointed to his grandfather's *waqf*, the *Waqf* of Mūsā al-Raṣāṣ for being "the most smart" among the most deservings. JS 264: 48.

335 For example, Sayyid ʿAbd al-Wahhāb and Ṣāliḥ were appointed as the *jibāyat* and *tawliya* of Birka Khātūn *Waqf* in Khaṭṭ Dāwūd Neighborhood with a daily salary of 3 *akçe*. In another example, Sayyid Khalīl ibn Abū al-Wafāʾ was appointed as trustee, *nāẓir*, *shaykh*, and *qāriʾ ḥadīth* for the Dār al-Ḥadīth *Waqf* in the same neighborhood. VGMA, 1119: 110/49. Sayyid Abū al-Mawāhib, the son of the deceased official's brother-in-law's sons, was appointed as the shaykh, trustee, and minister of *qirāʾat* al-*ḥadīth* of the Dār al-Qurrāʾ al-Sallāmiyya *Waqf*, also located in Khaṭṭ Dāwūd. VGMA, 1109: 6/158. Shaykh Maḥmūd was appointed as the *turba-dār* and trustee of the Banī Nūn Tomb. VGMA, 1109: 6/122. Al-Sayyid Ṭaha al-Rawḍayn ibn Sayyid Sulaymān al-Dajjānī was appointed as the trustee and *imām* of the Martūmā Mosque-ʿUmarī *Waqf* in the Rīsha neighborhood of Jerusalem. VGMA, 1109: 6/125.

336 For example, "Vakf-ı mezbûr tevliyetinin iki senelik irsâliyesi 5500 guruşun mültezimlerinden tahsiliçün nazır arzıyla emir. 24 Cemâziye'l-evvel 1187." VGMA, 723: 488. "Vakf-ı mezbûrun ve Şam haremeyn ve Sadaka-i Mısriyyun tevliyetlerinin mâl-ı mîrî olan 10300 guruş vefat iden mütevellisi Şeyh Muradzadenin terekesine vâzihu'l-yed olunandan tahsiliçün emir. 12 Şevval 1188." VGMA, 723: 489.

337 For example. "Şâm-ı Şerîfde sekban başların sakin oldukları hane harab olmağla mesârifi vakfı mezbûrun [Sahratullah-ı Müşerrefe] tevliyeti doksan dört ve beş seneleri zabt itdikleri zimmetlerinde olan akçeden mahsûb itmek üzere mütevellisi Şeyh Marazzade Seyyid Hüseyin Efendi mağrifetiyle tamir olunmak içün nazır arzıyla emr virilmişdir. 21 Muharrem 1188." VGMA, 723: 489.

338 Yediyıldız, "Müessese-Toplum," 171–80; al-Madanī, *Awqāf al-Quds*, 58–61.

339 In an edict for the *Waqf* of Khasseki Sultan (H. 1218/ M. 1803) it is ordered that the officials would be officially declared by *mutawallī* not with the *arz* and petition: "... Vakf-ı mezbūrda vākiʿ olan tevcihātının arz ve arz-ı hāl ile olunmayub mütevellisi inhāsı olmadıkça cihāt sādır olunmamak içündür. İşbu fermān-ı ʿālişānın unvanın mūcibince

of Jerusalem do not interfere in the affairs of the *waqf*, the *qāḍī*s were prevented from interfering with the powers of the *mutawallī*s by compiling some detailed articles with the desire of the *nāzir*".[340] The *mutawallī* was obliged to ensure that the production of *waqf* properties continued, that they were well preserved and repaired, and that those that were destroyed or in disrepair were replaced with better ones. However, all these changes were to be officially ratified by the local *qāḍī*, who was responsible for the general welfare of each *waqf* within his jurisdiction.[341] Depending on the size of the *waqf*s, there are different information on the conditions required of the *mutawallī*s. The *mutawallī*s carried out all these duties in accordance with the conditions of the *waqf* themselves or the temporary conditions that emerged over time, or they were assisted by officials such as the deputy *mutawallī*, *chief mutawallī*, *jābī*, *kābız*, *müşrif*, *kātib* and *muhasib*.[342]

In the Khasseki Sultan *Waqf*'s *atīq* treasury books (1118–1255 AH/1707–1840 CE), twenty-five appointment records show 16 dismissals (*rafʿ*), nine due to death, and one for deed renewal. Dismissals often stemmed from irregularities, with the trusteeship seized by the Navy Shipyard Commander between 1137–1139 AH/1723–1725 CE.[343] More generally, among the *waqf* officials of the city of Jerusalem, the *mutawallī*s were the most numerous. Almost every *waqf* had a *mutawallī*. Of the 673 entries in the *ḥurūfāt* book included in the scope of this study, *mutawallī*s were appointed in 232 of them. Among these, it was determined that there were around 128 *mutawallī*s who held more than one position

amel oluna deyu ketb kılınan mubarek hatt-ı hümāyūn-ı şevketmakrūn kaydı bilā sene şer virilmesine vakf-ı mezbūrun müetevellisi Ali Rüşdi zīde mecdihu istid'ā itmekle. Fī 22 Zilkade 1218 tarihinde bā fermān-ı Şerif kaydı balāsına şerh virildi. Emr-i şerif sitāde. Bā arz-ı Hafız Ahmed Ağa mütewellī-i vakf ve bā fermān-ı şerīfe. Fī 16 Şevval 1218." VGMA, 523: 2. In an appointment record (1194) in *ḥurūfāt* Book, the appointment of chief clerk was done by the *tezkire* of *mutawallī*. VGMA, 1111: 54/56. Yet, in an earlier edict sent to the same *waqf*, it was commanded that the salaries of officials must not be done by the tezkire of *mutawallī* without warrant. "… vakf-ı mezbūrun bilā berāt mütewellī tezkiresiyle ihdās olunan vezāifin men' içündür. Emr-i şerif sitāde. Bā arz-ı es-Sayyid al-Hac Mehmed Ağa mütewellī-i vakf ve bā fermān-ı ʿālī. Fī 25 Zilhicce Sene 1190." VGMA, 523: 2.

340 VGMA, 723: 488.

341 For example, in a court record (1116 AH/1704 CE) the *mutawallī* of the *Waqf* of ʿAlāʾ al-Dīn al-Baṣīr, Sayyid Muḥammad Sunʿullāh al-Khālidī, asked the Jerusalem *qāḍī* for the repair of the house close to Bāb al-Nāẓir of the *waqf*. JS 202: 272. The *mutawallī* of the *Waqf* of Ṣalāḥiyya *Madrasa*, Sayyid Jār Allāh Efendi al-Luṭfī, asked the permission of the *qāḍī* to repair al-Khiḍr Bazaar. JS 213: 82. The *mutawallī* of the *Waqf* of Qādiriyya *Madrasa*, al-Sayyid Ḥasan Effendi al-Marāshī, asked the permission of the *qāḍī* for repair.

342 The administrative officials in *waqf* stated as *mutawallī*, *nāzir*, *kātib*, *jābi* under the heading of "An Zābıtān-ı Vakf-ı Şerif" in VGMA. VGMA, 1005: 7.

343 VGMA, 523–524.

at the same time. In seventy of these, the duties of trusteeship and supervision were carried out together.[344] In twenty-six records, the office of *tawliya* was a share-based one, and the *mutawallīs* were appointed with varying proportions of shares.[345] In eight records, deputy *mutawallīs* were appointed. The reason for the high number of *mutawallīs* should be sought in the influence it would provide in the society, as well as the fact that it would provide a continuous income for the generation of the *mutawallīs* or the children of the *mutawallīs*, and that it was a ready-made profession or a comfortable source of livelihood. In the city of Jerusalem and throughout the empire, trusteeship was seen as an attractive profession in all periods. In fact, from time to time, there were struggles between sons and other officials for the position of *mutawallī*.[346]

As mentioned earlier, the standard of living and the prices of the time were taken into consideration when determining the fees of *mutawallīs*. However, as a result of centuries of trusteeship, developments such as the increase in prices, the decrease in the sources of *waqf* income, or the large number of generations of *mutawallīs* led to a decrease in wages or a widening of the differences between wages. The negative developments in *mutawallī* salaries over time were also reflected in the performance of duties and services. It is even recorded in archival documents that from time to time the officials committed

344 For example, the appointment of *mutawallī* and *nāẓır* executed together to the *Waqf* of the Mosque of Omar in the Jewish Quarter. See VGMA, 1107: 2/161; 1107: 2/168; 1107: 2/292.

345 For example, in 1141 AH/1728 CE, the biological children were appointed to the duty of *tawliya* instead of the one taking the share of one-eighth of the *Waqf* of Ḥaḍrat ʿIshmāwīl Nabī. VGMA, 1139: 87/21. In 1212 AH/1797 CE, Sayyid Shaykh Muḥammad al-Dajjānī was appointed to the duty of *tawliya* with one-third of the share of the *Waqf* of Ḥaḍrat Maryam Turba-i Sharīf. VGMA, 552: 37/14. The half share *tawliya* was the most recorded share. In 1221 AH/1806 CE, *niṣf tawliya* of the *Waqf* of Qarqāshandī Maktab near Dayr al-ʿAmūd in the Quarter of Afranj in Jerusalem was given to brothers al-Sayyid Mūsā, the biological son of the late official, and al-Sayyid ʿAbd al-Dāʿī. VGMA, 553: 38/21. In 1228 AH/1813 CE, the *berāt* was renewed due to its being lost. VGMA, 555: 25/3.

346 For example, the trouble between the official and his cousins due to *tawliya* and *nazāra* of Shaykh Manṣūr *Ribāṭ* in Jerusalem was reflected to Damascus. Ahkām Register: ʻŞam vālisi vezīre ve Kudüs-i Şerīf ḳāḍi sına hüküm ki: Sādāt-ı Kirām'dan Sayyid Ali bin Sayyid Arif -zīde şerefehū- Südde-i Saʿādetime gelüb Kudüs-i Şerīf'de vākıʿ Sahratullahü'l-Müşerrefe altında kā'in Şeyh Mansūr Revākı Vakfı'nın tawliya ve nezāreti berāt-ı şerīfemle bunun üzerinde olup ʿuhdesine lāzım gelen hıdmetini edā idüb bir vechile müdāhale olunmak īcāb itmez iken yine Kudüs-i Şerīf sākinlerinden amucaoğulları Şeyh Mehmed ve Şeyh İbrāhim ve Şeyh Sālih ve Şeyh Halil ve Şeyh Süleyman nām kimesneler kendü hallerinde olmayup hevāsına tābi kimesneler ile yekdil ve hılāf-ı şerʿ ve bilā-berāt [ve] sened tawliyai umūrına fuzūlī müdāhale ve teʿaddīden hālī olmadıkların bildirüp merkūmların ol vecihle olan müdāhale ve teʿaddīsi menʿ u defʿ olunmak bābında emr-i şerīfim recā eylediği ecilden mahallinde şerʿle görülmek içün yazılmışdır. Fī Evā'il-i Ramazan sene [1] 197.' BOA, ADVNS.AHK.ŞM (3): 146/3.

significant abuses.[347] In a later edict, it was commanded that the *waqf* income which was not collected by deputy *mutawallī* would be collected by Navy Shipyard Commander.[348] Uncollected *waqf* revenues also caused losses to the *waqfs*. The *qāḍī*, the *mubāshir* and the governor of Jerusalem made efforts to correct these corruptions related to the *mutawallīs*. On the other hand, it is understood that the inspectors, who were appointed to control the *mutawallīs* of the *waqfs*, did not or could not perform this duty properly. This can also be attributed to the fact that the same person served as *mutawallī* and inspector in most *waqfs*.

There are also rulings written to the vizier of Damascus, the Emir of Hajj, the vizier of Damascus, and the *qāḍī* of Jerusalem regarding the problems caused by the *mutawallī* of the *waqf* by threatening to take the land or the manors belonging to the *waqf* into his own name and sell them to someone else. For example, a woman named Jawdat bint ʿĀʾisha, a beneficiary of a Masjid al-Aqṣā and Ṣaḥrat Allāh *Waqf* house, was ordered to put an end to this and return the house to its rightful owner after the death of her mother, Aisha, and the person appointed as *mutawallī* was persecuting her with the threat of taking over the house and selling it to someone else.[349] It is understood that in most cases these measures taken by the state were insufficient and the abuses of the *mutawallīs* could not be prevented. The most important reason for this should be sought in the fact that usually well-established families or the rulers themselves performed the duty of trusteeship.

---

347 'Bābü's-Saʿāde Ağaları nezāretinde olub ber vech-i nāib-i müteveffā-yı Kapu Ağası Hıdır Mehmed Ağa'nın uhdesinde olan Kuds-i Şerīfde vākiʾ Khasseki Sultan tevliyeti ber vech-i hasbī tevliyet ve imāretlerinden ibaret olub imāretler içün külliyetli muʿayyenāt ve vezāif olunmakdan ise tevliyet-i merkūmeye mutasarrıf olanlar tevliyet-i merkūmeye evkāf-ı mezkūrenin kāffe-i hisselerden ve muʿayyenātı ahz ise kendi menāfiğleriçün imāretlere ve mahal-i sāireye vakfın taʿyin eylediği seneleri vech-i lāyıkı üzere virmeyüb evkāf-ı mezkūre harabe müşrīf ve imāretleri muʿattal olmak hasebiyle fi mā baʿd tevliyet-i merkūmenin imāretine [...] ve şart-ı vākıf icrāsıyla nizāmına [...] olmak içün āherden kimesne müdahale itmeyüb tawliya-i merkūmenin bi'l-cümle tevābi'i ve levāhıkiyle Darbhāne-i ʿĀmire tarafından zabt ve idare ve mesārif ve ʿavāidi Qadīmi vechile ...' VGMA, 523: 9.

348 "... kāimmakam-ı mutawallīsi olan Ahmed Efendi'nin Evkaf kasabātı ve kurāları ve ahalileri zimmetlerinde gerek tahsil idemediği ve gerek ʿan-nakdin karzen virüb tahsil idemedüğü mebāliğin tahsili içündür. Emr-i şerif sitāde. Bā takrīr-i Ahmed Ağa Emīn-i Darbhāne-i ʿĀmire ve bā-fermān-ı ʿālī- Fī 29 Rebiulahir 1203." VGMA, 523: 8.

349 BOA, ADVNS.AHK.ŞM (1): 288/2.

4.1.1 Women as *Mutawallī*

As Baer has noted, "In the long run, the *waqfs* served to rework property, in the sense that property that had passed into the hands of women through inheritance or other means was gradually returned to the control of male beneficiaries and male administrators. In this way, the *waqfs* actually weakened the economic position of women as a group."[350]

There were no legal restrictions preventing women from managing *waqfs*. Hürrem was authorized to appoint *mutawallīs* for the Khasseki Sultan *Waqf* in Istanbul.[351] Although she had a deputy in Jerusalem, she retained administrative control of the *waqf* as long as she lived, as well as the authority to make changes to the *waqfiyya*.[352] Baer has observed that women founders in 16th-century Istanbul tended to appoint more male than female administrators to the *waqfs* that they signed.[353] However, the examples he gives do not include imperial *waqfs*. Meriwether reveals that the majority of *waqf* administrators in Aleppo during the later period of her research were men, but the number of women is higher in her figures than in those of Gabriel Baer.[354] As for the endowments analyzed in the case of Jerusalem, none of the endowments established by male *waqfs* appointed a woman as *mutawallī*. On the other hand, in nineteen *waqfs* established by women, it was observed that the trusteeship was stipulated to the children of the endower after the death of the endower according to the *al-arshad fa al-arshad*[355] method. However, six endowers stipulated that their daughters should be the *mutawallīs* of their endowments after them. Four endowers stipulated that their sons,[356] two stipulated that their brothers,[357] one stipulated that her husband,[358] one stipulated that her brother's son,[359] and three stipulated that men other than sons should be the *mutawallīs* of their *waqfs*.[360]

In some 18th-century *waqfs* established in Jerusalem, the endower stipulated that his wife or daughters should reside in the endower's house after his

350 Baer, 'Women and *Waqf*, pp. 9–27.

351 VGMA, 608–2: 222/177.

352 VGMA, 608–2: 235/178.

353 Baer, "Women and *Waqf*," 13.

354 Meriwether, "Women and Waqf," 140–50; Fay, "Women and Waqf," 28–47.

355 "Tevliyeti vâkıfın mutlaka evlâdının erşedine meşrûta olan vakfın tevliyetine, vâkıfın gerek zükûr ve gerek inâs evlâdından hangisi en ziyâde reşid ise ol kimse müstehik ve meşrûtunleh olur." Ömer Hilmi Efendi, *İthāf al-Akhlāf*, 86–87.

356 JS 232: 87; 253: 253; 252: 141–142; 276: 88.

357 JS 247: 80–81; 242: 186.

358 JS 241: 123.

359 JS 243: 183–184.

360 JS 209: 253; 227: 391; 255: 53–54.

death until they married.[361] Qāsim Beg al-Tarjamān's, stipulated that wives or daughters reside in endowed houses, with income allocations (e.g., 100 *qurūsh* to his wife Laṭīfa).[362] Another *waqf*, Abdullah ibn al-Dāwudī, also allocated to his wife from the income of his *waqf*.[363] Muḥammad bin Budayrī[364] and Khālidiye bint Maḥmūd al-Khālidī[365] stipulated that the income of the *waqf* should be divided according to *sharīʿa* inheritance ratios (*mislü hazzi'l-ünseyeyn*), with-two shares for the male and one share for the female. On the other hand, Ismāʿīl ibn Hibbat Allāh al-Nāmrī stipulated that the income of the endowment should not be given to daughters.[366]

This treatment of women was to some extent a reflection of the male-dominated Muslim social structure in Ottoman Jerusalem. The opinions of the *imāms* and the rules of law on this issue were very clear. Any condition imposed by the *waqf* that violated *sharīʿa* law, including inheritance law, was considered invalid. Some *imāms* even went further and considered the *waqf* in such cases as *ghayr-i ṣaḥīḥ wa ghayr-i lāzim*. It was the *qadi*'s responsibility to ensure that the *sharīʿa* rules were strictly observed. Imam Abu Hanifa held that, as in the case of a will, a *waqf* could be established with 1/3 of the revenues of the endower and all of the remainder.[367]

There are various answers to the question of why men were preferred as administrators. First of all, most of the Ottoman imperial *waqf*s were huge institutions, and the properties donated to them were spread over long distances. Successful *mutawallī*s were chosen from among high-ranking military leaders or religious officials, all of whom were men. Both administrators and civil servants had to move from place to place as part of their duties, to gain experience in familiarizing themselves with the complex, managing personnel, and collecting taxes, as well as participating in on-the-job training, none of which was easily accomplished by women. Nevertheless, examples from Cairo during the Mamluk period show that in settings where the ruler came to power not within the framework of dynastic order but as a result of competition for the throne, it was decided that women would serve better and bring wealth and status to the ruler, taking into account other issues.[368]

361 JS 202: 12–13; 202: 186.
362 JS 213: 93–96.
363 JS 244: 182.
364 JS 272: 147.
365 JS 313: 199.
366 JS 221: 410.
367 Al-Alami, "*The Waqfs of the Traditional*," 156.
368 Fay, "Kadınlar ve Waqf," 31.

Since Mamluk women rarely lived longer and were relatively free of the violence that plagued Mamluk men, they served on an equal footing with the *mutawallī*s of large institutions; they were, after all, to some extent shields for the large institutions and those they supported.[369] In the Jerusalem *imāret*, members of the leading families of the region were appointed as administrators. However, there is no record of a woman from one of these prominent families being given this position.[370] Secondly, when women were among the beneficiaries of the great imperial *waqf*s, they were in a less advantageous position than men. Yes, they had access to magnificent mosques, hospitals, soup kitchens and Sufi lodges, and they also benefited from fountains and bridges. But they could not be salaried religious scholars or students in *madrasas*, and they were rarely in a position to enjoy the hospitality of caravanserais. It was also rare for them to work as unskilled laborers in such institutions.

In the period under review, women established *waqf*s in Jerusalem, and they were able to appoint themselves or their daughters after their deaths as *mutawallī*s or other beneficiaries of the *waqf*.

4.2 *Local Elites as* Mutawallīs *of Family* Waqfs

In addition to being founders of *waqf*s, Jerusalem's elite families are mentioned in the records in various contexts. A large proportion of these families appear before the court as *mutawallī*s of *waqf*s established by their fathers or grandfathers. For example, the trusteeship of Sayyid Aḥmad Dajjānī Waqf's trusteeship passed to Sayyid Yaḥyā,[371] the son of the endower, in 1167 AH/1753 CE and to to Sayyid Muḥammad ibn Sayyid ʿAlī (al-Dajjānī) Khalīfa upon the death of Sayyid Yahya in 1175 AH/1761 CE.[372] These people were also appointed to the Shaykhdom of Nabi Dāwūd'sTomb with the same appointment record. In another family *waqf*, Sayyid Muḥammad Efendi, one of the children of the heirs, was appointed to the supervision of the Sunʿ Allāh Effendi al-Khālidī *Waqf* descendant of Khālidī bin Walīd on 1164 AH/1750 CE, which was stated to be legitimate to the children.[373] In 1196 AH/1781 CE, Shaykh Muḥammad

369 ibid., 31.

370 Although al-Asali mentioned a woman administrator appointed with *berāt*, there is no record of that in the *atīk* books involving appointment records and its reasons between the years of 1118–1255 AH/1706–1839 CE. For further information, see Kamāl ʿAbd al-Jalīl al-ʿAsalī, *Wathāʾiq Maqdisiyya Tārīkhiyya* (Amman: Jāmiʿat al-Urduniyya, 1983), 311–12; VGMA, 523–524.

371 VGMA, 1112:1/ 203.

372 VGMA, 1110: 131/104.

373 VGMA, 1112: 1/139.

Sunʿ Allāh al-Khālidī was appointed as the trustee and supervisor.[374] Upon the death of the incumbent, Mūsā ibn Sunʿ Allāh, the son of the *aslah* and *arshad* (the most righteous and the most mature) son of the endower, was appointed in 1208 AH/1793 CE.[375] In another example, in 1192 AH/1778 CE, his brother-in-law Sayyid ʿAbd al-Qādir Shaykh Sajjāra Bisṭāmī was appointed as the trustee, supervisor and *shaykh* of Shaykh ʿAbdullāh al-Bisṭāmī Sufi Lodge *Waqf* upon the childless death of the endower.[376] Approximately twenty years after this date, in 1212 AH/1797 CE, Sayyid ʿAbd al-Qādir Shaykh Sajjāra Bistamī was given a new *berāt* (appointment deed) due to the loss of his deed.[377] In 1203 AH/ 1789 CE, his son ʿAbd al-Ḥaqq al-Jāʿūnī, preacher to the Mosque of the Fortress of Jerusalem, was appointed as the supervisor and scribe of Shaykh Khalil al-Jāʿūnī and his wife Şerife Alime bint Muḥammad bin Aba Şerif and Shaykh Kemaleddin Aba Şerif *Waqfs*.[378] In 1234 AH/1788 CE, upon the death of Abdulhak al-Jāʿūnī, the same duties were assigned to Sayyid Shaykh ʿAbd al-Raḥmān ibn ʿAwnī, the eldest son of the heir from the Jāʿūnī family, preacher to the Mosque of the Fortress of Jerusalem.[379]

Gabriel Baer, in his study covering the period between 1805 and 1814, stated that the members of Jerusalem's elite families constituted about half of the new *mutawallī* appointments with a ratio of eight out of fifteen.[380] In some of the appointments made during the period in question, ʿAbd al-Ṣamad al-ʿAlamī was appointed as the *mutawallī* of his grandfather Abū al-Faḍl's *waqf* on 1222 AH/1807 CE, replacing the dismissed daughter of the *waqf*. Two months later, Muḥammad Ḥusayn al-Khālidī, a clerk at the *Qāḍī* Court of Jerusalem, was appointed *mutawallī* of the *waqf* of Ahmad Beg al-Tarjamān, a relative of his grandmother. Another al-Khālidī succeeded him in 1813. Three members of the Nimrī family served as *mutawallīs* of their grandfathers' *waqfs*. The grandfathers of the Nimrī family and one of the *mutawallīs* in question also served as chief architect in Jerusalem. In 1810, Ibrahim Beg al-Tarjamān applied to the *qāḍī* for the allocation of the trusteeship fee, which was not specified in the *waqf*. In 1811, Hassan al-Jāʿūnī, who was the chief of the *cebecis*[381] in Jerusalem, was appointed as *mutawallī* of two *waqfs* established by his grandfather Hassan

374 VGMA, 1111: 54/92.
375 VGMA, 551: 99/ 27.
376 VGMA, 1111: 54/33.
377 VGMA, 552: 37/16.
378 VGMA, 551: 99/1.
379 VGMA, 555: 25/19.
380 Baer, "The Dismemberment," 299–300.
381 In the Ottoman army, they were *kapıkulu* cavalry soldiers who were in charge of procuring and protecting weapons and taking them to the front in time of campaign.

al-Jāʿūnī. In 1814, Bashir al-Jāʿūnī was appointed *mutawallī* of another family *waqf*. Muḥammad al- Daqqāq's daughter Khadija served as *mutawallī* and caretaker of her maternal grandfather's *waqf*. In 1227 AH /1812 CE, Ṣāliḥ al-Danaf was appointed as *mutawallī* and caretaker of his father's endowment; in 1813, Muḥammad Ṭāhir al-Ḥusaynī, the *muftī* of Jerusalem, was appointed as trustee of the endowment of his grandfather Abdullatif al-Ḥusaynī, who had been the *naqīb al-ashrāf* of Jerusalem; and in 1813, Abdullah al-Dajjānī was appointed as *mutawallī* of the Dajjānī family endowment.[382]

In conclusion, in the family *waqf*s established and maintained in the city of Jerusalem, the *waqf* usually preferred a member of his own family as the administrator, and preferably the sons of the male lineage.[383]

4.3 *Local Elites as* Mutawallīs *in Charitable* Waqfs

The importance of Jerusalem's leading families is greater in terms of charitable *waqf*s established by others rather than by their own families and not connected to their own families. The new appointments of members of Jerusalem's leading families as trustees of Jerusalem's other charitable *waqf*s are much larger than those made to family *waqf*s.[384] However, in terms of increasing the prestige and efficiency of the management of charitable *waqf*s, the dominant position of Jerusalem's leading families in this field, compared to other Jerusalemites, reinforces their influence in the social and political sphere. This is also true for other positions in the charitable *waqf*s that were passed down from father to son.

First of all, in the local environment, the family was the most important structure for the transmission of offices from one generation to the next. Over time, families belonging to Jerusalem's wealthy classes acquired vested rights within the *ʿulamāʾ* network and managed to transform them into a semi-official position. Thus, the al-Jārullah and al-Ḥusaynī families established a kind of monopoly on the office of *muftī*, while the Jamāʿīs held the position of orator of the al-Aqṣā Mosque for generations starting from the Ayyubid period under Saladin. The same is true for the offices of *nāʾib* or *raʾīs al-kuttāb* in the courts. Rather, they can be characterized as factions vying for various offices and ultimately dependent on the decisions taken by Istanbul. It is noteworthy that no effort to ensure the appointment of "local" candidates succeeded. It is also noteworthy that the inheritance of certain offices could be exploited in some cases. The inheritance of offices was not limited to large families with vested

382 Baer, "Jerusalem's Families," 111–13.

383 ibid., 113.

384 ibid., 116–17.

rights to official and semi-official positions. Smaller *ʿulamāʾ* also acquired their positions, often through family succession. In some cases, these transfers could be regulated in the endowments by leaving the duties of *mutawallī* or teacher to the descendants of the founder or a particular scholar. This ensured or at least encouraged the perpetuation of a particular family tradition. In many cases, positions passed from father to son, from one brother to another, from uncle to nephew, and so on. These transfers were then confirmed by the *qāḍī* with a *berāt-ı sultanī* (appointment deed). The transfer of trusteeships from father to son in some foundations controlled from Istanbul or the privileged positions held by prominent families in Jerusalem in some offices such as the office of *naqīb al-ashrāf*, which had to be appointed by the Ottoman sultan, also support this situation.[385] For a scholar at the beginning of his career, for example, a position by inheritance often provided only a foothold in the system from which he could climb to other positions. In the end, he was creating his own set of duties, which would be redistributed through succession to his sons or through the *qāḍī*'s redistribution of duties. While succession played an important role in the reproduction of the *ʿulamāʾ* network of relations, it never produced a closed system outside the control of central authorities.[386]

In the 18th century, partly due to the inheritance of offices, it became common practice to divide them between two or more scholars in halves, thirds, quarters, or even twelfths. Scholars thus collected a series of partial salaries, the sum of which would provide them with sufficient income. These could be important posts such as trusteeship of large *waqf* complexes, head of the *muezzin* or chief *imām* of Masjid al-Aqṣā, etc., as well as lower positions. Members of the Jārullah (Luṭfī, Abū al-Luṭf) family held the *muftī*'s office, one of the most important positions in Jerusalem, and the *tawliya* of the Ṣalāḥiyya *Madrasa* from the 8th century onwards. In addition, in the 18th century, they were appointed as the Shaykh of the Evhādiyya *Madrasa*,[387] Sayyid Jār Allāh Khalīfa was appointed as the reciter[388] for the soul of Sultan Suleiman in the Kāmiliyya *Madrasa*,[389] and as the minister, *shaykh*[390] and trustee[391] of the

385 "Fī-mā-baʿd muhdes cihāt tevcīh olunmayub olanların dahī birisi fevt oldukda evlād-ı var ise evlādına yok ise vakfa māhir olmak üzere fermān-ı ʿālī sādır olmuşdur. Emr-i şerīf sitāde. Bā-arz-ı ... Ağa-i Dārü's-Saʿādeti'ş-Şerīfe en-nāzır ve bā fermān-ı ʿālī. Fī 2 Rebiuʿl-ahir 1181." VGMA, 523: 2. For more detailed order, see VGMA, 814: 11.

386 Van Leeuwen, *Bir Osmanlı*, 138.

387 VGMA, 1140: 245/47; 1107: 2/1; 1107: 2/188.

388 VGMA, 1107: 2/189; 1109: 6/31.

389 VGMA, 1107: 2/190.

390 VGMA, 1112: 1/76; 1112: 1/155; 1112: 1/189.

391 VGMA, 1112: 1/156.

Duwaydāriyya *Madrasa*. They also took over the trusteeship and supervision of the *Ṣadaqāt-i Ḥukmiyya Waqf*.[392]

Some of the duties held by the members of the 'Alamī family, another important *'ulamā'* family of Jerusalem, were as follows: Wafā' al-'Alamī served as the *mutawallī* of the *Ḥaramayn Waqf* and other members of the 'Alamī family served as *mutawallī*s of the Bīmaristan al-Ṣalāḥiyya *Waqf* for generations: *shaykh, nāzīr, mutawallī,* doorkeeper[393] at the Sufi Khanqāh al-Ṣalāḥiyya; Ṣalāḥiyya *Madrasa*; clerk, *shaykh, nāzīr, mutawallī*[394] at the Malik Ṣalāḥ al-Dīn *Waqf*; *imām, shaykh, mutawallī, nāzir, jābī,* clerk[395] at the Ḥamrā *Madrasa*; *mutawallī, jābī*[396] at the As'adiyya Lodges; at the Qādirīyya Lodges as lodger, *shaykh*;[397] at the Ya'qūbiyya Mosque and Lodges as *mutawallī, nāzir, shaykh,* scribe;[398] at the Khātūniyya *Madrasa* as *mutawallī, nāzir*;[399] and at the Geylāniyya Tomb *Waqf* as *nāzir*.[400] The transfer of partial duties was valid for the *imām*ship of small mosques, *kārī*ship, preachership, *ferraşlık* (cleanership) etc.[401] The example of the 'Alamīs indicates that the duties were transferred between scholars through *ferağ* (waiver), in exchange for a certain price.[402]

392 VGMA, 1107: 2/9; 1107: 2/23; 1091: 77/10; 1091: 77/17:Malikiyya, Zamīniyya, Jawhariyya, Kāmiliyya, 'Uthmāniyya, Qādiriyya, Bāsiṭiyya, Ḥanafiyya, Karīmiyya, Maymūniyya Madrasas and Ribāṭ-i Manṣūrī, Hangāh-i Bāsiṭiyya, Hangāh-i Mawsiliyya, Hangāh-i Jawhariyya, Ṣadaqāt al-Ḥukmiyya, Jāmi' al-'Umarī *waqf*s. For detailed information, see Eroğlu Memiş, *Hurûfât Defterleri*, 182–85.

393 VGMA, 1128:68/19; 1112: 1/133; 1125: 64/13; 1160: 116/16; 1110: 131/116; 1110: 131/116; 1160: 116/8.

394 VGMA, 1128: 68/25; 1128: 68/19; 1128: 68/41.

395 VGMA, 1128: 68/26; 1110: 131/73; 1110: 131/87; 1110: 131/90; 1110: 131/113; 1108: 1/67; 1125: 64/7; 1160: 116/57; 1114: 10/1.

396 VGMA, 1160: 116/10; 1110: 131/92; 1107: 2/175; 1112: 1/132; 1110: 131/114; 1125: 64/10.

397 VGMA, 1107: 2/110; 1128: 68/41; 551: 99/50.

398 VGMA, 1107: 2/110; 1128: 68/41; 551: 99/50.

399 VGMA, 1107: 2/164; 1109: 6/46.

400 VGMA, 1109: 6/102; 1110: 131/107; 1125: 64/9; 1114: 10/2.

401 For example, apart from Makdīsi, they were appointed as *imām, cābi,* administrator in the *waqf* of the mosque and *zāwiya* around *'Ishmāwīl* tomb. VGMA, 1107: 2/173; 1110: 131/115; 1125: 64/8; 1125: 64/11. "Kudüs-i Şerīfde vāki' Geylāniyye Medresesi'nde yevmī bir pāre ile kātib ve yevmī bir pāre ile müsebbih ve yine Fārisiye Medresesinde yevmī 3 akçe ile meşārik ve yine ... Dāvudda bir pāre ile kāri' ve bir bāb hāne ile Cami-i ... (Meğāribe)Receb ve Şaban ve Ramazan-ı Şerīfde kāri-i hadīs ve Kur'an ve ... meşrūta diğer hāneye ve Fārisiyye Medresesinde ... ile Şeyh ve kā'immakām-ı mütewellī ve kātib Şeyh Feyzullah fevt karındaşı Şeyh Halile ināyet." VGMA, 1091: 77/3.

402 Other duties carried out by the 'Alamī family are as follows: Maymūniyya, Lu'lu'iyya *madrasa*s and the foundations of Jāmi' 'Umarī, Ṣaḥrat Allāh al-Musharrafa, Maqām Nabī 'Ishmāwīl (Samūyīl), *Awqāf* Qāḍī Quds 'Abdullāh Effendi, Waqf Ibrāhīm al-Rūmī, Jāmi'

Sayyid Muḥammad al-Ḥusaynī of the al-Ḥusaynī family was appointed as the trustee, *nāzīr*, and Shaykh of the Jabībiyya and Tāziyya *Madrasa*s in place of the deceased official.[403] In addition to the duties of trusteeship, supervision, shaykhdom, *tebrīz*, and tombkeeping[404] at the *madrasa* of Afdāliyya, they also continued to serve as *muftī* due to the loss of most of the male members of the Jārullah family due to illness.[405] For generations, members of the Ḥusaynī family undertook the duties of trusteeship, supervision and cibâyet of the offices of the Nabi Moses, Lut and Yunus Tomb *Waqf*s. They also managed the Khasseki Sultan *Waqf* for a period. In the period under review, ʿUmar al-Ḥusaynī was also appointed as the trustee of the Salmān al-Fārisī Tomb *Waqf* built by the trustee of Jerusalem in Mount Olive.[406]

Shaykh Sunʿ Allāh al-Khālidī, a member of the Khālidī family, served as the trustee and supervisor of the Dār al-Hadīth *Waqf* and as the trustee and supervisor of the Dār al-Qurrā al-Sellāmiyya Waqf,[407] as well as serving as the chief clerk of the Jerusalem Court[408] for many years.[409]

Members of the Imām family held the *imāmate* of the al-Aqṣā Mosque, the trusteeship of the Amīniyya *Madrasa*, and the management of the Tashṭīmūriyya Lodges.[410] Members of the Nimrī (evlād-ı Nammar) family were often officially appointed as chief architects of charitable *waqf*s in Ottoman

al-ʿAshara (bi'l-Aqṣā). For detailed information, see Eroğlu Memiş, *Hurūfāt Defterleri*, 182–85.

403 VGMA, 1107: 2/95–97.

404 "Medresetü'l-Mâlikiyye el-ma'rûf bi-Kubbetü'l-Efdâliyye ve Zâviye-i Mefârikiyye-i Seyyid Ömer el-Mücerred Ebu'l-Madanī al-Gavsî ve Tevâbi'i Vakıfları ..." VGMA, 1107: 2/78.

405 Al-Alami, "Waqfs," 153.

406 Other foundations in which the Ḥusaynī family held various positions are as follows: Ṣalāḥiyya, al-Sallāmiyya, Ṭūlūniyya, Ḥusayniyya, Tashṭimuriyya, Gaylāniyya, Khasakiyya *madrasas*; Ḥamrā' Ribāṭ, Bistāmiyya and Adhhamiyya lodges, *Maqām* al-Shaykh Ḥasan, *Waqf* al-Shaykh Muḥammad al-Karīmī, *Waqf* al-ʿAbd al-Ghanī Effendi, *Waqf* al-Salmān Effendi, *Waqf* al-Wālī Quds Muḥammad Pasha, *Waqf* al-Ḥāfiẓ Pasha, *Waqf* al-Murād Ḥilmī, *Waqf* al-ʿAbd al-Raḥmān Effendi, *Waqf* al-ʿAbbās Āghā. For detailed information, see Eroğlu Memiş, *Hurūfāt Defterleri*, pp. 182–85.

407 VGMA, 1107: 2/63.

408 VGMA, 1107: 2/199; 1110: 131/6; 1113: 35/28; 1113: 35/29; 1142: 84/7.

409 Other foundations in which the Khālidī family held various positions are as follows: Jīlāniyya, Fārisiyya, Qādiriyya, Khātūniyya, and Zamīniyya *madrasas*, Qalāwūn Masjid, and *Awqāf* al-ʿAbd al-Qādir al-Baṭīrī. For detailed information, see Eroğlu Memiş, *Hurūfāt Defterleri*, 182–85.

410 Al-Alami, "Waqfs," 154–55.

Jerusalem. They were also in charge of the *Waqf* Qanāt al-Sabīl (Foundation for Waterways).[411]

The Dāwudī-Dajjānīs were the trustees of numerous mosque and mausoleum *waqfs*. First of all, they are the trustees of the *Waqf* of the Nabi Dāwud in Jerusalem. Shaykh Sayyid Muḥyī al-Dīn al-Dajjānī was appointed as the trustee of the *Waqf* of the Nabi Dāwūd's *Maqam* and the trustee of the *Waqf* of Dār al-Qurrā al-Sellāmiyya.[412] In 1810, Shaykh Khalīl al-Dajjānī was appointed trustee and minister of two mosques in the villages of 'Allar and Bayt Nūbā.[413] Another al-Dajjānī, Darwīsh ibn Suleiman, was appointed a year and a half later as the trustee of a shaykh's mausoleum in 'Amvas, paying the previous trustee, a member of the Daqqāq family, his full salary.[414] Muḥammad Wafā al-Dajjānī was appointed trustee of another *waqf* shrine along with 'Abd al-Raḥīm al-Jāʿūnī.[415]

The al-Jāʿūnī family also held intergenerational positions in the administration of some other endowments. In April 1811, Mūsā and 'Abd al-Bāʿādī al-Jāʿūnī were appointed trustees of the *Waqf* of Muḥammad al-Nāṣirī ibn Aḥmad al-Ṭawrī (Abū Ṭūr), replacing their father Muṣṭafā, imam of the Dome of the Rock. In 1813, two other members of the al-Jāʿūnī family were appointed as trustees of the Bāṣitiyya *Madrasa*.[416]

Members of the Abū Suʿūd family were the trustees of the Jāmi ʿUmarī *Waqf* in the Jewish Quarter, while members of the Danaf (Anṣārī) family were the guardians of the Dome of the Rock Mosque for generations and managed the two *waqf* mosques in Bittā near Jerusalem.[417] The Daqqāq family held various positions at the Qādiriyya *madrasa*, the Suyūtī Mosque, and the Yūsuf Ağa al-Rūmī endowments.[418] The 'Asalī family held various positions at the

411 It is a charitable foundation established for the repair and maintenance of the fountains and waterways in Jerusalem.

412 VGMA, 1107: 2/60.

413 JS 294: 50.

414 JS 294: 109.

415 JS 292: 87. Other foundations where the Dajjānī family held various positions are as follows: Ṣalāḥiyya, Gaylāniyya, Muzhiriyya, Awhādiyya, Fakhriyya, Zamīniyya *madrasas* and *Ribāṭ* Ḥamawī, Jāmiʿ ʿUmarī, *Awqāf* Maqbara al-Yahūd, Maqām Sayyidinā Dāwūd, *Waqf* Qanāt al-Sabīl, *Waqf* 'Abd al-Karīm Chorbajī, *Waqf* Muṣṭafā Pasha, and *Awqāf* Ṣaḥrat Allāh al-Musharrafa. For detailed information, see Eroğlu Memiş, *Hurūfāt Defterleri*, pp. 182–185.

416 JS 294: 164; 297: 41.

417 JS 292: 115; 295: 28.

418 VGMA, 515: 95/ 150.

Maymūniyya and Qādiriyya *madrasa*, and the Khāṣṣekī Sulṭān and Turgut Agha *waqf*s.[419]

The families, mostly from the *ʿulamāʾ* class, of which some examples are given here, took active and long-term roles in the management of various religious-educational *waqf*s in the Ottoman period. In addition to their administrative duties, they served for generations in other charitable and public *waqf*s, of which there are numerous examples. For example Ibrāhīm Fakhr al-Dīn al-Jāʿūnī was appointed as the chief orator of the Masjid al-Aqṣā.[420] However, Abī Jamāʿa applied to the Sharīʿa Court claiming that the position of the chief orator of Masjid al-Aqṣā had been held by his sons since the reign of Ṣalāḥ al-Dīn al-Ayyūbī.[421] After examining the situation, the Ottoman administration decided to return the position to the Jamāʿa family.[422] Other officials who assumed the position of orator at al-Aqṣā Mosque were Abū al-Hudā ibn Muḥammad Effendi,[423] the Ḥanafī *Muftī* of Jerusalem, ʿAbd al-Raḥmān al-ʿAfīfī,[424] and Jār Allāh Effendi.[425]

In another appointment record, the Māliki Imam Muḥammad al-Muwakkit was appointed as the chief *imām* of the Masjid al-Aqṣā Mosque.[426] Shaykh ʿUthmān ibn ʿAlī al-ʿAlamī,[427] Khalīl Effendi,[428] ʿAbd al-Raḥīm ibn Mūsā Effendi Qāḍī al-Ṣalṭ,[429] Shāfiʿī Muftī Muḥammad Effendi,[430] and Fatḥ Allāh Qudayya[431] were appointed as the *imām*s of the mosque in question. Likewise, the chief *muezzin* positions were held by Shaykh Kamāl Fatḥ Allāh[432] and Kamāl al-Dīn Qudsiyya.[433] Although some other prominent families such as Budayrī, Daqqāq, Danaf, Quṭayna, Nashāshībī, and Nuṣayba served as trustees of charitable *waqf*s in Jerusalem, there is no record of them during the period covered by this study.

---

419 VGMA, 515: 75/82; 95/150.
420 JS 201: 354.
421 JS 202: 106.
422 JS 221: 17.
423 JS 205: 44.
424 JS 202: 141.
425 JS 209: 63.
426 JS 215: 54.
427 JS 214: 210.
428 JS 255: 175.
429 JS 274: 129.
430 JS 273: 104.
431 JS 205: 259.
432 JS 201: 429.
433 JS 211: 89.

In his study based on the Jerusalem *Sharīʿa* Registers between 1805 and 1814, Gabriel Baer identified twelve new appointments of trustees to charitable *waqf*s. Two of these appointments were made from the Ottoman ruling elite, while 60% of the rest were made by members of the city's leading families. It is noteworthy that the proportion of these appointments to charitable *waqf*s was higher when compared to those made to family *waqf*s. These data, although limited in number, show that the city's prominent families had a wide sphere of influence over the charitable *waqf*s.[434]

Apart from these, the number of families who worked in non-religious jobs is quite small. The most respected of these families were the Ḥadūta and Suʿdī branches of the ʿAlamī family, which were engaged in soap production, flour milling, and harvest management. In the *waqfiyya*s belonging to the ʿAsalī family were also described them as merchants.

The active and long-term positions of the families, some of which are presented here, in the management of various religious-educational *waqf*s in the Ottoman period frequently led them to establish new *waqf*s. It seems that the constant income provided to the family through these positions was the source of a significant amount of wealth to be transferred to the *waqf*s to be established by the family. It is also important to note that some families owned properties in the same neighborhood as the properties of the *waqf*s they served in. One of the best examples of this situation is the ʿAlamī *waqf*s. Most of the properties they owned and endowed were concentrated in the Naṣāra neighborhood, where the *Khānqāh* al-Ṣalāḥiyya and the Ḥamrā *madrasa* were also located. In another example, the properties belonging to the Jār Allāh family endowments are also located near the Ṣalāḥiyya *madrasa*. In a third example, the *waqf*s of the Imām family were located in the vicinity of the Tashṭīmūriyya lodges.[435]

4.4 *Local Elites as* Waqf *Beneficiaries*

It is possible to count family members as beneficiaries of the *waqf* before the poor (*ahl al-bayt, jins, āl*).[436] As can be seen in the examples given above, these families not only managed the *waqf*s, but were also the main beneficiaries. The institution of *waqf*, which allowed for the control of the *waqf* while he was still alive, and the wide scope of freedom it provided in determining and even defining the beneficiaries of his estate after his death, made it attractive to the influential families of Jerusalem.

434 Baer, "Jerusalem's Families," 110.

435 Al-Alami, "Waqfs," 153.

436 Van Leeuwen, *Bir Osmanlı*, 55.

Ḥasan Effendi ibn ʿAbd al-Laṭīf al-Ḥusaynī *waqf* is a good example of a property endowed to a family (*waqf ahlī, waqf dhurrī*). The beneficiaries were the founder of the family and his descendants. The payment would continue until his descendants died out. After that, the shops would be transferred to the *waqf*. Ḥasan Effendi, a member of the Ḥusaynī family, left his *waqf* on the condition that he himself would run the business in his lifetime. All rents and rural surplus produce were to be allocated to him and his descendants as long as they lived. The income beneficiaries identified in detail were his daughter's sons, as-Sayyid ʿUmar Effendi and ʿAlī and his sister's sons, his father, as-Sayyid ʿAbd al-Salām Effendi, his wife, the former *naqīb al-ashrāf* of Jerusalem, the sons of Naqībzāda as-Sayyid ʿAbd al-Laṭīf, Sayyid ʿAbdullāh Effendi, as-Sayyid Rāghib Effendi, Sayyida Nābihān, and Naqībzāda as-Sayyid ʿAbd al-Laṭīf's daughters, Sayyida Maḥbūba, Sayyida Ismāʿ and her brother's two daughters, Sayyida Amīna and Sayyida Fāṭima, and after them the sons of Sayyid ʿAbd al-Salām and ʿAbd al-Laṭīf, and the sons of the *waqf*, the sons of his daughter, the sons of his daughter, the sons of his sons, and the sons of his sons, until the generation ceases without daughters. After them, it was made conditional on the relatives of the *waqf*, and when the generation from them ceased, it was made conditional on the daughters of the *waqf*, and after them, it was made conditional on *Simāt* (Public Kitchen) Nabī Mūsā. He also set the following condition: The reconstruction costs of the houses and other properties, the maintenance and repair of the mills, and the fencing of very large gardens in the countryside were to be covered by the income of this *waqf*. For the first two or three years, even if all the income of the *waqf* was spent on such repairs, these works had to be carried out. As was customary, he appointed the "*mawqūfūn ʿalayhā*" as the administrator of the *waqf* and determined the salaries to be paid to the *waqf*'s officials.

The *waqf* established by Ḥasan Effendi is particularly interesting because it clearly reveals the management of rural and urban properties. Ḥasan Effendi, who was a *naqīb al-ashrāf*, divided the revenues of the *waqf* in a different way, while stipulating that the same people were responsible for its supervision. According to the rules of inheritance, his sons should receive two shares and his daughters one share, but he conditioned the shares of the daughters on their being cut off from their relatives.[437] In another *waqf* established by the Ḥusaynīs, ʿAbd al-Laṭīf Effendi al-Ḥusaynī (Ḥasan Effendi's father), deputy *naqīb al-ashrāf* and Shaykh al-Ḥaram in al-Quds, stipulated that his wives Fāṭima bint ʿAbd al-Ḥayy al-Dajjānī and Amīna bint Ibrāhīm Çelebi al-Nāmrī

437 JS 278: 112.

should live in the houses he endowed, and that this right would end if his wife married after his death. He also made it clear that his numerous rural and urban properties could not be exchanged or rented for more than three years.[438] The fact that ʿAbd al-Laṭīf Effendi's wives were also women from the prominent Dajjānī and Nāmrī families of Jerusalem is also important as an example of the relations established between the local elite through marriage ties.[439]

These *waqfs* were set up as a kind of trust fund for the family and were placed under the management of the head of one of the branches of the family; it was he who determined the terms of management and lease. The prohibition on long-term leases was a wise move, as it prevented one of the main causes of the disposal of endowed property. According to *sharīʿa* law, the administrator of a *waqf* could lease *waqf* properties for a short or long term. The long term was sometimes as long as ninety years. The fixed amount set as rent would often shrink due to the depreciation of the currency. Since the *waqf* administrator had little say in the repair of the leased property, it quickly fell into disrepair. The Ḥusaynīs wanted to ensure that this would not happen and made the lease agreements conditional on a short term.

Almost all of the newly established *waqfs* in Jerusalem during the period covered by this study were family *waqfs*, and most of them only had provisions regarding the *mutawallīs*. All managerial positions in the *waqf* were to be held by the sons of the *waqf*, and these positions were to be held mostly by male members of the family, in accordance with the *al-arshad fa al-arshad* method. Under no circumstances could they buy or sell property on behalf of the *waqf*.[440]

Some of the accounting records in the registry also record the lists of the sons who received a share of the *waqfs*' revenues and the shares they received.[441] For example, in the accounting record submitted to the court by Ibrāhīm Qāmiʿ, the trustee of Ḥusayn Qāmiʿ *waqf*, it is recorded that the income and expenses of the *waqf* were balanced and the surplus income was distributed among the sons of the *waqf* as nine shares, regardless of the order of their lineage.[442] In another similar example, Tarjumānzāda al-Sayyid Ibrāhīm Bey ibn

438 249: 63–64.

439 Ze'evi, a.g.e., s. 89–94.

440 In the period under study, 109 *waqfs* from 300 new *waqfs* in Jerusalem was left to the *waqf* administration by this way.

441 For example, in the *şecere* (family tree) record (1226/1811) belonging to the *Waqf* of endower Muḥammad Muʿarrā bin Musa, it is noted that the income of the house located in Hatt Merziban was shared among the children of the *waqf*. JS 290: 8; For a family tree see Appendix 6.

442 JS 297: 33.

Ḥājj Ṣāliḥ Bey, the trustee of the Qāsim Bey al-Tarjumān *waqf*, stated in the accounting record submitted to the court that the excess income of the foundation was distributed among 12 people in the amount of 100 *qurūsh* each.[443] These examples, which can be multiplied, show that family members were the beneficiaries of *waqf*s in the distribution of *waqf* revenues.

4.5 *Office Sales*

The ties between the charitable *waqf*s in Jerusalem and the city's leaders were not limited to administrative duties. The sale of offices was another important issue in this context. The sale of offices was a common practice at least by the end of the 16th century, if not earlier. The trade in office, which Muṣṭafā ʿĀlī mentions with disgust and condemnation, was the main subject of complaint in the 17th-century *naṣīḥatnāmes*.[444] The leaflet of Koçi Bey, an advisor to the sultans, is a good example of how the crisis that plagued the empire in the 17th century was perceived by some sections of the Ottoman elite. The essence of Koçi Bey's views is the belief that merit was no longer the criterion for government appointments and that the widespread trade in office throughout the empire led to corrupt and incompetent rulers.[445] For the old bureaucrat nobility, for whom Koçi Bey was the spokesman, this development posed a direct threat to their existence and to the survival of the Islamic state as they understood it. However, the social evolution of the ruling class in the 17th and 18th centuries was driven by the trade of office, which enabled social mobility and the emergence of a new kind of political and economic elite. The expansion and monetisation of the Ottoman economy in the 17th century prepared the preconditions for this transformation in the social hierarchy of the empire.[446] Whereas in the old arrangement the office was defined as a service in return for patronage, the new system was in the nature of a contract whereby two parties agreed to organise the sale of a commodity owned by the state. For posts and salaries, there was a right to use and dispose of them, and this right could be divided into shares and transferred to others.[447]

---

443 JS 297: 34.

444 Khoury mentions that in the evaluation of this development, historian Naima was more realistic and he suggested applicable solutions against the monopolization of state sources (*Osmanlı Imparatroluğu'nda*, 137).

445 Aksüt, *Koçi Bey Risalesi*.

446 Khoury, *Osmanlı İmparatroluğ'nda*, 138.

447 The rivalry for the sake of rank helped agricultural lands to gain value and this caused the rise in the price of ranks whose duty is to collect tax. In the first half of the century when the value of money is rather stable, the value of *malikāne* rose approximately 80%. The value of rural *malikāne*s rose beyond double in tenfold and twenties of the

As it has been mentioned many times before, three major charitable *waqf*s were of special importance for the Jerusalemites: Al-Aqṣā Mosque, the Dome of the Rock and the Khasseki Sultan *Waqf*. The revenues of the Masjid al-Aqṣā and Ṣaḥrat Allāh *Waqf*s were endowed for the sustenance of the sayyids, *ʿulamāʾ* and poor dervishes in the city. Their income was high and the salaries paid were considerable. As already noted, the number of attendants of the Masjid al-Aqṣā and Dome of the Rock mosques between 1121–1149 AH/1709–1737 CE was approximately 461, while the number of those living from the Khasseki Sultan *Waqf* in the same period was no less large. In the 16th century there were forty-six posts, rising to 495 by the thirties of the 19th century. It is unlikely that the increase in the number of posts was also affected by the general population growth. In fact, at the end of the 18th century, the city's population does not seem to have exceeded the mid-16th century figure of 12–14 thousand.[448]

The local elite families of Jerusalem, who monopolised various functions, especially the administration of the charitable *waqf*s, sold the offices to another elite family. Some of these families enjoyed patrilineal rights to certain posts in the aforementioned charitable *waqf*s. For example, in February 1812, one of the guards of the Dome of the Rock sold the position of *mudarris* in the Tankiziyya *Madrasa* to the sons of Ali al-Khālidī for 50 al-Asadī piasters. The income from the sold portion constituted 1/3 of the salary of the person in question. The other part of this salary was carried out by their father ʿAlī al-Khālidī. A year later, in March 1813, Badr al-Ḥusaynī, the son of the former *Naqīb al-ashrāf* of Jerusalem, sold the *ḥāfiẓ* (one who chants) office to Sulaymān Quṭayna, to whom part of the two houses were endowed. The price of this office sale was 1650 *kurūsh*, and Badr al-Ḥusaynī's agent in this transaction was another member of the Khālidī family.[449] In each of these two transactions, at least two prominent family members were involved.

nineteenth century. It should be noted that the next rise is the result of the loss of value in the money. Khoury, *Osmanlı İmparatroluğ'nda*, p. 138; Pamuk, *The Ottoman Empire and European Capitalism, 1820–1913: Trade, Investment, and Production* (Cambridge: Cambridge University Press, 1987), 969. Pamuk concludes that Ottoman money is rather stable between 1690 and 1760. He states the major loss of the value of Ottoman money was in the period of Mahmud II (1808–1839), thus, the price of *malikane* sales is misleading at that period. Pamuk, *The Ottoman Empire*, 970.

448 Urban population is impossible to know exactly due to lack of official record. Thus, researchers often look at the records of travelers. For example, Volney states that the population was 12 or 14 thousand in 1784. German scientist and traveller Seetzen claims that population was about 12 thousand at the beginning of nineteenth century. al-Asali, "Jerusalem," 220.

449 Baer, "Jerusalem's Families," 117.

The al-Khālidī family, on the other hand, passed down the trusteeship of the Dār al-Qurrā' al-Sallāmiyya *Waqf* in the Silsila neighbourhood of Jerusalem, which they purchased from the Imam family in 1789 for 360 *zolotas*, from father to son for generations. In another noteworthy example, in May 1814, the sons of Mūsā al-Khālidī purchased the office of *qāri' al-ḥadīth* and the management of the *waqf* established for this office from the imam of al-Aqṣā Mosque for 1,850 *zolotas*.[450]

With the sale of offices, not only the number of posts increased more than threefold, but also the posts lost their original meaning. In the 16th century, when they were first opened, they were seen as a sign of the sultan's benevolence and generosity, and were given to those who deserved them and to those in need. By the 18th century, these posts had been appropriated by families; as mentioned above, they could be sold, divided into shares and held, and disposed of as the holders saw fit.[451] When a post became vacant due to the death of the salary holder, it would remain vacant until a new person could apply to the government and be allocated. Moreover, there was no correlation between the position sought and the obligation received. What was allocated to the person was often not the post but the salary. A member of the Jamā'a family or a sayyid could request to be appointed as a sweeper, even if he had no intention of doing the job.[452]

4.6 *Other Tasks Undertaken by the Jerusalem's Elite Families*

In addition to these transactions, there are other data on the offices mentioned above that were passed down from generation to generation. For example, in May 1812, Yūsuf al-Nāmrī was appointed by the *qāḍī* to supervise the water supply of the al-'Ayn Bath and the wells in Jerusalem, with a daily salary of 4 'Uthmānī *akçe* to be paid from the *waqf* of the Masjid al-Aqṣā and Tankiziyya *madrasa*. He was appointed in place of his deceased father, who took over from his grandfather, who had held the position for more than a hundred years.[453]

Secondly, these family members were members of the committees established by the *qāḍī*, where decisions were taken on issues such as whether the repairs of *waqf*s were carried out efficiently, the approval of expenditures submitted by the purchaser of *waqf* property rights, and the determination of the

450 Baer, "Jerusalem's Families," 117.

451 See VGMA, 1111: 54/56 for the appointment of an official with the request of the trustee to replace an official who died without children.

452 VGMA, 1109: 6/75.

453 Baer, "Jerusalem's Families," 110.

amount of rent in long-term leases.[454] In addition to the *muhzır* and *çuhadar*, the clerk and the chief architect were also permanent members of these committees. The clerk's office was monopolised by the Khālidī family, and the architect's office by the Nimrī family. However, in addition to the employees of these two offices, many other members of these two families served on these committees. Sometimes a member of the Daqqāq family was appointed clerk, while a member of the Jāʿūnī family was appointed chief architect, and other Daqqāqs and Jāʿūnīs served on these committees. This situation did not change when the aforementioned families became trustees of such *waqf*s or received rights to the dispersed *waqf* properties.[455] A special and noteworthy example of this situation can be given: When the Ottoman official ʿAlī Agha acquired a very large *khuluww* of the property of the Al-Aqṣā Mosque and Dome of the Rock *Waqf*s, the committee set up to investigate the property included representatives of many of Jerusalem's leading families. In addition to the usual Khālidī, Nāmrī, and Daqqāq families, the committee included two members of the Ḥusaynī family who were *naqīb al-ashrāf* and *muftī*, one Abū Suʿūd, one Nuṣayba, and one Quṭayna, and members of other families.[456]

In a document dated 1226 AH/1811 CE, it is recorded that Khālidīzāda Sayyid Muḥammad Ḥusayn Effendi applied to the court as the trustee and representative of his grandfather Shaykh Maḥmūd al-Khālidī *waqf*. He requests the renewal of the *khuluww* contract of the house consisting of 2 floors and 2 rooms belonging to the *waqf*, which previously had a *khuluww* contract. As a justification, he states that the *waqf* does not have the funds to repair the house in question. The *qāḍī* approves the renewal of the *khuluww* contract and sets up a commission to determine the cost of repairing the houses. The chief architect of Jerusalem, ʿAbd al-Raḥīm al-Nāmrī, accompanied by his brother Bakr and his sister's son Khalīl, Sayyid Muḥammad Effendi al-Daqqāq, Sayyid Muḥammad ʿAlī Effendi al-Khālidī, Sayyid Yūsuf Effendi al-Shihābī, Sayyid Muṣṭafā al-Khālidī, Sayyid Ibrāhīm Beg al-Tarjumānī, and Ḥājj Yūsuf Agha al-Jāʿūnī were appointed by the Qāḍī of Jerusalem to determine the costs. In another similar example dated Rajab 1209/February 1795, Ṣāliḥ ibn al-Ḥājj Muḥammad Quṭayna, as the trustee of his grandfather Sayyid ʿAbdullāh *waqf*, requests permission from the *qāḍī* to repair the house, which he owns with a share of 6 *qīrāṭ* ¾ of the *waqf*, with the help of *khulū*. In the committee established by the *qāḍī* to determine the equivalent of the house before the repair, members of prominent families of Jerusalem such as Muṣṭafā Sunʿ Allāh al-Khālidī, ʿAbd al-Laṭīf Agha al-Dasūqī,

454 Baer, "Jerusalem's Families," 111.

455 Baer, "Jerusalem's Families," 117; JS 294: 88; 295: 28–29; 291: 92–3; 297: 118, 129.

456 JS 295: 73–74.

Jerusalem architects Ḥājjī ʿAbd al-Raḥīm and his brother Bakr al-Nāmrī, Sulaymān al-Qirṭās, Aḥmad al-Ḥusaynī, Khalīl al-Luṭfī took part.[457]

In conclusion, most of the prominent families of Jerusalem continued their traditional influence and wealth in the city, which they had possessed since the Ayyūbī and Mamlūk periods, through *waqfs* in the Ottoman period. They re-endowed the assets of various charitable public *waqfs* by establishing *waqfs*. They reinforced and activated their sphere of disposal over the *waqfs* through the appointment of their own family members as *waqf* administrators and beneficiaries, as well as through long-term leases. These rights, which were acquired through the sale of offices, were bought and sold among prominent families with an active position in the city's *waqf* network. In the case of Jerusalem, strong *ʿulamāʾ* families who tried to monopolise certain positions came to the fore and sometimes succeeded. However, the main families that succeeded in obtaining important positions did so not only through their power base in Jerusalem, but also through their connections with various groups in Istanbul. The strengthening of their positions in Jerusalem was tolerated by the state, but their official status was not secured through pressure from local factions. The appointments of Jerusalem notables were made under the control of the central authority. In a period when centralised control was reinforced through the appointment of officials and officials with strong local ties, the families were allowed to build a power base that would create a balance within local power structures, thus ensuring control of the system.

5 Ottoman State as the Distributor of *Waqf* Resources

With the understanding of patronage, *waqf* duties and salaries were used to acquire loyal servants from among the learned and respected, that is, the *ʿulamāʾ*, who served as spiritual and scholarly advisors, and to protect the existing ones from the rulers.[458] It should also be noted that the Ottoman administration needed prominent figures in provincial cities as intermediaries between the central administration and the local population. Therefore, the social and economic priorities of many of the prominent figures were supported by the Ottoman State. The Ottoman central government also recognized that the tax exemption known to the city's leading families allowed them to accumulate a large portion of their income and build up a significant surplus, which was often invested in other businesses. In the city's *waqf* network,

457 JS 297: 99.
458 Zilfi, *Women in the Ottoman*, 25–69.

the leading families received a share of the *surra* revenues sent from Istanbul for their duties at Masjid al-Aqṣā and the Dome of the Rock, as well as a share of the *jizya* collected from *dhimmi*s (non-Muslim subjects).[459] Thus, although the center and the local still remain the dominant units of analysis here, what complicates this schema is the fact that the relations between the center and its local bases were not simply characterized by the supremacy and domination of the former over the latter.[460] Rather, there was an interaction between imperial and provincial actors, a constant negotiation in which the balance of power between the two was not always clearly defined.[461]

In this part of the study, firstly, the importance of belonging to the elite households of the city of Jerusalem in the management of *waqf* properties will be discussed. Secondly, it will be discussed that the duties of the officials who received their salaries from the *waqf*s of Masjid al-Aqṣā and Dome of the Rock mosques were determinative in benefiting from the *surra*s sent to Jerusalem. The distribution of the *jizya* tax collected from non-Muslims in Jerusalem will also be analysed in large charitable foundations.

5.1 *The Rental Transactions of* Waqf *Properties*

Waqf institutions were allowed to rent out their properties under certain conditions. This was a well-established practice to generate income for the *waqf*, especially in times of economic hardship. *Waqf mutawallī*s rented out houses, shops and workshops in towns and villages or farms in rural areas. The rental income was used for the day-to-day administration of the *waqf*, especially if the *waqf* included a soup kitchen and *madrasa*.[462]

The method of collecting *waqf* revenues in the form of tax-farming was already in practice before the 17th and 18th centuries. Especially in *waqf*s with large income sources, this method was more favorable.[463] However, in the period we have analysed, this practice became more widespread in the

---

459 At the beginning of the seventeenth century, ʿAbd al-Qādir ibn Karīm al-Dīn al-Ḥusaynī, who was not a male heir at the time of his death, was the *muftī* of Jerusalem from the Ḥusaynī family, which was the *naqīb al-ashrāf* of Jerusalem. The duty of *muftī* passed to the ʿAlamī and Jār Allāh families, one of the prominent families of Jerusalem. However, the female lineage of ʿAbd al-Qādir was able to continue the name Ḥusaynī and the Sharif family. Ḥusaynīs held several religious duties such as *naqīb al-ashrāf* and *shaykh al-ḥaram*. At the end of the 18th century, Ḥusaynīs regained the post of *muftī*. Apart from taking a few breaks, they continued this duty until the twentieth century. Khadduri, *Arab Contemporaries*, 69.

460 Kappler, 285–86.

461 Yaycıoğlu, 'Provincial Power Holders," 446–47.

462 Ze'evi, *Kudüs*," 143.

463 Akdağ, *Türkiye'nin İktisadi*, 268.

operation of the *waqf*s. In this period, it is seen that the villages, which constituted the income items of the *waqf*s, were assigned to individuals as a unit of *mālikāne-muqāta'a*, and they, in turn, operated these *mālikāne*s by assigning them to others for a year with the practice that became a routine of the period. On the other hand, Jerusalem's notables, merchants, or other aspiring elite groups were unable to become large-scale refugees. Perhaps, in the minds of local notables, state land and tax collection were still seen as the sphere of influence of the ruling elite. With few exceptions, they did not intend to lease large tracts of land. They preferred to buy the land and invest in urban crafts.[464]

Waqf properties were leased according to local procedures.[465] The leading families of Jerusalem played a dominant role in the fragmentation and leasing of such *waqf* properties, and perhaps they earned significant revenues from the transactions in which they were involved. Between the years 1805–1814, 63 documents in the registers relate to *khuluww, ḥikr, icāre-i tavīle,* and *istibdāl* transactions. In more than half of these documents, the members of the aforementioned families obtained the right to become tenants of the fragmented *waqf* properties. In addition, in twenty-five of these transactions, members of the same families are the trustees of the transferred *waqf*s.[466]

Muḥammad Ṭāhir al-Ḥusaynī, who was the *muftī* of Jerusalem and also the trustee of the ʿAbd al-Laṭīf al-Ḥusaynī *waqf* (former *naqīb al-ashrāf* of Jerusalem), was granted permission to repair and renovate a large dilapidated bazaar belonging to the ʿAbd al-Laṭīf al-Ḥusaynī *waqf* on the basis of *khuluww*. In fact, this property belonged to another *waqf* and it was rented by ʿAbd al-Laṭīf al-Ḥusaynī with *ḥikr*. *Khuluww* was inaugurated on the *waqf* property and it endowed as a part of the *waqf*. When it was rented in return for *waqf*'s repair, *ijrā misl* was identified as annually 40 *zoloṭa* by common consent. The important thing is that the property acquired with *khuluww* by ʿUmar al-Ḥusaynī, actually, rented by ʿAbd al-Laṭīf al-Ḥusaynī as another *waqf*'s property with

464 Ze'evi, *Kudüs*, pp. 146–47.

465 Ze'evi, *Kudüs*, p. 148.

466 The total amount of debts designated as *kḥulūww* and *istibdāl* for the repair of *waqf* properties is recorded in the register as 83,138 *kurūsh*. The share of the families in this total is 57,540 *kurūsh*, that is, approximately 70 percent. The remainder was divided between two Ottoman administrators (7,928 *kurūsh*, approximately 10 percent), with the rest distributed among the inhabitants of Jerusalem (17,670 *kurūsh*, or 21 percent). Baer, "Jerusalem's Families," p. 114. Among the 57,540 guruş portion belonging to these families, nine of the leading families of Jerusalem acquired property through this method. In particular, two transactions recorded in the registers are significant because they constitute the majority of the total sum of 83,138 guruş. In the first of these, the Jārullāh, ʿAlamī, Khālidī, and Budayrī families were involved (31,755 *kurūsh*), while in the second, the Ḥusaynī family was involved (10,500 guruş). Baer, "Jerusalem's Families," p. 115; KŞS 295: 209–210; 228–229.

khuluww and re-endowed as a *waqf*. In the same month, another Ḥusaynī established a *dhurrī waqf* composed of rented properties through *khuluww* with the value of 3,687.5 *kurūsh* by Yāfā Muftī Muḥammad Ṣāliḥ Effendi.[467]

In the period covered by this study, the most comprehensive *istibdāl* transaction in terms of the receiver of *waqf* property was carried out by Muḥammad Ḥusayn al-Khālidī, a member of the Khālidī family and the clerk of the Jerusalem Court.[468]

These examples are important in terms of showing the extent to which the practice of *khuluww* reached in Jerusalem in the early years of the 19th century. On the other hand, these transactions, in which the *waqf* acquired a partially fragmented structure, were a profitable transaction for both the buyer of the rights to the dilapidated waqf property and the *waqf mutawallī*. From the point of view of the *mutawallīs*, long-term leases or leases with the *khuluww* method were found to be logical due to the inability to rent *waqf* properties for a short period of time or the lack of resources to restore waqf properties. From the buyer's perspective, in addition to the greater economic benefits, the social and political influence gained was also decisive in these gains.[469]

It is clear that the leading families of Jerusalem had a clear advantage over other Jerusalemites in the acquisition of these benefits and rights over *waqf* properties. As is evident in some cases, there was a family connection between the recipients of such rights and the trustees of the *waqfs*. The most striking example of this is the aforementioned sale of huge amounts of *khuluww* and the endowments of the al-Ḥusaynīs, who were the *naqīb al-ashrāf* of Jerusalem. However, other examples are also possible. For example, Muṣṭafā al-Khalīlī received the right to treat the repairs to the Qāsim al-Tarjumān *waqf* from his maternal great-great-grandfather, Qāsim al-Tarjumān, as a debt of the *waqf* from the administrators of the same *waqf* from another lineage. In another example, two members of the Daqqāq family obtained the right of *khuluww* of the *waqf* property established by their grandfather and managed by another Daqqāq. Yūsuf al-Jāʿūnī, on the other hand, received the *ḥikr* of the *waqf* property, whose administrator was another al-Jāʿūnī. Two weeks later, the new trustees of the *waqf* granted the right of *khuluww* on the *waqf* property to Esma, the daughter of another member of the Khālidī family. Such connections are unlikely to have been established for other Jerusalemites who did not belong to a prominent Jerusalem family.[470] Thus, these examples indicate

467 Baer, "Jerusalem's Families," 116.
468 ibid., 116.
469 ibid., 116.
470 ibid., 117.

that it is important to be a member of notable families of Jerusalem for taking the operation right of the *waqf*s and sustaining it. Thus, fortune and prestige acquired thanks to *waqf*s were used for new benefits.

5.2 *The* Surra/Surre *of Jerusalem*

Surra is an Arabic word and its dictionary meaning is "money pouch". In fact, *surra* has many meanings. Such as; "a pouch in which things like money and gold are placed and tied tightly,"[471] "to cover something with a cloth to ensure that it is protected and invisible,"[472] and the like. As a term, it is a term used to describe the gifts of money, gold and the like, that are usually sent to *Ḥaramayn* (Mecca and Medina) every year before the pilgrimage period.[473] In finance and accounting, it is a word used for fifty thousand *akçe*, that is, half a load.[474]

The Ottomans inherited the sending of *surra* from the Abbasids,[475] and it was given more importance in the Ottoman Empire and became a tradition. The first sending of *surra* to Mecca and Medina by the Ottomans started during the reign of Yıldırım Bayezit (1389–1402) and this tradition continued until the collapse of the state. With the conquest of Egypt and Hejaz, *surra* began to be sent regularly every year. However, the earliest document related to *surra* is dated Ṣafar 967/November 1559. There is no information about the *surra*s sent before this date.[476] During the reign of Çelebi Sultan Mehmed II, *surra* was sent to *Ḥaramayn* twice between 1413 and 1421. The amount of *surra* sent by Çelebi was thirty-five thousand *filori* and it was made a procedure to send this amount every year.[477]

---

471 Ibn Manẓūr, Lisān al-ʿArab, ed. ʿAlī Shīrī (Beirut: Dār Iḥyāʾ al-Turāth al-ʿArabī, 1988), 7:323, s.v. "Sarīr."

472 Atalar, *Osmanlı Devleti'nde*, 1.

473 Buzpınar, Tufan Şīt, "Surra," in *Türkiye Diyanet Vakfı İslâm Ansiklopedisi*, vol. 37 (Istanbul: Türkiye Diyanet Vakfı Yayınları, 2009), 567–569, 567.

474 Sertoğlu, *Osmanlı Tarih Lügatı*, 318.

475 The first sending of *surra* to Ḥaramayn (Mecca and Medina) took place during the reign of Abbasid Caliph al-Mahdī bi'llāh (158–169 AH/775–785 CE). During the reign of al-Muqtadir Bi'llāh (295–320 AH/908–932 CE), it started to be sent regularly every year. See Buzpınar, "Makamat-ı Mübareke," 567. The amount of surra sent by al-Muqtadir Bi'llāh was 315,426 filori gold. Atalar, *Osmanlı Devleti'nde*, 3. This tradition started by the Abbasids was continued by the Ayyubids and Mamluks. The purpose of sending *surra* was to meet the needs of the people living in holy places, to meet the needs of the poor, to pay homage to the sayyids and sharifs, and to provide the needs of those who came for pilgrimage.

476 Güler, *Osmanlı Devleti'nde*, 199–200.

477 İbrahim Ateş, "Osmanlılar Zamanında," 116.

In the Ottoman Empire, there were generally two different sources of income for the *surra*. One of these was the special gifts of the Sultan of the period (which were given to people whose names were determined in advance), and the other was the *waqf*s established to provide income for the *surra*. The *Ḥaramayn waqf*s in particular were one of the most important sources of revenue for the *surra*. Many *waqf* founders established *Ḥaramayn waqf*s or the servants of the mosques in the cities of Mecca and Medina, the janitors of the Prophet's tomb, those who came from various places to these two cities for pilgrimage or to settle there, the *sādāt* who lived there, and the poor who lived in the pilgrimage sites, with a direct stipulation in their endowments. There was also a sub-unit of the *Ḥaramayn waqf* called the "Surra Waqfs", even though they served the same purpose.[478] In addition, some *waqfiyya*s stipulated that if it became impossible for the *waqf*s to continue their services for various reasons, the revenues of the *waqf*s would be sent to *Ḥaramayn*. The annual revenues of these *waqf*s were collected by the central government and delivered together.[479] . In addition to this, in the Ottoman lands, a share was also allocated for surre from the *waqf* revenues of members of the dynasty, some members of the state officials, the state treasury, *Khazīna-i Khāṣṣa* and personal donations.[480] Apart from those in Istanbul and Edirne, such *waqf*s were concentrated in Western and Central Anatolia.[481]

Ottomans sent *surra* to Jerusalem which they regarded as the third sacred city after Mecca and Medina. When Aşıkpaşazāde mentioned Murad II, he wrote "every year, he sent 3500 filori to Jerusalem and Hebron, and Medina and Kabetullah (Mecca)." Yet, it is not certain that it is the *surra* that elucidated in this study's context.[482] In the period of Yavuz Sultan Selim, with the annexation of Jerusalem in 1517, made much help and benevolence. However, the oldest *surra* book belonging to Jerusalem was dated 1593.[483]

478 Atalar, *Osmanlı Devleti'nde*, 221.
479 Yediyıldız, *XVIII. Yüzyılda*, 234; Başol, *Kentleşme, Ekonomi*, 179.
480 Buzpınar, "Makamat-ı Mübareke," 568.
481 Suraiya Faroqhi, *Hacılar ve Sultanlar*, 34–58.
482 Atalar *Osmanlı Devleti'nde Surre-i Hümāyūn*, 12.
483 Fişne, *XVIII. Yüzyıl*, 14.

In her study, Rahime Fişne analyzed the books of the years 1113 AH/1701–1702 CE[484] and 1124 AH/1712–1713 CE,[485] which contain the *surra* records sent from Istanbul to Jerusalem; she found that the main source of the *surra*s sent to Jerusalem in both dates was Sultan allocations.[486] He also identified various foundations that were allocated a share for the surrender of Jerusalem.[487]

In the evaluation section of the study, he states that the places and officials to whom the *surra* was sent were the same in both books. In the present study, in order to make a comparison with the aforementioned *surra* books from the beginning of the century, the records of four *surra* books dated 1177 AH/1763–64 CE, 1186 AH/1772–73 CE, 1197 AH/1782–83 CE and 1207 AH/1807–808 CE, in which the records were recorded at ten-year intervals, were analyzed.[488] Accordingly, first of all, the amounts of *surra*s and their distribution were continuous. Namely, the salary of the sweeper – *Ḥaḍrat Pādishāh-i ʿĀlamaynā – ḥallallallāhu taʿālā – Khilāfata wa Salṭanata dar Ṣaḥrat Allāh-i Musharrafa* – that is, the sweeper of the Dome of the Rock, is fifty coins in all of the books.[489] The amount of *surra* sent to *Meşāyihu'l-Harem-i Kudüs* is fifty-eight coins in the books, and in the share sharing made in 1113 AH/1701–1702 CE and 1124 AH/1712–1713 CE, although the amount of shares did not change, the number of those who received shares increased over time. The share distribution made between 1113 AH/1701–1702 CE and 1124 AH/1712–1713 CE is as follows:

While the number of Ḥaram *shaykh*s in the *surra* record dated 1124 AH/1712–1713 CE was seven, the number of *shaykh*s in the accounting record dated 1121 AH/1709–1710 CE was also seven. However, in an eighth record, the *shaykh* of the Ḥaram is recorded as holding the position with a 1/3 share.[490]

The share allocation made in 1177 AH/1763–1764 CE is as follows:

484 The *surra* was sent to Jerusalem from Istanbul during the reign of Sultan Mustafa II. This is evident from the first page of the book, which reads "Defter-i Taksîmât-ı Surre-i Şerîfe-i Hakâniyye-i Rûmiyye-i Cedîde-i berâ-yıı ahâli-i Jerusalem-i Sharīf Şerefallahu Teâlâ ilâ yevmi'l-ahirati der-vācib-i sene-i sâlis ʿaşar ve mi'e ve elf". BOA, EV.HMK.SR: 556/2b.

485 He was sent from Istanbul to Jerusalem during the reign of Sultan Ahmed III.

486 Fişne (XVIII. Century), in her study analyzing the ledgers of the years 1113 /1701–1702 and 1124/1712–1713, provides information on the shares allocated from the Sultan's allocations for the surrender of Jerusalem in these years. Accordingly, 400 *hasene* coins were allocated from Sultan Selim Khan's Mosque *Waqf* in Edirne, 243 from the *Imâret-i Amire* and Mosque *waqf* (Valide Gülnuş Sultan) in Üsküdar, 246 *hasene* coins from the Nurbanu Sultan *waqf*s (Valide Gülnuş Sultan), the mother of Murad III, 18 gourds from the Darüssaʿade Agha Merhum Mehmed Agha *Waqf*, and 140 gourds from the Darüssaʿade Agha Merhum Abbas Agha *Waqf*. For detailed information, see Fişne, *XVIII. Century*, 17–18.

487 Fişne, *XVIII. Yüzyıl*, 17–18.

488 BOA, EV.HMK.SR: 1971; 2224; 2546; 2855.

489 BOA, EV.HMK.SR: 1971; 2224; 2546; 2855.

490 BOA, EV.HMH.d: 1632/25.

TABLE 13 'Cemaat-i Meşāyihü'l-Harem'[a]

First share holders	Second share holders			Third share holders
Sayyid Muḥammad ibn Sayyid Abdü'r-rahīm Müfti-i Hanefī der Kuds-i Şerif sikke 18	Shaykh Abdü'r-rezzāk ve Shaykh Muḥammad Effendi ve Sayyid Mustafa ibn Sayyid Muḥammad ve Shaykh Şihābü'd-dīn ibn Ali sikke 20			Shaykh Yunus ibn Shaykh Bedrü'd-dīn Gudayya ve Shaykh Nurullah ibn Shaykh Abdü'r-rahmān sikke 20
	Hisse-i Abdü'r-rezzāk sikke 5	Hisse-i Shaykh Muḥammad sikke 5	Hisse-i Sayyid Mustafa ve Şihābü'd-dīn Ber-vech-i iştirāk sikke 10	

a BOA, EV.HMK.SR: 556.

TABLE 14 'Cemaat-i Meşāyihü'l-Harem'[a]

Evlād-ı Shaykh Fazlullah ibn Shaykhu'l-harem Nureddin 'Alemī ve evlād-ı Shaykh Musa Fityanī veled-i Sayyide Saliha ve Sayyid Muḥammad ve Sayyid Ali veledān-ı Shaykh Osman 'alemī ve Shaykh Abdulhak Cemā'ī. Sikke 18.	Evlād-ı Shaykh Muḥammad ve Shaykh Osman ber vech-i iştirak ve evlād-ı Shaykh Abdullah ve evlād-ı Shaykh Abdulvehhab Sihabī ve Eyyid Ahmed ibni Shaykh Ahmed Muhaddis ve evlād-ı Shaykh Abdullah ve evlād-ı Şeyy Abdulvehhab ibni Şihabeddin ber vech-i iştirak er-rub' ve evlād-ı Sayyid Feyzullah 'Alemī ve evlād-ı Sayyid Muḥammad Emin ibni Sayyid Muhibbeddin es-sümün. Sikke 20.	Shaykh Muḥammad ibni Shaykh Nurullah en-nısıf ve Shaykh Hurī ve Shaykh İsmail ibn-i Shaykh Yunus en-nısıf. Sikke 20.
Hisse-i Evlād-ı Fazlullah *sikke* 3	Hisse-i evlād-ı Abdulvehhab rub'-ı 1 sikke-i hasene	Hisse-i Huri sikke 7,5.
Hisse-i Evlād-ı Osman *sikke* 7	Hisse-i evlād-ı Abdullah rub' 1 sikke-i hasene	Hisse-i İsmail 2,5.
Hisse-i Evlād-ı Musa *sikke* 3	Hisse-i Sayyid Ahmed Muḥammad rub'- 3,5 sikke-i hasene.	
Hisse-i Evlād-ı Abdulhak *sikke* 5	bervech-i iştirāk sikke 10	

a BOA, EV.HMK.SR: 1971/3.

As can be seen in Table 13, the first portion of 18 coins of the *surra* allocations made to the Shaykhate of the Jerusalem *Ḥaram al-Sharīf* in 1177 AH/1763–1764 CE was shared by five members of the leading families of Jerusalem instead of the *Muftī* of Jerusalem.[491] The second share of twenty coins was shared by nine members of the leading families of Jerusalem.[492] In the last share, the share ratio was maintained and one more person was added to the share.[493] This can be attributed to the new officials who were appointed to these posts by way of share allocation. On the other hand, it could also be the case that more people benefited from the *surra* through the allocation of shares independent of the duties in question.

In the book dated 1186 AH/1772–1773 CE, both the share rates and the number of officials remained unchanged.[494] In the *Surra* book dated 1197 AH/1782–1783 CE, the share ratios, the number of officials and even the number of officials did not change.[495] Finally, in the *surra* ledger dated 1207 AH/1792–1793 CE, the amount of *surra* allocated for the Shaykhate of *Ḥaram al-Sharīf*, the number of beneficiaries and the names of the officials were recorded exactly the same.[496]

As in the case of new officials appointed to *waqf*s, the central government had a decisive position in the allocation of *surra*. Again, as in the records of the appointment of *waqf* officials, the Ottoman administration supported the transfer of *surra* allocations from father to son. In the ruling dated 1148 AH/1735 CE, the issues regarding the allocations are recorded in detail.[497] According to this

---

491 Divided as "Evlâd-ı Şeyh Fazlullah ibn-i Şeyhu'l-harem Nureddin ʿAlemî ve evlâd-ı Şeyh Musa Fityanî veled-i Seyyide Saliha ve Seyyid Muḥammad ve Seyyid Ali veledân-ı Şeyh Osman ʿAlemî ve Şeyh Abdulhak Cemâʾî (Der kenar: Evlâd-ı Fazlullah- 3; evlâd-ı Osman- 7; evlâd-ı Musa- 3; Abdulhak 5 sikke)". BOA, EV.HMK.SR: 1971/2.

492 "Evlâd-ı Şeyh Muḥammad ve Şeyh Osman ber vech-i iştirak ve evlâd-ı Şeyh Abdullah ve evlâd-ı Şeyh Abdulvehhab Sihabî ve Seyyid Ahmed ibn-i Şeyh Ahmed Muhaddis ve evlâd-ı Şeyh Abdullah ve evlâd-ı Şeyy Abdulvehhab ibn-i Şihabeddin ber vech-i iştirak er-rubʿ ve evlâd-ı Seyyid Feyzullah ʿAlemî ve evlâd-ı Seyyid Muḥammad Emin ibn-i Seyyid Muhibbeddin es-sümün. Evlâd-ı Abdulvehhab ve evlâdı Abdullah rubʿ- 1 sikke-i hasene; Seyyid Ahmed Muḥammad rubʿ- 3,5 sikke-i hasene." BOA, EV.HMK.SR: 1971: 2.

493 "Şeyh Muḥammad ibn-i Şeyh Nurullah en-nısıf ve Şeyh Hurî ve Şeyh İsmail ibn-i Şeyh Yunus en-nısıf. Huri 7,5; İsmail 2,5." BOA, EV.HMK.SR: 1971/ 2.

494 The two changes of officers in the records are recorded as; "… Şeyh Hurî ve Şeyh İsmail ibn-i Şeyh Yunus en-nısıf." BOA, EV.HMK.SR: 1971/2. yerine "Yunus Efendi ibn-i Şeyh İsmail ve evlâd-ı Seyyid Yunus en-nısıf.". BOA, EV.HMK.SR: 2224/2.

495 BOA, EV.HMK.SR: 2546/2.

496 BOA, EV.HMK.SR: 2855/2.

497 The conditions of allocation were also stated in an imperial order dated 1148/1735 as follows: 'Kuds-i Şerīf'de vāki' Mescid-i Aksā ve Sahratullah-ı Müşerrefe Evkāflarından ve gerek taraf-ı saltanat-ı seniyyeden belde-i mübāreke ahalilerinden irsāl olunan surraden

ruling, the shares of the deceased *surra* owner were to be given to his children, to his brother if he did not have children, to his relative if he did not have a brother, and the shares of those who died without children were to be given to those who deserved them upon the request of the *Qāḍī* of Jerusalem.

The new beneficiaries assigned to the shares of the deceased in Jerusalem *surra*s were listed at the top of the relevant record. For example, under the heading "Cemā'at-i E'imme-i Sahratullah-ı Müşerrefe, Mescid-i Aksā ve Meğāribe Camii'", the record 'Evlād-ı Şeyh Musa ve Yahya ve Şeyh Muḥammad bin Yahya Fityanī ve evlād-ı Şeyh Nurullah bin Abdulhak ve evlād-ı Ahmed imam-ı Sahratullah ve evlād-ı Şeyh Salahaddin' had two notations. The first one reads, "'Evlād-ı Şeyh Musa ve Yahya ve Şeyh Muḥammad bin Yahya Fityanī ve evlād-ı Şeyh Nurullah bin Abdulhak ve evlād-ı Ahmed imam-ı Sahratullah ve evlād-ı Şeyh Salahaddin'. In the first one, it states 'mezkūr evlād-ı Şeyh Salahaddin feragat kerde. Becayeş Seyyid Halil ibni Seyyid Ebu'l-Mevāhib amed. Bā inha-i Ahmed Efendi ḳāḍi -yı Kuds-i Şerif ve bā arz-ı Beşir Ağa en-nāzır 17 Cemaziyelevvel 1177–2 sikke 15 pāre"[498] means a new person was

ve zikr olunan evkafın gerek sikke ve gerek Osmanī surra ve cihāt-ı sāireden cüz'iyye ve külliye her birine ... sükkānı üzerlerinde olub berevāt-ı Padişahī ile mutasarrıf olanlardan biri fevt oldukda evlādına evlādı olmadığı suretde karındaşına yahud karındaşı olmadıkda akrabasına virilüb bu suretde fevt olan gerek ricāl ve gerek nisā her bilā veled fevt olduklarında evkāftan düşen cihāt mutawallī bulunanların arzlarıyla ve cānib-i 'aliyyeden giden surraye mutasarrıf olanlardan bilā veled fevt oldukda kādı-i Kuds-i Şerif arzıyla erbāb-ı istihkākdan olanlara virilüb ferağ ve intikālātı dahi vech-i meşruh üzere mutawallī-i vakf bulunanların ve surra ashabı kādı-i Kuds-i Şerif arzlarıyla ferāğat olunub ref' iktizā eyledikde yine ber-minvāl-i meşrūh virilüb İstanbul'da sākin ve Kuds-i Şerife varmayub ba'zıları cihāt-ı vakf ashābının menzili yoğ iken açıktan arz u hal ve sehvan berāt ile ahalinin cihāt ve surraleri kimesneye kayd olunub şurūt-ı merkūma ... olunmak bābında sākin-i belde-i tayyibe fukaraları arz-ı hāl ve vech-i meşrūh üzer emr-i 'ālişān ... ve Haremeyn-i Şerifeyn Muhasebesine ve .. Kalemine kayd olunması niyaziyle istid'ā-yı itmeleriyle ... mezkūr içün zikr olunan evkāf-ı şerīfelerden hayāt-ı mahlūliye vāki' oldukda evlādlarına ve bilā veled vāki' oldukda müstehikkīne virilmek üzere mutawallī-i arz ve 'Asitāne-i Sa'ādete gelüb arzlarıyla tevcih olmak bābında ... emr-i 'ālī sādır olduğunda mahallinden vaz u der kneār olunmakla minvāl-i meşrūh amel ve hareket ve surra ve cihāt mahlūlü vāki' oldukda evlād-ı ve evlādı olmadığı suretde akrabasına ve bilā akraba vāki' oldukda müstehıkkīne virilmek .. mutawallī-i vakf arzı ve surra vāki oldukda Kuds-i Şerīf ḳāḍi sı arzıyla virilüb ve ferağ ve intikāl dahi minvāl-i meşrūh üzere virilüb arz-ı hāl ile virilmek ve iş bu şurūta murāca'a olunub arzlarıyla sādır olan emr-i 'ālīşān mucibince idare ve Haremeyn-i Şerifeyn Muhasebesine ve Mukāta'a Kalemine dahi kayd olunub muğāyir-i emr-*i 'ālīşāna bir ferd* hareket itdirilmemek bābında hükm-i hümāyun virilmek ricāsına i'lām eylemeğin mevāhim-i hükm ve bu fermān-ı 'ālī sādır olmağın vech-i meşrūh üzere emr-i şerīf-i 'ālīşān yazılmak içün iş bu tezkire virildü. 11 Rebiu'l-evvel 1148.' VGMA, 814: 11.

498 BOA, EV.HMK.SR: 1971/3. There are many examples for the similar applications for resigning from the duty. For example, see BOA, EV.HMK.SR: 1971/15–21.

appointed in the place of the person who waived the aforementioned allocation with the consent of the *Qāḍī* of Jerusalem and the supply of the minister.

The second *marginal note* on the same record reads as follows: "Mezkūr Ahmed İmam evlādından Abdülkerim müteveffā şode. Becāyeş Seyyid Abdurrahman ibn-i Şeyh Abdülkadir 'ammīzādesi amed. Ba inhā-i ve ba arzı Beşir Ağa. 3 sikke 12 pare.",[499] meaning the late person's share was given to the son of uncle. Similarly, upon the death of Abdülkerim, son of Shaykh Ahmed, one of the deceased pharmacists "Evlâd-ı Shaykh Ahmed and evlâd-ı Shaykh Ali veledân-ı Salahaddin and Shaykh Abdülkerim bin Shaykh Ahmed 'Alemî", it was allocated to his uncle's son Seyyid Abdurrahman ibni Seyyid Abdülkadir.[500] In only four of the fifty-five notes in the ledger, the allocation changed hands upon the death of the *surra* owner, while in the other fifty-one records it changed hands upon the surre owner's renunciation.[501] In most cases, the entire surrender was waived, but in some cases, some of it was waived.[502]

1122 AH/1787 CE, Shaykh Majid al-Dajjānī submitted a petition stating that he was the Shaykh of Shaykh Mansur Lodging, one of the residents of Jerusalem, and that the poor of the said lodging were given 20 *akçe*s per day from the Damascus Province with a certificate, but this fee was not given in the years 1114 AH/1702–1703 AD and 1117 AH/1705–1706 AD and 1118 AH/1706–1707 AD and 1119 AH/1707–1708 AD. In the continuation of the petition, the Shaykh requested that the amounts determined for the recorded years be given from the Damascus *surra*.[503] In another example, in the ruling dated Shawwal 1161/1748 sent to the *Qāḍī* of Jerusalem, the *juzhān* and *sulehā* (the reciters of the Qur'an and the righteous) in Sahratullah *Waqf* with an annual surcharge of 2 coins from the *mujāvirīn* community and 1.5 coins from the Sultan Selim Khan *Waqf* in Edirne with an annual surcharge of 1.5 coins from the Sultan Selim Khan

499 BOA, EV.HMK.SR: 1971/3.

500 "Mezkûr Şeyh Ahmed evlâdından Abdülkerim müteveffâ şode. Becâyeş Seyyid Abdurrahman ibn-i Seyyid Abdülkadir 'ammîzâdesi amed. Bâ inhâ-i ve bâ arz-ı Beşir Ağa en-Nâzır. 5 Muharrem 1177." BOA, EV.HMK.SR: 1971/15.

501 BOA, EV.HMK.SR 1971: 2–49.

502 E.g. "Ali Effendi, one of the sons of the aforementioned Musa Fityanî, waived only one year of *südüs* coins. Becâyeş. Evlâd-ı Seyyid Ali Cârullah amed. Bâ-inhâ-i İbrahim Efendi Kâdı-yı Jerusalem-i Şerîf and Hacı Mehmed … Aga en-Nazir 29 Rajab 1187." "Sayyid Khalil and Sayyid Mehmed of Sayyid Abu'l-Mawāhib's son, only two coins per year … ferâgat-kerde. Becâyeş. Sayyid … Sayyid Abdulhay Jamâ'î amed. Bâ-inhâ-i Hacı Mustafa Kâdı-yı Jerusalem-i Şerîf and bâ-arzı Beşir Ağa en-Nâzır, fî 15 Cemâziye'l-awwal 1178." BOA, EV.HMK.SR: 1971/3. In the first of the two examples given here, the *surra* owner waived 1/7 of his *surra* share, while in the second example, another *surra* owner waived two coins of his share.

503 VGMA, 233: 11.

Waqf in Edirne were in the possession of Sayyid Hashim al-Imam and Shaykh Abdullah al-Azharī, but a person named İbrahim, a resident of Jerusalem, intervened and did not pay their wages for 3 years.[504]

When the records in the *surra* book dated 1177 AH/1763–1764 AD are analyzed, it is seen that most of the *surra*s sent to Jerusalem were allocated to the officials in the holy places in Jerusalem such as Masjid al-Aqṣā, Sahratullah, and Jami al-Maghāriba *Waqf*s:

TABLE 15 Officials having share from *surra*

Duty	**Number of people**	**Number of official (person)**	**Amount of *surra* (hasene sikke/ para)**
Ferāşet	1	2	50
Meşāyihu'l-Harem	3	12	58
Hatips in Mescid-i Aksā	4	22	56
Imams in Cāmi-i Meğāribe and Al-Aqṣā Mosque and Sahratullah	12	47	50
Guests in Mescid-i Aksā	37	64	58
Servants in Sahratullah-i Müşerrefe	27	47	56
Servants in Mescid-i Aksā	20	38	156
Muezzin of Harem-i Şerif	31	59	55,5
Clerks and Others	22	34	37
Porters of Harem-i Şerif	25	41	25
Mebleıyn in Harem-i Şerif	20	27	20
Readers in Harem-i Şerif'	12	21	13
Friday Preachers in the gathering-place of Mescid-i Aksā	15	20	7,5
Tax Collectors of *Waqf*	8	13	8
The reader of thirty pages of Kur'an for the soul of Sultan Süleyman	91	93	62 sikke 15 para
The reader of thirty pages of Kur'an for the soul of Sultan Selim Han	33	134	400
The reader of thirty pages of Kur'an for the soul of Valide Sultan	35	103	243
Total	**396**	**777**	**1270,15**

504 BOA, ADVNS.AHK.ŞM (1): 191/3.

When the data in Table 15 is evaluated, first of all, for example, the number of holders of the *Ḥaram Shaykh* position, which was stated as three people, is twelve people with various shares. This shows that the allocations became share-based over time and the number of beneficiaries increased. Secondly, *imāms* and clerks received the largest share among the officials. For example, three clerks received a total of 14 coins, while one imam received 13 coins. On the other hand, the *muʿarrif* and *musaddirīn* shared 1.5 coins, while the janitors of al- Aqṣā Mosque and Ṣaḥratullāh shared one coin between them. Those in charge of reciting the Qur'an at al- Aqṣā Mosque on Fridays also received twenty coins, or half a coin. The servants other than the clergy who received the highest share were the sweeper, or cleaners. The two cleaners working in Sahratullah were given a total of fifty coins.

When the values given in Table 15 are compared with the ledger entries dated 1124 AH/1712–1713 CE, it is determined that there was a miscalculation. Namely, the 50 coins of *surra* allocated for the *ferāşet* was confused with the 58 coins of *surra* allocated for the Shaykhs of the Ḥaram. As a result of this confusion, Sayyid Muḥammad ibn Sayyid ʿAbd al-Raḥīm Ṣaḥrat Allāh, the Ḥanafī Muftī of Quds al-Sharīf, who was mentioned among the Shaykhs of the Ḥaram, was stated as the cleaners.[505] As a result, the amount of *surra* was underestimated by 50 coins. Secondly, it was found that the amount of *surra* sent to Jerusalem did not change. Thirdly, it was observed that the reciters of *eczāʾ* (part from Qur'ān) for Nurbanu Sultan's soul, who were recorded in the book dated 1124 AH/1712–1713 CE, were not included among the officials in the *surra* book dated 1177 AH/1763–1764 CE. In terms of the number of officials, it was found that the number of officials increased in the middle of the century compared to the beginning of the century. For example, while the number of *khaṭībs* was eleven in the book numbered 556, this number increased to twenty-two in the book numbered 1791. Again, the number of *imāms*, which was twenty-nine, increased to 48 in the book numbered 1791. Towards the end of the century, in the *surra* book dated 1207 AH/1792–1793 CE, it was found that these numbers increased even more.[506] This indicates an increase in the number of officials, which is important as it shows that the demand for positions that were highly advantageous in terms of salary, tax exemption and social prestige increased.

Despite the increasing number of officials, the amount of *surra* did not change, but the shares increased and the share per share decreased. At the beginning, middle and end of the century, the amount of *surra* allocated to orators remained constant at fifty-six coins. However, at the beginning of the

505 It is assessed that this situation was related to misreading. See Fişne, *XVIII. Yüzyıl*, 22.

506 BOA, EV.HMK.SR: 2885/3–4.

century, this share was shared among eleven people, while in the middle of the century this number increased to twenty-two and at the end of the century to twenty-three. Similarly, the number of imams increased from twenty-nine at the beginning of the century to forty-seven in the middle and fifty-six at the end of the century. This shows that in parallel with the increasing number of officials in the *waqf*s, the number of shareholders sharing the surre revenues also increased.

5.2.1 Local Elites Receiving a Share from the *Surra*

When we evaluate the local elites who were included in the *surra* book dated 1177 AH/1763–1764 CE and who received a share from the *surra* of Jerusalem due to their duties in the *waqf*s, it was possible to make a classification as follows. ʿAlamīs, ʿAsalīs, Jāʿūnīs, Jamāʿīs, Dāwūdīs, Fennānīs, Gifarīs, Harajīs, Harirīs, Harzajīs, Ḥusaynīs, ʿIzzīs, Luṭfīs, Muwaqqits, Samadīs, Salmūnīs, and Surūrīs are the most common family names in the records. Among these families, the highest number of records belong to the ʿAlamīs, ʿAsalīs, Ḥusaynīs, Dāwūdīs, Jāʿūnīs, Jamāʿīs, and Muwaqqits. Thirty-one *surra*s were given to the ʿAlamīs, three to the ʿAsalīs, twelve to the Jāʿūnīs, fifteen to the Jār Allāh, sixteen to the Jamāʿīs, twenty-eight to the Dāwūdīs, eight to the Fityānīs, five to the Ḥusaynīs (Wafāʾīs), and twenty to the Muwakkits. In fact, not only the names of family members but also the names of their children were written several times.[507]

The names of the members of the ʿAlamī and Dāwūdī families are usually mentioned among the *imāms*, *muʾadhdhin*s, *juzhāns*, and congregants of the mosques of al-Aqṣā, Ṣaḥrat Allāh, and Jāmiʿ al-Maghāriba, as well as various positions in the *Ḥaram al-Sharīf*. However, there are also those who were servants, janitors, and auxiliary personnel. Almost all of the Ḥusaynīs listed in the ledger are included in the section of those who read the *juzʾ*. Another group, the ʿAsalīs, are seen to have performed religious duties. From this we can see that the only purpose of the *surra* was not only to bestow favors on the poor, but also to show favor to the city's dignitaries. Secondly, the city's dignitaries also received a significant share of the *surra* for Jerusalem thanks to the important duties they performed in mosques such as the al-Aqṣā Mosque and the Dome of the Rock, which formed the center of the Jerusalem *waqf* network. The principle of succession applied by the Ottoman central government, both in terms of duties and *surra*s, also ensured that these rights were passed down from generation to generation. Thus, as another advantage of working

507 BOA, EV.HMK.SR: 1971/2–49.

in *waqf* positions, *surra* revenues contributed to the wealth and influence of these families.

5.3 Jizya (*Poll-Tax*) *Revenues*

Jizya, which means "tax *ḥaraj*"[508] in the dictionary, is an Islamic tax and refers to the tax collected from non-Muslims within the framework of the law of *dhimmi* status in Islamic states.[509] In return for the rights granted to *dhimmis*[510] in Islamic law, the most important obligation required of them is to pay a tax called *jizya*, which is a certain amount per person per year, under certain conditions.[511] Like other taxation practices based on Islamic law, *jizya* took its final form after a long period of development both theoretically and in practice.[512]

In the Ottoman Empire, *jizya* was collected from every non-Muslim male who had reached the age of puberty, was physically and mentally sound, and had a separate labor force and owned at least with the value of 300 *akçe* of movable property.[513] Women, children and disabled were not charged *jizya*. In addition, those who fulfilled special military obligations such as *voynuk*s, *martalo*s and *eflak*s were exempted from *jizya* in return for their service.[514]

Jizya was of two types: *maktūʿ* and *ʿalā al-ruʾūs* (per capita). *Maktūʿ jizya* was the *jizya* that was determined by peace at the time of conquest and generally applied to non-Muslim states subject to the state. *ʿAlā al-ruʾūs jizya* was a tax levied on individuals, taking into account the financial situation of the taxpayers. In Jerusalem, the *jizya* tax was collected from the Jews and Christians, who were the People of the Book, at a fixed rate per person. While there was no direct contact or negotiation with the individuals in the collection of the tax, the tax collected within the community was expected to be delivered in one lump sum.

---

508 Şemseddin Sami, *Kāmūs al-Aʿlām*, 476.

509 Özel, "Avarız ve Cizye Defterleri," 35.

510 *Dhimmi*: "It is a term used for a non-Muslim who has entered into the Muslim covenant and trust, or in other words, who has accepted the subjection of the Islamic government in accordance with the procedure." Pakalın, *Osmanlı Tarih Deyimleri*, 663.

511 Eryılmaz, *Osmanlı Devleti'nde*, 23.

512 Nedkoff, " Osmanlı İmparatorluğu'nda Cizye," 615. In the Ottoman Empire, when a *jizya* was to be imposed on a region or a person, the legitimacy of the *jizya* was shown by stating in the edicts, certificates, decrees, orders, insignia and similar documents that the origin of the matter came from Islamic law, how it was applied in the early years of Islam and how much tax was collected. Ercan, "Taxes Paid by Non-Muslims," 372.

513 Çağatay, "Osmanlı İmparatorluğu'nda Reayadan Alınan Vergi ve Rüsumlar," 495.

514 İnalcık, "Cizye," 45.

In the Ottoman Empire, the system based on the Ḥanafī madhhab jurisprudence was accepted and practiced. Accordingly, non-Muslims were divided into *ednā*, *evsat*, *ʿalā'* classes according to their income status.[515] The officials specifically in charge of collecting the *jizya* were elected from among the *emin'* and *mutemed* (trustworthy) people, and most of the time they were tax farmers, who were called *jizyedār*.[516]

In Jerusalem, the *jizya* tax collected from Jews and Christians was sent to the State Treasury and then used to fund prominent charitable causes.[517] In this practice, after the collection of the *jizya* was completed, the *jizyedār* would take the *jizya* revenues to the Jerusalem Sharīʿa Court and the share of the *waqfs* in question would be allocated from the total revenue.[518] In Jerusalem, exceptionally, some of the *jizya* revenues were sent to the al-Aqṣā Mosque, Dome of the Rock and Khasseki Sultan *Waqfs*.[519] In these *waqfs*, *jizya* taxes were paid as wages to the *ʿulamā'* of the *waqf*.[520] As a matter of fact, in the 18th century, imperial decrees made allocations from *jizya* revenues to Masjid al-Aqṣā and the Dome of the Rock.[521]

As can be seen in Table 16 of the later allocations as they appear in Ziyād ʿAbd al-ʿAziz al-Madanī, the largest allocation was made to the Sahratullah *Waqf*.

From the revenues obtained; 20,150 *kurūsh* was allocated to Sahratullah, 288 kurus to Khasseki Sultan *Waqf*, 120 *kurūsh* to *Zāwiya* al-Mawlawiyya, 98 *kurūsh* to *Zāwiya* al-Uzbakiyya and 75 *kurūsh* to *Zāwiya* al-Qādirīyya. On the other hand, in a decree sent to the Governor of Damascus and the *Qāḍī* of Jerusalem, the Qādirīyya and Uzbekiyya lodges and the *Zāwiya* al-Mawlawiyya in Jerusalem were each allocated a daily food fee of twenty-five right *akçe* to be

515 In Cohen's study on the social and economic life of the Jews in Jerusalem in the 16th century, it is stated that, as an exception, the *jizya* was paid by everyone at a minimum of 80 *akçe* (by the end of the century it was 90 *akçe*), i.e. one gold piece. These revenues were first sent to the Damascus Treasury and then to the Imperial Treasury. However, the *jizya* income of 85 Jerusalem Jews was earmarked for the Al-Aqsā Mosque. It is also stated that this practice continued regularly from the mid-16th century onwards. Also, for some of the problems experienced by the Jewish community regarding the jizya taxes paid, see Cohen, *Jewish Life*, 21–27.

516 Çağatay, "Osmanlı İmparatorluğu'nda," 495.

517 JS 276:34–41.

518 JS 272:34–41.

519 Al-Madani, "al-Awqāf al-Islāmiyya," 41.

520 Ze'evi, "Küdüs," 70.

521 JS 274:36; 276:34–41; 280:17.

TABLE 16 *Waqf* having share from the poll-tax income (1212/1798)[a]

Year	Number of the document			Total document	Total (*kurūsh*)
	Aʿlā	Awsat	Adnā		
1205	370	2792	1740	4902	24211
1209	173		682		
	1903 *kurūsh*	16282 *kurūsh*	18752 *kurūsh*		

a al-Madanī, "Awqāf al-Quds," 41.

paid from the Jerusalem *jizya*.[522] This practice indicates that allocations were made from *jizya* revenues to various *waqf*s in times of need.

5.4 *Other Privileges*

The leading families of Jerusalem could purchase loaves of bread and soup from the Khāṣṣekī Sulṭān *Imāret* (public kitchen) twice a day, once in the morning and once in the evening. In a register dated 1773, in addition to the families listed under the headings "*ʿulamā*'" and "*sādāt*" as residents of Jerusalem, the poor and pilgrims were also included in the list of beneficiaries of the *imāret*.[523] While the *waqf* lists the poor and pilgrims as beneficiaries of the *imāret*, the names of members of the Ḥusaynī, ʿAlamī, Khālidī, Muwakkīt, and Jār Allāh families were also included.[524] For example, Qur'an reciters, who were not

522 "Şam vâlisi Mîr-i hac vezîr ve Kudüs-i Şerîf kadısına hüküm ki: Kıdvetü'l-'ulemâ'i's-sâlikîn Şeyh Muḥammad es-Sâlih ibn-i eş-Şeyh Halîl el-Kadrî *-zîde salâhahû*-gelüp şeyh-i mezkûr medîne-i Kudüs-i Şerîf'de vâkı' Kadiriye Zâviyesi'nin şeyh ve zâviyedârlığının berât-ı şerîfemle mutasarrıf olup bundan akdem Kudüs-i Şerîfde tarîk-i Nakşibendî'ye mahsus Özbekiyye Zâviyesi ve tarîk-i Mevlevihane'ye mahsus Mevlevihane'nin nâ'ibleri ashâb-ı hayrât Evkâf-ı vâridât ta'yînine muvaffak olamayup îrâdları olmadığından nâşî ihtâr-ı arzdan gelen züvvârın ve misâfirîn bi'l-cümle fukarâ-i sâbirînden olup zâviyelerinde müddet-i ikâmetin ve eyyâm-ı ziyâretlerinde mertebesi ta'âmiyeleri olmayup niceleri bi'z-zarûrî su'âle ve niceleri aç oldukları halde giceledikleri mülhafık ve vücûhuyla mahall-i merhamet ve sezâvâr-ı âtıfet olmalarıyla Kudüs-i Şerîf cizyesi malından almak üzre zikr olunan üç aded zâviyelerin her birlerine yevmî yiğirmi beş sağ akçe ta'âmiye vazîfe ta'yîn ve yedlerine başka başka berevât-ı âlişânım ihsân olunmağla ..." BOA,ADVNS.ŞM (1): 77/1.

523 JS 253/ 81–82.

524 Singer, "The Privileged Poor," 265. Under the heading "Eczâ-i hân der makâm-ı Hazret-i Dâvud", the earliest date they are recorded in the list of *imāret* is 1002/1593–94.

listed in the endowment, were added to the lists at the end of the 16th century.[525] Similarly, families who were recorded among the beneficiaries of the *imāret* at a later date than the *waqf* were added to the lists due to their positions in the *waqf*s of Jerusalem. However, as Oded Peri has repeatedly pointed out, they were not only a form of repayment for their support of the Ottoman administration, but also a guarantee that the state would continue to grant them such privileges.[526] This reciprocity between local elites and the central administration, the different dimensions and examples of which are given above, was ensured through numerous practices put into effect by the Ottomans. However, while these practices provided a motivation for local elites to cooperate with the central authority, they also created a system of interdependence that resulted in greater reliance on and trust in the same local elites.[527]

Secondly, some prominent families of Jerusalem were exempted from taxes endowed by Ottoman sultans or rulers. In the 17th century in the *Sanjāq* of Jerusalem, direct links were established between the tax payers and the ruling and notable elite who benefited from the tax. Peasants, merchants, tradesmen or members of minorities had to pay their taxes directly to the janissaries, sipahis and *ʿulamāʾ*.[528] One way out of the circle of tax payers was to join a privileged class that did not have to pay taxes or preferably was one of the tax beneficiaries. The gentry were exempt from taxes, but received nothing from the state treasury. Rulers and their retinues, *sipahi, janissaries*, other members of the army and *ʿulamāʾ* were all tax beneficiaries.[529] In the 18th century, the situation was not much different.

The leading families of Jerusalem were also the beneficiaries of direct allocations of *waqf ghayr ṣaḥīḥ* (unauthenticated endowments), such as the endowment taxes of some villages in Palestine. Although this is not mentioned in the registers, it is evident from other records. The Dajjānī, Nuṣayba, and Ḥusaynī families were the recipients of such revenues.

525 Singer, "The Privileged Poor," 265. The earliest date that they were recorded in the soup kitchen list under the heading of '*Eczā-i hān der makām-ı Hazret-i Dāvud*' was H. 1002/ M. 1593–94.

526 Peri, "Waqf and Ottoman," 182–84.

527 Singer, "The Privileged Poor," 260–61. Singer mentions a similar correlation was set by Khoury in the Mosul example in the section of taxmen and province community.

528 Ze'evi, "Küdüs," 70.

529 ibid., p. 70.

6 Conclusion

In this third part of the study, the question of how Jerusalem's elite families established their influence within the *waqf* system is attempted to be answered by considering other actors within the Jerusalem *waqf* network. First of all, at the beginning of the 19th century, the population of Jerusalem was approximately 10,000, of which 5,000 were Muslims.[530] In his study, Gabriel Baer calculates the proportion of these families in the population of Jerusalem to be approximately 15–20%, assuming that each hamula consisted of 10–15 families and each family consisted of five people.[531] In our opinion, this ratio is even higher because the number of elite households included in our study is higher. On the other hand, as mentioned earlier, the proportion of private property owned by these families is much smaller. What is clear, however, is that the activities of these families in relation to *waqf*s were much broader than the proportions of both their population and personal property. However, this also varies according to different areas of activity.

From the Ayyubid and Mamluk periods onwards, prominent families with a prestigious position in Jerusalem society held various positions, especially the trusteeship of charitable endowments, and thus control of endowment properties, thereby monopolizing the mechanisms of endowments that provided both social prestige and economic power. This power and influence within the city's network of *waqf*s reinforced their wealth and influence in the city's network of relations and ensured their continuity through practices such as the reendowment of the properties of charitable *waqf*s, the increase in the number of officials who remained in the same family through share assignments, the sale of offices between certain families through the sale of offices, and the long-term leasing of *waqf* properties to certain families. First, the number of Jerusalem's leading families as founders of *waqf*s is striking. In fact, the number of new *waqf*s established by both Ottoman state officials and other Jerusalemites is less than half of those established by these families. Second, Jerusalem's elite families saw the *waqf* primarily as a means for private rather than charitable and strictly defined charitable purposes. The control of *waqf* revenues while the *waqf* was alive was not jeopardized by the process of *waqf* establishment. Importantly, the *waqf* was also seen as a tool for transferring the right of use of properties not owned by the *waqf* to the beneficiaries. Throughout the study, there is no evidence that the *waqf* was used by the elite traditional families of Jerusalem as a method of protection from state

530 Ben-Arieh, "The Population," 50–53.

531 Baer, "Jerusalem's Families," 118.

intervention or confiscation. Third, a detailed analysis of the *waqfiyya* reveals that the size of the endowment was quite significant in the modest number of *waqfs* established by the leading families of Jerusalem. The number of newly appointed trustees in these family *waqfs* was relatively small. This suggests that the participation and shares of Jerusalem's leading families were larger in the old and continuing *waqfs* than in the newly established *waqfs*. This is to be expected from families whose wealth is derived from long-standing positions.

Fourth, the source of the influence of the local elite in Jerusalem was, to some extent, of course their wealth. However, this is far from being the main reason, as the position of these families in the *waqf* system is dominant compared to their share of private property in the city. This high position played a crucial role in their appointment as trustees and other important officials of charitable *waqfs*. In many cases, their position in society was maintained through the coercive power of custom and the influence of tradition, as well as through the approval of the *qāḍī* to pass on from generation to generation within the same family the privileged position of trustees that had been held by their grandfathers many years earlier. Certain offices became the priority of certain families and their sale was possible, but the social consensus limited the sale of these offices to other prestigious family members. Tenants acquired such rights for reasons that required financial resources, such as the repair and maintenance of *waqf* properties or the planting of trees. However, these rights were not transferred as a result of public tension. The trustees of the charitable or spiritual *waqfs* had a say in the selection of beneficiaries. It was even seen as advantageous for both the trustees and the tenants in terms of the restoration of *waqf* properties.

Fifth, the *surra* and *jizya* revenues sent to Jerusalem also contributed to the wealth of these families through their intergenerational roles in large charitable *waqfs* such as the Al-Aqṣā Mosque, the Dome of the Rock, and the Khasseki Sultan *Waqf*. The daily food provided by the Khasseki Sultan *Waqf* is also evaluated in this context. The prominent families of Jerusalem were also beneficiaries of direct allocations of unauthenticated endowments, such as the endowment taxes of certain villages in Palestine. Again, this is mentioned as another dimension that contributed to the wealth of these families.

CHAPTER 5

The Impact of the Center on Provincial Relations: *Waqf* Applications in Jerusalem

In the context of the far-reaching reforms in Syria and Egypt after the Ottoman conquest, it was imperative to abolish the Mamluk system and centralize the administration in various fields. This centralization policy, of course, required the establishment of a large bureaucracy that would allow the central authorities to oversee and control administrative processes in the provinces. This bureaucracy would consist of both civil servants organized into hierarchical categories and departments, and administrative units and archives where documents, surveys and records would be processed and collected.[1] In the previous chapters, we have discussed land registries, the most detailed and important set of documents related to administrative mechanisms, the records of *sharīʿa* courts, and the centralized control of the *waqf*s.

This section will address the question of how the Ottoman central administration, as reflected in documents, used the centrally organized *waqf* sphere to shape networks of relations in Jerusalem in order to control the *waqf* system, strengthen its control over local groups, and promote economic development. In order to understand what kind of relations existed between the state and society, a close look will be taken at the actors in the provinces within the framework of the practices related to the *waqf*s of Jerusalem. The complaints of the people of Jerusalem from different social strata about the *waqf*s as reflected in the daily interactions in and around the court will be analyzed in terms of their practices and their voice and representation on behalf of others.

On the other hand, as historical sources, these documents should be approached with caution. As a textual genre that, at first glance, comes one step closer to the truth and offers a more precise picture of the legal practice of *waqf*s, there are physical problems, such as differences in the way *sharīʿa* court registers are kept, discontinuities between some existing volumes, or sometimes the cited documents are not where they should be. Furthermore, the context is shaped by the judicial and political systems of the Ottoman administration, which means that the concepts were, at least in part, created by the state. These concepts may have clashed with some regional customs or

1 İnalcık, "Osmanlı Arşivlerinin," 31–44.

 | DOI:10.1163/9789004743441_006

practices, thus preventing people from expressing their claims in court. Thus, people may have avoided the obligation to express their disputes in the terms of state officials or to conform their transactions to the formats permitted by legal scholarship or the state, preferring instead to compromise or to resolve their problems according to traditional custom.

In addition to the *sharīʿa* court registers, we will also refer to the *aḥkām* registers, which are the continuation of the complaint books, one of the most important sources for the determination of problems related to *waqf* practices.[2] Indeed, the *aḥkām* registers are an important series of sources that cover the problems about *waqf*s. Frequently consulted to understand the relations between the center and the actors in the provinces, the *aḥkām* books, which record the judgments issued by the Jerusalemites on the *arzuhāl* (petitions) and *arz-ı mahzar* (collective petitions) submitted to the Imperial Council regarding the problems experienced by the *waqf*s, will be examined in terms of the way the center produced solutions to the problems in the provinces.[3] As one of the technical means of communication between the provinces and Istanbul since the classical period of the Ottoman Empire, petitions and collective petitions had a major role in shaping the society and politics in the city and establishing political balances.[4]

Considering the above-mentioned issues regarding the sources, in this part of the study, we will present an analysis of various transactions and sample cases related to *waqf*s as recorded in various edicts and rulings in various books on Jerusalem, especially in the Jerusalem *sharīʿa* court registers. The case studies are organized in three groups: First, the extent to which the complaints submitted to the Imperial Council reflect the 'network of relations' around the *waqf* network in the remote Ottoman province of Jerusalem. Secondly, the interventions made by various segments of society in many areas related to *waqf*s, such as the management of *waqf*s, the operation of *waqf* properties, the collection of revenues, officials, wages, and the repair and maintenance of *waqf*s, will be identified.[5] In the complaints indicating violations of *waqf* law by various segments of society, conflicts of authority issues were at the heart of the disputes. Based on the social structure of Jerusalem, these violations,

2 Studies on *waqf*s made according to the *ahkām* registers are limited. For example, see *İstanbul Ahkām Defterleri İstanbul Vakıf Tarihi* and "Kudüs'teki İslami Vakıf." These two studies are transcription studies and include an evaluation regarding consisting of the classification of the provisions according to the subjects in their introductory chapters.

3 Tuğluca, "*Osmanlı'da Devlet Toplum*"; Gümrükçüoğlu, "Şikāyet Defterlerine," 175–206.

4 Lafi, "Petitions and Accomodating Urban Change," 1–4.

5 For a study in which complaints about *waqf* are evaluated under the headings 'organization, services and servants and income', see Tuğluca, *Osmanlı'da Devlet Toplum*, 215–47.

interventions and interference are analyzed under the headings of interventions by the ruling elite and *re'āyā* (ordinary people). Finally, the limits of state taxation will be discussed in the context of the *waqf*s of Jerusalem. In conclusion, the impact of the central government on provincial relations and the interaction of provincial actors with each other in the period covered by the study are again evaluated in the context of *waqf* practices. It should be noted that the following analysis focuses on different types of treatment and does not aim to show the frequency of similar cases.

1 Network of Relations in *Waqf* Practices

In the Ottoman system of government, where the principle of *dāire-i adliye* (circle of justice) was adopted and justice was at its center, the sultan protected the rights of his people, whom he regarded as God's trust, thereby strengthening the source of the state's legitimacy. For example, according to Halil İnalcık, justice is the foundation of this administrative tradition and justice is to protect the *re'āyā* from oppression.[6] Justice also meant that the people could directly present their complaints to the sovereign and that injustices could be redressed by his order.[7] The administration of legitimacy in the context of justice, was implemented through judicial institutionalizations such as the *Mezālim Dīvānı*[8] (Atrocities Court), *Dīvān-ı Hümāyun* (Imperial Council), *adaletnāmes* (justice decrees).[9] As one of the organizational tools that institutionalized the legitimacy of the power provided by the Circle of Justice, the petitions sent to the Imperial Council were instrumental in the rapid resolution of problems that could not be solved locally since the early periods of the Ottoman state.[10]

An *arzuhāl* is a type of petition that anyone from the ruling class or the common people, Muslim or non-Muslim, could write from a lower to a higher authority to express a wish or complaint.[11] In the Ottoman Empire, applying to the Imperial Council with a petition was an ancient institution with deep

6 Inalcık, *State Ideology*, 71–72.

7 Inalcık, "Şikāyet Hakkı," 33.

8 *Mezālim Dīvānı* is the court in which the people stood before the Sultan or a powerful representative, expressing their complaints and, if necessary, their losses were covered. See Darling, "Do Justice," 3–19.

9 Inalcık, *State Ideology*, 71.

10 Aydıner, "Rāgıb Paşa," 404.

11 Inalcık, *Osmanlı'da Devlet, Hukuk*, 50.

historical roots going back to the earliest days of the empire.[12] Individuals or groups from all segments of society had the right to submit written applications to the imperial bureaucracy regarding various social, economic, moral and legal issues. Petitioning was a traditional way for urban or rural people to persuade the imperial bureaucracy to intervene in their cause in order to eliminate excessive taxation or any form of persecution. The fact that the Imperial Council was open to all also contributed to the effective use of this institution by the subjects.[13]

In order to reflect the practices and problems that developed in daily life around the *waqf*s of the city of Jerusalem, in this part of the study, the provisions or rulings sent from Imperial Council will be analyzed from different perspectives and in a multidimensional manner, under the headings of the central government's relations with the people and the ruling-local elites, the ruler-local elites' relations with the people, and finally, the communities' relations with each other, and various social processes will be tried to be defined.

1.1 *Central Administration – Ordinary People*

The *reʿāyā* of Jerusalem utilized the grievance mechanism as a means of claiming their rights, albeit in limited numbers.[14] As can be seen in the many examples in the *Aḥkām* books, recent studies that examine political processes from the perspective of ordinary people and treat the subjects of the empire as individuals who have a say in determining their own destiny have stood against the perception of politics as a sphere of action monopolized by state elites and ending where the institutional boundaries of the state end.[15]

For example, the petition sent by Ḥadīce and ʿĀ'isha to the Imperial Council in 1155/1742 was recorded in the Damascus *Aḥkām* Books as the first complaints made by two women from Jerusalem regarding *waqf*s. The women in question

---

12 Öztürk, "Sosyo-Ekoomik Tarih Kaynağı Olarak Ahkām Defterleri," 611.

13 Uzunçarşılı, *Osmanlı Devleti'nin Merkez ve Bahriye Teşkilātı*, 13.

14 As mentioned earlier, in the current study, the petitions and collective petitions sent by the people of the city of Jerusalem were examined only in relation to *waqf* issues during the period between 1742 and 1830. In this sense, it is far from a holistic study of the registers. The study focuses on the central-provincial relations that developed around the Jerusalem *waqf*s examined in the context of the city of Jerusalem, the nature of the relations between various community segments and what issues in the countryside in particular regarding the *waqf*s were experienced. We also tried to understand the central government's approach to relations and issues in the countryside through *waqf*s and in terms of analyzing the provisions in response to the petitions and collective petitions submitted to the Imperial Council. The work is limited to the provisions sent to the city of Jerusalem.

15 Faroqhi, "Political Activity," 35.

stated that the Khāṣṣekī Sulṭān *waqf* had kept the inn called *Khān al-Usārī* located near the *dabbāgh* in the Yahūd neighborhood of Tripoli by paying an annual rent of 150 *kurūsh* each, and that the silk collected in Tripoli was stored in the said inn. However, while the governors should not have interfered neither in the collection of this silk nor in the rooms in the inn, they reported that the governors of Tripoli had been interfering with the inn for five or ten years. Upon further investigation, it was observed that the inn had been harassed by the *sarıca*s and *sekban*s (mercenaries) during the time of Seyfoğlu[16] and that the inn had been ruined over time and the silk collected at the inn had started to be collected elsewhere.

After the *waqf* inn was damaged in this way and became completely unusable, it was leased to Samsoncıbaşı Meḥmed on the condition that he would repair and restore it, pay 150 Esedī *kurūsh* annually to the *Rikāb-i Hümāyūn*, and carry out the collection of silks in the said inn as in the past. An order written in Rajab 1065/1655 stipulated that no one from the *ahl al-ʿurf* (military branch of ruling class like *mīr-mīrān*, his assistants, other state administrators, *nāẓir*s, and fortress guards) should interfere with the rented inn, and this order was renewed in 1153/1740. This time, it was understood that the inn in question was given as a mansion to the relatives of the governor and the poor merchants were not allowed to stay and were sent to distant places. Taking into account the other orders sent more than once over time, it was ruled that the implementation was to be carried out in accordance with the order issued upon the request of the chief eunuch.[17]

From the content of the ruling briefly summarized here, it is understood that the Ottoman registration system was kept meticulously at the center and the *reʿāyā* were subjected to the oppression of the *ahl al-ʿurf*. In the solution of this issue that developed in the provinces of Jerusalem far from the Ottoman Empire, the central administration sent a decree to the governor of Tripoli and the *Qāḍī* of Jerusalem, and it was decided to examine the situation in accordance with the registered decrees and to resolve it on the spot in accordance with the law. Therefore, with this matter referred to the *Qāḍī* of Jerusalem, the

16 Inalcık emphasized the tendency of *beys* to drop representing the sultan's executive power relying on their power sourcing from *sarıca-sekbans* and *levend* legions (paid soldiers) they started to feed from the end of the sixteenth century. As reflected in the *sijills* and *ahkāms* of the period covered by the study, the state no longer struggled only due to the increased demands of the center and security problems, but also with the illegal taxes collected and other waywardly practices these administrators engaged in. For other similar examples of such irregularities by administrators dating back to the early sixteenth century, see also Inalcik, *Osmanlı'da Devlet, Hukuk*, 75–190.

17 BOA, ADVNS.AHK.ŞM (1): 7/1.

official authority of *qāḍī* in the provinces allowed the state to have the final say in all matters related to *waqf*s, and the central administrator aimed to make it possible for the state to protect its interests in the field of *waqf*s.[18]

On the other hand, the function of making an impartial judgment, taking into account the conditions in the locality and conducting investigations to fulfill the *ʿurf* and *sharīʿa* was assigned to the *qāḍī*. This practice, which aimed at the fulfillment of laws and regulations, prevented bureaucrats from the center from making wrong and arbitrary decisions on behalf of the Sultan, which would be contrary to the principle of justice and law.[19]

In *waqf* matters, the *reʿāyā*, mostly in judicial matters and mostly in interpersonal disputes, applied directly to the Imperial Council for the problems they could not solve in the local court. For example, in a provision dated 1207/1792, it is recorded that the mill, which was one of the revenues of the Meḥmed Pasha *waqf*, the grandfather of Shaykh ʿAbdullāh, in Jerusalem, had been seized by Meḥmed ibn al-Harūn, the tenant of the *waqf* of Zakariyā, for several years and that he insisted on not paying the two-year rent when demanded.[20] Sayyid Ahmad, Sayyid Dāwud, Sayyid Khalīl and Sayyid Aḥmad, Sayyid Dāwūd, Sayyid Khalīl, and Sayyid Ibrāhīm reported that their grandfather al-Ḥājj ʿAlī had rented out a house (*bāb hane*) in Jerusalem for a certain amount of annual rent and that al-Ḥājj Meḥmed had not paid the rent and embezzled it. In the ruling sent in response, it was stated that the unpaid rent revenues should be delivered to the *waqf* and the estate should be left to its rightful owner. In the case of applications to the center, the ruling usually included the sultan's order that the claim be heard by the court according to the *sharīʿa* and *ʿurf* in order to ensure justice.[21]

However, the number of applications made by *reʿāyā* to the Imperial Council regarding *waqf*s in Ottoman Jerusalem was quite limited, which can be attributed to the city's distance from Istanbul and the economic situation in the city in the 18th century. Between 1742 and 1830, the number of complaints filed by the *reʿāyā* regarding *waqf*s was twenty, which constituted 12% of all applications.[22] One of the effective methods used by the public to convey their

---

18 For a similar analysis see Van Leeuwen, *Bir Osmanlı*, 133–40.

19 İnalcık, "Şikāyet Hakkı," 40.

20 BOA, ADVNS.AHK.ŞM (4): 178/2.

21 Inalcık, "Şikāyet Hakkı," 36.

22 There are 51 records about Jerusalem *waqf*s in the 814 numbered book titled "Ahkām-ı Mecca and Medina and Egypt and 33 records in the 815 numbered book with the same title at the Directorate General of *Waqf*s Archives (VGMA). In other books of VGMA, the number of records is as follows: 317 (1 record), 318 (1 record) 319 (11 entries), 320 (5 records), 321 (4 records), 324 (3 records), 359 (2 records). While the provisions contained

complaints was to go to Istanbul in person and submit their petitions. Those who could not come to Istanbul could send their letters or petitions through an official or a merchant traveling to the capital.[23] Those who acted as intermediaries in sending the petitions to Istanbul would assist the petitioner in the process and use this benevolence in power relations in the city.[24]

For centuries, the Sultan used this mechanism to prevent or correct injustices between individuals and injustices committed by those representing his authority by abusing this authority. The grand vizier was responsible for ensuring that the people's petitions reached the sultan and that the necessary action was taken as a result of his reading them. In this respect, the petition, one of the methods of communication between the ruler and the ruled, was a technical tool that demonstrated the power and legitimacy of the state in the provinces. It was also a way of regulating power relations.[25]

TABLE 17 The means of submission of petitions about the *waqf* affairs of Jerusalemites to the Imperial Council (1742–1830)

Means of petition submission	**Ruling elite (*ʿaskerī*)**	**Ordinary people (*reʿāyā*)**	**Total**	**%**
By bringing in person to Istanbul	98	9	107	61.1
By sending a letter to Istanbul	7	–	7	4
By *iʿlâm* (court order)	6	–	6	3.4
By sending *ʿarż* (chief eunuch's petition)	18	–	18	10.3
By sending *ʿarż-ı ḥâl* (individual petition)	26	10	36	20.6
By sending *ʿarż-ı maḥżâr* (collective petition)	–	1	1	0.6
Total	155	20	175	100

in the Damascus *Ahkām* books were written on the petitions and collective petitions sent by the Jerusalemites, the provisions in VGMA were based on the petitions concerning *waqf*-related issues sent by Chief Eunuch, ruler of the Ḥaramayn *Waqfs*.

23 Singer, *Kadılar, Kullar*, 159.

24 Lafi, "Istanbul," 1–4.

25 Lafi, "Istanbul," 1–4.

Table 17 above reveals the ways in which Jerusalemites made their complaints about the *waqf*s to the center. Accordingly, 61% of the complaints made to the center were made in person. The fact that these people were mostly members of the *ʿaskerī* (ruling elite) class may suggest that they traveled to and from Istanbul through their relations with the center or that they used the complaint mechanism easily for this reason alone. On the other hand, according to Hülya Taş, the *ʿaskerī* class was in a more advantageous position in the exercise of the right to file a complaint due to their power arising from their status and the financial means provided by the sources of income entrusted to them by the sultan.[26] Tuğluca, on the other hand, cites the Imperial Council's function as an administrative court for *ʿaskerī* class as another reason for this situation. Although the *ʿaskerī*s had the opportunity to take their administrative-financial and legal problems to the *qāḍī* court, they generally preferred to take them to the Imperial Council.[27] As a result, *ʿaskerī*s used the complaint mechanism more frequently than *reʿāyā* in matters related to *waqf*s.

Waqf trustees made the most applications to the Imperial Council (eighty-five complaints), followed by *waqf* officials (twenty-seven complaints).[28] Among the trustees, most of whom were local residents, sixty-three of them came to the Imperial Council in person to lodge their complaints.

Reʿāyā, on the other hand, rarely traveled to Istanbul. In the first record in which collective complaints about the *waqf*s were submitted, the Muslim inhabitants of Jerusalem applied with a petition, some of the inhabitants of the village named Niẓā came and the poor of the Ṣaḥrat Allāh and Khalīl al-Raḥmān sent a petition.[29] Two women applied, the first with a petition and

26 Taş, 'Osmanlıda 'Şikâyet', 186–204.

27 Tuğluca, *Osmanlı'da Devlet Toplum*, 60.

28 For example, the *mutawallī* and tombkeeper of *Sādād* al-Maghāriba Abū Madyan al-Ghawth *Waqf*, Sayyid ʿAbdullāh al-Maghribī have petitioned six complaints in which he went to Istanbul and complained about issues related to his *waqf*, one being in Ramaḍān, two in Shawwāl, and three in Dhū al-Ḥijja 1197 AH/1783 CE. See BOA, ADVNS.AHK.ŞM (3): 137/1; 147/3; 148/1; 152/2; 153/3; 156/2; 156/3. At the same time, Tashṭimūriyya Tomb *Waqf mutawallī*, *nāẓir*, and tombkeeper Sayyid ʿAbdullāh al-Maghribī submitted his petition regarding the tomb as the seventh complaint subject. See BOA, ADVNS.AHK.ŞM (3): 156/1. In another petition, Jerusalem Castle orator Sayyid ʿAbd al-Ḥaqq ibn Sayyid ʿAbd al-Raḥmān have submitted his four complaints about officer fees and interventions into his duty by going to the Imperial Council. BOA, ADVNS.AHK.ŞM (3): 29/3; 29/4; 32/1, 35/2. And fifthly petitioned about his grandfather Shaykh Khalīl al-Jāʾūnī *Waqf mutawallī* did not pay the rent of one house belonging to the *waqf*. BOA, ADVNS.AHK.ŞM (3): 32/2.

29 BOA, ADVNS.AHK.ŞM (1): 174/3.

the second by coming.[30] The first two of the three applications made by the children of the endower (*awlād al-wāqif*) were made with a petition and the third was made by coming.[31] Al-Shaykh Yūnus from the righteous persons (*ṣulaḥā'*) applied by going, and al-Ḥājj Meḥmed from the *re'aya*, whose titles and nicknames were not clarified, applied with a petition; also 'Alī, Sayyid Mūsā, Ibrāhīm, and 'Abdullāh ibn Mūsā ibn 'Abd al-Wahhāb submitted their complaints by going to the Imperial Council.[32] In matters related to *waqf*s, it seems that Christians were the most common non-Muslims to file complaints with petition, while Jews came to the Imperial Council to settle their affairs. The applications made by way of petition in the provisions were made by sending or submitting the petition. In other provinces of the Ottoman Empire, the most common method used by complainants to solve their problems was to go in person and explain their problems. In a study conducted by Tuğluca based on the *'Atīq* Complaint Books between 1683–1689, it was recorded that 73% of the complainants sought solutions to their problems by going in person.[33]

Among the provisions sent from Jerusalem to the Council, there are two complaints by women regarding the *waqf*s. The first of these complaints involves the activities of the *ahl al-'urf* and the second involves the activities of the trustees of the *waqf* against the complainants.[34]

Non-Muslims filed complaints mostly about judicial matters. Some Jews who applied to the Imperial Council filed complaints about the tenancy of property that belong to the outbuilding of a *waqf* or the interference with their own *waqf*s.[35] In the applications made by Christians, the most common compliants were about the excessive income demanded from the visitors of the Church of the Holy Sepulchre, some of whose income belong to the Khasseki Sultan *Waqf*, and the irregularities of the church janitors appointed by Khasseki Sultan *Waqf*.[36] The common point of the complaints, one concerning the *waqf*s property and the other concerning its charity, is that each religious group sought justice by applying to the Imperial Council.

In the resolution of complaints sent to the Imperial Council, it is worth noting that in administrative matters, the people to whom the judgements were addressed were the *ahl al-'urf*, whereas in a judicial matter, the judgement was

30 BOA, ADVNS.AHK.ŞM (1): 7/1; 288/2.
31 BOA, ADVNS.AHK.ŞM (3): 34/1; 105/3; 149/2.
32 See respectively. BOA, ADVNS.AHK.ŞM (3): 47/4; (2): 47/1; (2): 56/ 2; (2): 154/2; (7): 99/4.
33 Tuğluca, *Osmanlı'da Devlet*, 49.
34 BOA, ADVNS.AHK.ŞM (1): 7/1; (1): 288/2.
35 BOA, ADVNS.AHK.ŞM (1): 43/1; (5): 79/1.
36 BOA, ADVNS.AHK.ŞM (2): 30/4; (2): 31/4; (2): 289/3; (5): 80/3; (5): 86/1.

referred to the *qāḍī*.[37] In matters that directly concerned the *qāḍī* – which were mostly judicial matters – the judgement was sent to him as the *sharīʿa* judge of the local administration; and in administrative and military matters, the judgement was also sent to administrative superiors such as the governors and *sanjāq beys* for execution. In the case of banditry, for example, the judgement would be addressed to both the *qāḍī* and *sanjāq bey*.[38] In administrative and military matters, the phrase "it is written to be acted upon regarding to the law" is used for the execution of the judgement,[39] whereas for matters falling under the jurisdiction of the *qāḍī*, the phrase "it is written to be dealt with by the *sharīʿa* in the localilty" is used.[40]

An important issue in the provisions to the complaints is whether the provisions are final or not. We observe that some matters were referred to the local authority as the final decision-making authority. Feridun Emecen draws attention to the fact that the complainants may have acted deliberately. As a matter of fact, the centre was not in a position to judge the parties. In such cases, the centre tried to resolve the matter by referring it to the local authorities.[41] The ratio of *ʿurfī* (customary) and *sharʿī* (religious) matters in the provisions regarding Jerusalem was equal. In customary matters, it was requested to *menʿ u defʿ olunması* (prohibit and defeat) the acts of aggression and interventions,[42] whereas in shari' cases, it was requested *hilāf-ı şerʿ ile adl olunmaması* (not to do justice in violation of sharīʿa),[43] *hilāf-ı kadīme teʿaddī olunmaması* (no to commit acts of aggression in violence with the old law),[44] *hilāf-ı/muğāyir-i şart-ı vākıf muamele olunmaması* (no to treat in violation of/contrary to the terms of the endower),[45] *muğāyir-i vakfiye-i maʿmūlün bihā olunmaması* (no to treat in violation of the conditions situated in the *waqfiyya*).[46] In cases where there was a dispute over a previous *firman* or an imperial decree, reference

37 Inalcık, *Osmanlı'da Devlet*, 54.

38 E.g. see BOA, ADVNS.AHK.ŞM (1): 29/3; 245/4; (2): 156/1; (2): 286/3; (2): 314:5; (5): 54/3); VGMA, 324/83–84.

39 See BOA, ADVNS.AHK.ŞM (1): 28/5; 49/2; 51/2; (2): 76/3; 156/1.

40 See BOA, ADVNS.AHK.ŞM (1): 150/3; 181/2; (2): 76/2; 108/3; (3): 5/1; 76/2; (4): 32/1; 105/3; (5): 20/1; 27/1; (6): 14/4; 43/4; (7): 6/3; (7): 91/2.

41 Emecen, 'Osmanlı Divanının', p. 107–139.

42 See BOA, ADVNS.AHK.ŞM (1): 133/3; 133/4; (2): 6/3; 76/2; 154/2; 222/5; 303/2; (3): 5/1; 18/1; 38/3; 47/4; (4): 34/1; 57/1; 59/3; 70/1; 110/3; (5): 13/1; 79/1; 86/1; 127/1; (6): 170/1; (7): 6/3; 97/2; 100/1.

43 See BOA, ADVNS.AHK.ŞM (2): 30/4; 184/2.

44 BOA, ADVNS.AHK.ŞM (1): 40/2; 135/2; (2): 50/1; 147/1; (3): 120/4; 146/3; (4): 62/2; 152/6; (5): 79/1.

45 See BOA, ADVNS.AHK.ŞM (2): 222/4; (4): 34/1; 186/1; (5): 127/1; (6): 90/2; (7): 99/4.

46 See BOA, ADVNS.AHK.ŞM (3): 41/2; (4): 29/3.

was made to it and the execution of the provisions was requested. This situation was frequently observed in interventions in the trusteeship and duties of a *waqf*.[47]

1.2 *Central Administration and Local-Administrative Elites*

The petitions submitted to the Imperial Council are very important in terms of showing the interaction between the leading families of Jerusalem and the central authorities in Istanbul. The scholars belonging to the *ʿulamāʾ* families of Jerusalem increased their opportunities by penetrating the networks in Istanbul to establish relations with the notables and famous *ʿulamāʾ* and by resorting to petitions or intermediaries to strengthen their position.

Many applications were made to the Imperial Council from Jerusalem's local elite households who were in charge of the majority of Jerusalem's charitable *waqf*s. For example, one of the prominent families of Jerusalem, al-Sayyid al-Shaykh Muṣṭafā ibn Shaykh Abū al-Faḍl al-ʿAlamī, a member of the ʿAlamī family, trustee of *Madrasa al-Ḥamrā waqf* and also Shaykh, trustee, and inspector of *Khānqāh al-Ṣalāḥiyya*, submitted three complaints to the Imperial Council. Shaykh ʿAbd al-Qādir ibn Mawlānā Shaykh Muḥammad al-ʿAlamī, another member of the ʿAlamī family, also filed a complaint as the trustee of the *waqf* of the *Madrasa al-Maẓhabiyya*.[48]

Sayyid ʿAbdullāh, one of the leading local families of Jerusalem, one of the Maghribīs, the trustee of *Sādāt al-Maghāriba*, Abū Madyan al-Ghawth *Waqf*, and Abū Hurayra *Waqf*, came to the Imperial Council and submitted his complaint.[49] Another Maghribī, Shaykh ʿAbdullāh al-Maghribī, who was the trustee and inspector of the *waqf* of Sayyid ʿUmar al-Mujarrad, trustee and inspector of the *Zāwiya al-Maghāriba Waqf*, and trustee, inspector, and tombkeeper of the *Waqf* of *Tashṭīmūriyya* Tomb, came to the Imperial Council and submitted his complaints regarding the *waqf*s he managed and performed other duties.[50]

Sayyid ʿAbd al-Ḥaqq ibn ʿAbd al-Raḥmān, a member of another prominent family of Jerusalem, clerk of the Fortress Mosque of Jerusalem and trustee of the *waqf* of his grandfather Shaykh Khalīl al-Jāʿūnī, came to the Imperial Council and submitted his complaints.[51] These examples, the number of which could

47 See BOA, ADVNS.AHK.ŞM (1): 202/3; 212/5; 277/1; (2): 27/1; 150/2; 222/6; (3): 31/4; 32/2; 115/4; (4): 85/3; 110/3; 162/2; (5): 5/1; 10/4; 96/3; (6): 34/1; 58/2; 138/2.

48 See BOA, ADVNS.AHK.ŞM (5): 20/1.

49 See BOA, ADVNS.AHK.ŞM (3): 46/1; (3): 137/1; (4): 163/2.

50 See BOA, ADVNS.AHK.ŞM (3): 147/3; 148/1; 152/2; 153/3; 156/1; 156/2; 156/3.

51 See BOA, ADVNS.AHK.ŞM (4): 29/3; 29/4; 32/1; 32/2; 35/2). For other examples see Apart from these; Khālidī (BOA, ADVNS.AHK.ŞM (3): 120/4; (3): 135/2; (4): 85/3); ʿAsalī (BOA,

be increased, undoubtedly indicate that wealthy *ʿulamāʾ* families were in a much more advantageous position than others. They were able to pay for their services and create links between the relationship networks of the *ʿulamāʾ* and the relationship networks of merchants and moneylenders. Wealthy families could maintain their patronage relations in Istanbul for generations.[52] On the other hand, "local elites", who had the position of "intermediary" between the central administration and the people in the local base, were also patronising the local people and creating the sphere of authority in their own name.[53]

The rate of complaints sent to the Imperial Council regarding the *waqf*s of Jerusalem by the local elite, which we categorise as the "ruling class" in Jerusalem, is approximately 88 per cent. This shows that the leading local elites of Jerusalem were the most effective users of the complaint mechanism. Approximately 63 per cent of this rate went in person to submit their complaints. Sending a letter, on the other hand, was a method preferred mostly by the ruling elite. In six of the seven records, the *Qāḍī* of Jerusalem sent letters, while in one record, the Chief Eunuch, who was also the inspector of the charitable and public *waqf*s, notably the *Waqf*s of Masjid al-Aqṣā, Dome of the Rock and Khasseki Sultan, among the *waqf*s annexed to the *Ḥaram al-Sharīf*, sent letters. After a certain date, it was also detected that the *Qāḍī* of Jerusalem sent an *iʿlām* (sharīʿa court decision). The number of decisions submitted by the *Qāḍī* of Jerusalem was five.[54] Almost all of the *aḥkām* (imperial order) records in the Registers of Mecca, Medina, and Egypt, of the same period contained the provisions written upon the requests of the Chief Eunuch as the inspector of the *Ḥaramayn Waqfs*.[55]

Within the realm of the study, the *waqf* officials called *ahl al-murtaziqa* were also evaluated within the scope of the ruling class. Complaints made by *waqf* officials (approximately 18%) and mainly *waqf* trustees (approximately 57%) constituted the majority of the complaints made by the ruling class regarding *waqf*s in Ottoman Jerusalem (approximately 75%). With the exception of the Khasseki Sultan Waqf,[56] which was appointed by the Ottoman administration,

ADVNS.AHK.ŞM (4): 125/2); Abu'l-Lutf (Lutfī/Jārullah) (BOA, ADVNS.AHK.ŞM (5): 127/1); Daudī (BOA, ADVNS.AHK.ŞM (6): 134/1); Najjarī (BOA, ADVNS.AHK.ŞM (6): 170/1) family *waqf* administrators submitted their complaints by going to the Imperial Court.

52 Van Leeuwen, *Bir Osmanlı*, 133–54.

53 Canbakal, *17. Yüzyılda Ayıntāb*, 20.

54 See Table 17.

55 E.g. see VGMA, 814; 815.

56 Eighteen applications were made from Khasseki Sultan *Waqf* trustees during the period covered by the study. Four applications were made by the deputy trustees of the *waqf*. Among them, al-Ḥājj Khalīl, who was the former *Has Odabasi*, made three applications

the trustees of the *waqfs* were from the local people, while some of them, for example, were both truestees and inspectors of eleven *waqfs*;[57] in seven of the other twelve records, it is recorded that they applied as trustees as well as tomb keeper and inspector; in two of them, *mudarris* (scholar) and *zāwiyadār* (*shaykh* of Sufi lodge);[58] in one, tomb keeper;[59] *shaykh* and inspector[60] and *shaykh*.[61] The trustees of the *waqf*, of which many examples will be given below, mostly complained to the center about the management of *waqfs* and disputes over taxation, while the *re'āyā* of the *waqfs* also complained about the unfair taxes demanded from them. The biggest factions in Jerusalem were *waqf* staff and trustees. Being a member of the board of trustees of a *waqf* in a city meant having a say in the administration of that city.[62] These individuals, like local ruling officials, played an active role in the collection of *waqf* revenues. Thus, they were sometimes at odds with the villagers. The whole or part of a village could be part of a *waqf*, and in Jerusalem, the right to collect the revenues of the *waqf* could be granted to someone through the tax-farming procedure.

The Chief Eunuch, who was the Inspector of the *Ḥaramayn al-Sharīfayn waqfs*, frequently sent petitions. In the provisions recorded in the *Aḥkām* Registers of Mecca, Medina, and Egypt, there are numerous provisions relating to *waqfs*. For example, in a petition dated Rabīʿ al-Awwal 1163/February 1750, submitted by the Chief Eunuch Bashir Agha to the Imperial Council, he reported that the beneficiaries of the *waqfs* of Masjid al-Aqṣā, Dome of the Rock, and Ḥalīl al-Raḥmān in Jerusalem were demanding excessive salaries and creating new appointments by *ʿaskarī* and *dīwānī* certificates and *qāḍī*'s *ḥujja*. At the same time, they also demanded accounting fees from the *waqf* by obtaining a *ḥujja* from the *qāḍī* for some vacant posts.[63] Upon notification

with desire to the Imperial Council (BOA, ADVNS.AHK.ŞM (1): 191/1; 226/6; 232/2), and Abdullah, who is also the Trust of Jaffa Customs, made two applications.BOA, ADVNS.AHK.ŞM (1): 245/4; 288/1. *Sābıkan Bābu's-Sa'āde Ağaları* olan el-Hac Halil Ağa (BOA, ADVNS.AHK.ŞM (2): 184/2); Ali Ağa (BOA, ADVNS.AHK.ŞM (2): 196/1; 314/5), Mehmed Ağa (BOA, ADVNS.AHK.ŞM (2): 320/3; (BOA, ADVNS.AHK.ŞM (4): 92/1) They applied to the Imperial Council for various reasons.

57 E.g. see BOA, ADVNS.AHK.ŞM (6): 170/1; (7): 6/3; 97/3.

58 E.g. see BOA, ADVNS.AHK.ŞM (1): 155/1; (5): 96/3.

59 BOA, ADVNS.AHK.ŞM (1): 232/1.

60 BOA, ADVNS.AHK.ŞM (2): 173/4.

61 BOA, ADVNS.AHK.ŞM (5): 53/1.

62 Ergenç, "Osmanlı Klasik," 111; Canbakal, *17. Yüzyılda Ayıntāb*, 88.

63 "… Kudüs-i Şerif eyaletinde vāki' Hazreti Halilurrahman salavatullah ala nebiyyinā ve Alayh ve Mescid-i Aksā ve Sahrātulla-ı Müşerrefe Evkāfından bazı kimesneler divan ve askeri beratlarıyla ve kadı hüccetleriyle vezāif ve cirāye ve ziyāde ta'yināt ihdās idüb Haremeyn-i Şerifeyn Muhasebesi defterlerinde kaydı ve yedlerinde arz ile maliye

of the situation, it was reported that while the *qāḍīs* did not interfere with the trustees, they forbade the *waqf* officials from making new appointments, that no tax called accounting tax should be demanded from the trustees, and that the *waqfs* in question were freely disposed of in accordance with the laws and practices. It was ordered that the trustees of the *waqfs* should not be interfered with or offended in any way. This demand to protect the functioning and management order of *waqfs* shows that the supervision of *waqf* affairs in the provinces was carried out meticulously. Moreover, the fact that *waqfs*, even if they were the *Ḥaramayn*, or in some cases, the Sultan *waqf*, and even under the administration of the Chief Eunuch were not included in public affairs and was the subject of private complaints was due to the legal nature of the *waqf*. Theoretically, the state has no right of disposal over the *waqf*.[64]

Many complaints about the *waqfs* arose from the disregard of the principle of "*serbestiyet* (tax exempiton)" of the *waqfs*. When local authorities, due to taxation and security problems, intervened the *waqf* in violation of the principle of "tax exemption" and made demands on the *re'āyā* of the *waqf*, the inspector, and sometimes the trustee of the *waqf* omplained against them and asked for judgment from the sultan. For example, in 1147/1734, Sayyid Fatḥ Allāh, the *mutawallī* of Nabī Dāwūd *Zāwiya waqfs*, reported that while the taxes of *waqf's* villages Sāwiya, Majdal Yāyā, Birrāya, and Bayt Sayrāl should not be interfered with by the members of *ahl al-'urf*, they were interfered with in violation of the laws and practices. The decision of the Imperial Council on that matter was to prohibit the intervention of the *ahl al-'urf* in these *waqf* villages.[65] In this case, the *ahl al-'urf* whom the trustee of the *waqf* complained about had been reduced to the status of an oppressor, and the provision sent by the central government ordered the termination of the unjust interventions to the *waqf* in order to establish justice.

It has been observed that the problems of authority, which constitute the source of the tension between the central government and the ruling and local elites, are concentrated in the management of *waqfs*, the collection of revenues and taxes, which constitute the main subject of the complaints. The more active use of complaint mechanism by the elites of the city, who saw themselves as intermediaries between the central government and the people,

---

tarafından berevātı yoğiken kadılara istid'ā ile cirāye muhdes vezāifesiyle mütevelli-i vakfın rencide ve vakfın külli gadr eylediklerinden gayrı kadıların umur-ı vakıfda ve mütevellilerin muhasebesinde kat'a müdahaleleri yoğiken mahlūlātdan arza varub ve muhasebesini gördüm deyu mütevelli olanlar rencide ve harc-ı muhasebesi namıyle akça taleb ve gadr itmeleriyle ..." VGMA, 814: 106/1.

64 İnalcık, "Şikāyet Hakkı," 39.

65 VGMA, 814: 4.

was determined by the status, economic levels and relative distance of the complainants from the court.

1.3 *Ruling-Local Administrative Elites and the People*

The wealthy and influential local families of Jerusalem were seeking alliances with the local Ottoman elites. Dror Ze'evi mentions about the tendency of the ruling elite in seventeenth century Jerusalem, especially its second generation, to integrate into the local notables and, in parallel, for civil groups to purchase of the way that led to military groups.[66] In the eighteenth century, these tendencies were furthered by localization and reinforced by the sale of offices and the central government's approval of the successşon of offices passed down from generation to generation.

While recognize that they belong to a different group, local notables saw themselves as equal to or even higher than the ruling elite, with the exception of *sanjāq bey*, his deputy, and the *qāḍī* who was also usually appointed from Istanbul and formally included in a higher position. The records in the *sharīʿa* court registry pointed out that *qāḍī* and his court shared this view. In the long hierarchy lists of participants in special events, the local notables were at the top of the peer list. In the records, their names appear immediately after the *qāḍī* and the *sanjāq bey* or his senior representative, and before all of other high-ranking janissaries and fief holders.[67]

Although it permitted mobility from one elite to another, thorugh marriage, religious education or the purchase of titles, the demarcation line separating the two elite groups was strictly drawn. This line was partly maintained by the central government's strict monitoring and extensive files on the administrative data of Jerusalem *waqf*s. This is not limited to sultan *waqf*s, as is often the case with the Khasseki Sultan *Waqf*, whose *mutawallī*s were occasionally summoned Istanbul to inspect the files.[68] The organization of the *waqf*s of Jerusalem and the centralization of the appointments, as well as the official authority of the Jerusalem *qāḍī*, enabled the state to be desicive in all matters concerning the *waqf*s. In addition to strict bureaucratic centralisation, central control was consistently reinforced through the appointment of civil servants and officials with strong local ties.[69]

On the other hand, while the central administration allowed for interpretation between the two elites, the line between the elite and the unprivileged

66 Ze'evi, *Kudüs*, 89–90.

67 Cohen, *Osmanlı Kudüs'ünde*, 205.

68 Yediyıldız, *XVIII Yüzyılda*, 160.

69 Van Leeuwen, *Bir Osmanlı*, 175.

population was rigid and difficult to cross. Of course, there were many merchants and artisans who did not belong to the elite, but even within the elite there were those who could not cross this very clear demarcation line marked by tax exemption and other privileges. For those who did cross this line, however, the new status brought with it many advantages.[70]

As reflected in the imperial edicts and decrees, there were many instances in Jerusalem society during the period covered by the study in which "the local elites who had gained power, oppressed the ordinary people with the activities of bullying in cooperation with the military-administrative elite from time to time."[71] For example, it was ordered by edicts sent repeatedly to the governor of Damascus, the *qāḍī* of Jerusalem, and mutasallims (deputy *sanjāq* bey) of Gaza and Ramla that the barley taken from the town of Lod, one of the villages of the Khasseki Sultan *Waqf* and its villages every year by the governors of Damascus, should no longer be demanded, that the governors of Damascus and the other *ahl al-ʿurf* should not cause any difficulties to the *reʿāyā* of the *waqf* in this regard, and that the village should be built with the barley revenues from now on.[72] Upon the persistence of the problem, a later edict was sent to the governor of Damascus and the governors of the Province of Damascus and Tripoli in order to provide a solution to the problem, which was to demand the six hundred *keyl* of Ghazzawī barley that was deducted from the town of Lod from the towns in the province of Damascus and Tripoli. The issue of giving the five hundred *keyl* of barley, which was recorded to have been given to the governors of Damascus when they came to Jerusalem, to the *waqf* was also the subject of the next edict of the same date.[73] As can be seen in many examples to be given below, the indigenous people complained about the interventions of the members of *ahl al-ʿurf* who had fallen to the status of a bully. This situation can also be interpreted as the participation of the people in the administration.

The biggest concern of the *reʿāyā* with the *ahl al-ʿurf* was the collection of *waqf* revenues and tax disputes. In addition to the peasants who sometimes declared that they were poor and could not pay the *tekālīf-i şākka* (onerous exactions)[74] tax, the common complaints of the urbanites who thought that this tax was completely against the old law (*kanūn-ı ḳadīm*) and that they should

70 Ze'evi, *Kudüs*, 91–92.

71 Singer, *Kadılar, Kullar*, 166–67.

72 VGMA, 523: 11/18, 20, 22, 26.

73 VGMA, 523: 11/30, 32.

74 '*Tekālīf-i şakka*': Taxes were collected by *beylerbeys* and *sanjāq* governors under the names '*nal-baha, kaftan baha, selāmiye, devriye*' etc. These type of coercions were seen in the previous periods as well.

not pay it were the common people.[75] In some cases, it is even observed that in order to collect this tax, *mutasallim, voyvoda* and deputy *qāḍī* were in alliance. Terms such as *ashāb-ı ağraz, muzırrun-nās* are used to define these people.[76] In some provisions *waqf* employees are defined as *ashāb-ı ağraz*, while in some provisions there are people with the title of *sayyid* among these people.[77] It has been observed that the complainants used these general phrases as if to point out the cruelty and injustice done without targeting anyone. The people of Jerusalem filed complaints to the centre in order to be protected from the harassment of these people, whose identity and occupation were not clear, from the calamities that befell or might befall them. A trustee who wanted to prevent unfair interventions in *waqf* revenues and *waqf* properties or a *waqf* official who could not receive his salary from the *waqf*, or a villager who wanted to prevent excessive tax demands, often complained about *ashāb-ı ağrāz* in order to prevent unfair practices arising from confusion of authority, and in some cases to ensure themselves.[78] The fact that their complaints were predominantly related to taxes reinforces the idea that they mostly settled their individual cases with local court.

In order to legitimize their petitions, both petitioners and the officials frequently stated that the requested practice was in accordance with the precedent. For this purpose, expressions such as *te'āmül-i kadīm* (a custom or tradition that has been going on for a long time), *ḳadīmü'l-eyyām* (from the old days), *kadīmden olageldiği üzere* (as it was from the past), *mu'tād-ı kadīm üzere* (as it was customary), *kadīmīsi üzere* (as it used to be) were used.[79]

A tactic frequently used by *waqf* administrators to strengthen their claims was to mention the founder's will (*şart-ı vākıf mūcibince*). On the other hand, an arrangement that was not approved by these dignitaries was usually labelled as "contrary to the conditions set by the founder" (*mugāyir-i şart-ı vākıf*).[80] This language of approval and disapproval, used in common by central government officials and petitioners, prohibited all kinds of abuses related to *waqfs*, while officials tended to base their intervention on the will of the founder. It was also

75 See BOA, ADVNS.AHK.ŞM (3): 39/4; 110/4; 156/3.
76 BOA, ADVNS.AHK.ŞM (1): 2/2.
77 See BOA, ADVNS.AHK.ŞM (4): 32/1; (4): 35/2.
78 See BOA, ADVNS.AHK.ŞM (1): 77/1; 155/1; 232/1; (2): 163/2; 173/4; 183/4; 246/5; (3): 5/1; 38/3; 152/2; 156/1; (4): 29/4; 59/3; 125/2; (5): 9/1; 89/2.
79 See BOA, ADVNS.AHK.ŞM (1): 7/1; 37/3; 174/3; 226/6; (2): 6/3; 30/4; 31/4; 76/2; (3): 37/1; 66/3; (6): 34/1; 170/1.
80 See BOA, ADVNS.AHK.ŞM (1): 232/1; (2): 13/3; 50/1; 173/4; 222/4; (3): 41/2; 46/1; 64/3; 115/4; (4): 1/1; 29/3; 32/1; 34/1; 35/2; 70/1; 105/3; 159/2; 186/1; (5): 11/1; 34/1; 41/2; 90/2; 127/1; (6): 90/2; (7): 91/2; 99/4.

thanks to this common language that both officials and the petitioners recognized that the duty to fulfill the will of the endower belong to the Sultan.[81]

As a result, it can be said that an important heading in the unjust intervention and oppression of the *reʿāyā* was the *tekalif-i şakka* demanded by the ruling elite. Local elites, on the other hand, oppressed the people by demanding excessive revenues in the collection of *waqf* revenues. In Jerusalem, local elites as *waqf* trustees or officials complained mostly about the unjust interventions made by the *reʿāyā* in their duties. The ruling elite, on the other hand, complained most about the *reʿāyā* who did not pay *waqf* revenues or taxes. In this multidimensional and intertwined "network of relations" that develop around the *waqfs*, the reasons for the legitimacy and continuity of the Sultan's power in resolving the issues were pointed out, encouraging phrases were sent, and decrees were sent ordering the mobilisation of all measures for the establishment of justice. The responsibility for the realisation of the old practices and the will of the endower rested with the Sultan.

1.4 *Inter-communal Relations*

> "When it is known to you, the aforementioned *Mawlānā*, that I absolutely do not consent to the oppression and cruelty of the poor and other individuals in my times of happiness and prosperity, in the name of the Prophet, act and behave in accordance with the provisions of my noble imperial orders, which was issued in the past and is still honorable, and be detained and punished in the event of a contrary situation."[82]

The above statements in the ruling written in response to the petition submitted by the Greek Patriarch Antimos to the Imperial Council on Rabiʿ al-Awwal 1212/1797, stating that local and foreign clergymen, nuns, priests, etc. whom visited the Church of the Holy Sepulchre in Jerusalem could not receive the necessary attention and were treated unfairly despite paying the taxes demanded at the church gate, are meaningful in terms of reflecting the Sultan's perspective on his subjects. In the eyes of the Muslim and non-Muslim residents of Jerusalem, the Sultan, unlike his local representatives, was a

81 Faroqhi, 'Political Activity," 6–7.

82 "... eyyām-ı saʿādet-encāmımda reʿāyā fukarasına ve sāir bir ferde zulm u teʿaddī olundığına katʿa rızā-yı şāhānem olmadığı sen ki Mevlānā-yı mūmā ileyhsin maʿlūmun oldukda ber-vech-i muharrer mukaddemā ve hālā şeref-pezīr sudūr iden evāmir-i şerīfem mūciblerince ʿamel ve hareket ve hilāf-ı hālet vukūʿında tevkīʿ ve mübāʿadet olunmak bābında." BOA, ADVNS.AHK.ŞM (5): 80/3.

benevolent authority. The prosperity of Jerusalem was a symbol of power that directly affected the prestige of the Sultan as the caliph of the Islamic world. Among the Jerusalemites who did not like the decision of the *qāḍī*, who was the highest judicial authority in the Ottoman provinces, or who appealed directly to the center, thirteen records have been identified concerning *dhimmis* who were the subject of complaints by Muslim *re'āyā* for their interference in the *waqfs*. On the other hand, three Jews went to the Imperial Council and complained about the interventions made by Muslims in the *waqf* properties they owned. Almost all of the five applications made by Christians to the Imperial Council were related to the taxes levied on the Church of the Holy Sepulchre, the income of which belonged to the *Waqf* of Khasseki Sultan, or the janitor of the Church of the Holy Sepulchre appointed by the Khasseki Sultan *Waqf*. *Waqf* practices, irregularities and interventions in *waqfs* in Jerusalem during the period covered by this study will be analyzed in terms of inter-communal relations. The central government's perspective on the relations between different religious groups within *waqf* network of Jerusalem will also be evaluated in this context.

1.4.1 Intervention to Muslim *Waqfs* by the Non-Muslim *Re'āyā*

It is reflected in the provisions that some non-Muslims caused losses to the *waqf* by not paying the revenues belonging to Muslim *waqfs*. For example, in Ṣafar 1172/1758, al-Ḥājj Meḥmed, the *mutawallī* of the Khasseki Sultan *Waqf*, reported that the *dhimmīs* residing in the villages of Bethlehem and Beth Jala and the villages subject to the District of Ramla should have paid 8.5 sacks of *akçe* to the *waqf*, but they were left in their possession.[83]

Damage to the *waqf* by encroaching on the *waqf* properties for various reasons and the construction of buildings on the *waqf* lands by various people without permission are among the problems that were the subject of many provisions in the ledgers.[84] In a provision dated Shawwāl 1156/1743 written to the *qāḍī* of Jerusalem, 'Abd al-Fattāḥ, *mutawallī* of the *waqf* of 'Umar Masjid in Jerusalem, complained that some Greeks belonging to the Greek church had invaded six rooms belonging to the *waqf* and damaged the *waqf* by encroaching on the ranges of the *waqf* land. In the investigation made upon the complaint, it was reported that an order was issued on the subject in 1151/1738, and this time it was reported that the damages of the *waqf* should be compensated by referring to that order.[85] In another provision dated Dhū al-Qa'da 1173/1760,

83 BOA, ADVNS.AHK.ŞM (2): 108/3.

84 BOA, ADVNS.AHK.ŞM (1): 51/2; (2): 166/1; (3): 137/1; 147/3; (4): 62/2; (5): 20/1.

85 BOA, ADVNS.AHK.ŞM (1): 51/2.

it was recorded that a group of *dhimmīs* whose names were known around the *Waqf* of Mosque of ʿUmar and *Waqfs* of *Madrasa al-Khamra*, had built a toilet at the bottom of the wall of the Waqf and caused the wall to rot and collapse. It was decided to take necessary action to prevent this situation, which was reported by the *mutawallī* of the *waqf*, Sayyid Muṣṭafā al-ʿAlamī from the *sādāt* (descendants of the Prophet).[86]

In another example, dated Rajab 1195/1781, the tombkeeper of the Tomb of Shaykh Meḥmed near the Tomb of Prophet Dāwūd, Shaykh Esʿad ʿAlī ibn Saʿīd ʿĀrif, reported that the revenues of a land in Jerusalem 50 *zirāʿ* in length and 30 *zirāʿ* in width were given to the tombkeeper of the said tomb and that non-Muslims from the people of Jerusalem were bullying and persecuting him by throwing away the toilet drain and garbage on the plot.[87] Similarly, in a provision dated Ṣafar 1197/1783, the *mutawallī* of the *Waqf* of Karkashandi Mosque in Dayr al-ʿAmūd neighborhood in Jerusalem reported that the local Franks caused the mosque to be ruined by throwing their garbage around the mosque.[88]

In some cases, non-Muslim subjects seized land belonging to Muslim *waqfs* contrary to the laws and practices. For example, the owner of the partial trusteeship and supervision of *Manjikiyya Madrasa Waqf* in Jerusalem with the certificate of *shaykh al-Islām*, Shaykh Yūsuf ibn Shaykh Muṣṭafā, came and reported that the olive garden in the neighborhood called Ḥaḍrat Khiḍr, which was registered in the *waqfiyya*, was seized by a *dhimmī* named Avirko in the region and that he was bullying to rent it to someone else equivalent of its rent.[89]

In another provision dated Rabīʿ al-Awwal 1208/1793, Shaykh ʿAbd al-Qādir ibn Shaykh Meḥmed al-ʿAlamī, the *mutawallī* of the *Muẓhariyya Waqf* of Jerusalem, reported that a *dhimmī* from the Efrenc community, one of the residents of Jerusalem, had interfered with the *waqf*'s inn called Efrenc inn.[90] An examination of the Accounting Books of Anatolia in the Imperial Treasury section reveals another dimension of the issue. Namely, it was understood that the trusteeship and inspection of the *waqf* was held by Shaykh ʿInāyat Allāh with a daily salary of 4 *akçe*, but upon the withdrawal of this person, it was assigned to Shaykh ʿAbd al-Qādir ibn Shaykh Meḥmed al-ʿAlamī by a petition of the *qāḍī* of Jerusalem on an earlier date. It was ruled that the request of the current

86 BOA, ADVNS.AHK.ŞM (2): 166/1.
87 BOA, ADVNS.AHK.ŞM (3): 64/3.
88 BOA, ADVNS.AHK.ŞM (3): 121/3.
89 BOA, ADVNS.AHK.ŞM (4): 62/2.
90 BOA, ADVNS.AHK.ŞM (5): 20/1.

mutawallī of the *waqf*, who reported the situation, should be resolved on the spot in accordance with the law. In the decree dated Rabīʿ al-Thānī 1181/1767, which was submitted to Jerusalem, it was stated that the *waqf* inspector was instructed to take the properties of the *Waqf* of Dome of the Rock, such as mills, ovens, vegetable gardens, and baths near the monastery of the Armenian community, back which were seized by non-Muslim communities.[91]

It is also reflected in the provisions that non-Muslims damaged the *waqf*s and the places belonging to the *waqf*s with the structures they built in the *waqf* ranges under their control. In Ramaḍān 1197/1783, Shaykh ʿAbdullāh al-Maghribī, *mutawallī* of the *Waqf* of Abū Madyan al-Ghawth located in Jerusalem's Maghāriba neighborhood, reported that some *dhimmī*s whose names were known constructed unnecessary buildings on the lands rented by the *Waqf* every year from the *Waqf* property without permission and acted to damage the *Waqf*.[92]

In the provisions, it was also recorded that non-Muslims who rented *waqf* properties did not pay the rents they were supposed to pay to the *waqf*. On Jumādā al-Thānī 1197/1783, the named non-Muslims did not pay their annual rents of 75 piasters each for the vineyards, gardens, and plots of land in the village of ʿAyn Kārim, one of the properties of the *Waqf* of Abū Madyan al-Ghawth since 1190/1776, and thus, they embezzled them and caused the *waqf* to incur losses.[93] In a provision registered on Shawwāl 1206/1792, Süleymān Khalīfa, *mutawallī* of the *Waqf* of Dome of the Rock, reported that a *dhimmī* named Abraham walad al-Abraham, who rented three gardens from the property of the *Waqf* with the method of *ijāratayn*, did not pay the rent of 586 *kurūsh* for the year 1200/1785 to the *Waqf* in his lifetime, and upon his death without children, a resident of Jerusalem collected the aforementioned *Waqf* income from the estate of the deceased, also did not pay, and seized the *Waqf* gardens and caused losses to the *Waqf*.[94] On the same date, the *mutawallī* of the *Sādāt al-Maghāriba* Abū Hurayra *Waqf* reported that the registered *dhimmī* tenants of the vineyard, garden, and land in the village of ʿAyn Kārim in Jerusalem had not paid the annual rent of 75 *kurūsh* since the year 1190/1776.[95]

---

91 "Musakkafâtından Kudüs-i Şerîf derūnunda Ermeni tāifesinin Manastırı kurbunda tāhūneler, furun ve hakūre ve hamam-z'zeheb ber takrīb tāife-i mesfūrlar zabt itmeleriyle taraf-ı vakfdan zabtiçün inspector arzıyla emr virilmişdir. 17 Rebiu'l-ahir 1181." VGMA, 763: 489/30.

92 BOA, ADVNS.AHK.ŞM (3): 147/3.

93 BOA, ADVNS.AHK.ŞM (3): 137/1.

94 BOA, ADVNS.AHK.ŞM (4): 163/1.

95 BOA, ADVNS.AHK.ŞM (4): 163/2.

When the provisions recorded in the Imperial Council were consulted, it was ruled that an order was issued in 1197/1783 for the payment of the rents, and upon the non-payment of the rents, it was ruled that the matter was resolved in accordance with the law by referring to the order issued again. On Dhū al-Qaʿda 1208/1794, the *mutawallī* of the *Waqf* of the Dome of the Rock was informed that the house of the *Waqf* in Jerusalem had been seized by a Jew named Abraham Ara'il for several years and that he had been bullying them when the rent was demanded.[96]

It was also decided by many provisions that due to inappropriate behavior of non-Muslims in Muslim holy places and around *waqfs*.[97] A provision written to the Jerusalem *Qāḍī* relates to this issue. In this provision, it is mentioned that some Jews drank wine and engaged in inappropriate acts around the tomb where the mother of Joseph was buried and that this should be prevented.[98] In another example, a petition was submitted by the Jerusalemite Muslims to Istanbul in which it was stated that *dhimmis* mentioned by name have kept entering the masjid in the Mount of Olives named Masjid al-Asʿad[99] although they were repeatedly warned not to enter and kept entering by force and harassed the Muslims contrary to law and practices.[100]

The continuity of the *waqf* system, which was of great importance in terms of establishing social peace and unity in Islamic states and which provided the most valuable examples within the Ottoman Empire, was made possible with the establishment of financial resources for these *waqfs*. The non-Muslim *reʿāyā* living in the towns and lands allocated to the *Waqfs* were held responsible for fulfilling their obligations. The fact that, for various reasons, the non-Muslim *reʿāyā* left their old towns and migrated to other places caused losses to the *waqfs* to which they were attached. The provisions identified on the subject belong to the villages of the Khasseki Sultan *Waqf*, and the first one is dated Muḥarram 1170/1756. Since some of the *dhimmīs* in Bethlehem and Beth Jala, villages of Khasseki Sultan *Waqf*, left their homes and settled in other

96 BOA, ADVNS.AHK.ŞM (5): 16/1.

97 BOA, ADVNS.AHK.ŞM (1): 41/3; (3): 64/3; (4): 152/5.

98 BOA, ADVNS.AHK.ŞM (4): 152/5.

99 It is considered that the mosque belonged to the *waqf* variously recorded in the *Hurūfāt* registers as *Zāwiya Qādiriyya* (so-called), *Zāwiya Esʿād Bey Waqf* in Tūr-i Sīnā, *Shaykh al-Islām Esʿād Efendi, Esʿād Efendi, Esʿādiyya, Qādiriyya* and *Zāwiya Qādiriyya*. From these records, it is understood that the mosque was built by *Shaykh al-Islām Esʿād Efendi* and was named after him.

100 BOA, ADVNS.AHK.ŞM (1): 41/ 3.

places in Jerusalem, causing great losses to the Waqf, it was adjudicated that these *dhimmī*s should be returned to their original homes by officers.[101]

In a record dated Jumādā al-Awwal 1208/1793, the then trustee of the Khasseki Sultan *Waqf* at that time, Ḥāfiẓ Aḥmad of Rhodes, reported that some of the Muslim and non-Muslim subjects from the *Waqf*'s villages belonging to the Khasseki Sultan *Waqf* had left their old towns and migrated to other places. If they were not registered in *ʿawāriḍ* households in the places where they went, they were ordered to return to their old towns with the help of the *zābiṭ*s, and if they were registered, they were ordered to pay *ispenç* (animal tax) taxes to the *ẓābit*s of the village where they were registered.[102]

In some situations, Muslims and non-Muslims allied to cause losses to the *waqf* revenues. In the first record dated Dhū al-Ḥijja 1170/1757, Khasseki Sultan *waqf mutawallī* al-Ḥājj Maḥmūd reported that Muslims named Muṣṭafā Ece, Mūsā Hindī, Mūsā Birgil, and non-Muslims named Mīkhāʾīl, Maḥrūda, and Khalīl Marāghim, who were foreigners, provoked the people and prevented them from paying the taxes.[103]

1.4.2 Interventions by Muslim *Reʿāyā* against Non-Muslims

In a provision dated Jumādā al-Thānī 1156/1743, it was recorded that although some of the Jews – recorded with their names – had paid the fees of *ijāratayn* taxes to the related *waqf*s, the *mutawallī*s of the Dome of the Rock and Khātūniyya *waqf*s in Jerusalem had bullied them by demanding some extra taxes. The provision decided that the issue should be resolved on the spot and that interventions made by the *mutawallī*s which were contrary to the deeds would be prevented.[104] In a record on Rabīʿ al-Awwal 1212/1797, a *dhimmī* named Khāniya had built a house on a *waqf* land with the permission of the *mutawallī* in 1200/1785 in order to pay the *muqāṭaʿa*s of the *waqf* year to year. Upon the death of Khāniya, the *mutawallī* of the *waqf* confiscated the house. Khāniya's son's application to take the house in question, which he inherited from his father, into his own name, was ruled to be evaluated on the spot in accordance with the law.[105]

The second group that oppressed non-Muslim *reʿāyā* by being a vigilante was the *ahl al-ʿurf* elites. On Shawwāl 1164/1751, the deputy *mutawallī* of Jerusalem's *Waqf* of Khasseki Sultan and Amīn of Jaffa, ʿAbdullāh, sent a petition stating

101 BOA, ADVNS.AHK.ŞM (2): 56/2.
102 BOA, ADVNS.AHK.ŞM (5): 5/1.
103 BOA, ADVNS.AHK.ŞM (2): 76/3.
104 BOA, ADVNS.AHK.ŞM (1): 43/1.
105 BOA, ADVNS.AHK.ŞM (5): 79/1.

that the Greek and Armenian groups, who were on their way to visit the Holy Sepulchre Church in Jerusalem, which was among the revenues of the *waqf*, were passing through the places mentioned on the way in Anatolia, and that the *ahl al-ʿurf* leaders[106] there were unfairly demanding taxes and preventing them from traveling to Jerusalem. They demanded that the Christian pilgrims be put on a ship to reach Jerusalem safely, preventing them from being harmed and enabling them to fulfill their pilgrimage. In the investigation made upon the request received by Imperial Council, it was ruled that the Armenian community should not be persecuted and their property should not be seized on the road in 1146/1733, and similarly, this time, it was ruled to prohibit the activities of these economic usurpers, which were carried out in violation of laws and practices.[107]

A similar complaint regarding the unfair fees demanded from the Greek and Armenian people coming to Holy Sepulchre was reported by the Greek Patriarch Bartalos in Muharram 1169/1755.[108] In the ruling sent on Rabīʿ al-Awwal 1177/1763, it was reported that the unjust practices of the *ahl al-ʿurf* leaders continued, that they collected unfair revenues from the Greek and Armenian groups who came to the Holy Sepulchre, and that the pier masters on the way also committed cruelty in unison with the ship captains. The orders sent in 1146/1733 and 1164/1750 were pointed out, and it was ruled that the interventions of the customary people should be prevented. In a later ruling dated Rabīʿ al-Awwal 1212/1797, Antimos, the Greek Patriarch of Jerusalem, petitioned that local and foreign clergymen, nuns, priests, etc., who visited the Holy Sepulchre Church in Jerusalem could not receive the necessary attention despite paying the taxes demanded at the church gate and that they suffered injustice.[109]

The janitorial service of the Holy Sepulchre Church also caused some disputes that were reflected in the rulings. In the period covered by this study,

---

106 In the decree dated Shawwāl 1164, the *ahl al-ʿurf* contingent responsible for the safety of non-Muslim *reʿāyā* traveling to Jerusalem is described as follows: "... *Anadolu vâlisi vezîre ve Erzurum vâlisi vezîre ve Diyârbekir vâlisi vezîre ve Sivâs vâlisi vezîre ve Maraş beğlerbeğisi* [ ] *Paşa'ya ve Amed ve Erzurum kadılarına ve Sivâs ve Adana kadıları ve Kütahya ve Konya ve Maraş nâ'iblerine ve zikr olunan eyâletlerden Kudüs-i Şerîfe varup gelince yol üzerlerinde vâkıʿ sâir küzât ve nüvvâb -zîde fazlühüm- ve mütesellimler ve yeniçeri serdârları ve kethüdâ yerleri ve Adana'da Şark-pâre ağası* [...] *ve Ayntâb kâ'im-makâmı* [...] *ve sâir zâbıtân ve aʿyân ve* [...] *ve iş erlerine* [...]". See BOA, ADVNS.AHK.ŞM (1): 245/4.

107 BOA, ADVNS.AHK.ŞM (1): 252/2.

108 BOA, ADVNS.AHK.ŞM (2): 30/4.

109 BOA, ADVNS.AHK.ŞM (5): 80/3.

in order to prevent disputes between the church families, the janitor of the church was undertaken by officials from the Khasseki Sultan *Waqf*. In the three provisions recorded on the subject, those who interfered with the *waqf* officials who duly fulfilled their duties without a certificate of authorization were seized as partners (*'ale'l-iştirāk*).[110] In the decree dated Jumādā al-Thānī 1212/1797, it was reported that people other than the people appointed as janitors at the gate of the Holy Sepulchre Church entered the church and harassed the church visitors and oppressed them in various ways such as taking their candles from their hands and beating their belongings. Accordingly, it was ruled that people other than the gatekeepers at the Holy Sepulchre gate were prohibited from entering the church and interfering with the visitors.[111]

From time to time, non-Muslim *re'āyā* were also interfered with by Muslim *re'āyā*. In a ruling dated Shawwāl 1197/1783 recorded in the Damascus *Aḥkām* on daily life, a person who was the representative of the Jewish community applied to the Imperial Council with an *i'lām* (court decision) and stated that the Jewish community could grind their flour in any mill they wished with *sharī'a* permission, but some people opposed this situation and bullied them to grind only in a certain mill. In the decree sent to the *qāḍī* and trustee of Jerusalem, it was reported that the mentioned mill and its revenues belonged to a *waqf* and that an imperial decree was written to prevent the interventions made to the mill without a deed, unless there was a deed for the Jews to grind their flour there.[112]

1.4.3 Relations between the Non-Muslim *Re'āyā*

In the applications made by Christians to the Imperial Council, Istanbul was informed about the changes to be made in the use of religious places and the necessary permission was requested. In the petition submitted by the Greek Patriarch Bermenebas on Ṣafar 1169/1755 regarding the Holy Sepulchre Church, the revenues of which were delivered to the Khasseki Sultan *Waqf* officials, the *imāret* and *rikābiyya* income to the *mutawallī* of Khasseki Sultan *Waqf*, the Greek Patriarch Bermenebas stated that the building of the Anastasis Church (tomb) was old and the Efrenc community wanted to renovate the tomb with stones brought from their own country contrary to the practices and that they wanted to take the old stones back to their own country and that this situation

110 BOA, ADVNS.AHK.ŞM (4): 135/2; (5): 19/1; (6): 34/1.

111 BOA, ADVNS.AHK.ŞM (5): 86/1.

112 BOA, ADVNS.AHK.ŞM (3): 153/1.

had been previously reported by the Governor of Jaffa and the *mutawallī* of the *waqf*.[113]

It is recorded that in the decree dated 1155 AH/1742 CE on the subject, the Efrenc community was ordered not to construct buildings in the Holy Sepulchre Church and to keep the stones of the tomb in Jaffa and not to take them to their hometowns, contrary to the practices, but he requested that the decree be renewed due to the change of the sultan. The *Qāḍī* of Jerusalem also declared in 1152/1739 that there was no dispute between the Frank, Greek, and Armenian communities, that they agreed to visit the places they visited according to the old practices, and that the communities should not interfere in each other's areas. This provision also provides information on the background of the request of the Efrenc. The two cellars near the garden of the Efrenc priests in Jerusalem, where they kept their crops, and the two rooms where the visitors from France stayed were dilapidated, and they had been discovered by the *qāḍī* two years ago and repaired in accordance with the judgment, but it was ordered that this privilege granted to the French State should not be an example for other states. In fact, with the decree sent in 1154/1741, it was ruled that no further repairs of this kind would be permitted even to the French side, but in 1155/1742, the Efrenc community rebuilt the tomb of Jesus. The request of the Efrenc community to rebuild the tomb of Jesus and to keep the old stones in Jaffa and then take them back to their homeland was referred to the previous orders, and it was stated that no repair and maintenance would be allowed without an order of the governor, a mandate of the trustee, and a certificate of survey.

In November 1810 (Dhū al-Qaʿda 1225), Butros, son of Yaqub, wrote a letter to Istanbul stating that Seyhun, Nofu Malkor, and Yaqub, who owned the houses in the Maronite Quarter that had been inherited from his father, had improperly occupied eight of these houses and demanded the removal of this occupation. The order from Istanbul to the *Qāḍī* of Jerusalem stated that the houses should be given to their rightful owners after the necessary investigations were carried out.[114] In 1822, the houses of Jews named Asak, Fuad and Ravibid were illegally seized and an investigation was requested.[115] In another petition written to Istanbul, Basık, son of Rafael, reported that his house in the Jewish neighborhood in the castle in Jerusalem was in need of repair and he had it repaired without harming anyone, but some people interfered with it and asked for the unnecessary interventions to be stopped. Thereupon, an

113 BOA, ADVNS.AHK.ŞM (2): 31/4.

114 BOA, ADVNS.AHK.ŞM (6): 117/4.

115 BOA, ADVNS.AHK.ŞM (7): 80/4.

order was sent to the *Qāḍī* of Jerusalem to initiate the necessary investigation, to investigate what kind of house the repaired house was and what was the reason for the interference.[116]

In conclusion, this part of the study has attempted to evaluate the extent to which complaints, which were used to prevent injustice in order to establish justice in the Ottoman Empire, were an important tool in terms of strengthening the Sultan's legitimacy in the eyes of the people in terms of *waqf* practices. Approaching the issue from a different angle, this study analyzes the "network of social relations" through that lens. In this way, it is seen that the Sultan created an opportunity to prevent and correct injustices among his subjects and the abuse of authority by those who represented him. By engaging in direct communication with the people who applied to the *Imperial Council* as a place to seek their rights, the Sultan reinforced his image as a benevolent authority who, unlike his local representatives, ruled with justice in the eyes of his subjects. On the other hand, the petitions analyzed here show that there were tensions between various segments of society over *waqf* issues for various reasons.

2 Interventions in *Waqfs*

Interventions in *waqfs* by various segments of society are quite common in the applications made to the Imperial Council. In this part of the study, these interventions will be analyzed in terms of the local actors who intervened. Abuses against *waqfs* and their justifications will be evaluated through case studies. The measures taken by the central government to prevent or prohibit these abuses will also be questioned in terms of the effectiveness of the central government in the provincial apparatus. In the Ottomans, the justice and complaint system was administered by the bureaucracy. The Ottoman bureaucracy was also subject to established rules and customs.[117] In this section, in addition to the *aḥkāms* of the period that falls within the field of study, a large number of documents on the subject in registers and edicts are also included.

2.1 *Interventions in* Waqfs *by the Ruling Elite*

During the period covered by this study, various interventions were made to *waqfs* by members of the ruling elite, primarily *mutawallīs*, other *waqf* officials, *tīmār* holders, and members of the *ahl al-ʿurf*. These interventions, which

116 BOA, ADVNS.AHK.ŞM (7): 84/1.

117 Inalcık, "Complaint Right," 38–39.

developed around conflicts of authority, often disrupted the functioning of the *waqfs* and caused them to suffer financial losses.

2.1.1 Disputes between *Mutawallīs*

There were disagreements among the *mutawallīs* of *waqfs*, most of whom belonged to prominent Jerusalem families, which we consider as part of the "ruling elite" of Jerusalem. In the first instance, the dispute stemmed from the fact that one person was the *mutawallī* of more than one *waqf*. Namely, Khalīl Abū al-Wafā al-Dajjānī, Abū al-Mawāhib, Abū al-Hudā Ṣāliḥ Meḥmed al-Imām, and Bahā' al-Dīn 'Abdullatīf disagreed over the trusteeship and supervision of the Sharāf al-Dīn al-Ḥaqqārī *Waqf* and the trusteeships of the Lefte Village Masjid *Waqf*, the Shaykh Aḥmad *Waqf*, and the Shaykh 'Alī al-Ḥaqqārī *Waqf*. The dispute was referred to the court, and as a result, Abū al-Hudā Ṣāliḥ Meḥmed al-Imām was appointed as the *mutawallī* of the 'Ammār *Waqf*; Khalīl Abū al-Wafā was appointed as the *mutawallī* of the Lefte Village *Waqf*; and Shaykh Bahā' al-Dīn was appointed as the trustee of the Shaykh Aḥmad *Waqf* (Abū Dīs and Ṭūr Villages).[118]

In another registry record, when the trusteeship of the Bereket Khan *Waqf* became vacant from Shaykh Mūsā, Shaykh Tājuddīn intervened in the trusteeship by causing difficulties. However, the records of the Ottoman central administration recorded that the position was entrusted to 'Abdurraḥmān, the brother of the current trustee.[119] In this case, it was the records kept at the center that were decisive. Namely, as mentioned earlier, the appointment of a deceased trustee's son, or in his absence, a relative, or in his absence, the appointment of a person deemed appropriate by the *qāḍī*, is a procedure reflected in many records. Consequently, disputes between the administrators of the *waqfs* were resolved by examining the records in Istanbul upon notification of the issues and drafting rulings in line with the analyzed records.

In some cases, a *mutawallī* of a *waqf* interfered with the revenues of another *waqf* by claiming that the assets belonging to the *waqf* were the assets of the *waqf* under his administration. For example, Chief Eunuch al-Ḥājj Bashīr Agha, inspector of *Ḥaramayn Waqfs*, sent a letter to the Imperial Council in which he presented eighteen *qīrāṭ* land shares in the village named Berikun in the district of Jerusalem, which were endowed to the mosques of Masjid al-Aqṣā and Dome of the Rock for the maintenance of the waterways built by Sultan Suleiman Khan, and the shares of Tamīm al-Dārī *Waqf*. The fields of six *qīrāṭ* land shares from the al-Dārī *Waqf* have been dilapidated and empty for

118 JS 209: 7.

119 JS 214: 115.

several years, and the *waqf* lands called Maʿrisāt al-Sabīl and Umm Selhune, whose income and taxes belong to the *Waqf* of Qanāt al-Sabīl, have been used for fifteen years by people named ʿAbdurraḥmān and Tājuddīn, the sons of Abū al-Suʿūd, and Muḥammad, the son of Hindī, one of the leading families of Jerusalem, in violation of the condition of the *waqfiyya*.

It was recorded that they unnecessarily appropriated the land within the borders of the said Berikun village by claiming that it was from the *Waqf* of the Masjid in Bethlehem, of which they were the trustees. It was reported that they caused the Sultan Suleiman *Waqf* to be canceled because they caused difficulties and did not pay for the waterways. In the ruling sent to the *Qāḍī* of Jerusalem upon the aforementioned petition dated 1166/1752, it was ordered that the trustee of the Sultan Suleiman *Waqf* should seize the 18-*qīrāṭ* share of the village named Berikun and 6 *qīrāṭ* shares of Tamīm ad-Dārī *Waqf* and the revenues of the mentioned lands should be seized by the *mutawallī* of the Sultan Suleiman *waqf* and should be used for the repair and maintenance of the waterways.[120] In a similar example, in 1212/1797, it was reported that six *kitʿa* gardens belonging to the Zulḳādiriya *Madrasa Waqf* in Jerusalem were seized by the trustees of the Salāḥiyya *Madrasa*s, and an inn, six shops, and the shops and inn of the foundation in the Marʿaş neighborhood of Aleppo were seized by some people from the economic elite.[121]

In addition, *waqf* administrators intervened with the property of other *waqf*s that bordered their *waqf*s, causing them to incur losses. For example, in a registry record dated 1133/1721, Khalil Ahmad al-Dajjānī, one of the prominent families of Jerusalem and the trustee and inspector of al-Sayf al-Dīn al-Haqqārī

---

120 "… Kudüs-i Şerif kazasına tābi Berikun nām karyenin on sekiz kırat hissesi vakf-ı rāh-ı āb ve altı kırat hissesi vakf-ı Temimü'd-dārī el-Ensāri Vakfı'ndan olduğu derkenar olub defterhāne-i ʿāmire derkenarı mūcibince karyeteyn-i mezbūreteyn arāzisinden hāsıl olan mahsūlāt Sultan-ı müşārunileyhin vakfı mütevellisi tarafından zabt ve şart-ı vākıf üzere suyolları masārıfına sarf ve mezburānın sinīn-i māziyeden beru zimmetlerinde güzeşte mahsulāt dahi vakıf içün tahsil ve rāh-ı āb mütevellisine teslim ettirilmek bābında bundan akdem emr-i ālişān sādır olmuşiken birkaç seneden beru zikr olunan suyollarına kurā-i mezbūre hisseleri ve arāzi-i mezkūre mahsulātı sarf olunmadığından vakf-ı mezbūr suyolları günden güne harab ve mā-i mezkūreye İbādullahın kemal üzere eşedd-i ihtiyacları olduğunu hālā Kudüs-i Şerif kadısı efendi arz ve i'lām ve ahāli-i Kudüs-i Şerif muhzır-ı birle inhā ve istirhām etmeleri kazā-i mezbūre tabi Berikun nām karyenin on sekiz kırat hissesi ve altı kırat hissesi dahi vakf-ı temimü'd-dāri el-Ensāri defterhāne-i āmire derkenarı mucibince karyeteyni mezbūreteyn arāzisinden hāsıl olan mahsulāt Sultan-ı müşārunileyhin vakfı mütevellisi tarafından zabt ve şart-ı vākıf üzere su yolları masārıfına sarf ve ḳadimi ve ola geldüğü vecih üzere ta'mir ve termīme ve tathīre muhtac olan mahalleri gereği gibi ta'mir ve tathir olub …" VGMA, 814: 130. For a similar decree on the same topic: VGMA, 323: 303.

121 BOA, ADVNS.AHK.ŞM (5): 96/3.

Waqf, came to the *Shari'a* court and reported that half of the revenues of Lefte Village belonged to al-Sayf al-Dīn al-Haqqārī *Waqf* and half to Sahratullah *Waqf*, but the trustee of Sahratullah *Waqf* took more than his share and caused losses to al-Sayf al-Dīn al-Haqqārī *Waqf*. The deputy judge ruled that the trustee of Sahratullah *Waqf* should be prohibited from taking this excess.[122]

Sometimes the damages caused to the *waqf* by the former trustee were complained to the Imperial Council by the new trustee. Thus, in a ruling sent in 1156/1743, 'Abdulfattāḥ, who was the trustee of the Masjid al-Sharīf *Waqf* of Ḥaḍrat 'Umar al-Khaṭṭāb in Jerusalem in accordance with the conditions of the *waqfiyya*, submitted a petition to the Imperial Council and reported that the former trustee of the *waqf* did not maintain the repairs of the *waqf* and left the masjid in need of repair in a dilapidated state in order to earn more income. It was also noted that he had caused losses to the *waqf* by illegally selling some of the land belonging to the *waqf* to other people.[123]

Irregularities in *istibdāl*, *khuluww al-shar'ī*, and other long-term leases were indicative of this situation. In a way, it was used as a means of irregularity. In addition to the misuse of *waqf* property, this example also shows that *waqf* administrators neglected parts of the *waqf* in need of repair and maintenance.[124] In another petition sent on 1173/1760, Sayyid Mūsā, one of the residents of Salḥāne neighborhood in Jerusalem, came to the Imperial Council and asked for the problem to be solved because the wall of the school next to the residence he owned was about to collapse and the trustees of the school, Yūsuf and Raḥmān, were not willing to repair it..[125]

In another example, the trustees of the Sahratullah and Ḥalīl al-Raḥmān *Waqfs* reported that the poor people were persecuted and oppressed when they demanded the wages and daily sustenance of the *waqf* employees, while they were supposed to be paid their salaries and distributed bread and soups as was the custom. In the decree sent in response to this, it was ruled that the

122 JS 212: 331.

123 "... Kudüs-i Şerīfde vākı' Hazret-i Ömer el-Hattāb -radıyallāhu te'ālā anhu- Hazretleri'nin mescid-i şerīfi ile mescid-i evkāflarının meşrūtiyet üzre mütevellīsi olan Abdülfettāh nām kimesne Südde-i Sa'ādetim'e arz-ı hāl idüp sābıka evkaf-ı mezbūrun mütevellīsi olan [ ] nām kimesne tama'-ı hāmından nāşī mescidleri harāb ve vakf-ı mezbūrun ba'zı arsasın hilāf-ı şer'le vākıf ve mugāyir-i vakfa ve fetvā-yı şer'le [ ] ve [ ] ve [ ] nām kimesnelere bey' idüp mesācid-i vakfa gadr olmağla mesācid vakfının tahrīr ve ma'rifet-i şer'le keşf ve der-i devlet-medāra arz ve i'lām olunmak içün ..." BOA, ADVNS.AHK.ŞM (1): 49/2.

124 al-Madanī, *Awqāf al-Quds*, 77.

125 BOA, ADVNS.AHK.ŞM (2): 154/2.

wages of the *waqf* officials should be paid in accordance with their certificates and the soups should be cooked and distributed as was the custom.[126]

2.1.2 Interventions by *Waqf* Officials

In addition to the trustees, some other *waqf* officials other than the trustees, who are also considered as part of the "ruling elite," also intervened in the management of the *waqfs*. Edicts were also sent to the trustees to prevent interventions by *waqf* officials. In a decree dated Dhū al-Ḥijja 1171/1757 regarding the trusteeship of Sahratullah *Waqf*, the trustee was ordered not to be harassed by the *waqf* officials after paying the wages of the *waqf* officials. In another decree dated 1181/1767, it was reported that the trusteeship was granted to Sayyid Süleymān for the year one hundred and five and that the order of freedom was given with the supply of the inspector to prevent the intervention of the previous trustees. In a third decree dated 1189/1775, a decree was written to prevent the interventions of the *waqf* officials, who claimed that the wages of the *waqf* officials were not made in accordance with the Receb Pasha order, against the interventions they would make to the trustee upon their request to make the accounting of the *waqf* together.[127]

In another ruling dated 1173/1760, Sayyid Muṣṭafā ibn Abū al-Faḍl al-ʿAlamī, the trustee of the Ḥamra *Madrasa Waqf* in Jerusalem, reported that he had obtained the necessary permission from the *Qāḍī* of Jerusalem and paid the money needed for the repair from his own property in 1170/1756, as some parts of the *waqf* had fallen into ruin over time and needed repair. The trustee, who wanted to take the money he spent for the repair of the *waqf* from the revenues of the *waqf*, was interfered with and prevented by some people from *waqf* officers, *ashāb-i aghrāḍ*, and the trustee requested that this intervention, which was contrary to the *fatwa* issued by the *shaykh al-Islām*, be prevented.[128] The fact that Sayyid Muṣṭafā ibn Abū al-Faḍl al-ʿAlamī, a member of the al-ʿAlamī family, one of the leading *ʿulamāʾ* families of Jerusalem, personally came and strengthened his hand in the decision by obtaining the *fatwa* of the *shaykh al-Islām* is important in terms of showing that the relations between the *ʿulamāʾ* and Istanbul were strong.

There are also records indicating that *waqf* administrators intervened against *waqf* officials who caused losses to *waqfs* in various ways, such as renting out the properties of the *waqfs* improperly or embezzling them. For example, in 1143/1730, Mustafa İbrahim Çelebi, the clerk of the Khasseki Sultan

---

126 BOA, ADVNS.AHK.ŞM (1): 174/3.
127 VGMA, 763: 488/4; 489/27; 490/50.
128 BOA, ADVNS.AHK.ŞM (2): 163/2.

Waqf, was sued for renting out a house from the Turgut Paşa *Waqf* to Jews. Due to the loss incurred by the Turgut Pasha *Waqf*, the deputy judge canceled this lease.[129]

In another registry record dated 1116/1704, Shaykh ʿAbd al-Qādir, one of the Maghribīs, the trustee of the Abū Madyan al-Ghawth *Waqf*, was accused of stealing the property of the Maghribī Shaykh ʿAbd al-Qādir *Waqf*.[130] In another register dated 1127/1715, ʿAbdurraḥmān Abū al-Suʿūd Efendi al-Dāwūdī of the Dāwūdī family, the chief trustee of the *Waqf*s of Jerusalem, Ramla, Nablus, Majdal, and Jenin, was alleged to have caused losses to the *waqf* by embezzling the property of the *waqf* by some trustees. The chief minister, who was present before the Jerusalem Court, was informed that the accounts of the *waqf* had been submitted by the trustees in question to be checked.[131]

As can be seen in the examples given above, *waqf* officials, particularly the *mutawallī*s, who were among the "ruling subjects" of Jerusalem, caused the *waqf*s to be dilapidated and incur losses in various ways, such as embezzling *waqf* properties, renting them out improperly, interfering with the assets of other *waqf*s, or failing to carry out the repairs and maintenance that the *waqf*s needed. In some cases, *waqf* administrators who failed to pay the wages of *waqf* officials victimized them.

2.1.3 Interventions by the *Sipahi*s (Fief Holders)

It is observed that the *sipahīs* were not content with collecting the *dīwānī* (traditional taxes) shares at their disposal and also collected the revenues of the *waqf*. Disputes that turned into jurisdictional conflicts over *waqf*-fief areas are frequently mentioned in the records. For example, the *sipahīs* Jaʿfar ibn ʿAql and Khalīl claimed that the land called *Kapu Uçurumu*, which was operated by the trustees of the Nabī Ishmawil *Waqf*, Feyẓullāh al-ʿAlamī and ʿAbdulbāqī al-ʿAlamī, on a fief basis, was unjustly seized. These trustees, on the other hand, claimed that the land in question had been *waqf* land for 200 years. As a result of the investigation of the trustees' claims, which were supported by the *fellāḥīn* (rural residents), it was decided that the land in question was in the possession of the fief owners and that the unjust interventions of the trustees of the *waqf* should be abandoned.[132]

The *mutawallī* of the *Waqf*s of Masjid al-Aqṣā and Dome of the Rock reported that the *waqf* revenues of the village of ʿAyn Sinyā, whose revenues were among

129 JS 225: 6.
130 JS 202: 276.
131 JS 209: 109.
132 JS 210: 101.

the incomes of prayers and scribes of the two mosques, were intervened into by ʿAyn Sinyā *zeʿāmet* holders, namely Ṣāliḥ Bey, Muṣṭafā Bey, and Meḥmet Bey ibn ʿOsmān.[133] The *zeʿāmet* (fief) owner Murād Agha ibn Meḥmed applied to Jerusalem's *Sharīʿa* Court in 1193/1779 and claimed that the 23 *qīrāṭ* of the revenues of the Upper and Lower Tab Village belonged to the Shaykh Jarrah *Waqf* and some other parts belonged to the Muḥarramiya *Madrasa Waqf*. The defendant claimed that the revenues of both villages belonged to the owners of the fief. The plaintiffs, on the other hand, stated that the two villages were *waqf* and that only the *ʿushr* was paid to the fief holders as tax in accordance with the decree, but that the tax on summer and winter olives was also among the revenues of the *waqf*. In the *sharīʿa* court, it was decided that only the *ʿushr* of the *waqf* village should be paid to the *sipahīs* and that the *zeʿāmet* (fief) owner should not interfere with the *waqf*.[134]

The authorities repeatedly issued instructions for the owners of *tīmārs* and *zeʿāmets* (fiefs) not to interfere with the *waqf* lands. In the registry record dated 1131/1719, a ruling was sent to the governor of Damascus, the deputy judge, and the *Qāḍī* of Jerusalem stating that the villages of Bayt Inān, al-Tīybe, ʿAyn Yebrud, Dajjāniyya, ʿAyn ʿArīk, and Lefte were from the Waqf of Masjid al-Aqṣā and Sahratullah. Accordingly, it was ordered not to interfere with the *waqf reʿāyās*.[135]

Again, in 1201/1786, the *mutawallīs* of Ḥusayn [...] *Waqf* went to the Imperial Council and reported that the crops of the 12 *kīrāt* shares belonging to the *waqf* were seized by the fief owner Sayyid Aḥmed and his partner. In the reply sent to the Governor of Damascus and the *Qāḍī* of Jerusalem, it was understood after the investigation that 12 *qīrāṭ* of the income of the village subject to the complaint belonged to the *waqf* and 12 *qīrāṭ* to the fief owners, and it was ordered to continue the practices in this manner.[136]

2.1.4 Interventions by *Ahl al-ʿurf*

The fact that the *waqf* revenues collected from the *waqf* villages remained in the possession of the members of the ruling elites (*ahl al-ʿurf*) and that these amounts could not be collected in any way was the subject of a significant number of provisions and edicts sent to Jerusalem. When the revenues of the village named Kālūn, which was one of the revenues of the villages of Khasseki Sultan *Waqf* in Jerusalem, which were collected in accordance with the charter

133 JS 229: 1.
134 JS 261: 26.
135 JS 214: 151.
136 BOA, ADVNS.AHK.ŞM (4): 110/3.

of the years 1164 and 65/1750–51, remained in the possession of the tax-farmers, the *mutawallī* reported the uncollected *waqf* revenues. In the imperial edict dated 1210/1795, Ḥāfiẓ Aḥmad Agha, the *mutawallī* of the *waqf*, sent a supply for the collection of 1250 *kurūsh*, which were the revenues of the inns, roofed buildings, and *waqf* villages in Tripoli, which remained in the possession of the governors of Damascus.[137]

In another imperial edict dated 1212/1798 sent upon the *mutawallī*'s request, the revenues of the *waqf* for the years 1210 and 1211/1796–1797 were ordered to be collected from the governors of Damascus. Numerous edicts are also recorded for the collection of the revenues of the villages of the Sahratullah *Waqf* from the tax-farmers who were in arrears.[138] A large number of edicts were registered regarding the collection of revenues of the Dome of the Rock *Waqf* villages from the tax-farmers.[139]

In addition to the uncollected *waqf* revenues from the *ahl al-ʿurf*, the damages caused by the same class to the *waqfs* were also recorded. As recorded in Ziyād ʿAbd al-ʿAzīz al-Madanī, in the registry record of Jerusalem dated 1116 AH/1705 CE, it was determined that the soldiers interfered with and damaged the *waqf* lands. In another charge dated 1116 AH/1705 CE, it is recorded that they damaged the lands of the ʿĪsāwiyya Village lands belonging to the Khasseki Sultan *Waqf* and Nabī Mūsā *Waqf*, the *waqf* lands belonging to the *imāms* and *khaṭībs* of Masjid al-Aqṣā and Sahratullah mosques, the land of Shaykh Muḥammad al-Qırımī *Waqf*, and other *waqf* lands allocated to orphans and the poor.[140] Another act of brutality committed by the soldiers in 1231 AH/1815 CE was reported by al-Shaykh Ḥasan in Istanbul. In the Shaykh Bahāʾ al-Dīn Naqshbandī Sufi Lodge in Jerusalem, a group of soldiers forcibly stayed and continued their tyranny by evicting the poor and dervishes from the sufi lodge. In the decree sent to the *qāḍī* and *mutasallim* of Jerusalem, it was ruled that the situation should be checked on the spot and the matter should be resolved on the spot.[141]

---

137 VGMA, 523: 10/41.

138 VGMA, 523: 10/46.

139 *Fermāns* have been sent; for the collection of the 5552,5 *kurūsh* belonging to the *waqf* for the year of hundred and eighty that was left with *multazim* Sayyid Suleiman (VGMA, 763: 489/39); for the collection of the revenues of *muqāṭaʿa* in Aleppo for the years of seventy eight and nine that was left with *Gayrizade* and for the collection of revenues of houses and other buildings in Egypt. VGMA, 763: 489/35, 37, 38, 40. Again other *fermāns* were sent for the collection of *waqf*'s 5500 *kurūsh* held by *multazims*. VGMA, 763: 489/42, 43, 44.

140 al-Madanī, *Awqāf al-Quds*, p. 77–78.

141 BOA, ADVNS.AHK.ŞM (6): 170/1.

In a different dimension of the economic exploitation by the *ahl al-ʿurf*, village shaykhs caused losses to the *waqfs* by demanding different practices in the collection of the revenues of the *waqf* villages. In the ruling dated 1163 AH/1750 CE, although the villages of Ḥalīl al-Raḥmān and Masjid al-Aqṣā and Sahratullah *Waqfs* were exempt from taxes and delivered the other fees and revenues to the *waqf* officers, the shaykhs of Banī Zayd village interfered with the olive oil collected from the villages and prevented its collection. As the olive oil collected in kind to be burned in the mosques of the aforementioned *waqfs* could not be collected, the shaykhs of Banī Zayd were ordered not to interfere in the affairs of the people and not to disturb the order of the *waqfs*.[142] In the summaries of six edicts sent between Rabīʿ al-Awwal 1174 and Ṣafar 1191 AH/1760–1777 CE on the subject, when the inhabitants of the *waqf* villages wanted to pay the olive oil belonging to the *waqf* in cash instead of in kind, the *mutawallī* submitted the situation to Istanbul and ordered that the payments be made in kind and not to offer cash.[143]

In conclusion, it can be said that the ruling elites of Jerusalem, due to their power arising from their status and the financial means provided by the sources of income entrusted to them by the sultan, intervened in the *waqfs* in various ways, some of which are mentioned above. Some of these interventions, which were characterized by jurisdictional issues, were brought to the *qāḍī* court, while others that did not reach a conclusion in the *qāḍī* court were brought to the Imperial Council.

2.2 *Interventions by the* Reʿāyā

As one of the keys to entry into the ruling elite, the appointment of *waqf* officials with an appointment deed in return for a certain service, and especially the influence and reputation that would come with the management of a *waqf* in a city, made the management of *waqfs* attractive to the *reʿāyā* of Jerusalem. The number of interventions made by *reʿāyā* in the management of *waqfs*, often in the initial and new *mutawallī* appointments, is numerous. The interference of the *reʿāyā*, who often fraudulently obtained the appointment, has been described as unnecessary bullying. In order to prevent such a situation, a ruling dated 1196 AH/1782 CE states that the *mutawallī* of the Nabī Ṣāliḥ Tomb *Waqf* voluntarily left his duty to his son with a certificate, and it was ordered to prevent unnecessary interventions by the *reʿāyā* to the *waqf* matters.[144]

---

142 VGMA, 814: 106–2. For another provision on the same subject see VGMA, 814: 111.

143 VGMA, 763: 488/15;17; 29; 41; 51; 55.

144 BOA, ADVNS.AHK.ŞM (3): 102/5.

In another example, after mentioning the appointments made for the trusteeship of the Ṣalāḥiyya Bīmaristān (hospital) *Waqf* in order, Sayyid Jūdullāh al-ʿAlamī from the same family,[145] who claimed that the duty, which had been held by the ʿAlamī family for generations, was given to Yūsuf Khalīfa with a daily wage of 4 *akçe* in the year 1197 AH/1783 CE, although the wage for the trusteeship was actually 6 *akçe*, and that he was the owner of 2 *akçe*, presented a shareholding certificate. Upon examination of the Account Book of Anatolia and *Ḥaramayn* records (namely *Jizya* and *Mevkūfāt* and *Baş Mukātaʿa* and *Mukabele-i Süvārī* and *Istanbul* and *Küçük Rūznāmçe* and *Ḥaslar* and *Büyük Kala* and *Maden Kalemleri* and *Ḥaramayn mukātaʿasī* and *Rūznāmçe-i ʿAskerī*), it was understood that the presented certificate was forged, and it was ruled that this person was prohibited from interfering in the affairs of the *waqf*.[146] In another ruling dated Ramaḍān 1197 AH/1783 CE, Sayyid ʿAlī ibn Sayyid ʿĀrif, one of the *sādāt*, who fulfilled the duty of the trusteeship and supervision of the Shaykh Manṣūr Rawak *Waqf* under the Sahratullah *Waqf* with a deed, was interfered with unnecessarily by his uncle's sons and bullied them.[147] In a provision

145 "... Salāhaddin Timarhānesi Vakfı'nın yevmī dört akçe vazīfe ile tawliyai Muhyiddin Halīfe'nin üzerinde iken ref'inden elli dokuz tārihinde 'İmādeddin bin Müslim'e tevcīh ve tedāvül-i ... ile tevcīh olunarak bin kırk yedi senesinde Ömer mahlūlünden Sayyid Abdülbākī'ye tevcīh ve anın dahı mahlūlünden bin doksan üç tārihinde Şeyh Mustafa ve Şeyh Ali ve Şeyh Abdurrahim el-'Alemī'ye tevcīh olundukdan sonra Şeyh Mustafa'nın hissesi kasr-ı yedinden doksan beş senesi Receb'inde müşterekleri Şeyh Ali ve Şeyh Abdurrahim ibn-i Şeyh Ömer el-'Alemī'ye tevcīh olunup dört akçe ile berāt virildikden sonra ref'inden bin yüz beş senesinde el-Hac Muslihiddin'e anın dahı ref'inden yüz altı senesi Muharrem'inde el-Hac Muslihiddin bin Muhyiddin Ser-Etibbā'-i Kudüs-i Şerīfe ve anın dahı ref'inden sene-i merkūme Receb'inde sāhib-i evvelleri mezbūrān Şeyh Ali ve Şeyh Abdurrahim ibkā olundukdan sonra Şeyh Abdurrahim'in iki akçe hissesi yüz yedi tārihinden oğlı Şeyh Abdurrahman'a ve anın dahı mahlūlünden bin yüz altmış tārihinde evlāddan Şeyh Abdurrahman'a tevcīh ve ba'dehu seksen bir senesi zāyi den berāt ve kasr-ı yedinden seksen dört senesinde 'ammī-zādesi Şeyh Ali el-'Alemī 'ye tevcīh ve mezkūr Şeyh Ali bin Şeyh Ömer el- el-'Alemī'nin üzerinde kalan iki akçe ile nısf hissesi mahlūlünden on dokuz senesinde evlāddan Şeyh Ali el-'Alemī 'ye ve anların mahlūllerinden elli üç senesinde oğlı Şeyh Ali el-'Alemī 'ye tevcīh olundukdan sonra tawliya-i mezbūr bilā-berāt Şeyh Ali el-'Alemī evlādından Abdurrahmān'ın 'uhdesinde olmağla mahlūlünden dört akçe ile temāmen tawliya-i mezbūr Kudüs-i Şerīf kādısı arzıyla oğlı eş-Şeyh Abdülhamid el-'Alemī'ye doksan yedi senesi Muharrem'inde ba'de't-tevcīh kasr-ı yedinden sene-i mezbūre Safer'inde Yusuf Halīfe'ye tevcīh ve hālā berātı üzerinde oldığı Anadolı Muhāsebesinden ihrāc olunmağla bu def'a merkūm Yusuf Halīfe Südde-i Sa'ādetim'e takdīm eylediği arz-ı hālinde ber-vech-i muharrer tawliya-i mezbūre yevmī dört akçe vazīfe ile bā-berāt-ı ālişān mutasarrıf olup ..." BOA, ADVNS.AHK.ŞM (3): 139/1.

146 BOA, ADVNS.AHK.ŞM (3): 139/1. For another provision regarding the same subject dated Shaban 1201/1787 see BOA, ADVNS.AHK.ŞM (4): 128/1.

147 BOA, ADVNS.AHK.ŞM (3): 146/3.

dated 1163 AH/1750 CE, it was noted that the *mutawallī* and tombkeeper of the *Waqf* of Nabī Dāwūd ibn Nabī Suleiman was performed by Sayyid Mūsā with loyalty. He was also the Shaykh of the sufi lodge of the *waqf*. The revenues of the *waqf* villages of Ṣawba and Tulfa were stipulated for feeding the travelers and the visitors of the tomb and the sufi lodge. On the other hand, when some named people from foreigners and *ashāb-i aghrāḍ* (malicious people) interfered in the *tawliyya* of the *waqf* without their certificate and bullied them, it was ordered that these interventions, which were against laws and practices, should be prohibited and the *mutawallī* should not be offended.[148]

In the ruling dated 1169 AH/1756 CE sent to the *Qāḍī* of Jerusalem, it was stated that al-Hajj Mehmed Mezīd had stipulated in his *waqfiyya* that the attendant who put water in the fountains at the gate of the Jerusalem castle every day had the right to dispose of his house in Jerusalem in return for his service, and that the brothers named İbrahim and Yusuf Hicazī were fulfilling this duty from *eben ʿan cedd* (from grandfather to father) with their certificates in their hands.[149] However, Aḥmad, the son of ʿAlī, a resident of Jerusalem, seized the *waqf* estate in violation of the laws and practices.[150]

Similarly, in 1174 AH/1760 CE, Sayyid Muṣṭafā al-ʿAlamī al-Fārisī, one of the *Sādāt al-Kirām*, who was the holder of two shares of the trusteeship, inspectorship, and Shaykhdom duties of the Melik Salāḥ al-Dīn Khanqāh *Waqf*, came to the court and stated that although he was doing the *waqf*'s work in full, paying the wages of the *waqf*'s officials and fulfilling the other conditions of the *waqf* in accordance with the conditions of the *waqfiyya*, he reported that Sayyid Mūsā and Sayyid ʿAbdulghanī and from the *ashāb-i aghrāḍ* interfered in the affairs of the *waqf* in violation of the condition of the *waqfiyya* and the certificate and that they offended him. Upon this situation, the Anatolian Accounting books were checked, and in the said books, two shares of the trusteeship, inspectorship, and Shaykhdom aspects of the *waqf* were owned by the applicant to the court, Sayyid Muṣṭafā al-ʿAlamī al-Fārisī, and the other shares were jointly owned by Sayyid Muṣṭafā and Sayyid ʿAbdussamed and Sayyid Ebūssuʿūd al-ʿAlamī from the same family. Therefore, it was recorded that a

148 BOA, ADVNS.AHK.ŞM (1): 232/1.

149 *eben ʿan cedd*: from (since) father, from grandfather: points out that the task has been carried out by the same family for generations. E.g. See BOA, ADVNS.AHK.ŞM (2): 50/1.

150 BOA, ADVNS.AHK.ŞM (2): 50/1.

certificate of *ibkā*[151] was granted to Sayyid Mustafa al-'Alamī al-Fārisī, who performed the *waqf*'s affairs in the best way.[152]

In another provision of the same date, it was recorded that unnecessary interventions were made by some people from the *ashāb-i aghrāḍ* against Sayyid Khalīl Bistāmī, who was the *mutawallī* and the guardian of the Shaykh ʿAbdullāh Bistāmī Mausoleum *Waqf* in Jerusalem and who did his job properly.[153]

Despite a high number of interventions in the management of *waqfs* during the period covered by the study, interventions in other duties or officials were reflected in the provisions in a very limited manner.[154] Compared to the number of interventions made to the *mutawallīs*, the number of interventions in other duties or officials was small and due to the priorities brought by the duty of *tawliyya*, it was more demanded, claimed and was the subject of more disputes reflected in the provisions.

Interventions were also made by the *reʿāyās* to the *mutawallīs* of the *waqf* in the collection of the *waqf* fees and customary taxes. In various provisions regarding the *waqfs* of Jerusalem, interventions were made in the collection of *waqf* revenues by the *waqf mutawallīs* by themselves or in the right of tax-farming that delayed to their deputies. In a provision dated 1206 AH/1791 CE, Sayyid Saʿīd and Sayyid Ṣāliḥ, joint *mutawallīs* of the *Waqf* of Adhamiyya Sufi Lodge, reported that when they wanted to collect the *waqf*'s revenues and customary taxes, some people from the *ashāb-i aghrāḍ* intervened in violation of the laws and practices.[155] There are many examples on the subject, which will be examined in more detail under the heading of collection of *waqf* revenues and taxes, since the scope of this study is the eighteenth century.

It is noteworthy that in the examples given so far, most of which are selected from the *aḥkāms*, almost all of the interventions in the management of *waqfs* are concentrated on the charitable (*khayrī*) *waqfs*. This must have been due to the fact that complaints were made to Istanbul and the existence and credibility of the records in Istanbul regarding the *waqfs* of Jerusalem, especially

151 In the dictionary, *ibkā* means that the officers who perform their services every year for a year, will be allowed to stay in that place for a year again before the end of this period if their performances were favorited, and in Arabic it means to keep it continuous, continuously ... (Pakalın, *Osmanlı Tarih Deyimleri*, 12). Records indicate that people continue their existing duties, i.e. same people remained appointed.

152 BOA, ADVNS.AHK.ŞM (2): 173/4.

153 BOA, ADVNS.AHK.ŞM (2): 183/4. For further examples on the subject see BOA, ADVNS.AHK.ŞM (3): 58/4; 68/2; 76/2; 120/4; 121/4; (4): 59/3; 125/2; (5): 27/1; 41/2; 53/1; 95/1; (6): 14/45; (7): 6/3.

154 For example, see BOA, ADVNS.AHK.ŞM (2): 50/1; (3): 46/1; (4): 128/2; (5): 9/1; (6): 43/4.

155 BOA, ADVNS.AHK.ŞM (4): 162/2.

those related to officials, wages, estates, and properties. It is possible that the problems experienced regarding the management of the family (*dhurrī*) *waqf*s were limited to unnecessary interventions in the family. On the other hand, the management of charitable *waqf*s was subject to interventions from almost all segments of society.

On the other hand, there are examples of lawsuits filed by the beneficiaries against the judges and the *mutawallīs* in the *sijill* registry records of Jerusalem. The source of the interpersonal disputes between the *mutawallīs* and beneficiaries was the disputes over the sharing of the revenues of the *waqfs*. For example, there was a dispute between Asʿardī Ṣāliḥ, the *mutawallī* of Asʿardiyya *Waqf* in the vicinity of Masjid al-Aqṣā, Aḥmet Çelebi and his brother, and Shaykh Majd al-Dīn ʿAbd al-Ghanī al-Asʿardī as the beneficiaries of the *waqf* regarding the sharing of the income.[156] In another case, ʿUmar Ibrāhīm al-ʿAjamī claimed that he was a descendant of Muḥammad al-Qaṭmānī and that he fulfilled the condition of the sequence of generation (*baṭn*) and demanded a share of the income of the *waqf*.[157] In some cases, the issue was whether or not the individuals were sons of the *waqf*. In such cases, it was necessary to prove whether the plaintiffs were actually among the founder's descendants or not. Proof was made by examining the *waqfiyya*, the affirmation (*ikrār*), or testimony (*ishhād*). In a case recorded in the registry, upon ʿUmar Ibrāhīm's demand for a share of the *waqf*'s income claiming to be a son of the *waqf*, the *mutawallī* of the *waqf* stated that the income of the *waqf* was exclusive to the endower's own son. Since ʿUmar Ibrāhīm could not prove this, he was banned from interfering in the management of the *waqf*.[158]

ʿAlī Agha, known as a *ashāb-i khayrāt* (benevolent person) from the Jewish Quarter in Jerusalem, endowed places such as one room from a *khan*, four shops, and stipulated that the management of the *waqf* was to be entrusted first to his sons, then to his daughters, then to his freed slaves when he was no longer descended from his sons, and to the *mutawallī* of the Khalīl al-Raḥmān *Waqf* when he was no longer descended from his freed slaves.[159]

Upon the assignment of the *mutawallī* duty to Meḥmed Khalīfa, the *mutawallī* of the Ḥalīl al-Raḥmān *Waqf*, after the endower's son ceased to be son, Sayyid Bashīr, Sayyid Ismāʿīl, and Sayyid Ḥasan first objected to the appointment on

---

156 JS 214: 42.

157 JS 218: 8.

158 JS 218: 8.

159 "... evlād-ı zükūruna ve baʿdehū evlād-ı ināsına ve baʿde'l-inkırāz utekāsına ve utekāsı inkırāzından sonra nezāretlerinde olan evkāfdan Hazret-i Halīlü'r-Rahmān salavatu'llāhu alā nebiyyinā ve ʿaleyhi's-selām ve Sahrātullāhü'l-Müşerrefe evkāf-ı şerīfine mütevellī olanlara ..." BOA, ADVNS.AHK.ŞM (4): 1/1.

the grounds that they were descendants of the daughter and were in another province. In the replying provisions, it was ruled that there was no record of the *waqf* in the Imperial Council and other records, and therefore the matter should be resolved on the spot. This situation had been the subject of more than one complaint as it shows that the appointment was made in accordance with the condition of the *waqf*.[160] In some cases, the *mutawallī* of the *waqf* did not want to give the income of the children of the *waqf* as an excuse for his expenditures. For example, in the provision dated 1199 AH/1784 CE, Sayyid ʿAbd al-Ḥaqq came and reported that his grandfather, Shaykh Ḥasan al-Jāʿūnī, had stipulated in the *waqfiyya* of the *waqf*, that the income of the *waqf* was to be given to him while he was alive and to his sons after his death. When Sayyid ʿAlī, the *mutawallī* of the *waqf*, refused to pay the income of the son on the grounds of the expenses he had incurred for the *waqf*, Sayyid ʿAbd al-Ḥaqq, who claimed to be the son of the *waqf*, reported the situation, and the ruling sent to the *Qāḍī* of Jerusalem stated that the situation should be examined and resolved on the spot.[161]

The fact that the beneficiaries of the *waqf* were not satisfied with their shares and caused difficulties in order to get more shares is another subject of dispute reflected in the records. In a record dated 1196 AH/1782 CE, Sayyid ʿAlī from *sādāt*, who was the *mutawallī* of the Shaykh Aḥmad Reyḥānī *Waqf* in Jerusalem "on the basis of sonship," reported that although the income of the *waqf* was divided equally to the sons and daughters in accordance with the conditions of the *waqfiyya*, the sons of the *waqf* did not agree with their shares and started bullying by demanding more income. In the ruling sent on the subject, it was ordered to prevent the sons of the *waqf* from demanding excessive income contrary to the terms of the *waqfiyya*.[162]

160 BOA, ADVNS.AHK.ŞM (4): 105/3; (5): 90/2.

161 BOA, ADVNS.AHK.ŞM (4): 32/1.

162 "Şam vālisine ve Kudüs-i Şerīf mollasına hüküm [ki]: Kudüs-i Şerīf'de vākı Şeyh Ahmed Reyhānī nām sāhibü'l-hayr vakfının evlādiyet ve meşrūtiyet üzre mütevellīsi olan Sādāt-ı Kirām'dan . . ikrām es-Sayyid Ali zīde şerefehu Bābü's-Sa ādetim'e arz-ı hāl idüp vakf-ı mezbūrun hāsıl olan gallesi evlād-ı zükūr ve ināsına ale's-seviye şart ve ta yīn olundığı vakfiye-i ma'mūl-bihāsında mukayyed ve bu dahı evlād-ı vakfdan ve hālā berāt-ı şerīfemle vakf-ı mezbūrun bā-meşrūt mütevellīsi olup hāsıl olan galle-i vakfdan ber-mūceb-i vakfiye-i maʿmūlun bihā evlād-ı zükūr ve ināsın hisselerini şart-ı vākıf üzre edāda kusūrı yoğiken evlād-ı vakfdan ma'lūmü'l-ism kimesneler şart-ı vākıf üzre hisselerini ahz u kabz ādemi kanā'at ve mugāyir-i şart-ı vākıf ziyāde talebiyle teaddī ve rencideden hālī olmadıkların bildirüp merkūmların mugāyir-i şart-ı vākıf ziyāde hisse mutālebesiyle zāhir olan teaddīleri maʿrifet-i şerʿle men olunmak bābında hükm-i hümāyūnum recā itmeğin mahallinde şerʿle görilmek içün emr yazılmışdır. [Fī] evāsıt-ı Z sene [1]196." BOA, ADVNS.AHK.ŞM (3): 115/4.

In some instances, some of the *reʿāyās* interfered in the management of the *waqfs* by claiming that they carried the conditions of *tawliya* stipulated by the *waqfiyya* for the sons. In a ruling dated 1197 AH/1783 CE, upon the death of Shaykh Ibrāhīm, who had been entrusted with the management and the supervision of the Shaykh Muḥammad Sunʿullah al-Khālidī *Waqf* in Jerusalem, the duty was entrusted to Shaykh Muḥammad Sunʿullah al-Khālidī, but a resident of Jerusalem named Sayyid ʿAlī intervened in the management of the *waqf* by claiming that he was also a son of the *waqf* and seized its revenues by force in 1191 AH/1777 CE. Upon the notification of the situation by the newly appointed *mutawallī* of the *waqf* (grandson of Shaykh Muḥammad Sunʿullah al-Khālidī), the ruling sent to the *qāḍī* of Jerusalem ordered the banning of this person who interfered in the management of the *waqf* and the seizure of the *waqf* revenues.[163]

In another ruling dated 1240 AH/1824 CE, the persons named Ibrāhīm, ʿAbdullāh ibn Mūsā ibn ʿAbd al-Wahhāb reported that their deceased grandfather Ibrāhīm had endowed the income of the shops he owned in Jerusalem on the condition that it would be divided among his sons, but that his children al-Ḥājj ʿAbdurraḥīm, Khalīl, Ṣadīq, and Meḥmed Ṣadīq, who were his sons, did not agree to their shares and wanted to take the whole amount. The decision ruled that the matter should be resolved in accordance with the law in the local area, and it was decided to divide the shares in accordance with the condition of the *waqfiyya*.[164]

Another dimension of the problems between the *mutawallīs* and beneficiaries regarding the income of the *waqf* was the right of *suknā* (residence).[165] According to a ruling dated 1199 AH/1785 CE, Shaykh Kamāl al-Dīn endowed a mansion in Jerusalem, which he owned as property, and conditioned his right of residence to those who recited verses (*al-shifā al-sharīf*) from the Qur'an. Shaykh ʿAbd al-Wahhāb, Shaykh Muḥyī al-Dīn, and Shaykh Khalīl were jointly disposing of the right of residence. Due to their successive deaths

163 BOA, ADVNS.AHK.ŞM (3): 135/2.

164 BOA, ADVNS.AHK.ŞM (7): 99/4.

165 A right that is mentioned in the *waqfiyyas* and which can be counted within the concept of the right to usufruct is the right of residence. The endowers have allocated their homes or shops, sometimes to their wives, daughters, sometimes to their sons for generations, and sometimes to servants who have served in their dignitaries in exchange for their duties. The persons to whom these ranges are allocated have the right to reside in these places. Like other rights, this right has its place in the issue of the right to usufruct, as the right to reside can be conditional on generations of children and some of the tasks determined in *khayrāt* institutions continue today. Ömer Hilmi Efendi, *Ithaf-ül-ahlāf*, 51, 53, 108.

and lack of children, the duty was entrusted to Sayyid ʿAbd al-Ḥak ibn Sayyid ʿAbd al-Raḥmān, who was from *sādāt* and was the scribe of the Mosque of Jerusalem Fortress, upon his request, with the permit and deed of the *shaykh al-Islām*. The aforementioned Sayyid ʿAbd al-Ḥaqq ibn Sayyid ʿAbd al-Raḥmān, the scribe of the Mosque of Jerusalem Fortress, was also the *mutawallī* of his grandfather Shaykh Khalīl al-Jāʿūnī's *Waqf* and belonged to the Jāʿūnī family, one of the leading families of Jerusalem. As mentioned earlier, the fact that Sayyid ʿAbd al-Ḥaqq, who belonged to an *ʿulamāʾ* family, traveled to Istanbul and was deemed worthy of the right of residence by the *shaykh al-Islām* is important in terms of showing the extent of his relations with the central administration. However, in the relevant record, it is stated that Sayyid Bakr and Sayyid Meḥmed, residents of Jerusalem, had appropriated the right of residence of the mansion in violation of the condition of the *waqfiyya* and the appointment decision. In response, Sayyid ʿAbd al-Ḥak ibn Sayyid ʿAbd al-Raḥmān, who reported the situation, demanded that he be given the residence of the mansion in return for his position as the scribe at the Jerusalem Fortress Mosque and that interventions in the *waqf* be prohibited. The ruling written upon the request stipulated that the matter should be resolved in the local court in accordance with *sharīʿa* law.[166]

Lawsuits filed by legal representatives (agents) who carried out transactions on behalf of beneficiaries, sometimes women and children, for a fee were also common. The terms of the power of attorney and its ratification were sometimes included in the transaction records. Disputes were usually resolved through ordinary legal means, especially through personal testimony. For example, in a ruling dated 1224 AH/1809 CE, Meḥmed ibn al-Shaykh Ḥasan Ḥamdī, who was both the descendant of the *waqf* and the *mutawallī* of the *waqf* of Interpreter Aḥmed Beg ibn Rajab in Jerusalem as per the conditions of the endowment, and 14 people whose names were known and who were also descendants of the *waqf* in question, appeared before the court and sued their father and the Jerusalem's *mutasallim* Qāsim Beg, who was the guardian of young children named Ibrāhīm and Yūsuf, who were among the descendants of the *waqf*. The property house of 1.5 *sehm* (share) out of 16 *sehm*, the property vineyard outside the house, and the partial property bakery was endowed in 1144 AH/1731 CE, it was stipulated that the income of the *waqf* should be divided equally among the children of the endower. Upon the death of Nafīsa Khānim, the daughter of the endower, her shares passed to her sons Ibrāhīm and Yūsuf, and since they were too young, their father *mutasallim* Qāsim Beg

166 BOA, ADVNS.AHK.ŞM (4): 35/2.

became their proxy. In violation of the conditions in the *waqfiyya*, Qāsim Beg had unnecessarily seized the endowment's assets for 15 years and spent the income for his own affairs. Upon this, the *mutawallī* of the *waqf* then sent a notification to the Imperial Council and reported the situation.[167] As a result of the investigation, it was determined that the situation was correct and it was ruled that the said properties and revenues be given to the children of the endower, who were the principal owners.[168]

An example of a room built on a plot of land, which was not mentioned in the *waqfiyya* and was probably disposed of by the *muqāṭaʿa/hikr* method, can be found in a ruling dated 1240 AH/1824 CE. After the death of Shaykh Mūsā ibn ʿAbd al-Wahhāb, who had built a room for himself from his own property with the approval of the *mutawallī* on the land belonging to the *waqf* of the former chief architect Ibrāhīm in Jerusalem, the former *mutawallīs* of the *waqf* intervened, claiming that the room in question was built for the *waqf*. In the case, which was decided to be heard on the spot in accordance with the *sharīʿa* law, the *fatwa* issued by the *shaykh al-Islām* on the subject was also pointed out.[169]

Since the forcible intervention of local people or bandits in shares and places allocated to the *waqf* officials in return for their services and resulting damage to the *waqfs* revenues were common problems, there are many examples in the registers. These people, who were recorded as *ashāb-i aghrāḍ* in the rulings, interfered unjustly and unnecessarily with *waqf* officials who fulfilled their duties properly. In 1174 AH/1760 CE, Ibrāhīm Khalīfa and ʿAlī ibn Meḥmed, who jointly carried out the bookkeeping service of the Khasseki Sultan *Waqf*;[170] in 1193 AH/1779 CE, they interfered unjustly and unnecessarily against the *waqf* official in Lod; in 1193 AH/1779 CE to Abū Ismāʿīl al-Shaykh Meḥmed al-Ḥāfiẓ, who was the *mutawallī* and preacher of Mosque of ʿUmarī and its poor in Lod and the clerk of the Jāmiʿ al-Kebīr and its poor; to Shaykh al-Ḥājj Dāwūd, who was the tombkeeper of Anberin and Yaʿqūb Baḥtiyārī mausoleums and their *Waqf* in Sırıq Alazor Kary; to 1199 AH/1784 CE to Sayyid ʿAbdulkerīm, Shaykh ʿAbdulwahhāb, and Shaykh ʿAbdullāh who were the servants and doorkeepers to Sahratullah *Waqf* in return for a half *akçe* per day from the *Waqf* of ʿĪsā al-Nabī[171] and, to whom the duty of oratory of the Mosque in the castle of Jerusalem was entrusted;[172] 1208 AH/1794 AD to Derviş Mehmed[173] after the death of Sayyid

167 BOA, ADVNS.AHK.ŞM (6): 90/1.
168 BOA, ADVNS.AHK.ŞM (7): 90/2.
169 BOA, ADVNS.AHK.ŞM (7): 100/1.
170 BOA, ADVNS.AHK.ŞM (2): 180/2.
171 BOA, ADVNS.AHK.ŞM (4): 29/4.
172 BOA, ADVNS.AHK.ŞM (4): 128/2.
173 BOA, ADVNS.AHK.ŞM (5): 7/2.

Meḥmed in 1208/1794, the sole administrator of the Naqshbandī *Zāwiya* near the *Ḥaram al-Sharīf*; again, Shaykh Ḥasan, who had fraudulently taken over the sole administrator position of the Naqshbandī *Zāwiya*, was dismissed and replaced by Shaykh Selāmī, and Shaykh Ḥasan later unjustly interfered with Shaykh Selāmī again, are some of the unnecessary and unjust interventions made to the *waqf* officials..

In a different example dated 1173 AH/1760 CE, Sayyid Meḥmed, *mutawallī* of Ḥalīl al-Raḥmān and Sahratullah *Waqfs*, stated that the people of villages of the *waqf*, whose names were known, did not want to give the olive oil they had to give to the *waqf* for the year 1175 AH/1762 CE, whereas the specified amount of olive oil was given to *waqf* employees as wages. Thereupon, it was ruled that the *waqf* villagers who caused difficulties should be warned and the amount remaining in their dues should be collected.[174] The following year, another ruling was sent regarding the uncollected olive oil, pointing to the order dated 1173 AH/1760 CE and stating that the *reʿāyā* insisted on not paying the specified amount of olive oil on the basis of leading notables who were acting as a landlord.[175]

Persistent non-payment of rents by those who rented *waqf*'s residential or commercial and agricultural assets is one of the most common interventions of the *reʿāyās* in the *waqf* transactions. For example, in a record dated 1116 AH/1704 CE, Ḥājj ʿAbdullāh, *mutawallī* of al-Ḥājj Muḥammad Asīle *Waqf*, sued ʿAbdulkerīm Çorbacı, who rented the house in the Ṣahyūn neighborhood, for not paying the rent of the *waqf*.[176] In the decree dated 1195 AH/1781 CE sent to the *Qāḍī* of Jerusalem, the *nāʾibs* of Gaza, Ramla, Jaffa, and *mutasallims* of Gaza, Ramla, Jaffa; Mīr Behrām, who was the descendant of the *waqf* and the *mutawallī* Dervish Pasha *Waqf* in accordance with the condition of the *waqf*, reported that the tenants did not pay the rent income of the *waqf* property in Jerusalem, Gaza, Ramla, and Jaffa and their sub-districts by practicing landlordism. The *mutawallī* demanded that the rent revenues, which had been in the possession of the tenants since 1190 AH/1776 CE, be delivered to the *waqf* and was ordered to resolve the issue on the spot in accordance with the law.[177] In another *sijill* record dated 1197 AH/1783 CE, Meḥmed Surūrī and Muṣṭafā al-Jāʿūnī, *mutawallīs* of the Aḥmed el-Sawrī *Waqf*, claimed that the hamlet of Samīra was the land of the *waqf* land and the head of Muḥzırs Ibrāhīm had not

174 BOA, ADVNS.AHK.ŞM (2): 150/2.
175 BOA, ADVNS.AHK.ŞM (2): 174/4.
176 JS 202: 270.
177 BOA, ADVNS.AHK.ŞM (3): 60/4.

paid the rent to the *waqf*.[178] In a ruling dated 1199 AH/1784 CE, *mutawallīs* of the Shaykh Khalīl al-Jāʿūnī *Waqf*, ʿAbdulfattāḥ and Sayyid ʿAbdulḥak reported that a man named ʿAbdullatīf had appropriated a number of *waqf* properties registered in the *waqfiyya* and did not pay the rent and died in the meantime. The heirs of the deceased ʿAbdullatīf were demanded to pay the amount remaining in his possession, they again refused to pay, and the *mutawallīs* applied to the Imperial Council with a petition. Upon the request of the *mutawallīs*, who stated that they had also received a fatwa from *shaykh al-Islām*, it was ruled that the matter be resolved in accordance with the *fatwa*.[179]

It was also common for various people to encroach on the lands and estates to the *waqf* or to embezzle them. For example, in a *sijill* record dated 1208 AH/1794 CE, Dāwūd Mūsā sued the *mutawallī* of his grandfather Muḥammad ibn Ḥasan al-Istebanī's *Waqf*, Ḥasan al-Shawā. The claimant declared that although Ḥasan as-Shawā, who was the guardian of his sister Fāṭūn and her two sons, had been cultivating the land belonging to Ṣalāḥiyya *Waqf* for 10 years, but had not paid anything to the *waqf*. With the testimony of the witnesses, it was revealed that the land in question was the land of the *waqf* and the intervention of Ḥasan as-Shawā, the representative of Fāṭūn and her two sons, was prevented.[180]

In 1202 AH/1787 CE, it was reported that the *waqf* land belonging to the mosque under the management of Sayyid ʿAbd al-Wahhāb, the *mutawallī* of the Ṣalāḥiyya Mosque in Jerusalem, was forcibly seized by some of the residents of Jerusalem.[181] In another ruling of the same date, it was reported that the land in the town called Burj ʿArab, one of the towns of Shaykh Mūsā ʿUsayr Waqf registered in the book, was unjustly seized by some people.[182] On the same date, when Sayyid Meḥmed and Sayyid Ibrāhīm opposed Abū Yūsuf al-Sayyid Meḥmed al-Masīḥ, who was the owner of the rooms called "kebīr-u revan" built by Shaykh Manṣūr Miṣrī in Jerusalem, they bullied and caused losses to the revenues of the *waqf* in violation of the conditions of the *waqfiyya*.[183] In the ruling dated 1218 AH/1803 CE, Sayyid Meḥmed and Sayyid Aḥmed, who lived in Jerusalem, were in possession of a part of a house in the Jewish quarter, which they had endowed and left the administration and income to their

178 JS 264: 9.
179 BOA, ADVNS.AHK.ŞM (4): 32/2.
180 JS 275: 48.
181 BOA, ADVNS.AHK.ŞM (4): 143/3.
182 BOA, ADVNS.AHK.ŞM (4): 152/2.
183 BOA, ADVNS.AHK.ŞM (4): 186/1.

descendants, and a person named Meḥmed caused damage to the endowment with his unjust intervention contrary to the conditions of the *waqfiyya*.[184]

Some members of the *reʿāyās* caused damage to the *waqf* by turning the *waqfs* lands into dumps and toilets. In the first ruling dated 1200 AH/1786 CE, the mausoleum of Shaykh Muḥammad Munsī, located near the Tomb of Prophet Dāwūd Nabī, states that although the income of the land whose boundaries were specified in the *waqfiyya* was stipulated to the mausoleum, the inhabitants of Jerusalem and some poor people wanted to turn the land into dumps and toilets, and upon notification of the situation, two separate orders were issued in 1195, 1196 AH/ 1780–1781 CE. In both cases, the lost certificate was renewed.[185] In a second decree dated 1208 AH/1794 CE, the lost certificate was renewed for the third time.[186]

It is also common for some members of the *reʿāyās* to build a wall around the *waqf* land and damage the *waqf*. Sayyid ʿAlī, who was the *mutawallī* of the Shaykh Aḥmad and Necatī *Waqf* in Jerusalem on the basis of sonship and legitimacy, reported that the *waqf* suffered damages when some people whose names were mentioned seized the land of the *waqf* and built a wall on it.[187] Among the rulings, it was also observed that the *waqfs* suffered losses as a result of unauthorized construction of buildings on *waqfs* or lands whose income was allocated to the *waqf*. For example, in the ruling dated 1173 AH/1760 CE, it is stated that some people built a stone wall and a sidewalk called *balāṭ* on the *waqf* land seized in accordance with the *waqfiyya* of the *Waqf* of *Khānqāh* Ṣalāḥiyya, causing damage to the *waqf*.[188] In a ruling dated 1197 AH/1783 CE, Shaykh ʿAbdullāh, the *mutawallī* and *nāẓir* of the *Waqf* of *Zāwiya* Maghāriba, reported that some people built houses without permission in the ʿAyn Karīm village of the *waqf*, where agriculture and animal husbandry were practiced, and where the taxes and fees belonged to the *waqf*, and that they caused losses to the *waqf* by preventing the cultivation and harvesting of the land.[189]

In order for the *waqf* to continue to function smoothly, the *reʿāyās* should not leave the land where they were registered. However, there are also provisions stipulating that the *reʿāyās* of the *waqf* should be returned to their former places due to the damage caused to the *waqf* as a result of the *reʿāyās* leaving their places of residence and migrating to other places. In the first ruling dated

184 BOA, ADVNS.AHK.ŞM (5): 127/1.
185 BOA, ADVNS.AHK.ŞM (4): 70/1.
186 BOA, ADVNS.AHK.ŞM (5): 11/1.
187 BOA, ADVNS.AHK.ŞM (4): 152/6.
188 BOA, ADVNS.AHK.ŞM (2): 161/4.
189 BOA, ADVNS.AHK.ŞM (3): 156/2.

1200 AH/1786 CE, it was recorded that some of the *reʿāyās* and their sons registered in the book of the *waqf* villages of Sultan Suleiman's and Sultan Selīm Ḥan son of Khāṣṣekī Sulṭān's mosque, *imāret*, and *khanqāh* in Jerusalem left their places and settled in other places[190] and in another ruling dated the same date for the same *waqf*, it was recorded that the reason for this situation was that the management of the *waqf* was entrusted to the tax-farmer and the people migrated to other places because the tax-farmer did not protect or uphold the *waqf*.[191]

On the same date, in the summary of the edict sent to Jerusalem upon the request of the Bābüssaāde Agha, it was ordered to resettle the migrated *reʿāyā* of the *waqf*.[192] In a provision dated 1208 AH/1793 CE on the same subject, Ḥāfiẓ Aḥmed of Rhodes, the Agha of the *Bābüssaāde*, reported that some Muslim and non-Muslim *reʿāyās* from the villages of the *waqf* registered in the ledger had migrated to other places.[193] In the provisions in question, subjects who had settled and registered to the *ʿawāriḍ* (taxable households) were allowed to remain on the condition that Muslims should pay the *raʿiyya* taxes and non-Muslims should pay *ispençe* taxes, while unregistered others should be settled in their old villages. In the aforementioned decrees, the Muslims who had settled in the places where they went and were registered in the *awāriḍ* (extraordinary taxes) household were allowed to stay on the condition that they paid the *raʿiyyat* tax (traditional taxes) and the non-Muslims paid the *ispenç tax* (traditional tax levied on non-Muslims), while the others were ordered to be transferred to their old villages and settled in their houses.

In another example, a ruling dated 1194 AH/1780 CE deals with a letter sent by *ʿulamāʾ*, *ṣulaḥāʾ*, preachers, and other poor people residing in Jerusalem through ʿUmar ʿIzzet regarding the oppression of the people by Mūsā, ʿAlī, and ʿAbdullāh, known as ʿAkab, who lived in a village on Mount Derzī, with the support of the *ahl al-ʿurf* people. In the letter in question, the aforementioned people made the people miserable and caused them to migrate by imputing crimes to the people and demanding money. When the Imperial Council's Office was asked, it was determined that these people were oppressing the people, and it was ruled that these people should not go to the *qāḍī*, deputy judge (*nāʾib*), *mutasallim*, *voyvoda*, *subaşı*, and other members of the *ahl al-ʿurf*, and that the oppression should be prevented.[194]

---

190 BOA, ADVNS.AHK.ŞM (4): 67/3.
191 BOA, ADVNS.AHK.ŞM (4): 67/4.
192 VGMA, 523: 10/14.
193 VGMA, 523: 10/14.
194 BOA, ADVNS.AHK.ŞM (3): 18/1.

In a case that may be the opposite of this situation, an edict was sent for the transfer of a person named Suʿūdī to the peninsula of Cyprus for bullying the *reʿāyās* of Khāṣṣekī Sulṭān *Waqf* in the town of Lud.[195]

3 Conclusion

The above-mentioned section on the interventions by the *reʿāyās* in the *waqfs* has made it possible to identify the issues of conflict between the parties in Jerusalem regarding the *waqfs*. The *reʿāyās*, sometimes claiming injustice, often intervened in the functioning of the *waqfs*, causing them to suffer losses. For the *reʿāyās*, who learned to use the system to their advantage, applying to the Sultan with a petition, even from a distance, was a way out. On the other hand, it is difficult to say that everyone in the society who felt that they were subjected to unfair practices applied. However, it is possible to say that this mechanism, which prioritized the individual within the framework of the Ottoman legal system, functioned appropriately, at least in the case of Jerusalem.

Overall, it is clear that the central authorities tried to keep the administration of the *waqfs* under strict control. The examples cited above show that not only was the appointment system strictly scrutinized, but extensive files on the administrative data of the Jerusalem *waqfs* were kept in Istanbul. This situation was not limited to the *salāṭīn waqfs* whose trustees were summoned to Istanbul from time to time to inspect the files. The organization of the *waqfs* of Jerusalem allowed the central authorities to exercise strict control over their administration. This is primarily the result of the systematic incorporation of the administration of the *waqfs* and the network of *ʿulamāʾ* into the bureaucratic, economic, and administrative structure of the state. This conclusion, based on the records analyzed in this study, contradicts the view that central control over the relations between the Ottoman authorities and the provinces decreased and local powers increased their independence. It can be argued that central control was strengthened not only through strict bureaucratic centralization measures but also through the continuous appointment of officials and officials with strong local ties. In this case, the control of the system was achieved through a careful policy of appointments and by allowing families to build a power base that would create a balance within local power structures.[196] The *waqfs* were an important mechanism for this. This is because *waqfs* were

195 VGMA, 523: 10/13.

196 For a similar assessment of the Damascus *waqfs*, see Van Leeauwen, *An Ottoman*, pp. 133–163.

a means of shaping and integrating networks of relationships and institutions, as well as a mechanism for supporting and controlling local networks of relationships, and at the same time, by incorporating the economic networks of state officials into its administration, it ensured the control of the *waqf* institution as a mechanism to help implement its policies.

4 Collection of *Waqf* Revenues and Limits of State Taxation

All states before the Industrial Revolution exhibited an economic activity largely dependent on land. Land-dependent economic activity also led to the emergence of a ruling class dependent on the production obtained from the land. In this system, in return for the salaries of civil servants in the service of the state, some revenues from the region where they served were transferred to these people. The ruling class-producer class relationship shaped around the system called '*dirlik*' constituted the essential element of state functioning. Producing more than what could be consumed, the so-called social surplus product, was a vital issue as it would determine how and in what form the cycle between the dominant element and the producer would take place.[197]

Relations between Ottoman officials and local peasants were based on *sharīʿa* law and custom. *Sharīʿa* regulated the tax levied on agricultural produce and the *jizya* levied on non-Muslims (*dhimmis*). In addition to these, the content of detailed laws was determined by local customs established by Ottoman officials who conducted the first provincial surveys and administered the various provinces of the empire.[198] Agricultural relations point to tensions between social groups and provide clues to changes yet to emerge.

In addition to the fiefs, which remained officially *mīrī* land, i.e., state land, and whose cultivators enjoyed certain rights, the land tenure system also included land endowed by its owners for public good, religious purposes, or individuals. In the *Sanjāq* of *al-Quds*, *waqf* land accounted for a large proportion of cultivated land, perhaps the largest category, estimated at 60% in the 17th century, as cited in Ze'evi. The Ottomans left the Mamluk *waqf*s untouched, adding to them throughout the 16th and 17th centuries. Apart from fiefs and *waqf*s, there was some private land, mostly in towns, villages, and their environs.[199]

In the 17th and 18th centuries, one of the dominant issues was the decline in the importance of the system based on fiefs in the face of the tax-farming

197 Taşkın, "Rüsum-ı Örfiye," 55–73.
198 Singer, *Kadılar, Kullar*, 61–62.
199 Ze'evi, *Kudüs*, 3.

system. Alongside the fief, the institution of *waqf* was a common mechanism for the control and administration of rural and urban wealth and the redistribution of economic surplus. *Waqfs* could be endowed by any property owner. The endowment of property as a *waqf* is based on the Islamic principle that distinguishes between the actual possession of property (*raqaba*) and the right to utilize it (*tasarruf*). In this respect, *waqf* and fief were very similar. Both systems clearly distinguished between absolute ownership and the right to benefit from it. A person establishing a *waqf* could choose any person or group – himself, his family, the urban poor, a school, a mosque, or a religious order – to benefit from it. However, the only beneficiaries of the fief were members of the ruling elite. Beneficiaries of *waqf* revenues could also be entitled to a portion of the income of the *waqf*. The beneficiaries of the *waqf* did not own the property; they could not dispose of it or exchange it for something else through sale or other means, except with the permission of the *waqf*'s *mutawallī*. The beneficiaries of *waqf* revenues could be changed by the court in accordance with the conditions specified in the *waqfiyya*, while fief holders with fiefs could be changed by the sultan's decree or, in some cases, by the *beylerbeg* (governor of provinces).[200]

In the 16th century, tax-farming was already a common system in parts of *Bilād al-Sham* province; according to Abū Ḥusayn, the economy of the entire province was rising on the basis of tax-farming. On the other hand, in the district of *al-Quds* and neighboring districts until the end of the 17th century, tax-farming was limited to a very small area and accounted for only a small portion of the taxes collected. Most of the area was divided into *tīmārs* (fiefs).[201]

A comparison of a sample of 25 villages selected from 17th-century registers with their status in the previous century, according to the *al-Quds* land registry records, reveals that the status of most villages remained unchanged, and none of them is mentioned as part of tax-farming. For example, the village of Bayt ʿImrīn, which appears in the list of fiefs in the *tahrirs*, was referred to as a *zeʿāmet* a century later. While the registry refers to the village of Bayt Ṣafāfa as part of a fief, the *tahrir* record describes it as part fief and part *waqf* land. This may be because the conditions for the conversion of *dirliks* into *muqāṭaʿa* were not met.

In the *Sanjāq* of Jerusalem, direct links were established between those who paid taxes and the ruling and notable elite who benefited from them. Peasants, merchants, artisans or non-Muslim subjects had to pay their taxes directly.

200 For further information regarding the comparison see Ze'evi, *Kudüs*, 134–35. Also see Heffening, "*Waqf*," 1096–1102.

201 Ze'evi, *Kudüs*, 136.

Negotiations between tax payers and tax beneficiaries, pressures for more complete tax collection and demands for prompt payment were a very important part of the local reality, possibly leading to struggles and conflicts between segments of society.[202] As a matter of fact, the collection of *waqf* revenues and taxes, as well as the unlawful demand for new taxes were the main activities of the landlords, which are widely reflected in the documents analyzed in this study. In this section of the study, firstly, general information on the taxes collected from the *re'āyā* in the 18th century will be presented, and then the taxes collected from the *waqf*s of Jerusalem and the practices related to these taxes will be examined in turn.

4.1 *Collection of* Waqf *Revenues*

The conditions of the *re'āyā* of *waqf* lands were not much different from those of the inhabitants of other areas (i.e., areas under the fief system or areas that had become *muqāṭa'a*). Each *waqf* had a *mutawallī*, either appointed by the founder or, according to the terms of the *waqfiyya*, subsequently appointed by the state or the *qāḍī*. This person was the sole responsible administrator of the institution. The *mutawallī* had the authority to appoint the *jābī*, the collector of the *waqf*'s income. If the *mutawallī* was unable to perform this task, he appointed a deputy *mutawallī* in his place. In this way, he would manage the affairs.[203]

First of all, it should be noted that *waqf* revenues were collected in cash and in kind. In particular, the majority of the revenues from the towns, hamlets and salt flats were collected in the form of wheat, barley, chickpeas, lentils, and salt. In addition, *revgān-ı zeyt* (olive oil) was collected from some sources within the city, especially ground rent.[204]

The *mutawallī*s of the *waqf*s with more than one town and hamlet usually followed two ways of collecting *waqf* revenues at harvest time. The first was to collect the revenues themselves or through their assistants, and the second, due to the difficulties in collecting the revenues, was through the tax-farming method.[205] The method of collecting *waqf* revenues in the form of tax-farming

202 ibid., 70.

203 Akdağ, *Türkiye'nin İktisadi*, 66–69. For example, with the petition of Sulṭān Suleiman and Khāṣṣakī Sulṭān *Awqāf*'s inspector Āghā of *Bābüssaāde*, Muṣṭafā Āghā, *tawliya* of the *waqf* was taken from the former *Bābüssaāde* Āghā Sayyid Muḥammad Āghā and transferred to then *waqf*'s clerk and "ahālī-i mürtezikanın muhtarı" al-Ḥājj 'Alī for two years by proxy. It was reported that during this period the mentioned *āghā* will be fulfilling his pilgrimage. BOA, ADVNS.AHK.ŞM (2): 285/1.

204 For example, see VGMA, 523: 9/18, 20, 21, 22, 26, 30, 31, 32; 763: 488/15, 17, 51, 55, 57, 61.

205 Demirel, *Osmanlı Vakıf-Şehir*, 108–10.

was already practiced before the 17th and 18th centuries. This method was more appropriate especially for *waqf*s with large income sources.[206] However, this practice became more widespread in the operation of *waqf*s in the period we have analyzed.

In this period, it is observed that the villages constituting the income items of the *waqf*s were entrusted to individuals as a *mālikāne-mukāta'a* unit, and they, in what became a routine practice of the period, managed these *mālikāne*s by entrusting them to others for a year. The archival records on these practices, which differ from the classical period, will provide a better explanation of the subject. As seen in the records of this period, the task of collecting the taxes of the *re'āyā* in the lands connected to the *waqf* was carried out by tax-farmers rather than *waqf* officials such as the *mutawallī* or *jābī*. These tax-farmers were appointed for one year by the original *mālikāne*'s beneficiaries. On the other hand, the *mutawallī*s were often appointed by the district governors. In a ruling on the process of appointing the *mutawallī*: al-Ḥājj Muḥammad demanded from the *mutawallī* of the *waqf*, the former Khāṣṣ Odabaşı al-Ḥājj Khalīl, that he be entrusted with the collection of the dues and crops, the payment of the wages of the officials, and the collection of other dues belonging to the *waqf*, which were determined by law and records in the year 1169 AH for Lod and the villages connected to it from the Sulṭān Sulaymān and Khāṣṣekī Sulṭān *Waqf*s in Jerusalem.

The duty of being the *mutawallī* of the *waqf* was given to al-Ḥājj Muḥammad with a certificate approved and sealed by the *mutawallī* of the *waqf*. In a decree dated 1169 AH/1755 CE written to the Governor of Damascus and the *Qāḍī* of Jerusalem: "Sulṭān Sulaymān and Khāṣṣekī Sulṭān demanded that the harvest of Lod and the customary taxes, as required by law and records of the related villages, be granted for the year 1169 AH for one year." Although no title is given for al-Ḥājj Muḥammad, the name suggests that he was a member of the custom. The relevant ruling also specifies the limits of the authority of the tax-farmer: The *muqāṭa'a* was free since the *waqf* was one of the imperial *waqf*s. It is stated that no one else can interfere in the revenues of the ordinary taxes of the *waqf* villages and lands and that he would collect the tithe tax and other ordinary taxes belonging to the *waqf* from the ordinary people residing there.[207]

206 Akdağ, *Türkiye'nin İktisadi*, 68.

207 "Şam vālisi ve mīrü'l-hāc vezīre ve Kudüs-i Şerīf mollasına hüküm ki: El-Hac Mehmed zīde kadruhü gelüp Kudüs-i Şerīfde vākı' merhūm Sultan Süleyman ve Khasseki Sultan -tābe serāhümānın- evkāflarından Lūt ve tevābi'i karyelerin bin yüz altmış dokuz senesi Martı ibtidāsından Şubātı gāyetine varınca bir sene tamāmına değin zabt ve vākı olan mahsūlāt ve rüsūmatın kanūn ve defter mūcebince ahz u kabz ve re'āyā vü berāyā ve fukarā ve zu afāyı hımāyet u sıyānet ve ol tarafda imāret-i āmirenin umūrını rü'yet ve mürtezika-i

In an imperial edict dated 1173 AH/1759 CE sent to *al-Quds*, it was reported that the trusteeship of the Khāṣṣekī Sulṭān *Waqf* was given to the person who was the tax-farmer of the Khāṣṣekī Sulṭān *Waqf* in accordance with the *temessuk* (trust deed) given by the *mutawallī* of the *waqf* and that an order was issued to prevent interference by other people.[208] In another decree dated Dhū al-Ḥijja 1192 AH/1778 CE, upon the request of al-Ḥājj Muḥammad Āghā, the *mutawallī* of the Khāṣṣekī Sulṭān *Waqf*, it was ruled that the claim of the former tax-farmer of the *waqf* that he had incurred losses be heard before the inspector.[209]

This meant that the owner of this *mālikāne* was responsible only to the center in his own *muqāṭaʿa* region, without being subject to the province or *sanjāq*, and had the authority of custom (the right to collect customary taxes and maintain order and security in the relevant region) under the supervision of the *qāḍī*.[210] At the *sanjāq* level, such *mālikane*s were usually given to *pashas*.[211] However, as mentioned above, they could also choose to grant this right to others. These tax-farmers were mostly local notables. Thus, local delegation of the right to collect taxes was a common phenomenon in the vicinity of Jerusalem Perhaps this practice was even more common in the case of *waqf* lands. The objective difficulties of tax collection may have created similar situations across the empire. But this local practice was different from the tax-farming, which in later centuries was often cited as the cause of the oppression of peasants and gradually replaced the *tīmār* (fief).[212]

---

vakfın hıdmetleri mukabelesinde müstahak oldukları vazīfelerin virmek ve serbestiyet üzre zabt ü rabt itmek içün taraf-ı vakfdan kendüye der-uhde ve iltizām ve bu dahi ilzām ve taraf-ı āhardan bir vechle müdāhale olunmayup mukaddem ve mu'ahhar temessüki dahı zuhūr ider ise amel ve ihtiyār olunmamak üzre zabtiçün vakf-ı mezbūrun hatt-ı hümāyūn-ı şevket-makrūnumla ma'nūn berāt-ı āliṣānımla ber-vech-i te'yīd mütevellīsi olan sābıka Has Odabaşı el-Hac Halīl zīde mecdühū tarafından memhūr ve ma'mūl temessük virildüğün bildirüp yedinde olan temessüki mūcebince vakf-ı mezbūr karyeleri sene-i mezbūrede kendüye zabt ve vākıf olan a'şār ve rüsūmatı kanūn ve defter mūcebince ahz u kabz itdirilüp mugāyir temessük āhardan bir ferde bir vech ile müdāhale ve muʿāraza itdirilmemek bābında hükm-i hümāyūnum recā itdüği ecilden vech-i meşrūh üzre amel olunmak içün yazılmışdır.Fī Evā'il-i Za Sene [1]168." (BOA, ADVNS.AHK.ŞM (2): 27/1. For a provision on the subject see BOA, ADVNS.AHK.ŞM (2): 47/1.

208 "Emr-i hümāyūn mūcibince tawliya-i mezbūr mezkūr tarafından virilen temessükü mūcibince mültezimi olan kimesneye buyurulub taraf-ı aherden müdahale olunmamak içün emr-i şerif virilmişdir. Emr-i şerif sitāde. Bā-arz u hāl-i Yakub Ağa mütevelli-i sābık ve bā fermān-ı 'ālī- Fī 18 Rebiulahir 1173." VGMA, 763: 490.

209 VGMA, 523: 9/12.

210 Ergenç, "XVIII. Yüzyılda," 92.

211 Ergenç, "XVIII. Yüzyılda," 93.

212 Ze'evi, *Kudüs*, 25.

This change in the fiscal classification of *sanjāq*s led to the emergence of a provincial administration dominated by the *mutasallims* (deputies of the members of the *ahl al-ʿurf* of the customary authority) who were not subject to each other's supervision. The authority of the *ahl al-ʿurf* passed into the hands of influential provincial officials through these transfers.[213] These practices, which the state resorted to due to its circumstances and needs, led to the transformation of the administrative chain it had established to realize central authority into what Özer Ergenç calls disconnected links. Each link is directly connected to the center. Naturally, since the state could not tightly control so many links or administrative units over its vast territory, the administrative structure was more decentralized than centralized.[214]

On the other hand, it can be said that the number of those who had a say in the collection of *waqfs*' revenues increased in the 18th century with the aforementioned management by proxy. Moreover, the fact that instead of the people who we can call "the real owners of the business," those who exercised this authority on their behalf became administrators caused problems. The most common complaint in this regard concerns irregularities committed by the *mutawallī*s of the Sulṭān Suleiman Khān and Khāṣṣekī Sulṭān *Waqfs*. For example, Āghā of *Bābüssaāde* Suleiman Āghā reported that the trusteeship of the Sulṭān Suleiman Khān and Khāṣṣekī Sulṭān *Waqf* in Jerusalem, the former Ḥāṣṣ Odabaşı al-Ḥājj Khalīl, which had been allocated to Ismāʿīl, the accountant of the *waqf*, was this time assigned to his brother al-Ḥājj ʿUmar on the surety of al-Ḥājj Suleiman, the Amīr of Yāfā, but the aforementioned Sulaymān's brother al-Ḥājj ʿUmar did not pay the revenues of the *waqf* and kept them in his possession. The *waqf*'s inspector attributed the non-payment of the *waqf*'s revenues for the year in question to this situation and ordered the collection of the *waqf*'s revenues from al-Ḥājj ʿUmar with a decree sent to the governor of Damascus and the *qāḍī* of Jerusalem.[215]

In another ruling dated 1161 AH/1748 CE, it was stated that another *mutawallī* named Muḥammad was appointed to the trusteeship of the *waqf* upon the death of al-Ḥājj ʿUmar, the brother of al-Ḥājj Suleiman, the Amīr of Yāfā, who had been acting as the *mutawallī* after Ismāʿīl Effendi, the accountant of the

---

213 'Referral of authority' was not only limited to the eighteenth century. Ergenç, shown with the examples he gave from the end of the sixteenth century that in addition to the tax revenues of '*havass-ı hümāyun*' some sources of revenues of state officials '*has*' and '*ze'āmet*'s were also managed this way. Ergenç, "Osmanlı Şehirlerindeki," 1269. However, we can state that the extent of this situation widened to cover not only to the second person but to the third and fourth at the end of the sixteenth century.

214 Ergenç, "XVIII. Yüzyılda," 94.

215 BOA, ADVNS.AHK.ŞM (1): 186/1.

former Khāṣṣ Odabaşı al-Ḥājj Khalīl. In the related provision, Muḥammad, the acting *mutawallī*, was asked to collect the uncollected fees, such as *rikāb-i hümāyūn* coin, script and accounting fee, and other dues, from the estate of the deceased al-Ḥājj ʿUmar, to have the parts of the *waqf* in need of repair and maintenance for the year 1161 AH/1748 CE, to pay the wages of the *waqf* officials, and to operate the public kitchen.[216] However, it is understood from another provision written later that the aforementioned revenues could not be collected by the acting *mutawallī* al-Ḥājj Muḥammad. In the aforementioned provision, the original *mutawallī* of the *waqf*, the former Khāṣṣ Odabaşı al-Ḥājj Khalīl, sent a petition to the Ottoman central administration, stating that some of the *rusūmāt* (traditional taxes) that were supposed to be collected by al-Ḥājj ʿUmar from the villages and hamlets of the *waqf* were being withheld by certain individuals, and some remained in the possession of the *reʿāyā*. In the reply to this petition, the *mutawallī*'s deputy, al-Ḥājj Muḥammad, was asked to collect the remaining crops and traditional taxes in full.[217]

In the *waqf* where revenues could not be collected, the situation of appointing a "deputy of the deputy" also arose. Namely, al-Ḥājj ʿUmar, who was appointed as the *mutawallī* of the *waqf* for both the trusteeship of the *waqf* and the collection of revenues, appointed al-Ḥājj ʿAlī Effendi as the acting *mutawallī* this time. In the aforementioned decree, it was reported that al-Ḥājj ʿAlī Effendi, who was appointed as the acting *mutawallī*, fulfilled his duty duly, collected the revenues of the *waqf* as usual, and did not have a penny in his possession, while Muḥammad Āghā from Egypt, a resident of *al-Quds*, who was appointed as the acting *mutawallī* eight months after him, forcibly and unjustly confiscated a room of flooring and one thousand two hundred *kurūsh*. Thereupon, the central government ordered the collection of one room of flooring and one thousand two hundred *kurūsh*, which were forcibly and unjustly confiscated.[218] In a later ruling, it is understood that the *mutawallī* of the *waqf*,[219] the former Sultan's private chamberlain al-Ḥājj Khalīl applied to Imperial Council for the compensation of the damage caused to the *waqf* by the three thousand *kurūsh* remaining in the possession of the *mutawallī*'s deputy, Egyptian Mehmed Agha.[220]

As can be seen from the examples given above, the authority in the *waqf* was shared between the deputy *mutawallī*s and the tax-farmers who had been

216 BOA, ADVNS.AHK.ŞM (1): 191/1.
217 BOA, ADVNS.AHK.ŞM (1): 191/2.
218 BOA, ADVNS.AHK.ŞM (1): 206/1.
219 BOA, ADVNS.AHK.ŞM (1): 206/1.
220 BOA, ADVNS.AHK.ŞM (1): 233/2.

granted the collection of taxes from the *muqāṭaʿa* areas. However, in addition to the authority problems between these two, these officials also intervened in other *waqfs*. For example, in a ruling dated Rajab 1168 AH/1755 AD, the *mutawallī* of the Sayf al-Dīn al-Ḥaqqārī *Waqf*, as-Sayyid ʿAlī, reported that half of the income of the village, whose name we cannot read, belonged to the Sayf al-Dīn al-Ḥaqqārī *Waqf* and the other half to the Dome of the Rock *Waqf*, and that the *mutawallīs* had been collecting the revenues and taxes of the *waqf* jointly since the past; however, contrary to these practices and the conditions of the *waqfiyya*, the tax-farmer of the Dome of the Rock *Waqf* was taking more than his share and causing losses to the *waqf*.[221]

On the other hand, although the increase of tax-farming in the 18th century provided considerable convenience to *waqf* officials or hereditary officials, it also led to the destruction of revenue sources by tax-farmers. At this point, the problems in the collection of revenues come to the fore, and it is necessary to explain what kind of difficulties arose during the collection of *waqf* revenues. There is no doubt that there were some interventions in the collection of *waqf* revenues, especially in the 18th and 19th centuries. In addition to the weakening of centralized control, the distinct characteristics of *al-Quds* and its surroundings by local powers seem to have increased this issue.

4.2 *Taxation Limits of Central Authority*

Villages that were part of the *waqfs* established for the tombs and monuments of *Ḥaramayn al-Sharīfayn*, namely *Makka* and *Madīna*, the *waqfs* of the *Qubbat al-Ṣakhra* in *al-Quds* and the Ibrāhīm Mosque in *al-Khalīl*, and the great Ottoman dynastic *waqfs*, including the public kitchens, were to be disposed of under the tax exemption (*bi-wajh al-sarbastiyya*) principle in accordance with the stipulations of Ottoman traditional law.[222] This meant the freedom of *waqf* villages, not their complete exemption from taxation. It is the exemption of *waqf reʿāyā* from taxes such as *ʿawāriḍ*, which were imposed in extraordinary circumstances. However, villages belonging to *waqfs* established for other purposes, including those from the Mamluk period, did not benefit from such exemptions.[223]

In a decree dated Rabīʿ al-Awwal 1163 AH/1720 AD sent to the *Qāḍī* of Jerusalem, it was stated that the villages of the *waqfs* of Khalīl al-Raḥmān,

221 BOA, ADVNS.AHK.ŞM (2): 13/3.

222 For information on the Jerusalem Code of Laws (*Kudüs Kanunnāmesi*) at the beginning of the TTD (Tapu Tahrīr Registers (Land Registry Records)) 516 and 515 see Singer, *Kadılar, Kullar*, 49.

223 Singer, *Kadılar, Kullar*, 56.

Masjid al-Aqṣā, and Ṣaḥrat Allāh were exempt from *ʿawāriḍ* taxes, that other taxes due should be paid to the *waqf*, and that this should be done by the *mutawallī* of the *waqf*, and that the villagers should not be harassed by tax collectors or tax revenue owners other than the *waqf*'s collectors in this process.[224] In addition to this general provision, many imperial decrees recorded that regarding the *serbestiyyet* (free disposal) of Kafr Rūḥā, one of the villages of Khalīl al-Raḥmān and Ṣaḥrat Allāh *Waqf*.[225]

Another *waqf* that was freely disposed of and often violated due to conflicts of authority in the provisions were the villages of the *waqf* of Khasseki Sultan mosque and public kitchen.[226] The *waqf*'s town Lud and its villages were also reported to be exempt from all taxes.[227] A provision was sent to the governor of Sidon to prevent the *waqf* from being bullied by taking the tithe taxes of the Kākūn village of the *waqf* in the vicinity of Sidon, as written in the recordsIn order to prevent any interference with the *waqf*'s *mutawallī* Aḥmad Āghā's petition sent in Rabīʿ al-Awwal 1207 AH/1792 CE, the people and villages of the town of Lud had been freely disposed of for a long time, and it was necessary to notify them again in accordance with the orders of tax exemption given in the past.[228] A short time later, this time upon the request of ʿAbdullāh Āghā, the inspector of the *waqf*, another order was sent to prevent any interference

224 "… Kudüs-i Şerif eyâletinde bulunan Hazreti Halilürrahmān, Mescid-i Aksā ve Sahrātullah-ı Müşerrefe Evkāfı kurâları mefrūzu'l-kalem ve maktū'u'l-kadem min külli'l-vücūh ve tekālif-i örfiye ve şakka ve avārız-ı dīvaniyyeden muāf olub üzerlerine edāsı lāzım gelen hukuk ve rüsūmların cānib-i vakfa edā ve zābit-i vakıf ma'rifetiyle zabt ru'yet ve re'āyāsı rencide ve tecridden himaye olunub āherin dahl ve te'addisi men' ve def' olunmak bābında …" VGMA, 814:106–2; 814: 111; 814: 280; 323: 286; 324: 56; 763: 488/16.

225 VGMA, 763: 488/6; 489/ 26, 27,28, 33.

226 "… Kudüs-i Şerīf'de vākı' merhūm ve mağfūrün-lehā Khasseki Sultan tābet serāhānın cāmi'-i şerīf ve imāret-i Evkāfı karyeleri mefrūzü'l-kalem ve maktū'ü'l-kadem min-külli'l-vücūh serbest olup öteden berü serbestiyet üzre zabt olunagelüp umūr-ı vakf-ı re'āyāya āhardan bir vechile dahl ve ta' arruz olunmak īcāb itmez iken …" BOA, ADVNS.AHK.ŞM (1): 186/2; (2): 9/1; 12/2; 27/1; 314/5.

227 "… Kudüs-i Şerīfde vākı' merhūm ve mağfurün-lehā Sultan Süleyman Hān ve Khasseki Sultan tābet serāhümānın cāmi'-i şerīf ve tekye ve imāret-i āmireleri Evkāfından taht-ı kazānıza tābi Lūt kazāsı ve tevābi i karyeleri mefrūzü'l-kalem ve maktu ü'l-kadem min-külli'l-vücūh serbest olup vākı olan cürm-i cināyet ve resm-i arūsāne ve kul ve cāriye müjdegāneleri ve sāir bād-ı hevālarına mīr-mirān ve mīr-livā ve mütesellim ve voyvoda ve serdār ve sāir ehl-i örf ta'ifesi taraflarından hılāf-ı kanūn bir dürlü dahl ve ta arruz olunmak īcāb itmez iken vāliler ve mütesellim ve voyvoda ve sāir ehl-i örf ta'ifesi taraflarından rüsūm-ı serbestiyete hılāf-ı kanūn fuzūlī müdāhale ve re'āyā-yı vakfı ahz u haps teklīfi ile te'āddī ve ahvāl-i fukarā diger-gūn ve perākende ve perīşān olmalarına bā'is ve bādī olmalarıyla rüsūm-ı serbestiyesine ehl-i örf tāifesi taraflarından hılāf-ı kanūn bir dürlü dahl ve ta'arruz olunmamak bābında …" BOA, ADVNS.AHK.ŞM (2): 166/1; 183/3.

228 VGMA, 523: 8/33.

with the *reʿāyā* of the *waqf* the edict dated Ṣafar 1209 AH/1794 CE, the *reʿāyā* of the *waqf* in the town of Lud and other villages, as well as the *reʿāyā* in the lands of Jenin and Gaza, were added to the edict, and these villages and their inhabitants were declared free from taxation.[229] The villages named Sāwiya, Majdal Yābā, Yarāya, and Baliyya Siberli in the district of Jerusalem belonging to the Dāwūd Nabī Zāwiya *waqf* were also exempt from extraordinary taxes.[230]

The waterways built by Sulṭān Suleiman for the *Masjid al-Aqṣā* and *Qubbat al-Ṣakhra* mosques in Jerusalem were in need of repair. The details of the *waqf* shares subject to taxes such as *ʿushr* (religious tax) and *rusūm* (customary tax) are given, and it is stated that Bayt Laḥm, Bayt Jālā, ʿAyn Silwān, Ṣur Bahir, Bayt Ṣaḥūr, ʿAnūldī, Mizraʿat Irṭās, and the village of *Qanṭara* are located in the vicinity of the waterways endowed by Sulṭān Sulaymān for the Masjid al-Aqṣā and Dome of the Rock mosques. For this reason, the people of these villages must pay their tithe and other customary taxes in exchange for securing the waterways, in accordance with the laws and records, to the administrators of the *waqf*. In return for their services, they were exempted from the *takālīf ʿurfiyya*, *shāqqa*, and *dawr akçesi*, which should have been paid to governors and *mutasallims* of Damascus and *mutaṣarrifs* and *mutasallims* of Jerusalem and Nāblus, and other taxes demanded locally. Thus, it was ruled that the villagers in the vicinity of the waterways of the *waqf* would continue to pay their *sharīʿa* taxes and be exempt from customary taxes. The security of the waterways was also ensured through various local tax exemptions.

---

229 "… Lud Kasabası ve sāir tevābi'inde olan kurā re'āyāsıyla Cebel ve Gazze topraklarında olan re'āyā-yı Vakfın serbestiyeti içündür. Vakfı mezbūr mütevellisi Ahmed Ağa arzuhāl sunub işbu emr-i şerifin bālāsı mūcibince amel oluna deyu istid'ā kılınan hatt-ı hümayun-ı şevketmakrūn kayd olunmak babında istida-yı inayet 'amel istid'āsı kaydı balāsına şerh virilmiştir. 16 Rebiulevvel 1209. Emr-i şerif sitāde. Bā arz-ı Abdullah Ağa-i Bābü's-Sa'āde en-nāzır ve bā telhīs ve bā fermān-ı 'ālī- Fī 26 Safer 1209." VGMA, 523: 9/38.

230 "Kudüs-i Şerifde nakībü'l-Eşrāf kāiymakāmı Hazret-i Davud Nebī salavatullah-ı 'alā nebiyyinā aleyhisselām Hazretleri'nin Zāviye-i Şerīfeleri Evkāfının berāt-ı şerīfim ile mütevellīsi olan kıdvetu'l-Sādātı'l-Kirām Sayyid Fethullah-zīde şerefehū- südde-i sa'ādetime arzuhāl idüb Hazreti müşarun ileyhā Zāviyeleri Evkāfından Kudüs-i Şerif kazasında vāki' Sāviye ve Mecdel Yaya ve Yerrayā ve .. nām karyeler mefrūzü'l-kalem ve maktū'ü'l-kadem min-külli'l-vücūh serbest olup rüsūm-ı serbestiyetlerine mīr-mirān ve mīr-livā ve mütesellim ve voyvoda ve serdār ve sāir ehl-i örf tā'ifesi taraflarından müdahale olunmamak üzere yerinde birkaç kıt'a evāmir-i şerīfe ve buyuruldular ve … muğāyir-i rüsūm-ı serbestiyesine ehl-i örf tāifesi tarafından müdahale ve devr ve sāir … ile te'āddī olunmağla men'i içün emr-i şerīfim virilmek ricāsına istirham ve Selātīn-i 'İzām evlaf karyeleri mefruzu'l-kalem ve maktu'ü'l-Kadem serbest olmak kānun-u mukarrer olmağın … Hazreti müşārun ileyhin Evkaf karyelerinin rüsūm-ı serbestiyetlerine dahl Mir-Mirān, Mīr Livā, voyvoda ve sāir ehl-i örf tarafından müdahale olunmamak … Evahir-i Saferu'l-hayr sene seb'a ve erba'īn ve mie ve elf. 1147." VGMA, 814: 4.

4.2.1 Taxes Collected from *Re'āyā* in the Eighteenth Century

As of the late 16th century, the Ottoman Empire took many measures in the tax system and related administrative system (which we have already discussed) due to economic difficulties and military needs. In addition to the increase in taxes regularly and continuously paid by the *re'āyā*, new taxes were also imposed on the *re'āyā*. The collection of these taxes did not only affect the life of the *re'āyā* in material terms. In addition to the administrative staff, the involvement of local notables (and their proxies) in tax collection meant an increase in the number of those who had control over the *re'āyā*.

In the Ottoman Empire, taxes were categorized under two headings: *shar'ī* (religious) and *'urfī* (customary). We can list religious taxes as *ḥarāj*, *'ushr*, *jizya*, etc., and customary taxes as *rusūm 'urfiyya* (*raiyyet rusūmu* (*çift*, *ispenç*)). However, in the 18th century, the taxes collected by the state from society were not limited to these. Taxes such as *bād-i hawā'* (*'arūs*, *jurm*, *jināya*, etc.), *imdādiyya* (*imdād-i ḥaḍariyya* and *safariyya*), *'awāriḍ dīwāniyya*, and *takālīf 'urfiyya* (*'awāriḍ akçesi*, *nüzūl bedeli*, *sürsat*, etc.), and expenses incurred on the people of the sub-district named *salyāne* were other taxes levied on the *re'āyā* during extraordinary or severe conditions like war, drought, or famine. In addition, the *re'āyā* also paid illegal taxes collected by authorities in the provinces by force.

4.2.1.1 *Rüsūm-ı Şer'iyye* (*Religious Taxes*)

In the Ottoman Empire, the term *shar'ī* taxes refers to the tax paid by the farmer as rent from crops or other animal products obtained from the cultivation of state-owned land or its grass or water. Religious taxes were considered as the state treasury's income and were demanded within the framework of *sharī'a* provisions. Taxes such as *jizya*, *kharāj*, and *'ushr* were also accepted as religious taxes. It should be added here that since Islam emerged in a political environment, it had encountered a number of taxes applied in previous religions and societies. From this point of view, the Islamic tax system did not emerge suddenly but was institutionalized in later periods. Even the *jizya*, one of the basic taxes, began to be collected in the 9th year of the *hijra*.[231]

The general framework of *shar'ī* taxes is the tax called *'ushr* (tithe), which is levied on products produced by the people, especially grains. It was also demanded outside agricultural production. Originally a tax familiar to the Muslim and Christian worlds since the Middle Ages, it was considered *shar'ī* since it had been levied by all Islamic states since the early years of Islam.

231 Yeniçeri, *İslamda Devlet Bütçesi*, 32–33.

According to Ottoman jurists, the tithe is *harac-ı mukāseme*, meaning that it was taken in kind. In other words, since the state is the real owner of the land, it has the right to share the income with the people, who are considered as tenants.[232]

4.2.1.2 ʿUshr (*Tithe*) *Tax*

Tithe is a religious tax levied on crops at a certain rate. Calculated as a percentage of the total value of agricultural production in many *waqf* villages in the Jerusalem land registry books, it was another type of tax levied in addition to the *qism* and *kharāj* (part and tribute). According to the *Kanunnāme* of 967 AH/1560 CE and the *taḥrīr* books, villages belonging to the *waqf* of the *Ḥaramayn al-Sharīfayn*, Jerusalem, and Hebron did not pay tithe tax.[233] In Jerusalem, *waqf* such as Qubbat al-Ṣakhra, Masjid al-Aqṣā, Khalīl al-Raḥmān (Sayyidunā Khalīl) *waqf* in Hebron[234] and the Tombs of Moses, Yunus and Lut in Jerusalem and the public kitchen of Khasseki Sultan did not pay the tithe taxes.[235]

On the other hand, various *madrasa*, *ribāṭ*, inns, and tomb *waqf* around Jerusalem, most of which were established during the Mamluk period, and villages that were part of other property *waqf* did pay the tax. When the Ottomans conquered these lands, they preserved the *waqf* but taxed their revenues through the levy of *ʿushr*.[236]

Fifty-three villages, 32% of all villages in the *sanjāq*, were in this situation. Of these, like Bayt Sakāyā, fourteen *qirāṭ* (a *qirāṭ* is 1/24 of anything) were counted. The tax (revenue) to be collected from a village, such as pieces of land or trees, is divided into qararīt. There were also villages allocated to the Ṣaḥrat Allāh *waqf*, where ten *qirāṭ* were divided among three smaller *waqf*, half of which paid the tithe and the other half did not. The land registry book clearly stated that "all revenues other than the Dome of the Rock *Waqf* share will be subject to tithe."[237]

232 Ünal, "Öşür," 534.

233 "… ve külliyen Haremeyn-i Şerifeyn ve Kudüs-i Şerif ve Halilürrahman … hazretlerinin Evkaf-ı Avārız-ı divaniye ve tekalif-i örfiyeden ve öşürden defter-i atikde muaf ve müsellem kayd olunmağın defter-i cedid de dahi kemakan muaf ve müsellem kayd olundu." TKGMA, TTD 516.

234 Because this *waqf* or a part of it was a soup kitchen it is also called *Khalil İbrahim Table*. Al-Ḥanbalī, *al-Uns al-Jalīl*, 98; Cohen and Lewis, *Population and Revenues*, p. 73.

235 For tombs of Musa, Yunus and Lut see Uriel Heyd, *Ottoman Documents on Palestine*, 76, 155, 158.

236 Powers, "Revenues of Public," 163.

237 TKGMA, TTD 289: 55.

Villages that were not affiliated with any *waqf* also did not pay tithe. This group of seventy-six villages constituted 46 percent of the villages in the *Sanjāq* of Jerusalem. Most of the villages that were not part of a *waqf* were relatively small, with no more than twenty-five households, and poorer. Thus, it appears that the tithe was collected only from *waqf* lands.[238]

The establishment of a large new *waqf* in Jerusalem in the name of Hürrem Sulṭān, the wife of Sulṭān Sulaymān, led to significant changes in the distribution of taxes. In addition to some agricultural revenues in the *sanjāq* of Jerusalem, which had previously been allocated to the *sanjaqbey*, the *waqf* also took over agricultural revenues in other *sanjāq*. In the villages of Bayt Jala, Bethlehem, Bayt Iksa, Bayt Likyā, and Bukayʿat al-Dān, *mīr-i liwāʾ* (commander of the brigade) was later applied to other incomes. The *waqf*, established in the early 1550s, is mentioned for the first time in the fourth land registry book. In the 16th century, other small *waqf* were established, usually by private owners from Jerusalem.[239] The *waqf* of Ṣalāḥ al-Dīn Ayyūbī's descendants received one-third of the state's share of grain tax and taxes on other crops.[240]

The collection of the *ʿushr* tax from the *waqf* villages was an important issue in the decrees sent to Jerusalem. For example, in a ruling dated 1156 AH/1743 CE, a bailiff was appointed to collect and deliver taxes from the inhabitants of the villages Bethlehem and Bayt Jala, which were among the villages of the Khāṣṣekī Sulṭān *Waqf* under the supervision of the Chief Eunuch Ibrāhīm Āghā, in the years 1155 and 1156 AH.[241] In another ruling sent on 1177 AH/1763 CE, the agricultural and livestock farmers in a village of the Khāṣṣekī Sulṭān *Waqf* in Jerusalem, whose name we cannot read, did not want to pay the required *ʿushr* and caused losses to the *waqf* due to their demands such as "we want to give this amount of object called *maqṭūʿ* per couple." Upon the notification of the situation with a petition by the *waqf*'s inspector, it was ruled to collect the *ʿushr* recorded in the law and records.[242]

In another example, the *mutawallī* of the *Miṣriyyūn Waqf* in Jerusalem, Shaykh Mūsā, recorded that the owners of the land in Jerusalem, one of the properties of the *waqf*, had been regularly submitting the *waqf*'s tithe every year. However, in 1190 AH/1776 CE, Sayyid ʿAbd al-Laṭīf and ʿAlī Beg, residents of

---

238 Singer, *Kadılar, Kullar*, 86.

239 Powers, Revenues of Public', 199.

240 This *waqf* is known more determinately as *the Şeyh Ahmed and Şeyh Ali el-Hakkarī Waqf* in page 29 of the 516 numbered TTD (Land Registry Records). It was not on Powers' list of Jerusalem *waqfs* under the name Saladin, namely three *waqfs*, a *madrasa*, a *khānqāh* and one *bīmāristān*. Powers, "Revenues of Public," 166–9.; Singer, *Kadılar, Kullar*, 86.

241 BOA, ADVNS.AHK.ŞM (1): 58/6.

242 BOA, ADVNS.AHK.ŞM (2): 320/3.

Jerusalem, interfered with the revenues of the *waqf* under the name of *dawr-i kayl* and *dar-anbār* and seized them by force, contrary to the laws and practices. In addition, a *fatwā* was issued by the *shaykh al-islām* on this issue, and accordingly, it was ruled in 1194 AH/1780 CE that the entire amount of the *ʿushr* crop should be collected and delivered to the *waqf*.[243]

4.2.1.3 Jizya

As mentioned earlier, *jizya* was a head tax levied on Christians and Jews and in some cases paid to the *ʿulamāʾ* of al-Aqṣā and the Dome of the Rock as fees.[244] The proceeds of the *jizya* were sent to *Bayt al-Māl* (Central Treasury) and then disbursed to prominent charitable causes.[245] In Jerusalem, exceptionally, some of the *jizya* revenues were sent to the *Waqf*s of the Masjid al-Aqṣā, Dome of the Rock, and Khasseki Sultan.[246] In this practice, after the collection of the *jizya* tax was completed, the *jizyedār* (the collector of *jizya*) would take the *jizya* revenues to the Jerusalem *Sharīʿa* Court and the share of these *waqf*s would be allocated from the total revenue.[247]

In addition to the *jizya* tax, within the scope of customary taxes, it was also observed that visitors to the Church of the Holy Sepulchre in Jerusalem paid a certain tax, and problems arose regarding this tax, which were sometimes reported to the central government. As a matter of practice, those who visited the Church of the Holy Sepulchre were required to pay the taxes to the *mutawallī* of the *waqf* and then visit the church without paying anything else. In a ruling dated 1129 AH/1716 CE, however, other fees were demanded contrary to usual practices, and this situation was requested to be investigated by Khalīl Āghā, the *mutawallī* of the *waqf*, who collected the taxes from the visitors of the Holy Sepulchre.[248] In another ruling dated 1166 AH/1752 CE, it was recorded

---

243 BOA, ADVNS.AHK.ŞM (3): 40/5.

244 Ze'evi, "Küdüs," 70.

245 JS 276: 34–41.

246 al-Madanī, *Awqāf al-Quds*, 41.

247 al-Madanī, *Awqāf al-Quds* 41.

248 "Kudüs-i Şerīf kadısına [hüküm] ki: Kudüs-i Şerīfde Rum patriği olan Bartalos nām patrik ʿarz-ı hāl sunup Kudüs-i Şerīfde mütemekkin Rum ve Ermenī patrikleri vekilleri ve sāir ruhbān tāifesine bundan akdem Meclis-i Şerʿe varup medīne-i mezbūreye züvvārları vardıklarında Kamāme ta'bīr olunan kenīseye duhūl içün kapusunda Qadīmden berü mu'tād olan vergilerin vakıf mütevellīlerine edā ve kenīse-i mezbūreye duhūl idüp lākin yerlü ve yabancı ruhbān ve rāhibe ve papas ve huddām-ı manastırdan bir şey ahz olunmak muʿtād olmamağla vakf-ı mezbūr mütevellīsi olup hāzır-ı bi'l-meclis olan Halīl Ağa nām kimesneden husūs-ı mezbūr su'āl olunup ba'de'l-yevm dahī hılāf-ı mu'tād mesfūrūnun duhūllerine bir şey ahz olunmamak üzre ʿarz olunmasın iltimās ve fi'l-vākı' husūs-ı mezbūr su'āl-i muharrer üzre oldığı mütevellī-i merküm dahı iʿtirāf itmekle

that the fee for visiting the Holy Sepulchre Church was fifty *akça* per person as *rasm-i qilla* (head tax), and that these revenues were given to the *waqf* of Dome of the Rock, Masjid al-Aqṣā, and Masjid al-Maghāriba.[249] In the rest of the ruling, it is stated that the said income was paid as *resm-i manastır* (monastery tax) to the *mutawallī* of the *Waqf* of the Tomb of Prophet Lūt and recorded as income to the Dome of the Rock *Waqf*.[250]

On the other hand, non-Muslim subjects were most disturbed by the demands for money under various names made by administrators in the region. For instance, during the registration of the orders issued for the Greek monasteries in the registry of the monasteries, a fee of ten *kurūsh* was initially charged under the name of *kaydiyya* (registration fee), but later this amount was increased to five hundred and a thousand *kurūsh*. In the event of the death of a visitor to Jerusalem and its environs, additional income was demanded from his relatives under the name of *izn tadhkira* (official permission/document fees) when he was to be buried.[251]

---

fī-mā-ba'du Kamāme Kapusu'nda mesfūrūn husūs-ı mezbūr içün rencīde olunmamak bābında Kudüs-i Şerīf kadısı arz eyledikde hılāf-ı Qadīm te'addī olunmamak üzre Dīvān-ı Hümāyūn tarafından bin yüz otuz beş senesinde emr-i şerīf virildiği mukaddemā sādır olan emr-i şerīf mūcebince bu def'a dahı emr-i şerīfim memhūr arz-ı hāliyle istid'ā ve Kudüs-i Şerīf ve tevābi'i Rūmiyān Patrikliği mesfūr rāhibin üzerinde olup ruhbān tāifesinin ve sāir Rum re'āyālarının Kudüs-i Şerīf'de āyinlerine müte allık umūrlarını arz eyledikde i tibār olunmak üzre berātı şurūtunda mutasarrıf oldığı Piskopos Kalemi'nden derkenār olmağla mukaddemā sādır olan emr-i şerīf ve şurūt-ı berāt mūcebince Dīvān-ı Hümāyūn tarafından emr-i şerīfim tahrīri bābında bi'l-fi'l Başdefterdārım olan Mustafa Halīmī dāme 'ulüvvühū i'lām itmeğin Başdefterdārım mūmā-ileyhin i'lāmı mūcebince 'amel olunmak içün yazılmışdır. Fī evāsıt-ı M sene [1]129." BOA, ADVNS.AHK.ŞM (2): 30/4.

249 "... Dārü's-Sa'ādeti'ş-Şerīfe Ağası olub hālā Ḥarameyn-i Şerifeyn Evkāfı nāzırı olan Beşir Ağa -dāme uluvvehū- divān-ı hümāyuna arz gönderüb taht-ı nezāretlerinde olmağla Kudüs-i Şerifde vāki Mescid-i Aksā ve Sahrātullahi'l-Müşerrefe evkāfdan yine Kudüs-i Şerif Sancağında Sahrātullahi'l-Müşerrefe ve Mescid-i Aksā ve Cāmi-'u'l-Meğāribe deyu defter-i evkāfda yazıldığı mahalde mahsūl-ı aded Ziyaretciyān-ı efrenciyandır Deyr-i Kamāme beher nefer ellişer tamamen fi sene üç bin akçe yazu ile muharrer kalemiyle tahrir ve mahsul kitabı gallātdır ..." VGMA, 814: 132.

250 "... Nefs-i Kudüs-i şerif ma'a mevadd ve kura ve mezari'i sāire ile vakfiyet üzere mukayyed olduğu defter-i hakānīden derkenār ve Kamāmeye vāridāt-ı Ziyaretciyān-ı Efrenciyān ber-mūceb-i defter-i hakānī beher neferden elli akçe resm-i kılle deyū cānibi vakıfdan ahz ve kabz oluna gelmişiken birkaç seneden beru ve bir mezkūr ziyadetine vāridat-ı tāife-i mezbūrenin beher neferinden defter-i hakānī mūcibince icāb ve iktiza eden ellişer akçeyi manastır-ı mezkūr ahalileri beyinlerinde tevzi' ve taksim defterleri mūcibince ziyaretçilerden tahsil ve hazreti Lūt Aleyhisselām mütevellisine resm-i manastırları eda edüb Sahrātullahi'l-Müşerrefe Vakfı'na hāsıl kayd olunan ..." VGMA, 814: 132.

251 BOA, ADVNS.AHK.ŞM (7): 186/1.

In addition, while Jews coming to Jerusalem were initially charged one and a half *kurūsh ʿakāriyya* and no other money was demanded from them, later on they were charged three hundred *kurūsh* each under the name of *qudūmiyya* (toll taxes) and twenty *kurūsh* each month under the name of *mushāhada* (short stay office). Again, the heirs of deceased members of the Greek, Armenian, and Jewish communities were charged extra money under the name of *rasm-i qisma* (fees paid to civil servants for the affairs of the deceased). Upon this, orders were sent from Istanbul stating that the heirs of the deceased should not demand more than twenty-five *kurūsh* and that the rights of minor heirs should be carefully protected.[252] However, it is understood from the large number of orders with the same content sent to the region at certain intervals that the necessary orders were not followed.[253]

Besides, it is also observed that administrators and officers demanded excessive revenues from the non-Muslim population under the pretext of exploration. In addition, in case of the death of Armenian priests in the Church of the Holy Sepulchre,[254] it was an old custom for them to be buried in their own cellars inside the church, and while this was not supposed to be interfered with, administrators and officers interfered with the burial of deceased priests inside the church and again demanded money. When this situation was reported to Istanbul by the priests in the church, administrators and officials were warned not to interfere.[255] When the congregations in the region notified Istanbul of their discomfort with the excessive demands for money, the necessary investigations were made and the congregations were informed with new edicts that the rights previously granted to them were protected. Necessary orders were also sent to the *Qāḍī* of Jerusalem regarding these issues.

4.2.1.4 Rusūm ʿUrfiyya (*Customary Taxes*)

Customary taxes, on the other hand, are the payment by the *reʿāyāʾ* of the expenditures for the duties of all the service members of the government.[256] Taxes other than those accepted as religious, such as *jizya*, *ḥarāj*, and tithe taxes, were included in this group. The amount and type of these taxes may have differed in the *Kanunnāme* issued for each of the Ottoman *sanjāq* separately. This was because the climate, vegetation, and animal breeding conditions of each

252 BOA, ADVNS.AHK.ŞM (6): 25/3; 53/2; (7): 127/1.

253 BOA, ADVNS.AHK.ŞM (6): 107:2; 108/1; 157/2; 183/3; 193/2; (7): 9/4; 27/2; 39/1.

254 The church, also called "Saint Sepulchre", "Merkad-ı Isā", "Holy Tomb Church", "Kiyame Church" and "Church of The Apocalypse", is mentioned in the records of the Ottoman State as "Kumāme or Kamāme Church". *Kamāme* means rubbish, garbage.

255 BOA, ADVNS.AHK.ŞM (6): 132/3.

256 Akdağ, *Türkiye'nin İktisadi*, 190.

region led to different ways of life. In this case, a different taxation procedure could emerge for each *sanjāq*. For example, *rijāliyya* remained a tax item only in Nablus and its environs.[257]

Similar taxes were levied in certain regions of the Ottoman tax system, not in the country as a whole. Over time, some of these taxes were replaced by taxes within the Ottoman tax system. For example, taxes such as *ʿādat-i dawriyya, ḥimāya, māl-i sulṭān*, which had been levied in the Palestine region since the Mamluk and Ayyubid periods, remained in force for a certain period after the Ottoman rule was established, but were later abolished.[258]

4.2.1.5 ʿAvārız *Taxes*

On the other hand, *ʿavārız* taxes were levied in extraordinary circumstances upon the decision of the Imperial Council and the order of the Sultan. Initially levied only to meet the needs of the army in times of war, they were later collected to alleviate the hardship of the treasury due to reasons such as the distribution of *ulufe* (salaries). Some of the main *ʿavārız* taxes were to provide the necessary war materials and auxiliary forces for the army, to provide laborers, wagons and animals, to transport and sell certain crops (*sürsat*), and to participate in the administrative expenses of the campaign with money under the name of *avārız akçesi* or the fee (*ʿavārız bedeli*).[259] *ʿAvārız* taxes were collected in kind, as a service or as a fee. As we have explained above, the *ʿavārız* group of taxes became customary, that is, traditional, over time. From the 18th century onwards, they were collected directly for the needs of governors and *sanjaqbeys*.[260] As of the 17th century, the revenues of governors and sanjaqbeys were insufficient for them. At this time, the fief system was being replaced by the *mālikane* system, and the has of the *sanjaqbeyi* (head of *sanjāq*) and *beylerbeyi* (head of province) were in the process of being absorbed into this system. On the other hand, the expenditures incurred by the *umarān* in the provinces for the gate people they had to feed had a negative impact on their economic situation. In particular, the insufficiency of their material resources to fulfill their military obligations[261] caused the state to seek an additional source of

257 *Taşkın, Osmanlı İdaresinde Safed*, 55–73.

258 BOA, TD: 427; BOA, TD: 1038.

259 Barkan, "Avārız," 14.

260 For the first applications of these taxes also named imdādiyye see Cezar, "Osmanlı Maliyesinde," 69–102.

261 In the seventeenth century apart from *beylerbeyi, sanjaqbeyi* and *mutasallims*; the *janissaries, cebecis*, artillerymen, *altıbölükhalkı, kale dizdarı kethüdası* and his privates and *timarlı* (fief-holder) soldiers were on average receiving 7–10 *akçe* salaries. Tımarlıs also had tax revenues from their *dirliks* yearly amounting to 500–2000 *akçe*. This meant a daily

income for them.[262] The *'avārīz* collected in Palestine was paid to the *yerliyye* battalion in Damascus.[263]

In the eighteenth century, the taxes paid by the *re'āyā* were not limited to these. From the foundation period onwards, the *re'ayā* were also liable for *raiyyet rüsumu* and the *bād-ı hevā* taxes.[264] *Raiyyet rüsumu* was a tax on the farmer *re'āyā*. It was levied at a rate determined according to the land the *re'āyā* owned and whether they were married or not.[265] It was paid to whomever it was allocated by the state. Depending on where the *re'āyā* lived, it was paid to the owner of the *dirlik* (fief) or, in the case of *muqāṭa'a* land, to the owner of the *malikane* (or his *multazim*). *Bād-ı hevā* (*niyābet*) taxes, on the other hand, were taxes such as *resm-i arūs* (marriage and nuptials tax), *cürm u cināyet* (crime and homicide tax), farm deed, house deed, *kul* ve *cāriye müjdegānisi* (servant and concubine tax), etc., which were collected on an *ad hoc* basis.

There were also taxes collected from urban production and trade. These taxes were collected under the names of of *Mizān-ı harīr muqāta'a*, Stamp and

---

income of 2–7 *akçes*. At this period, one bread was 1 *akçe*, a *vukiyye* (1,2 kilos) of lamb meat was 8 *akçes*. Accordingly, it can be said that they did not have enough income even for their own livelihoods. However, at the end of the seventeenth century, 91% of the money spent for the army was allocated to the cost of *ulufe*. In other words, the state was in no condition to cover defense costs. This continued in the eighteenth century. In 1721, 15,324 janissaries stationed in Istanbul, Edirne and Gallipoli had a daily total of 56,022 *akçe*. That was 3–4 akçes a day. Furthermore, there was no centralization in the collection of state revenues. The army's expenses were provided in complex ways. For example, in 1763, the salaries of the soldiers serving to the Belgrade Castle Guard Musa Pasha were covered by the *nüzul* and *avarız* prices of villages around Berkofça. Alexandria's *jizya* revenues were allocated to the meat expenses of Vidin Castle janissaries. The total of these tax revenues depended on time. Then it was another time-consuming procedure to transfer the income to these expenses. Bkz. Oğuzoğlu, "XVIII. Yüzyılın," 295–303.

262 Cezar examined the issue in detail and highlighted that while the creation of *imdadiyye* tax is closely related to the *timar* areas becoming *muqāṭa'as*, it cannot be interpreted as a result of the elimination of the "*khāṣṣ* revenues". Because, as it is known, in the period we examined (even after the issuance of these taxes) these come under the name *khāṣṣ*.

263 Ze'evi, *Kudüs.*, 70.

264 For detailed information see İnalcık, "Osmanlılarda Raiyyet," 1–14.

265 In the Ottoman Empire, rural society's taxes were collected in a schematic tax system called *çift* (meaning a pair, double, couple). First of all, a pair means a pair of oxen, and all the fields that a pair of oxen can rake are called *çiftlik* (farm). The peasant families with the farm are formulated as a couple. Families with half the land of this land come from *nim-çift*s, then farmers who are landless and their taxes were determined on the basis of the family labor, i.e. the *bennāk*s, and then the singles (the *mucerred*s) who are not married but produce a source of income. The size of a farm site was stable within the borders of the *sanjāq*, but it differed from *sanjaq* to *sanjaq*. See İnalcık, "Osmanlılarda Raiyyet," 1–14.

Customs *Muqāṭaʿa*, *Bāc-ı bazār-ı galle-i muqāṭaʿa*, and so on.[266] There were also *ihtisab* taxes collected in the markets of Jerusalem and allocated to soldiers stationed in the fortresses and fortresses of the *Sanjāq*, and customs taxes collected in the port of Jaffa and allocated to the preparation of the pilgrimage caravan to Mecca.[267]

The *maʿsara*s, the workshops where grapes, sesame seeds, olives, etc. were pressed, were generally taxed at 12 *akça*. However, the type of product pressed in the *maʿsara*s determined the amount of this tax. Mills, which were used to produce flour, a staple of consumption, were also taxed at certain rates. The mill tax, also known as *resm-i ʿasiyāb* or *resm-i tahûn*, was 60 *akçe* for each stone of a full-year mill and 30 *akçe* for each stone of a half-year mill.[268] With two edicts dated Rabīʿ al-Awwal and Shawwāl 1191 AH/1777 CE, the tax on tobacco harvested from the lands of Khalīl al-Raḥmān and Ṣaḥrat Allāh *Waqf* was ordered to be collected by the *waqf*.[269]

On the other hand, complaints about the *ʿavārız* and *imdadiyye* taxes reflected in the Jerusalem *Aḥkām* indicate that these taxes could not be collected in full. People could resort to various means to avoid paying the taxes. In cases of such irregularities, the tax administrators would apply to the Imperial Council and file a complaint. When the state heard about such cases, it ordered the collection of the tax, even if it was late.[270] In a ruling dated 1163 AH/1749 CE, the *mutawallī* of the Sultan Suleiman and Khasseki Sultan *Waqf*s reported that the *reʿāyā* in the village named Bayt Jala, one of the villages of the *waqf muqātaʿa*, did not pay the *ʿushr*, *resm-i ispençe*[271] and other taxes they were required to pay in violation of the laws and records.[272] In a ruling dated Safer 1168/November-December 1754, it is reported that the Sultan Suleiman and Khasseki Sultan *Waqf*s suffered damages as a result of a person named

---

266 Ergenç, *XVI. Yüzyılın*, 237–38.

267 Ze'evi, *Kudüs*, 70.

268 Taşkın, *Osmanlı İdaresinde*, 155–56.

269 VGMA, 763: 490/57; 490/61.

270 Özkaya, *Osmanlı İmparatorluğunda Āyanlık*, 51–54.

271 The *Ispençe* officially is a tax that was not imposed throughout the Ottoman Empire, but only on Christians per household. The earliest record of this tax dates back to the reign of Bayezid I and is a 25 *akce* tax levied on non-Muslim men with married households. İnalcık, "İspence," 177. It has been stated that the *İspençe* corresponds to the resm-i *çifte* levied on Muslims, as well as the *bennāk* taxes. There is no precise definition of the qualifications of those who were obliged to pay the *İspençe*. In many places it was levied on all non-Muslim *reʿāyā* regardless of whether they were married or not, while in some places it was levied only on married non-Muslim men. However, in order for this tax to be collected, the *reʿāyā* had to own 300 *akce* of movable property. Louis Fekete, "Turkish Tax Surveys," 313.

272 BOA, ADVNS.AHK.ŞM (1): 226/6.

Qāsim Diyār, who claimed to be a janissary, provoking the people and encouraging them not to pay their taxes.[273] In another similar ruling, the *re'āyā* in the towns of Khasseki Sultan *Waqf* did not pay their taxes such as *resm-i bennâk*[274] and when the *mutawallī* Rūḍūsī Aḥmad demanded the taxes, some of them caused problems by claiming to be janissaries and caused losses to the *waqf*.[275]

4.2.2 Unpaid Taxes

The failure of the *waqf re'āyās* to pay the taxes they were required to pay according to the law and records under various pretexts was the subject of the edicts and orders sent to Jerusalem.[276] The most frequently mentioned provisions in the Damascus *Aḥkām* Books are those related to the *Waqf* of Khasseki Sultan Public Kitchen and such as unfair interventions from outside, persecution of the *waqf*'s *re'āyās*, problems with the income items that sustained the *waqf*, and damages incurred when the *waqf*'s *re'āyās* resisted and did not pay the taxes they were supposed to pay or migrated.[277]

A ruling dated Rajab 1161/June-July 1748; some people from the inhabitants of the town of Lut, one of the towns of the Khasseki Sultan Mosque and *Imāret Waqfs* in Jerusalem, which had been freely appropriated, prevented the collection of taxes by sowing discord among the *waqf*'s *re'āyā* and prevented

---

273 BOA, ADVNS.AHK.ŞM (2): 12/2.

274 "The taxes referred to as *bennāk* (also spelled *benlāk*) applied to married re'āyā who did not possess a *çiftlik* and were able to cultivate a plot smaller than a *nīm-çift*. The *bennāk* were categorized in two groups: *Ekinlü Bennāk* and *Caba* (*Kara*) *Bennāk*. Those who held less than half a *çift* of land were known as *Ekinlü Bennāk*, and they paid one *akçe* for every two *dönüm* of the land they cultivated. When this levy exceeded the standard *12-akçe bennāk* tax, the payment was no longer collected as the *bennāk resmī* but instead as a tax referred to as *resm-i dönüm*, assessed per *dönüm* of cultivated land.

The *Caba Bennāk*, on the other hand, were married re'āyā who did not hold land under a tapu deed. They typically worked as laborers on the *tapu*-holding lands of others, or they cultivated land obtained without a deed from the *sipāhī*, for which they paid the *resm-i dönüm*." Taşkın, "Rüsūm-ı Örfiye," 59–60.

275 BOA, ADVNS.AHK.ŞM (5): 10/4.

276 Of the 55 imperial decrees (*fermān*) sent to the Khasseki Sultan *Waqf* between 1173–1223 AH/1759–1808 CE, approximately 19(about 35%) concern issues related to the collection of taxes owed to the waqf, the status of villages exempt from taxation, and various acts of interference and usurpation committed against these waqf villages. Similarly, of the 61 *fermāns* sent between 1167–1191 AH/1753–1777 CE to the Ḥalīl al-Raḥmān, Masjid al-Aqsā, and Dome of the Rock *Waqfs*, approximately 15 (about 25%) concern the same matters. Furthermore, among the 212 decrees(*ḥükm*) issued to Jerusalem between 1742–1830, 41 (about 19%) pertain to the collection of taxes allocated to waqfs, the condition of tax-exempt villages, and interventions or acts of oppression (*mütegallibelik*) directed toward these waqf lands and their inhabitants. For detailed discussion, see VGMA, 523: 8–10; VGMA, 763: 488–490.

277 See BOA, ADVNS.AHK.ŞM (2): 180/1.

the collection of taxes, and the food that should have been collected for the public kitchen could not be cooked in the public kitchen and food could not be distributed to the poor and orphans. Upon the situation communicated by the *waqf*'s inspector, the Chief Eunuch, the Ottoman government issued a decree to prevent those who sowed discord among the *re'āyā* by first warning them and then, if they did not heed the warnings, by taking them to task.[278] In another ruling dated 1163 AH/1749 ADCE the *mutawallī* of the *waqf*, the former Khāṣṣ Odabaşı al-Ḥājj Khalīl, reported that the *re'āyā*s of the village of Beit Jālā, one of the villages of the Khasseki Sultan *Waqf*'s *muqāta'a*, had not paid taxes such as *'ushr* and *ispenç* for three years, and that the deductions made from the *waqf*'s crops prevented the functioning of the public kitchen, and ordered the collection of these taxes again.[279] In a similar case, al-Ḥājj Muḥammad was in charge of collecting the *'ushr* and *rusūm* of the *re'āyā* of Bethlehem, Bayt Jala, and Bayt Iksa under the Khasseki Sultan *waqf* and the named places in the district of Ramla for the years 1169–1170 AH/1755–1756 CE, and when the *re'āyā* made excuses and refrained from making payments, it was ordered to collect all the receivables.[280]

Again, Mehmed, who was appointed to manage the *waqf* by proxy and to collect the revenues, went to the Imperial Council to report the situation after the inhabitants of the villages of Bethlehem and Beit Jālā and (there are 3 more village names) in Jerusalem and Ramla had difficulties in paying the required portion of the tithe, crops and taxes for the years 1161, 1162 and 1163 AH (1747, 1748, 1749 CE). The Ottoman administration, in turn, ruled to collect the amount due from the *waqf re'āyā*s and to ensure that their taxes were paid on time every year.[281] However, it is understood from the provisions sent later on that the shortage continued. 1167 AH/1753 CE, those living in the towns of the Khasseki Sultan *Waqf* and the towns in the districts of Jerusalem and Ramla were ordered not to pay their taxes such as tithe due to the drought in the years one thousand sixty-one, sixty-two and three. In the aforementioned years, when the collection of this tax was demanded at the beginning of Rabī' al-Awwal 1165 AH upon the request of Muḥammad, the tax-farmer, they resisted, and it was ruled that it should be collected by the *mutawallī* al-Ḥājj Khalīl In another example, it was recorded that the *re'āyā* did not deliver the taxes belonging to the *waqf* by obeying some bandits and caused losses to the

278 BOA, ADVNS.AHK.ŞM (1): 186/2. For a similar situation see BOA, ADVNS.AHK.ŞM (2): 76/3.

279 BOA, ADVNS.AHK.ŞM (1): 226/6; for another provision dated 1165/1751 about the taxes that could not be collected see BOA, ADVNS.AHK.ŞM (1): 226/6.

280 BOA, ADVNS.AHK.ŞM (1): 110/2.

281 BOA, ADVNS.AHK.ŞM (1): 252/4.

waqf. For example, on Muḥarram 1158 AH/1745 CE, the *Qāḍī* of Jerusalem sent a letter stating that the *reʿāyā* of the villages named Bethlehem and Bayt Jala, whose revenues belonged to the Khāṣṣekī Sulṭān Public Kitchen and Sulṭān Qāytbāy *Waqf*, did not pay their taxes by obeying a bandit named Qarā Kamāl. The number of *reʿāyā* in the village of Bethlehem, which was 287, was recorded as 239 in the village of Bayt Jala. The village of Bethlehem was all *waqf*, with a total income of 36,000 *akça*, of which 27,000 *akça* belonged to the Khāṣṣekī Sulṭān Public Kitchen and 9,000 *akça* to the Sulṭān Qāytbāy *Waqf*; the village of Bayt Jala was also all *waqf*, with a total income of 30,000 *akça*, of which 24,500 *akça* belonged to the Khāṣṣekī Sulṭān Public Kitchen and 5,500 *akça* to the Sulṭān Qāytbāy *Waqf*. It was ruled that payments should be made in this manner.[282]

Another ruling dated Rabīʿ al-Ākhir 1200 AH/January-March 1786 CE states that some of the residents of some of the towns in Jerusalem that belonged to Sulṭān Sulaymān Khān, Khāṣṣekī Sulṭān, and Sulṭān Salīm II, the *Khanqāh al-Maʿmūra Waqf*, should be returned to their homes in order to eliminate the damages caused by the migration of some of the residents to other places. In the ruling dated 1206 AH, this time, some foreigners provoked the people and started an insurrection, which resulted in twenty-nine *reʿāyā* and those living in the towns of *Waqf Madrasa* Mālikiyya not to pay their due fees and customary taxes and causing losses to the *waqf*.[283] In another example, it was ruled that the *reʿāyā* of Ṣaḥrat Allāh and its adjacent towns and the towns of Jabal al-Nablus with the *Waqf* of Khalīl al-Raḥmān and the *reʿāyā* of the towns subject to the Jabal Nablus district should collect the religious and customary taxes that could not be collected due to some reasons.[284]

In the light of the information provided so far, it can be said that the *waqf* subject to provisions, edicts, and other orders regarding taxes in 18th-century Ottoman Jerusalem were mostly charitable, public *waqf* such as Masjid al-Aqṣā, Ṣaḥrat Allāh, and Khāṣṣekī Sulṭān *Waqf*, which were under the supervision of the Chief Eunuch Āghā. On the other hand, what the situation was like for the charitable *waqf* with smaller incomes and the family *waqf* is an issue that should not be overlooked when describing the network of *waqf* in Jerusalem.

In the 1739 accounting record of the *Maghāriba Waqf*, a charitable *waqf*, it is recorded that a total of 406 *zolota* of taxes were paid under three items within the expenses: fellahin tax (32 *zolota*), tithe tax (332 *zolota*), and partial tithe for the fief holders (42 *zolota*). In addition, the taxes demanded for the bureaucratic

282 BOA, ADVNS.AHK.ŞM (1): 86/4.
283 BOA, ADVNS.AHK.ŞM (4): 160/2.
284 BOA, ADVNS.AHK.ŞM (2): 147/1.

procedures carried out during the accounting of the *waqf* were also included in the last section of the accounting record where income and expenses were balanced. In this section, 10 *zolota* were charged for the accounting tax, three *zolota* for the clerk, one *zolota* for the *rasliyya*, three *zolota* for the *waqf* clerk, and one *zolota* for the accounting book.[285] Similarly, in the accounting record dated 1168 AH / 1755 CE of the al-Shaykh Khalīl al-Jāʿūnī *Waqf*, which was a zurrî foundation, it is recorded that five *zolota*s were paid as accounting tax and fees, and fifteen *zolota*s were paid as bookkeeper, *resliyye* and registration expenses.[286]

Among the later accounting records in the registers: In the accounts of the Ḥusayn Qāmiʿ *Waqf* dated Rajab 1229 AH/1814 CE and the Qāsim Bey al-Tarjumān *Waqf* dated Muḥarram 1229 AH/1813 CE, the fee was recorded as 3 *zolota*; in the accounts of the al-Ḥājj Ibrāhīm al-Shāfiʿī *Waqf* dated Rajab 1231 AH/1816 ADCE the fee was recorded as three *zolota* and the *kalemiyye* (recording fee) as one *zolota*.[287] These accounts show that in the period covered by this study, an average of three *zolota*s of accounting tax was levied and additional taxes were demanded depending on the size of the *waqf*.

4.2.3 Illegally Collected Taxes and Bullying

In the 18th century, taxes collected by provincial authorities in violation of the law (*bidʿa*) were another source of economic burden on the *reʿāyā*. *Takālīf-i shāqqa* (salguns-irregular taxes) were among the most important taxes collected by force by these powers, which were composed of the *ahl al-ʿurf* (military branch of the ruling elite), *ahl al-ʾilm* (*ʿulamāʾ*-scholars), and *aʿyān* (local notables). However, in the 17th and 18th centuries, *takālīf-i shāqqa* and other irregular tax collections became a 'disaster' for society.[288] Although the state took measures to oppose them and prevent their collection, it failed to implement them. This situation can be considered not only as a result of localization in the provinces, but also as an effect of the unfavorable economic conditions of the period on "officials."

In the Ottoman Empire, a tax was levied in return for every service provided to the *reʿāyā*. Civil servants collected these taxes while performing the services related to their specialty. This was how they made a living. Most of the people with appointment deeds did not actually receive a salary from the state. The taxes they were authorized to collect for themselves were defined in the laws.[289] The tax laws of the state did not change much from the 16th

---

285 JS 224: 185–187.

286 JS 264: 149.

287 See respectively. JS 297: 33; 34; 299: 27.

288 İnalcık, *Osmanlı İmparatorluğu'nun Ekonomik*, 96.

289 Ergenç, *XVI. Yüzyılın*, 141; Özkaya, *Osmanlı İmparatorluğunda Āyanlık*, 46.

to the 18th century. However, there was a process of of *tīmār* areas becoming *muqāta'as* in the collection of taxes. This process meant that the tax revenues that had been transferred to military and civil administrators at their posts were also included in the central treasury. Although the fief system was not completely abolished, the income of local administrators, who now had to directly feed their own soldiers, decreased. Apart from the *'imdād-ı seferiyye'* (taxes paid during wartimes) and *'imdād-ı hazariyye'* (taxes paid during peace times), taxes that the state allocated to this sector, local administrators sought ways to supplement their income through illegal means.

Beylerbeys and *sanjaqbeys* paid *resm-i caize*[290] when they were appointed to office, they also gave gifts and money to the grand vizier and other state officials, and those appointed to large provinces paid a sum of money to the *darphāne*.[291] In addition, the terms of office of *qāḍīs*, *beylerbeys* and *sanjāq mutasarrifs* were very short, and they were often left without duties and salaries. They tried to take advantage of the existing conditions as much as possible during these short terms of office, which were ripe for abuse.[292]

The state, on the other hand, was trying to maximize the revenues of the treasury as much as possible due to its increasing expenditures. Therefore, it often wanted to 'force' the tax capacity of the *re'āyā* only for the central treasury and the army. On the other hand, it also tried to maintain the "principle of protection of the *re'āyā*," which was the foundation of the Ottoman order, and to keep these two factors in balance.[293] In this context, the state tried to prevent the lawless practices of the military, which were as destructive as banditry or even more destructive.[294] Another reason behind the increasing tax demands on the *re'āyā* was the decrease in the revenue that should have reached the state budget due to the changing fiscal and administrative order. These were processes that affected each other.

290 'Cāize' is the money given to rank-sellers by whomever bought the rank. See Pakalın, *Osmanlı Tarih Deyimleri*, 255.

291 Oğuzoğlu, "Osmanlı Şehirlerindeki," 18.

292 Özkaya, *Osmanlı İmparatorluğunda Āyanlık*, 19–20.

293 In the Ottoman economic worldview, the maximization of taxation (*fiskalizm*) played a dominant role. In particular, the *avārız* taxes—which the state expanded and rendered continuous during periods of fiscal strain—functioned, in effect, as the state's own extraordinary levies (*salgun*). Their purpose was to raise the amount of revenue accumulated in the treasury to the highest possible level. However, the imposition of *salgun* by officials for their own benefit was considered an infringement upon the absolute legal authority of the Ottoman sultan. According to the established law, no one other than the sultan possessed the right to dispose of land or re'āyā. The re'āyā were the producers and thus constituted the principal source of state revenue. İnalcık, *Osmanlı İmparatorluğu'nun Ekonomik*, 98–99; Genç, *Osmanlı İmparatorluğu'nda Devlet*, 43–52, 50–51.

294 Özkaya, *Osmanlı İmparatorluğunda Āyanlık*, 90.

In the 18th-century *Sanjāq* of Jerusalem, the interventions of the *ahl al-ʿurf* were especially concentrated in the areas of *waqf*.[295] In these records, it is seen that they unnecessarily interfered with the taxes paid by the *waqf reʿāyās*, confiscated their food and beverages, and demanded taxes by force. Due to their unnecessary interference with *waqf reʿāyās* and *ḥilāf-i qānūn* (in violation of the old practices) tax collection, they were complained about either directly by the *reʿāyās* or by the *waqf mutawallī*.[296]

In the imperial edicts and decrees sent to Jerusalem during the period covered by this study, it was determined that activities such as unnecessary interventions in *waqf reʿāyās*, *ḥilāf-i qānūn* (in violation of the old practices) tax collection, or economic usurpation were carried out by different groups. In this section of the study, these interventions by *waqf* officials, fief holders, *ahl al-ʿurf*, and *ʿulamāʾ* will be analyzed under separate headings.

4.2.3.1 *Unfair Tax Claims of* Waqf *Officials*

There are also cases where *waqf* officials forcibly demanded excessive taxes from *waqf reʿāyās* under various pretexts. Numerous rulings were sent to Jerusalem regarding the collection of the money unjustly demanded from the *reʿāyā* by the officials and what should be done to prevent such incidents. For example, in some villages of the Ṣaḥrat Allāh and Shaykh Mūsā al-Ḥaqqārī *Waqf*s in Jerusalem, the *mutawallī*s of the *waqf*s bullied the *reʿāyā*s of the *waqf*s by demanding excessive taxes contrary to the law and records, while the people whose names were known in some villages of Jerusalem were paying the taxes they were supposed to pay, such as tithe and customary taxes. A decree was sent to the Governor of Damascus and the *Qāḍī* of Jerusalem to prevent the damages suffered by the *waqf reʿāyā*s due to the extortionate demands[297]

295 Ahmet Tabakoğlu, "XVII ve XVIII. Yüzyıl Osmanlı Bütçeleri," 389–414.

296 This situation could be seen clearly in the provision dated 1173/1760. In an imperial order directed at the *Qāḍī* of Jerusalem it is said: "… Kudüs-i Şerīfde vākıʿ merhūm ve mağfurün-lehā Sultan Süleyman Hān ve Khasseki Sultan -tābet serāhümā-nın Cāmi-i Şerīf ve Tekye ve İmāret-i ʿĀmireleri Evkāfından taht-ı kazānıza tābiʿ Lūd kazāsı ve tevābi'i karyeleri mefrūzü'l-kalem ve maktuʿü'l-kadem min-külli'l-vücūh serbest olup vākıʿ olan cürm-i cināyet ve resm-i arūsāne ve kul ve cāriye müjdegāneleri ve sāir bād-ı hevālarına mīr-mirān ve mīr-livā ve mütesellim ve voyvoda ve serdār ve sāir ehl-i örf tā'ifesi taraflarından hilāf-ı kanūn bir dürlü dahl ve taʿarruz olunmak īcāb itmez iken vāliler ve mütesellim ve voyvoda ve sāir ehl-i örf tā'ifesi taraflarından rüsūm-ı serbestiyete hilāf-ı kanūn fuzūlī müdāhale ve reʿāyā-yı vakf-ı ahz u haps teklīfi ile teʿāddī ve ahvāl-i fukarāa diger-gūn ve perākende ve perīşān olmalarına bāʿis ve bādī olmalarıyla rüsūm-ı serbestiyyesine ehl-i örf tā'ifesi taraflarından hilāf-ı kanūn bir dürlü dahl ve taʿarruz olunmamak bābında …" BOA, ADVNS.AHK.ŞM (2): 156/1.

297 BOA, ADVNS.AHK.ŞM (1): 158/2.

In another example, Ibrahim, the clerk of the Khasseki Sultan *Waqf*, collected taxes from the trustees of the *waqf* and performed his duty properly, but for a couple of years, the trustees objected and did not make payments, causing the *waqf* to incur losses.[298]

There are also examples of *waqf* trustees interfering with the shares of other *waqfs* in the collection of shared revenues and taxes belonging to *waqfs*. In a ruling dated 1228 AH/1813 CE, the revenues and taxes of the village of Bayt Ṣafāfā, which were allocated among various *waqfs* in shares, were interfered with by the trustees of other *waqfs* in violation of laws and practices.[299] The daily books (*rūznāmçe*), accounting (*icmāl*), detailed land surveys (*mufaṣṣal*) and other *waqf* registers located in the Ottoman Imperial Archives (*Dafṭarḫāne-i ʿĀmire*) were consulted and the shares of each *waqf* and the amount of taxes to be collected were reported.[300] Similarly, in another record dated 1228 AH/1813 CE, it

---

298 BOA, ADVNS.AHK.ŞM (2): 290/2.

299 "... Sulehādan ve Sādāt-ı Kirāmdan Şeyh ' Abdülbākī evlādından Sayyid Mehmed ve karındaşı Sayyid Ahmed zīde şerefhümā gelüp Kudüs-i Şerīf sancağında ve nāhiyesine tābi' Beyt-i Safāfe karyesinin hāsıl-ı kısm mine's-sülüs hınta ve şa'ir on altı kırat sekiz bin dört yüz akçe yazusından on yedi kırat fī on üç kırat min kırat altı bin yüz kırk akçesi timār ve bākī şürekā hissesi ve altı kırat fī on bir kırat min kırat ve iki bin iki yüz altmış akçesi Kudüs-i Şerīfde Münhale? Medresesi Vakfı resm-i mukırr ve nebh ve bād-ı hevāsı timār ve karye-i Beyt-i Safāfe el-mezbūre ve gayrıdan üç bin dört yüz akçe timāra mutasarrıf Sayyid Mehmed veledi Sayyid Abdülrahmān'ın müşterekiyle kaydına dāhil oldığı ve'l- öşr an māli'l-vakfı yine Kudüs-i Şerīf'de Edhemiyye Zāviyesi'ne tahrīr oldığı ve Gazze sancağında Remle nāhiyesinde kıt'a-i arz-ı Vādiyü'l-arāle'nin mahsūlātı . Kudüs-i Şerīf'de Edhemiyye Zāviyesi Vakfı ve el- öşr an māli'l-vakfı dahı müşterekiyle Remle nāhiyesinde . nām karye ve gayrıdan altı bin akçe timāra mutasarrıf Mustafa veledi Süleyman'ın kaydında idüği Defter-i Hākanī'de mukayyed ve merkümān Sayyid Mehmed bin Sayyid Ahmed zikr olunan Edhemiyye Zāviyesi Vakfı'nın bā-berāt-ı ālişān mütevellīleri olmalarıyla sālifü'z-zikr Beyt-i Safāfe karyesini ber-mūceb-i Defter-i hākanī Münhale? Medresesi Vakfı mütevellīsi ve merhūm Sayyid Mehmed veledi Sayyid Abdurrahman ve müşterekiyle ve kıt a-i arz-ı Vādiyü'l-arāle el-mezbūreyi dahı merküm Mustafa veled-i Süleyman ve müşterekiyle Edhemiyye Zāviyesi Vakfı tarafından zabt ve karye-i Beyt-i Safāfe? el-mezbūrenin el-öşr an māli'l-vakfıyla kıt a-i arz-ı Vādiyü'l-arāle el-mezbūrenin mahsūlātını ahz u kabz murād eylediklerinde hılāf-ı Defter-i hākanī ve mugāyir-i kanūn fuzūlī müdāhale ve gadr sevdāsında oldukların inhā ..." BOA, ADVNS.AHK.ŞM (6): 138/2.

300 "... ber-mukteżā-yı Defter-i Hākanī karye-i Beyt-i Safāfa el-mezbūrenin kısm-ı mine's-sülüs mahsūlātının on yedi kıratıyla yine bir kıratında on üç kıratı cānibine 'ā'id mahsūlātıyla rüsūmātı merkūm Sayyid Mehmed veled-i Sayyid Abdurrahmān ile sāir müşterekleri taraflarından ve altı kıratıyla yine bir kıratının on bir kıratı cānibine 'ā'id mahsūlātı Kudüs-i Şerīfde vāki' Münhaliyye Medresesi Vakfı tarafından ve'l-'öşr 'an māli'l-vakfı dahi yine Kudüs-i Şerīf'de vāki' Edhemiyye Zāviyesi Vakfı tarafından ve kıt'a-i arz Vādiyü'l-Arāle el-mezbūrenin mahsūlātı dahı kezālik Kudüs-i Şerīf'de vākı Edhemiyye Zāviyesi Vakfı tarafından ve'l-'öşr an māli'l-vakfı dahi merkūm Mustafa veled-i Süleyman ile sāir müşterekleri taraflarından ve beyt fī mahalle-i Bābü'l-'Amūd ... el-mezbūre dahi

was reported that they were interested in seizing the revenues of the village of Abu Muʿīn.[301] As a result of the analysis of the records, the shares of each *waqf* from the revenues were distinguished in detail.[302]

On the other hand, the *mutawallīs* (mostly the deputy *mutawallī*), who were in charge of collecting *waqf* revenues and taxes, were also subjected to difficulties in order to prevent the collection of revenues from the *reʿāyā*, who were defined as *ashāb-ı ağrāz* (malicious people). For example, in Shawwal 1197 AH/1783 CE, although the *Zāwiya* Maghāriba *Waqf* in the ʿAyn Kārim town of Jerusalem and various lands and places in Jerusalem belonged to the *Khanqāh* al-Ṣalāḥiyya *Waqf*, the *mutawallī* of the lodging *waqf*, Shaykh Abdullah, was subjected to difficulties and problems while collecting the tithe tax and customary taxes belonging to the *Waqf*. Upon the notification of the situation by Shaykh ʿAbdullāh, the *zāwiyedār* and *mutawallī* of the Zāwiya

kezālik Edhemiyye Zāviyesi Vakfı tarafından zabt olunmak iktizā eylediğin hālā Rikāb-ı Hümāyūnum'da Defter Emīni olan es-Sayyid Abdurrahīm Mecid -dāme mecdühū- arz itmeğin sen ki vezīr-i müşārün-ileyhsin arzı mūcebince amel olunmak bābında mütemerrid şurūtı derciyle emr-i ālī yazılmışdır. Fī Evāhir-i Receb Sene [1]228." BOA, ADVNS.AHK.ŞM (6): 138/2.

301 "... merkümān Sayyid Musa ve Sayyid Abdülbedī ? Nasrī Mehmed bin Ahmed el-Tūrī Vakfı'nın askerī rūznāmçesinden virilen berāt-ı şerīfemle ber-vech-i iştirāk mütevellīleri olmalarıyla karye-i Ebū Mu īn el-mezbūreyi ber-mūceb-i Defter-i hākanī Ribāṭ el-Mansūr Vakfı mütevellīsi ve hisse-i merküm mutasarrıfı ve merküme Sayyid Mustafa ve müştereki ve hass mutasarrıfıyla ve karye-i . el-mezbūreyi dahı Hüseyniye Medresesi Vakfı mütevellīsi ve merküm Abdullah ve müşterekiyle zabt ve karye-i Ebū Mu īn el-mezbūrenin dört kıratı cānibine ā'id mahsūlātıyla karye-i . el-mezbūrenin üç kıratıyla bir kıratın sülüsi cānibine 'ā'id mahsūlātı Nasrī Mehmed bin Ahmed el-Tūrī Vakfı tarafından kanūn ve defter mūcebince ahz u kabz murād eylediklerinde hılāf-ı Defter-i hākanī ve mugāyir-i kanūn fuzūlī müdāhale ve gadr sevdāsında oldukların inhā ..." BOA, ADVNS.AHK.ŞM (6): 136/1.

302 "... karye-i Ebū Muʿīn hālī ez-ra'iyyet el-mezbūrenin kısm mine's-sülüs mahsūlātın dört kıratı cānibine 'ā'id mahsūlātı Nasrī Mehmed bin Ahmed el-Tūrī Vakfı tarafından ve bir buçuk kırat ve rubʿ kıratı cānibine 'ā'id mahsūlātı Ribāṭ el-Mansūr Vakfı tarafından ve üç kıratıyla üç rubʿ kıratı cānibine 'ā'id mahsūlātı hisse-i mevkūf deyu tahrīr olundığına bināen mutasarrıfı tarafından on dört buçuk kıratı cānibine 'ā'id mahsūlātı ve'l-'öşr 'an māli'l-vakfı ve rüsūmāt-ı sāiresi merkūm Sayyid Mustafa veled-i Sayyid İsmail ile sāir müşterekleri taraflarından ve ber-vech-i nakd bin iki yüz elli akçesi dahi Hāss-ı Hümāyūn mutasarrıfı tarafından ve karye-i ... el-mezbūrenin kısm mine's-sülüs mahsūlātının sekiz kıratı cānibine 'ā'id mahsūlātı Hüseyniyye Medresesi Vakfı tarafından ve üç kıratıyla bir kıratın sülüsi cānibine 'ā'id mahsūlatı Nasrī Mehmed bin Tūrī Vakfı tarafından ve on iki kıratıyla bir kıratın sülüsānı cānibine 'ā'id mahsūlāt ve'l-'öşr 'an māli'l-vakfı ve rüsūmāt-ı sāiresi merkūm Abdullah bin Hasan ile sāir müşterekleri taraflarından zabt olunmak iktizā eylediğin hālā Rikāb-ı Hümāyūnum'da Defter Emīni olan es-Sayyid Abdürrahim ... -dāme mecdühū- 'arz itmeğin sen ki vezīr-i müşārün-ileyhsin arzı mūcebince amel olunmak bābında mütemerris ve şurūt-ı derciyle emr-i 'ālī yazılmışdır. Hāmī. Fī Evā'il-i Receb Sene [1]228." BOA, ADVNS.AHK.ŞM (6): 136/1.

Maghāriba *Waqf*, an investigation conducted at the Imperial Archives revealed that the *waqf*s had separate proportions of the revenues of the village of ʿAyn Kārim and that the collection should be made separately. It was even recorded that the amount to be delivered from the village to the lodges that year was mistakenly written as 2,942 *akçe* when it should have been 9,442 *akçe*.[303]

In the ruling dated Ramadan 1234 AH/1819 CE regarding the same *waqf*, Suleiman Mehmed and his partners, who demanded the granting of the *Zāwiya* Maghāriba *Waqf*, 1/3 of the revenues of ʿAyn Kārim village, 1/3 of which belonged to the Malik Ṣalāḥ al-Dīn *Waqf*, 1/3 of the revenues of Tūrat al-Jawz village, 1/3 of which belonged to the Saljūqiyya *Madrasa Waqf*, and ¼ of the revenues of various hamlets, were deemed appropriate to collect the revenues and taxes and to give 1000 *akçe* to the central government in return as *khāss-ı şāhī*.[304]

In another ruling, it was reported that the tithe tax and customary tax revenues of the ʿAyn Silwān village, which was the property of the Ṣalāḥiyya *Madrasa Waqf*, were 4,500 *akçe* in terms of the revenues of the *waqf*, which should have been handed over to the Head of Commander of Jerusalem since it was his property, but foreigners interfered with it and the *Ḥaramayn* Accounting Books were consulted for the revenues of the *waqf*. In the accounting book records, it was ruled that the amount of 5000 acres, which included 4.5 Egyptian coins per day, three rubʿs of trusteeship shares, 50–60 foot soldiers *reʿāyā* in the district, and the revenues of the Ṣalāḥiyya *Madrasa* property, ʿAyn Silwān Village, together with the *hass-ı mir-livâ* and other customary taxes that amounted to 5000 coins, should be handed over to the Head of the Commander.[305] The

303 BOA, ADVNS.AHK.ŞM (3): 152/2.

304 BOA, ADVNS.AHK.ŞM (7): 6/2.

305 "... Hazīne-i ʿĀmirem'de mahfūz Haremeyn Muhasebesi defterlerine nazar olundukda Kudüs-i Şerīf'de Hangāh-ı Salāhiyye Medresesi Vakfı'nın yevmī dört buçuk Mısrī para ile üç rubʿ hisse tawliyai mezkūrdan Sayyid Ali el-Takī birāder Sayyid ... ve Sayyid Ahmed ve Sayyid ... ve bir rubʿ hissesi dahi mezkūr Sayyid Mehmed ile es-Sayyid Mustafa ve es-Sayyid Abdullah ve es-Sayyid Ahmed'in iştirāken bā-işāret-i ʿaliyye üzerlerinde oldığı mestūr ve Defterhāne-i ʿĀmirem'de mahfūz defter-i icmāl ve Mufaṣṣal ve evkāfa mürācaʿat olundukda Kudüs-i Şerīf nāhiyesine tābiʿ Vakf-ı es-Sultan el-Melik en-Nāsır Yusuf bin Eyyūb Ali Medresesine der-Kudüs-i Şerīf deyü yazıldığı mahallin tahtına kıtʿa ve karye-i ʿAyn-ı Silvān tābiʿ-i Kudüs-i Şerīf maʿa kurā-i mevādd-ı sāire ... deyu defter-i evkāfda muharrir kalemiyle tahrīr-i defter olmuşdur ve yine nāhiye-i mezbūre elli altmış nefer reʿāyā ile karye-i ʿAyn-ı Silvān Vakf-ı el-Melik en-Nāsır es-Sultan Salāhaddin Yusuf bin Eyyūb Ali Medresesi bi'l-Kudüs-i Şerīf el-ʿöşr hass-ı mīr-livā ve hāsıl-ı ... el-ʿöşr ʿan hamīle-i münhasıl ve ʿan ... ʿani'l-māli'l-vakf ʿani'l-harāc ve resm ... maʿa gayr-i el-ʿöşr maʿa rüsūm ve bād-ı hevā dört bin akçe yazu maʿa ziyāde ber-vech-i maktū der-ʿuhde-i Mevlānā İshak el-Müderris ... Sultan Salahaddin el-mezbūr fī sene beş bin akçe ber-mūceb-i ... mīr-livā olanlara teslīm eyle deyü defter-i Mufaṣṣalda muharrir kalemiyle tahrīr ve defter-i icmālde el-ʿöşr maʿa

mutawallī, supervisor and tomb keeper of the *waqf* of Tomb of Tāshtīmuriyya Shaykh ʿAbdullāh reported that although he was responsible for collecting the revenues of *waqf* shops, marketplace and six revenue items recorded in the books, some people from certain malicious ones (*aṣḥāb-i aghrāḍ*) had created troubles to be able to prevent the collection of these tithe tax and other ordinary taxes.[306]

4.2.3.2 *Usurpation by the* Sipahis (*Fief Holders*)

Another group that caused difficulties in the collection of *waqf* revenues and taxes were the owners of *zeʿāmet* and *tīmār*.

According to a decree dated 1156 AH/1743 CE sent to the *Qāḍī* of Jerusalem, while the *waqf*, was collecting the tithe and other taxes of the village named ʿAlem, a *sipahi* from the fief owners in the vicinity of the village intervened and collected the *waqf* taxes himself. Upon the notification of this situation contrary to the law and practices, it was ruled that the intervention of the *sipahi* should be prohibited and the practices should continue in accordance with the law.[307]

The *zāʿim* and *sipahi*s of the nearby *timar* and *zeʿāmet* villages intervened in the villages of Khasseki Sultan's public kitchen in Jerusalem, which were within the boundaries of the villages subject to the *Sanjāq* of Jerusalem and its sub-districts, on the grounds that the *waqf* villages were part of the *timar* and *zeʿāmet* (fief) villages, and forcibly seized their revenues. After an investigation to determine whether the villages were *waqf* or fiefs, it was understood that the revenues should be paid to the *waqf* and the *zāʿim* and *sipahi*s who interfered with the *waqf* revenues were prohibited from interfering.[308] In another ruling, the tithe tax and customary taxes of places such as the *waqf* share owned by Ṣalāḥ al-Dīn Ayyūbī in the hamlet of *Khān* al-Karīm in Jerusalem and the *waqf*

---

rüsūm dört bin beş yüz akçe yazu ile Mīr-livā-i Kudüs-i Şerīf hāssından olmak üzre tahrīr-i defter olmuşdur bu takdīrce ber-mukteżā-yı Defter-i Hākanī sāl-be-sāl ber-vech-i maktū mīr-livā olanlara beş bin akçe virmek üzre karye-i ʿAyn-ı Silvān el-mezbūrenin ve'l-ʿöşr ʿan hāmileri münhasıl ʿani'l-... ve ʿan māli'l-vakf ʿani'l-harāc mahsūlātıyla rüsūmātı müşārün-ileyh Melikü'n-Nāsır Sultan Selahaddin Yusuf bin Eyyūb'un Kudüs-i Şerīfde olan Medresesi Vakfı tarafından zabt olunmak iktizā eylediğin ..." BOA, ADVNS.AHK.ŞM (3): 129/2.

306 BOA, ADVNS.AHK.ŞM (3): 156/1.

307 BOA, ADVNS.AHK.ŞM (1): 37/3.

308 BOA, ADVNS.AHK.ŞM (2): 76/2; 290/2.

share belonging to the Madhhabiyya *Madrasa*, and the persons to whom they were allocated were defined in detail.[309]

ʿAbd al-Ḥayy and al-Shaykh ʿAbdullāh were jointly the *mutawallī*s of the Madhhabiyya *Madrasa Waqf* with a charter, and they restrained the aforementioned hamlet with the *mutawallī* of the Malik Ṣalāḥ al-Dīn *Waqf* and the *mutasarrif* of the *mīr-livā-i khass*, and the town of Bayt Sāḥūr Wādī with the share holder of the Muḥyī al-Dīn share and the aforementioned *sipāhi* and others jointly, and they restrained the hamlet. They declared that they wished to keep and dispose of the harvest corresponding to eight *qirāṭ* 337 *akçe*s belonging to the *madrasa waqf* from the aforementioned town and twelve *qiraat* two thousand *akçe*s from the town of Bayt Sāḥūr Wādī in accordance with the law and the book. However, the aforementioned *sipāhi*s were not satisfied with their share and reported that they were unnecessarily interfering and bullying with the crops belonging to the madrasa *waqf*. The shares checked from the *ruznāmçe, icmāl* and *mufaṣṣal* books in the Imperial Archives were confirmed, and it was ruled to prevent the unjustified interventions of the *sipāhi*s.[310] Another ruling was issued in 1206 AH/1791 CE to prevent the unjust intervention of the *sipāhi*s, who were the mutual owners of fiefs, in the hamlet belonging to the Mazhabiyya *Waqf*.[311] Sayyid Ahmed son of Sayyid Ali, who was the *mutawallī* of the Ahmed Altıncı *waqf*, who was the owner of 8300 *akçe*s of *timar* in Kaluca town in Jerusalem, was not satisfied with the tithe and other customary taxes that he was supposed to collect and coveted the excess and caused losses to the *waqf*.[312]

309 "... Kudüs-i Şerīf Sancağında ve Nāhiyesinde mezraʻa-i Hānü'l-karīm nām-ı diğer Hān-ı ... der-nezd-i Kudüs-i Şerīf hāsıl-ı kısm-ı mine'r-rubʻ hisse-i Vakfü'l-Melik Selāhaddin Ali der-Kudüs-i Şerīf on altı kırāt altı yüz altmış üç akçe ve hisse-i Vakf-ı Medrese-i Mezhebiyye der-Kudüs-i Şerīf sekiz kırāt üç yüz otuz yedi akçe el- öşr an māl-i vakf hass-ı mīr-livā yüz akçe yekūn bin akçe ve yine Kudüs-i Şerīf nāhiyesine tābiʻ Beyt-i Sahūrü'l-Vādī ... vakf nefer otuz yedi hāsıl-ı kısm mine's-sülüs on beş kırāt hınta ve şaʻīr ve harāc-ı isticār dört bin akçeden hisse-i Vakf-ı Medrese-i Mezhebiyye on iki kırāt iki bin akçe ve hisse-i Muhyiddin on iki kırāt iki bin akçe el-ʻöşr ʻan cümle münhasıl ve zeʻāmet ve timārının üç yüz akçe ve resm-i ... dört yüz akçe ve bād-ı hevā yüz akçe yekūn el-ʻöşr ve rüsūm-ı bād-ı hevā bin sekiz yüz akçe yazular ile defter-i Mufaṣṣalda muharrīr kalemiyle başka başka tahrīr ve defter-i icmālde beyt-i Sahurü'l-Vādī karyesinin el- öşr rüsūm-ı bād-ı hevā diyü bin sekiz yüz akçe ma a gayrhi yazılup dört bin sekiz yüz akçe yekūnundan iki bin beş yüz akçesi ifrāz ve tamāmen karye-i Beyt-i Sahurü'l- ... ve gayrıdan dört bin beş yüz akçe timāra mutasarrıf Yusuf ve Ahmed ve ... Halīl'in ve bākīsi müştekī kaydlarında oldığı Defter-i hākanīde mukayyed ..." BOA, ADVNS.AHK.ŞM (4): 150/1.

310 BOA, ADVNS.AHK.ŞM (4): 150/1.

311 BOA, ADVNS.AHK.ŞM (4): 160/3.

312 BOA, ADVNS.AHK.ŞM (5): 30/2.

There are also provisions on the *re'āyā* who owned the *ze'āmet* and *timar* of the *waqf* land in the *sanjāq* and sub-district of Jerusalem, and on the tithe and other customary of *waqfs* such as the *Madrasa* Madhhabiyya *Waqf*, Muḥyī al-Dīn *Waqf*, and Çeharkes *Waqf*, as well as on the unjust intervention in the Maghhabiyya *Waqf*.[313]

4.2.3.3 *Usurpation by the* ahl al-'urf

In the period we have examined, some members of the *ahl al-'urf* were engaged in tax collecting, preventing the collection of taxes or attempting to tax the people themselves. Although the oppression of the people by the tyrants was emphasized, such individuals also found favor with the people who did not want to fulfill their heavy tax obligations. They became their supporters and strengthened their power.

In the *Sanjāq* and district of Jerusalem, Ibrāhīm son of 'Alī, who was the owner of a village named Ṣūr Bāhir and a fief of two thousand *akçe* in the *sanjāq* and district of Jerusalem, was interfered with by the *sanjāq* and *waqf* mutualists in the collection of the revenues of the *waqf* and the revenues including the revenues such as tithe and other customary taxes. When the Land Registry records were analyzed, it was ruled that the collection of the hamlets, which were described in detail in the relevant record, and the revenues and taxes of the *waqf* were to be collected by Ibrāhīm son of 'Alī, the fief holder, and that the other *ahl al-'urf* members were not to interfere.[314]

In another similar example, after the childless death of 'Alī son of Ḥasan, the *mutawallī* of a six thousand *akçe* fief in the town of Bayt Ṣafāfā in Jerusalem, 'Abdullāh son of Sa'īd, to whom the duty was entrusted, was unnecessarily interfered with by the Regiment Leader of Jerusalem and his followers, who forcibly seized the *waqf* revenues and taxes.[315]

In another example of bullying of *waqf re'āyās* of Ramla, Ludd, and the related towns of Sulṭān Sulaymān Khān and Khāṣṣekī Sulṭān *awqāf* were forcibly distributed livestock and were put in a difficult situation by demanding their salaries. Although they paid the taxes of the villages that were freely owned to the governors of Damascus in full, the governors and *mutaṣallim* (deputy governor) of Damascus demanded 70–80 *kurūsh* for the animals that were forcibly distributed by the governors and *mutaṣallim* of Damascus, which

313 For example, see: BOA, ADVNS.AHK.ŞM (4): 160/3; 150/1.

314 BOA, ADVNS.AHK.ŞM (2): 56/4.

315 BOA, ADVNS.AHK.ŞM (4): 57/1.

were 20 *qurūsh* each, and caused the *re'āyās* to be miserable and migrate to other places due to the amounts they could not pay.[316]

In another ruling, it is stated that the *re'āyā* of the town of Lud and subordinate towns of Sultan Suleiman Khan and Khasseki Sultan *Waqfs* in Jerusalem were exempted from extraordinary taxes (such as *cürm-i cināyet, resm-i arūsāne, kul ve cāriye müjdegāneleri* and *bād-ı hevā*). Although they were exempt from these taxes, the governor of the Damascus province, the governor of Damascus *sanjāq* and his deputy, tax collector, Regiment Leader and other people from the *ahl al-'urf* elites demanded these taxes as an innovation and made the people miserable. Upon the notification of the situation by the Chief Eunuch, as the inspector of *Ḥaramayn Waqfs*, an order was issued to prevent the intervention of the *ahl al-'urf* in the aforementioned *waqf* villages with reference to the order issued by Sultan Murad Han for the tax exemption of the villages belonging to the sultan *waqfs*.[317] The edict sent in 1181 AH/1767 CE for the non-humiliation of the Khasseki Sultan *Waqf* villages' *re'āyā* was renewed on Muharram 1183/1769 ordering that the *re'āyā* would not be humiliated by the deputy *mutasallims* against the principle of tax exemption.[318]

In another imperial decree dated the same date (24 Muharram 1183), it was understood that the *mutasallims* of the *waqf* Ramla and Gaza were demanding fees.[319] A new imperial decree was sent stating that the *waqf re'āyā* would not be humiliated with this unlawful revenue demands.[320] This time, the revenues of the same *waqf*, *voyvodas* who were from the *ahl al-'urf* elites and were holders of *muqāta'as* in Gaza and Ramla appointed criers (*mübaşir*) by fraud and demanded fees under the name tax for the service of criers (*hıdmet-i mübaşiriyye*).[321] Again, former Chief Eunuch Mehmed, the *mutawallī* of the

316 BOA, ADVNS.AHK.ŞM (2): 9/1.

317 "... İmdī Selātīn-i İzām Evkāfı karyeleri mefrūzü'l-kalem ve maktū'ü'l-kadem min-külli'l-vücūh serbest hāriçden kat'ā dahl olunmak cā'iz değildir kanun üzere 'amel olunmak için Hudāvendigār-ı esbāk 'ammī-zādem merhūm ve mağfūrün-leh Sultan Mahmud Hān -tābe serāhü- zemānında emr-i şerīf virilüp tecdīdin recā itmekle vech-i meşrūh üzre 'amel olunmak emrim içün yazılmışdır." BOA, ADVNS.AHK.ŞM (2): 156/1. Benzer bir örnek için bkz. BOA, ADVNS.AHK.ŞM (2): 314/5.

318 "... Kāimmakām-ı mütesellimler tarafından hala serbestiyet şurūtuna muğāyir re'āyā-yı vakf rencīde olunmamak içündür. Emr-i şerīf sitāde. Bā arz-ı ... Ağa-i Dāru's-Sa'ādeti'ş-Şerīfe en-nāzır ve bā-fermān-ı 'ālī- Fī 3 Şa'ban 1183." VGMA, 523: 10/4,5.

319 "... Remle ve Gazze mütesellimleri taraflarından vakf-ı mezbūr re'āyālarını akçe talebiyle rencīde itdirilmemek içündür. Emr-i şerīf sitāde. Bā arz-ı Mehmed Ağa mütevelli-i vakf ve bā-fermān-ı şerīfe- Fī 24 Muharrem 1183." VGMA, (523: 10).

320 "... Re'āyā-yı vakf rencide itdirilmemek içündür. Emr-i şerif sitāde. Bā arz-ı Mehmed Ağa mütevelli-i vakf ve bā fermān-ı şerīfe- Fī 21 Receb1184." VGMA, 523: 8.

321 BOA, ADVNS.AHK.ŞM (2): 189/3.

Khasseki Sultan *Waqf*, reported that although the *mutawallī* of the *waqf* duly collected the the tithe and customary taxes that should have been collected from the *re'āyā* in the villages of the *waqf* according to the book, the *mutasallims* of Jerusalem and members of *ahl al-'urf* elites of Jerusalem demanded unfair taxes from the *re'āyā* and bullied them.[322] It was also stated that the revenues of the 'Īsawiyya village, one of the villages of the of Khasseki Sultan *Waqf*, were divided into three shares of *hisse-i mülk* (personal property), *waqf* and *sanjaqbey* (*mir-liva hassı*), and that six *qīrāṭ* shares of this division belonged to Sa'd al-Dīn's sons as personal property. Despite the order taken by the fathers of the property owners in 1193 AH/1779 CE in order to prevent the intervention of the the *ahl al-'urf* in the personal property, in 1209 AH/1794 CE, upon the intervention of the the *ahl al-'urf* in this share again, *waqf mutawallī*s Sayyid Sa'īd, Sayyid Ṣāliḥ, Sayyid Ḥusayn, Shaykh 'Abd al-Raḥmān, and Sayyid Abū Bakr, from the *sādāt*, came and presented the situation. In the aforementioned record, it was recorded that the total amount of the *waqf*'s revenues with tithe and other extraordinary (*bad-ı heva*) taxes was 4300 *kurūsh*.[323]

Shaykh Abū Ḥamza bin Ṣāliḥ 'Ukayl, the reciter of the mosque built 'Umar ibn al-Khaṭṭāb in Jerusalem, and his son Jānābi submitted a petition and stated that they were persecuted by demanding taxes from people who did not have any land or property in Jerusalem. In the ruling dated 1194 AH/1780 CE, it was ordered not to demand the *'avārız* tax from people who did not own land in Jerusalem and not to intervene with the demand of *tekālif-i şākka* by the *ahl al-'urf* elites without an order.[324] In another example, in the village of 'Ayn Kārim, one of the villages of the Maghāriba Sufi Lodge *Waqf*, it was reported that the *ahl al-'urf* elites demanded unjust *tekālif-i örfiye* from the *re'āyā* who were registered in *'avārız hāne*.[325]

---

322 "... Dīvān-ı Hümāyūn Kalemi'nden muktezāsı lede's-su'āl kurā-i mezbūre ahālī ve re'āyāları evāmir-i 'aliyyemle vārid olan tekāliflerin emr ve defter mūcibince cem'ine me'mūr olanlara edā eylediklerinden sonra ehl-i örf tāifesi taraflarından bilā-emr-i şerīf tekālif-i şakka talebi ve sāir gūne bed ve mezālim ve . . ile te'addī ve rencīde olunmamaları içün emr-i şerīfim i'tāsı iktizā eylediği tahrīr olunmağla vech-i meşrūh üzre 'amel olunmak fermānım olmağın imdi; eyyām-ı 'adālet mülūkānemde vazīfe-i cenāb . . olan re'āyā fukarāsına ve bir ferde bir vechle zulm u te'addī olundığına kat'a rızā-yı dāverānem olmayup vücūh-ı mezālim ve te'addiyātdan her hālde hımāyet u sıyānetleri min-külli'l-vücūh āsūde-nişīn esīr-i istirāhat olmaları matlūb-ı Pādişāhānem olmağla ..." BOA, ADVNS.AHK.ŞM (4): 92/1.

323 BOA, ADVNS.AHK.ŞM (4): 193:2.

324 BOA, ADVNS.AHK.ŞM (3): 39/4. For a similar demand and practices see also: BOA, ADVNS.AHK.ŞM (3): 110/4; 156/3.

325 "... karye-i 'Īsāviyye vakf-ı 'imāret Kudüs-i Şerīf hāsıl-ı kısım mine's-sülüs on kırāt hınta ve şa'ir ve mahsūl ... harāc isti'cār ve galle altı bin akçe senedin hisse-i vakf Ahmed Muhyiddin Ali iki kırāt ve rub' kırāt altı yüz seksen beş akçe ve hisse-i mülk-i Sa'adeddin ... altı kırāt

Finally, the olive oil revenues of the sub-district of Banī Zayd, which was among the villages of Masjid al-Aqṣā and Sahratullah *Waqf* and was exempt from the extraordinary taxes such as *tekālif-i örfiye*, *şakka* and *avārız-ı dīvāniye* and only had to pay taxes specified by the law and regulations, was intervened by the sub-district's *shaykhs*.[326]

---

bin beş yüz akçe ve hisse-i mülk-i İskender iki buçuk kırāt altı yüz yiğirmi beş akçe ve hisse-i mülk-i Halīl ... Mehmed yarım kırāt yüz yiğirmi beş akçe ve hisse-i vakf-ı imāret der-Kudüs rub' kırāt on iki kırāt üç bin altmış beş akçe el-'öşr 'an māli'l-vakf ve'l-mülk iki yüz doksan üç akçe ve resm-i ... ve bād-ı hevā yekūn hisse ma'a'l-'öşr resm dört bin üç yüz akçedir hisse-i vakf-ı 'imāret Kudüs-i Şerīf üç bin dört yüz akçe ve hisse-i mīri ber-vech-i nakd ber-mūceb-i defter-i atīk fī sene dokuz akçe yazu ile defter-i Mufaṣṣalda muharrīr kalemiyle tahrīr olundığı Defter-i Hākanī'de mukayyed ve mūmā-ileyhim mezkūr Sa'adeddin ... evlādından olmalarıyla merküm Sa'adeddin ... mülk tarafına tahrīr olunan altı kırāt hisseye mülkiyet üzre bā-hüccet-i şer'iyye mutasarrıflar olup karye-i mezbūreyi ber-mūceb-i Defter-i Hākanī hisse-i mülk ve vakf ve hass mutasarrıflarıyla zabt ve hāsıl-ı kısm mine's-sülüs mahsūlünden Sa'adeddin ... mülki tarafına 'ā'id altı kırāt hissesi mülkiyet üzere ahz u kabz murād eylediklerinden bir vechle müdāhale īcāb itmez iken evkāf ve emlāk-ı mezkūre ve hass mutasarrıfları Defter-i Hākanī mūcebince taraflarına 'ā'id olan hisse ... ahz u kabzına kana'at itmeyüp ziyādeye tecāvüz ile ..." BOA, ADVNS.AHK.ŞM (4): 191/4.

326 "Kudüs-i Şerīf Kadısına ve Valisine hüküm ki; İftihārü'l-havass ve'l-mukarrabīn mu'temedi'l-mülūk ve's-selātīn muhtāru'l-izzu ve't-temkīn bi'l-fi'il Dāru's-Sa'ādeti'ş-Şerīfe Ağası olub Haremeyn-i Şerifeyn Evkāfı nāzırı olan Hacı Beşir Ağa -dāme 'uluvvehū- Dīvān-ı Hümayun'a arz gönderüb taht-ı nezāretlerinde olmağla Kudüs-i Şerīf eyāletinde vāki' Hazreti Halilurrahman -salavatullah ala nebiyyinā ve aleyhi's-selām- ve Mescid-i Aksā ve Sahratullah-ı Müşerrefe Evkāfı kurāları mefrūzu'l-kalem ve maktū'u'l-kadem min külli'l-vücūh ve tekālif-i örfiyye ve şakka ve avārız-ı dīvaniyyeden muaf olub üzerlerine edāsı lāzım gelen hukuk ve rüsūmların cānib-i vakfa eda ve zābiti vakıf ma'rifetiyle zabt u ru'yet ve re'āyāsı rencīde ve tecrīdden himāye olunub āherin dahl ve te'addisi men' ve def' olunmak bābında şerefsüdūr iden emr-i 'ālīşāna muğāyir Benī Zeyt Nāhiyesi meşāyihleri mücerred re'āyāya tahrīr itdirilmemek içün tahrīri ve cānib-i vakfa hāsıl kayd olunan revgan-ı zeyt mahsūlün vakt ve zemaniyle edaya te'allül ve muhalefet izhāriyle ta'tīline sebeb ve bādī ve ihtilāl-i umūra mü'eddī oldukları mütevelli-i vakf inhā itmekle nāhiye-i mezkūrenin revgan-ı zeyt mahsūlü cevāmi-i lātifede i'kād olunan kanādil içün aynī vakfa īrad kabul olunduğu mestūr ve mukayyed olub zeyt *mahsūlü vakfin akdem umūru olub* re'āyāya ihtilallari sāire dahī sirāyet ile vakfa mūcibi gadr olduğu zāhir ve āşikar olmağla nāhiye meşāyihlerinin ol-makūle muğāyir-i nizām-ı kadīm ve hilāf-ı serbestīsine ve men' ve hareketleri men' ve def' ve cānib-i vakfa āid ve rāciğ olan zeyt mahsūlüne aynī ve vakfa zemaniyle taraf-ı vakfa teslīm itdirmeyüb fi mā ba'd umūr-ı re'āyāya dahi ve ta'arruz ve nizām-ı vakfa te'addīden bī-gāyed tevakkī ve mücānebet itmeleri tefhīm ve .. olunmayub tekrar tasaddī iderler ise .. ve iclā olunub ... arz ve i'lām olunmak ve re'āyā-yı vakfa serbestiyet üzere zabt-ı birle zabt ve ru'yet ve [taraf-ı] āherden bir ferd dahl ve te'addī itdirilmemek bābında hükm-i hümayun virilmek ricāsına i'lām eylemeyin mūcibince hüküm deyu fermān-ı 'āli sādır olmağın vech-i meşrūh üzere emr-i şerīf yazılmak içün işbu tezkire virildi. 18 Rebiu'l-evvel Sene 1163." VGMA, 814: 106–2.

In the ruling dated 1164 AH/1750 CE, it was reported that the shaykhs of the aforementioned towns interfered with the *waqf* again and provoked the *re'āyā* of the *waqf*.[327] The olive oil, which was requested in kind to be burned in the lamps of the Masjid al-Aqṣā and Sahratullah mosques, was also the subject of edicts sent to Jerusalem in 1190 AH/1776 CE and 1191 AH/ 1777 CE.[328]

The various interventions and interference in the collection of revenues and taxes belonging to the *waqf*s of Jerusalem, of which we have given some examples above and of which we have been able to identify only those that were recorded, reflect the contradictions within the administrative order in 18th century Jerusalem. In a sense, the state had to deal with the effects of this localization while localizing the administration in the provinces. This is confirmed by the fact that the administrative-local elites, defined as those who made decisions on behalf of the city, were also the source of the bullying movements.

In the *waqf* villages, the interference of the ruling elite to the tax exemptions through issuing new taxes and oppressing the *re'āyā* were reported to the central government by the *waqf mutawallī*s or inspectors. In the orders sent by the state in response to the abuses reported by *mutawallī*s or inspectors of *waqf*s, or by submitting a petition or a collective petition, orders were given to prohibit those who collected taxes illegally and oppressed the *re'āyā*. Most of the time, the state merely reminded them of the law and warned them, and if necessary, warned them again. There are not many records indicating that these officials were dismissed or exiled. From the *re'āyā*'s point of view, the free status of the *waqf* villages seems to have been the *re'āyā*'s only defense against the attempts of officials and *a'yān* to collect money from the *re'āyā* for their own account. These unlawful practices led to the impoverishment of the villagers and their abandonment.

In addition, the autonomous behavior of some provincial administrators in the period we have analyzed led the state to rely more and more on the *a'yān* both to break their power and to enforce their orders. In the period we have examined, the *a'yān* sometimes joined forces with officials to exploit the *re'āyā*, sometimes supported the *re'āyā* to oppose the rulers, and sometimes

---

327 VGMA, 814: 111.

328 "… Nāhiye-i Benī Zeyd kurāları mahsullerinden mu'ayyen olan revgan-ı zeyt aynī teslim olub bedeli aynī teklif olunmamak içün emir. 29 Cemaziye'l-ahir 1190." VGMA, 763: 490/51. "… Benī Zeyd nāhiyesi kurālarının mu'ayyen olan yetmiş kantar revgan-ı zeyt tamamen tahsīl içün emir virilmişdir. 23 Safer 1191." VGMA, 763: 490/55.

participated in the city administration as intermediaries between the *reʿāyā* and the center.[329]

5 Conclusion

In conclusion, the documents we have included in this fourth part of our study, although they cannot be separated from historical influences, help us to understand the types of treatments, complaints and mechanisms that were part of the long development process of the *waqf* institution, how they worked, their problems and the methods by which they were tried to be solved. It was possible to see which legal apparatuses were in use and which local variations were accepted as part of *waqf* practice. The documents also show the extent to which the administration of *waqf*s was integrated into the state system. They also provide indications of the interests, conflicts and plans of officials, various factions and individuals. In fact, the documents reflect a representation of the daily workings of the *waqf* sphere. On the other hand, there are very few records concerning peasants and provincial officials, or the situation of Christians and Jews, indicating the state's control over agricultural production cycles. Sometimes, as reflected in the records, *waqf*s in the city had extensions in the surrounding areas and even in other parts of the province. Their administration, the adjudication of transactions, the control of financial and other financial aspects, the appointment system, and the assessment of claims all took place in the city center and were to some extent dominated by the Jerusalem elite. The *mutawallī*s of the *waqf*s, their officials, and sometimes their positions in the commissions or committees established for the affairs of the *waqf*s attest to this situation.

There is no record among the documents analyzed that clearly indicates the disintegration or breakdown of the *waqf* system. The conclusions reached are broadly similar to those reached by Richard Van Leeuwen in his study of the *waqf*s of Damascus. For example, the registers and rulings show no obvious internal conflicts resulting from external influences, only the obvious corruption of the *mutawallī*s and other actors intervening in the *waqf*s and their interventions to reorganize or improve the system.[330] None of the types of cases is so dominant as to give the impression that the balance within the system has become unstable, such as when the position of parties, such as beneficiaries

329 Özkaya, *Osmanlı İmparatorluğunda Āyanlık*, 29.

330 Van Leeuwen, *An Ottoman*, 186–93.

or *mutawallīs*, is seen to have deteriorated to the point of undermining the functioning of the system.

The examples given indicate that the central state's relationship with the *waqfs* was not based on a reorganization effort, but rather on the incorporation of *waqfs* into administrative structures.[331] Some examples show that *waqfs* were an integral part of the fiscal system and that disputes between *waqfs* and the state were mostly related to the collection of taxes and the division of authority between administrative representatives and *waqfs*. In general, the representatives of the *waqfs* were given priority and were protected against possible usurpation of authority and rights by local administrators. However, the state also took drastic measures when the revenues of the central treasury were at stake.

331 Van Leeuwen, *An Ottoman*, 191.

Conclusion

This study attempts to answer the question to what extent the *waqf*s of the city of Jerusalem were decisive in the urban space, urban society and the city's relations with the central government by focusing on the years 1703–1831. An attempt has been made to define Jerusalem society within the framework of the *waqf* practices of the Ottoman central government in the provinces, the political and social hierarchy, the power of the city elites and their relations with ordinary people.

In this study, the similarities and differences between Jerusalem as a provincial city and other Ottoman provincial cities are highlighted. After the Ottoman conquest, new *waqf*s were established in Jerusalem, which continued to increase in importance within the framework of the pilgrimage organization of the Ottoman central administration, and in some cases, allocations were made from the *waqf*s, or when the founders of the *waqf*s ceased to be descended from their children, it became one of the blessed places where the *waqf* revenues were directed. Gifts were sent to the region with *surra* regiments to be distributed during the pilgrimage season, various grants were made, and allocations were made to *waqf* employees. In Jerusalem, one of the few cities where the charitable activities of the Ottoman sultans were directed, the Khasseki Sultan public kitchen founded by Hürrem Sultan, the wife of Suleiman the Magnificent, served as a *waqf-imāret* to feed the hungry for the four hundred years of Ottoman rule in the region. The *imāret* provided free bread and food to many poor and needy people, including widows, orphans, the elderly, the sick and the infirm, as well as students, Sufis, travelers and pilgrims. *Waqf* employees also ate at the *imāret*, and many *'ulamā'* and scholars were among its beneficiaries. In fact, feeding the poor and needy and allocating funds from the *imāret* to prominent members of society was an important aspect of the *waqf-imāret* complexes of the Ottoman administration.[1] On the other hand, the city of Jerusalem in the early modern period was neither a center of commercial activity or industrial production, nor a regional center of political power. Of course, Jerusalem, like other urban settlements, had certain administrative, military and economic functions, but religion was in many ways the main factor driving the city's development.

In the first part of this study, we tried to determine the extent to which *waqf*s played a decisive role in the formation of urban space in the case of Jerusalem, since they were the *waqf* of the institutions that determined the development

1 Kazancıgil, *Edirne İmaretleri*; Singer, "İmâret," 72–74; Peri, "Waqf and Ottoman Welfare Policy," 167–86.

 | DOI:10.1163/9789004743441_007

of Jerusalem as an urban entity: first as a center of authority, second as a center of knowledge, third as a marketplace, and fourth as a spiritual center. *Waqfs* were an important means of imparting values to space that were rooted in tradition and a system of religious symbols. *Waqfs* were also an important tool for determining the status of properties, sanctifying them, and establishing and protecting their position in the urban fabric. Finally, *waqfs* served as a mechanism to coordinate between private interests and private initiatives and the interests of the urban community. It is through these functions that *waqf* networks have created the model that underpins urban development.

The mosques of Masjid al-Aqṣā and Dome of the Rock, which are of central importance for the *waqfs* of Jerusalem, the numerous Ayyubid and Mamluk *waqfs* within the *Ḥaram al-Sharīf*, and the numerous churches and synagogues shaped the skyline of the city. On the other hand, when we look at the period under study in terms of architectural activities, it is not possible to say that this period was very bright. Religious buildings in the *Ḥaram al-Sharīf* continued to be repaired frequently. However, apart from a few fountains built in the city, the largest structure built in and around Jerusalem was the castle on the road to Bethlehem. Similarly, the number of *madrasas* in Jerusalem declined markedly. Of the forty-nine *madrasas*, for example, dating from the Mamluk period, only forty-four were still teaching in the 18th century.

The grants of sultans or courtiers were centered around the *Ḥaram al-Sharīf*, the city's most important sanctuary. Therefore, the religious character of the city shaped its relationship with the ruling will as a dominant factor. The influence of religion also determined the composition of the local elite and the general contours of the city's physical structure. Indeed, the city's economy was largely based on the services provided to visitors who came to the city for religious purposes.

Since the urban structure was so encompassed by the phenomenon of *waqf*, the spiritual element should likewise be seen as an important tool in integrating the urban society. City life was largely organized by *waqf* networks. They represent the essence of the temporal-spatial organization that shaped social life and social relations. There is probably no person in Jerusalem whose life was not shaped by the *waqf* system, whether in the form of schools, mosques, commercial districts, public baths, coffee houses or other social gathering places, or in the form of salaries, grants and allocations. According to Richard Van Leeuwen, if the concept of the Islamic city were to be resurrected under another guise, the primary criterion to be evaluated would be the extent to which urban structures were shaped by *waqfs*.

In this study, it was argued that the primary function of *waqf* was their integrative role in social, economic, and political life. As discussed in the third chapter, as the provincial agents of Ottomanization, charitable-public *waqf* assumed important functions. This is because the *waqf* were one of the Ottoman institutions that connected with the center in Istanbul, and although their relationship with the palace was never severed, their appointments were ultimately made with the agreement of the local notables. The Khāṣṣekī Sulṭān *Waqf* and the Masjid al-Aqṣā and Qubbat al-Ṣakhra foundations; the Bīmāristān Ṣalāḥiyya, Muḥammadiyya, Osmaniyya, Ḥusniyya, Arghūniyya, Mencikiyya, Maymūniyya, Zülkādiriyya, Tāziyya, Emīniyya, and Ṣalāḥiyya *madrasa*; and the Bāsṭiyya, Jawhariyya, Tenkiziyya, and Malik Ṣalāḥ al-Dīn *Khānqāh*s were the main charitable-public *waqf* that made these relations possible in Jerusalem. Those of the Ottoman subjects in the provinces who were appointed to managerial positions in the sultanate's *waqf* saw their own interests in the continuity and stability of Ottoman rule. Such an identification increased their loyalty to the Ottoman Empire as well as their interests in their own regions.

The findings of this study show that most of the office holders were locals belonging to families that had been residents of Jerusalem for at least several generations. They held office either by direct appointment or by acting as proxies for state-appointed officials who were absent from their posts. In this process, methods such as shareholdings, the creation of new posts, succession from father to son, and the sale of offices were also frequently used. Jerusalem's local elite, mostly composed of *ʿulamāʾ*, were connected to the capital through various privileges granted by the center. From a different perspective, the existence of a large ruling elite layer was also an expression of the level of integration between the city as a whole and the imperial center.

In the case of Jerusalem, *waqf*s established by the ruling elite, such as governors and dignitaries, which in the case of Jerusalem range from modest and local *waqf*s, correspond to economic conditions and policies that reflect the general state of the city's development. *Waqf*s established by individuals or families, on the other hand, are the accumulation of the professional lives and achievements of individuals and generations, and thus constitute the source of family wealth. These categories of *waqf* have different historical functions and reflect different roles within the power structures to which they all ultimately belong. The *ʿulamāʾ*, are associated with all these types of *waqf* and represent, perhaps together with the state, the main force that integrates them into a single system.

Economic and administrative conditions led to the further development of *waqf* legislation to regulate competition over *waqf* properties and to incorporate newly emerging practices. The 18th century practices of *khuluww al-shāriʿ*, *istibdâl* and *hikr/hukr* are the ultimate examples of this situation. The elaboration of rules enhanced the practical aspects of the *waqf* concept, established the basis of the *waqf* as an independent institution, and protected its status. Simultaneously, the importance of *waqf*s in the policies of the state or, more specifically, the ruling elite increased. Not only did the economic potential of *waqf*s increase, generating new revenue streams, but they also became a mechanism for strengthening the state apparatus by shaping networks of relations and contributing to their subordination to state interests. The state's efforts to penetrate and control *waqf* networks were probably the main force shaping the development of the institution.

As explained with examples in the fourth and final part of this study, the political and financial ties that brought the provinces and the center closer together were established through the *waqf*. As is the case with many charitable *waqf*s in the provinces, the sultan had to support them even after the establishment phase was completed. Allowing the buildings to fall into disrepair could lead the people to believe that the dynasty and the palace had lost their power.

Another level of ties with the center was of a financial nature: The *waqf*s sent their surpluses to Istanbul or, as in the case of the allocation of *jizya* revenues, received funds when they were in need. This connection opened a channel for constant communication from Constantinople, as well as for the flow of complaints and petitions from Jerusalem.

Another focal point of interaction between the center and the city was direct taxes, the collection of which involved some degree of negotiation. As for the distribution of these taxes and other local costs among the city's inhabitants, or decisions on other aspects of city administration, these were a matter of local agreements and alliances, and the state apparently did not interfere in these matters. If the inhabitants of the city were dissatisfied with the decisions taken locally, they could always request the intervention of the state, and such requests were frequent during the period covered in this study. Moreover, the center often referred the resolution of various disputes to the decision-makers in Jerusalem.

*Waqf*s were also a means of strengthening state control. This was made possible by monitoring the economic infrastructure of social and political groups and their *waqf* properties, using *waqf*s as a basis for economic expansion, requiring an inventory of properties and the creation of records attached to legal and administrative archives. These records were maintained by the bureaucracy and legal organization, enabling the state to implement its policies and monitor transactions.

In conclusion, from any perspective, *waqf*s were institutions intertwined with the political, social, economic and cultural fabric in which they were embedded. When considered as a network, *waqf*s represented one of the main forms of organizational expression for society as a whole. They were so numerous and widespread that they radically shaped economic activity, property rights, urban-village relations and the appearance of cities. Religious rituals and education were almost entirely supported and shaped by their activities. From the most private and self-interested foundations to the most public and far-reaching undertakings, *waqf*s were collectively framed as acts of benevolence.

This historical process of changes in *waqf* law and practices in the early modern period such as the division of duties with shares, sale of offices, long-term leases of *waqf* properties, *khuluww al-shari'*, presented in the case of the *waqf*s of Jerusalem, took on a different dimension in the following century, culminating in the transformation of *waqf* properties into private property. As a result of this process, which accelerated in the second half of the nineteenth century and especially after the promulgation of the Land Law of 1858, many of the properties allocated to the *waqf*s of Jerusalem were legally or illegally sold, looted or converted into private property; and in some cases, most of the charitable *waqf*s disappeared.[2] On the other hand, the growing interest of Europeans in Jerusalem in the second half of the nineteenth century led them to acquire property in order to consolidate their presence in the city. European countries sought to acquire these properties through outright purchase, various forms of lease, or through agreements or gifts from Ottoman sultans within the framework of political and economic power relations. The processes by which the *waqf*s of Jerusalem, most of which were charitable in nature, were transformed into private property and could be bought and sold provide important clues about the current status of the *waqf*s.

2 For a detailed review describing the conversion of *waqf* properties in the city of Jerusalem to private ownership, see Sroor, *Fondations*, 461.

Glossary

ʿaʿyān al-umarāʾ notable commanders (elite military-administrative leaders)
ʿalā al-ruʾūs jizya tax based on financial capacity
ʿaqaba a steep road or buildings in the Old City of Jerusalem
ʿarḍ petition
ʿarḍ al-maḥḍar collective petitions
ʿakār endowed (*waqf*) properties
ʿaskerī military-administrative elite class
ʿaskarī rūznāma/askeri ruzname daily books of the ruling class
ʿatīq/atik old treasury records
ʿulamāʾ religious scholars
ʿurf customary law or sultanic authority
ʿushr tithe (10% tax on agricultural products)
adaletnāme sultanic order against abuses of power
aḥkām register of imperial orders
ahl al-sharīʿa experts in Islamic law (ʿulamāʾ)
ahl al-ʿurf administrative/military officials
ahlī awqāf family endowments
ajr mithl fair compensation for unauthorized property use
akāʾid core tenets of Islamic principles
akçe Ottoman silver coin (currency unit)
amīr al-ḥajj commander of the pilgrimage caravan
amīn/emin person in charge of services
arpalık supplementary salary for officials
arwām Ottoman Turks, Rumi, Anatolian
ashrāf descendants of the Prophet
asitane major sufi lodge
awqāf taḥrīr *waqf* land registry books
awlād children, descendants
aʿyān local notables
bā-muʿayyana specified, designated
bāb door, gate
babüssaāde ağası chief eunuch
bar wajh ḥasbī voluntary/ unpaid services
berāt official certificate of appointment
berevāt certificates of appointment (plural of berāt)
beşe junior military officer, janissary cadets
beylerbeyi governor-general of province

bīmāristān hospital (often charitable)
bint daughter
bölükbaşı commander of a janissary division (bölük)
cābī tax or revenue collector
cemaziyelahir Jumada al-Thani (6th month of the Hijri calendar)
çavuş sergeant or envoy
çelebi honorific for educated men (Sufis, scholars, or merchants)
çift-hane sistemi land-allotment system for family subsistence farming
çuhadar High ranking servant in the Inner Palace
cürm-i cinayet fine for homicide
daire-i adliye judicial system for equitable governance
dār house, building
dabbāgh tanner
dhimmī protected non-Muslim subjects (under Islamic rule)
divān-ı hümāyūn Imperial Council
dīwānī calligraphic script for official documents
dizdār fortress commander
effendi title for bureaucracts, scholars, or gentlemen
faqīh Islamic jurist, reciter, khalīfa, mullā
farmān imperial decree
farrāsh janitor or palace attendant
fatwā Islamic legal opinion issued by a mufti
fī sabīl Allāh for the sake of God
fiqh Islamic jurisprudence
fuqahā' Islamic jurists
ghayr ṣaḥīḥ invalid
ḥaddād blacksmith
ḥāfiẓ one who memorized the Quran
ḥākim al-sharīʿa sharia judge (qāḍī)
ḥammām public bathhouse
ḥāra urban neighborhood
Ḥaramayn the two Holy Sanctuaries (Mecca and Medina)
has odabaşı chief steward of the sultan's private quarters
ḥāṣil harvest revenue
ḥujjat al-sharʿī notarized legal document
ḥurūfāt appointment registers for officials
ḥikr long-term lease
hijrī Islamic lunar calendar
iʿlām court verdict document
ibqā' to sustain/maintain a legal status
ijmāʿ consensus of Islamic scholars

ikrār legal acknowledgment
imām prayer leader (in a mosque)
imāra/imaret public soup kitchen
infāq charitable spending for God's sake
ispençe fixed land tax on Christian peasants (re'āyā)
ishhād legal witnessing
istibdāl exchange/sale of waqf property
iṣḥā agent or representative
jābī/cabi tax collector
jadīd/cedid new
jizya poll tax on non-Muslim adult males
kalāmiyya bureaucratic scribal class
kapıkulu sultan's standing army (Janissaries, *sipahi*s)
kārkhāna workshop
kātib scribe or clerk
kasr thawāb increasing spiritual rewards
kethüdā-yeri deputy commander of the imperial cavalry
khalīfa caliph
khān/han caravanserai (travelers' inn)
khānqāh Sufi lodge
khāṣṣ imperial of elite-owned land
khasseki sultan Imperial concubine who bore a son (mother of a şehzade)
khātim reading the entire Quran
khayrāt charitable acts or endowments
khayrāt charities system
khayrī awqāf public-benefit endowments
khuluww permanent lease
kulliyya religious-social complex
levend irregular mercenaries
liwā' sanjāq, provincial subdivision
madrasa Islamic college
maḥalla urban neighborhood
maḥmās grinder
mālikāne lifetime tax-farming rights
mālikāne sistemi lifetime tax-farming system
maqāmāt mubāraka sacred sites
marqad tomb
masjid small mosque (for daily prayers without Fridays sermons)
mawlānā honorific title for Islamic scholars/Sufi masters
mawlid celebration of the Prophet Muhammad's birth
mazbut state-administered

mazraʿa cultivated farmland
memşā public toilet
menzilhane lodging station
meşihat shaykhdom or office of the sheikh al-Islam
mawlawi Mawlawi sufi order (following of Rumi)
mawlawkhāne Mawlawi lodge (Sufi center of rituals/teaching)
mezālim divānı atrocities court
minbār pulpit in a mosque
muʿallimkhāna school
muʿīd assistant to *mudarris*
muʾadhdhin call to prayer
mudarris professor in a madrasa
mufredat textbooks or curriculum manuals
mughāyir al-qānūn al-qadīm wa-l-ʿurf contrary to established law and custom
muḥāsaba accounting books
muḥaṣṣil deputy tax collector
muḥtasib market superintendent
muḥḍir officer summoning court parties
mühimme imperial decree registers
mulla local Islamic scholar
mülhak semi-autonomous waqf (managed privately but state-supervised)
muqātaʿa leased revenue collection
murattib organizer
musallā open-air prayer ground
mutaṣallim deputy governor
mutawallī waqf trustee
muʾtamad trusted agent
muwakkithane timekeeping office (determined prayer times)
nāʾib deputy judge
naqīb al-ashrāf official for sayyid and sharifs
nasihatname advice literature (for rulers/officials)
nāẓir inspector
niṣf half
nuqūd cash
pīr shaykh, sufi master
postnişin shaykh of Sufi lodge
qāḍī judge
qāḍī ʿaskar/kadiasker chief judge
qadīm old, customary
qānūn qadīm established legal norms

qānūnnāma/kanunname sultan's law code
qaḍā' qāḍī's jurisdiction
qiṭ'at arāḍī delimited agricultural plot
qismat 'askariyya inheritance distribution for ruling elite
qiyās comparison
qurūsh/kurush coin
Qur'ān holy book of Islam
qurrā' Qur'ān reciters
re'āyā/reaya ordinary people, tax-paying subjects, both Muslim and non-Muslim
ra'īs al-kuttāb head of editorial affairs
rasm 'arūsāna marriage tax
ribāṭ military buildings on border
rijāliyya high-ranking statesmen
riqābiyya gifts to sultan at Nevruz
riyāsat al-a'imma chief imam
riyāsat al-mu'adhdhinīn head of mu'adhdhins
ru'ūs tadhkira summary document for civil service appointments
rub' quarter
rusūm shar'iyya religious taxes
rusūm 'urfiyya customary taxes
ṣadaqa material aid to needy
ṣadaqa mawqūfa charity organization, waqf
sabīl fountains
salhane abattoir
sancakbeyi head of sanjāq
sanjāq/sancak provincial sub-administrative unit
sarica-sekban irregular salaried soldiers
sayyid wa sharīf descendants of Prophet
sekban mercenary soldier
serdar commander of janissaries
shaykh sufi master of tribal leader
sharī'a religious, moral, legal provisions of Islam
sijill court register
sikka coin
sipahi timar holder
sūfī people adopting Sufi lifestyle
sūq bazaar
sūra chapter of Qur'ān
surra grants, money, gifts
ṣulaḥā' righteous persons

ṣāliḥāt charities
tabhāne hostel
tabrīz demonstration
tadhkira summary document
taḥrīr tax revenue records
takālīf shaqqa mandatory taxes
tekke-zaviye sufi lodge
tamassuk official letter
tanẓīmāt reform period starting in 1839
taṣarruf right of use
thuluth one in three
thumun one in eight
tilāwa reading Qur'ān
timar fief system
timarhane mental asylum
topçu Ottoman artilleryman
türbe funerary monuments
valide sultan mother of sultan
wakāla commercial inn, caravanserai
waqf pious endowment
waqfiyya endowment deed
wāqif founder of waqf, endower
waẓīfa stipend or regular payment
wujūh al-balad urban notables
yadd amīn kutub librarian
yawmī daily wage
zaʿāma large revenues-generating estated (20,000+ akçe annually)
zahab gold
zakat alms
zāwiya/zaviye small sufi lodge
zirāʿa agriculture/ cultivation
zolota Polish money, isolette
dhurrī descendants, in *waqf* context: family beneficiaries
dhū al-qaʿda eleventh month in Hijri calendar

Appendix

TABLE A1 Jerusalem *Madrasa* records (1703–1831)

No.	Quarter name	*Madrasa* name	Endower	Founding date	First and last recording dates	VGMA (register: page/order)	Total record
1	Bābu'l-Hadīd	Arğūniyye	Seyfeddin Arğun el-Kāmilī	758/ 1356	Şaban 1167	1112: 1/203	1
2	Harem-i Şerif	Bāsıtıyye (Hangāh-ı Bāsıtıyye)	Kadı Zeyneddin Abdulbasīt bin Halil el-Dimeşkī	834/ 1430	Şaban 1143 – Cemaziyelevvel 1108	1107: 2/235	5
3	-	Belāsiyye ve İsmāiliyye	-	-	16 Receb 1207	515: 65/69	1
4	Kudüs-i Şerīf	Belediyye	-	-	10 Safer 1158	515: 51/53	11
5	Kudüs-i Şerīf	Birke (Börke) Han	-	-	Şevval 1132 – Muharrem 1134	110: 2/280	3
6	Kudüs-i Şerīf	Cebībiyye	-	-	Şevval 1121 – Safer 1120	1107: 2/95	3
7	-	Ceharkesiyye	-	-	Cemaziyelevvel 1207	515: 65/70	1
8	Harem-i Şerif	Dengiziyye (Tenkiziyye)	Şam naibi Emir Tenkiz el-Nasīrī	729/ 1328	Rebiulevvel 1137 – Zilkade 1228	1119: 110/32	10

TABLE A1 Jerusalem *Madrasa* records (1703–1831) (*cont.*)

No.	Quarter name	*Madrasa* name	Endower	Founding date	First and last recording dates	VGMA (register: page/order)	Total record
9	Derūn-i Mescid-i Aksā	Zāviye-i Habībe Medresesi	Ribāṭ-ı Alāeddin Emīr Alemüddin Sencere'd-Devādār es-Sālihī	-	Şaban 1111	1160: 116/84	1
10	Bāb-ı Hatta	Düveydāriyye (Hanefiyye Medresesi Mülhakatından Düveydāriyye Medresesi Zāviyesi)	Ribāṭ-ı Alāeddin Emīr Alemüddin Sencere'd-Devādār es-Sālihī	695/ 1295	Şaban 1111 – Cemaziyelevvel 1160	1160: 116/40	8
11	Kudüs-i Şerīf	Efrādiyye	-	-	Şaban 1110	1140: 245/48	1
12	Hatt-ı Davudda	Es-Sellāmiyye (Mevsıliyye)	Şeyh Mecdeddin Abdulmelik bin Ebubekir el-Musilī	-	Cemzaiyelevvel 1137	1119: 110/48	1

TABLE A1 Jerusalem *Madrasa* records (1703–1831) (*cont.*)

No.	Quarter name	*Madrasa* name	Endower	Founding date	First and last recording dates	VGMA (register: page/order)	Total record
13	Kudüs-i Şerīf	Evhādiyye	Melik el-Evhād Necmeddin Yusuf bin el-Melik Muazzam İsa bin el-Ādil tarafından	697/ 1297	Şaban 1110 – Muharrem 1131	1140: 245/47	3
14	Kudüs-i Şerīf	Fārisiyye	Emir Fārisī bin el-Emir Kutlu Melik bin Abdullah	755/ 1354	Safer 1120 – Receb 1138	1107: 2/163	7
15	Kudüs-i Şerīf	Ferhādiye	-	-	Cemaziyelevvel 1143	515: 56/58	8
16	Harem-i Şerif	Fenāriyye	Şihabeddin et-Tulūnī	800/ 1398	Cemaziyelevvel 1130	1107: 2/234	1
17	Tāziyye Medresesi yakınında	Geylāniyye (Hālidiyye)	-	753/ 1352	Zilkade 1123 – Cemaziyelevvel 1201	1107: 2/166	8
18	Kudüs-i Şerīf	Hanefiyye (Medreseti'l-Mu'azzamiyye)	El-Melik Mu'azzam İsa	606/ 1209	Zilhicce 1143 – Cemaziyelevvel 1163	1109: 6/69	9

TABLE A1 Jerusalem *Madrasa* records (1703–1831) (*cont.*)

No.	Quarter name	*Madrasa* name	Endower	Founding date	First and last recording dates	VGMA (register: page/order)	Total record
19	Kudüs-i Şerīf	Hangāh-ı Cevheriyye	Cevher el-Kunuk-bay el-Zimām	843/1439	Muharrem 1131 – Şaban 1143	1109: 6/22	2
20	Akabutü's-Sitt	Hasekiyye	Haseki Hürrem Sultan	1552	Cemaziyelahir 1126 – Muharrem 1147	1107: 2/184	12
21	Kudüs-i Şerīf	Hātuniyye	Şemseddin Muḥammad bin Seydeffin, el-Kazāniyye el-Bağdadiyye'nin kızı Ugul Hatun	755/ 1354	Cemzaiyelahir 1136 – Muharrem 1147	1119: 110/18	12
22	Nāzır Kapısı'nın kuzeyi	Hüsniyye	Emir Hüsameddin Ebu Muḥammad el-Husn bin Nasreddin	-	Cemāziyelahir 1126 – Rebiulahir 1181	1108: 1/64	2

TABLE A1 Jerusalem *Madrasa* records (1703–1831) (*cont.*)

No.	Quarter name	*Madrasa* name	Endower	Founding date	First and last recording dates	VGMA (register: page/order)	Total record
23	Kudüs-i Şerīf'de Karbun Mahallesi	Imādiyye	Şeyh 'Imadeddin Abdulhāfız Bediran bin Seyyid bin Tırkān	837/ 1434	Ramazan 1130 – Muharrem 1162	1112: 1/103	2
24	Kudüs-i Şerīf	Kāmiliyye	-	-	Şaban 1125 – Muharrem 1144	1107: 2/189	3
25	Bāb-ı Hatta	Kerīmiyye	-	700/ 1301	1104	1160: 116/132	1
26	Kudüs-i Şerīf	Medrese-i Hatun el-Osmānī	-	-	Muharrem 1116	515: 54/57	63
27	Nasāra	Medrese-i Hamrā (Hangāh-ı Salāhīde; Medrese-i Elhamr; Salāhiyyetü'l-Hamrā)	-	-	Receb 1112 – Rebiulevvel 1184	1107: 2/19	25
28	Kudüs-i Şerīf	Medrese-i Hangāh-ı Serāhiyye	-	-	Rebiulevvel 1111	1160: 116/39	1

TABLE A1 Jerusalem *Madrasa* records (1703–1831) (*cont.*)

No.	Quarter name	*Madrasa* name	Endower	Founding date	First and last recording dates	VGMA (register: page/order)	Total record
29	Hatta Kapısı ile Esbat Kapısı arasında	Medrese-i Kādiriyye	Misr Hatun'un babası Nasreddin Muḥammad el-Ğādirī	836/ 1433	Ramazan 1130	1107: 2/245	1
30	Kudüs-i Şerīf	Medrese-i Kāmiliyye Vakfı	-	-	Zilkade 1139	1128: 68/15	1
31	Kudüs-i Şerīf Mağaribe Mahallesi	Medrese-i Malikāniyye dimekle ma'ruf Ğalabiye Zāviyesine mutasarrıf Es-Seyyid Ömer Evkafları	Es-Seyyid Ömer Evkafları	-	Şaban 1111	1160: 116/42	1
32	Kudsi Şerif	Medrese-i Şārānī Vakfı	-	-	Rebiulahir 1203	1113: 35/33	1

TABLE A1 Jerusalem *Madrasa* records (1703–1831) (*cont.*)

No.	Quarter name	*Madrasa* name	Endower	Founding date	First and last recording dates	VGMA (register: page/order)	Total record
33	Davud Sokağı, Zincir Kapısı (Bāb-ı Silsile)	Medrese-i Tāziyye	Emir Tāz	-	Şevval 1121	1107: 2/97	1
34	Şeref Mah. Zincir Kapısı (Bāb-ı Silsile)	Medrese-i Taştimuriyye Evkafı	El-Eşref es-Seyfi Taştimur el-ʿAlāī	784/ 1382	Şaban 1137 – Ramazan 1137	1119: 110/55	2
35	Mağaribe Mahallesi	Medresetü'l-Mālikiyye el-Ma'rūf bikubbeti'l-Efdāliyye (Efzāliyye)	Melik Efdal Nūreddīn Ebi'l-Hasan ʿAli bin Sultan Salāhaddīn	589/1193	Cemaziyelahir 1121 – Muharrem 1140	1107: 2/78	3
36	Şeref Kapısı üzeri	Melikiyye	El-Melike Kutluktimur	757/ 1356	Muharrem 1127 – Safer 1134	1107: 2/217	7
37	Kudüs-i Şerīf	Mencikiyye	Emir Mencik Paşa bin Abdullah (Mehmed es-Seyfi Mencik el-Eşrefi)	730/ 1368	Rebiulahir 1118 – Zilkade 1123	1107: 2/167	3

TABLE A1 Jerusalem *Madrasa* records (1703–1831) (*cont.*)

No.	Quarter name	*Madrasa* name	Endower	Founding date	First and last recording dates	VGMA (register: page/order)	Total record
38	Bābü's-Sāhira yakınları	Meymūniyye	Emir Fāris al-Dīn Ebu Said Meymūn bin Abdullah el-Kasrī	593 /1196	Receb 1123 – Rebiulevvel 1149	1107: 2/140	10
39	Kudüs-i Şerīf	Musliyye	-	-	Receb 1119 – Şaban 1143	1107: 2/279	9
40	Kudüs-i Şerīf	Osman bināsı Medrese Vakfı	-	-	Cemaziyelahir 1129	1107: 2/226	1
41	Kudüs-i Şerīf	Osmaniyye (Isfahāniyye)	Isfahan Şah Hatun (Hanım)	840/ 1436	1104 – Cemaziyelahir 1156	1112: 1/12	7
42	Kudüs-i Şerīf	Salāhiyye	Sultan Selahaddin	588/ 1192	Muharrem 1111 – Rebiulevvel 1148	1140: 245/51	14
43	Kudüs-i Şerīf	Sebātiye (Mesatīn)	-	-	1104	1160: 116/127	1
44	Kudüs-i Şerīf	Si'irdiyye	Abdulgāni el-Si'irdī	952/ 1545	1112	1160: 116/105	1

TABLE A1 Jerusalem *Madrasa* records (1703–1831) (*cont.*)

No.	Quarter name	*Madrasa* name	Endower	Founding date	First and last recording dates	VGMA (register: page/order)	Total record
45	Kudüs-i Şerīf	Şeyhuniyye	Emir Seyfeddin Katişa bin Ali bin Muḥammad	761/ 1359	Cemaziyelevvel 1201	1113: 35/18	1
46	Hatta Kapısı	Tulūniyye	Şihābeddin Ahmed bin en-Nāsırī Muḥammad et-Tulūnī ez-Zāhirīye	800/ 1398 yılından önce	Cemaziyelevvel 1130 – Cemaziyelevvel 1130	1107: 2/232	2
47	Kudüs-i Şerīf	Ümmiyye	-	-	19 Şevval 1139	515: 36/12	1
48	Kudüs-i Şerīf	Yākubiyye	-	-	Safer 1139	1128: 68/4	1
49	Kudüs-i Şerīf	Zeyniyye	-	-	Cemaziyelevvel 1180	1108: 1/59	1
50	Harem-i Şerif	Zülkādiriyye	-	-	Rebiulevvel 1132 – Ramazan 1159	1107: 2/267	3
Total							278

FIGURE A1 *al-Ḥaram al-Sharīf* (National Library of Australia, nla pic. an23479017-v[1])

FIGURE A2 Bāb al-Qaṭṭānīn (Van Berchem, 1927, p. 737)

TABLE A2 *Masjid* records of Jerusalem (1703–1831)

No.	Quarter name	*Waqf* name	First and last recording dates	VGMA (register: page/ order)	Total record
1	Kudüs-i Şerīf	Şeyh Muḥammad Safī Mescidi	Muharrem 1140	1128: 68/34	1
2	Cebel-i Tūr	Şeyh Mansur Mescidi	1112 – Rebiulevvel 1164	1160: 116/104	2
3	Bābu'l-'Amūd	Bābu'l-'Amūd Vakfı dimekle ma'rūf Mescid-i Harāb	Rebiulevvel 1146	1109: 6/52	1
4	Kudüs Kalesi dāhilinde Tağ Mahallesi	Halime Hatun Mescidi Vakfı	Rebiulevvel 1111	1160: 116/37	1
5	Mescid-i Aksā havlisinde Kubbet-üs Sahra binası ittisalinde	Halvetu'l-Bekrī Mescid-i Şerifi Vakfı	Safer 1197	1111: 54/98	1
6	Mescid-i Aksā'nın havlisinin kenarında mebnā	Kadı Şuveyke Mescidi	Safer 1197	1111: 54/97	1
7	Kudüs-i Şerīf	Melik Seyfeddin bin Asīr ve Bedreddin ve Seyfeddin bin Asīr Mescid-i Şerifi	Rebiulahir 1137	1119: 110/39	1
8	Ermeni Manastırı ve Kale kurbu	Mescid Vakfı	Muharrem 1133	1107: 2/284	1
9	Kudüs-i Şerīf	Mescid Vakfı Necmeddin Ebū Muḥammad Abdurrahim Et-Tebārī dimekle ma'ruf Vakıf	Zilkade 1208	551: 99/29	1

TABLE A2 *Masjid* records of Jerusalem (1703–1831) (*cont.*)

No.	Quarter name	*Waqf* name	First and last recording dates	VGMA (register: page/ order)	Total record
10	Kudüs-i Şerīf	Mescid-i Beyt-i Terkeman olarak bilinen mescid	Şevval 1123	1107: 2/148	1
11	Yahudi Mahallesi	Mescid-i Ömerī vakfı	Zilkade 1113 – Safer 1174	1107: 2/292	7
12	Kudüs-i Şerīf	Palasī Mescidi Vakfı	Receb 1132	1107: 2/275	1
13	Kudüs-i Şerīf	Sinan Ağa Mescidi Vakfı	Şevval 1117 – Receb 1119	1107: 2/12	4
14	Deyrü'l-'Amūd	Sultan Kalavun Elfī binā eylediği Mescid-i Şerif	Ramazan 1159	1112: 1/62	1
Total					24

TABLE A3 Mosque records of Jerusalem (1703–1831)

No.	Quarter name	*Waqf* name	First and last recording dates	VGMA (register: page/ order)	Total record
1	Kudüs-i Şerīf	Sultan Kayıtbay Camii	Şaban 1103	1160: 116/31	1
2	Harem-i Şerif	Mescid-i Aksā	Safer 1140 – Cemaziyelevvel 1147	1109: 6/72	22
3	Harem-i Şerif	Kubbet-üs Sahra-ı Müşerrefe	Şevval 1123 – Receb 1199	1107: 2/150	29
4	Kudüs-i Şerīf	1. Camii'l-Beytūni 2. Camii'l-Beyādi 3.Cami-i Sencel 4. Cami-i Devāim 5.Cami-i Şufūt	Rebiulevvel 1184	1125: 64/5	1

TABLE A3 Mosque records of Jerusalem (1703–1831) (*cont.*)

No.	Quarter name	*Waqf* name	First and last recording dates	VGMA (register: page/ order)	Total record
5	Meğāribe Mahallesi	Cāmi-i Meğāribe	Şevval 1105 – Rebiulahir 1138	1091: 77/3	3
6	Kudüs-i Şerīf	1-Cami-i Bel'ayn Sükkānü'l-Erbaīn 2- Cami-i Sağīr Ömerī Evkafı	Şaban 1181 – Receb 1231	555: 25/11	2
7	Yahudi Mahallesi	Berekāt Han Camii Vakfı	1104	1160: 116/119	1
8	Cebel-i Şīmalī	Beyrut (Bīrun) Şeyh Yusuf Camii Vakfı	Safer 1153	1109: 6/119	1
9	Kudüs-i Şerīf	Cami-i A'silīn Vakfı	Safer 1104	1160: 116/114	1
10	Kızılca Mahallesi kurbunda	Cami-i Kavsī	1104	1160: 116/124	1
11	Nasārā Mahallesi	Cami-i Ömerī dimekle marūf Tahte'l-Minareti'l-Habeş Camii	Cemaziyelahir 1112 – Cemāziyelevvel 1139	1128: 68/5	2
12	Kudüs-i Şerīf	1. Cami-i Term-i Es'iyye 2. Camiu'l-Ma'd Leys-i Cerrāh 3.Cami-i Çebsīt Vakfı	Rebiulahir 1163	1112: 1/118	1
13	Kudüs-i Şerīf	Camiu's-Suyūfī Evkafı	Şevval 1131	1107: 2/258	1
14	Mār Yakub kurbu	Camiu'ş-Şerifeyn	Ramazan 1159	1112: 1/61	1
15	Kudüs-i Şerīf	Cami-u'l-Hayāt	Cemāziyelevvel 1139	1128: 68/6	1
16	Kudüs-i Şerīf	Hz. Nebiyullah Cami-i Şerifi	Receb 1191 – Cemaziyelevvel 1197	1111: 54/9	1

TABLE A3 Mosque records of Jerusalem (1703–1831) (*cont.*)

No.	Quarter name	*Waqf* name	First and last recording dates	VGMA (register: page/ order)	Total record
17	Nasāra Mahallesi	Kalavun Camii Vakfı	Cemaziyelevvel 1130	1107: 2/243	1
18	Efrenc Mahallesi Deyru'l-'Amud kurbunda	Karkaşandī Camii	Cemaziyelahir 1153 – Zilhicce 1196	1109: 6/129	4
19	Kudüs-i Şerīf	Mahalle Camii (Sarīm Camii)	Muharrem 1112	1160: 116/50	1
20	Rīşe	Martūmā Cami-i Ömerī Vakfı	Safer 1153	1109: 6/125	1
21	Musalliye	Musalliye Mahallesi Camii	Şevval 1117	1107: 2/10	1
22		Esad Efendi Camii	26 Safer 1110 – 1257	515: 96/154	4
23	Kudüs-i Şerīf	Pazar Cami-i Şerifi (Sinan Vakfı'ndan Camii'l-Bāzār)	Rebiulevvel 1111 – Safer 1136	1119: 110/13	3
24	Kalavun Mahallesi	Rıdvan Bey Vakfı Şeyh Mehmed Karkaşendī diye vakf eylediği dārın süknası ve bina eylediği Cami ve Muallimhane	Cemaziyelevvel 1157	1112: 1/26	1
25	Kudüs-i Şerīf	Sinan Ağa Cami-i Vakfı	Rebiulevvel 1111 – Rebiülevvel 1207	1160: 116/36	2

TABLE A3 Mosque records of Jerusalem (1703–1831) (*cont.*)

No.	Quarter name	*Waqf* name	First and last recording dates	VGMA (register: page/ order)	Total record
26	Kudüs-i Şerīf	Şeyh Ebu Fakih Cami-i Şerifi İki Kıt'a Hanesi Evkafı	Rebiulevvel 1125 – Gurre-i Muharrem 1174	1110: 131/108	2
27	Meğāribe kurbunda	Şeyh İsmail Ezrak Camii Vakfı	Safer 1104 – Şevval 1123	1107: 2/145	2
28	Kudüs-i Şerīf	Şeyh Lu'Lu' Cami-i Vakfı	Rebiulahir 1123 – Gurre-i Muharrem 1174	1110: 131/109	2
29	Medādīn	Şeyh Mehmed Hicāziye Camii Vakfı	Şaban 1122	1107: 2/123	1
30	Haddādīn	Şeyh Muḥammad bin Mücadiye mensub Cami Vakfı	Şaban 1143 – Ramazan 1217	1109: 6/6	3
31	Kudüs-i Şerīf	Şeyh Şehabeddin Camii Vakfı	Şaban 1122	1107: 2/126	1
32	Kudüs-i Şerīf	Tayyibe Camii Vakfı	Şaban 1154	1109: 6/148	1
33	Kudüs-i Şerīf	Yusūfiyye Camii	Şaban 1102	1160: 116/14	1
Total					97

TABLE A4 Sufi lodges records of Jerusalem (1703–1831)

23.834 mm	Quarter name	*Waqf* name	Founding date	First and last recording dates	VGMA (register: page/ order)	Total record
1	Meğāribe	Mağribīler Tekyesi	-	Zi'l-ka'de 1102 – Rebiülahir 1250	1160: 116/18	6
2	Kudüs-i Şerīf	Melik Selahaddin Tekyesi	-	Gurre-i Safer 1174	1110: 131/116	1
3	Harem-i Şerif yakını	Özbekler Tekkesi (Zāviye-i Nakşibendiyye)	-	1206–1293	515: 100/169	1
4	Kudüs-i Şerīf	Seyyid Şahbaz, Şeyh Mezīd, Şeyh Muharrem Senāu'd-dīn ve Seyyid Celāl Tekyesi	-	Muharrem 1115	1160: 116/92	1
5	Kubbet-üs Sahra	Şeyh Mansur Tekyesi Vakfı	-	Şa'ban 1162	1112: 1/112	1
6	Kudüs-i Şerīf	Tarīk-i Rüfāiye Tekyesi	-	23 Şa'ban	1110: 131/15	1
7	Kudüs-i Şerīf	Tekrurī Tekyesi	-	Ramazan 1162 – Şevval 1168	1112: 1/113	2
8	Sa'diyye Mahallesi	Vakf-ı Hüdaverdi Bey Mir Liva-i sabık-ı der Mevlevihane-i Kudüs	1133/ 1730–1731	7 Receb 1211	515: 44/36	1

TABLE A4 Sufi lodges records of Jerusalem (1703–1831) (*cont.*)

23.834 mm	Quarter name	*Waqf* name	Founding date	First and last recording dates	VGMA (register: page/ order)	Total record
9	Harem-i Şerif yakını	Vakf-ı Tekye-i eş-Şeyh Seyyid Şihab ve Şeyh Farid ve Şeyh Merdem Bahaeddin ve Seyyid Celal meşruta Hindiyān der-Kuds-i Şerif	832/ 1429	12 Safer 1195 – 19 Zilkade 1195	515: 94/145, 1160: 116/92	3
Total						17

TABLE A5 *Zāwiya* records of Jerusalem (1703–1831)

No.	Quarter name	*Waqf* name	First and last recording dates	VGMA (register: page/order)	Total record
1	Kudüs-i Şerīf	Davud Nebī Zāviyesi	Şaban 1208	551: 99/45	1
2	Kudüs-i Şerīf	Edhemiye (Şeyh İbrahim Edhem) Zāviyesi	21 Cemaziyelahir 1193 – 9 Zilkade 1256	515: 72/77	4
3	Mescid-i Aksā	1. Rāk Mansur Bey Zāviyesi ve 2. Habib Düzürde Zāviye-i Mansur Bey	Şaban 1118	110: 2/47	1
4	Kudüs-i Şerīf	Yākubiyye dimekle ma'rūf Zāviye	Zilkade 1135 – Rebiülevvel 1207	551: 99/36	6

TABLE A5 *Zāwiya* records of Jerusalem (1703–1831) (*cont.*)

No.	Quarter name	*Waqf* name	First and last recording dates	VGMA (register: page/order)	Total record
5	Cevvalde Mahallesi	Karkaşandī Zāviyesi	Şaban 1154	1109: 6/151	1
6	Kudüs-i Şerīf	Lu'lu' Gazi Zāviyesi	Safer 1192 – Cemaziyelevvel 1239	1111: 54/18	3
7	Kudüs-i Şerīf	Bistāmiye Zāviyesi Vakfı (Şeyh Abdullah El-Bistamī Zāviyesi Evkafı)	Cemāziyelahir 1126 – Safer 1212	1107: 2/213	3
8	Kudüs-i Şerīf	Kameriyye	-	515: 41/27	1
9	Meğāribe Mahallesi	Zāviye-i Mefārikiyye-i Seyyid Ömer al-Mücerred Ebu'l-Medenī al-Gavsī ve Tevābi'i Vakıfları	Cemaziyelahir 1121	1107: 2/78	1
10	Kudüs-i Şerīf	Mi'rac-ı Makam ve Burak Zāviyesi (Muḥammad el-Mustafa Mirac Yeri ve Burak-ı Şerif Zāviyesi)	Cemaziyelahir 1112 – Muharrem 1146	1160: 116/56	2
11	Kudüs-i Şerīf	Mehmed Paşa Zāviyesi	Muharrem 1111 – Şaban 1111	1140: 245/56	2
12	Kudüs-i Şerīf	Sadriyye Zāviyesi	-	515: 89/122	1
13	Sahil-i Er Sūkında medfun	Seyyid Ali bin Ali Zāviyesi Evkafı	Muharrem 1167 – Cemzaiyelahir 1193	1216: 15/7	2
14	Kudüs-i Şerīf	Sultaniye Vakfı Zāviyesi	1104	1160: 116/116	1

TABLE A5 *Zāwiya* records of Jerusalem (1703–1831) (*cont.*)

No.	Quarter name	*Waqf* name	First and last recording dates	VGMA (register: page/order)	Total record
15	Kudüs-i Şerīf	Şeyh Alaeddin Ali Zāviyesi	-	515: 76/83	3
16	Kudüs-i Şerīf	Şeyh Abdulkadir-i Geylanī Zāviyesi	Cemaziyelahir 1157	1112/1/32	1
17	Kudüs-i Şerīf	Şeyh Celaleddin Zāviyesi	Safer 1115	1160/116/94	1
18	Kudüs-i Şerīf	Şeyh İsmail Ezrak, Şeyh Muḥammad Masbūtī, Şeyh Haydar Evkafı Zāviyesi	Şaban 1111	1160/116/41	1
19	Hārretü'ş-Şeref Mahallesi	Şeyh İsmail Zāviyesi vakfı	Cemaziyelevvel 1123	1107/2/158	1
20	Kudüs-i Şerīf	Şeyh Salāhaddin Zāviyesi	Zilhicce 1102 – Rebiulevvel 1103	1160/116/20	2
21	Şeref Mahallesi	Şeyh Suyūfi (Subūti) Zāviyesi	Safer 1139	1128/68/3	1
22	Kudüs-i Şerīf	Şeyh Muḥammad el-Kırımī Merkadi Zāviyesi Vakfı (Veliyullah-ı Teala Şeyh Muḥammad el-Kırımī Merkad-ı Şerifi Zāviyesi Evkafı)	Zilhicce 1144 – Receb 1167	1109/6/36	2
23	Kudüs-i Şerīf	Tāhiriyye ve Kāsımiyye Zāviyesi	-	515: 84/106	1
24	Kudüs-i Şerīf	Zāviye-i Bedriyye Evkafı	Muharrem 1111	1160/116/46	1
25	Kudüs-i Şerīf	Zāviye-i Hanefiyye	Cemaziyelahir 1121	1107/2/79	1

TABLE A5 *Zāwiya* records of Jerusalem (1703–1831) (*cont.*)

No.	Quarter name	*Waqf* name	First and last recording dates	VGMA (register: page/order)	Total record
26	Kudüs-i Şerīf	Zāviye-i Salāhiyye (Zāviye-i Hangāh-ı Salāhī)	Şevval 1163 – Safer 1204	554/25/1	3
27	Harem-i Şerif civarı	Vakf-ı Zaviye-i Köstendilī Şeyh İbrahim Efendi 'an meşayih-i tarikat-ı Rufai der	Gurre-i Zilkade 1259	515: 101/171	1
Total					48

TABLE A6 *Khanqāh* records of Jerusalem (1703–1831)

No.	Quarter name	*Waqf* name	First and last recording dates	VGMA (register: page/order)	Total record
1	Kudüs-i Şerīf	Hangāh-ı Cevheriyye Evkafı	Zilkade 1143 – Rebiulevvel 1171	1109: 6/24	3
2	Kudüs-i Şerīf	Bāsıtiyye Hangāhı Vakfı	Cemaziyelahir 1103 – Muharrem 1140	1160: 116/27	6
3	Kudüs-i Şerīf	Hangāh Evkafı	Şaban 1118	1107: 2/35	2
4	Kudüs-i Şerīf	Hangāh-ı Cerrāhiyye Evkafı	Muharrem 1143	1139: 87/41	1
5	Kudüs-i Şerīf	Hangāh-ı Evhādiyye Vakfı	Şaban 1125	1107: 2/188	1
6		Hangāh-ı Fahriyye		515: 92/ 139	5
7	Kudüs-i Şerīf	Hangāh-ı Melikiyye Vakfı	Cemaziyelevvel 1146	1109: 6/60	1

TABLE A6 *Khanqāh* records of Jerusalem (1703–1831) (*cont.*)

No.	Quarter name	*Waqf* name	First and last recording dates	VGMA (register: page/order)	Total record
8	Kudüs-i Şerīf	Hangāh-ı Mencikiyye Evkafı	Cemaziyelahir 1157	1112: 1/30	1
9	Kudüs-i Şerīf	Hangāh-ı Musliyye Evkafı	Safer 1131 – Cemaziyelevvel 1157	1112: 1/24	2
10	Kudüs-i Şerīf	Hangāh-ı Serahiyye Vakfı	Rebiulevvel 1111	1160: 116/38	1
11	Kudüs-i Şerīf	Hātuniye Hanğahı	19 Rebiulevvel 1090 – 26 Zilkade 1146	515: 72/78	8
12	Kudüs-i Şerīf	Hilye Hangāhı (Vakf-ı Hangāh-ı Hilye)	-	515: 38/18	1
13	Kudüs-i Şerīf	Melik Salahaddin'in vakf eylediği Hangāh-ı Salāhiyye Evkafı (Hangāh-ı Melik Salahaddin Evkafı (Hangāh-ı Salāhī)	Şaban 1095 – Rebiülevvel 1207	1160: 116/8	17
14	Cebel-i Tūr-ı Sinada	Merhum Es'ad Efendi Hangāhı	Şaban 1124	1160: 116/10	1
Total					50

TABLE A7 *Ribāṭ* records of Jerusalem (1703–1831)

No.	Quarter name	*Waqf* name	First and last recording dates	VGMA (register: page/order)	Total record
1	Kudüs-i Şerīf	Ribat-ı Alāeddin	-	515: 83/101	2
2	Kudüs-i Şerīf	Ribāṭ-ı Bayram Çavuş ve Mektebi	Şevval 1112	1160: 116/59	1
3	Kudüs-i Şerīf	Ribāṭ-ı Hamavī	Evāhir-i Receb 1129	515: 84/105	3
4	Kudüs-i Şerīf	Ribāṭ-ı Kalamiye	-	515: 87/112	2
5	Kudüs-i Şerīf	Ribāṭ-ı Kürdī	-	515: 87/114	1
6	Kudüs-i Şerīf	Ribat-ı Mansūrīn	Zilhicce 1143	1109: 6/25	1
7	Kudüs-i Şerīf	Ribāṭ-ı Sānī Vakfı	Receb 1123	1107: 2/137	1
8	Bābü'l-Hattā kurbunda	Ribāṭı'l-Mardīn	Şevval 1117 – Muharrem 1167	1107: 2/11	2
9	Bābü'l-Hatta	Ribāṭi'l-Marte	Cemaziyelevvel 1108	1140: 245/7	1
10	Bābü'l-Kattanīn	Ribati'l-Temcūn Vakfı	Ramazan 1135	1119: 110/4	1
11	Bābü'l-Kattanīn	Ribatı'l-Hücūr Vakfı	Şevval 1135	1107: 2/320	1
Total					16

TABLE A8 *Maqam/Merkad al-Sharif* records of Jerusalem (1703–1831)

No.	Quarter name	*Waqf* name	First and last recording dates	VGMA (register: page/order)	Total record
1	Kudüs-i Şerīf	Hz. Musa, Hz. Yunus, Hz. Lut Makam-ı Şerifeleri Vakfı	Zi'l-ka'de 1113 –	1107/2/120	4
2	Kudüs-i Şerīf medfun	Hz. 'Amber Peygamber Makam-ı Şerifi Vakfı	Ramazan 1178 – Şa'ban 1196	1111.54.81	2
3	Kudüs-i Şerīf	Yūşā Evkafı	Şa'ban 1110	1140/245/46	1

TABLE A8 *Maqam/Merkad al-Sharif* records of Jerusalem (1703–1831) (*cont.*)

No.	Quarter name	*Waqf* name	First and last recording dates	VGMA (register: page/order)	Total record
4	Kudüs-i Şerīf	Seyyid Ebu Türāb Makamı	Muharrem 1112	1160/116/48	1
5	Nasārā Mahallesi	Makam-ı Mescid-i Hızır Aleyhisselam vakfı	Zi'l-ka'de 1221 Yevm 17	553/38/22	1
6	Kudüs-i Şerīf	Şeyh Alaaddin el-Baytarī Makamı	Rebiu'l-ahir 1162	1112/1/109	1
7	Kudüs-i Şerīf	Davud en-Nebī Merkadi	Muharrem 1139 – Şa'ban 1208	1110/131/104	8
8	Kudüs-i Şerīf	Hz. Aziz Nebī Merkadi Vakfı	Muharrem 1122	1107/2/109	1
9	Kudüs-i Şerīf	Hz. Musa ve Hz. İsa Peygamberlerin Merkadlari	Şa'ban 1118	1107/2/33	1
10	Davud Nebī kurbunda 'Arz-ı Sıhyonda	Şeyh Muḥammad Mensī Merkadi Vakfı	Şa'ban 1167 – Receb 1199	1112/1/202	3
Total					23

TABLE A9 Tomb records of Jerusalem (1703–1831)

No.	Quarter name	*Waqf* name	First and last recording dates	VGMA (register: page/order)
1	Kudüs-i Şerīf	Hz. Şemuyil En-Nebī Türbesi Vakfı	Cemaziyelevvel 1157	1112: 1/28
2	Kudüs-i Şerīf dāhilinde	Şeyh Abdullah Bistamī Türbe-i Şerifi Vakfı	Safer 1174	1110: 131/85
3	Kudüs-i Şerīf	Şeyh Abdullah Ennamī Türbesi	Safer 1169	1110: 131/34
4	Hudud-ı Hūd	Şeyh Ahmed Cādigī Türbesi Vakfı	Rebiulahir1118	1107: 2/31

TABLE A9 Tomb records of Jerusalem (1703–1831) (*cont.*)

No.	Quarter name	*Waqf* name	First and last recording dates	VGMA (register: page/order)
5	Hayādire Mahallesi	Şeyh Haydar (Velī) Türbesi	1104 – Şevval 1148	1160: 116/122
6	Hārratü'ş-Şeref	Şeyh İbrahim el-Erzak Türbesi	Muharrem 1131	1107: 2/252
7	Bābü's-Sihr Mahallesi Şeyh Ferid Zāviyesi Kurbunda	Şeyh Murad Türbesi Vakfı	Safer 1140	1139: 87/10
8	Bostancı Mahallesi	Şeyh Musa el- 'Ālemī Evkafı ve Türbe-i Şerifi	Cemaziyelahir 1112	1160: 116/55
9	Bābü'l-Hatta Mahallesi	Şeyh Türbesi Vakfı	Zi'lhicce 1140	1139: 87/5
10	Cey'ul Batīh kurbunda	Şeyh Yakub Türbe ve Makamı	Gurre-i Muharrem 1174	1110: 131/111
11	Dercetü'l-'Ayn nām Mahalde	Ahmed Mehmed Çalık Türbesi vakfı	Cemaziyelahir 1129	1107: 2/228
12	Kudüs	Belāsī Türbesi Vakfı	Şaban 1154	1109: 6/149
13	Kudüs-i Şerīf	Benī Aziz Türbe-i Şerifi	Cemaziyelahir 1156	1112: 1/13
14	Kudüs-i Şerīf	Ben-i Nūn Türbesi	Safer 1153	1109: 6/122
15	Kudüs-i Şerīf	Bereket Kasım Hatun Türbesi Evkafı	Şaban 1113	1160: 116/66
16	Kudüs-i Şerīf	Berekethan Türbesi Evkafı	Zilkade 1113	1160: 116/74
17		Cālikiyye Türbesi		
18	Kudüs-i Şerīf	Cerrah Türbesi Vakfı	Cemāziyelevvel 1126	1107: 2/209
19	Hattı Davud	Geylāniyye Türbesi	Safer 1104 – Cemaziyelevvel 1201	1160: 116/109
20	Kudüs-i Şerīf	Hüdaverdi Sa'ādeddin Türbesi	1104 – Safer 1104	1160: 116/118

TABLE A9 Tomb records of Jerusalem (1703–1831) (*cont.*)

No.	Quarter name	*Waqf* name	First and last recording dates	VGMA (register: page/order)
21	Kudüs-i Şerīf	Melik Seyfeddin bin Asīr ve Bedreddin ve Seyfeddin bin Asīr Türbesi ve Mescid-i Şerifi Evkafları	Rebiulahir 1137	1119: 110/39
22	Bābü'l-Hatta	Ribatı'l-Mārevī (Maridī) Türbe-i Şerifi Evkafı	Cemzaiyelevvel 1137 – Receb 1166	1119: 110/50
Total				4

TABLE A10 Praying and reciting *waqfs* of Jerusalem (1703–1831)

No.	Quarter name	*Waqf* name	Office name	First and last recording dates	VGMA (register: page/ order)	Total record no
1	Kudüs-i Şerīf	Kubbet-üs Sahra-ı Şerifde Sabah namazından sonra merhum Turgut Ağa ruhu için tilāvet olunan ecza-ı şerīfe için	eczāhān	Zilhicce 1029 – Receb 1199	1160: 116/3	2
2	Kudüs-i Şerīf	Şeyh Kemaledin bin Şerif Vakfı (nın Mescid-i Aksā Şerefallahu Teālā vazifesi)	kırāat-ı şifā-i şerif	Rebiulahir 1107 – Muharrem 1205	1160: 116/5	3
3	Bāb al-'Amud	Merhum Husrev Rumī için vakf eylediği	kāri-i ma teyessera	Şaban 1058 – Şevval 1139	1160: 116/7	2
4	Kudüs-i Şerīf	Üç dükkān	kırāat-ı ma teyessera	C.evvel 1103	1160: 116/25	1

TABLE A10 Praying and reciting *waqf*s of Jerusalem (1703–1831) (*cont.*)

No.	Quarter name	*Waqf* name	Office name	First and last recording dates	VGMA (register: page/ order)	Total record no
5	Bāb al-'Amud	Merhum Yusuf Vakfı	kırāat-ı ma teyessera	Zilhicce 1111	1160: 116/47	1
6	Kudüs-i Şerīf	Sultan Haseki Vakfından Kubbet-üs Sahrai'l-Müşerrefede	cüzhān	1112	1160: 116/101	1
7	Kubbet-üs Sahra	Hatun Sultan Evkafı	kāri-i aşır	Safer 1104	1160: 116/110	1
8	Al-Quds	Beyt-i 'Ibādullah vakfı olan Mısır tarafında evkafdan	eczāhān	1104	1160: 116/121	1
9	Mecelle Sūkı Beyti'l-Me'bizde		kıraāt-ı ma teyessera	1104	1160: 116/128	1
10	Kudüs-i Şerīf	Tavaşī Ağa Vakfından	cüzhān	1104	1160: 116/130	1
11	Kudüs-i Şerīf	Kubbet-üs Sahraa Meşruta Sinan Paşa Vakfı	cüzhān	Şevval 1117	1107: 2/21	1
12	Kudüs-i Şerīf	Nasreddin el-Vücūh Evkafı	kurrā-i Kur'an	Şaban 1118	1107: 2/34	1
13	Bābü'l 'Amūd Mahallesi	Haser ve Yusuf Vakfı	kāri-i ma teyssere	Şaban 1118	1107: 2/50	1
14	Hatt-ı Davud	Merdāne Vakfı	kāri-i Kur'an	Zilhicce 1121	1107: 2/71	1
15	Bābü'l-Kattānīn Mahallesi		kāri-i Kur'an	Receb 1121	1107: 2/84	1
16	Kudüs-i Şerīf	Çavuş Zevcesi Vakfı	yasinhān, tebarekehān	Rebiulahir 1122	1107: 2/117	2
17	Kubbet-üs Sahra Müşerrefe	Ömer Efendi ruhu içun	aşırhān	Rebiulahir 1125	1107: 2/179	1

TABLE A10 Praying and reciting *waqf*s of Jerusalem (1703–1831) (*cont.*)

No.	Quarter name	*Waqf* name	Office name	First and last recording dates	VGMA (register: page/ order)	Total record no
18	Kubbet-üs Sahra Müşerrefe	Bayram binası hücre	cüzhān	Rebiulahir 1125	1107: 2/180	1
19	Kubbet-üs Sahra Müşerrefe	Hoca Muḥammad Zor ruhu için	cüzhān	Rebiulahir 1125	1107: 2/182	1
20	Murde'a Vakfından (Ayn-ı Hadīd Mezraası)	Mescid-i Aksāda Kur'an tilāvetine meşruta	kāri-i Kur'an	Rebiulevvel 1126	1107: 2/194	1
21	Kudüs-i Şerīf	Haseki Sultan Vakfı (Davud Aleyhisselam Makam-ı Şerifi'nde cüz okunmasına meşruta)	aşırhān	Cemaziyelevvel 1130	1107: 2/240	1
22	Hatt-ı Davud Mahallesi		kıraat-ı ma teyessera	Receb 1123 – Receb 1132	1107: 2/278	2
23	Kudüs-i Şerīf	Kubbet-üs Sahra vakfı	kāri-i ma teyessera	Zilhicce 1133	1107: 2/297	1
24	Mescid-i Aksā Kapılarından Bab-ı Hadid kapısı	Bab-ı Hadīd Hane Vakfı	kāri	Rebuüîlevvel 1134	1107: 2/309	1
25	Hatt-ı Davud Mahallesi	Merdāne Hatun Vakfı	kāri-i ma teyessera	Muharrem 1135	1107: 2/315	1
26	Kudüs-i Şerīf	Hasekiye Vakfı	fetihhān	Şevval1135	1107: 2/321	1
27	Hārrat'uş-Şeref	Şeyh Muḥammad Palasi ve şeyh İsmail azrek kurbunda	kāri-i ma teyessera	Şevval 1135	1107: 2/322	1

TABLE A10 Praying and reciting *waqf*s of Jerusalem (1703–1831) (*cont.*)

No.	Quarter name	*Waqf* name	Office name	First and last recording dates	VGMA (register: page/ order)	Total record no
28	Hārratü'ş-Şeref	Hane Vakfı	kāri-i ma teyessera	Şevval 1136	1119: 110/6	1
29	Kudüs-i Şerīf	Haseki Sultan Evkafından	duāgū	Cemaziyelahir 1136	1119: 110/21	2
30	Kudüs-i Şerīf	Küçük Ahmed Paşa Evkafından Kubbet-üs Sahrai'l-Müşerrefede	cüzhān	Cemaziyelevvel 1103 – Rebiulahir 1137	1119: 110/34	8
31	Kudüs-i Şerīf	Küçük Ahmed Paşa Evkafından Kubbet-üs Sahrai'l-Müşerrefede	cüzhān, duāgū	Rebiulahir 1137	1119: 110/43	1
32	Kudsi Şerif	Kubbet-üs Sahra-ı Müşerrefede Mustafa Paşa Vakfı	cüzhān	Zi'lhicce 1140	1139: 87/6	1
33	Harem-i Şerif sathında olub		kurrā	Şaban 1143	1109: 6/8	1
34	Kudüs-i Şerīf	Şeyh Mehmed Pervez Evkafı	cüzhān	Ramazan 1146	1109: 6/66	1
35	Kudüs-i Şerīf	Mescid-i Aksā ve Kubbet-üs Sahra Müşerrefe	kāri-i hadīs	Safer 1140 – Cemaziyelevvel 1147	1109: 6/72	2
36	Bābü'l-Kattānīnde Dāru's-Satı	Meryem Hatun Vakfı (Dāre'l-Satı dimekle marūf)	kāri-i Kur'an	Rebulahir 1148	1109: 6/87	1
37	Kudüs-i Şerīf	Sultan Süleyman Han Evkafı'ndan (Kubbet-üs Sahrai'l Müşerrefe) Vakfı Sultan Süleyman ruhu için	cüzhān	Şaban 1125 – Rebiulevvel 1149	1109: 6/96	3

TABLE A10 Praying and reciting *waqf*s of Jerusalem (1703–1831) (*cont.*)

No.	Quarter name	*Waqf* name	Office name	First and last recording dates	VGMA (register: page/ order)	Total record no
38	Kudüs-i Şerīf	Sultan Süleyman Han Evkafından (Kubbe-i Kubbet-üs Sahrai'l Müşerrefe) Vakfı	Esma-i Hüsnā okunması için cüzhān	Rebiulevvel 1149	1109: 6/99	1
39	Hārratü'l-Haddadīn Mahallesi	Hüdāvirdi Vakfı	kāri-i tefsir	Cemaziyelevvel 1157	1112: 1/25	1
40	Vadiyi'l-Tavvāhīn kurbunda	Abdullah nām sahibu'l-hayr tilāvet-i Kur'an olunmak içün vakf eylediği menzil süknāsı	Tilāvet-i Kur'an	Ramazan 1159	1112: 1/60	1
41	Hatt-ı Davud'da Bābü't-Tevvabīn Mahallesi	-	kırāat-ı ma teyessera	Şevval 1163 – Muharrem 1167	1112: 1/130	2
42	Kısmet-i Askeriye	-	fetihhān	Şa'ban 1193 – Safer 1229	1142: 124/1	5
43	Kısmet-i Askeriye	-	sure-i mülk-hanlık	Rebiu'l-ahir 1220	1142: 124/2	2
44	Kısmet-i Askeriye	-	yasinhān	Şevval 1220	1142: 124/3	2
45	Kubbet-üs Sahra-ı Müşerrefe	Vakf-ı Eczāhānān-ı İbrahim bey bin Karaman	eczāhān	-	515: 47/46	30
46	Kubbet-üs Sahra-ı Müşerrefe	Vakf-ı Eczāhānān-ı Zeyneb Hatun	eczāhān	-	515: 48/47	7

TABLE A10 Praying and reciting *waqfs* of Jerusalem (1703–1831) (*cont.*)

No.	Quarter name	*Waqf* name	Office name	First and last recording dates	VGMA (register: page/ order)	Total record no
47	Kubbet-üs Sahra-ı Müşerrefe	Vakf-ı Eczāhānān-ı İbn-i Ibade der Kubbet-üs Sahra eczāhānān-ı vakt-i zuhur	eczāhān	-	515: 49/49	12
48	Kubbet-üs Sahra-ı Müşerrefe	Vakf-ı Eczāhānān-ı Medrese-i Belediyye	eczāhān	10 Safer 1158	515: 52/53	11
49	Kubbet-üs Sahra-ı Müşerrefe	Vakf-ı En'ām-ı Müezzinān velede-i Çelebi Efendi Defterdar	müezzinān	24 C.evvel 1211	515: 49/50	3
50	Kubbet-üs Sahra-ı Müşerrefe	Evlad-ı Mehmed Bey Türbesi Eczāhānları Vakfı	eczāhān	-	515: 90/129	5
51	Kubbet-üs Sahra-ı Müşerrefe	Vakf-ı Eczāhānān-ı Hamza Kāşif	eczāhān	-	515: 92/135	4
Total						140

TABLE A11 Other *waqf* records in Jerusalem (1703–1831)

No.	Quarter name	*Waqf* name	First and last recording dates	VGMA (register: page/ order)	Total record
1	Kudüs-i Şerīf	1. Melik Seyfeddin İsa 2. Bedreddin ve Seyfeddin İsa Evkafı	Rebiulahir 1137	1119: 110/45	1

TABLE A11 Other *waqf* records in Jerusalem (1703–1831) (*cont.*)

No.	Quarter name	*Waqf* name	First and last recording dates	VGMA (register: page/order)	Total record
2	Kudüs-i Şerīf	1. Şeyh Halil Cā'ūnī Vakfı ve 2. Zevcesi Şerife Aişe binti Şeyh Muḥammad Vakfı ve 3. Şeyh Kemaleddin Ebā Şerif Vakfı	Şa'ban 1203 – Rebiülahir 1234	551: 99/2	3
3	Kudüs-i Şerīf	Abdülmelik el-Musullī Vakfı	Şevval 1117	1107: 2/7	1
4	Kudüs-i Şerīf	Ahmed Eş-Şurbī (Nurī) Vakfı	Muharrem 1222	553: 38/23	1
5	Kudüs-i Şerīf	Ahmed Sedrī Vakfı	1104	1160: 116/131	1
6	Kudüs-i Şerīf	Alaeddin Basrī Vakfı	Receb 1119	1107: 2/58	1
7	Kudüs-i Şerīf	Ali Evkafı	Rebiulahir 1137	1119: 110/33	1
8	Kudüs-i Şerīf	Ali Hoca Vakfı	Rebiulahir 1126	1107: 2/200	1
9	Jabal Sharkī	Bayezid-i Bistamī Vakfı	Cemaziyelevvel 1157 – Safer 1159	1112: 1/29	2
10	Kubbet-üs Sahra	Bayram binası hücre	Rebiulahir 1125	1107: 2/180	1
11	Kudüs-i Şerīf	Bayram Çavuş Batur	Rebiulevvel 1122	1107: 2/74	1
12	Hatt Davud Quarter	Birke Hatun (Birkehan) Vakfı	Cemāziyelevvel 1126 – Muharrem 1134	1107: 2/266	3
13	Kudüs-i Şerīf	Celaleddin Vakfı	Receb 1192 – Şaban 1227	1111: 54/37	2

TABLE A11 Other *waqf* records in Jerusalem (1703–1831) (*cont.*)

No.	Quarter name	*Waqf* name	First and last recording dates	VGMA (register: page/ order)	Total record
14	Kudüs-i Şerīf	Cemaleddin Es-Sāmid Musa Evkafı (Veliyullah)	Receb 1159 – Şevval 1167	1112: 1/58	3
15	Kudüs-i Şerīf	Çarıklı Vakfı	Receb 1119	1107: 2/54	1
16	Kudüs-i Şerīf	Durgut Ağa Vakfı	Zilkade 1138	1091: 77/13	1
17	Kudüs-i Şerīf	Ebu Medyen El-Gavs El-Mücerred Evkafı	Şevval 1111	1160: 116/44	1
18	Armenian Quarter	El-Hac Ömer Evkafı	Ramazan 1113	1160: 116/69	1
19	Kudüs-i Şerīf	Halil bin Şemseddin el-'Aselī Vakfı	Receb 1201	1113: 35/20	1
20	Kudüs-i Şerīf	Halil Evkafı	Şaban 1111	1160: 116/83	1
21	Cāmi' al-Arab	Hasanlar Vakfı	Cemāziyelevvel 1126	1107: 2/202	1
22	Kudüs-i Şerīf	Hz. Halid bin Velid Silsilesinden olub merhum eş-Şeyh Sun'ullah Efendi el-Hālidī Vakfı	Rebiu'l-ahir 1164 – Şevval 1208	1112: 1/139	4
23	Kudüs-i Şerīf	Hz. Kadem-i Şerif	Şa'ban 1111	1160: 116/81	1
24	Kudüs-i Şerīf	Husrev Er-Rūmī Vakfı	Şa'ban 1058 – Şevval 1139	1128: 68/12	2
25	Bāb al-'Amūd	Husrevī Yusuf Vakfı	Zi'l-hicce 1111 – Receb 1123	1107: 2/141	3

TABLE A11 Other *waqf* records in Jerusalem (1703–1831) (*cont.*)

No.	Quarter name	*Waqf* name	First and last recording dates	VGMA (register: page/ order)	Total record
26	Quarter of Hārrat al-Haddadīn	Hüdāvirdi Vakfı	Cemaziye'l-evvel 1157	1112: 1/25	1
27	Kudüs-i Şerīf	İbrahim Ağa Vakfı	Şa'ban 1122	1107: 2/128	1
28	Kudüs-i Şerīf	'İmādiyye [Medrese] ve Şeyh İmadeddin Abdu'l-Hāfız Vakıfları	Şa'ban 1121	1107: 2/91	1
29	Kudüs-i Şerīf	İsmail Ezrak Evkafı	Ramazan 1113	1160: 116/68	1
30	Kudüs-i Şerīf	Kasriyye Evkafı	Muharrem 1111	1140: 245/55	1
31	Kudüs-i Şerīf	Küçük Ahmed Paşa Evkafı	Cemaziye'l-evvel 1103 – Muharrem 1177	1160: 116/24	8
32	Kudüs-i Şerīf	Lu'lu' Gazi Evkafı	Cemzaiye'l-ahir 1136 – Cemaziye'l-evvel 1239	1119: 110/23	12
33	Kudüs-i Şerīf	Mağribīler Vakfı	1104 – Cemzaiye's-Sanī 1109	1140: 245/28	3
34	Kudüs-i Şerīf	Melik Salahaddin ve Şeyh Ali ve Şeyh Ahmed el-Hakkāri Evkafları	Rebiu'l-ahir 1137	1119: 110/38	4
35	Neighborhood of Hatt Davud	Merdāne Hatun Vakfı	Zi'l-hicce 1121 – Muharrem 1135	1107: 2/315	2
36	Kudüs-i Şerīf	Merhum Seyfeddin el-Hakkārī Evkafı	Rebiu's-Sani 1109 – Şevval 1117	1160: 116/64	3

TABLE A11 Other *waqf* records in Jerusalem (1703–1831) (*cont.*)

No.	Quarter name	*Waqf* name	First and last recording dates	VGMA (register: page/ order)	Total record
37	Sūk Davud Aleyhisselamda medfun	Merhum Taştimur 'Alāī Evkafı	Rebiu'l-evvel 1162	1112: 1/106	1
38	Bāb al-Qattānīn, Dāru's-Satı	Meryem Hatun Vakfı (Dārü'l-Satı dimekle marūf)	Rebu'l-ahir 1148	1109: 6/87	1
39	Kudüs-i Şerīf	Murad Paşa Evkafı	Şa'ban 1111 – Ramazan 1146	1160: 116/85	4
40	Kudüs-i Şerīf	Muslī Çavuş Zevcesi Vakfı	Muharrem 1122 – Gurre-i Rebiu'l-ahir 1122	1107: 2/106	2
41	Kudüs-i Şerīf	Mütevelli Şeyh Harrāc Evkafı	Zi'l-ka'de 1113	1160: 116/73	1
42	Kudüs-i Şerīf	Nasirī Muḥammad ibni Ahmed Es-Sutūrī Vakfı	Receb 1197 – Zi'l-ka'de 1221	1111: 54/108	2
43	Kudüs-i Şerīf	Nasreddin el-Vücūh Evkafı	Şa'ban 1118	1107: 2/34	1
44	Kudüs-i Şerīf	Nasuh Vakfı	Zilkade 1135 – Şevval 1137	1107: 2/323	2
45	Kudüs-i Şerīf	Osmaniyye vakfı	Cemaziyel evvel 1133	1107: 2/289	1
46	Kudüs-i Şerīf	Peymānī Hatun Vakfı	Muharrem 1132	1107: 2/265	1
47	Al-Masjid al-Aqṣā	Revvāk Şeyh Mansur Bey dimekle ma'rūf	Muharrem 1140 – Cemaziye'l-ahir 1242	1128: 68/29	9
48	Kudüs-i Şerīf	Sākūtī el-Hac İbrahim Vakfı	Zi'l-ka'de 1196	1111: 54/88	1
49	Kudüs-i Şerīf	Sarīhu's-Site Sırzī Evkafı	Muharrem 1122	1107: 2/108	1

TABLE A11 Other *waqf* records in Jerusalem (1703–1831) (*cont.*)

No.	Quarter name	*Waqf* name	First and last recording dates	VGMA (register: page/ order)	Total record
51	Kudüs-i Şerīf	Seyyid Ali bin Ali Evkafı	Zi'l-hicce 1102	1160: 116/22	1
52	Kudüs-i Şerīf	Meşīhat-ı Sādātü'l-Meğaribe Seyyid Mansur Evkafı	Şa'ban 1110	1140: 245/49	1
53	Kudüs-i Şerīf	Sitti Meryem binti Ömer	Rebiu's-Sani 1109	1140: 245/27	1
54	Kudüs-i Şerīf	Suritānī Vakfı	Rebiu'l-evvel 1121	1107: 2/73	1
55	Kudüs-i Şerīf	Şemseddin ibni Kutbu'l-Ensarī Vakfı	Receb 1110	1140: 245/40	1
56	Kudüs-i Şerīf	Şeyh Ahmed al-Atravanī Vakfı	Şa'ban 1122	1107: 2/127	1
57	Kudüs-i Şerīf	Şeyh Ahmed el-Müsbit Vakfı (Veliyullah)	Ramazan 1146	1109: 6/67	1
58	Kudüs-i Şerīf	Şeyh Ahmed el-Yemen Vakfı	Safer 1122	1107: 2/111	1
59	Kudüs-i Şerīf	Şeyh Ahmed Paşa Evkafı	Safer 1112	1160: 116/62	1
60	Kudüs-i Şerīf	Şeyh 'Ālemī Vakfı		1139: 87/36	1
61	Kudüs-i Şerīf	Şeyh Cerrah Evkafı	Şa'ban 1111 – Cemaziye'l-evvel 1157	1160: 116/82	5
62	Kudüs-i Şerīf	Şeyh Efendi Vakfı	Cemaziye'levvel 1141	1139: 87/28	1
63	Kudüs-i Şerīf	Şeyh Ğānemi'l-Mukaddes Vakfı	Receb 1130 – Cemaziye'l-ahir 1157	1107: 2/229	3

TABLE A11 Other *waqf* records in Jerusalem (1703–1831) (*cont.*)

No.	Quarter name	*Waqf* name	First and last recording dates	VGMA (register: page/ order)	Total record
64	Kudüs-i Şerīf	Şeyh Hasan bin Macid Vakfı	Şevval 1117	1107: 2/18	1
65	Kudüs-i Şerīf	Şeyh Kemaleddin Ebī Şerif Vakfı	Rebiu'l-ahir 1107 – Muharrem 1205	1113: 35/3	3
66	Kudüs-i Şerīf	Şeyh Lūd ve Şeyh Ali Attarī Vakfı	Şa'ban 1138	1091: 77/7	1
67	Kudüs-i Şerīf	Şeyh Mehmed Pervez Evkafı	Ramazan 1146	1109: 6/65	2
68	Hārratü'ş-Şeref Mahallesi	Şeyh Palas Vakfı	Muharrem 1131	1107: 2/251	1
69	Kudüs-i Şerīf	Şeyh Sayd Vakfı	Safer 1120	1107: 2/67	1
70	Kudüs-i Şerīf haricinde	Şeyhülislam el-Burhan ibni Şerif Vakfı	Cemaziye'l-evvel 1108	1140: 245/8	1
71	Kudüs-i Şerīf	Şeyhülislam Es'ad Efendi Vakfı	Şevval 1105 – Şevval 1163	1160: 116/147	2
72	Kudüs-i Şerīf	Tavaşī Mehmed Ağa Vakfı	1104 – Rebiülevvel 1207	1160: 116/130	7
73	Kudüs-i Şerīf	Şeyh Ahmed et-Tennurī Vakfı	Rebiu'l-evvel 1116	1107: 2/3	1
75	Kudüs-i Şerīf	Abdullah Efendi ve İbrahim Çavuş Vakfı (Değirmen Vakfı)	Safer 1131	1107: 2/253	1
76	Kudüs-i Şerīf	Çakmak Sultan	-	515: 36/10	1

TABLE A11 Other *waqf* records in Jerusalem (1703–1831) (*cont.*)

No.	Quarter name	*Waqf* name	First and last recording dates	VGMA (register: page/ order)	Total record
77	Kudüs-i Şerīf	Muhyiddin Muslu, Sadreddin Muslu ve evlād-ı Muhyiddin Muslu	3 Receb 1173 – 9 Receb 1233	515: 36/11	3
78	Kudüs-i Şerīf	Mehmed Bey	-	515: 39/21	2
79	Kudüs-i Şerīf	Behram Kethüda	-	515: 39/22	2
80	Kudüs-i Şerīf	Yusuf bin Eyyub	3 C.ahir 1146 – 6 Cemaziyelevvel 1227	515: 40/23	1
81	Kudüs-i Şerīf	Şeyh Sekbani	-	515: 40/24	1
82	Kudüs-i Şerīf	Şeyh Muḥammad el-Geylani	-	515: 40/25	1
83	Kudüs-i Şerīf	Mir Mehmed Bey	-	515: 41/29	2
84	Kudüs-i Şerīf	Davud Paşa Mirimiran-Mısır	-	515: 42/30	4
85	Kudüs-i Şerīf	Şeyh Ömer Mahmud	-	515: 42/31	2
86	Kudüs-i Şerīf	Temīm ed-Dārī	-	515: 42/32	2
87	Kudüs-i Şerīf	İbrahim Paşa	-	515: 44/38	12
88	Kudüs-i Şerīf	Mirimiranı Vilayet-i Maarra Mustafa Paşa	-	515: 45/40	12
89	Kudüs-i Şerīf	Üveys Paşa	-	515: 46/42	21

TABLE A11 Other *waqf* records in Jerusalem (1703–1831) (*cont.*)

No.	Quarter name	*Waqf* name	First and last recording dates	VGMA (register: page/ order)	Total record
90	Kudüs-i Şerīf	Hoca İbadullah Ankaravī	-	515: 47/43	4
91	Kudüs-i Şerīf	Sinan Subaşı	-	515: 47/44	9
92	Kudüs-i Şerīf	Fatma binti Zeyneb Hatun	-	515: 49/48	2
93	Kudüs-i Şerīf	Tavūsiyye Hatun	-	515: 52/54	1
94	Kudüs-i Şerīf	Cārullah Efendi	-	515: 77/86	5
95	Kudüs-i Şerīf	Şeyh Ahmed en-Nūrī	18 C.evvel 1112 – 29 Zilkade 1221	515: 82/97	7
96	Kudüs-i Şerīf	Bedreddin Hatib	-	515: 83/102	1
97	Kudüs-i Şerīf	Bedreddin Mehmed Ebu Kasım el-Hakkārī ve Seyfeddin bin İsa Evkafından Mektebi Muallim Şerefeddin İsa	22 Rebiulevvel 1137 – 16 Receb 1218	515: 85/108	3
98	Kudüs-i Şerīf	İbrahim Ağa	-	515: 86/111	1
99	Kudüs-i Şerīf	Şeyh kemal ve Şeyh Burhaneddin ve Şeyh Nasureddin	-	515: 89/119	1
100	Kudüs-i Şerīf	Hoca Bayram İsfī ve Mesnūhī	-	515: 89/120	1
101	Kudüs-i Şerīf	Abdulaziz	-	515: 89/123	1

TABLE A11 Other *waqf* records in Jerusalem (1703–1831) (*cont.*)

No.	Quarter name	*Waqf* name	First and last recording dates	VGMA (register: page/ order)	Total record
102	Kudüs-i Şerīf	Kansuncu ve Mehmed Beranhan	-	515: 89/124	1
103	Kudüs-i Şerīf	Hane-i ibn-i Salih	-	515: 91/130	1
104	Kudüs-i Şerīf	Şeyh Ahmed Servi veled-i İbrahim	20 Rebiulevvel 1108	515: 91/138	1
105	Kudüs-i Şerīf	Abdusselam Bey	-	515: 92/136	2
106	Kudüs-i Şerīf	Şeyh Alaeddin el-Basri	25 Rebiülahir 1169	515: 94/143	1
107	Kudüs-i Şerīf	Seyyidi Ali Alim	5 Safer 1265	515: 94/144	1
108	Kudüs-i Şerīf	Meşihat-ı Taife-i Tuccar ʿan Sakinān-ı Kudüs	10 Muharrem 1032	515: 94/147	1
109	Kudüs-i Şerīf	Abdulkadir el-Harirī	-	515: 94/148	1
110	Kudüs-i Şerīf	Şeyh Sehban Şeyh Yusuf	8 Muharrem 1167	515:98/ 158	1
111	Kudüs-i Şerīf	Subhi Mehmed ibni en-Neca ibni Alaeddin Ebu Yemen	28 Cemaziyelahir 1131	515: 99/164	1
112	Kudüs-i Şerīf	Şeyh Selim	-	515: 100/166	1
113	Kudüs-i Şerīf	Seyyid es-Salih er-Rufai	-	515: 100/167	1
Total					258

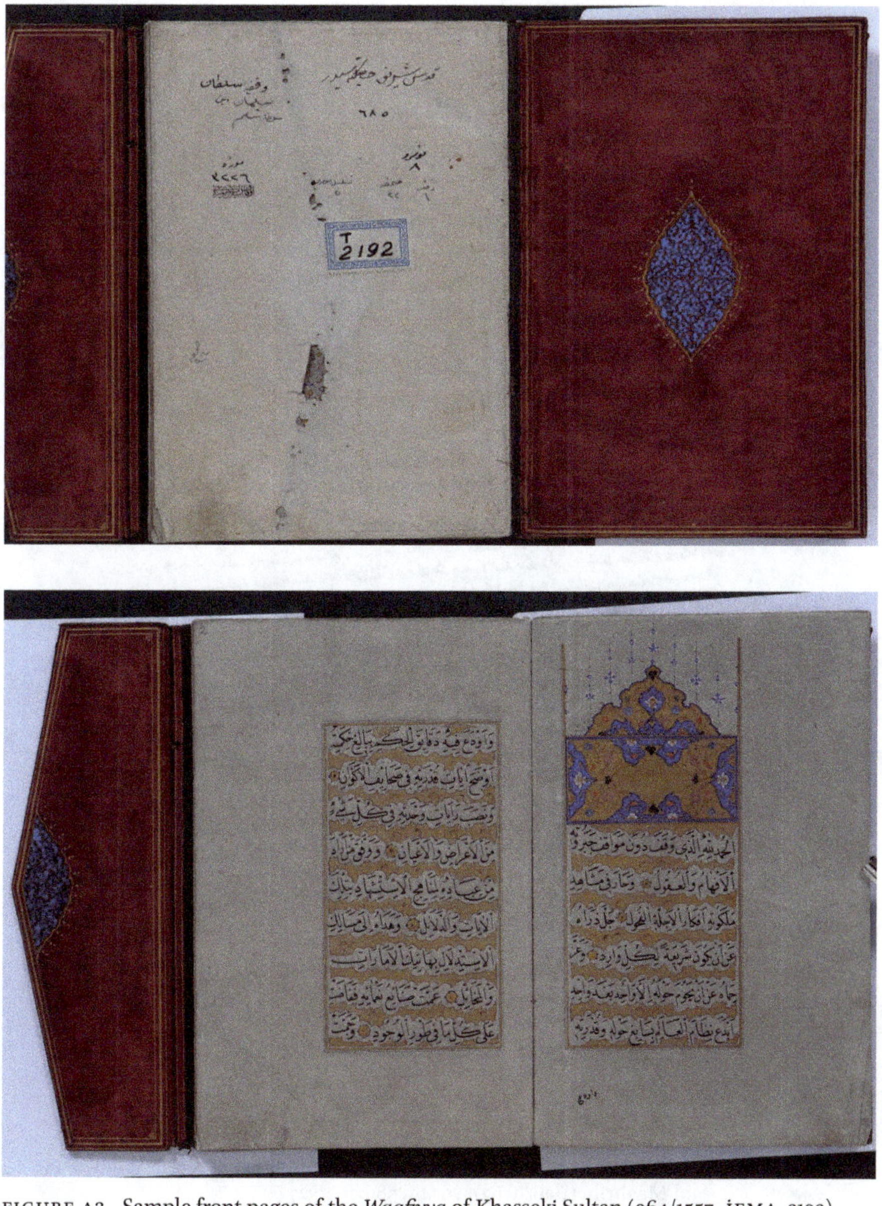

FIGURE A3 Sample front pages of the *Waqfiyya* of Khasseki Sultan (964/1557- İEMA, 2192)

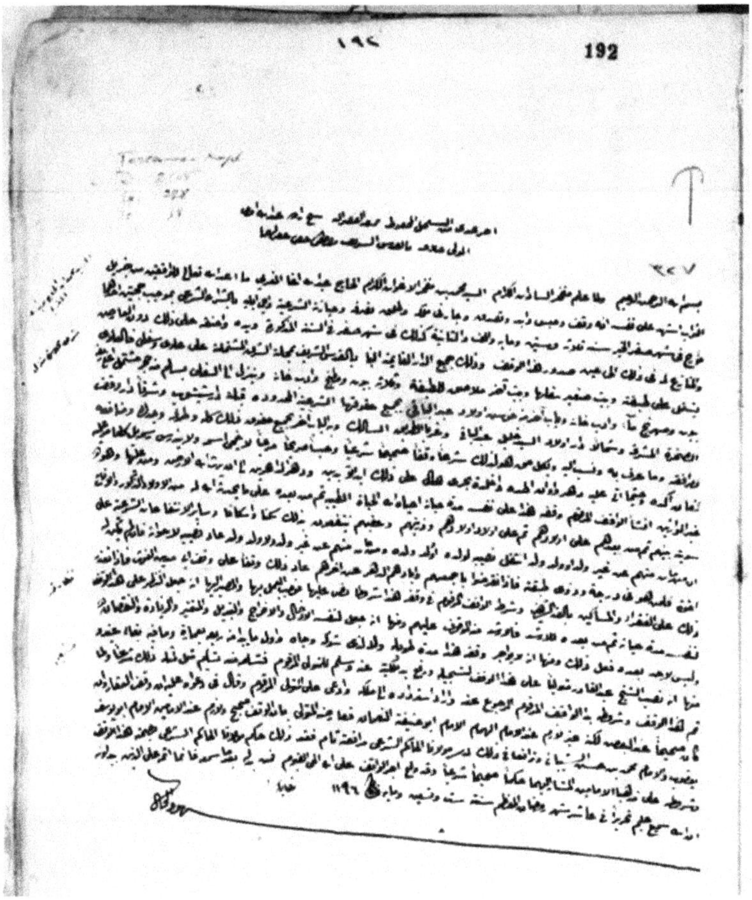

FIGURE A4 Copied record of the *Waqfiyya* of Sayyid Mehmed ibn Hajj Abdullah al-Maghribī (1196/ 1763), VGMA, 589: 192/327

FIGURE A5 Copied sample of the *Waqfiyya* of Patriarch Minas from Armenian community of Jerusalem, 1113/1701, JS 199

TABLE A12 List of the compiled *waqfiyyas*/*hujjats* in a register housed in the archive of *the Iḥyā' al-Turāth wa'l-Shu'ūn al-Dīniyya* in Abu Dis

No.	*Waqf of* ... / *Waqf Hujja* of ...	Sayfa
1	Muḥammad b. İbrahim al-Bībī	1
2	Muḥammad b. eş-Şeyh Muḥammad Bībī el-İmām	4
3	Vehbe Hacı Salih	6
4	Muḥammad Hüseyin Ebu	9
5	Sinan Paşa	10
6	Muḥammad Emin al-Hüseynī	11
7	Halil Abdurrahaman al-Cā'ūnī	12
8	Barbara Şehāde Ebū Lihye 'alā evlād-ı evlādihā evlādı Abdurrahman al-Qutb	13
9	Ebū Medyen al-Gavs (Gavs)	14
10	Vakf-ı Eş-Şeyh Muḥammad Muḥammad al-Hüseynī	15
11	'An vakf-ı Salih İbrahim el-Berk ve Abdulkadir Abdullah el-Dāvūdī	17
12	Abdullatīf Mūsā er-Rasās	18
13	Halīl Abdullah el-Hıdmī	
14	Mevā'ıduhā seken el-Meğāribe bi'l-emākin el-vakfiyye ve't-ta'mīr 'āid ala's-sākin	
15	Ahmed Reşīd Bey Vāli-i Vilāye-i Ankara	21
16	El-Haham Hārun bin İbrahim eş-Şecārī el-Mūsevī	22
17	Muḥammadi's-Sā'dī	25
18	İsmāil bin el-Hāc Şākir bin Ahmed ez-Zürrī	28
19	Selāse-i Yehūd Mūsevī	30
20	Merhūmīn Muḥammad Emin Paşa Ebī Lābbūt ve neclehū (oğlu) Mahmūd Muḥammad Emīn Paşa	34
21	Feyzullah el-'Alemī	41
22	Būlīs 'Ataullah Ceryīs el-Lātīnī	42
23	... fī karyei't-Tūr	43
24	Muḥammad Kāmil Muḥammad Tāhir el-Huseynī	44
25	Sened-i īcār vakf-ı Sinān Paşa el-kāin bi-Yafa	47
26	El-Medresetu'l-Tenkīziyye	50
27	El-Medresetu'l-Hālidiyye	56
28	Eş-Şeyh Muḥammad Quttūnī	59
29	Tevliyet-i vakf-ı el-mir'etu Hābe binti Şemuyil es-Siknācī	61
30	Tevliyet-i Vakf-ı Muḥammad bin Mustafa ...	62
31	Vakf-ı el-Hāce Mahbūbe	65

TABLE A12 List of the compiled *waqfiyyas*/*hujjats* in a register housed (*cont.*)

No.	*Waqf of …/ Waqf Hujja* of …	Sayfa
32	Muḥammad Emīn el-Huseynī	66
33	Hucce-i bey' (satış sözleşmesi)	
34	El-Hāc Hasan Efendi Müftī el-Sāde el-Hanefiyye bi'l-Kuds-i Şerīf	68
35	Hasan el-Huseynī li-emlāki Necībe Abdullah el-Melāh	69
36	Hasan el-Hüseynī li-emlāki Emine Abdullah el-Melāh	71
37	Abdullah Efendi el-Huseynī	72
38	El-Hāc Abdullatīf Efendi nakību's-Sa'dāti'l-Eşrāf bi'l-Kuds-i Şerīf	74
39	Feyzullah el-'Alemi 'ala Cāmi-i ve Türbe-i Bedir bi karye-i Müşerrefāt	76
40	Musa Rubil el-Mevsūyi's-Siknācı	77
41	Hāssā Yağkūb Zaklin es-Siknācı	78
42	El-hevāce Şalom Şehīr es-Siknācı	79
43	El-Haham Eyzer bin Şemuyil bin Lebīb es-Siknāci	80
44	El-Hevāce Lebīb bin Nesīm el-Mūsevī	81
45	İsrāil bin Mā'īr ve Mürdehāy bin Şem'ūn es-Siknāciyyīn	82
46	Sūret hasır ırt Yūdā eş-Şūn Hanāniyye bin İsrāil el-Mūseviyye	82
47	El-Hac Yusuf 'Avayda	85
48	El-Haham Şemuyil Murdehāy es-Siknācı	86
49	Hucce Turkiyye	87
50	Süleyman Efendi en-Neşeşībī	90
51	Mustafa Ağa bin el-merhūm Ali Efendi	93
52	İsā Muḥammad Ebu Sibiteyn mine't-Tur	96
53	Elhevāce Musā Rubil Es-Siknācı	97
54	Daru'l-eğneym	99
55	El-Hāce Şemse min Cenīn	101
56	Huccet-i īcār el-kurā el-vakfiyye el-vākı'a bi-kadā Yafa ve'l'ā'ida li-vakf Sinan Paşa	102
57	El-Hāc Ahmed Süleyman Baba ed-Dabbağ ledeyhi ve veledeyhi Muḥammad Musa mine'l-Kuds	103
58	El-Hāce 'Ali Ağa Topçu	106
59	El-Haham Hırşil Melānişṭayn ve zevcetehū es-Siknāciyeyn	107
60	İsrāil Zelman es-Siknāci	108
61	Şemuyil Dāvud Haruş Muğrabī	109
62	Hāyem Rôşenfild es-Siknācı	110
63	Şemuyil Liyuvī Siknāci	111

TABLE A12 List of the compiled *waqfiyyas*/*hujjats* in a register housed (*cont.*)

No.	*Waqf of ...* / *Waqf Hujja* of ...	Sayfa
64	Salih Abdulcevād el-'Aselī	112
65	Salih Abdulcevād el-'Aselī	114
66	Salise Salih Abdulcevād el-'Aselī	115
67	Rābi' Salih Abdulcevād el-'Aselī	117
68	Süleyman Eendi el-Quttīni	118
69	Tevliyet-i Vakf Seyyidi Ebī Medyen el-Gavs kuddise sırrahu'l-aziz	120
70	Tevliyet bi-ismi'l-Hāc Rāğıb Efendi el-Hālidi 'alā vakfey Sun'ullah Efendi El-Halidi ve Musa Efendi el-Halidi	121
71	Muḥammad bin el-'Aselī	123
72	Muḥammad bin el-'Aselī	126
73	Eş-Şeyh Ğabāyīn	126
74	Tevliyet-i el-Hac Derviş el-Benān	127
75	İ'lāmı'ş-Şer'ī ... Eş-Şeyh Muḥammad ed-Dāvūdī Sübliyā	127
76	Mevlānā Muḥammad Paşa Muhāfızı'l-Kuds	128
77	Eş-Şeyh Nureddin Hamza er-Rūmī el-Hanefī	130
78	Kāsım bin Ed-Decānī	133
79	Ömer el-Hüseynī	134
80	Hücce isbāt vakfiyye ... bi-bābu'l-'amūd Bāsim Sinābeddin	136
81	Zeyneddin el-Yamanlı	
82	Da'va Esas 1979 Karar 38	137
83	Da'va Esas 52 Sicil 52	130
84	Akrār bin Süleyman abdullah ... min Dimeşk bi vakafe cidde'l-a'lā Lala Mustafa Paşa bi-evkāfı 'Adīde	141
85	Salih bin Seyyid Ahmed ...	142
86	Sūret-i tevliyet-i Yusuf Derviş Necmi ..	143
87	... min Vakfı'l-Halilī	144
88	Abdulkadir bin Eş-Şeyh Ahmed eş-Şehīd bi-ibni Dāvūd el-Makdīsī	145
89	Eş-Şeyh Abdullah ed-Dāvūdī	148
90	Eş-Şeyh Abdullah İbrahim	149
91	Eş-Şeyh Abdullah İbrahim ed-Dāvūdī	150
92	Eş-Şeyh Abdullah İbrahim ed-Dāvūdī	151
93	Sūret-i Vekāle	152
94	Sūret-i fetvā el-munzam min eş-Şeyh Hüseyin Ebu'-Su'ūd li-vakf Ebi'l-Fazlu'l-'Alemī	

TABLE A13 List of distribution the newly endowed *waqf* asset in the city center by neighborhoods (1703–1831)

No.	Neighborhood names	Assets	Total	%
1	Bāb al-Hıtta	22 ev, 6 kırat 1 ev, 8 kırat 1 ev, 12 kırat 1 ev, 16 kırat ev, 18 kırat ¾ hisseli ev, 11 kırat boş (Khuluww) ev, 1 ahır, 1 mahmās (öğütücü), 1 fırın, 10 dükkān, 10 kırat ¼ hisseli 1 dükkān, 12 kırat 1 dükkān, 15 kırat 1 ev, 3 kırat boş (Khuluww) dükkān, 12 kırat boş (Khuluww) dükkān, 1 hakūre, 6 kırat 2 sebze bahçesi, 18 kırat 2 sebze bahçesi, 2 kırat 1/3 hisseli ev, 10 kırat ½ hisseli ev,	-22 ev -6 hisseli ev -1 ahır, -1 mahmas -1 fırın, -10 dükkan -5 hisseli dükkān -1 sebze bahç. -4 hisseli sebze bahç. Toplam: 51	8
2	Nasāra	9 ev, 1 oda, 1 kat, 6 kırat 1 beyt, 4 kırat 9/10 hisseli 1 büyük ev,12 kırat 2 ev, 4 kırat 9/10 hisseli 3 ev, 9/10 ve ½ kırat 3 ev, 9 kırat 2 ev, 17 kırat 4/7 hisseli ev, 18 kırat 2/3 hisseli ev, 18 kırat 4 ev, alt katta 1 beyt, 1 kırat 1/3 hisseli beyt, 10 kırat ½ hisseli ev, 6 dükkān, 1 yeni berber dükkānı, 1 küçük dükkān, 1 kahve dükkānı, 12 kırat 2 dükkān, 4 kırat 9/10 hisseli 2 dükkān, 12 kırat 1 sabun imalathanesi, 1 mağaza, 1 fırın. 4 kırat 9/10 hisseli 1 fırın, 9 kırat hakure, 1 derbekūne.	-9 ev, 1 oda, 1 kat, 1 beyt, hisseli 1 beyt, -19hisseli ev -9 dükkan, -4 hisseli dükkan, -1 sabun imalathane, -1 mağaza, -1 fırın, -1 hisseli fırın, -1 hisseli sebze bahçesi -1 derbekune Toplam: 50	7,9

TABLE A13 List of distribution the newly endowed *waqf* asset (*cont.*)

No.	Neighborhood names	Assets	Total	%
3	Yahud	6 ev, 11 kırat 1 ev, 8 kırat 1 ev, 22 kırat 2 ev, 4 kırat 9/10 hisseli 1 ev, 11 kırat 1/5 hisseli 1 ev, 12 kırat 4 ev, 14 kırat 1/5 hisseli 1 ev, 13 kırat 1/5 hisseli 1 ev, 12 kırat 2 ev (Ebī Şāmāt Sok.) 1 ev (Ebī Şāmāt Sok.), 11 kırat 1 beyt, 12 dükkān, 8 kırat 6 dükkān, 12 kırat 1/6 hisseli değirmen, 1 sabun imalathanesi, .), 1 tuğla imalathanesi (Ebī Şāmāt Sokağı).	-6 ev -15 hisseli ev -1 hisseli beyt -12 dükkan -6 hisseli dükkan -1 hisseli değirmen -1 sabun imalathanesi -1 tuğla imalathanesi Toplam: 43	7,8
4	Rīsha	16 ev, 6 kırat 3 ev, 18 kırat 1 ev, 7 kırat ½ hisseli ev, 1 boş (Khuluww) ev, 7 dükkān, 9/10 ve ½ kırat 2 hakure.	-16 ev -6 hisseli ev -7 dükkan -2 hisseli sebze bahçesi Toplam:31	4
	Hatt Davud (Bāb al-Silsila)	5 ev, ahşap 1 ev, 1 boş (Khuluww) ev, 2 kırat 1 ev, 7 kırat 1 ev, 10 kırat 1 ev, 10 ½ kırat 1 ev, 12 kırat 3 ev, 14 kırat 1 ev, 15 kırat ¼ hisseli 1 ev, 7 dükkān, 4 kırat 9/10 hisseli 2 dükkān, 2 ev Benī Haris (Kale yakınında), 2 kırat ½ hisseli ev, 6 kırat imalathane.	-9 ev -10 hisseli ev -7 dükkan -2 hisseli dükkan -1 hisseli imalathane Toplam:29	4

TABLE A13 List of distribution the newly endowed *waqf* asset (*cont.*)

No.	Neighborhood names	Assets	Total	%
	Bāb al-ʿAmūd	36 ev, büyük 1 ev, 2 beyt, 1 küçük ev, 1 ev (Bābu'S-Sahira), harabe 1 ev, 1 kemerli ev, 23 kırat 1 ev, 13 kırat ½ hisseli 1 ev, 20 kırat 1 ev, 6 kırat 1/6 hisseli 1 ev, 16 kırat 1/5 hisseli 1 ev, 6 kırat 1 ev, 3 kırat 1 ev, 1 eyvan, 18 kırat 1 ev, 8 kırat 1 ev, 4 kırat 1 ev, 7 kırat 3/5 hisseli 1 ev, 19 kırat 1 ev, 7 kırat 1 ev, 15 kırat 1/3 hisseli 2 ev, 12 kırat ½ hisseli 1 ev, 10 kırat 1 ev, 18 kırat 1ev, 12 kırat 4 ev, 6 kırat ½ hisseli kemerli 1 ev, 1 kırat 1/3 hisseli 1 ev, 19 kırat 1 ev, 9 kırat 1 ev, 13 kırat 1/3 hisseli tabaka, 12 kırat 1 ev (Bābu's-Sāhire), 21 kırat 1 ev, 2 kırat ½ hisseli ev (Tekye Yokuşu)3 dükkān. 12 kırat bağımsız 1 dükkān, 6 kırat 1 dükkān, 4 kırat 1 dükkān (Sūkı'd-Dār), 18 kırat 3/5 hisseli dükkān, 13 kırat 2/3 hisseli 1 kahve kileri, 13 kırat 2/3 hisseli 1 fırın dükkānı, 1 dokuma dükkānı, 1 fırın, 18 kırat 3/5 hisseli büyük kiler, 2 sabun imalathanesi, 21 kırat 1/5 hisseli sabun imalathanesi, 2 kırat ½ hisseli sabun imalathanesi, 4 karārit 4/5 ve nīf hisseli sabun imalathanesi, 8 kırat imalathane, 2 kerm (Bābu'S-Sahira), 2 hakure (Bābu'S-Sahira), 1 hakure, 3 kırat 3/5 hisseli sebze bahçesi, 2 hakūre.	-41 ev -2 beyt -1 eyvan -29 hisseli ev -1 hisseli tabaka -3 dükkan -4 hisseli dükkan -1 hisseli kahve kileri -1 hisseli fırın dükkanı -1 dokuma dükkanı -1 fırın -1 büyük kiler -2 sabun imalathanesi -3 his-seli sabun imalathanesi -1 hisseli imalathane -2 üzüm bağı (kerm) -5 sebze bahçesi -1 hisseli sebze bahçesi Toplam: 98	15

TABLE A13 List of distribution the newly endowed *waqf* asset (*cont.*)

No.	Neighborhood names	Assets	Total	%
5	Sa'diyya	1 ev, 1 kırat ½ hisseli ev, 12 kırat 1 ev, 6 kırat 1 ev, 5 kırat 3/5 hisseli 1 sebze bahçesi, 8 kırat (bed) arazi.	-1 ev -3 hisseli ev -1 hisseli sebze bahçesi -1 hisseli arazi Toplam: 6	
6	Maghāriba	11 ev, 4 oda, 13 kırat ½ hisseli 1 ev, 6 kırat 2 ev, 6 kırat 1/3 hisseli 1 ev, 12 kırat 2/3 hisseli 1 ev, ½ hisseli 1 ev, 2 hakūre, 1 yeni boş (Khuluww) öğütücü.	-11 ev -4 oda -6 hisseli ev -2 sebze bahçesi -1 öğütücü Toplam: 24	3,1
7	Sharaf	32 ev, 2 büyük ev, 1 kemerli ev, harab 1 ev, 3 katlı bir ev, 1 boş (Khuluww) ev, 1 eyvan rakabesi, 1 nısıf sarnıç, 1 kırat 1/8 hisseli 1 ev, 21 kırat 1 ev, 23 kırat 2 ev, 13 kırat 1 ev, 23 kırat 1 boş (Khuluww) ev, 7 kırat 1/3 hisseli 1 ev, 12 kırat 5 ev, 6 kırat 7 ev, 9/10 kırat ½ hisseli 2 ev, 2 kırat 2/3 hisseli 1 ev, 12 kırat 6/7 hisseli 1 ev, 2 kırat ½ hisseli 1 ev, 14 kırat ½ hisseli 1 ev, 1 kırat 7/8 hisseli 1 ev, 8 kırat ½ hisseli 1 ev, 12 kırat 2 ev, 5 kırat 3/5 hisseli 1 ev, 4 kırat 4/5 hisseli 1 ev, 8 kırat 1/3 hisseli ve nısıf hisseli 1 ev, 1/9 hisseli 1 ev, 18 kırat 1 ev, 2 kırat 2/3 hisseli 1 ev, 9 kırat 9/10 hisseli 1 ev, 13 kırat 1/5 hisseli 1 ev, 4 kırat ½ hisseli 1 ev, 1 dükkān, 6 kırat 1 fırın, 13 kırat ½ hisseli 1 fırın, 13 kırat ½ hisseli 1 fırın, 2 kırat	-38 ev -1 eyvan rakabesi -1 hisseli sarnıç -38 hisseli ev -1 dükkan -4 hisseli fırın -3 sebze bahçesi -3 hisseli sebze bahçesi -2 hisseli imalathane -1 fahūre Toplam: 92	12

TABLE A13 List of distribution the newly endowed *waqf* asset (*cont.*)

No.	Neighborhood names	Assets	Total	%
		½ hisseli 1 fırın, 3 hakūre, 12 kırat 1 sebze bahçesi, 2 kırat 1 hakūre, 3 kırat ½ hisseli 1 hakūre, 6 kırat 1 imalathane, 9/10 kırat ½ hisseli imalathane, 1 fahūre (çanak çömlek, çömlekçilik).		
12	Aqabat al-Sitt	2 ev, Haremlik, selamlık bölümlerinden oluşan 1 ev, 1 büyük ev, 22 kırat 1 ev, 15 kırat 3/5 hisseli 1 ev.	-4 ev -2 hisseli ev Toplam: 6	
13	Bāb al-Hadīd	3 ev, 1 büyük ev, 2 kırat 1/3 hisseli katlı 1 ev, 4 kırat 2 ev.	-4 ev -3 hisseli ev Toplam: 7	
	Vādi al-Tavvāhīn -Hatt	10 ev, 22 kırat 1 ev, 1 kırat 1/3 hisseli 1 ev, 3 kırat 1 ev, 3 kırat 1/3 hisseli 1 ev, 22 kırat 1 ev, 3 mağaza, 1 fırın.	-10 ev -5 hisseli ev -3 mağaza -1 fırın Toplam: 19	3
16	Aqabat al-Zāhiriyya	7 ev, 12 kırat 4 ev, 8 kırat 1 ev, 3 kırat 2 ev, 21 kırat 1 ev, 3 kırat 1 ev, 17 kırat 1 ev, 12 kırat şadırvanlı 1 hakūre, 1 hakūre, 1 sabun imalathanesi.	-7 ev -10 hisseli ev -1 şadırvanlı sebze bahçesi -1 sebze bahçesi -1 sabun imalathanesi Toplam:20	3
17	Javvalda (Bāb al-Halīl)	1 ev, 1/8 kırat 1 ev, 2 hakūre, 18 kırat 1 hakūre, 18 kırat hakūre, 1 mezraa, 6 kırat kıt'a arazi.	-1 ev -1 hisseli ev -2 sebze bahçesi -2 hisseli sebz. bahç. -1 mezraa -1 hisseli arazi Toplam:8	

TABLE A13 List of distribution the newly endowed *waqf* asset (*cont.*)

No.	Neighborhood names	Assets	Total	%
18	Kanātır al- Hıdır	3 ev, 1/8 kırat ve nısıf hisseli 1 ev, 8 kırat ½ hisseli 1 ev, 2 kırat 1/6 hisseli 1 ev, 3 kırat 1/3 hisseli 1 ev, 1/8 kırat ve nısıf hisseli 2 beyt, 10 kırat 2/3 hisseli sebze bahçesi, 1 boş (Khuluww) sebze bahçesi, 16 kırat arazi.	-3 ev -4 ev hissesi -1 hisseli beyt -1 sebze bahçesi -1 hiss. Sebze bahç -1 hisseli arazi Toplam:11	1,5
22	Tebāne	12 ev, katlı 1 ev, 7 kırat 1 ev, 1 kırat ¾ hisseli 1 ev, 3 tabaka,3 kırat 2 dükkān.	-13 ev -2 hisseli ev -3 tabaka - 2 hisseli dükkan Toplam:20	3
27	Hatt Merzibān (Bāb al-Qattānīn)	8 ev, 3 katlı 1 ev, 6 kırat 1 ev,6 kırat 1/6 hisseli 1 ev, 18 kırat 2 ev, 10 kırat ½ hisseli 1 ev, 5 kırat 1 ev, 4 kırat 4/5 hisseli 1 ev, 6 kırat 3 mağzilin, 12 kırat hakure, 5 kırat hakure arzı, ¼ kırat hisseli değirmen, 1 kahvehāne, 9 kırat ½ hisseli 1 dükkān.	-9 ev -7 hisseli ev -3 mağaza -1 hisseli sebze bahçesi -1 his.sebze bahç.arazi -1 hisseli değirmen -1 kahvehāne -1 hisseli dükkan Toplam:21	3
20	Various Locations	Kasīla Yokuşu (1 ev); Sebt Yokuşu (1 ev, 1 evin Khuluwwı); Tabbāhīn Çarşısı (Büyük Çarşı) 1 ev, 1 dükkān, 14 kırat hisseli dükkān, 12 kırat hisseli ev, 1 kırat 1/9 hisseli ev, 3 dükkan Khuluwwı); Sudan	Toplam: 32	5

TABLE A13 List of distribution the newly endowed *waqf* asset (*cont.*)

No.	Neighborhood names	Assets	Total	%
		Yokuşu (4 kırat 1/3 hisseli ve yarım hisseli ev, 19 kırat yarım hisseli ev); Hattı Kırımī (7/8 kırat hisseli evin Khuluwwı); Sarāyā Yokuşu (2 dükkān ve pay); Şevvāyīn Mahallesi (2 ev, 6 kırat 1 ev); Hayādire (12 kırat 2 ev, 12 kırat 1 hakūre, 5 kırat 2 hakūre, 1 mengene); Melāt Sokağı (1 ev, 9 kırat 1 ev); Sahyūn el-Cevāniyye (1 ev, 12 kırat 1 ev); Re'si'l-Kasīla (4 kırat 7/8 hisseli 1 ev, 4 kırat 7/8 hisseli sebze bahçesi, 3 kırat 2/9 hisseli 1 ev); Maslah (6 kırat 2 ev, 18 kırat 1 ev, 1 dükkān).		
21	Neighborhood Not Specified	9 ev, 1 ev (Duveyye), 1 ev (Niyābe), 1 ev (Benī Merra), 1 ev (Şeyh Reyhan Hattı), 1 ev (Azzām Sokağı), 1 yeni kat (Küçük Kemer), 4 kırat 1 ev (Bezbezet Sokağı), 12 kırat 1 ev (Hūşu'l-Murūb), 16 evin 22 kırat hissesi, 8 kırat ev (rakabesi değirmene), 6 kırat 1 ev, 9/10 ve ½ kırat 2 ev, 3 dükkān, 11 dükkānın 22 kırat hissesi, 9/10 ve ½ kırat 2 dükkān, 1 mağsara hissesi (imalathane), 7 kırat 4 hakure, 18 kırat sebze bahçesi, 1 kırat ½ hisseli 1 hakūre (Vād Mah.),1 kıt'a arazi (İbrahim arazisi), 11 kırat arazi, 12 kırat mezraa (Bābu'l-Esbat Mah.), 1 boş (Khuluww) değirmen (Ermeni Mah.).	-15 ev -22 hisseli ev -3 dükkan -13 hisseli dükkan -1 imalathane -6 hisseli sebze bahçesi -1 kıta arazı -2 hisseli arazi -1 değirmen Toplam: 64	10,1
Total			630	100

TABLE A14 Distribution of the assets of newly established *waqfs* outside the city in Jerusalem according to neighborhoods (1703–1831)

No.	Neighborhood name	*Waqf* assets	Total
1	Yusūfiyye Arzı	Zeytinlik	1
2	Baka'a	1 kermin Khuluwwhakkı medresetu'l-belediyye, Khuluww-ı sūkı'l-kattānīn ve karyeti'l-Ceyb Vakf-ı Sultan Īnal 9/10 ve ½ kıratı mezraa.	2
3	Tabl (Tabele) Vadisi	8 kırat 1 mezraa.	1
4	Silvan Village	8 kırat 1 mezraa, 16 kırat 1 mezraa, 12 kırat 2 mezraa.	-4 hisseli mezraa Toplam:4
5	'Isāviyye Village	4 kırat 2/3 hisseli arazi, 1 ev, 1 arazi.	-1 ev -1 arazi -1 hisseli arazi Toplam:3
6	Beyt-i Safāfa	6 kırat 1/6 hisseli zeytinlik, 8 kırat mezraa, 2 kırat mezraa,.	-1 hisseli zeytinlik -2 hisseli mezraa Toplam: 3
7	Arz-ı Masrara	3 mezraa, 6 kırat mezraa, 15 kırat mezraa, 9 kırat mezraa, 4 kırat ½ hisseli mezraa, 1 su deposu.	-3 mezraa -3 hisseli mezraa -1 su deposu Toplam:7
8	Sur Bahīr Village	6 kırat hisseli bed.	1
9	Beyt-i İksā Village	6 kırat mezraa.	1
10	Ebu Sūr Village	5 tek mezraa.	5
11	Ceyb Village	3/2 mezraa.	1
12	Seyfi Mencik Land	1 mezraa.	1
13	Mount Olive	Boş (Khuluww) 1 mezraa, mezraa, 16 kırat mezraa, 1 küçük ev.	-2 mezraa -1 hisseli mezraa -1 ev Toplam:4
14	Ṣalāḥiyya Land	1 mezraa, yarım hisseli boş (Khuluww) mezraa, 18 kırat mezraa, 4 kırat mezraa, 12 kırat mezraa, 15 kırat mezraa, 9 kırat arazi, 12 kırat sebze bahçesi.	-1 mezraa -6 mezraa -1 hisseli sebze bahçesi Toplam:8
15	Vādi al-Jawz	1 kerm.	1

TABLE A14 Distribution of the assets of newly established *waqfs* outside the city (*cont.*)

No.	Neighborhood name	*Waqf* assets	Total
16	Kermi'l-Esved	15 kırat mezraa.	1
17	Simār Land	12 kırat mezraa.	1
18	Kadūm Vadisi	1 Mezraa, 6 kırat mezraa, 9 kırat kerm.	2
19	Deyr-i Sinne (Sene) Land	Mezraa,	1
20	Savāne	12 kırat mezraa.	1
21	Shaykh Jarrah District	17 kırat arazi.	1
22	Matarabiye Land	6 kırat arazi.	1
23	Maqam Nabī Davud (Outside the city walls)	7 kırat ½ hisseli ev, 10 kırat ½ hisseli arazi, 1 ev, 12 kırat sebze bahçesi.	-1 ev -1 hisseli ev -1 hisseli sebze bah. -1 hisseli arazi Toplam:4
24	Except for Jerusalem, no location specified	2 köyde 4 kırat hisse, 4 kırat hisseli 2 mezraa, 2 kırat kıt'a arz, 1 hakūre, 5 kırat ¼ hisseli mezraa (Nekağ arazisi), 20 kırat mezra (Kudüs dışında Mağbediye arazisi), 1boş (Khuluww) arazi, Cerrahiyye Arazisi, Kudüs haricinde Bātın-ı Şerif arazisi, Kudüs haricinde arazi, Kudüs dışında Bedreddin bin Cemā'ā Vakfı ile komşu bir saray, 12 kırat sebze bahçesi,	-
25	Jaffa	Bostan ve hāsılı.	1
26	al-Khalīl	2 tabaka, 'Ayn Sāre yakınında 1 kerm.	3
Total			59

TABLE A15 Distribution of *waqfs* founders' nicknames in Jerusalem (1703–1831)

Endower	Nicknames	No.	%	Endower	Nicknames	No.
Family names	'Akilik	1	16,3	Family names	'Alemī	6
	Akkaş	1			'Aselī	3
	'Akkal	1			Bālī	1
	'Alavun	1			Beradī	1
	Asker	1			Cā'ūnī	13
	Bāballah	1			Cemā'ī	1
	Bāz	1			Dāvūdī (el- Ensārī)	3
	Denef (el-Ensārī)	4			Decānī	1
	Derviş	1			Decānī (el-Ğuşe)	2
	Devīk	1			Hakavī	1
	Felāha	1			Hakimī	1
	Harb	1			Halidī	2
	Hucac	1			Halilī	3
	Kalibu	1			Hatenī-Kadı	2
	Karniye	1			Hayrī	1
	Kutb	2			Hevārī	2
	Kuttīne (Kutayna)	4			Hılvanī	2
	Kuttīne-Çelebi	1			Hüseynī	5
	Kuveyder	2			Hüseynī-Danizāde	1
	Rasās	5			Hüseynī-İmam	1
	Rekāt	1			'Izravī	2
	Semūm	2			Kımi'	5
	Serendah	1			Kırmī	1
	Şevā	1			Lutfī	1
	Tantūre	2			Mağribī	8
	Tavīl	1			Mağribī-Tavīl	1
	Tenekeci	1			Nastī-Usta	1
	Tercemān	2			Nimrī	3
	Tūkān	2			Nu'acī	3
	'Uzmā	1			Remlī	1

TABLE A15 Distribution of *waqfs* founders' nicknames in Jerusalem (1703–1831) (*cont.*)

Endower	Nicknames	No.	%	Endower	Nicknames	No.
	Zuheyman	1			Şekki Mekkī	5
Total	31	47			Şihabī	1
Family names	Ebu'l-Lutf	1	2		Terhī	2
	Ebu Şerif	1			Zemānī	2
	Ebu Cibne	1		Total	34	88
	Ebu'n-Nasr-Şurafā	2		Family names	Halebī	2
	Ebu'l-Hevā	1			Keşmirī	2
Total	5	6			Hicazī- Debbağ	1
Family names	ibn-i Kadbān	1	3,6		Remlī	1
	İbn-i Hamid- es-Sūfī	1			Cibālī (Kadın)	2
	İbn-i Ğanem	2			'Akkavī	2
	İbn-i Muğsele	1			İskenderānī	1
	İbn-i Saliha	1			Dīsī	1
	İbn-i Cūd	1			Şāmī	2
	İbn-i Hoca	1			Kūfī	1
	İbn-i Habiş	2		Total	10	15
	İbn-i Kadı-yı Salt	1		Family names with 'evlād' form	Tanbağa	1
Total	9	11			ed-Derviş es-Safadī	1
Nicknames in the form of bint	Alaybeyzāde	1	18,7		Mu'avin ez-Zağir es-Sa'dī	1
	Bahş	1				
	Bedevī	1		Total	3	3
	Beşāra	1		Nicknames in the form of ethnicity	Rūmiyye	1
	Cahşe	1			Kurdī	2
	Dürzī	1			Turk	1

TABLE A15 Distribution of *waqfs* founders' nicknames in Jerusalem (1703–1831) (*cont.*)

Endower	Nicknames	No.	%	Endower	Nicknames	No.
	Ebu Lahye kızı	2			Boşnak	1
	Habeşzāde	1		Total	4	5
	Harb	1		Nicknames of *ahl al-'urf*	Ağa-Dizdār	1
	'Aselī	1			Ağa – Mağribī	2
	Havaş	1			Baş ağa	1
	Hılvanī	1			Beşe- 'atiyye	1
	Hīkel	1			Bey- 'Aselī	1
	Hatun-'Aselī	1			Bey- El-Emīr	1
	Hatun- Nemrī	1			Bey- Alaybeyzāde	1
	Felāha	1			Bey- Hindiyye	1
	Efendi kızı	1			Bey	1
	İmam	1			Beşe- Kal'avī	1
	Kadı-yı es-Salt	1			Beşe- Kutb	1
	Kuttīne, Şeyhu'l-Hanbelī	2			Beşe- Iskāfī	1
					Beşe- Mukaddem	1
	Mağribī- Tavīl	1			Çavuş	1
	Mesnah	1			Kāimmakan-ı Kuds	1
	Mücahid	2			Miğmarbaşı- Nammar	2
	Müftü-yi Kuds	1			Mütesellim-i Kuds	1
	Saydavī	1			PAşa	1
	Saltī	1			Topçu	1
	Serendah	1			Topçubaşı	1
	Şeyh kızı	2			Vezīr, Muhafız-ı Dimeşk-i Şam ve'l-Kuds-i Şerif ve Gazze ve Nablus ve Emīru'l-Hac eş-Şāmī	1

TABLE A15 Distribution of *waqf*s founders' nicknames in Jerusalem (1703–1831) (*cont.*)

Endower	Nicknames	No.	%	Endower	Nicknames	No.
	Şeşberk	1				
	Tanbağa	1				
	Tafeş	1				
	Tevvābīn	1				
	Zevcet-i Paşa	1				
	Unknown	19				
Total		56		Total		39
ʿulamāʾ		3		*ʿulamāʾ*	Reisü'l-küttāb (Halidī)	9
		1			Kāimmakam-ı Nakībü'l-eşraf	3
		2			El-Muvakkıt	1
		4			Çelebi- Nimrī	1
		1			Sirāc	1
		1			Müftü-yi bi-İskele-i Yafa-Hüseynī	1
		1			Şeyh-Cağbe	2
		1			Hādim'i Mescid-i Aksā- Neşāşibī	1
		1			Nakību'l-eşraf	2
		1			Nakību'l-eşraf-'Alemī	1
		1			Nakību'l-eşraf-Şeyhü'l-Harem-Hüseynī	1
						43
Re'āyā					Debbağ	1
						2
Unknown Endowers						300

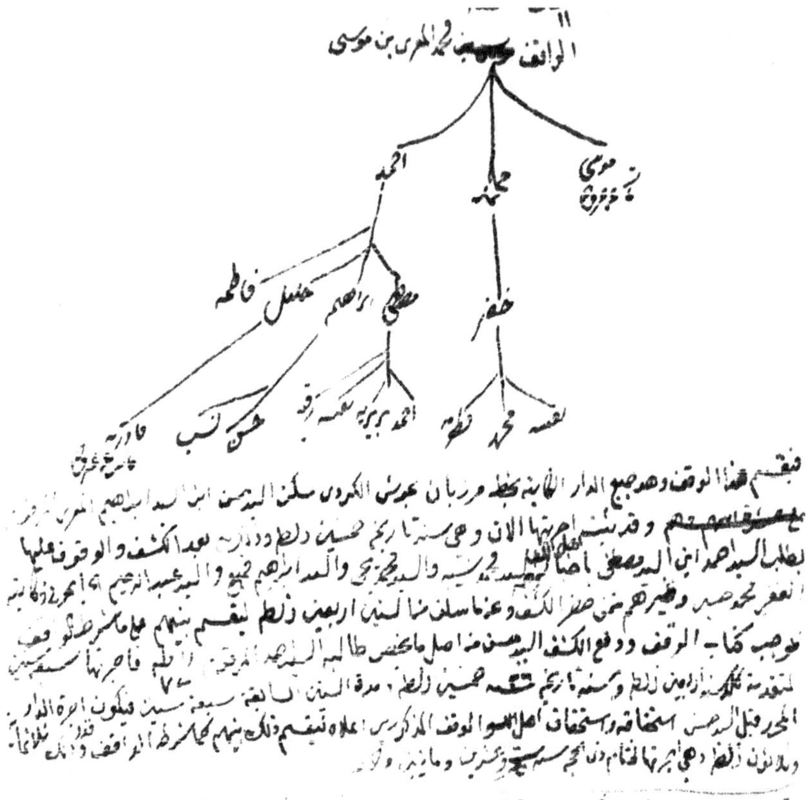

FIGURE A6 Sample of a family tree regarding sharing of *waqf* revenues (JS, 290: 8)

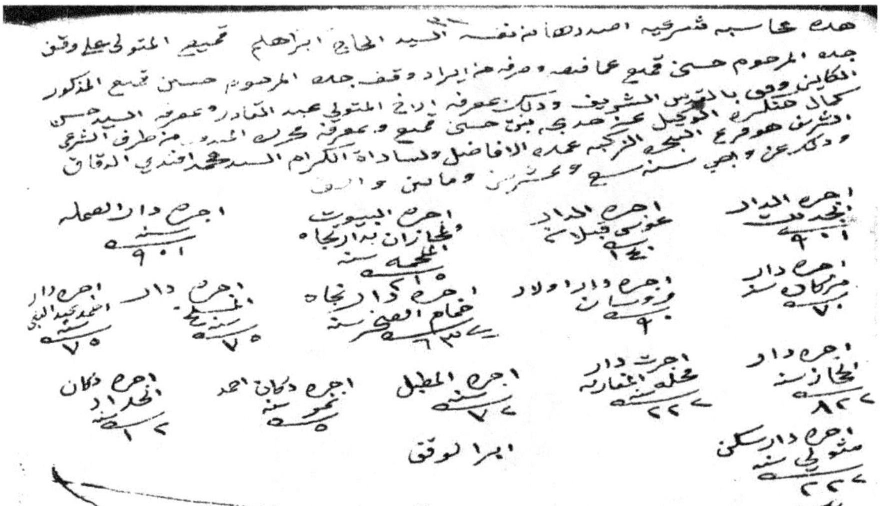

FIGURE A7 Account register of the *Waqf* of Husayin al-Qımiʿdated 1127/1715 (JS, 297: 33)

FIGURE A8 Qubbat al-Yusuf (Berchem 1927, s. 1092)

Bibliography

Archival Resources

Palestine

The Archive of the *Iḥyā᾿ al-Turāth wa'l-Shu᾿ūn al-Dīniyya*

Jerusalem Sharīʿa Court Sijils (JS)

201/231; 202/12–13, 12, 786, 295, 274, 375; 203/181, 399; 205/108–110; 207/82–83, 117–121, 122–123, 129–130, 144, 213–214, 340, 343–344, 345, 257; 208/81–82, 105; 209/249, 253, 261–62, 267–68, 279–80, 448, 484–1, 484–2; 212/ 7–8, 48–49, 31–32, 51–52, 91–94; 213/ 31–32, 51–52, 91–94, 95, 97, 174; 214/144, 219; 216/15; 217/340–41, 359–60; 218/18, 20–21, 22–3, 29, 32–3, 44, 129–30, 147, 156, 470, 154, 253, 277–78, 346–47, 276, 390, 486, 487; 220/33–4, 145–46, 200, 410–12; 221/19, 48, 301, 410–11, 331, 604, 590, 596, 602; 222/66; 223/58, 66, 107–1, 107–2, 161, 172–73, 279–81, 288–89, 311–13, 372, 425; 225/73, 88, 125–27, 203, 226–27, 227–28; 226/50; 227/144, 123, 179, 192, 289–90, 340–43, 289, 391; 228/3–4, 224; 229/43–4, 52, 61; 230/ 4, 42, 128, 147, 168, 174, 187, 210, 240–41; 231/ 204, 310, 323, 312, 251; 232/ 87, 205–206, 207, 532; 233/135–36, 203; 234/34; 235/123, 180–81, 183–84, 217–19, 262–63, 318, 320–22; 236/35, 55, 117–18, 89–90, 376, 382; 239/ 15, 16–7, 50; 238/26, 129; 241/39–41, 85, 123, 129–30, 130–31, 141–42, 146, 147–48; 242/133–36, 164–67, 184–1, 184–2, 186, 185–86; 243/ 23, 27, 36–7, 147, 283, 183–84, 50, 98, 276, 275, 122; 244/135, 179, 181, 190; 245/4, 16, 55–6, 60; 246/ 25, 116, 116–17, 118–19, 89, 136; 247/19, 48–9, 71–2, 80–81, 109–110; 248/54–55, 61; 249/31, 63–4, 70–71, 137–38; 250/17–18, 18–20, 22–24, 39–40, 126–27, 130, 137–38; 251/39, 108–109, 111–14, 131–33, 134–35, 139–141, 150–51; 252/ 8–9, 35–36, 53, 80, 68, 138, 141–42, 143–45; 253/24–25, 70–71, 253, 279; 254/1, 36, 49, 71, 74, 139, 161, 306–307, 355, 443–44, 457, 518, 505–506; 255/47, 53–4, 102–103, 116, 120–21; 256/118–19, 134, 151–52; 257/65, 99; 258/122, 259: 118, 154, 170–71, 228–29; 260/8, 25, 70–73; 261/20, 107–108, 108–109; 262/59, 73, 108–109; 264/45–46, 64–65, 88–90, 138–39; 166, 96–97, 158–59; 267/156–57, 152–54, 159–60; 269/119–120, 128–29, 134; 272/134–35, 147; 273/13–14, 134–35, 36–7, 102, 114; 274/13–4, 156–59; 275/134, 93, 102–103; 276/74–5, 84–5, 88, 141; 277/23–25, 149–51, 182; 278/112; 279/145–46, 147; 288/89, 280/87–89; 281/12–14, 167, 80; 282/119; 283/3, 118–19; 285/119, 89; 290/1, 4, 38; 292/16; 293/188; 295/ 232; 297/52, 53–54, 86, 33, 34, 86, 41, 164; 298/52, 67, 52, 169, 314/123; 290: 1,4, 8, 38, 124, 308; 299/21; 301/109; 302/93; 305: 3, 42, 305; 307/124; 308/106, 124, 155; 309/72; 311/33; 329: 101–103.

Turkey

Archive of General Directorate of Foundations (VGMA)

Waqfiyya Registers

583: 28/20, 583: 29/21, 583: 29/22, 583: 212/179, 587: 91/115–16, 589: 192/327, 589: 192/328, 589: 194/330, 589: 195/331, 589: 196/332, 608: 235/178, 608: 1/55–63, 608–1: 224/240, 608–2: 15/7, 641: 117/14, 730: 36/15, 731: 65/44, 741: 290/164, 745: 309/102, 745: 315/105, 747: 274/219, 779: 140/131, 1626: 1–18, 731: 44/1–6, 608: 2/1–3, 1647/1–68.

***Aḥkām* (Desicions) Registers**

814/4, 814/11, 814/13, 814/44–45, 814/49–1, 814/49–2, 814/66, 814/70, 814/74, 814/86, 814/89, 814/90, 814/91, 814/93, 814/95, 814/103, 814/106–1, 814/106–2, 814/111, 814/112, 814/121, 814/127, 814/130, 814/131, 814/132–1, 814/132–2, 814/133, 814/134, 814/138, 814/150, 814/156, 814/162, 814/166, 814/182, 814/186, 814/191, 814/197, 814/201, 814/217, 814/219–1, 814/219–2, 814/227, 814/229, 814/256, 814/259, 814/265, 814/270, 814/273, 814/279, 814/280, 814/281, 814/288, 814/289, 814/290, 814/291, 814/292, 814/307, 815/7, 815/11–1, 815/11–2, 815/16, 815/29, 815/32, 815/42, 815/45, 815/46–1, 815/46–2, 815/77, 815/82, 815/100–1, 815/100–2, 815/117, 815/120, 815/127, 815/130, 814/144, 815/146, 815/172, 815/180, 815/184, 815/186, 815/203, 815/204, 815/207, 815/211, 815/212, 815/215, 815/216, 815/219, 815/223, 815/226, 815/231, 815/243, 317/221, 318/119, 319/31, 319/110, 319/125, 319/131, 319/185, 319/197, 319/206, 319/213, 319/231, 319/297, 319/299, 319/345, 320/23, 320/90, 320/198, 320/201, 320/292, 320/364, 321/124, 321/96, 323/23, 359/83, 359/94.

***Atīq* (Old Treasury) Registers**

3/ 374, 3/375, 3/376, 3/377, 3/378, 3/379, 3/380, 523/1–23, 524/1–26, 528/1, 528/2, 528/3.

***Cedīd* (New Treasury) Registers**

160/337, 160/344, 160/337, 160/345, 160/337, 160/346, 160/337, 160/347, 160/352, 160/356, 160/381, 160/438, 160/447, 160/513, 160/515, 160/522, 160/527, 160/543, 160/641, 160/646, 160/655, 160/699, 160/710, 160/726, 160/754, 162/113, 162/115, 162/126, 515: 23/1, 515: 33/1, 515: 34/6, 515: 35/7, 515: 35/9, 515: 36/10, 515: 36/11, 515: 36/12.

***Hulāsā* (Summation) Registers**

604/4–1, 604/4–2.

***Ḥurūfāt/ 'Askerī Rūznāmçe* (Appointment) Registers**

551/99, 552/37, 553/38, 554/25, 555/25, 556/39, 557/43, 1091/77, 1107/2, 1108/1, 1109/6, 1110/131, 1111/54, 1112/1, 1114/10, 1115/1, 1119/110, 1125/64, 1128/68, 1139/87, 1140/245, 1142/85, 1159/97, 1160/117, 1216/15.

***Tafsīl* (Detailed) Registers**

233/11, 763/82, 359/83, 359/94, 359/225.

Ottoman Imperial Archives (BOA)

Damascus *Aḥkām* (Desicions) Registers (ADVNS.AHK.ŞM)

1: 7/1, 22/3, 28/5, 29/3, 37/3, 41/3, 43/1, 44/2, 49/2, 51/2, 58/6, 77/1, 85/4, 87/2, 155/1, 158/2, 174/3, 186/1, 186/2, 191/1, 191/2, 191/3, 206/1, 210/2, 212/5, 226/6, 232/1, 233/2, 245/4, 252/2, 252/4, 279/4, 288/1, 288/2, 289/4;

2: 9/1, 12/2, 13/3, 27/1, 30/4, 31/4, 47/1, 50/1, 56/2, 56/4, 76/3, 108/3, 110/2, 147/1, 150/2, 154/2, 156/1, 161/4, 162/1, 163/2, 166/1, 173/4, 174/4, 180/1, 180/2, 183/4, 184/2, 187/4, 189/3, 196/1, 285/1, 289/3, 290/2, 314/5, 320/3;

3: 4/2, 5/1, 18/1, 39/4, 40/5, 46/1, 47/4, 58/4, 60/4, 64/3, 66/3, 68/2, 76/2, 102/3, 102/5, 108/4, 110/4, 114/4, 115/4, 120/4, 121/3, 121/4, 127/1, 135/2, 137/1, 137/3, 138/4, 139/1, 146/3, 147/3, 148/1, 152/2, 153/1, 153/2, 153/3, 156/1, 156/2, 156/3;

4: 1/1, 29/3, 29/4, 32/1, 32/2, 34/1, 35/2, 57/1, 58/4, 59/3, 62/2, 67/3, 67/4, 70/1, 85/3, 92/1, 93/2, 105/3, 106/1, 110/3, 125/2, 128/1, 128/2, 129/3, 135/2, 143/3, 144/1, 149/2, 150/1, 152/2, 152/4, 152/5, 160/2, 160/3, 162/3, 163/1, 163/2, 178/2, 186/1, 191/4, 193/2;

5: 5/1, 7/2, 9/1, 10/4, 11/1, 13/1, 16/1, 19/1, 20/1, 27/1, 30/2, 34/1, 41/2, 53/1, 54/3, 79/1, 80/3, 86/1, 89/2, 90/2, 95/1, 96/3, 127/1, 129/2;

6: 14/4, 34/1, 43/4, 58/2, 70/3, 90/2, 134/1, 136/1, 138/2, 170/1;

7: 6/2, 6/3, 91/2, 97/2, 99/4, 100/1.

***Evkāf* (*Awqāf*) Registers (EV.d)**

10001, 12567/75, 12567/80, 13301/2, 13301/3, 13301/85, 13270/22, 13872/26, 14588/2, 21908/1–3.

***Evkāf-ı Haremeyn Muhasebeciliği* (*Awqāf* Account Registers of Ḥaramayn) (EV.HMH.d)**

386/1–4, 387/1–8, 705/ 1–8, 718/1–13, 1258/2, 1427/1–11, 1431/1–12, 1472/1–3, 1619/1–7, 1632/ 1–34, 2060/1–16, 5241/2, 5243/1–13, 6314/1–6, 6364/18, 6563/27.

Mektūbī (Correpondence) Registers (EV.MKT)

19/1, 723/10, 795/29, 2553/193, 749/50, 1193/36.

***Kalemi Cihāt* (Office of Correspondence of Official Duties) Registers (EV.MKT.CHT)**

581/200.

Evkāf Muhasebe (*Awqāf* Account) Registers (EV.MH)

104/114, 154/107, 1865/251.

Evkāf Haremeyn Mukāta'ası Surre (Surra *of Awqāf* Ḥaramayn Mukāta'a) Registers (EV.HMK.SR.d)

1971, 2224, 2546, 2855.

Land Registry and Cadastre Information System (TKGMA)

***Evkāf Taḥrīr* (*Awqāf* Land Registry) Registers**

516, 515 (253), 517 (253), 514 (539)/5–23, 518 (446), 519 (503).

Archive of the Museum of Islamic Arts (İEMA)

2192.

National Library of Turkey

Suriye Vilayeti Salnamesi (1288/ 1871–1872: 149–168)

The Holy Books

Kur'an-ı Kerim ve Yüce Meāli, (Elmalılı Hamdi Yazır), Tasdik No: 500, İstanbul, 1995.

Published Works

ʿAbd al-Mahdī, ʿAbd al-Jalīl Ḥasan. *Al-Madāris fī Bayt al-Maqdis fī l-ʿAṣrayn al-Ayyūbī wa-l-Mamlūkī.* Amman: Maktabat al-Aqṣā, 1981.

Abacı, Nurcan. "Osmanlı Kentlerinde Sosyal Kontrol: Araçlar ve İşleyiş." In *Şinasi Tekin'in Anısına Uygurlardan Osmanlı'ya,* edited by Günay Kut and Fatma Büyükkarcı Yılmaz, 101–10. Istanbul: Simurg Kitapçılık, 2005.

Abacı, Nurcan. "SNA (Social Network Analysis) and Ottoman History: A Social Network Analysis of Mountain and Immigrant Villages of Bursa (Late Ottoman/Early Republic)." Paper presented at the 12th International Congress of Ottoman Social and Economic History, Retz, Austria, July 11–15, 2011.

Abouali, Diana. *Family and Society in a Seventeenth-Century Ottoman City: The ʿAlamis of Jerusalem.* PhD diss., Harvard University, 2003.

Abou-El-Haj, Rifaʿat ʿAli. *Formation of the Modern State: The Ottoman Empire, Sixteenth to Eighteenth Centuries.* Albany: State University of New York Press, 1991.

Abu-Manneh, Butrus. "Jerusalem in the Tanzimat Period: The New Ottoman Administration and Notables." *Die Welt des Islams,* new ser., 30, no. 1/4 (1990): 5–6.

Abu-Manneh, Butrus. "The Ḥusaynīs: The Rise of a Notable Family in 18th Century Palestine." In *Palestine in the Late Ottoman Period: Political, Social, and Economic Transformation,* edited by David Kushner, 93–109. Leiden: E. J. Brill, 1986.

Akarlı, Engin D. "Provincial Power Magnates in Ottoman Bilad al-Sham and Egypt, 1740–1840." In *La vie sociale dans les provinces arabes à l'époque Ottomane,* edited by Abdeljelil Tamimi, 41–56. Zaghouan: Centre d'Études et de Recherches Ottomanes, Morisques, de Documentation et d'Information, 1988.

Akdağ, Mustafa. "Osmanlı Tarihinde Āyanlık Düzeni Devri, 1730–1839." *Tarih Araştırmaları Dergisi* 8, no. 12 (1974): 51–61.

Akdağ, Mustafa. *Türkiye'nin İktisadi ve İçtimai Tarihi.* Vol. 2. Ankara: Türk Tarih Kurumu Yayınları, 1971.

Akgündüz, Ahmet. "Osmanlı Hukukunda Vakıflar, Hükümleri ve Çeşitleri." In *Türkler*, vol. 10, 447–60. Ankara: Yeni Türkiye Yayınları, 2002.

Akgündüz, Ahmet. *İslam Hukukunda ve Osmanlı Tatbikatında Vakıf Müessesesi*. Ankara: Türk Tarih Kurumu Yayınları, 1988.

Akgündüz, Ahmet. *Osmanlı Kanunnâmeleri ve Hukukî Tahlilleri*. Vol. 7. Istanbul: Osmanlı Araştırmaları Vakfı, 1994.

Aksüt, Ali Kemali. *Koçi Bey Risalesi*. Istanbul: Vakit Yayınları, 1939.

al-Alami, Muhammed Ali. "The Waqfs of the Traditional Families of Jerusalem during the Ottoman Period." In *Ottoman Jerusalem: The Living City, 1517–1917*, edited by Sylvia Auld and Robert Hillenbrand, 145–58. London: Altajir World of Islam Trust, 2000.

Alkan, Mustafa. *Adana Vakıfları: İnsan, Vakıf ve Şehir*. Ankara: Türk Tarih Kurumu Yayınları, 2014.

Alkan, Mustafa. "Türk Tarihi Araştırmaları Açısından Vakıf Kayıtlar Arşivi." *Vakıflar Dergisi* 30 (2007): 1–34.

Armağan, A. Latif. "XVIII. Yüzyılda Hac Yolu Güzergâhı ve Menziller." *Osmanlı Araştırmaları* 20 (2000): 73–118.

Arnon, Adar. "The Quarters of Jerusalem in the Ottoman Period." *Middle Eastern Studies* 28, no. 1 (1992): 1–65.

al-ʿĀrif, al-ʿĀrif. *Al-Mufaṣṣal fī Tārīkh al-Quds*. Jerusalem: Fawzī Yūsuf, 1961.

al-ʿĀrif, ʿĀrif. *Tārīkh al-Ḥaram al-Qudsī*. Jerusalem: Maṭbaʿat Dār al-Aytām al-Islāmiyya al-Ṣināʿiyya, 1947.

al-ʿĀrif, ʿĀrif. *Tārīkh Qubbat al-Ṣakhra al-Musharrafa wa-l-Masjid al-Aqṣā wa-Mulakhkhaṣ Tārīkh al-Quds*. Jerusalem: Maktabat al-Andalus, 1955.

al-Asali, Kamil Jamil. "Jerusalem under the Ottomans, 1516–1831." In *Jerusalem in History*, edited by Kamil Jamil al-Asali, 200–24. London: Scorpion Publishing, 1989.

al-Asali, Kamil Jamil. "The Cemeteries of Ottoman Jerusalem." In *Ottoman Jerusalem: The Living City, 1517–1917*, edited by Sylvia Auld and Robert Hillenbrand, 279–84. London: Altajir World of Islam Trust, 2000.

al-Asali, Kamil Jamil. "The Libraries of Ottoman Jerusalem." In *Ottoman Jerusalem: The Living City, 1517–1917*, edited by Sylvia Auld and Robert Hillenbrand, 285–89. London: Altajir World of Islam Trust, 2000.

ʿAsalī, Kāmil Jamīl. *Ajdādunā fī Tharā Bayt al-Maqdis: Dirāsa Athariyya Tārīkhiyya li-Maqābir al-Quds wa-Turābihā wa-Ithbāt bi-Asmāʾ al-Aʿyān al-Madfunīn Fīhā*. Amman: al-Majmaʿ al-Malakī li-Buḥūth al-Ḥaḍāra al-Islāmiyya, 1981.

al-ʿAsalī, Kāmil Jamīl. *Maʿāhid al-ʿIlm fī Bayt al-Maqdis*. Amman: Jāmiʿat ʿUmmāl al-Maṭābiʿ al-Taʿāwuniyya, 1981.

al-ʿAsalī, Kamāl ʿAbd al-Jalīl. *Wathāʾiq Maqdisiyya Tārīkhiyya*. Amman: Jāmiʿat al-Urduniyya, 1983.

Atalar, Münir. *Osmanlı Devleti'nde Surre-i Hümâyûn ve Surre Alayları*. Ankara: Diyanet İşleri Başkanlığı Yayınları, 1991.

Ateş, İbrahim. "Osmanlılar Zamanında Mekke ve Medine'ye Gönderilen Para ve Hediyeler." *Vakıflar Dergisi* 13 (1981): 159–74.

Auld, Sylvia, and Robert Hillenbrand, eds. *Ottoman Jerusalem: The Living City, 1517–1917*. 2 vols. London: Altajir World of Islam Trust, 2000.

Avcı, Casim. "Kudüs." In *Türkiye Diyanet Vakfı İslâm Ansiklopedisi*, vol. 26, 327–29. Ankara: Türkiye Diyanet Vakfı, 2002.

Avcı, Yasemin. *Değişim Sürecinde Bir Osmanlı Kenti: Kudüs (1890–1914)*. Ankara: Phoenix Yayınevi, 2004.

Ayar, Ali Rıza. "Abdurrahman Eşref Efendi'nin (öl. 1738) 'Mir'ātü's-Safā' Adlı El Yazmasının Tanıtılması." In *Uluslararası Avrasya Sempozyumu, 4–7 Ekim 2017*, 777–86. Amasya: Amasya Üniversitesi, 2017.

Aydıner, Mesut. "Rāgıb Paşa." In *Türkiye Diyanet Vakfı İslâm Ansiklopedisi*, vol. 34, 403–06. Istanbul: Türkiye Diyanet Vakfı, 2007.

Ayverdi, Ekrem Hakkı. *Osmanlı Mīmārīsinin İlk Devri*. Vol. 1. Istanbul: İstanbul Fetih Cemiyeti Yayınları, 1966.

Baer, Gabriel. "Jerusalem's Families of Notables and Waqf in the Early 19th Century." In *Palestine in the Late Ottoman Period*, edited by David Kushner, 109–11. Leiden: E. J. Brill, 1986.

Baer, Gabriel. "The Dismemberment of Awqaf in Early 19th Century Jerusalem." In *Ottoman Palestine, 1800–1914: Studies in Economic and Social History*, edited by Gad G. Gilbar, 299–319. Leiden: E. J. Brill, 1990.

Baer, Gabriel. "The Waqf as a Prop for the Social System (16th–20th Centuries)." *Islamic Law and Society* 4, no. 3 (1997): 264–97.

Baer, Gabriel. "Women and Waqf: An Analysis of the Istanbul Tahrir of 1546." *Asian and African Studies* 17, no. 1 (1983): 9–27.

Bakhīt, Muḥammad Adnān. *The Ottoman Province of Damascus in the Sixteenth Century*. Beirut: Librairie du Liban, 1982.

Bakhīt, Muḥammad ʿAdnān. "Dirāsa fī Maṣādir al-Infāq ʿalā Madāris al-Quds al-Sharīf wa-Miṣr wa-Fātiḥa ʿalā Ḍaw' Daftar Taḥrīr (T.D. 131) (932/1525–939/1531–1533)." In *Al-Mu'tamar al-Dawlī al-Sābiʿ li-Tārīkh Bilād al-Shām: Awqāf Bilād al-Shām min Bad' al-Futūḥāt al-Islāmiyya ilā Nihāyat al-Qarn al-ʿIshrīn*, vol. 3, edited by Muḥammad ʿAdnān Bakhīt, 1–42. Amman: University of Jordan Press, 2008.

Baltacı, Cahit. *XV–XVI. Asırlarda Osmanlı Medreseleri: Teşkilât ve İşleyiş*. Istanbul: İrfan Matbaası, 1998.

Barbir, Karl K. *Ottoman Rule in Damascus, 1708–1758*. Princeton, NJ: Princeton University Press, 1980.

Barkan, Ömer Lütfi. "Avārız." In *İslâm Ansiklopedisi*, vol. 2, 27–30. Ankara: Millî Eğitim Bakanlığı, 1979.

Barkan, Ömer Lütfi. “Osmanlı İmparatorluğu'nda Bir İskân ve Kolonizasyon Metodu Olarak Vakıflar ve Temlikler I: İstilâ Devirlerinin Kolonizatör Türk Dervişleri ve Zâviyeler.” *Vakıflar Dergisi* 2 (1942): 279–386.

Barkan, Ömer Lütfi. “Şehirlerin Teşekkül ve İnkişāf Tarihi Bakımından: Osmanlı İmparatorluğunda İmāret Sitelerinin Kuruluş ve İşleyiş Tarzına Ait Araştırmalar.” *İstanbul Üniversitesi İktisat Fakültesi Mecmuası* 23, no. 1–2 (1962–63): 239–96.

Barkan, Ömer Lütfi. *Osmanlı Devleti'nin Sosyal ve Ekonomik Tarihi: Tetkikler-Makaleler*. 2 vols. Edited by Hüseyin Özdeğer. Istanbul: İstanbul Üniversitesi, 2000.

Barkan, Ömer Lütfi. *Türkiye'de Toprak Meselesi*. Istanbul: Gözlem Yayınları, 1980.

Barkey, Karen. *Bandits and Bureaucrats: The Ottoman Route to State Centralization*. New York: Cornell University Press, 1994.

Barnes, John Robert. *An Introduction to Religious Foundations in the Ottoman Empire*. Leiden: Brill, 1987.

Basuğuy, Bedrettin. *Selahaddin-i Eyyubi Devrinde İlmi Faaliyetler*. Istanbul: Hivda İletişim, 2009.

Başol, Şamettin. *Kentleşme, Ekonomi ve Sosyal Hayat Yönleriyle 17. Yüzyıl Bursa Vakıfları*. PhD diss., Gazi Üniversitesi, Sosyal Bilimler Enstitüsü, Tarih Anabilim Dalı, 2008.

Bates, Ülkü. “Women as Patrons of Architecture in Turkey.” In *Women in the Muslim World*, edited by Lois Beck and Nikki Keddie, 243–60. Cambridge, MA: Harvard University Press, 1978.

Baykara, Tuncer. *Anadolu'nun Tarihī Coğrafyasına Giriş 1: Anadolu'nun İdarī Taksimatı*. Ankara: Türk Kültürünü Araştırma Enstitüsü, 1988.

Baykara, Tuncer. *Osmanlı Taşra Teşkilâtında XVIII. Yüzyılda Görev ve Görevliler (Anadolu)*. Ankara: Vakıflar Genel Müdürlüğü Yayınları, 1990.

Ben-Arieh, Yehoshua. *Jerusalem in the 19th Century: The Old City*. Jerusalem: Yad Izhak Ben-Zvi Institute; New York: St. Martin's Press, 1984.

Ben-Arieh, Yehoshua. “The Population of the Large Towns in Palestine During the First Eighty Years of the Nineteenth Century According to Western Sources.” In *Studies on Palestine during the Ottoman Period*, edited by Moshe Ma'oz, 49–69. Jerusalem: Magnes Press, 1975.

Berger, Maurits. “Khayr.” In *Encyclopaedia of Islam*, 2nd ed., vol. 4, 1151–53. Leiden: Brill, 1978.

Ben-Bassat, Yuval. *Petitioning the Sultan: Protests and Justice in Late Ottoman Palestine*. Leiden: I.B. Tauris, 2013.

Bilgin, Aydın. *Osmanlı Bürokrasisinde Dīvān-ı Hümāyūn Defter Formlarının Ortaya Çıkışı ve Gelişimi, (XV–XVI. yüzyıl)*. PhD diss., Marmara Üniversitesi, Türkiyat Araştırmaları Enstitüsü, Bilgi ve Belge Yönetimi Anabilim Dalı, 2003.

Bilmen, Ömer Nasuhi. *Hukūku İslāmiyye ve Istılāhāti Fıkhiyye Kāmūsū*. Vol. 4. Istanbul: Bilmen Yayınevi, 1951.

Bodman, Herbert L. *Political Factions in Aleppo, 1760–1826*. Chapel Hill: University of North Carolina Press, 1963.

Bostancı, Işıl Işık. *19. Yüzyılda Filistin (İdari ve Sosyo-Ekonomik Vaziyet)*. PhD diss., Fırat Üniversitesi, Sosyal Bilimler Enstitüsü, Tarih Anabilim Dalı, 2006.

Bozkurt, Gülnihal. *Gayrımüslim Osmanlı Vatandaşlarının Hukuki Durumu*. Ankara: Türk Tarih Kurumu Yayınları, 1996.

Bozkurt, Nebi. "Dârü'lhadis." In *Türkiye Diyanet Vakfı İslâm Ansiklopedisi*, vol. 8, 527–29. Istanbul: Türkiye Diyanet Vakfı, 1993.

Bozkurt, Nebi. "Dârü'lkurrâ." In *Türkiye Diyanet Vakfı İslâm Ansiklopedisi*, vol. 8, 543–45. Istanbul: Türkiye Diyanet Vakfı, 1993.

Bozkurt, Nebi. "Mescid-i Aksā." In *Türkiye Diyanet Vakfı İslâm Ansiklopedisi*, vol. 29, 269–70. Istanbul: Türkiye Diyanet Vakfı, 2003.

Braude, Benjamin, and Bernard Lewis. "Introduction." In *Christians and Jews in the Ottoman Empire*, edited by Benjamin Braude and Bernard Lewis, vol. 2, 1–33. New York: Holmes & Meier Publishers, 1982.

Buhl, F. "Kudüs." In *İslâm Ansiklopedisi*, vol. 6, 952–64. Istanbul: Kültür ve Turizm Bakanlığı – Milli Eğitim Basımevi, 1977.

Burgoyne, Michael H. "The Gates of Haram al-Sharīf." In *Bayt al-Maqdis:* 'Abd al-Malik's *Jerusalem*, edited by Julian Raby and Jeremy Johns, vol. 1, 105–24. Oxford: Oxford University Press, 1992.

Burgoyne, Michael H. *Mamluk Jerusalem: An Architectural Study*. London: World of Islam Festival Trust, 1987.

Büssow, Johann. *Hamidian Palestine: Politics and Society in the District of Jerusalem, 1872–1908*. Leiden: Brill, 2011.

Buzpınar, Şit Tufan. "Makamat-ı Mübareke Meselesi ve Kırım Harbi." In *Savaştan Barışa: 150. Yıldönümünde Kırım Savaşı ve Paris Antlaşması (1853–1856): Bildiriler*, edited by İsmail Mangaltepe and Zafer Gölen, 181–92. Istanbul: İstanbul Üniversitesi Edebiyat Fakültesi Yayınları, 2007.

Buzpınar, Şerif Tufan. "Surre." In *Türkiye Diyanet Vakfı İslâm Ansiklopedisi*, vol. 37, 567–69. Istanbul: Türkiye Diyanet Vakfı, 2009.

Canaan, Taufik. "Water and 'The Water of Life' in Palestinian Superstition." *Journal of the Palestine Oriental Society* 9 (1929): 57–66.

Canbakal, Hülya. *17. Yüzyılda Ayıntāb: Osmanlı Kentinde Toplum ve Siyaset*. Istanbul: İletişim Yayınları, 2009.

Canbakal, Hülya. "On the 'Nobility' of Urban Notables." In *The Provincial Elites in the Ottoman Empire: Halcyon Days in Crete V*, edited by Antonis Anastasopoulos, 39–50. Rethymno: Crete University Press, 2005.

Canbakal, Hülya. "The Ottoman State and Descendants of the Prophet in Anatolia and the Balkans (c. 1500–1700)." *Journal of the Economic and Social History of the Orient* 52, no. 3 (2009): 542–78.

Cezar, Yavuz. "Osmanlı Maliyesinde XVII. Yüzyılın İkinci Yarısındaki 'İmdadiyye' Uygulamaları." *İstanbul Üniversitesi Siyasal Bilimler Fakültesi Dergisi*, no. 2 (1984): 69–102.

Chateaubriand, François René de. *Kudüs Yolculuğu*. Translated by Osman Peltek. Vol. 3. Ankara: Türk Tarih Kurumu Yayınları, 1949.

Chateaubriand, François-René. *Paris-Kudüs Yolculuğu*. Vol. 3. Translated by Oğuz Peltek. Ankara: Milli Eğitim Basımevi, 1949.

Cohen, Amnon. *Economic Life in Ottoman Jerusalem*. Cambridge: Cambridge University Press, 1989.

Cohen, Amnon. *Jewish Life under Islam: Jerusalem in the Sixteenth Century*. Cambridge, MA: Harvard University Press, 1984.

Cohen, Amnon. "On the Realities of the Millet System: Jerusalem in the Sixteenth Century." In *Christians and Jews in the Ottoman Empire: The Functioning of a Plural Society*, vol. 2, edited by Benjamin Braude and Bernard Lewis, 7–18. New York: Holmes & Meier, 1982.

Cohen, Amnon. *Osmanlı Kudüs'ünde Loncalar*. Translated by N. Elhüseyni. Istanbul: Tarih Vakfı Yurt Yayınları, 2003.

Cohen, Amnon. *Palestine in the 18th Century: Patterns of Government and Administration*. Jerusalem: Magnes Press, 1973.

Cohen, Amnon. "The Walls of Jerusalem." In *The Islamic World: From Classical to Modern Times; Essays in Honor of Bernard Lewis*, edited by C. E. Bosworth and Charles Issawi, 467–77. Princeton, NJ: Darwin Press, 1989.

Cohen, Mark R. *Poverty and Charity in the Jewish Community of Medieval Egypt*. Princeton, NJ: Princeton University Press, 2005.

Conrad, Lawrence I. "The Khālidī Library." In *Ottoman Jerusalem: The Living City, 1517–1917*, edited by Sylvia Auld and Robert Hillenbrand, 191–209. London: Altajir World of Islam Trust, 2000.

Conrad, Lawrence I., and Barbara Kellner-Heinkele. "Ottoman Resources in the Khalidi Library in Jerusalem." In *Aspects of Ottoman History: Papers from CIEPO IX, Jerusalem*, edited by Amy Singer and Amnon Cohen, 159–71. Jerusalem: Magnes Press, 1994.

Cuneo, Paolo. "The Urban Structure and Physical Organization of Ottoman Jerusalem in the Context of Ottoman Urbanism." In *Ottoman Jerusalem: The Living City, 1517–1917*, edited by Sylvia Auld and Robert Hillenbrand, 211–20. London: Altajir World of Islam Trust, 2000.

Çadırcı, Musa. *Tanzimat Döneminde Anadolu Kentleri'nin Sosyal ve Ekonomik Yapıları*. Ankara: Türk Tarih Kurumu Basımevi, 1991.

Çağatay, Neşet. "Türk Vakıflarının Özellikleri." In *X. Türk Tarih Kongresi, 22–26 Eylül 1986, Kongreye Sunulan Bildiriler*, vol. 4, 1615–27. Ankara: Türk Tarih Kurumu Basımevi, 1993.

Çakan, İsmail Lütfi. "En Faziletli Üç Mescid." *Altınoluk Dergisi*, no. 18 (1987): 8–11.

Çakar, Enver. "Kanuni Sultan Süleyman Kanunnāmesine Göre 1522 Yılında Osmanlı İmparatorluğu'nun İdarī Taksimatı." *Fırat Üniversitesi Sosyal Bilimler Dergisi* 12, no. 2 (2002): 261–82.

Çakar, Enver. "XVI. Yüzyılda Şam Beylerbeyiliği'nin İdarī Taksimatı." *Fırat Üniversitesi Sosyal Bilimler Dergisi* 12, no. 1 (2003): 351–66.

Çelebi, Evliya. *Seyahatnāme*. Vol. 9 (1672–72). Istanbul: Devlet Matbaası, 1935.

Çetin, Osman. *Selçuklu Müesseseleri ve Anadolu'da İslamiyet*. Istanbul: Marifet Yayınları, 1981.

Çiftçi, Cafer. *Bursa'da Vakıfların Sosyo-Ekonomik İşlevleri*. Bursa: Bursa Kültür Sanat ve Turizm Vakfı Yayınları, 2004.

Çizakça, Murat. "Cash Waqfs of Bursa, 1555–1823." *Journal of the Economic and Social History of the Orient* 38, no. 3 (1995): 313–54.

Çizakça, Murat. "İktisat Tarihi Açısından Vakıflar." *Vakıflar Dergisi* 80, no. Yıl Özel Sayısı (2018): 75–92.

Darling, Linda T. "'Do Justice, Do Justice, For That Is Paradise': Middle Eastern Advice for Indian Muslim Rulers." *Comparative Studies of South Asia, Africa and the Middle East* 22, nos. 1–2 (2002): 3–19.

De Jong, Frederick. "The Sufi Orders in Nineteenth and Twentieth-Century Palestine." *Studia Islamica* 58 (1983): 149–81.

Demirel, Ömer. *Osmanlı Vakıf-Şehir İlişkisine Bir Örnek: Sivas Şehir Hayatında Vakıfların Rolü*. Ankara: Türk Tarih Kurumu Yayınları, 2000.

Demirkol, Erdem. *II. Abdülhamid Döneminde Kudüs'te Kilise İmar ve İnşa Faaliyetleri*. Master's thesis, Marmara Üniversitesi Türkiyat Araştırmaları Enstitüsü, Türk Tarihi Anabilim Dalı, 2007.

Devellioğlu, Ferit. *Osmanlıca-Türkçe Ansiklopedik Lûgat*. Ankara: Aydın Kitabevi Yayınları, 2002.

Doumani, Beshara B. *Family Life in the Ottoman Mediterranean: A Social History*. Cambridge: Cambridge University Press, 2017.

Doumani, Beshara. "Palestinian Islamic Court Records: A Source for Socioeconomic History." *MESA Bulletin* 19, no. 2 (1985): 155–71.

Doumani, Beshara. *Rediscovering Palestine: Merchants and Peasants in Jabal Nablus, 1700–1900*. Berkeley: University of California Press, 1995.

Douwes, Dick. *The Ottomans in Syria: A History of Justice and Oppression*. London: I. B. Tauris, 2000.

Dow, Martin. "The Hammams of Ottoman Jerusalem." In *Ottoman Jerusalem: The Living City, 1517–1917*, edited by Sylvia Auld and Robert Hillenbrand, 519–24. London: Altajir World of Islam Trust, 2000.

Durmuş, Muhammed Emin. *Osmanlı Vakıf Hukukunda Mukâtaa*. Istanbul: İktisat Yayınları, 2021.

Emecen, Feridun M. "Fodula." In *Türkiye Diyanet Vakfı İslâm Ansiklopedisi*, vol. 13, 167–70. Istanbul: Türkiye Diyanet Vakfı, 1996.

Emecen, Feridun M. "Kuruluştan Küçük Kaynarca'ya." In *Osmanlı Devleti ve Medeniyeti Tarihi*, edited by Ekmeleddin İhsanoğlu, vol. 1, 5–61. Istanbul: İslam Tarih, Sanat ve Kültür Araştırma Merkezi, 1994.

Emecen, Feridun M. "Osmanlı Divanının Ana Defter Serileri: Ahkām-ı Mirī, Ahkām-ı Kuyūd-ı Mühimme ve Ahkām-ı Şikāyet." *Türkiye Araştırmaları Literatür Dergisi* 3, no. 5 (2005): 107–39.

Ercan, Yavuz. "Osmanlı İmparatorluğu'nda Gayrimüslimlerin Ödedikleri Vergiler ve Bu Vergilerin Doğurduğu Sosyal Sonuçlar." *Belleten* 55, no. 213 (1991): 371–401.

Erdoğan, Emine. *XVI. Yüzyılda Kudüs Merkez ve Nahiyesinde Nüfus ve Etnik Yapı*. Master's thesis, Gazi Üniversitesi, 1998.

Ergenç, Özer. "Osmanlı Klasik Dönemindeki A'yān ve Eşrāf Üzerine Bazı Bilgiler." *Osmanlı Araştırmaları* 3 (1982): 105–18.

Ergenç, Özer. "Osmanlı Şehirlerindeki Yönetim Kurumlarının Niteliği Üzerinde Bazı Düşünceler." In *VIII. Türk Tarih Kongresi, Ankara, 4–15 Ekim 1976, Kongreye Sunulan Bildiriler*, vol. 3, 1265–74. Ankara: Türk Tarih Kurumu, 1981.

Ergenç, Özer. "Osmanlı Şehrindeki Mahallenin İşlev ve Nitelikleri Üzerine." *Osmanlı Araştırmaları* 4 (1984): 69–78.

Ergenç, Özer. "Şehir Tarihi Araştırmaları Hakkında Bazı Düşünceler." *Belleten* 52, no. 203 (1988): 667–83.

Ergenç, Özer. *Osmanlı Klasik Dönemi Kent Tarihçiliğine Katkı: XVI. Yüzyılda Ankara ve Konya*. Ankara: Ankara Enstitüsü Vakfı, 1995.

Ergenç, Özer. *XVI. Yüzyılın Sonlarında Bursa: Yerleşimi, Yönetimi, Ekonomik ve Sosyal Durumu Üzerine Bir Araştırma*. Ankara: Türk Tarih Kurumu, 2006.

Ergenç, Özer. "XVIII. Yüzyılda Osmanlı Taşra Yönetiminin Māli Nitelikleri." *Journal of Turkish Studies/Türklük Bilgisi Araştırmaları*, Raiyyet Rüsūmu, Essays Presented to Halil İnalcık on His Seventieth Birthday by His Colleagues and Students 10 (1986): 87–96.

Ergene, Boğaç. *Local Court, Provincial Society and Justice in the Ottoman Empire: Legal Practice and Dispute Resolution in Çankırı and Kastamonu (1652–1744)*. Leiden: Brill, 2003.

Ergin, Osman Nuri. *Türk Şehirlerinde İmaret Sistemi*. Istanbul: Cumhuriyet Matbaası, 1939.

Eroğlu Memiş, Şerife. "'*Nebzetü'l-Menāsik*': al-Nakshbandī al-Murādī'nin Hac Rehberi'nde Kudüs Bahsi." In *Dini, Tarihi ve Edebi Açıdan Kudüs*, edited by İbrahim Çelik et al., 169–99. Istanbul: DBY Yayınları, 2018.

Eroğlu Memiş, Şerife. "17. ve 18. Yüzyıllarda Edirne'de Vakıf Kurucularının Toplumsal Statülerine İlişkin Bazı Tespitler." *Vakıflar Dergisi* 36 (2011): 67–87.

Eroğlu Memiş, Şerife. "A Table in the City of Hebron in the xviiith Century: Simāt al-Khalīl." *Journal of Historical Research* 40, no. 69 (2021): 188–233.

Eroğlu Memiş, Şerife. "Between Ottomanisation and Local Networks: Appointment Registers as Archival Sources for Waqf Studies, the Case of Jerusalem's Maghariba Neighborhood." In *Ordinary Jerusalem, 1840–1940: Opening New Archives, Revisiting a Global City*, edited by Angelos Dalachanis and Vincent Lemire, 75–99. Leiden: Brill, 2018.

Eroğlu Memiş, Şerife. "Ḥurūfāt ya da 'Askerī Rūznāmçe Defterlerinde Eṣnāf Teşkilātı Atama Kayıtları ve Önemi: Qaḍā'-i al-Quds al-Sharīf Örneği." In *Osmanlıdan Günümüze Filistin Sempozyumu: Bildiriler*, vol. 1, 41–71. Ankara: Türk Tarih Kurumu, 2013.

Eroğlu Memiş, Şerife. "Osmanlı Toplumsal Tarihi Kaynaklarından Hurūfāt ya da 'Askerî Rūznāmçe Defterleri: Kazā-i Kudüs-i Şerif Örneği." *Vakıflar Dergisi* 39 (2013): 115–46.

Eroğlu Memiş, Şerife. "Sürdürülebilir Gelişmede Vakıfların Tarihi Rolü: Ebū Medyen al-Ghawth Zāwiya." *Keşkül Dergisi*, no. 46 (2018): 78–85.

Eroğlu Memiş, Şerife. "Tarihi Bir Vesika Olarak Hac Seyahatnameleri: Moralı Bahtî'nin Manzûme fî Menâsiki'l-Hacc Örneği." In *xviii. Türk Tarih Kongresi Bildirileri, 1–5 Ekim 2018*, vol. 2, 601–16. Ankara: Türk Tarih Kurumu, 2022.

Eroğlu Memiş, Şerife. *Kudüs-i Şerif*. Istanbul: Yeditepe Yayınevi, 2017.

Erünsal, İsmail E. *Osmanlı Vakıf Kütüphaneleri: Tarihi Gelişimi ve Organizasyonu*. Ankara: Türk Tarih Kurumu Yayınları, 2008.

Eryılmaz, Bilal. *Osmanlı Devleti'nde Gayrimüslim Tebaanın Yönetimi*. Istanbul: Risale Yayınları, 1996.

Eyice, Semavi. "Hamam (I. Tarih ve Mimari)." In *Türkiye Diyanet Vakfi İslâm Ansiklopedisi*, vol. 15, 402–30. Istanbul: Türkiye Diyanet Vakfı, 1997.

Faroqhi, Suraiya. "A Great Foundation in Difficulties: Or Some Evidence on Economic Contraction in the Ottoman Empire of the Mid-Seventeenth Century." In *Mélanges Professeur Robert Mantran*, edited by Abdeljelil Temimi, 109–21. Zaghouan: Centre d'Études et de Recherches Ottomanes, Morisques, de Documentation et d'Information, 1988.

Faroqhi, Suraiya. "Agricultural Crisis and the Art of Flute-Playing: The Worldly Affairs of the Mevlevi Dervishes (1595–1652)." *Turcica* 20 (1988): 43–70.

Faroqhi, Suraiya. "Kentlerde Toplumsal Yaşam." In *Osmanlı İmparatorluğunun Ekonomik ve Sosyal Tarihi*, edited by Halil İnalcık and Donald Quataert, vol. 2, 699–730. Istanbul: Eren Yayıncılık, 2000.

Faroqhi, Suraiya. "Political Activity Among Ottoman Taxpayers and the Problem of Sultanic Legitimation (1570–1650)." *Journal of the Economic and Social History of the Orient* 35, no. 1 (1992): 1–39.

Faroqhi, Suraiya. "Sayyid Gazi Revisited: The Foundation as Seen Through Sixteenth- and Seventeenth-Century Documents." *Turcica* 13 (1981): 90–122.

Faroqhi, Suraiya. "The Tekke of Hacı Bektaş: Social Position and Economic Activities." *International Journal of Middle East Studies* 7, no. 2 (1976): 183–208.

Faroqhi, Suraiya. *Hacılar ve Sultanlar, 1517–1638*. Istanbul: Tarih Vakfı Yurt Yayınları, 1995.

Faroqhi, Suraiya. *Osmanlı Dünyasında Üretmek, Pazarlamak, Yaşamak*. Istanbul: Yapı Kredi Yayınları, 2003.

Faroqhi, Suraiya. *The Ottoman Empire and the World Around It, 1540s to 1774*. London: I.B. Tauris, 2004.

Fay, Mary Ann. "Kadınlar ve Waqf: 18. Yüzyıl Mısır'ında Mülkiyet, İktidar ve Toplumsal Cinsiyetin Nüfuz Alanı." In *Modernleşmenin Eşiğinde Osmanlı Kadınları*, edited by Madeline C. Zilfi, 28–47. Istanbul: Tarih Vakfı Yurt Yayınları, 2000.

Fekete, Lajos. "Türk Vergi Tahrirleri." Translated by Sadrettin Karatay. *Belleten* 11, no. 42 (1947): 299–328.

Fişne, Rahime. *XVIII. Yüzyıl Başlarında Kudüs Surresi (Transkripsiyon ve Değerlendirme)*. MA thesis, Afyon Kocatepe Üniversitesi, Sosyal Bilimler Enstitüsü, 2012.

Fotić, Aleksandar. "The Official Explanations for the Confiscation and Sale of Monasteries (Churches) and Their Estates at the Time of Selim II." *Turcica* 26 (1994): 33–54.

Frenkel, Yehoshua. "Awqāf in Mamlūk Bilād al-Shām." *Mamlūk Studies Review* 13, no. 1 (2009): 149–66.

Frenkel, Yehoshua. "Political and Social Aspects of Islamic Religious Endowments (Awqāf): Saladin in Cairo (1169–73) and Jerusalem (1187–93)." *Bulletin of the School of Oriental and African Studies* 62, no. 1 (1999): 1–20.

Genç, Mehmet. "Klasik Osmanlı Sosyal-İktisadî Sistemi ve Vakıflar." *Vakıflar Dergisi* 42 (2014): 15–31.

Genç, Mehmet. *Osmanlı İmparatorluğu'nda Devlet ve Ekonomi*. Istanbul: Ötüken Neşriyat, 2000.

Gerber, Haim. "A New Look at the Tanzimat: The Case of the Province of Jerusalem." In *Palestine in the Late Ottoman Period*, edited by David Kushner, 30–45. Jerusalem: Yad Izhak Ben-Zvi, 1986.

Gerber, Haim. *Economy and Society in an Ottoman City: Bursa, 1600–1700*. Jerusalem: Hebrew University, 1988.

Gerber, Haim. "The Jews of the Ottoman Empire in the Sixteenth and Seventeenth Centuries: Economy and Society." In *The Jews of the Ottoman Empire*, edited by Avigdor Levy, 49–60. Princeton, NJ: Darwin Press, 1994.

Ghūsha, Muḥammad Hāshim Mūsā. *Ḥārat al-Saʿdiyya fī al-Quds*. Ramallah: Sharikat Maṭbaʿat Bayt al-Maqdis, 1999.

Ghūsha, Muḥammad Hāshim. *Al-Awqāf al-Islāmiyya fī al-Quds al-Sharīf: Dirāsa Tārīkhiyya Muwaththaqa*. Istanbul: IRCICA, 2009.

Gil, Moshe. *Documents of the Jewish Pious Foundations from the Cairo Geniza*. Leiden: Brill, 1976.

Goitein, Shelomo Dov. *A Mediterranean Society: The Jewish Communities of the Arab World as Portrayed in the Documents of the Cairo Geniza*. Vol. 2. Berkeley: University of California Press, 1971.

Göçek, Fatma Müge. *Rise of the Bourgeoisie, Demise of Empire: Ottoman Westernization and Social Change*. New York: Oxford University Press, 1996.

Göloğlu, Sabiha. "Depicting the Islamic Pilgrimage Sites: Mecca, Medina, and Jerusalem in Late Ottoman Illustrated Prayer Books." In *Proceedings of the 15th International Congress of Turkish Art, Naples, 14–16 September 2015*, edited by Michele Bernardini, Alessandro Taddei, and Michael Douglas Sheridan, 323–38. Ankara: Republic of Turkey Ministry of Culture and Tourism, 2018.

Gül, Muammer. "Kudüs ve Tarih İçinde Aldığı İsimler." *Fırat Üniversitesi Sosyal Bilimler Dergisi* 11, no. 2 (2001): 305–12.

Güler, Mustafa. *Osmanlı Devleti'nde Haremeyn Vakıfları (16. ve 17. Yüzyıllar)*. Istanbul: Çamlıca Yayınları, 2011.

Gülsoy, Ufuk, Vahdettin Engin, et al. *Bir Medeniyetin İzdüşümü: Vakıflar*. Istanbul: Vakıflar Genel Müdürlüğü Yayınları, 2012.

Gümrükçüoğlu, Saliha Okur. "Şikâyet Defterlerine Göre Osmanlı Teb'asının Şikayetleri." *Ankara Üniversitesi Hukuk Fakültesi Dergisi* 61, no. 1 (2012): 175–206.

Güneş, Hasan Hüseyin, and Mehtap Kuş. "Kudüs Mevlevihanesi ve Vakfiyeleri Üzerine Metodik Bir İrdeleme." In *II. Uluslararası Sultan Divani Mevlevilik Sempozyumu Bildirileri, Afyon, 2013*, 118–26. Afyon: Afyonkarahisar Valiliği, 2013.

Güneş, Hasan H. *Kudüs Meğaribe Mahallesi*. Ankara: Vakıflar Genel Müdürlüğü Yayınları, 2017.

Gürbüz, Adnan. *Toprak-Vakıf İlişkileri Çerçevesinde XVI. Yüzyılda Amasya Sancağı*. PhD diss., Ankara Üniversitesi, Sosyal Bilimler Enstitüsü, 1993.

Halaçoğlu, Yusuf. *XIV–XVII. Yüzyıllarda Osmanlılarda Devlet Teşkilatı ve Sosyal Yapı*. Ankara: Türk Tarih Kurumu Yayınları, 1995.

al-Halili, Shams al-Dīn Muḥammad ibn Sharaf al-Dīn. *Tārīkh al-Quds wa-l-Khalīl*. Edited by Muḥammad Adnan al-Bakhīt and Nūfān Rajā' al-Sawāriyya. London: Mu'assasat al-Furqān lil-Turāth al-Islāmī, 2004.

Halm, Heinz. "The Reestablishment of Sunni Fiqh in Jerusalem under Ayyubid Rule." In *The Third International Conference on Bilad al-Sham: Palestine, 19–24 April 1980*, vol. 1, 245–60. Amman: University of Jordan, 1983.

al-Ḥanbalī, Mujīr al-Dīn. *Al-Uns al-Jalīl bi-Tārīkh al-Quds wa-l-Khalīl*. Vol. 2. Amman: Maktabat al-Muḥtasib, 1973.

Haarmann, Ulrich. "Mamluk Endowment Deeds as a Source for the History of Education in Late Medieval Egypt." *Al-Abḥāth* 28 (1980): 31–47.

Harman, Ömer Faruk. "Kudüs." In *Türkiye Diyanet Vakfi İslâm Ansiklopedisi*, vol. 26, 323–27. Ankara: Türkiye Diyanet Vakfı, 2002.

Hathaway, Jane. "Rewriting Eighteenth-Century Ottoman History." *Mediterranean Historical Review* 19, no. 1 (2004): 29–53.

Hathaway, Jane, ed. *Osmanlı İmparatorluğu'nda İsyan ve Ayaklanma*. Translated by Deniz Berktay. Istanbul: Alkım, 2010.

Heffening, Wilhelm. "Wakf." In *Encyclopaedia of Islam*, 1st ed., edited by Martijn Theodor Houtsma, Thomas Walker Arnold, René Basset, and Richard Hartmann, 4:1096–1103. Leiden: E. J. Brill, 1934.

Heyd, Uriel. *Ottoman Documents on Palestine, 1552–1615: A Study of the Firman According to the Mühimme Defteri*. London: Oxford University Press, 1960.

Heyd, Uriel. *Studies in Ottoman Criminal Law*. Edited by V. L. Ménage. Oxford: Clarendon Press, 1973.

Hillenbrand, Robert. "Introduction: Structure, Style, and Context in the Monuments of Ottoman Jerusalem." In *Ottoman Jerusalem: The Living City, 1517–1917*, edited by Sylvia Auld and Robert Hillenbrand, 1–25. London: Altajir World of Islam Trust, 2000.

Hodgson, Marshall G. S. *The Venture of Islam: Conscience and History in a World Civilization*. Vol. 2. Chicago: University of Chicago Press, 1974.

Hoexter, Miriam. *Endowments, Rulers and Community: Waqf al-Haramayn in Ottoman Algiers*. Leiden: Brill, 1998.

Hourani, Albert. "Ottoman Reform and the Politics of Notables." In *The Beginnings of Modernization in the Middle East: The Nineteenth Century*, edited by William R. Polk and Richard L. Chambers, 41–68. Chicago: University of Chicago Press, 1968.

Humphreys, R. Stephen. "The Expressive Intent of the Mamluk Architecture of Cairo: A Preliminary Essay." *Studia Islamica*, no. 35 (1972): 69–119.

al-Ḥusaynī, Ḥasan ibn ʿAbd al-Laṭīf. *Tarājim Ahl al-Quds fī Qarn al-Thānī ʿAshar al-Hijrī*. Edited by Salāma Ṣāliḥ al-Nuʿaymāt. Amman: al-Jāmiʿa al-Urduniyya, Maṭbaʿat Shākir wa-ʿAkshā, 1985.

Hütteroth, Wolf-Dieter, and Kamal Abdulfattah. *Historical Geography of Palestine, Transjordan, and Southern Syria in the Late 16th Century*. Erlangen: Fränkische Geographische Gesellschaft, 1977.

Ibn Manẓūr, Muḥammad ibn Mukarram. *Lisān al-ʿArab*. Vol. 7. Edited by ʿAlī Shīrī. Beirut: Dār Iḥyāʾ al-Turāth al-ʿArabī, 1988.

Imber, Colin. *Ebu's-suʿud: The Islamic Legal Tradition*. Stanford, CA: Stanford University Press, 1997.

İlhan, M. Mehdi. *Osmanlı Su Yollarının Sevk ve İdaresi*. Canberra: Australian National University Press, 2009.

İnalcık, Halil. "Capital Formation in the Ottoman Empire." *Journal of Economic History* 29, no. 1 (1969): 97–140.

İnalcık, Halil. "Centralization and Decentralization in Ottoman Administration." In *Studies in Eighteenth-Century Islamic History*, edited by Thomas Naff and Roger Owen, 27–52. Carbondale: Southern Illinois University Press, 1977.

İnalcık, Halil. "Cizye." In *Türkiye Diyanet Vakfı İslâm Ansiklopedisi*, vol. 8, 45–50. Istanbul: Türkiye Diyanet Vakfı, 1993.

İnalcık, Halil. "Istanbul: An Islamic City." *Journal of Islamic Studies* 1 (1990): 1–23.

İnalcık, Halil. "İspence." In *Türkiye Diyanet Vakfı İslâm Ansiklopedisi*, vol. 23, 177–78. Istanbul: Türkiye Diyanet Vakfı, 2001.

İnalcık, Halil. "Kanun." In *Encyclopaedia of Islam*, 2nd ed., vol. 4, 558–66. Leiden: Brill, 1978.

İnalcık, Halil. "Military and Fiscal Transformation in the Ottoman Empire, 1600–1700." *Archivum Ottomanicum* 6 (1980): 283–337.

İnalcık, Halil. "Osmanlı Arşivlerinin Türk ve Dünya Tarihi İçin Önemi." In *Osmanlı Arşivleri ve Osmanlı Araştırmaları Sempozyumu*, 31–44. Istanbul: Türk Tarih Kurumu, 1985.

İnalcık, Halil. "Osmanlı Fetih Yöntemleri." *Cogito: Osmanlılar Özel Sayısı*, no. 19 (1999): 104–19.

İnalcık, Halil. "Osmanlılarda Raiyyet Rüsumu." In *Osmanlı İmparatorluğu: Toplum ve Ekonomi*, 31–58. Istanbul: Eren Yayıncılık, 1996.

İnalcık, Halil. "Şikāyet Hakkı: Arz-ı Hāl ve Arz-ı Mahzar'lar." *Osmanlı Araştırmaları* 7–8 (1988): 33–54.

İnalcık, Halil. "State Ideology under Sultan Süleyman I." In *The Middle East and the Balkans under the Ottoman Empire: Essays on Economy and Society*, 70–94. Bloomington: Indiana University Press, 1993.

İnalcık, Halil. "The Nature of Traditional Society: Turkey." In *Political Modernization in Japan and Turkey*, edited by Robert E. Ward and Dankwart A. Rustow, 42–63. Princeton, NJ: Princeton University Press, 1964.

İnalcık, Halil. "The Ottoman State: Economy and Society, 1300–1600." In *An Economic and Social History of the Ottoman Empire*, vol. 1, edited by Halil İnalcık and Donald Quataert, 9–411. Cambridge: Cambridge University Press, 1997.

İnalcık, Halil. "The Rebuilding of Istanbul by Mehmed the Conqueror." *Cultura Turcica* 4, no. 1–2 (1967): 5–15.

İnalcık, Halil. "Weights and Measures." In *An Economic and Social History of the Ottoman Empire*, edited by Halil İnalcık and Donald Quataert, vol. 1, 975–1000. Cambridge: Cambridge University Press, 1997.

İnalcık, Halil. *Osmanlı'da Devlet, Hukuk, Adâlet*. Istanbul: Eren Yayıncılık, 2000.

İnalcık, Halil. *Osmanlı İmparatorluğu Klasik Çağı (1300–1600)*. Istanbul: Yapı Kredi Yayınları, 2005.

İnalcık, Halil, and Donald Quataert, eds. *An Economic and Social History of the Ottoman Empire, 1300–1914*. Cambridge: Cambridge University Press, 1994.

İnalcık, Halil, and Donald Quataert. *Osmanlı İmparatorluğu'nun Ekonomik ve Sosyal Tarihi, 1300–1600*. Vol. 1. Translated by Halil Berktay. Istanbul: Eren Yayıncılık, 2000.

Innes, Joanna. "'Networks' in British History." Special issue, *East Asian Journal of British History* 5 (2016): 51–72.

İpşirli, Mehmet. "Osmanlıda Vakıfların Tarihī Gelişmesi." *Sivil Toplum Düşünce ve Araştırma Dergisi*, no. 15 (July – September 2006): 61–72.

İpşirli, Mehmet, and M. Tamimi. *Evkâf ve Emlâkü'l-Müslimîn fī Filisṭīn*. Istanbul: İslam Tarih, Sanat ve Kültür Araştırma Merkezi, 1982.

Jennings, Ronald C. "Pious Foundations in the Society and Economy of Ottoman Trabzon, 1565–1640: A Study Based on the Juridical Registers Şer'i Mahkeme Sicilleri of Trabzon." In *Studies on Ottoman Social History in the Sixteenth and Seventeenth Centuries: Women, Zimmis and Sharia Courts in Kayseri, Cyprus and Trabzon*, 613–65. Istanbul: Isis Press, 1999.

Jennings, Ronald C. "The Office of Vekil (Wakil) in 17th Century Ottoman Shari'a Records." *Studia Islamica*, no. 42 (1975): 147–69.

Kahya, Hatice Kübra. "İstibdāl Uygulamaları Işığında Osmanlı Vakıf Hukukunun Dönüşümü." PhD diss., Istanbul University, 2021.

Kanat, Elif. *Kudüs'teki İslami Vakıf ve Eserlerle İlgili Şam Ahkam Defterlerinde Yer Alan Hükümler (1742–1830)*. MA thesis, Marmara Üniversitesi, Türkiyat Araştırmaları Enstitüsü, 2013.

Kara, Mustafa. "Tasavvuf." In *Doğuştan Günümüze Büyük İslâm Tarihi*, edited by Hakkı Dursun Yıldız, vol. 13, 529–64. Istanbul: Çağ Yayınları, 1989.

Karaman, M. Lutfullah. "Filistin." In *İslâm Ansiklopedisi*, vol. 13, 89–103. Istanbul: Türkiye Diyanet Vakfı Yayınları, 1996.

Kark, Ruth. "Conceptual Models of Developing Pre-Industrial Cities: An Examination of Their Applicability to 19th Century Palestine." *Geographical Research Forum*, no. 7 (1984): 18–27.

Kark, Ruth. "The Contribution of the Ottoman Regime to the Development of Jerusalem and Jaffa." In *Palestine in the Late Ottoman Period: Political, Social, and Economic Transformation*, edited by David Kushner, 46–58. Jerusalem: Yad Izhak Ben-Zvi, 1986.

Karpat, Kemal H. "Millets and Nationality: The Roots of the Incongruity of Nation and State in the Post-Ottoman Era." In *Christians and Jews in the Ottoman Empire*, edited by Benjamin Braude and Bernard Lewis, vol. 1, 141–69. New York: Holmes & Meier Publishers, 1982.

Karpat, Kemal H. *Osmanlı Nüfusu (1830–1914): Demografik ve Sosyal Özellikleri*. Istanbul: Tarih Vakfı Yurt Yayınları, 2003.

Kaya, Süleyman. "XVIII. Yüzyıl Sonlarında Üsküdar Vakıflarının Gelir Kaynakları." *Divan: Disiplinlerarası Çalışmalar Dergisi* 15, no. 29 (2010): 95–132.

Kaya, Süleyman. *Osmanlı Hukukunda İcâreteyn*. Istanbul: Klasik Yayınları, 2014.

Kayaoğlu, İsmet. "Vakfın Menşei Hakkındaki Görüşler." *Vakıflar Dergisi* 11 (1977): 47–55.

Kazıcı, Ziya. *Osmanlı'da Toplum Yapısı*. Istanbul: Bilge Yayıncılık, 2003.

Kazıcı, Ziya. *Osmanlılarda Vergi Sistemi*. Istanbul: Şamil Yayınevi, 1977.

Kermeli, Eugenia. "Ebū Su'ūd's Definitions of Church Waqfs: Theory and Practice in Ottoman Law." In *Islamic Law: Theory and Practice*, edited by Robert Gleave and Eugenia Kermeli, 141–56. London: I.B. Tauris, 1997.

Khadduri, Majid. *Arab Contemporaries: The Role of Personalities in Politics*. Baltimore: Johns Hopkins University Press, 1973.

Khayat, Habeeb Albert. "*Waqf in Palestine and Israel from the Ottoman Reforms to the Present*." PhD diss., American University, Washington, DC, 1962.

Khoury, Dina Rizk. "The Introduction of Commercial Agriculture in the Province of Mosul and Its Effects on the Peasantry, 1750–1850." In *Landholding and Commercial Agriculture in the Middle East*, edited by Çağlar Keyder and Faruk Tabak, 155–71. Albany: State University of New York Press, 1991.

Khoury, Dina Rizk. "The Ottoman Center versus Provincial Power-Holders: An Analysis of the Historiography." In *Türkiye Tarihi, 1603–1839*, edited by Suraiya Faroqhi, translated by Fethi Aytuna, 135–206. Istanbul: Kitabevi, 2011.

Khoury, Dina Rizk. *Osmanlı İmparatorluğu'nda Devlet ve Taşra Toplumu*. Translated by Ülkü Tansel. 3rd ed. Istanbul: İş Bankası Kültür Yayınları, 2008.

Kılıç, Mustafa. "Osmanlı Tarih Araştırmalarında Mühimme Defterlerinin Yeri ve 107 Numaralı Mühimme Defteri." *Cumhuriyet Üniversitesi İlahiyat Fakültesi Dergisi* 7, no. 2 (December 2003): 249–60.

Kılıç, Rüya. *Osmanlı'da Sayyidler ve Şerifler*. Istanbul: Kitap Yayınevi, 2005.

Knauf, Ernst Axel. "Ottoman Jerusalem in Western Eyes." In *Ottoman Jerusalem: The Living City, 1517–1917*, edited by Sylvia Auld and Robert Hillenbrand, 73–76. London: Altajir World of Islam Trust, 2000.

Koçi Bey. *Koçi Bey Risalesi*. Edited by Ali Kemali Aksüt. Istanbul: Vakit Kütüphanesi, 1939.

Kopraman, Kazım Yaşar. "Mısır Memlûkleri (1250–1517)." In *Doğuştan Günümüze Büyük İslâm Tarihi*, vol. 6. Istanbul: Çağ Yayınları, 1986.

Köprülü, Mehmet Fuat. "Vakıf Müessesesi ve Vakıf Vesikalarının Tarihi Ehemmiyeti." *Vakıflar Dergisi* 1 (1938): 1–6.

Köprülü, Mehmet Fuat. *İslam ve Türk Hukuk Tarihi Araştırmaları ve Vakıf Müessesesi*. Istanbul: Ötüken Yayınları, 1983.

Kreiser, Klaus. "The Place of Jerusalem in the Ottoman Perception." In *Ottoman Jerusalem: The Living City, 1517–1917*, edited by Sylvia Auld and Robert Hillenbrand, 53–57. London: Altajir World of Islam Trust, 2000.

Kuban, Doğan. "Anadolu Türk Şehri: Tarihi Gelişmesi, Sosyal ve Fiziki Özellikleri Üzerinde Bazı Gelişmeler." *Vakıflar Dergisi* 7 (1968): 7–71.

Kunt, İ. Metin. *Sancaktan Eyalete: 1550–1650 Arasında Osmanlı Ümerası ve İl İdaresi.* Istanbul: Boğaziçi Üniversitesi Yayınevi, 1978.

Kunter, Halim Baki. "Türk Vakıfları ve Vakfiyeleri Üzerine Mücmel Bir Etüd." *Vakıflar Dergisi* 1 (1938): 103–29.

Kupferschmidt, Uri M. "Palestinian Waqfs and the Supreme Muslim Council." Paper presented at the International Seminar on Social and Economic Aspects of the Muslim Waqf, Jerusalem, June 1979.

Kupferschmidt, Uri M. "The Supreme Muslim Council, 1921–1937: Islam under the British Mandate for Palestine." PhD diss., Hebrew University of Jerusalem, 1978.

Kuran, Timur. "The Provision of Public Goods under Islamic Law: Origins, Impact, and Limitations of the Waqf System." *Law & Society Review* 35, no. 4 (2001): 841–98.

Lafi, Nora. "Petitions and Accommodating Urban Change in the Ottoman Empire." In *Istanbul as Seen From a Distance: Centre and Provinces in the Ottoman Empire*, edited by Elizabeth Özdalga, Sait Özervarlı, and Feryal Tansuğ, 73–82. Istanbul: Swedish Research Institute, 2011.

Lapidus, Ira M. *Muslim Cities in the Later Middle Ages.* Cambridge: Cambridge University Press, 1967.

Lev, Yaacov. "Charity and Gift Giving in Medieval Islam." In *Charity and Giving in Monotheistic Religions*, edited by Miriam Frenkel and Yaacov Lev, 45–64. Berlin: Walter de Gruyter, 2009.

Lewis, Bernard, and Amnon Cohen. *Population and Revenue in the Towns of Palestine in the Sixteenth Century.* Princeton, NJ: Princeton University Press, 1978.

Little, Donald P. "Jerusalem under the Ayyūbids and Mamlūks, 1187–1516 AD." In *Jerusalem in History*, edited by Kamil Jamil al-Asali, 177–99. London: Scorpion Publishing Ltd., 1989.

Little, Donald P. "The Nature of Khanqahs, Ribats and Zawiyas under the Mamluks." In *Islamic Studies Presented to Charles J. Adams*, edited by Wael B. Hallaq and Donald P. Little, 91–105. Leiden: Brill, 1991.

al-Lukaymī al-Dimyāṭī, Muṣṭafā As'ad. *Laṭā'if al-Uns al-Jalīl fī Tahāyif al-Quds wa-l-Khalīl.* Edited by Khālid 'Abdīn al-Ḥamsharī. Acre: Mu'assasat al-Aswār, 2001.

Lutfi, Huda. *Al-Quds al-Mamlūkiyya: A History of Mamlūk Jerusalem Based on the Ḥaram Documents.* Berlin: Klaus Schwarz Verlag, 1985.

al-Māṣādirī, 'Abd al-Mun'im. *Nuẓum Dawlat Salāṭīn al-Mamālīk wa-Rusūmuhum fī Miṣr.* Vol. 1. Cairo: Cairo University Press, 1964.

al-Madanī, Ziyād 'Abd al-'Azīz. "Al-Awkāf al-Islāmiyya fī al-Quds: Dirāsa Ijtimā'iyya wa-Iqtiṣādiyya, 1212–1700/1336–1918." In *Seventh International Conference on Bilād al-Shām History: Waqfs in Bilād al-Shām from the Beginnings of Islamic Conquests to the End of the Twentieth Century*, edited by Muḥammad Adnan Bakhīt, vol. 3, 309–35. Amman: University of Jordan, 2008.

al-Madanī, Ziyād ʿAbd al-ʿAzīz Muḥammad. *Awqāf al-Quds fī al-Qarn al-Thāmin ʿAshar al-Mīlādī, 1112–1214/1700–1799*. Amman: Wizārat al-Thaqāfa, 2010.

Makdisi, George. *The Rise of Colleges: Institutions of Learning in Islam and the West*. Edinburgh: Edinburgh University Press, 1981.

Mandaville, J. E. "Usurious Piety: The Cash Waqf Controversy in the Ottoman Empire." *International Journal of Middle East Studies* 10, no. 3 (1979): 289–308.

Mandaville, Jon E. "The Jerusalem Shariʿa Court Registers: A Supplement and Complement to the Central Archives." In *Studies on Palestine during the Ottoman Period, edited by Moshe Maʿoz*, 517–24. Jerusalem: Magnes Press, 1975.

Mandaville, Jon E. "The Ottoman Court Records of Syria and Jordan." *Journal of the American Oriental Society* 86, no. 3 (1966): 311–19.

Mannaʿ, ʿAdel. "Eighteenth- and Nineteenth-Century Rebellions in Palestine." *Journal of Palestine Studies* 24, no. 1 (1994): 51–66.

Mannaʿ, ʿAdel. "Continuity and Change in the Socio-Political Elite in Palestine during the Late Ottoman Period." In *The Syrian Land in the 18th and 19th Century: The Common and the Specific in the Historical Process*, edited by Thomas Philipp, 69–89. Stuttgart: Franz Steiner Verlag, 1992.

Mannaʿ, ʿAdel. "The Sijill as a Source for the Study of Palestine during the Ottoman Period with Special Reference to the French Invasion." In *Palestine in the Late Ottoman Period: Political, Social, and Economic Transformation*, edited by David Kushner, 351–62. Jerusalem: Yad Izhak Ben-Zvi; Leiden: E. J. Brill, 1986.

Marcus, Abraham. *The Middle East on the Eve of Modernity: Aleppo in the Eighteenth Century*. New York: Columbia University Press, 1989.

Mardin, Şerif. *Din ve İdeoloji*. Ankara: Ankara Üniversitesi Siyasal Bilgiler Fakültesi Yayınları, 1969.

Masters, Bruce. "Arap Vilayetlerinde Yarı Özerk Güçler." In *Türkiye Tarihi 1603–1839*, edited by Suraiya Faroqhi, translated by Fethi Aytuna, 135–206. Istanbul: Kitabevi, 2011.

Masters, Bruce. *The Origins of Western Economic Dominance in the Middle East: Mercantilism and the Islamic Economy in Aleppo, 1600–1750*. New York: New York University Press, 1988.

McCarthy, Justin. *The Population of Palestine: Population History and Statistics of the Late Ottoman Period and the Mandate*. New York: Columbia University Press, 1990.

McChesney, Robert D. *Charity and Philanthropy in Islam: Institutionalizing the Call to Do Good*. Indianapolis: Indiana University Center on Philanthropy.

McGowan, Bruce. "The Age of the Ayans." In *An Economic and Social History of the Ottoman Empire*, edited by Halil İnalcık and Donald Quataert, vol. 2, 637–758. Cambridge: Cambridge University Press, 1997.

Meier, Astrid. "For the Sake of God Alone? Food Distribution Policies, Takiyyas, and Imarets in Early Ottoman Damascus." In *Feeding People, Feeding Power: Imarets in the Ottoman Empire*, edited by Nina Ergin, Christoph Neumann, and Amy Singer, 121–49. Istanbul: Eren Yayıncılık, 2007.

Meriwether, Margaret L. "Yeniden Kadınlar ve Waqf Üstüne: Halep, 1770–1840." In *Modernleşmenin Eşiğinde Osmanlı Kadınları*, edited by Madeline C. Zilfi, 140–50. Istanbul: Tarih Vakfı Yurt Yayınları, 2000.

Mert, Özcan. *18. ve 19. Yüzyıllarda Çapanoğulları*. Ankara: Kültür Bakanlığı Yayınları, 1980.

Miroğlu, İsmet. "Türk-İslâm Dünyasında Vakıfların Yeri." In *II. Vakıf Haftası, 3–9 Aralık 1984: Konuşmalar ve Tebliğler*, 121–29. Ankara: Vakıflar Genel Müdürlüğü Yayınları, 1985.

Moran, Berna. *Türk Romanına Eleştirel Bir Bakış*. Vol. 2. Istanbul: İletişim Yayınları, 2008.

Mu'assasat Iḥyā' al-Turāth wa-l-Buḥūth al-Islāmiyya. *Dalīl Madīnat al-Quds: Manārāt Maqdisiyya*. Jerusalem: Wizārat al-Awqāf wa-l-Shu'ūn al-Dīniyya, 2010.

al-Murādī, Muḥammad Khalīl. *Silk al-Durar fī Aʿyān al-Qarn al-Thānī ʿAshar*. Edited by Ekrem Hasan al-ʿUlabī. Vol. 4. Beirut: Dār al-Ṣādir, 2001.

Müller, Christian. *Der Kadi und seine Zeugen: Studie der mamlukischen Ḥaram-Dokumente aus Jerusalem*. Wiesbaden: Harrassowitz, 2013.

Myres, David. "Al-ʿImāra al-Āmira: The Charitable Foundation of Khāṣṣekī Sulṭān (959/1551)." In *Ottoman Jerusalem: The Living City, 1517–1917*, edited by Sylvia Auld and Robert Hillenbrand, 539–82. London: Altajir World of Islam Trust, 2000.

al-Nābulusī, ʿAbd al-Ghanī ibn Ismāʿīl. *Al-Ḥaḍra al-Unsiyya fī al-Riḥla al-Qudsiyya*. Beirut: Al-Maṣādir, 1990.

Nācī, Muʿallim. *Lughāt-i Nācī*. Istanbul: Çağrı Yayınları, 2006.

Natsheh, Yusuf. "Al-ʿImāra al-Āmira: The Charitable Foundation of Khāṣṣekī Sulṭān (959/1552)." In *Ottoman Jerusalem: The Living City, 1517–1917*, edited by Sylvia Auld and Robert Hillenbrand, vol. 2, 747–90. London: Altajir World of Islam Trust, 2000.

Natsheh, Yusuf. "Architectural Survey: Catalogue of Buildings." In *Ottoman Jerusalem: The Living City, 1517–1917*, edited by Sylvia Auld and Robert Hillenbrand, 963–95. London: Altajir World of Islam Trust, 2000.

Natsheh, Yusuf. "Al-Zāwiya al-Naqshbandiyya (1033/1623–24)." In *Ottoman Jerusalem: The Living City, 1517–1917*, edited by Sylvia Auld and Robert Hillenbrand, vol. 2, 904–13. London: Altajir World of Islam Trust, 2000.

Nagata, Yuzo. *Muhsinzāde Mehmet Paşa ve Āyanlık Müessesesi*. Izmir: Akademi Kitabevi, 1999.

Nagata, Yuzo. *Tarihte Āyānlar: Karaosmanoğulları Üzerine Bir İnceleme*. Ankara: Türk Tarih Kurumu Yayınları, 1997.

Necipoğlu, Gülru. "The Dome of the Rock as Palimpsest: ʿAbd al-Malik's Grand Narrative and Sultan Süleyman's Glosses." *Muqarnas* 25 (2008): 17–105.

Nedkoff, B. Christof. "Osmanlı İmparatorluğu'nda Cizye (Baş Vergisi)." *Belleten* 8, no. 32 (1944): 615–16.

Neuwirth, Angelika. "Jerusalem in Islam: The Entire Honorary Names of the City." In *Ottoman Jerusalem: The Living City, 1517–1917*, edited by Sylvia Auld and Robert Hillenbrand, 77–95. London: Altajir World of Islam Trust, 2000.

Noonan, F. Thomas. *The Road to Jerusalem: Pilgrimage and Travel in the Age of Discovery*. Philadelphia: University of Pennsylvania Press, 2007.

Ocak, Ahmet Yaşar. "Zaviyeler." *Vakıflar Dergisi* 12 (1978): 247–69.

Ocak, Ahmet Yaşar, and Suraiya Faroqhi. "Zāviye." In *İslâm Ansiklopedisi*, vol. 13, 477–80. Istanbul: Milli Eğitim Bakanlığı Yayınları, 1993.

Oğuzoğlu, Yusuf. "Change in the Ottoman State Order (1299–1918)." In *Fluctuations in the Ottoman Social Order*, edited by Yusuf Oğuzoğlu, 1–57. Harvard: Harvard University, 2006.

Oğuzoğlu, Yusuf. "Osmanlı Şehirlerindeki Askerilerin Ekonomik Durumuna İlişkin Bazı Bilgiler." In *Birinci Askeri Tarih Semineri Bildiriler*, vol. 2, 109–16. Ankara: Genelkurmay Askeri Tarih ve Stratejik Etüt Başkanlığı Yayınları, 1983.

Oğuzoğlu, Yusuf. "Osmanlı Şehirlerindeki Halkın Vergi Yükü Üzerine Bir Araştırma (1680–1700)." *Osmanlı Araştırmaları* 15 (1995): 139–56.

Oğuzoğlu, Yusuf. "XVIII. Yüzyılın İkinci Yarısında Osmanlı Ordusunun Durumu." *Osmanlı Araştırmaları* 20 (2000): 295–303.

Öcalan, Hasan Basri. *Bursa'da Tasavvuf Kültürü (XVII. Yüzyıl)*. Bursa: Gaye Kitabevi, 2000.

Orbay, Kayhan. "Vakıf Taamhoran and Fodulahoran Registers as Archival Sources for Imārets." In *Feeding People, Feeding Power: Imārets in the Ottoman Empire*, edited by Nina Ergin, Christoph K. Neumann, and Amy Singer, 31–44. Istanbul: Eren Yayıncılık, 2007.

Orbay, Kayhan. "Vakıfların Bazı Arşiv Kaynakları (Vakfiyeler, Şeriyye Sicilleri, Mühimmeler, Tahrir Defterleri ve Vakıf Muhasebe Defterleri)." *Vakıflar Dergisi* 27 (2005): 41–53.

Ortaylı, İlber. "Kadı." In *Türkiye Diyanet Vakfi İslâm Ansiklopedisi*, vol. 26, 70–75. Istanbul: Türkiye Diyanet Vakfı, 2001.

Öz, Mehmet. "Osmanlı Klasik Döneminde Anadolu Kentleri." *Türkiye Araştırmaları Literatür Dergisi* 3, no. 6 (2005): 57–88.

Özbaran, Salih. "Some Notes on the Salyane System in the Ottoman Empire as Organized in Arabia in the Sixteenth Century." *Osmanlı Araştırmaları* 6 (1985): 39–45.

Özcan, Abdülkadir. "Cülus." In *Türkiye Diyanet Vakfi İslâm Ansiklopedisi*, vol. 8, 108–14. Istanbul: Türkiye Diyanet Vakfı, 1993.

Özel, Oktay. "Avarız ve Cizye Defterleri." In *Osmanlı Devleti'nde Bilgi ve İstatistik*, edited by Halil İnalcık and Şevket Pamuk, 33–50. Ankara: Devlet İstatistik Enstitüsü, 2001.

Özergin, M. Kemal. "Eski Bir Rūznāmeye Göre İstanbul ve Rumeli Medreseleri." *İstanbul Üniversitesi Edebiyat Fakültesi Tarih Enstitüsü Dergisi* 4–5 (1973–74): 263–90.

Özkaya, Yücel. *Osmanlı İmparatorluğunda Āyanlık*. Ankara: Türk Tarih Kurumu Yayınları, 1994.

Özkaya, Yücel. *XVIII. Yüzyılda Osmanlı Kurumları ve Osmanlı Toplum Yaşantısı*. Ankara: Kültür ve Turizm Bakanlığı Yayınları, 1985.

Öztürk, Nazif. *Menşe'i ve Tarihi Gelişimi Açısından Vakıflar*. Ankara: Vakıflar Genel Müdürlüğü Yayınları, 1983.

Öztürk, Said. "Kayseri ve Çevresinin Sosyo-Ekonomik Tarihi İçin Önemli Bir Kaynak: Karaman Ahkām Defterleri." In *III. Kayseri ve Yöresi Tarih Sempozyumu Bildirileri (6–7 Nisan 2000)*, 147–60. Kayseri: Kayseri Belediyesi Yayınları, 2000.

Özvar, Erol. *Osmanlı Maliyesinde Malikāne Uygulaması*. Istanbul: Kitabevi Yayınları, 2003.

Özyürek, Ercan. *158 Uluborlu Şeriyye Sicil Defteri ve Bu Sicilin Uluborlu Kent Tarihindeki Yeri, 1311–1313 AH/1890–1892 CE*. Master's thesis, Süleyman Demirel Üniversitesi Sosyal Bilimler Enstitüsü, Isparta, 2002.

Pakalın, Mehmet Zeki. *Osmanlı Tarih Deyimleri ve Terimleri Sözlüğü*. 3 vols. Istanbul: Milli Eğitim Basımevi, 1946–1956.

Palestinian Academic Society for the Study of International Affairs (PASSIA). *Mescid-i Aksâ Rehberi (Harem-i Şerîf)*. Jerusalem: TİKA Yayınları, 2013.

Pamuk, Şevket. *Osmanlı-Türkiye İktisadî Tarihi, 1500–1914*. Istanbul: İletişim Yayınları, 2005.

Pamuk, Şevket. *The Ottoman Empire and European Capitalism, 1820–1913: Trade, Investment, and Production*. Cambridge: Cambridge University Press, 1987.

Pappe, Ilan. *The Rise and Fall of a Palestinian Dynasty: The Husaynīs, 1700–1948*. Berkeley: University of California Press, 2010.

Paşa, Mustafa Nuri. *Netâyicü'l-Vukûât: Kurumları ve Örgütleriyle Osmanlı Tarihi*. Vol. 2. Edited by Neşet Çağatay. Ankara: Türk Tarih Kurumu Yayınları, 1979–80.

Pedersen, Johannes. "Mescit." In *İslâm Ansiklopedisi*, vol. 8, 81–86. Istanbul: Milli Eğitim Bakanlığı Yayınları, 1993.

Peri, Oded. "Muslim Waqf and Collection of Jizya in Late Eighteenth-Century Jerusalem." In *Ottoman Palestine, 1800–1914: Studies in Economic and Social History*, edited by Gad G. Gilbar, 287–98. Leiden: E.J. Brill, 1990.

Peri, Oded. "The Waqf as an Instrument to Increase and Consolidate Political Power: The Case of Khasseki Sultan Waqf in Late Eighteenth-Century Jerusalem." In *Studies in Islamic Society: Contributions in Memory of Gabriel Baer*, edited by Gabriel R. Warburg and Gad G. Gilbar, 47–62. Haifa: Haifa University Press, 1984.

Peri, Oded. "Waqf and Ottoman Welfare Policy." *Journal of the Economic and Social History of the Orient* 35 (1992): 171–85.

Peri, Oded. "Waqf and Ottoman Welfare Policy: The Poor Kitchen of Hasseki Sultan in Eighteenth-Century Jerusalem." *Journal of the Economic and Social History of the Orient* 32, no. 2 (1989): 167–86.

Peirce, Leslie P. "Changing Perceptions of the Ottoman Empire: The Early Centuries." *Mediterranean Historical Review* 19, no. 1 (2004): 6–28.

Peirce, Leslie P. *The Imperial Harem: Women and Sovereignty in the Ottoman Empire.* New York: Oxford University Press, 1993.

Peters, F. E. *Jerusalem.* Princeton, NJ: Princeton University Press, 1995.

Peters, Rudolph. "Waqf." In *Encyclopaedia of Islam*, 2nd ed., vol. 11, 59–63. Leiden: Brill, 2002.

Petry, Carl F. "A Geniza for Mamluk Studies? Charitable Trust (Waqf) Documents as a Source for Economic and Social History." *Mamluk Studies Review* 2 (1998): 51–60.

Polat, İbrahim Ethem. *Kudüs Seyahatnamesi: Evliya Çelebi'nin İzinde.* Istanbul: Bengü Yayınları, 2011.

Powers, David S. "Revenues of Public Waqfs in Sixteenth-Century Jerusalem." *Archivum Ottomanicum* 9 (1984): 163–202.

Quataert, Donald. *Workers, Peasants, and Economic Change in the Ottoman Empire, 1730–1914.* Istanbul: Isis Press, 1993.

Rafeq, Abdul-Karim. "Changes in the Relationship between the Ottoman Central Administration and the Syrian Provinces from the Sixteenth Century to the Eighteenth Century." In *Studies in Eighteenth-Century Islamic History*, edited by Thomas Naff and Roger Owen, 53–73. Carbondale: Southern Illinois University Press, 1977.

Rafeq, Abdul-Karim. "Ottoman Jerusalem in the Writings of Arab Travelers." In *Ottoman Jerusalem: The Living City, 1517–1917*, edited by Sylvia Auld and Robert Hillenbrand, 63–73. London: Altajir World of Islam Trust, 2000.

Rafeq, Abdul-Karim. "The 'Ulamā' of Ottoman Jerusalem (16th–18th Centuries)." In *Ottoman Jerusalem: The Living City, 1517–1917*, edited by Sylvia Auld and Robert Hillenbrand, 45–52. London: Altajir World of Islam Trust, 2000.

Raymond, André. *Artisans et commerçants au Caire au XVIIIe siècle.* 2 vols. Damascus: Institut Français de Damas, 1973–74.

Raymond, André. *Osmanlı Döneminde Arap Kentleri.* Translated by Ali Berktay. Istanbul: Tarih Vakfı Yurt Yayınları, 1995.

Raymond, André. "The Ottoman Conquest and the Development of the Great Arab Towns." *International Journal of Turkish Studies* 1, no. 1 (1979–80): 84–101.

Roded, Ruth. "Quantitative Analysis of Waqf Endowment Deeds: A Pilot Project." *Osmanlı Araştırmaları* 9 (1989): 61–95.

Rosenthal, Franz, et al. "Hiba." In *Encyclopaedia of Islam*, 2nd ed., vol. 3, 342–350. Leiden: Brill.

Rozen, Minna. "The Naqīb al-Ashrāf Rebellion in Jerusalem and Its Repercussions on the City's Dhimmis." *Asian and African Studies* 18 (1984): 250–51.

Rosen-Ayalon, Myriam. "On Süleyman's Sabīls in Jerusalem." In *The Islamic World: From Classical to Modern Times; Essays in Honor of Bernard Lewis*, edited by C. E. Bosworth, Charles Issawi, Roger Savory, and A. L. Udovitch, 589–607. Princeton, NJ: Darwin Press, 1989.

Sabra, Adam. *Poverty and Charity in Medieval Islam: Mamluk Egypt, 1250–1517*. Cambridge: Cambridge University Press, 2000.

Sağlık, Şaban. "Malzeme ve Estetik Olarak Bir Taşra Estetiğinden Bahsedilir mi?" *Hece Öykü Dergisi*, no. 41 (2010): 68–78.

Sahillioğlu, Halil. "Ahkām Defteri." In *Türkiye Diyanet Vakfı İslâm Ansiklopedisi*, vol. 1, 551. Istanbul: Türkiye Diyanet Vakfı, 1988.

Sakaoğlu, Necdet. *Anadolu Derebeyi Ocaklarından Köse Paşa Hanedanı*. Ankara: Yurt Yayınları, 1984.

Salameh, Khadr. "Aspects of the Sijills of the Shari'a Court in Jerusalem." In *Ottoman Jerusalem: The Living City, 1517–1917*, edited by Sylvia Auld and Robert Hillenbrand, 103–35. London: Altajir World of Islam Trust, 2000.

Salebci, Hüseyin. "Tarih Boyunca Vakıflar." In *II. Vakıf Haftası, 3–9 Aralık 1984: Konuşmalar ve Tebliğler*, 107–12. Ankara: Vakıflar Genel Müdürlüğü Yayınları, 1985.

Salzmann, Ariel. "An Ancien Régime Revisited: 'Privatization' and Political Economy in the Eighteenth-Century Ottoman Empire." *Politics & Society* 21, no. 4 (1993): 393–423.

Salzmann, Ariel. *Tocqueville in the Ottoman Empire: Rival Paths to the Modern State*. Leiden: Brill, 2004.

Savaş, Saim. *Bir Tekkenin Dinî ve Sosyal Tarihi: Sivas Ali Baba Zaviyesi*. Istanbul: Dergâh Yayınları, 1992.

Schacht, Joseph. "Early Doctrines on Waqf." In *Fuad Köprülü Armağanı*, 443–52. Istanbul: Osman Yalçın Matbaası, 1953.

Schacht, Joseph. "Zakāt." In *Shorter Encyclopaedia of Islam*, 654–56. Leiden: Brill, 1953.

Schacht, Joseph, and Aharon Layish. "Mīrāth." In *Encyclopaedia of Islam*, 2nd ed., vol. 7, 106–13. Leiden: Brill, 1993.

Schilcher, Linda S. *Families in Politics: Damascene Factions and Estates of the 18th and 19th Centuries*. Stuttgart: Franz Steiner Verlag, 1985.

Schölch, Alexander. "Jerusalem in the 19th Century (1831–1917 AD)." In *Jerusalem in History*, edited by Kamil Jamil al-Asali, 228–48. Essex: Scorpion Publishing, 1989.

Selen, H. Sadi. "16. ve 17. Yüzyıllarda Anadolu'nun Köy ve Küçük Şehir Hayatı III." In *Türk Tarih Kongresi*, 589–97. Ankara: Türk Tarih Kurumu Basımevi, 1948.

Sertoğlu, Mithat. *Osmanlı Tarih Lügatı*. Ankara: Enderun Kitabevi, 1958.

Shaham, Ron. "Christian and Jewish Waqf in Palestine during the Late Ottoman Period." *Bulletin of the School of Oriental and African Studies* 54, no. 3 (1991): 460–72.

Shilo, Shmuel. "Wills." In *The Principles of Jewish Law*, edited by Menachem Elon, 652–58. Jerusalem: Encyclopaedia Judaica, 1975.

Singer, Amy. *Kadılar, Kullar, Kudüslü Köylüler*. Translated by Sema Bulutsuz. Istanbul: Tarih Vakfı Yurt Yayınları, 1996.

Singer, Amy. *Osmanlı'da Hayırseverlik: Kudüs'te Bir Haseki Sultan İmareti*. Translated by Dilek Şendil. Istanbul: Tarih Vakfı Yurt Yayınları, 2004.

Singer, Amy. "The Mülknāmes of Khāṣṣekī Hürrem Sulṭān's Waqf in Jerusalem." *Muqarnas* 14 (1997): 96–102.

Singer, Amy. "The Privileged Poor of Ottoman Jerusalem." In *Pauvreté et Richesse dans le monde musulman méditerranéen/Poverty and Wealth in the Muslim Mediterranean World*, edited by Jean-Paul Pascual, 257–69. Paris: Maisonneuve et Larose, 2003.

Somel, Selçuk Akşin. "Arap Eyaletleri ve Günümüz Arap Devletleri: Tarihsel Bir Perspektiften Genel Bir Bakış." *Yeni Türkiye*, no. 3 (1995): 597–615.

Stephan, St. H. "An Endowment Deed of Khāṣṣekī Sulṭān, Dated 30 Jumāda al-Ūlā 959 AH/24 May 1552 CE." *Quarterly of the Department of Antiquities in Palestine* 10 (1994): 170–94.

Stillman, Norman A. "Charity and Social Service in Medieval Islam." *Societas* 5 (1975): 105–15.

Sroor, Musa Uluslararası. *Fondations pieuses en mouvement: De la transformation du statut de propriété des biens waqfs à Jérusalem (1858–1917)*. Damascus: Institut Français du Proche-Orient; Aix-en-Provence: IREMAM, 2010.

Sroor, Musa Uluslararası. "Jerusalem's Islamic Archives: Sources for the Question of the Waqf in the Ottoman Period." *Journal of Palestine Studies* 34, no. 3/4 (2005): 82–90.

St. Laurent, Beatrice. "The Dome of the Rock: Restorations and Significance, 1540–1918." In *Ottoman Jerusalem: The Living City, 1517–1917*, edited by Sylvia Auld and Robert Hillenbrand, 415–24. London: Altajir World of Islam Trust, 2000.

Steih, Abdalqader. *Osmanlı Kudüs'ü (1700–1805)*. Istanbul: Taş Mektep Yayın Atölyesi / ORDAF, 2017.

Süreyya, Mehmet. *Sicilli: Osmani*. Istanbul: Matbaa-i Amire, 1891–93.

al-Sūwāriyya, Salīm Jūmā'a. *Al-Ḥayāt al-Ijtimā'iyya fī Madīnat al-Quds: 1750–1800*. Amman: Dār 'Ālam al-Thaqāfa lil-Nashr wa-al-Tawzī', 2009.

Şahin, Canay. "The Rise and Fall of an Āyān Family in Eighteenth-Century Anatolia: The Caniklizādes (1737–1808)." PhD dissertation, Bilkent University, 2003.

Şentop, Mustafa. "Osmanlı Yerel Yönetiminde Kadılık." In *İslam Geleneğinden Günümüze Şehir ve Yönetimler*, edited by Vecdi Akyüz, vol. 2, 281–87. Istanbul: İlke Yayınları, 1996.

Sāmī, Şemseddin. *Kāmūs al-A'lām*. Istanbul: Çağrı Yayınları, 1899–1900.

Tabakoğlu, Ahmet. "XVII ve XVIII. Yüzyıl Osmanlı Bütçeleri." *İstanbul Üniversitesi İktisat Fakültesi Mecmuası* 41, no. 1–4 (1985): 389–414.

Talhami, Ghada. "Jerusalem in the Muslim Consciousness." *The Muslim World* 86, no. 3–4 (1996): 222–87.

Tamari, Salim. "Waqf Endowments in the Old City of Jerusalem: Changing Status and Archival Sources." In *Ordinary Jerusalem, 1840–1940: Opening New Archives, Revisiting a Global City*, edited by Angelos Dalachanis and Vincent Lemire, 487–509. Leiden: Brill, 2018.

Tanman, Baha, and Ahmet Vefa Çobanoğlu. "Osmanlı Dönemi'nde Kudüs: Kent Dokusu, Mimarlık ve Çini Sanatına İlişkin Bir Araştırmanın İlk Sonuçları." In *Ortadoğu'da Osmanlı Dönemi Kültür İzleri Uluslararası Bilgi Şöleni Bildirileri (25–27 Ekim 2000, Hatay)*, vol. 2, 511–43. Ankara: Atatürk Kültür Merkezi Başkanlığı Yayınları, 2001.

Taş, Hülya. "Merkezi Mutlak Yönetim Modeli İçinde Yerel Unsurlar: Ankara Örneği." In *Selçukludan Cumhuriyete Şehir Yönetimi*, edited by Erol Özvar and Arif Bilgin, 191–203. Istanbul: Türk Dünyası Belediyeler Birliği Yayınları, 2008.

Taş, Hülya. "Osmanlıda 'Şikâyet Hakkı'nın Kullanımı Üzerine Düşünceler." *Memleket Siyaset Yönetim* 3 (2007): 186–204.

Taş, Hülya. *XVII. Yüzyılda Ankara*. Ankara: Türk Tarih Kurumu Yayınları, 2006.

Taşkın, Ünal. *Osmanlı İdaresinde Safed (1516–1600)*. Elazığ: Fırat Üniversitesi Yayınları, 2011.

Taşkın, Ünal. "Rüsūm-ı Örfiye." *Tarih Okulu* 14 (2013): 55–73.

Tekeli, İlhan. *Tarih Yazımı Üzerine Düşünmek*. Istanbul: Dost Kitabevi, 1998.

Tezcan, Baki. *The Second Ottoman Empire: Political and Social Transformation in the Early Modern World*. Cambridge: Cambridge University Press, 2010.

Tibawi, Abdul Latif. *The Islamic Pious Foundations in Jerusalem*. London: The Islamic Cultural Centre, 1978.

Toledano, Ehud. "The Emergence of Ottoman-Local Elites (1700–1900): A Framework for Research." In *Turkey: Middle Eastern Politics and Ideas; A History from Within*, edited by Ilan Pappé and Moshe Ma'oz, 145–62. London: I.B. Tauris, 1997.

Toledano, Ehud. "The Sancak of Jerusalem in the Sixteenth Century: Aspects of Topography and Population." *Archivum Ottomanicum* 9 (1984): 279–319.

Tomar, Cengiz. "Kudüs (Memlükler Dönemi)." In *Türkiye Diyanet Vakfı İslâm Ansiklopedisi*, vol. 26, 332–34. Istanbul: Türkiye Diyanet Vakfı, 2002.

Tomar, Cengiz. "Şam." In *Türkiye Diyanet Vakfı İslâm Ansiklopedisi*, vol. 38, 311–15. Istanbul: Türkiye Diyanet Vakfı, 2010.

Tural, Sadık. "615 Numaralı İstanbul Askeri Kassam Defterinin Değerlendirilmesi." Master's thesis, İstanbul Üniversitesi Sosyal Bilimler Enstitüsü, 1961.

Turan, Osman. *Selçuklular Tarihi ve Türk-İslam Medeniyeti*. Istanbul: Ötüken Yayınları, 1998.

Tuğluca, Murat. *Osmanlı Devlet-Toplum İlişkisinde Şikayet Mekanizması ve İşleyiş Biçimi*. Ankara: Türk Tarih Kurumu Yayınları, 2016.

Türk Dil Kurumu. *Türkçe Sözlük*. 10th ed. Ankara: Türk Dil Kurumu Yayınları, 2005.

Tütüncü, Mehmet. "Kudüs Mevlevîhânesi Tarihi ve Mimarisi." In *Uluslararası Düşünce ve Sanatta Mevlânâ Sempozyumu Bildirileri (Çanakkale, 25–28 Mayıs 2006)*, 699–723. Çanakkale: T.C. Kültür ve Turizm Bakanlığı, 2006.

Tütüncü, Mehmet. "Kudüs Tekke ve Zaviyeleri ve Sancakbeyi Mehmed Paşa." In *Uluslararası Türk Sanat Tarihi ve Arkeolojisi Sempozyumu: Prof. Dr. Rüçhan Arık-Prof. Dr. Mehmet Oluş Arık Armağanı (Konya, 25–27 Nisan 2006)*, 1–20. Konya: Selçuk Üniversitesi, 2007.

Tütüncü, Mehmet. *Turkish Jerusalem (1516–1917): Ottoman Inscriptions from Jerusalem and Other Palestinian Cities*. Haarlem, Netherlands: SOTA, 2006.

Uğur, Yunus. "Mahkeme Kayıtları (Şer'iye Sicilleri): Literatür Değerlendirmesi ve Bibliyografya." *Türk Araştırmaları ve Literatür Dergisi* 1, no. 1 (2003): 305–44.

Uluçay, M. Çağatay. *Padişahların Kadınları ve Kızları*. Ankara: Türk Tarih Kurumu Yayınları, 1980.

Unan, Fahri. "Osmanlılarda Medrese Eğitimi." In *Osmanlı*, edited by Güler Eren and Kemal Çiçek, vol. 6, 148–55. Ankara: Yeni Türkiye Yayınları, 2002.

Ülgen, A. Saim. "Hamam." In *İslâm Ansiklopedisi*, vol. 5, part 1, 186–91. Istanbul: Milli Eğitim Bakanlığı Yayınları, 1986.

Ünal, M. Ali. "Öşür." In *Osmanlı Tarih Sözlüğü*, 312–13. Istanbul: Paradigma Yayınları, 2011.

Uzunçarşılı, İsmail Hakkı. *Meşhur Rumeli Ayanlarından Tirsinikli İsmail, Yılık Oğlu Süleyman Ağalar ve Alemdar Mustafa Paşa*. Istanbul: Maarif Matbaası, 1942.

Uzunçarşılı, İsmail Hakkı. *Mekke-i Mükerreme Emirleri*. Ankara: Türk Tarih Kurumu Yayınları, 1972.

Uzunçarşılı, İsmail Hakkı. *Osmanlı Devleti'nin İlmiye Teşkilâtı*. Ankara: Türk Tarih Kurumu Yayınları, 1988.

Uzunçarşılı, İsmail Hakkı. *Osmanlı Devleti'nin Merkez ve Bahriye Teşkilâtı*. Ankara: Türk Tarih Kurumu Basımevi, 1948.

van Berchem, Max. *Corpus Inscriptionum Arabicarum: Jerusalem*. 5 vols. Cairo: Imprimerie de l'Institut Français d'Archéologie Orientale, 1922–49.

van Leeuwen, Richard. *Bir Osmanlı Şehri: Şam – Waqflar ve Şehir*. Translated by H. Ebru Aksoy. Istanbul: Küre Yayınları, 2012.

van Leeuwen, Richard. "The Maronite Waqf of Dayr Sayyidat Bkirki in Mount Lebanon during the 18th Century." In *Le Waqf dans l'espace islamique: Outil de pouvoir socio-politique*, edited by Randi Deguilhem, 259–78. Damascus: Institut Français de Damas, 1995.

van Leeuwen, Richard. *Notables and Clergy in Mount Lebanon: The Khazin Sheiks and the Maronite Church (1736–1840)*. Amsterdam: Institute for Near Eastern and Islamic Studies, 1992.

Verbit, Gilbert Paul. *A Ninth Century Treatise on the Law of Trusts: Being a Translation of al-Khaṣṣāf, Aḥkām al-Waqf.* Bloomington, IN: Xlibris Corp., 2008.

Weir, T. H., and A. Zysow. "Ṣadaḳa." In *Encyclopaedia of Islam,* 2nd ed., vol. 8, 708–16. Leiden: Brill, 1995.

Winter, Michael. "The Ashrāf and Niqābat al-Ashrāf in Egypt in Ottoman and Modern Times." *Asian and African Studies* 19 (1985): 193–216.

Winter, Michael. *Egyptian Society under Ottoman Rule, 1517–1798.* London: Routledge, 1992.

Yaşar, Şükran. *Osmanlı Tahrir Defterlerine Göre XVI. Yüzyılda Kudüs'ün Demografik Yapısı.* Master's thesis, Fırat Üniversitesi Sosyal Bilimler Enstitüsü, 1997.

Yaycıoğlu, Ali. "Provincial Power-Holders and the Empire in the Late Ottoman World: Conflict or Partnership?" In *The Ottoman World,* edited by Christine Woodhead, 436–52. London: Routledge, 2012.

Yaycıoğlu, Ali. "Sened-i İttifak (1808): Osmanlı İmparatorluğu'nda Bir Ortaklık ve Entegrasyon Denemesi." In *Nizam-ı Kadimden Nizam-ı Cedide: III. Selim ve Dönemi,* edited by Seyfi Kenan, 667–709. Istanbul: İSAM, 2010.

Yazbak, Mahmoud. "The Islamic Waqf in Yaffa and the Urban Space: From the Ottoman State to the State of Israel." *Adalah's Journal for Land, Planning and Justice* 2 (2010): 47–69.

Yediyıldız, Bahaeddin. "İslam'da Vakıf." In *Doğuştan Günümüze Büyük İslam Tarihi,* vol. 14, 329–48. Istanbul: Çağ Yayınları, 1989.

Yediyıldız, Bahaeddin. "Müessese-Toplum Münasebetleri Çerçevesinde XVIII Asır Türk Toplumu ve Vakıf Müessesesi." *Vakıflar Dergisi* 15 (1982): 23–53.

Yediyıldız, Bahaeddin. "Osmanlı Döneminde Türk Vakıfları ya da Türk Hayrat Sistemi." In *Osmanlı: Toplum,* edited by Güler Eren, vol. 5, 17–33. Ankara: Yeni Türkiye Yayınları, 1999.

Yediyıldız, Bahaeddin. "Sosyal Teşkilatlar Bütünlüğü Olarak Osmanlı Vakıf Külliyeleri." *Türk Kültürü* 19, no. 129 (1981): 71–85.

Yediyıldız, Bahaeddin. "Türk Vakıfları Enstitüsü Kurulmalıdır." In *I. Vakıf Şūrası (3–5 Aralık 1985): Tebliğler, Tartışmalar ve Komisyon Raporları,* 45–52. Ankara: Vakıflar Genel Müdürlüğü Yayınları, 1985.

Yediyıldız, Bahaeddin. "Vakıf." In *İslâm Ansiklopedisi,* vol. 13, 153–72. Istanbul: Milli Eğitim Bakanlığı Yayınları, 1986.

Yediyıldız, Bahaeddin. "Vakıf." In *Türkiye Diyanet Vakfı İslâm Ansiklopedisi,* vol. 42, 475–79. Istanbul: Türkiye Diyanet Vakfı, 2012.

Yediyıldız, Bahaeddin. "Vakıf İncelemelerinde Metod Araştırmaları." In *II. Vakıf Haftası, 3–9 Aralık 1984: Konuşmalar ve Tebliğler,* 51–62. Ankara: Renk Ofset Matbaacılık, 1985.

Yediyıldız, Bahaeddin. "Vakıf Müessesesinin XVIII. Asırda Kültür Üzerindeki Etkileri." In *Türkiye'nin Sosyal ve Ekonomik Tarihi (1071–1920)*, edited by Osman Okyar and Halil İnalcık, 119–24. Ankara: Meteksan, 1980.

Yediyıldız, Bahaeddin. "XVIII. Asır Türk Vakıflarının İktisadî Boyutu." *Vakıflar Dergisi* 18 (1984): 5–41.

Yediyıldız, Bahaeddin. *İslam ve Türk Hukuk Tarihi Araştırmaları ve Vakıf Müessesesi*. Istanbul: Ötüken Neşriyat, 1983.

Yediyıldız, Bahaeddin. *XVIII. Yüzyılda Türkiye'de Vakıf Müessesesi: Bir Sosyal Tarih İncelemesi*. Ankara: Türk Tarih Kurumu Yayınları, 2003.

Yeniçeri, Celal. *İslam'da Devlet Bütçesi*. Istanbul: İlim ve Kültür Yayınları, 1984.

Yıldız, Kenan. *1660 İstanbul Yangını ve Etkileri: Vakıflar, Toplum ve Ekonomi*. Ankara: Türk Tarih Kurumu Yayınları, 2017.

Yörükoğlu, Ömer. "Vakıf Müessesesinin Hukuki, Tarihi, Felsefi Temelleri." In *II. Vakıf Haftası, 3–9 Aralık 1984: Konuşmalar ve Tebliğler*, 113–24. Ankara: Vakıflar Genel Müdürlüğü Yayınları, 1985.

Yücel, Yaşar. "Osmanlı İmparatorluğu'nda Desantralizasyona (Adem-i Merkeziyet) Dair Bazı Gözlemler." *Belleten* 43, no. 171 (1979): 657–705.

Yücel, Yaşar, ed. *Kitâbu Mesâlih'l-Menâfi'i'l-Mü'minin*. In *Texts on the Ottoman State Order-II*. Ankara: Ankara Üniversitesi Dil ve Tarih-Coğrafya Fakültesi, 1980.

Yücel, Yaşar. *Osmanlı Ekonomi, Kültür, Uygarlık, Tarihine Dair Bir Kaynak: Esas Defteri (1640 Tarihli)*. Ankara: Türk Tarih Kurumu Yayınları, 1992.

Yücel, Yaşar, and Ali Sevim. *Osmanlı Klasik Dönemi'nin Üç Hükümdarı: Fatih, Yavuz, Kanuni*. Ankara: Türk Tarih Kurumu Yayınları, 1991.

Yüksel, Hasan. *Osmanlı Sosyal ve Ekonomik Hayatında Vakıfların Rolü (1585–1683)*. Sivas: Dilek Matbaası, 1998.

Zarcone, Thierry. *Kudüs'teki Orta Asyalı ve Hintli Sufi Hacılar*. Istanbul: Kabalcı Yayınevi, 2012.

Ze'evi, Dror. *Kudüs: 17. Yüzyılda Bir Osmanlı Sancağında Toplum ve Ekonomi*. Translated by S. Çağlayan. Istanbul: Tarih Vakfı Yurt Yayınları, 2000.

Zens, Robert. "Pazvantoğlu Osman Paşa ve Belgrad Paşalığı, 1791–1807." In *Osmanlı İmparatorluğu'nda İsyan ve Ayaklanma*, edited by Jane Hathaway, translated by Deniz Berktay, 141–65. Istanbul: Alkım, 2010.

Zilfi, Madeline C. *Women in the Ottoman Empire: Middle Eastern Women in the Early Modern Era*. Leiden: Brill, 1997.

Index

www.ingramcontent.com/pod-product-compliance
Lightning Source LLC
Chambersburg PA
CBHW071336230926
51849CB00002B/412
* 9 7 8 9 0 0 4 7 4 3 4 3 4 *